Harden's
Established 1991

2025
LONDON
restaurants

SURVEY DRIVEN REVIEWS OF 1.6K RESTAURANTS

Take your dining to the next level

Enjoy benefits at the UK's Best Restaurants

Join today at hardens.com

© **Harden's Limited 2024**

ISBN 978-1-9160761-8-1

British Library Cataloguing-in-Publication data:
a catalogue record for this book is available from the British Library.

Printed in the UK by the Short Run Press

Assistant editor: Bruce Millar

Harden's Limited
Missionworks, 41 Iffley Road, London W6 0PB

Would restaurateurs (and PRs) please address communications to 'Editorial' at the above address, or ideally by email to: editorial@hardens.com

The contents of this book are believed correct at the time of printing. Nevertheless, the publisher can accept no responsibility for errors or changes in or omissions from the details given.

No part of this publication may be reproduced or transmitted in any form or by any means, electronically or mechanically, including photocopying, recording or any information storage or retrieval system, without prior permission in writing from the publisher.

CONTENTS

Ratings & prices

How this guide is written

Survey results
Most mentioned   **11**
Nominations   **12**
Highest ratings   **14**
Best by cuisine   **16**

The restaurant scene   **18**

Openings and closures   **20**

Directory   **24**

Area overviews   **262**

Maps   **298**
- 1 – London overview
- 2 – West End overview
- 3 – Mayfair & St James's
- 4 – West Soho
- 5 – East Soho, Chinatown & Covent Garden
- 6 – Knightsbridge, Chelsea & South Kensington
- 7 – Notting Hill & Bayswater
- 8 – Hammersmith & Chiswick
- 9 – Hampstead, Camden Town & Islington
- 10 – The City
- 11 – South London (& Fulham)
- 12 – Docklands
- 13 – Shoreditch & Hoxton
- 14 – East End

RATINGS & PRICES

Ratings

Our rating system does not tell you – as most guides do – that expensive restaurants are often better than cheap ones! What we do is compare each restaurant's performance – as judged by the average ratings awarded by reporters in the survey – with other similarly-priced restaurants. This approach has the advantage that it helps you find – whatever your budget for any particular meal – where you will get the best 'bang for your buck'.

The following qualities are assessed:

F — Food
S — Service
A — Ambience

The rating indicates that, **_in comparison with other restaurants in the same price-bracket_**, performance is…

5 — Exceptional
4 — Very good
3 — Good
2 — Acceptable
1 — Poor

Prices

The price shown for each restaurant is the cost for one (1) person of an average three-course dinner with half a bottle of house wine and coffee, any cover charge, service and VAT. Lunch is often cheaper. With BYO restaurants, we have assumed that two people share a £7 bottle of off-licence wine.

Map reference – *shown immediately after the telephone number.*

Full postcodes – *for non-group restaurants, the first entry in the 'small print' at the end of each listing, so you can set your sat-nav.*

Website, Instagram – *shown in the small print, where applicable.*

Opening hours – *unless otherwise stated, restaurants are open for lunch and dinner seven days a week.*

Dress – *where appropriate, the management's preferences concerning patrons' dress are given.*

Sustainability – *if a restaurant or group has a star rating from the Sustainable Restaurants Association, this is shown.*

HOW THIS GUIDE IS WRITTEN

Celebrating our 34th year!
This guide is based on our annual poll of what 'ordinary' diners-out think of London's restaurants. The first such survey was in 1991 with a few over 100 people taking part. This year, the total number of reporters in our combined London/UK survey, conducted mainly online, numbered 2,500, and between them they contributed 30,000 individual reports.

How intelligent is AI?
At a time when the credibility of online reviews and influencer posts are under ongoing scrutiny, there is an ever-greater need for trusted sources such as the Harden's annual national diners' poll. In particular, the active curation by humans that we provide. For – while obviously folks can attempt to stuff the Harden's ballot too – our high degree of editorial oversight, plus our historical data about both the restaurants and those commenting, make it much harder to cheat. In this way Harden's can socially source restaurant feedback, but – vitally – curate it carefully. It is this careful curation that provides extra 'value-added' for diners.

How we determine the ratings
In general, ratings are arrived at statistically. We create a ranking akin to football leagues, with the most expensive restaurants in the top league and the cheaper ones in lower ones. Any restaurant's ranking *within its own particular league* determines its ratings.

How we write the reviews
The tone of each review and the ratings are guided by the ranking of the restaurant concerned, derived as described above. At the margin, we may also pay regard to the balance of positive votes (such as for 'favourite restaurant') against negative ones (such as for 'most overpriced'). To explain why an entry has been rated as it has, we extract snippets from user comments ("enclosed in double quotes"). Some well-known restaurants generate over a hundred reports, and a short summary cannot do individual justice to all of them. What we seek to do – *without any regard to our own personal opinions* – is to illustrate key themes in the collective feedback.

How do we find our reporters?
Anyone can take part. Register now at www.hardens.com if you have not already done so! In fact, we find that once people have taken part, they often continue to do so. With high repeat-participation, the end-result is really more the product of a very large and ever-evolving panel, or jury, than a random 'poll'.

Most of us want to spend our money with businesses who do good for both people and planet – but it can be hard to know which restaurants are really doing the work. Below, The Sustainable Restaurant Association shares some ways to identify a sustainable restaurant for your next dining experience.

1. How does the restaurant talk about sustainability?

Before you go, check the restaurant's website and social media. Ideally, a business should be setting clear, measurable sustainability targets and sharing their progress against these goals, whether it's reducing their carbon footprint, serving more plant-based foods or improving their sourcing standards. Transparency is always best practice.

2. Look for provenance on the menu.

Check the menus, looking for provenance – the stories behind the food. Is there a focus on local sourcing? Do they mention producers by name? Do they showcase seasonal ingredients? Transparency all the way from the farm or fishing vessel to your plate allows for better quality control and lets you know exactly what has gone into your meal, including farming methods, animal welfare and food miles.

3. Is there a good selection of plant-rich dishes?

If a menu shows a good proportion of interesting, considered plant-based options, this is generally a good indicator of a commitment to sustainability. The amount of meat that a restaurant buys and serves has a direct effect on a variety of sustainability metrics, including carbon emissions, water use, land use and pollution. Serving less meat and more plant-rich dishes also supports better public health and the much-needed transition to healthy, sustainable diets.

4. How do they minimise their footprint?

How else does the restaurant work to minimise their environmental impact? Check to see whether they've conducted a carbon footprint and set targets for reductions. Do they use clean energy sources for cooking, heating and transport? What steps do they take to reduce packaging – have they ditched single-use items like straws or paper napkins? How are they working to eliminate food waste?

5. Do they have third party certifications?

The easiest way to rest assured that a restaurant is doing what they say they're doing is to check for credible, reputable third-party sustainability accreditations. Think organic certification, Fairtrade or Rainforest Alliance for responsible sourcing practices, the MSC blue fish label when it comes to seafood, the Coolfood Pledge for reducing greenhouse gas emissions, or – for a comprehensive approach – the Food Made Good Standard, the only global sustainability certification that's tailored to the hospitality industry.

The Food Made Good Standard is unique in its holistic approach, assessing businesses across 10 criteria that encompass responsible sourcing, social sustainability and environmental impact. We make a point of rewarding action over intention so, when you see a restaurant sporting the Food Made Good logo, you know they're committed to sustainability in a tangible, measurable and transparent way.

Whether you're considering a fine dining restaurant or a cosy neighbourhood hangout for your next meal, the Food Made Good Standard is how you can rest assured that they're playing their part in building a more sustainable future for all of us.

Choosing sustainable restaurants is casting a vote for a better hospitality industry and supporting the development of a better food system. To be assured that a restaurant makes sustainability a priority and does good for both people and planet, look for the Food Made Good Standard logo on websites, social media, in windows and on menus, or check out the Food Made Good Directory for inspiration on where to eat next.

Interested in learning more about Food Made Good? Check out www.thesra.org, follow The Sustainable Restaurant Association on Instagram and LinkedIn and sign up to their newsletter for regular news and insights from the world of sustainable hospitality!

HOW THIS GUIDE IS WRITTEN

Wouldn't a random sample be better?
That's a theoretical question, as there is no obvious way, still less a cost-efficient one, to identify a random sample of the guests at each of, say, 5,000 establishments across the UK, and get them to take part in any sort of survey. People steeped in statistical market research tend be most keen on this idea. Other folks accept that having someone stand with a clipboard at Oxford Circus asking random people their opinion on London's most expensive restaurants is unlikely to glean useful data.

Do people ever try to stuff the ballot?
Of course they do! Sometimes with the aid of social media agencies. Many rogue entries are weeded out every year. But stuffing the ballot is not as trivial a task as some people seem to think: the survey results throw up clear natural voting patterns against which unfair 'campaigns' tend to stand out.

Aren't inspections the best way to run a guide?
This could be called the 'traditional' model of restaurant reviewing; and chefs seem particularly prone to tout this form of recognition as the one form of criticism that they will respect. And, doubtless the inspection model has its strengths. But a prime weakness is that it is so expensive it precludes too many visits. Take its most famous champion: Michelin. The tyre man has not historically claimed to visit each entry listed in its guide annually. Even once! But cost alone is not the only reason to query the inspection model. Another vital issue: who are its inspectors? Often catering professionals, whose tastes may be at odds with the natural customer base. On many entries of note, however, Harden's has dozens of reports annually from the folks who keep the restaurant in business. We believe that such feedback from paying customers, carefully analysed, is far more revealing and accurate than an occasional, so-called 'professional' inspection.

SURVEY MOST MENTIONED

Restaurants are ranked by number of mentions in our poll. (Last year's position is in brackets.) If two or more entries score equally, the food rating is used to 'break the tie'. Asterisks* indicate the first appearance of a new restaurant.

1 J Sheekey (1)
2 Chez Bruce (3)
3 Clos Maggiore (6)
4 Scott's (2)
5 Bouchon Racine*
6 The Wolseley (5)
7 Noble Rot (4)
8 Core by Clare Smyth (8)
9 Medlar (10)
10 Bocca di Lupo (11)

11 The River Café (7)
12 Sam's Riverside (18)
13 Andrew Edmunds (13)
14 Gymkhana (21)
15 Brasserie Zédel (9)
16 The Ritz (17)
17 La Poule au Pot (19)
18 The Delaunay (12)
19 Noble Rot Soho (15)
20 The Devonshire*

21 The Cinnamon Club (14)
22 Lasdun*
23 64 Goodge Street (-)
24 Mountain*
25 La Trompette (16)
26 The Ledbury (34)
27 Arlington*
28 The Ivy (39)
29 Bentley's (22)
30 Rules (26)

31 The Portrait Restaurant by Richard Corrigan (-)
32 Manzi's*
32 A Wong (20)
34 Galvin La Chapelle (27)
35 Bleeding Heart Bistro (-)
36 Hide (-)
37 The Tamil Prince (-)
38 Noble Rot Mayfair (-)
39 Sabor (-)
40 Scott's Richmond*

SURVEY NOMINATIONS

Top gastronomic experience

1. Core by Clare Smyth (1)
2. Chez Bruce (2)
3. The Ledbury (5)
4. Medlar (10)
5. The Ritz (8)
6. Bouchon Racine (3)
7. Mountain (-)
8. The Five Fields (6)
9. La Trompette (-)
10. Frog by Adam Handling (7)

Favourite

1. Chez Bruce (1)
2. Core by Clare Smyth (-)
3. Bouchon Racine (3)
4. Sam's Riverside (2)
5. Bocca di Lupo (7)
6. Medlar (8)
7. Sabor (-)
8. Andrew Edmunds (-)
9. The Ritz (-)
10. J Sheekey (10)

Best for business

1. The Wolseley (1)
2. Hawksmoor (3)
3. The Delaunay (2)
4. Bleeding Heart Bistro (10)
5. Scott's (4)
6. Cabotte (8)
7. The Ivy (-)
8. Hide (-)
9. 1 Lombard Street (-)
10. Galvin La Chapelle (7)

Best for romance

1. Clos Maggiore (1)
2. La Poule au Pot (2)
3. Andrew Edmunds (3)
4. Chez Bruce (8)
5. Scott's (9)
6. The Ritz (-)
7. Sessions Arts Club (5)
8. J Sheekey (-)
9. Core by Clare Smyth (4)
10. Galvin La Chapelle (6)

RANKED BY THE NUMBER OF REPORTERS' VOTES

Best breakfast/brunch

1. The Wolseley (1)
2. Dishoom (2)
3. The Delaunay (3)
4. Hide (-)
5. Côte (6)
6. Megan's (8)
7= The Wolseley City (-)
7= Granger & Co (4)
9. Breakfast Club (5)
10. The Ivy Grills & Brasseries (-)

Best bar/pub food

1. The Devonshire*
2. Harwood Arms (1)
3. Canton Arms (-)
4. The Anchor & Hope (2)
5. The Pelican (9)
6= The Eagle (4)
6= The Ladbroke Arms (8)
8. The Wigmore, The Langham (6)
9. The Guinea Grill (-)
10. The Drapers Arms (7)

Most disappointing cooking

1. Oxo Tower (Restaurant) (1)
2. The Wolseley (3)
3. Hawksmoor (-)
4= The Ivy (2)
4= Arlington*
6. Six by Nico (-)
7. The Ivy Asia (-)
8. Dinner by Heston Blumenthal, Mandarin Oriental (4)
9. Lasdun (-)
10. Quo Vadis (-)

Most overpriced restaurant

1. The River Café (1)
2. Sexy Fish (4)
3. Hawksmoor (-)
4. Gordon Ramsay (2)
5. Oxo Tower (Restaurant) (3)
6. Hélène Darroze, The Connaught Hotel (5)
7. The Ritz (-)
8. Lasdun (-)
9. Hide (-)
10. Alain Ducasse at The Dorchester (-)

SURVEY HIGHEST RATINGS

FOOD

SERVICE

£140+

1. Endo at The Rotunda
2. The Ledbury
3. La Dame de Pic
4. Da Terra
5. Core by Clare Smyth

1. Endo at The Rotunda
2. Ormer Mayfair
3. Core by Clare Smyth
4. The Ritz
5. The Ledbury

£100–£139

1. Lyle's
2. Chez Bruce
3. Min Jiang
4. Launceston Place
5. Pearly Queen

1. Clarke's
2. Noizé
3. Charlie's at Brown's
4. Chez Bruce
5. Wiltons

£80–99

1. Casa Fofó
2. Brat
3. The Silver Birch
4. BiBi
5. Pahli Hill

1. Cibo
2. Six Portland Road
3. Bouchon Racine
4. Cabotte
5. The Silver Birch

£60–£79

1. Café Spice Namaste
2. Barshu
3. Babur
4. Brigadiers
5. Smoking Goat

1. Café Spice Namaste
2. The French House
3. Brunswick House Café
4. Noble Rot Soho
5. Sabor

£59 or less

1. The Barbary
2. Xi'an Impression
3. Kolae
4. Bleecker Burger
5. Padella

1. The Barbary
2. Kolae
3. Plaza Khao Gaeng
4. Imad's Syrian Kitchen
5. Kokum

AMBIENCE

1. The Ritz
2. Core by Clare Smyth
3. Ormer Mayfair
4. Endo at The Rotunda
5. Sketch, Lecture Room

1. Clos Maggiore
2. Galvin La Chapelle
3. Hutong, The Shard
4. Arlington
5. Veeraswamy

1. The Summerhouse
2. Rules
3. Oslo Court
4. Bob Bob Ricard
5. Quo Vadis

1. Sessions Arts Club
2. Café Spice Namaste
3. La Poule au Pot
4. Andrew Edmunds
5. Ognisko Restaurant

1. Ciao Bella
2. The Barbary
3. Los Mochis
4. Mercato Metropolitano
5. The Eagle

OVERALL

1. Endo at The Rotunda
2. Pied à Terre
3. Core by Clare Smyth
4. Ormer Mayfair
5. The Ledbury

1. Galvin La Chapelle
2. Wiltons
3. Chez Bruce
4. Otto's
5. Noizé

1. Brat
2. Bouchon Racine
3. The Silver Birch
4. Oslo Court
5. Mountain

1. Café Spice Namaste
2. The French House
3. Smoking Goat
4. Sabor
5. Brunswick House Café

1. The Barbary
2. Plaza Khao Gaeng
3. Kolae
4. Kricket
5. Kiln

SURVEY BEST BY CUISINE

These are the restaurants which received the best average food ratings (excluding establishments with a small or notably local following).

Where the most common types of cuisine are concerned, we present the results in two price-brackets. For less common cuisines, we list the top three, regardless of price.

For further information about restaurants which are particularly notable for their food, see the area overviews starting on page 262.

British, Modern

£80 and over
1. The Ledbury
2. Core by Clare Smyth
3. The Five Fields
4. Aulis London
5. Behind

Under £80
1. The Anglesea Arms
2. The Camberwell Arms
3. The French House
4. Lorne
5. The Devonshire

French

£80 and over
1. La Dame de Pic
2. The Ritz
3. Otto's
4. Bouchon Racine
5. Noizé

Under £80
1. Les 2 Garcons
2. Casse-Croute
3. La Poule au Pot
4. Bleeding Heart Bistro
5. Ploussard

Italian/Mediterranean

£80 and over
1. Luca
2. Murano
3. Theo Randall
4. Olivomare
5. Caractère

Under £80
1. Bocca di Lupo
2. Pentolina
3. Eataly
4. Bruto
5. 500

Indian & Pakistani

£80 and over
1. BiBi
2. Pahli Hill
3. Yaatra
4. Veeraswamy
5. Gymkhana

Under £80
1. Café Spice Namaste
2. Babur
3. Brigadiers
4. Dastaan
5. Tayyabs

Chinese

£80 and over
1. A Wong
2. Min Jiang
3. Yauatcha
4. Imperial Treasure
5. Hunan

Under £80
1. Barshu
2. Xi'an Impression
3. Master Wei
4. Singapore Garden
5. Four Seasons

Japanese

£80 and over
1. Endo at The Rotunda
2. Nobu Portman Square
3. Chisou
4. Zuma
5. Roka

Under £80
1. Los Mochis
2. Jin Kichi
3. Oka
4. Sticks'n'Sushi
5. Shoryu Ramen

British, Traditional
1. The Ritz
2. Wiltons
3. St John

Vegetarian
1. Gauthier Soho
2. Bubala
3. Tendril

Burgers, etc
1. Bleecker Burger
2. Patty and Bun
3. Black Bear

Pizza
1. Crisp Pizza
2. Santa Maria
3. Base Face Pizza

Fish & Chips
1. Fish Central
2. Toff's
3. fish!

Thai
1. Smoking Goat
2. Kolae
3. Kiln

Steaks & Grills
1. The Devonshire
2. Blacklock
3. The Guinea Grill

Fish & Seafood
1. Behind
2. Pearly Queen
3. Smith's

Fusion
1. Akoko
2. Da Terra
3. Ikoyi

Spanish
1. Sabor
2. Cambio de Tercio
3. Moro

THE RESTAURANT SCENE

Steady (very) as she goes...

In the last 12 months, the guide has added 132 newcomers. This is a low level of openings, with only two years lower since 2010 (one of which was last year).

The rate of closures stands at 84. This is not exceptional by the standards of the frothy years of 2013-2017 when a brisk rate of closures was part and parcel of major growth overall. But by the level of most years post-2000, it's high.

Taking the two factors together and subtracting the closures from the openings gives net growth: this year's rate of 48 sits in a range that's low-to-middling since the guide started 34 years ago. It's the sixth-lowest rate since 2000.

An economist might say this low-growth scene is not a surprise. London's population is growing only slowly (about 1% a year). Tourist spend this year was down 5% quarter on quarter at the beginning of 2024. And, with the cost of living crisis, the casual dining sector in the UK only started to grow again in Q2 2024 after two years of decline, according to figures from CGA by NIQ and AlixPartners.

The old guard continue to bow out

Prior to the period 2015-2020, it was rare for well-rated restaurants to close. But market conditions have been sufficiently challenging of late that this is no longer the case, with many good, long-established players choosing this year to throw in the towel.

Just as last year's guide was published, we captured the news that Le Gavroche and Marcus Wareing at the Berkeley were to close. The following months have seen other lower profile, but well-rated names choosing to quit such as: L'Amorosa, Anglo, Cornerstone, Frenchie, Galvin at Windows, Mere, Odette's, Pidgin, and Plu.

The Devonshire leads the charge

The Top-10 lists on the preceding pages of the guide are generally dominated by long-established names, so it's exciting to see a new opening go straight to the top of one of our poll categories. Best Bar & Pub, no less, was awarded to Charlie Carroll and Oisin Rogers' The Devonshire.

Amongst other exciting new names to appear this year, the following stand out in terms of instant fame, or immediate acclaim within our annual diners' poll: Akara, Arlington, Brooklands, Counter 71, Josphine, Kolae, Mambow, Morchella, Mountain, The Park, Pearly Queen, 64 Goodge Street and The Wolseley City.

£100+? Now old news...

The average formula price of dinner for one at entries in the guide this year is £78.84 (c.f. £75.65 last year). This represents an increase of 4.2% in the past year: still above general price growth of 2.2% (according to the government's CPI for the 12 months to July 2024), but well down on the 9.2% noted the prior year.

Pricier restaurants (those charging over £100 per head) registered an average rise a little higher than the general average (at 5.1%). However, price inflation in the top tier is no longer charging ahead in the eye-catching way that it was in the previous couple of years.

The break-through of the psychologically important £100 per head price barrier and colonisation of new £100+ price points now seems to be moderating. There are currrently 211 restaurants in the guide whose formula price is over £100 per head. This is up 11% from last year's 191; and the number of entries in the £150+, £200+ and £250+ price categories are now expanding at a similar pace – not the mind-blowing 50%-80% expansions seen last year.

French cuisine – the future or the past?

In terms of cuisines, this year saw a high interest in classic French cooking amongst new openings. Modern British and Italian openings continue to be the most popular categories for newcomers (accounting for 27 and 11 openings respectively), with French cuisine replacing Japanese cuisine this year as the third highest category (with 10 newcomers).

But this resurgence in interest in the creamy classical flavourings of La Belle France conceals a long-term decline in its grip on the top tier of London cooking. Of the 61 restaurants with a formula price in the guide of over £150 per head, only 11 are French, compared with 14 that are Japanese. Over one third are modern British and the remainder reflect the huge culinary diversity of the capital (Californian, Chinese, Latino, Scandinavian, West African).

In this light, it's puzzling that chefs and the food press continue to obsess on the awards of a certain large, French tyre manufacturer. Half of London's six three-star awards from the folks in Clermont Ferrand are to famous French chefs, painting a picture of excellence that's now 'passé'.

Where's hot

In terms of location, Central London remained dominant, with 48 arrivals. In the 'burbs, East London led the way as it often has in recent years (with 29 openings) followed by West and South London (with 21 apiece). North London, as it so often does, came up in last place (with 13 newcomers).

These figures mask big differences in the level of aspiration of the various openings. For example, West London openings are, on average, aiming for price points similar to those in the West End; whereas those in East and North London are pitched at about two thirds of such a level, and those in South London are on average about half the price.

OPENINGS & CLOSURES

The listings below relate to the period from Autumn 2023 to Autumn 2024.

Only branches of small groups in the listings below contribute to the grand total figures. (It is beyond the scope of this book to track comings and goings at the large multiples.)

* temporarily closed as we to go to press.

Openings (132)
A Braccetto
Agora
Akara
Akira Back
Alley Cats *(W1, SW3)*
Ambassadors Clubhouse
AngloThai
Arlington
Azzurra
The Barbary *(W2)*
Baudry Greene
The Bear
Bébé Bob
Big Easy *(E20)*
Big Night
Bistro Freddie
Bleecker Burger *(SE1)*
Boca a boca
Bruno
The Butcher's Tap and Grill
Cafe Britaly
Cafe Francois
Café Petiole
Caldesi In Belsize *(NW3)*
Camille
Canton Blue
Carmel *(W1)*
Chakana
Chayote
Chez Roux
Chop Chop
Clap
Cloth
The Cocochine
Cornus
The Counter *(W1, W10)*
Crispin at Studio Voltaire
Crudough *(EC1)*
Dalla
Dear Jackie
Donia
The Dover
Dream Xi'an
Emilia's Crafted Pasta *(NW1)*
Faber
Fish & Bubbles
Florencio Pizza
Fonda
Field by Fortnum's
Forty Three Sichuan Kitchen
Forza Wine *(SE1)*
Frame
Francatelli
Gaia
Il Gattopardo
Gerry's Hot Subs
Goodbye Horses
Grasso
Hainan House
Harrods (The Georgian)
Henri
Hiden
Holy Carrot Portobello
Home SW13 *(SW13)*
Hotel Dalhousie
The Hound
The Hunan Man
Ibai
INÉ
Inis Café
It's Bagels
Ixchel
Jamie Oliver
Jang
JinCheng Alley
Jones & Sons *(E18)*
Josephine
Juno
Kachori

OPENINGS & CLOSURES

Kinkally
KöD (EC2)
Kolae
Kolamba East (E1)
Kricket (E14)
Lahpet Larder (SE1)
Lita
Lolo
Lucky Cat (EC2)
Lussmann's
La Maison Ani
Mambow (E5)
Marceline
Mary's
Mignonette
Mildreds (SW1)
Mistress
Morchella
Noci (EC1, SW11, TW10)
Oka (W11)
Oma
Ottolenghi (NW3)
La Palombe
El Pastor (SW11)
Pearly Queen
Piraña London
Plates
Pollini
Pravaas
River Café Café
Roe
Roti King (SE1, E1)
Sael
Saltine
Sesta
Shanghai Noir
Singapulah
Stem + Stem
Sunday in Brooklyn (W1)
Sune
Sushi Revolution (EC2)
Tabisca*
The Tamil Crown
tashas
temper (W2)
thirty7
Three Darlings
Three Uncles (W5)
Tollington's
UBA
Undercroft
Watan
Whyte's
Wild
Wilson's
Yasmin
YGF Malatang
YiQi
Yum Bug
Zest
Zia Lucia (SW6)

OPENINGS & CLOSURES

Closures (84)

Allegra
Alter
L'Amorosa
Ampéli
Anglo
The Beefsteaks @ M. Manze
Block Soho
Il Borro
Bossa
Bund
Ceviche Soho (W1)
Church Road
Coal Rooms
Copper & Ink
Cornerstone
Delhi Grill
Dipna Anand
The Duck Truck
E&O (W11)
Ekte Nordic Kitchen
Eline
Farmacy
The Fat Badger
Frenchie
Galvin at Windows
The Gate (W1, EC1)
The Gurkhas
Gustoso
Haché (SW4)
The Hampshire
Harvest
Haugen
Hawthorn
Haya
Hereford Road
Hicce
Hicce Hart
Holy Carrot (SW1)
Homeslice (W12)
Hush (W1)
Issho-Ni
Jiji
Jinjuu
Kaki
Kalimera
Ken Lo's Memories
Little Pizza Hicce
London Stock
Lure
M Restaurant (E14)
Maddox Tavern
Maene
Magenta
Marugame Udon (W1)
Mere
Supa Ya Ramen (E8)
Odette's
Only Food and Courses
Park Row
Pascor
Pidgin
Plu
Pollen Street Social
Rasa Street
Republic
Richoux (W1)
Romulo Café
Roof Garden, Pantechnicon
Saltie Girl
The Sea, The Sea (E8)
Seven Park Place
Social Eating House
Soffice London
Supa Ya Ramen (SE15)
Tila
Tokimeite
Tommi's Burger Joint (W1)
Townsend
Turnips
12:51
20 Berkeley
28-50 (SW3)
Vinoteca (N1)
VQ (EC3N)
Zaibatsu

DIRECTORY

Comments in "double quotation marks" were made by reporters.

F S A

081 Pizzeria SE15 £39 4 2 2
5th Floor, Peckham Levels, 95a Rye Lane   no tel   1–4D
Peckish for pizza down Peckham way? Andrea Asciuti's popular pitstop is a pint-sized, 20-cover premises (a lot of the business is for delivery) and punches well above its weight, with a superb selection of funky Neapolitan pizzas (from 72-hour fermented dough), panuozzo (Neapolitan street-food sarnies), tapas (e.g. arancina, deep fried aubergine balls, lobster croquettes) and puds (including Nutella pizza, natch). / SE15 4ST; 081pizzeria.com; /081pizzerialdn/; Mon-Sun 11 pm.

A Braccetto SW5 NEW
242 Earl's Court Road   020 7373 2797   6–2A
Close to Earl's Court station, this modern take on the classic Italian neighbourhood trat' was launched in March 2024 by the family who founded the Spaghetti House group back in the day (in 1955). It opened too late to generate much in the way of survey feedback, but the press have mostly found in its favour: in April 2024, The Observer's Jay Rayner didn't like the steak or pricey wine list, but found the antipasti and pasta lived up to the family's heritage, and both he and the Mail on Sunday's Tom Parker Bowles (in May) applaud the pizza: "thin and crispy… [with] an uncommon subtlety to the toppings". / SW5 9AA; a-braccetto.com; Mon-Sat 11 pm, Sun 10.30 pm.

A Cena TW1 £81 4 4 3
418 Richmond Road   020 8288 0108   1–4A
"Very good food" – but "no pizzas!", the menu is more ambitious – has been served for more than 20 years at this "friendly local Italian" near Richmond Bridge in St Margaret's – the last five under owner Tom Rowlandson, who trained with Skye Gyngell at Petersham Nurseries and has pushed standards ever higher. / TW1 2EB; acena.co.uk; acenarestaurant; Tue-Sat 10 pm.

A Wong SW1 £252 5 5 4
70 Wilton Rd   020 7828 8931   2–4B
"Probably the best Chinese gastronomic experience in the UK" – Andrew Wong "has changed the game for Chinese cuisine" in the West and "the progress he has made over the years is phenomenal" at this Pimlico HQ (which began life as his parents' restaurant, Kym's). "The hype is deserved" for food that's "exceptional, original, and utterly delicious": "he really sets the bar and showcases that Chinese gastronomy can go head-to-head against the likes of French and Japanese traditions when it comes to this level of cooking". ("You can see the refinement and constant drive to make each and every element of a dish better and better"). At lunch, "exquisite dim sum" is served à la carte (and there's also a lunchtime tasting option). In the evening, there's the "pure theatre" of a lengthy tasting menu for £200 per person ("I don't do tasting menus anymore, but this was a wise exception to my rule and an absolute triumph"). To a striking extent, no-one questions the quality here. Even so, some do bristle at the ultimate bill ("the food is exceptional, but you might prefer a week in Greece for similar money?"). "Still, despite the huge money, he's full, so there are plenty of takers". Top Tips – "Keep your eyes on instagram for last-minute bookings". And "if visiting, ensure you have a drink in the basement bar, which very much has an old HK vibe". / SW1V 1DE; awong.co.uk; a.wong_londonuk; Wed-Sat, Tue 8.30 pm.

The Abingdon W8 £70 3 4 4
54 Abingdon Rd   020 7937 3339   6–2A
"Not so much a gastropub as a restaurant attached to a stylish pub/wine bar" – this upscale local, tucked away off Kensington High Street, has been gradually transformed over 25 years by two generations of the Staples family. The food (which according to the website 'maintains the sensibility of a British gastropub, combined with techniques and flavours from the 21st century') is "consistently reliable", backed up by "excellent service and a very warm welcome". / W8 6AP; theabingdon.co.uk; theabingdon; Mon-Sat 10 pm, Sun 9 pm.

Acme Fire Cult E8 £56 2 3 2
The Bootyard, Abbot Street   no tel   14–1A
A live-fire restaurant at 40FT Brewery in Dalston, from Andrew Clarke and Daniel Watkins, where the BBQ offers "an emphasis on veg (although meat is also available)", and where beer by-products are used to make ferments and hot sauces. It's a "fun" and "innovative" place, but not always a consistent one. Top Menu Tip – "Coal Roast Leeks and Pistachio Romesco were amazing. Marmite/Pecorino on Sourdough a must". / E8 3DP; acmefirecult.com; acmefirecult; Tue, Wed 10 pm, Thu-Sat 11 pm, Sun 4 pm.

The Admiral Codrington SW3 £69 3 2 3
17 Mossop St   020 7581 0005   6–2C
In the traditional heart of posh Chelsea, this Sloaney backstreet boozer is nowadays part of Butcombe Inns, whose four siblings in the capital likewise occupy nice properties in expensive postcodes. With its small garden and cute dining room with retractable roof, it wins solid ratings but nothing like the attention it once enjoyed, and is primarily recommendable as a relatively affordable fallback in this pricey bit of town. / SW3 2LY; theadmiralcodrington.co.uk; theadcod; Wed-Sun 10.30 pm.

Afghan Kitchen N1 £38 3 2 2
35 Islington Green   020 7359 8019   9–3D
Since the early 1990s, this tiny, two-floor canteen on Islington Green has been a popular local pitstop. Don't expect anything foodie, but for a flavourful refuel at a good price, its small selection of simple curries is just the job. / N1 8DU; kubiti.blog; afghankitchenldn; Tue-Sat 10 pm.

Aglio e Olio SW10 £53 3 3 2
194 Fulham Rd   020 7351 0070   6–3B
A "reliable local" fixture for more than 25 years almost opposite Chelsea & Westminster Hospital, this "good-value", "buzzy" café serves "very good Italian food in a relaxed setting". It's "nothing fancy, but the sort of place you can take your children or your grandparents and everyone will feel very much at home". / SW10 9PN; aglioeolio.co.uk; Mon-Sun 11 pm.

Agora SE1 NEW
2-4 Bedale Street   no tel   10–4C
David Carter (of Smokestak fame) has gone Greek-with-a-twist with this March 2024 newcomer, which occupies the ground floor of the two-floor site in Borough Market that was previously Rabot 1745 (RIP) – (see also Oma, which is on the floor above, and can be entered separately). The street-level part of the operation (Agora is 'market' in Greek) is in modern taverna style, with a two-metre rotisserie, where whole lamb and pig are cooked on the spit to deliver Eastern Mediterranean street-food plates. It opened too late for survey feedback, but in his May 2024 review The Evening Standard's Jimi Famurewa loved its "almost illegally fun" atmosphere and "epic" dishes. / SE1 9AL; agora.london; Mon-Sat 10 pm.

Akara SE1 NEW £36 3 3 4
Arch 208, 18 Stoney Street   020 3861 5190   10–4C
"If you like Akoko you will like Akara" – Aji Akokomi's more casual (and much more affordable!) new spin-off to his increasingly famous Fitzrovia HQ occupies a shiny new unit in Borough Yards and opened in October 2023. Like the mothership, it's dedicated to putting a "refined" spin on West African culinary traditions. "The akara dumplings [for which it's named] are a must" and contribute to a menu of dishes which "whilst carrying some West African spice still remain delicate", (although some of the accompanying sauces are pretty fiery). The tasteful, upbeat interior is "open and airy with good table spacing, and service is very attentive". / SE1 9AD; akaralondon.co.uk; akara.london; Tue-Sat 11 pm, Mon 10 pm.

F S A

Akira at Japan House W8 £88 3 2 2
101-111 Kensington High Street   020 3971 4646   6–1A
"A showcase for good Japanese cuisine" – the first-floor restaurant in Kensington's Japan House cultural centre wins particular praise for its "lovely Japanese afternoon tea". Fans also say it's "consistently excellent" for more substantial meals – with a "sake menu that's worth a visit in its own right" – but it can also "feel expensive" for what is delivered. / W8 5SA; japanhouselondon.uk; japanhouseldn; Mon-Sat 8 pm, Sun 6 pm.

Akira Back W1 NEW
22 Hanover Square   020 7889 8888   3–2C
In the new Mandarin Oriental hotel in Hanover Square, Mayfair, the long-awaited European debut of Korean celeb chef Akira Back. His self-named main restaurant reinterprets Korean and Japanese dishes, while 'Dosa' is a 14-seat chef's table offering contemporary Korean dishes prepared using French techniques. Back is also behind the hotel's two bars, ABar Lounge and ABar Rooftop. / W1S 1JP; mandarinoriental.com; Mon-Thu 10 pm, Fri & Sat 11 pm, Sun 9 pm.

Akoko W1 £164 5 4 3
21 Berners Street   020 7323 0593   5–1A
"Easily my best and most enjoyable meal of the year" – Aji Akokomi's groundbreaking Fitzrovia passion project provides an "interesting take on food from different African countries" and is helping to break the glass ceiling for the level of esteem with which African cuisine is held generally. His latest chef – Ayo Adeyemi, appointed in 2022 – has settled into an impressive stride, providing "wonderful combinations" drawn from across West African traditions: "imaginative flavours that challenge without being overly spicy". It helps that the food is "all served up with a smile" by the superbly "welcoming" staff, who together with the "refined", sand-walled interior (with art commissioned for the restaurant itself, along with the crockery and cutlery) help create "a top-class experience". In early 2024, the team finally brought home the Michelin star so long overdue to the restaurant but slightly puzzlingly withheld from former chef, Theo Clench. (See also Akara). / W1T 3LJ; akoko.co.uk; akokorestaurant; Tue-Sat 11 pm.

Akub W8 £73 4 3 4
27 Uxbridge Street   07729 039206   7–2B
Fadi Kattan's "superb Palestinian food" has generated real excitement over his Notting Hill yearling "in a cute three-floor building". The vibrant menu itself is full of interest and unfamiliar dishes and divided into 'Mukabilat' (small plates) and 'Ra'Isiyat' (large plates) and uses British ingredients alongside more exotic imported foodstuffs. / W8 7TQ; akub-restaurant.com; akub.london; Tue-Thu 11 pm, Fri & Sat 11.30 pm, Sun 4 pm.

Al Duca SW1 £91 3 2 2
4-5 Duke of York St   020 7839 3090   3–3D
"Excellent Italian food and a good wine list", all at decent prices for central London, continue to carve a niche for this St James's trattoria. You wouldn't choose it to dazzle a fashionista, but it has a "pleasant if quiet ambience that allows conversation". / SW1Y 6LA; alduca-restaurant.co.uk; alducarestaurant; Mon-Sat 11 pm.

Alain Ducasse at The Dorchester W1 £319 2 2 3
53 Park Lane   020 7629 8866   3–3A
Über-chef Alain Ducasse's deluxe Mayfair outpost (one of 34 he owns around the world) opened in London in 2007 to instant acclaim from the folks in Clermont Ferrand, who immediately awarded it three Michelin stars for its luxurious modern French cuisine. It's an award that has always puzzled London's fooderati, who have never really rated the place. An appropriately comfortable room, its centrepiece is the (slightly weird) 'Table Lumière' – a private-ish table surrounded by a floor-ceiling curtain of 4,500 fibre optic

cables. Much nominated as a business favourite, it is a "great space for talks, with such well-spaced tables and there's an excellent set lunch menu" too. If you don't opt for the set lunch route, though, a visit is no bargain, and over one third of those who mention it in our annual diners' poll do so as their most overpriced meal of the year. What's also entirely absent are raves from more foodie reporters over the cooking, which is not terribly rated but can seem "expensive and average for all the hype". / W1K 1QA; alainducasse-dorchester.com; alainducasseatthedorchester; Tue-Sat 9.30 pm.

Alex Dilling Café Royal W1   £212   2 2 2
Café Royal, 68 Regent Street   020 7406 3333   4–4C
"Exceptional food with flavours to match" still features in some reports on ex-Greenhouse chef Alex Dilling's fêted two-year-old, overlooking Regent Street from the grand confines of the Café Royal, which soon after its launch was blessed with two Michelin Stars. However, feedback in our survey slumped badly this year. No-one says the food is bad, but half of reporters consider it "overpriced" and there's a theme in feedback of a rather "dull" feel to the enterprise: "lots of clever techniques but the flavour and feel fell short…"; "I've given 4 for food to acknowledge the skill, but this was a demonstration of skill without any soul…"; "all very 'comme il faut' but slightly underwhelming and a touch impersonal with well-drilled, but slightly impersonal, service". / W1B 4DY; hotelcaferoyal.com; alexdillingcaferoyal; Sat, Tue-Fri 9.30 pm.

Alley Cats   £31   3 3 3
22 Paddington Street, W1   020 3301 5305   2–1A **NEW**
342 King's Rd, SW3   020 7042 7177   6–3C **NEW**
Crispy NYC-style pizza is the mainstay at this walk-ins-only newcomer in Marylebone, where Sicilian-born chef Francesco Macri knocks out thin, 14-inch pizzas topped with imported Italian ingredients. According to our diners' poll it's not bad, but whether it's worth braving the queues inspired by its instant TikTok fame is more dubious. And as of August 2024, you can also grab a slice or some of their signature meatballs in tomato sauce on the King's Road in Chelsea, complete with gingham tablecloths, church pew-style seating, and episodes of 'The Sopranos' silently projected on an endless loop.

Aloo Tama SW1   £49   4 3 2
18 Greencoat Place   020 7834 9873   2–4C
"A gem!" – easily missed on the fringes of Westminster (not far from Vincent Square) – this welcoming Nepalese café realises its dumpling, noodles and other simple fare with a light touch. And if you need a lunchtime snack in Paddington, their truck in Merchant Square is also a handy option. / SW1P 1PG; alootama.com; alootamaofficial; Tue-Sat 10 pm, Sun 9 pm.

Amaya SW1   £101   4 4 3
Halkin Arcade, 19 Motcomb St   020 7823 1166   6–1D
"Very Belgravia in feel, cost and clientele… but that doesn't stop the food tasting good!" – this once-ground-breaking Indian venue is part of the accomplished MW Eats group (with siblings including Chutney Mary and Veeraswamy). Luxurious, if slightly "cavernous" in ambience – it was an early pioneer of grill-cooking presented tapas-style from the very visible open kitchen; and has maintained an impressive level of quality and luxury over its 20 years in operation (est 2004). "This is the place to take someone who thinks they don't like Indian food: some of the most delicious things ever come from their tandoor"… "as they should at the extortionate prices!" Top Menu Tips – "the black pepper chicken and the seabass are highlights". / SW1X 8JT; amaya.biz; amaya.ldn; Mon-Sat 10.30 pm, Sun 10 pm.

Amazonico W1   £145   2 2 4
10 Berkeley Square   020 7404 5000   3–3B
The "wonderful decor" at this jungle-themed Mayfair haunt combines with live music and cocktails to create a "great atmosphere". But the high-end

Latin-American-cum-Japanese cuisine comes at "gulp-inducing prices", and critics say the venue is "Instagram-worthy but not much else" – "a place to go to be seen". / W1J 6EF; amazonicorestaurant.com; amazonicolondon.

Ambassadors Clubhouse W1 NEW
25 Heddon St   no tel   4–3A

From the phenomenal JKS restaurant group, this large (140 cover) summer 2024 launch is located just off Regent Street and is focused on all things Punjabi. The menu highlights classic papads, chaats, kebabs, curries, pilaus, biryanis, tandoor-roasted breads, and desserts. The 140-cover restaurant spans two floors with a 40-cover outdoor verandah and three private dining spaces. A dedicated music series will launch from September. / W1B 4BH; Sun-Wed 11 pm, Thu-Sat 1 am.

The American Bar, The Stafford SW1   £90   3 3 3
16-18 Saint James's Place   020 7493 0111   3–4C

Ties festooned from the ceiling is the signature look of this veteran St James's location, which makes a civilised launch-pad for an evening in the West End. With help from Northcote's Lisa Goodwin-Allen, the menu – well-rated in reports – offers light US-inspired bites (ribs, jambalaya prawns, mac 'n' cheese). / SW1A 1NJ; thestaffordlondon.com; thestaffordlondon; Sun-Wed midnight, Thu-Sat 1 am.

Amrutha SW18   £37   3 4 2
326 Garratt Lane   020 8001 4628   11–2B

This "fantastic" Earlsfield venture offers 'vegan soul food' that is both "incredible value" and full of "lovely, interesting flavours" ("would never even have known it was vegan!"). Founded by school friends Arvin Suntaramoorphy and Shyam Kotecha, it takes an ethical approach to business, allowing guests to pay less if they are unsatisfied, and feeding the penniless for free in return for a couple of hours' labour. There's a spinoff branch in Honor Oak Park. / SW18 4EJ; amrutha.co.uk; amruthauk; Tue-Sat 10 pm, Sun 9 pm.

The Anchor & Hope SE1   £69   4 3 3
36 The Cut   020 7928 9898   10–4A

"Deserving its many plaudits" – this "model gastropub" near the Old Vic remains one of London's most popular food pubs and still "delivers on all fronts". "Service is engaging and lively" and provides "expert cuisine" that mixes Mediterranean dishes with those of more traditional British inspiration, alongside "very drinkable" wine. The interior is "noisy and busy but that's part of the buzzy ambience" and while "it's a biggish room, it's still best to book". / SE1 8LP; anchorandhopepub.co.uk; anchorhopecut; Mon & Tue 10 pm, Wed-Sat 10.30 pm, Sun 3.15 pm.

Andanza SE1   £54   3 3 2
66 Weston Street   020 7967 1972   10–4C

This tiny tapas bar, hidden away from the Borough Market crowds, has an enthusiastic following for its "tremendous Spanish food" and "delightful service" – and is "probably the most cramped restaurant that is still adorable". Top Menu Tip – "foie gras in Pedro Ximinez". / SE1 3QJ; andanza.co.uk; andanza.se1; Mon-Sat 11 pm, Sun 5 pm.

The Andover Arms W6   £56   3 4 4
57 Aldensley Rd   020 8748 2155   8–1C

"A very good neighbourhood gastropub" – this Hammersmith backstreet boozer is no longer No. 1 on TripAdvisor (as it was several years ago), to the great relief of the local residents. The relatively new management are "really helpful" and the "no-nonsense pub grub" is much jazzier than under previous regimes. Top Menu Tip – "Sunday lunch is very good with lots of families happily munching into a roast". / W6 0DL; theandoverarmsw6.com; theandoverarms; Mon-Sat 10 pm, Sun 9 pm.

FSA

Andrew Edmunds W1 £73 3 4 5
46 Lexington Street 020 7437 5708 4–2C

"The perfect place to eavesdrop and/or bring a lover… it just screams (murmurs?) romantique!" – this "legendary Soho institution" has navigated the sad loss of its owner and founder in September 2022, and remains one of the Top-20 most commented-on destinations in our annual diners' poll. Set in a "super-cosy", Dickensian townhouse, its effortless charm bewitches all of the many who comment on it; and "long may its handwritten menus, its candles in bottles on the table, its tiny tables in the wood-panelled room and charming service continue". "The range and quality of their legendary wine list at exceptional prices for London is the main gastronomic attraction, but their modern British food is pretty good too": "never fussy, but always very well done and incredibly tasty". "The church pew seating can get uncomfortable over a long sitting… nothing that another bottle of wine won't solve!". "I was worried it would decline after Andrew passed away, but the staff are doing his memory true service, continuing the Edmunds tradition of real hospitality: it is better than ever!" / W1F 0LP; andrewedmunds.com; andrew.edmunds; Mon-Sun 10.30 pm.

Angelina E8 £86 5 3 3
56 Dalston Lane 020 7241 1851 14–1A

"A wide variety of techniques" is behind food of "scrumptious flavour" and "rare visual beauty" at this "top-class experience": a stylish neighbourhood haunt with large, leafy pavement terrace discovered "off the beaten track" in Dalston. The cooking is usually described as 'fusion', which in effect means broadly Italian dishes presented Japanese kaiseki-style, with multiple small courses chosen each day by the chef, in response to the best available produce. / E8 3AH; angelina.london; angelina.dalston; Mon-Wed 11 pm, Sat, Thu & Fri 11.30 pm, Sun 10.30 pm.

Angler,
South Place Hotel EC2 £148 3 4 2
3 South Pl 020 3215 1260 13–2A

"Want to impress a client?" – this seventh-floor City rooftop venue from D&D London near Moorgate "is a destination restaurant that's worth the expense". "Technically precise and well-thought-out fish dishes" from chef Gary Foulkes "make Angler justify its Michelin star, with the kitchen showing a delicate touch and the confidence to sometimes elevate some humble fish species" as well as more luxurious options. The main drawback is "the very hotel-like vibe of the dining room", which feels "a bit bland (although this matters less for business lunching and dining"). And for non-suits, "you can't help but feel the food's a bit wasted here, especially on the business clientele who don't seem to be paying it much attention!" / EC2M 2AF; anglerrestaurant.com; angler_restaurant; Tue-Sat 9.15 pm; SRA-3 stars.

The Anglesea Arms W6 £67 5 4 4
35 Wingate Rd 020 8749 1291 8–1B

"More gastro than pub, but jolly good" – this well-known corner-boozer near Ravenscourt Park is "the best 'local' you could wish for" and regularly features in our list of London's top gastropubs. Not only it is superbly atmospheric – "with candles on the tables and a roaring fire in the winter" – but it produces "consistently outstanding food" from the menu scrawled at the end of the room. "Everything on menu is well-thought-through" and "it's hard to believe they can turn out such consistent brilliance from such a tiny kitchen". / W6 0UR; angleseaarmspub.co.uk; theangleseaarmsw6; Mon-Sun 10 pm.

The Anglesea Arms SW7 £65 2 3 3
15 Selwood Ter 020 7373 7960 6–2B

"Still a great haunt in South Kensington" – in summer the big front terrace of this well-located watering hole is a particular favourite for the kind of West

FSA RATINGS: FROM 1 POOR — 5 EXCEPTIONAL

Londoners who look like they're just back from Bali; and it also has a charming, traditional interior. As pub grub goes, it's "consistently good with decent ales". / SW7 3QG; angleseaarms.com; Mon-Sat 9 pm, Sun 8.30 pm.

AngloThai W1 NEW
22-24 Seymour Place   awaiting tel   2–2A
John & Desiree Chantarasak aim to offer a unique fusion of Thai and British cuisine at this Autumn 2024 newcomer in Marylebone. With 50 covers, it's their first bricks 'n' mortar site following numerous residencies and pop-ups and is backed by the MJMK Restaurants, who have been responsible for a number of high-quality launches in recent times. British-reared meats and biodynamic wines will be a feature. / W1H 7NL; anglothai.co.uk; Mon, Wed & Thu, Sun 10 pm, Fri & Sat 11 pm.

Anima e Cuore NW1   £63   2 2 2
129 Kentish Town Rd   07590 427171   9–2B
This Kentish Town fixture from Calabrian-born, Moroccan-heritage chef Mustapha Mouflih has achieved cult status over the past decade for its "mostly great" Italian cooking served in modest premises at very good prices – the bills held in check by "brilliant BYOB for corkage". Ratings have dropped this year, though, with several reporters "disappointed after reading good reviews". / NW1 8PB; animaecuoreuk; Wed-Sun 10.30 pm.

Annie's W4   £70   3 3 4
162 Thames Rd   020 8994 9080   1–3A
Brunching families by day, couples sipping cocktails by night are drawn to Lorraine Angliss's cute all-day local, which is celebrating its quarter century this year. Key to its appeal is the site – a cosily decorated corner in the picturesque heart of charming Strand-on-the-Green (but with no river views). This was Lorraine's first venture: her empire now includes four other places under the Little Bird and Rock & Rose brands. / W4 3QS; anniesrestaurant.co.uk; anniesrestaurant; Tue-Sat 10 pm, Sun 5 pm.

L'Antica Pizzeria da Michele   £65   4 2 2
44 Old Compton Street, W1   020 7434 4563   5–2A
199 Baker Street, NW1   020 7935 6458   2–1A
"Very, very large… thin-based crust… filled with toppings… excellent tastes" – the pizza satisfies all-comers to this pair of outlets from the veteran Naples operation that became famous through Elizabeth Gilbert's 2006 bestseller 'Eat Pray Love'. The first London outpost, on the tourist beat near Madame Tussauds and Sherlock Holmes in Baker Street, has been joined by a second in Soho. / anticapizzeriadamichele.co.uk; anticapizzeriadamicheleuk.

The Apollo Arms SW4   £69   3 2 3
13-19 Old Town   020 3827 1213   11–1D
This "large" and comfortably appointed pub in Clapham Old Town has made a "great addition to the local scene" since it reopened in 2023 under the team behind Ganymede in Belgravia and The Hunter's Moon in South Kensington. Culinarily, the aim is a 'Contemporary Twist on Traditional British Pub Cuisine', with brunch a feature. / SW4 0JT; apolloarms.co.uk; theapolloarms; Mon-Wed 11 pm, Thu-Sat midnight, Sun 10 pm.

Applebee's Fish SE1   £78   3 2 2
5 Stoney St   020 7407 5777   10–4C
"Amazingly fresh and beautifully cooked fish, plus great chips" is the straightforward offer at this family-run stalwart in the heart of Borough Market, which has plenty of outdoor seating for warmer months. Gripes? "Deserts are a little average". The family also run La Gamba tapas bar along the river at the Festival Hall. / SE1 9AA; applebeesfish.com; applebeesfishlondon; Mon-Thu 10 pm, Fri & Sat 11 pm, Sun 6 pm.

Apricity W1 — £106 — 3 3 3
68 Duke Street   020 8017 2780   3–2A

Chantelle Nicholson and her team work to admirable sustainable and low-waste principles at her Mayfair two-year-old, whose plaster walls, bare tables and "simple" decor are in keeping with its wholesome ethos. The menu celebrates British veg first and foremost, as well as regeneratively farmed meat and sustainably caught fish. All reports acknowledge it as a "friendly" spot with a kitchen that "delivers good results". / W1K 6JU; apricityrestaurant.com; apricityrestaurant; Tue-Sat 9 pm; SRA-3 stars.

Apulia EC1 — £72 — 3 3 3
50 Long Lane   020 7600 8107   10–1B

This "friendly Italian near the Barbican" has a good-sized fan club. It serves "food that is just that little bit different" – "the cooking seems to have taken a step up recently, and the place is often bustling". There's a "great and fairly priced list of Italian wines" – "and do leave room for the puddings". / EC1A 9EJ; apuliarestaurant.co.uk; apuliarestaurant; Mon-Sat 10.30 pm, Sun 9.30 pm.

Aqua Shard SE1 — £121 — 2 2 4
Level 31, 31 St Thomas St   020 3011 1256   10–4C

"The panorama is fantastic", of course, from this 31st-floor roost "at the top of the Shard". Reports from diners here, though, are often presented in terms of pros and cons, with the vista balanced by modern British food that can seem like "an afterthought"; or occasions of "mediocre" service. And to the most cynical, it's a case of "absolute hype and focus upon the view and the supposed glamour, which is actually fairly threadbare under the veneer". / SE1 9RY; aquashard.co.uk; aquashard; Mon-Sun 10.30 pm.

Arabica — £60 — 2 3 3
7 Lewis Cubitt Walk, N1   020 3747 4422   9–3C
3 Rochester Walk, SE1   020 3011 5151   10–4C

One of the success stories of Borough Market – this Levantine operation with an "interesting mix of Middle Eastern food" started out as a simple stall before trading up to a permanent restaurant that gets "very busy at lunchtime". It has a similarly well-rated offshoot in King's Cross. / arabicalondon.com; arabicalondon.

The Araki W1 — £398 — 4 4 2
Unit 4 12 New Burlington St   020 7287 2481   4–3A

When Matsuhiro Araki opened this nine-seat Mayfair venue in 2014, it broke the mould. He set the bar for the new omakase-style revolution that would sweep London; introduced the capital to a £300+ per head price point, which was almost double what anyone else was charging at the time; and became the world's first chef to have won three Michelin stars for a Japanese restaurant in both London and Tokyo. In 2019, he returned to the Far East, leaving his protégé Marty Lau and daughter Manae Araki in charge. The tyre man wasn't happy and removed all three stars in one fell swoop, not even leaving one to remain! Ever since – not helped by a multiplying number of new rivals offering a similar experience – media interest in the place has dwindled, yet each year it has inspired nothing but upbeat feedback in our annual diners' poll. This year is no exception, with (albeit limited) feedback praising "an intimate dining experience with exquisite and fine sushi" – and we've maintained a high rating on that basis. / W1S 3BH; the-araki.co.uk; the_araki_london; Tue-Sat 9 pm.

Arcade Food Hall — £36 — 2 2 2
103-105 New Oxford Street, WC1   020 7519 1202   5–1A
1st Floor, Circus Road South, SW11   11–1C

A "useful pitstop for a quick bite while out in the West End" – this food hall at the foot of Centre Point is, say fans, "so much better than similar places where there's a disorganised queue for food": here, "you order on your phone from your table, and a waiter brings your food from whichever stall you have picked". As for the food, "the variety is great" from some high-quality names, "but the quality is less consistent" – and "the noise can be just too much". Similar feedback too on its year-old, 500-seat sibling at Battersea Power Station, whose 13 different brands "provide great choice but are quite pricey". Backers the all-conquering JKS Restaurants look like they are onto a commercial winner in both places, but (inevitably?) neither site has lived up to the fooderati hype that's accompanied both launches. / arcadefoodhall.com.

Archway SW8 £74 4 4 3
Arch 65, Queen's Circus   020 37811 102   11–1C
Now into its second year, this "neighbourhood restaurant in the most unlikely of places" – a railway arch near Battersea Park – offers a "small and perfect Italianesque/Med menu served by staff who care that you are having a happy time (but without being intrusive)". Chef Alex Owens learnt her trade at the River Café, while owner Emily Few Brown runs the front of house. / SW8 4NE; archwaybattersea.co.uk; archwaybattersea; Wed-Sat 11 pm, Sun 4 pm.

Ark Fish E18 £59 3 2 2
142 Hermon Hill   020 8989 5345   1–1D
"Fine fish" from Billingsgate and "good wine" make for an "excellent fish 'n' chips meal" at this large South Woodford chippy. / E18 1QH; arkfishrestaurant.co.uk; ark_fish_restaurant; Tue-Thu 9.45 pm, Fri & Sat 10.15 pm, Sun 8.45 pm.

Arlington SW1 NEW £101 2 5 5
20 Arlington Street   020 3856 1000   3–4C
"Le Caprice vn 2.0!" – "Welcome back Mr Jeremy King" – "like a phoenix rising from the ashes", this "baby-bum-smooth" brasserie off Piccadilly has been resurrected by its former owner and is "virtually unchanged, except for the name!" The very many old regulars who comment say "it's wonderful to see" this in-crowd haunt "restored to its former glory", and declare "the magic is back!": "it feels just as before with the same, quite ritzy crowd" all packed into a setting that's "smart, sophisticated and comfortable" yet with "tables set close together". And even though legendary maitre d', Jesus Adorno didn't stay long, the service sets "an example of its type of how to do things right". But while most reports are full-on hallelujahs to its reincarnation, there are grumbles amongst a noticeable few that it "feels a bit like a weird time machine": "the food is stuck in the 1980s", when the die for the original menu was cast and "we've had enough of the Bang Bang chicken nostalgia – let's have a more modern menu!". The main sense overall, however? – "It looks and feels like the old Caprice. Hurrah!" / SW1A 1RG; arlingtonrestaurant; Mon-Sat 11 pm, Sun 10 pm.

Arros QD W1 £105 3 3 3
64 Eastcastle Street   020 3883 3525   3–1D
"A joy!" – paella cooked over a wood fire in the Valencian style, "so drier than some you may have had before" – is the headline attraction at this London outpost from superstar Spanish chef Quique Dacosta. But "sublime starters – beef cheeks, Atlantic squid and pork jowl" also really hit the spot on an "unexpected" menu. The location just off Oxford Street does little to attract custom, although it is a "good place to host in the private dining room". / W1W 8NQ; arrosqd.com; arrosqd; Mon-Thu 10.30 pm, Fri & Sat 11 pm, Sun 3.30 pm.

L'Artista NW11 £52 2 2 3
917 Finchley Rd   020 8731 7501   1–1B
For 40 years, this local landmark in Golders Green has inhabited the railway arch by the tube. Its simple pizza and pasta formula still wins recommendations for its "cheap 'n' cheerful" possibilities – especially with kids in tow – but it also gives rise to the odd report of a "very poor and disappointing" experience. / NW11 7PE; lartistapizzeria.com; lartistalondon; Mon-Sun midnight.

FSA

Artusi SE15 £66　3 3 2
161 Bellenden Rd　020 3302 8200　1–4D

After 10 years, this low-key pioneer of the Peckham gastro scene "continues to serve excellent, good-value food" from a curt but interesting Italian menu with two or three options for each course; fans say consistency is high and that you are "never disappointed". It takes its name from 19th-century cookery writer Pellegrino Artusi. / SE15 4DH; artusi.co.uk; artusipeckham; Tue-Thu 9.30 pm, Fri & Sat 10 pm, Sun 4 pm.

Assaggi W2 £121　4 4 2
39 Chepstow Pl　020 7792 5501　7–1B

"A perennial favourite" – Nino Sassu's quirky first-floor venue above a Bayswater pub is now in its 30th year serving "very well executed Italian food (fish is particularly good)". If it no longer excites the fooderati as it once did, reporters still extol the "warm welcome" of an "airy room with no music, just the pleasant murmur of fellow diners enjoying their food and conversation". / W2 4TS; assaggi.co.uk; assagginottinghill; Tue-Sat 9.30 pm.

L'Atelier Robuchon W1 £141　2 3 2
6 Clarges Street　020 8076 0570　3–4C

Part of the luxe international chain of the star French chef, who passed away five years ago: this Mayfair yearling took over the site of the more casual 'Comptoir Robuchon' and is a return to London for the 'Atelier' brand (whose former incarnation in Covent Garden closed five years ago). "The recent refurbishment has made the room much easier on the eye" and "it's great to watch the immense care given to cooking even a humble dish" by the assembled brigade. Most reports, though, focus on value with a widespread feeling that "while the food is good, it is very expensive for what you get". Perhaps the recent appointment of chef Qassim Bouhassoun will zhoosh it up a bit. / W1J 8AE; robuchonlondon.co.uk; latelierrobuchonmayfair; Mon-Sat 10.30 pm, Sun 9.45 pm.

The Atlas SW6 £59　3 4 4
16 Seagrave Rd　020 7385 9129　6–3A

One of London's earlier-wave of gastropubs, this "great local" can still feel like a discovery down a side street near West Brompton tube, despite being increasingly surrounded by the shiny new blocks built in the area. The Med-inspired cuisine remains a cut above. In summer "the terrace is fantastic in the sunshine" and its cosy interior is just the job on a cold day. / SW6 1RX; theatlaspub.co.uk; theatlaspub; Mon-Sat 9.30 pm, Sun 8.30 pm.

The Audley W1 £60　3 3 3
43 Mount Street　020 3840 9862　3–3A

Artfully restored by ArtFarm (the hospitality wing of the Hauser + Wirth Swiss art dealership), this wood-panelled and appropriately art-stuffed pub is celebrating its second year as a "quality local"; and although it's in the beating heart of 'Mayfair Village', it's not a bad value one either, with "lovely" service and "really good pub food" (even if the menu doesn't stretch much beyond Scotch eggs, sausages, shepherd's pie and the like). Upstairs is the Mount Street Restaurant (see also) and there are event spaces on the upper floors. / W1K 3AH; theaudleypublichouse.com; Audleypublichouse; Mon-Fri 11.30 pm, Sat midnight, Sun 10.30 pm.

Audrey Green WC2 £35　3 2 3
National Portrait Gallery, St Martin's Place　020 3822 0246　2–2C

"Decent coffee and breakfast options" are the pick of the offerings at the revamped NPG's new all-day café from the Aussie chain Daisy Green. Downstairs is Larry's Bar, a useful night-time spot for cocktails and small plates. / WC2H 0HE; npg.org.uk; nationalportraitgallery; Sun-Thu 5.30 pm, Fri & Sat 7 pm.

FSA RATINGS: FROM 1 POOR — 5 EXCEPTIONAL

F S A

Augustine Kitchen SW11 — £71 — 4 3 3
63 Battersea Bridge Rd   020 7978 7085   6–4C

"This hidden French gem" – "on Battersea Bridge Road of all places" – "doesn't look like much from outside, but the food is marvellous". Patron Franck Raymond "exceeds expectations" with cuisine from his hometown of Evian in the French Alps, served in a "modest" but "calm and civilised" setting. / SW11 3AU; augustine-kitchen.co.uk; augustines11; Tue-Sat 9 pm.

Aulis London W1 — £237 — 5 4 3
16a St Anne's Court   020 3948 9665   4–1D

"Wow factor = 10/10 – it's an incredible experience". This chef's table and development kitchen in a Soho alleyway is "the place to go for a taste of Simon Rogan's excellent and inventive cuisine" and does justice to the renown of his renowned Michelin three star HQ, L'Enclume, far away in the Lake District. "The decor was improved" in 2023 and you are served at a curved counter with 12 seats. Service is "very friendly" and you eat from a tasting menu designed by executive chef Oli Marlow and head chef Charlie Tayler for £185 per person, with much of the produce sourced from 'Our Farm' – Simon's business in the lakes. Practically all reports rate the culinary results as "exceptional". / W1F 0BF; aulis.london; aulissimonrogan; Tue-Sat 11 pm.

Avanti W4 — £54 — 3 3 4
South Parade   020 8994 9444   8–2A

"Excellent tapas, half a dozen paellas and good pizza as well" make this "homespun" local by Chiswick's Bedford Park a "pleasant but simple place to eat". It's "very good value", with an attractive terrace for warmer months. / W4 1LD; avantichiswick.com; avantichiswick; Mon-Sun 10 pm.

Ave Mario WC2 — £69 — 3 4 3
15 Henrietta Street   07933 624393   5–3C

"Mad but fun, and actually with pretty decent food" sums up the general view of this vast and operatic mock-Italian in Covent Garden from the Paris-based Big Mama group, which majors mostly in pizza and pasta. It's "definitely aimed at Instagrammers" and "groups of youngsters having fun" – but while it's "seriously over-hyped", at least that means nobody goes without knowing what they're in for. / WC2E 8QG; bigmammagroup.com; bigmamma.uk; Sun-Wed 10.30 pm, Thu-Sat 10.45 pm.

L'Aventure NW8 — £82 — 4 3 3
3 Blenheim Terrace   020 7624 6232   9–3A

La Patronne, Catherine Parisot, was just in her twenties when she started this "lovely" old-fashioned charmer in St John's Wood and has run it for over 43 years now. A very loyal clientele from all over London has discovered it over the years, and for them it's a huge "favourite" that's particularly "perfect for evenings 'à deux'". Her classic 'cuisine bourgeoise' is "old-fashioned French cooking at its best (you would struggle to match it in France)"; and features "a number of staples on the menu that have been on forever (her pea soup is unbeatable!"). Its ratings no longer scale the pinnacles they did some years ago, but the overall tenor of reports remains overwhelmingly positive: "so French, perfect food, perfect service, I love it!" / NW8 0EH; laventure.co.uk; Mon-Sat 11 pm.

Awesome Thai SW13 — £42 — 3 3 2
68 Church Rd   020 8563 7027   11–1A

"Deservedly popular Thai local with welcoming staff and very tasty (if not exactly distinguished) cooking", which opened a few years ago opposite the Olympic Cinema in Barnes. No reports on its Finchley sibling, but TripAdvisor says it's one of London's best! / SW13 0DQ; awesomethai.co.uk; Mon-Sat 10.30 pm, Sun 10 pm.

FSA RATINGS: FROM 1 POOR — 5 EXCEPTIONAL

Azzurra SW1 NEW £130
127-128 Sloane Street   020 3953 5838   6–1D
The ground floor unit of a new development north of Sloane Square, this new arrival opened in autumn 2023 courtesy of Hong Kong's Aqua group (best known for Hutong in the Shard). The inspiration, apparently, is the Amalfi coast and Sicily, although its glossy modern styling would be equally at home in Dubai or Singapore. Chelsea is not short of Italian restaurants – perhaps why despite its size and prominent location it has yet to inspire much in the way of survey feedback? / SW1X 9AS; azzurrarestaurant.co.uk; azzurrarestaurant; Sun-Wed 10 pm, Thu-Sat 10.30 pm.

Babur SE23 £63 5 4 3
119 Brockley Rise   020 8291 2400   1–4D
"Love having such a unique Indian locally" – this *"culinary stalwart of South East London is still going strong after nearly 40 years"*. *"Staff welcome you like an old friend"* and chef Jiwan Lal's cuisine is *"at least as good as that of the West End's fine dining establishments"*, in the view of many locals; and *"magnificent value for this level of cooking"*. Top Tip – *"good value buffet on the weekends"*. / SE23 1JP; babur.info; baburrestaurant; Mon-Sat 11 pm, Sun 10.30 pm.

Bacchanalia W1 £189 1 2 3
1 Mount Street   020 3161 9720   3–2B
"Is it where the vulgar go to look at each other?" – Richard Caring wasn't looking to please the good taste committee with his *"far OTT"* Mayfair scene, where staff clad in togas, winged statues and muralled nymphs overlooking the large dining room make it all a bit like a luxurious Mayfair production of 'Carry on Cleo'. The menu is a romp through a hotchpotch of Med-inspired crudo, seafood dishes, pasta – even schnitzel! – and if you aren't spending enough already, the menu encourages you to 'elevate your dish with… a decadent addition': meaning extra caviar or black truffle is available to sprinkle on all items. One fan recommends it for its romantic potential (*"the ladies enjoy dining here"*) but almost half of our feedback registers *"disappointment"*, so it would very much depend on the tastes of your dining companion… / W1K 3NA; bacchanalia.co.uk; bacchanalialdn; Mon-Sat 12.30 am, Sun midnight.

Bacco TW9 £76 3 2 2
39-41 Kew Rd   020 8332 0348   1–4A
Tipped as a "top venue for a pre-theatre meal (Richmond Theatre and Orange Tree nearby)", this longstanding Italian restaurant near the station combines "well-cooked food, kindly service" and a "very good wine list, at reasonable prices". / TW9 2NQ; bacco-restaurant.co.uk; Mon-Sat 9.30 pm.

Bageriet WC2 £21 3 2 2
24 Rose St   020 7240 0000   5–3C
Down a cute Covent Garden alley, this tiny Scandi café with a handful of seats outside in summer is sweet in more ways than one: "the renowned Princess Tarta is criminally delicious and can be personalised to order… 100% authentic too!" / WC2E 9EA; bageriet.co.uk; bageriet_london; Mon-Fri 6.30 pm, Sat 6 pm.

Bala Baya SE1 £74 4 4 4
Old Union Yard Arches, 229 Union Street   020 8001 7015   10–4B
"A really interesting menu" of *"modern Israeli food"* (including *"loads for veggies"*) is found at this lively railway arch venue on the South Bank from ex-Ottolenghi chef Eran Tibi – *"highly recommended"*. Top Menu Tip – *"the dumplings with date jus are fantastic"*. / SE1 0LR; balabaya.co.uk; bala_baya; Mon-Sun 11 pm.

F S A

Balham Social SW12   **£41**   3|3|3
2 Station Parade Road, Balham High Road   020 4529 8222   11–2C
"A heady mix of cocktails and curry, with friendly and informative staff" – this contemporary Indian on the site of former Balham favourite Lamberts (RIP) operates as a café by day but is "noisily popular in the evening", when it serves for "very good dishes with a modern and innovative twist on Indian favourites" in "an attractively decorated setting". / SW12 9AZ; balhamsocial.com; balham.social; Mon-Thu 10.30 pm, Fri & Sat 11 pm, Sun 10 pm.

Balthazar WC2   **£85**   1|2|3
4-6 Russell Street   020 3301 1155   5–3D
This "big, buzzy faux-Parisian brasserie" in the heart of Covent Garden certainly looks the part, but it "can get very busy" and "extremely noisy" as a result. It provides "lots of classic French cuisine", but with very mixed results: fans say it's "executed pretty well" but reviews overall are often jaundiced – for example: "dull food, impossible to chat… really bad experience and a ridiculous bill". / WC2B 5HZ; balthazarlondon.com; balthazarldn; Mon-Sat 10.45 pm, Sun 9.45 pm.

Baluchi,
Lalit Hotel London SE1   **£86**   3|3|3
181 Tooley St   020 3765 0000   10–4D
"The food is served with a bit of theatre" in this splendid old school hall not far south of Tower Bridge (Grade II listed and part of what was once St. Olave's Grammar School) – nowadays a contemporary Indian venue that's part of Lalit Hotel Group's flagship UK property. It's consistently well-reviewed in our annual diners' poll, but at less busy times can seem "quiet". / SE1 2JR; thelalit.com; TheLalitLondon; Mon-Sun 10 pm.

Bancone   **£60**   2|2|2
10 Lower James Street, W1   020 3034 0820   4–3C
39 William IV Street, WC2   020 7240 8786   5–4C
Borough Yards, Stoney Street, SE1   020 3034 1229   10–4C
"Delicious pasta at relatively affordable prices" inspires major loyalty to these "busy" pasta pitstops in Soho, near Trafalgar Square and in Borough Yards: for their legions of fans, "a staple option for a quick meal in London", even if "the narrow WC2 branch in particular is tight for space and can feel a little crowded and noisy". The experience, though, can tip into just feeling "rushed", "unimpressive" or "hyped", not least due to the "hit 'n' miss service". Top Menu Tips – "obviously the 'silk handkerchiefs' are best"; "Cacio Pepe is like you'll never find outside Rome at an unbelievable price". / bancone.co.uk; bancone.pasta.

Bang Bang Oriental NW9   **£55**   3|2|2
399 Edgware Road   no tel   1–1A
"If you're talking street food, then just go along and take it all in!" – this vast Oriental food court in Colindale offers "20+ options, huge flavours and huge portions". It's "so much fun" but can be "hit and miss between the different units" – and watch the prices as "certain dishes are more expensive than in the Golden Dragon restaurant downstairs". Top Tip – "bring Tupperware to take any left-over food home". / NW9 0AS; bangbangoriental.com; bangbangoriental; Sun-Thu 9.30 pm, Fri & Sat 10 pm.

Bao   **£41**   4|3|3
53 Lexington St, W1   07769 627811   4–2C
56 James Street, W1   no tel   3–1A
4 Pancras Square, N1   no tel   9–3C
13 Stoney Street, SE1   020 3967 5407   10–4C
Battersea Power Station, SW11   no tel   11–1C
1 Redchurch Street, E2   no tel   13–1B
"Eat in or take out, these buns are delicious" – the universally agreed take on this Taiwanese street-food operation founded 13 years ago by Shing Tat, his

wife Erchen Chang and sister Wai Ting Chung, now with six sites across the capital and part of the JKS Restaurants group. The "good-value" filled steamed buns "really make you want to go back" – "I called in 3 times in the same afternoon!" – while "the noodles are fab, too". The only real complaint concerns the settings, with some branches "far too cramped" given their popularity. / baolondon.com; bao_london.

Baozi Inn £38 3 2 2
24 Romilly Street, W1 020 7287 3266 5–3A
34-36 Southwark Street, SE1 020 8037 5875 10–4C
"Brilliant, lip-numbing" northern Chinese cooking has put this Soho fixture from Wei Shao firmly on the map, and it serves a flexible menu of skewers, noodles and rice, wok dishes and other dim sum options. Some feel its Borough Market offshoot is "weak" by comparison ("it's as if the Soho one benefits from the proximity of Chinatown but they don't expect anyone with any discernment in SE1!"). / baoziinn.com.

Bar D4100 SE15 £30 4 3 3
143 Evelina Road no tel 1–4D
"Top pizza and panuozzo with nice drinks" (from wines or slushy cocktails to pints for a fiver) put the crowd in a fun and easygoing frame of mind at this "relaxed and funky" little bar in Nunhead. (Their pizza is also a feature in The Perseverance pub in Bloomsbury). / SE15 3HB; dinnerforonehundred.com; Mon-Sun 11 pm.

Bar des Prés W1 £132 4 4 3
16 Albemarle Street 020 3908 2000 3–3C
"Superb!" Saint Germain comes to Mayfair at TV-chef Cyril Lignac's luxurious three-year-old, which – like his original Parisian venture – offers "the fusion of Japanese food with French expertise". In practice that means a selection of raw seafood; sushi and sashimi; salads; and Asian-inflected seafood mains, with the odd tidbit for meat-eaters such as Wagyu sando; all followed by French desserts. It took brickbats last year for seeming "fancy" and "flash", but this year inspired little but praise for "top-quality dishes". And "it's great fun to watch the guys behind the bar" all adding to the "excellent dining experience". / W1S 4HW; bardespres.com; bardespres; Mon-Sat 11 pm, Sun 10 pm.

Bar Douro SE1 £56 3 3 4
Arch 35b, 85b Southwark Bridge Rd 020 7378 0524 10–4B
This "hip, buzzy under-arch venue with counter seating" and distinctive blue-and-white tiling, near Borough Market, showcases "really interesting" wines and tapas-style dishes from Portugal. Founder Max Graham, from the Churchill port family, also has a second branch in the City in Finsbury Avenue Square, although this inspires no feedback (and is not listed). / SE1 0NQ; bardouro.co.uk; bardouro; Tue-Sat 10 pm, Sun 9 pm.

Bar Esteban N8 £67 3 2 3
29 Park Rd 020 8340 3090 1–1C
This "enjoyable tapas" bar in Crouch End (sibling to Stokie's Escocesa, see also) is suitably "cramped and authentic", and for a dozen years has been "a handy spot to have on the doorstep, with a very good Spanish wine list, mostly available by the glass". 'Esteban' was founded by Stephen Lironi, a Glasgow-born music producer, backed here by Spanish duo chef Pablo Rodriguez and manager Naroa Ortega. No complaints about the quality, although "the menu rarely changes". / N8 8TE; baresteban.com; bar__esteban; Tue-Thu 10 pm, Fri & Sat 11 pm.

Bar Italia W1 £45 2 3 5
22 Frith St 020 7437 4520 5–2A
"A real sense of being a little part of history in London" – with a side order of "proper cannoli and great coffee" – is the prime attraction of this "excellent"

24/7 coffee bar, an all-but-unique survivor of post-War Soho, founded in 1949 by the Polledri family who remain committed to its legacy. / W1D 4RF; baritaliasoho.co.uk; baritaliasoho; Mon-Sun 4 am.

The Barbary £83 5 4 4
16 Neal's Yard, WC2   no tel   5–2C
112 Westbourne Grove, W2   020 7870 5659   7–1B **NEW**
"Superb North African food is served in this dimly lit, bustly counter-style restaurant with bags of ambience" in Neal's Yard, Soho, opened in 2016 by Leyo and Zoe Paskin as a follow-up to their nearby hit Palomar: "the hype is fully justified" (although "the fixed bar seating can be mightily uncomfortable if you're tall"). And in September 2024 they are to expand to the Notting Hill/Bayswater border, with a 75-cover restaurant newcomer in a Grade II listed building on the corner of Westbourne Grove and Chepstow Road: it will feature a take on the popular kitchen counter format, in addition to an open-plan dining room and a cocktail bar.

The Barbary Next Door WC2 £52 4 4 2
16a Neal's Yard   no tel   5–2C
This "friendly", quirky counter bar sits on Neal's Yard, right next to The Barbary (see also). It's a tiny chip off the old block, serving Spanish and North African food washed down with a selection of beers, wine and cocktails: "amazing flavours in every dish and there's a great relaxed ambience". / WC2H 9DP; thebarbarynextdoor.co.uk; thebarbarynextdoor; Mon-Fri 10 pm, Sat 11 pm, Sun 2.30 pm.

Barbican Brasserie,
Barbican Centre (fka Osteria) EC2 £60 2 3 2
Level 2 Silk Street   020 7588 3008   10–1B
At the heart of the brutalist Barbican complex (with views of the internal lake) this arts-centre amenity is, fans say, "a better-than-you'd expect place": "a nice restaurant with good service and a range of choices to suit most tastes". Possibly this is true, but, arguably, this is also an indictment of the modest level of expectations of most Britons towards their institutions and top caterers (in this case, Searcy's). / EC2Y 8DS; osterialondon.co.uk; SearcysLondon; Mon-Wed, Sat 7 pm, Thu & Fri 9 pm.

La Barca SE1 £92 3 3 3
80-81 Lower Marsh   020 7928 2226   10–4A
This "classic" Italian with landmark status at the back of Waterloo station notches up its half-century this year, still knocking out a traditional menu with a good helping of old-school pizzazz (steak diane flambéed at your table!). "It looks unassuming from the outside, but the cooking will surprise you" (albeit the bill might too…). Top Menu Tip – "their alla Barca seafood spaghetti is delicious". / SE1 7AB; labarca-ristorante.com; labarca1976; Mon-Sat 10.30 pm.

Barge East E9 £68 3 3 4
Sweetwater Mooring, White Post Lane   020 3026 2807   14–1D
"A great summer spot with friends": this 120-year-old barge is permanently moored in Hackney Wick – near the Queen Elizabeth Olympic Park – and provides a "fabulous experience on the water that makes for a great fun night out". One reporter did quibble about the prices, but still said: "I loved our meal here – the concept is brilliant, with the interior of the barge turned into a cheerful dining room, and unusual dishes based on fish and foods grown in a kitchen garden by the mooring". / E9 5EN; bargeeast.com; bargeeast; Wed, Fri & Sat, Thu 11.30 pm, Sun 8 pm.

The Baring N1 £87 4 3 3
55 Baring Street   020 7359 5785   14–2A
This "buzzy pub" near the Regent's canal in Islington has a "brilliant" culinary reputation since it relaunched two years ago. "They take great care

to offer seasonal, fresh food cooked with real imagination and flair, but always reassuringly familiar" ("so good, I actually laughed!"). "Well-chosen wines", a "superb Sunday lunch", "no-frills good service" and a "dog-friendly approach, too" complete the deal. / N1 3DS; thebaring.co.uk; thebaring; Tue-Sat 9.30 pm, Sun 4 pm.

The Barley Mow W1 £99 233
82 Duke Street 020 4553 1414 3–2A

With its parquet floors and white Edwardian-style tiling behind the bar, this Mayfair boozer has undergone a fine restoration by the Cubitt House group. For a civilised pub meal in a pricey bit of town it's worth remembering – "the ground floor bar is fine for beer and pub snacks, but it is the more cosy upstairs dining room where the menu showcases seasonal British dishes" with a 'decadent French' twist from chef Chris Fordham-Smith. / W1K 6JG; cubitthouse.co.uk; cubitthouse; Mon-Sat 9.30 pm, Sun 8 pm; SRA-1 star.

Barrafina £70 443
26-27 Dean Street, W1 020 7813 8016 4–1D
10 Adelaide St, WC2 020 7440 1456 5–4C
43 Drury Lane, WC2 020 7440 1456 5–2D
Coal Drops Yard, N1 0207 440 1486 9–3C
2 Dirty Lane, SE1 020 7440 1486 10–4C

"Counter seats are the best" at the Hart Bros' "magical slice of Spain" – a "joyful" and thriving homage to Barcelona's famous Cal Pep, which since its 2007 launch has steadily appeared near the top of our annual diners' poll as one of London's most popular restaurant groups. Its branches have multiplied, but – to a miraculous extent – the formula has stayed the same. "At the bar, it's fun to watch the talented staff who were clearly enjoying their jobs, meticulously preparing the outstanding dishes": "brilliant small plates, with plenty of choice" and "packed with authentic flavours" ("particularly strong on fish and seafood"); plus "an excellent range of sherries" and wines. But, while it's maintained "impressive consistency over many years", it can feel "like a bar experience at restaurant prices" nowadays, and its ratings drifted south of their usual peaks this year. There's also the odd tale of caution in reports: "I've been almost every year since it opened. It's still great fun and pretty good, but the last three visits have fallen below the super-high quality of the past". Top Menu Tips – "love the Croquetes; the Cos salad with anchovy and crispy pancetta; and perfectly unctuous Tortilla". / barrafina.co.uk.

Barshu W1 £75 532
28 Frith St 020 7287 6688 5–3A

"Sublime" and "well-executed Sichuan dishes in all their spiciness" ("crazy Chinese cooking like I've never experienced anywhere else!") make this "a sensational go-to" foodie destination for its many long-term fans (who reckon it's "back to late-noughties form"). The decor is relatively "soothing" by the standards of the area, with no agreement over whether sitting upstairs or downstairs is best. / W1D 5LF; barshurestaurant.co.uk; barshurestaurant; Sun-Thu 10 pm, Fri & Sat 10.30 pm.

Base Face Pizza W6 £41 452
300 King Street 020 8617 1092 8–2B

"The slow-rise sourdough bases are like nothing ever tasted before" – this "small and friendly" three-year-old Hammersmith independent now has spinoffs in Barnes and Putney, and serves "unusual and unusually good pizza". Founder Tim Thornton is a jazz bassist whose lockdown project – baking pizzas to raise funds for the NHS – took over his life. "I went all the way to Naples and had what was supposed to be 'the best pizza in town', and I'm not sure it was any better than at Base Face!" / W6 0RR; basefacepizza.com; base.face.pizza; Tue-Sun 10 pm.

F S A

Baudry Greene WC2 NEW £68 3 4 4
20 Endell Street   no tel   5–2C
"A great new addition to Covent Garden as a 'cafe-bar', especially given the increased tendency to have groups that are a mix of drinkers and non-drinkers" – this Continental-style café is close to the Royal Opera House and brought to us by the team behind 10 Cases wine bar and Parsons fish restaurant in the same street. Breakfast features a Bavarian spread; there are high-quality salads and sandwiches for lunch; and in the evening savoury and sweet snacks accompany wine and cocktails. *"It gives everyone options and feels like a good balance of acting casual yet feeling luxurious and special"*. / WC2H 9BD; baudrygreene.co.uk; baudrygreene; Mon-Sat 10 pm.

Bayleaf N20 £26 3 3 3
1282 High Road   020 8446 8671   1–1B
This *"excellent high-end Indian restaurant"* in Whetstone has earned a more-than-local reputation for its *"imaginative cooking and great service"* in recent years, having started out as a takeaway. / N20 9HH; bayleaf.co.uk; bayleafofficial; Mon-Sun 10 pm.

The Bear SE5 NEW
296A Camberwell New Road   020 3015 5168   1–3C
Camberwell's gentrification continues apace with this revamped, classic neighbourhood boozer – brought back to life after being closed for six years. The tucked-away dining area showcases the talents of chef Joe Sharratt, formerly of Brixton hotspot Naughty Piglets, and seating possibilities include a counter next to the kitchen. No survey feedback as yet, but in his April 2024 review, The Evening Standard's Jimi Famurewa thought that – while some dishes *"did not work"* – other small plates were *"thrilling"*. / SE5 0RP; thebearcamberwell.com; Tue-Thu midnight, Fri & Sat 1 am, Sun 10 pm.

Le Beaujolais WC2 £65 2 2 4
25 Litchfield Street   020 7836 2955   5–3B
"Just off Cambridge Circus", this *"little piece of France in the centre of London"* dates from 1972 and hasn't changed much in the interim. *"Great-value wines and simple dishes"* are the draw: the latter might be Boeuf Bourguignon or Saucisses de Toulouse or one of a fine selection of cheeses. There's also a *"private members' restaurant downstairs"*. Anyone interested in gastronomy should probably head elsewhere, but for old-school character at affordable prices it's a big hit. / WC2H 9NJ; lebeaujolais.london; Sun & Mon 9.45 pm, Tue-Sat 10.45 pm.

Bébé Bob W1 NEW £62 3 4 4
37 Golden Square   020 7242 1000   4–2B
Open in September 2023 in Soho's Golden Square – this glam diner is a 'junior' offshoot of Deco-style Bob Bob Ricard nearby. Cut from a similar, amusingly OTT cloth, it follows the current fashion for rotisserie chicken (although – as at its sibling – there's plenty of caviar, blinis and Champagne on the menu, too). It can seem pricey, but otherwise is consistently well reviewed (and is memorably described by The Guardian's Grace Dent as *"boss-level KFC"* in her January 2024 critique). / W1F 9LB; bebebob.com; bebebob; Tue-Sat 11.30 pm.

Behind E8 £151 5 5 4
20 Sidworth Street   no tel   14–2B
"Epic!" – *"Andy Beynon and his team are so welcoming"* and deliver an *"absolutely amazing"* tasting menu experience at this funky-looking and *"super-stylish"* venue in Hackney (near London Fields). *"You sit at a long, curvaceous, blonde-wooden counter, and service is by the whole kitchen team who are clearly passionate about what they're doing"*. The menu revolves around *"inventive fish dishes"* from *"quality produce"* that are *"stuffed with*

really bold flavours". Top Menu Tip – "loved the aged trout with smoked beurre-blanc. Raw red prawn with prawn head and Riesling sauce. Loved it all". / E8 3SD; behindrestaurant.co.uk; behindrestaurant; Wed-Sat 11 pm.

Bellamy's W1 £81   3 4 4
18-18a Bruton Place   020 7491 2727   3–2B

"If it was good enough for Queen Elizabeth II, it's good enough for the rest of us!" – Gavin Rankin's "very civilised, old school" brasserie in a cute Mayfair mews has a "lovely old-fashioned vibe" (and was one of the few restaurants in the UK in which the late Queen ever ate out). "Peaceful and very enjoyable", it's one of those rare dining rooms where jacket and tie are still the norm (although the dress code is an unwritten one). Staff are "utterly professional" and "predictably discreet". "Start an evening with cocktails at the bar (next to the restaurant)" and then move next door for "classic French cuisine" that's "lovely" but won't scare the horses. Top Tip – "the counter bar is also a great spot in which to have a posh fish finger sandwich!" / W1J 6LY; bellamysrestaurant.co.uk; bellamysmayfair; Mon-Sat 10.30 pm.

Bellanger N1 £59   1 2 3
9 Islington Green   020 7226 2555   9–3D

"I used to be a regular, now I'm so sad". The June 2023 reformatting of this "very handsome-looking" Wolseley Group outpost on Islington Green (which had closed in 2019 and then reopened in 2020 after failing to sell the site) is not going well. It's a large site, evoking a fin-de-siecle Parisian haunt with a "newish design that's pleasant enough" and a fairly traditional, French brasserie-style menu. For too many, though, "since reopening after a further refresh results are dire". One reporter neatly summarises the mood: "This is written with huge sadness, as it was my favourite place for nearly any occasion in the Corbin & King days. Now it feels like a Café Rouge, with a cynical and over-priced menu and average service (I really feel for the staff, a lot of whom were there in the good old days). What a waste, and what a loss for Upper Street: it was such a godsend to have a grown-up restaurant in the area when it first opened, and then reopened". / N1 2XH; bellanger.co.uk; bellanger_n1; Mon-Sat 10 pm, Sun 9 pm.

Bellazul W1 £75   3 4 3
43 Blandford Street   020 7486 7340   3–1A

A "lively Mediterranean newcomer" which aims to import a little southern European sparkle to Marylebone. "Dishes range from simple pizzas to sophisticated options", with inspiration taken from Morocco to Greece and "the watchword is good-quality raw materials, well cooked". One reporter found it "a bit soulless on the lower ground floor but with good ground level and pavement tables". / W1U 7HF; /bellazulw1/; Mon-Sun 11 pm.

Belvedere W8 £78   2 2 4
off Abbotsbury Rd in Holland Park   020 7602 1238   8–1D

This gorgeous, seventeenth-century former aristocrats' ballroom has a stunning location – actually within Holland Park – but has defied various previous attempts to create a successful restaurant. And, two years on, it remains unclear whether George Bukhov-Weinstein and Ilya Demichev – the duo behind Goodman, Burger & Lobster and Wild Tavern – have done better, despite their lavish revamp. Even one reporter "very pleasantly surprised by the quality of the food" thought it "pricey". More common are those who find it "mediocre in every respect, apart from the beautiful setting" or say it's "just toooo expensive". / W8 6LU; belvedererestaurant.co.uk; belvedere_holland_park; Tue-Fri midnight, Sat 12.30 am, Sun 10.30 pm.

Benares W1 £96   4 4 3
12a Berkeley Square House,   020 7629 8886   3–3B

"Really classy Indian food with a modern twist" from head chef Sameer Taneja is "professionally served" at this Mayfair luminary, which remains near the "top of the pile" as one of the UK's best known and most respected 'nouvelle Indians'. It occupies a "large" first-floor space on Berkeley Square, and the setting gives a very stylish and sophisticated impression, well-suited to a special occasion. Top Tip – "superb tasting menu". / W1J 6BS; benaresrestaurant.co.uk; benaresofficial; Mon-Sat 10.30 pm, Sun 9.30 pm.

Bentley's W1 £106 3 4 4
11-15 Swallow St   020 7734 4756   4–4B

"I love Bentley's!" – "You always come away happy and well fed" from Richard Corrigan's carefully nurtured institution, which has a "lovely, old school feel that's not too formal"; and which celebrates its 108th year in 2024. "Choose upstairs or down depending on your preferred level of formality": "downstairs is jollier" – "the Oyster bar is an absolute favourite" – while "upstairs is more calm and quiet". In both locations, you can enjoy "consistently great" fish and seafood prepared in a traditional style. And in summer, the "gorgeous", big, heated terrace on the pavement outside comes into its own. Personable service is "attentive", but "you are left in peace" when required and this is a "great and reliable central London business choice". Top Menu Tip – "the dressed crab here is the best in town"; "wonderful oysters, and the specials are always worth checking out". / W1B 4DG; bentleys.org; bentleysoysterbar; Mon-Sat 9.45 pm, Sun 9 pm.

Berber & Q £67 4 4 2
Arch 338 Acton Mews, E8   020 7923 0829   14–2A
Exmouth Market, EC1   020 7837 1726   10–1A

"Sublimely executed feelgood nosh of the highest charcoal-grilled order" has attracted a "devoted fan base" for this Middle East/North Africa-inspired grill in a Haggerston railway arch, and its shawarma bar spinoff in Exmouth Market. Ten years on, its feedback – though consistently excellent – no longer scales the hyper-dizzying peaks it once did, perhaps because founder Josh Katz is increasingly focused on his newer, multi-site project, Carmel (see also). / berberandq.com; berberandq.

Berbere Pizza NW5 £45 3 3 2
300 Kentish Town Road   020 3417 7130   9–2C

A "top selection" of "authentic and unfussy" sourdough pizzas (made daily on site and proofed for 24 hours) with "interesting and tasty" toppings wins a thumbs up from north London fans of this "buzzy" two-year-old in Kentish Town. Along with a Clapham branch, it is the London outpost of a sizable Bologna-based group. / NW5 2TG; berberepizzeria.co.uk; berberepizzeria_ldn; Sun-Thu 10 pm, Fri & Sat 10.30 pm.

Berenjak £66 5 4 4
27 Romilly Street, W1   020 3319 8120   5–2A
1 Bedale Street, SE1   020 3011 1021   10–4C

Kian Samyani delivers "a flavour tsunami" – "huge portions" of "delicious and unusual" dishes inspired by the hole-in-the-wall kebab shops of Tehran – at his six-year-old Soho flagship, now backed by JKS Restaurants and with branches in Borough Market, Oxfordshire's Soho Farmhouse, Dubai and Sharjah. "They hardly miss a beat" on the food front – "perhaps the starters edge the mains" – while "attentive service" and "great atmosphere" also win praise. / berenjaklondon.com; berenjaklondon.

The Berners Tavern, London EDITION W1 £115 3 4 5
10 Berners Street   020 7908 7979   3–1D

"For first timers, the room [a converted banking hall] remains one of – if not the most – dramatic dining room in London and possibly the UK" at this Ian Shrager-designed hotel north of Oxford Street. Jason Atherton's smart brasserie cuisine more than holds its own nowadays, too, and it's a hit with expense-accounters as well as those on a big night out: "come for the business meeting, stay for the mac 'n' cheese and wine list – always a treat!". / W1T 3NP; editionhotels.com; bernerstavern; Mon-Sun 10 pm.

Best Mangal £53 3|3|3
619 Fulham Rd, SW6   020 7610 0009   6–4A
104 North End Rd, W14   020 7610 1050   8–2D
"Great Turkish food – either to eat in or take away" has earned a more-than-local reputation for this pair of Anatolian charcoal BBQs, on Fulham Broadway and near West Kensington station. (Note, 'Best Mangal 1996' in North End Road is a separate business). / bestmangal.com.

Bibendum SW3 £232 3|3|3
81 Fulham Rd   020 7589 1480   6–2C
"A superb location in the temple of Michelin House" – this famous destination occupies a space originally created by the late Sir Terence Conran in 1987 and was, in its time, an icon of London's restaurant renaissance. As a design classic, it can have an "amazing ambience" – particularly at lunch when it is lovely and light-filled – but strike unlucky and the space can also seem oddly characterless. Chef Claude Bosi has staged his own culinary renaissance here since 2017 and his intricate (some would say "over fussy") modern French cuisine has won the place an impressive two Michelin stars. But buoyed by such acclaim, prices have risen to a level that a very high proportion of reporters in our annual diners' poll now consider excessive, and – though its ratings are solid – enthusiasm for the place was muted in the commentary we received this year. / SW3 6RD; claudebosi.com; claudebosiatbibendum; Tue-Sat 9.30 pm.

Bibendum Oyster Bar SW3 £89 3|4|4
Michelin House, 81 Fulham Road   020 7581 5817   6–2C
Claude Bosi's "casual chic" alternative to his flagship upstairs occupies the foyer of the iconic Michelin Building on Brompton Cross and also aims to provide "superb food and the very best service", but in a more dressed-down manner to the mothership upstairs. Under Claude, the offering has expanded considerably from the old days when it only provided cold oysters, crab and other 'fruits de mer' – there's now an extensive menu incorporating hot fish mains and they'll even grill you a steak. Top Tip – "it's particularly enjoyable amongst the lush floral display in the front courtyard in warmer weather". / SW3 6RD; claudebosi.com; claudebosiatbibendum; Wed-Sat, Mon & Tue 9.30 pm.

BiBi W1 £93 5|4|3
42 North Audley Street   020 3780 7310   3–2A
"Sitting at the highly stylish open-kitchen counter of this Mayfair Indian is a wonderful experience" and often recommended as the best way to enjoy the "aromatic, exciting and intricate tasting menu" here, from chef Chet Sharma (the Chef's Selection is the only option in the evening; at lunchtimes there is also an à la carte menu). It's yet another hit from the formidable JKS Restaurants stable, and provides arguably "the best sophisticated Indian dining in town", outscoring both its stablemates Gymkhana and Trishna in our annual diners' poll… so "how it doesn't have a Michelin star, we just don't know". Top Tip – "The music and buzz made it impossible to hear the dishes being introduced, so please note that this isn't a romantic spot!" / W1K 6ZR; bibirestaurants.com; bibi_ldn; Tue-Sat 9 pm; SRA-1 star.

Big Easy £73 2|2|3
12 Maiden Ln, WC2   020 3728 4888   5–3D
332-334 King's Road, SW3   020 7352 4071   6–3C
Crossrail Pl, E14   020 3841 8844   12–1C
158 Westfield Ave, E20   020 4580 1176   14–1D **NEW**
Giant nachos, a bucket of beer and a platter of jumbo shrimp – if that sounds, good head off to these "large and vibrant" US-style 'Bar.B.Q & Crabshacks', which have multiplied in recent years from their age-old Chelsea home to colonise Covent Garden, Canary Wharf and Westfield Stratford. They are the kind of places you can make a reservation for 20 and they won't

blink. Top Menu Tip – "great lunch and weekend deals": e.g. "lobster, salad and chips with a glass of Prosecco for £15 in WC2 – what more could you ask for!" / bigeasy.co.uk; bigeasylondon.

Big Fernand SW7 £26 4 3 2
39 Thurloe Place   020 3031 8330   6–2C
«C'est ouf!». "Superb burgers at reasonable prices" – "a really good range with a focus on flavour" and using different French regional cheeses – win a big thumbs-up for the South Kensington outpost of this Gallic 'Maison du Hamburgé' chain (that's 50-strong in 'La Patrie'). Delivery is a big business here too: "appropriately packaged so none of the greatness is lost!"
/ SW7 2HP; bigfernanduk.com; bigfernand_uk; Mon-Sun 10 pm.

Big Night E9 NEW £18
177 Morning Lane   07983309028   14–1B
Taking over the former Nest site in Hackney's Morning Lane, this early 2024 newcomer is an informal venue offering communal dining on skewers of grilled meat and other small plates (as inspired by Japan's izakaya drinking dens, but using British recipes and ingredients). No reports as yet, but while testing influencer fave-raves, The Evening Standard's Joanna Taylor gave it a big thumbs-up, saying its shots-fuelled style "certainly manages to live up to its name even on Sunday evening". / E9 6LH; bignight.info; Thu-Sun midnight.

Bingham Riverhouse TW10 £88 2 3 3
61-63 Petersham Road   020 8940 0902   1–4A
South African chef, Vanessa Marx has taken the reins (from Steven Edwards) at this attractive dining room – part of a boutique hotel, beautifully situated with a riverside garden in Richmond. Her menu is eclectic with a selection of small and larger plates. But while the reception to it has been a little up-and-down ("exceptional food, let down by a few off-kilter moments…"; "less cohesive than the previous dining experience…"; "expensive…") its ratings overall are still pretty good all-round. / TW10 6UT; binghamriverhouse.com; binghamriverhouse; Tue-Sat 9 pm, Sun 3 pm.

The Biriyani Centre KT3 £25 5 4 3
94 Burlington Road   07305 141532   11–2B
"Hidden away in New Malden" – Radhika & Thiru Kamaraj's "tiny (14 seat) restaurant in a nondescript, small, suburban shopping parade" is a destination of curry pilgrimage for fans of subcontinental cuisine from several postcodes away. It helps that "the owners serving are delightful" in this small but "crisply decorated" room; however, it's the notably high standard of cooking with "bright, fresh flavours" and all at such "modest prices for a high quality of food" that pulls 'em in. Unlicensed – BYO for small corkage. Top Menu Tips – "excellent pani puris; very good 'Gobi 65' (cauliflower) and fine dum chicken and vegetable biryanis". / KT3 4NT; thebiryanicentre.co.uk; Mon-Sun 11 pm.

Bistro Aix N8 £65 3 3 3
54 Topsfield Pde, Tottenham Ln   020 8340 6346   9–1C
"Lovely food, lovely atmosphere and discreet staff" are the attractions at this "local" bistro, a Crouch End fixture for more than 20 years. "Love it! The rooms are like a maze", with white tablecloths adding a touch of style.
/ N8 8PT; bistroaix.co.uk; bistroaix); Mon-Sun 11 pm.

Bistro Freddie EC2 NEW £80 3 2 4
74 Luke Street   07729 3032   13–1B
Dominic Hamdy has followed up Soho's Bar Crispin with this fashionista-friendly Shoreditch bistro, where – as often happens in NYC – an old-school French formula somehow tickles the fancy of the hip crowd. It's very 'now', even though its cream walls and candles stuck into bottles would have looked retro 40 years ago, as would many of the traditional French inspirations on

chef Anna Sogaard's hand-scrawled menu (e.g. grilled bavette in peppercorn sauce; plaice meuniere in capers and dill). Top Tip – pie! / EC2A 4PY; bistrofreddie.com; bistro_freddie; Tue-Sun 08.30 pm.

Bistro Union SW4 — £66 — 3|4|3
40 Abbeville Rd   020 7042 6400   11–2D

This "buzzy, friendly, smart-casual local" in 'Abbeville Village' – sibling to Adam Byatt's Clapham star Trinity – thrives on a menu of "French-inflected food that delivers flavour and fun". "Friendly staff" and "cooking that never lets you down" make it many people's ideal of a "good neighbourhood restaurant". / SW4 9NG; bistrounion.co.uk; bistrounionclapham; Wed-Sat 8.30 pm, Sun 5 pm.

Black Bear Burger — £49 — 3|3|2
11-13 Market Row, SW9   020 7737 3444   11–2D
Market Halls Canary Wharf, Canada Square, E14   no tel   12–1C
Boxpark Shoreditch, 2-10 Bethnal Green Road, E1   no tel   13–2B
17 Exmouth Market, EC1   020 7837 1039   10–1A

"Sinfully good" burgers are delivered with "quick and efficient service" – and "genius free soft serve ice cream" (which accompanies your bill) – at this independent group with a handful of outlets around London. Former nurse Liz Down and her husband Stew started out in 2016 with a stall on Broadway Market, inspired by working holidays in the Canadian Rockies. Top Tip – "indulge in the guilty pleasure of their dry-aged beef glazed in miso with double cheese". / blackbearburger.com; black_bear_burger.

The Black Book W1 — £57 — 3|4|4
23 Frith Street   020 7434 1724   5–2A

"Wine is the star attraction in this luxurious hidden basement in Soho", with a "lengthy, well-thought-out list" from master sommeliers Gearoid Devaney & Xavier Rousset (who founded it as Trade, a club for industry insiders). "The light bites are not to be ignored", which "make this one of the better options for quiet drinks in the centre of town" – and late opening is another feature. / W1D 4RR; blackbooksoho.co.uk; theblackbooksoho; Tue, Wed 1 am, Thu-Sat 3 am.

Black Dog Beer House TW8 — £62 — 3|3|3
17 Albany Road   020 8568 5688   1–3A

"A traditional pub with great ales and good food" – this madeover free house in Brentford claims justifiably (if ungrammatically) to be 'a decent boozer doing it different!'. This includes an 'eclectic' food offering (from Moules Mariniere + fries to Sichuan Spiced Pork Ribs) and 14 kegs on tap (four with real ales, three with real ciders and the remainder natural wines). / TW8 0NF; blackdogbeerhouse.co.uk; blackdogbeerhouse; Wed-Sat 11 pm, Mon 10.30 pm, Sun 9.30 pm.

The Black Lamb SW19 — £64 — 3|2|2
67 High Street   020 8947 8278   11–2B

"It's good to have an independent option in Wimbledon village" and for the most part, this two year-old venture from the Gladwin family – their fifth shabby-chic London venue – is welcomed as "a decent venue in the culinary wasteland of the area"; and it espouses their 'Wild & Local' ethos, with "locally sourced and seasonally driven food". Notwithstanding the odd unfavourable comparison with its predecessor The White Onion (RIP), its scores are reasonable across the board. / SW19 5EE; theblacksheep-restaurant.com; theblacklamb_resto; Wed-Fri 10.30 pm, Tue 10 pm, Sat 11.30 pm, Sun 8.30 pm.

Black Salt SW14 — £51 — 3|4|2
505-507 Upper Richmond Road West   020 4548 3327   11–2A

"Top-class cooking" has earned a strong reputation for this three-year-old Indian in East Sheen – a spinoff from the brilliant Dastaan in Ewell, and similarly belying its "pedestrian" interior. A few reports this year, though, suggest success risks going to their heads a little ("a return visit and still worth the trip, but bills have risen – please don't price yourself out of the game!"). Top Tip – "the pork cheek vindaloo and the soft-shell crab remain things of beauty". / SW14 7DE; blacksaltsheen.com; blacksaltsheen; Tue-Thu 10 pm, Fri & Sat 10.30 pm, Sun 9 pm.

Blanchette W1 £88 3 2 2

Blacklock £55 3 3 4
24 Great Windmill St, W1   020 3441 6996   4–3D
16a Bedford Street, WC2   020 303 4139   5–3C
5 Frobisher Passage, E14   020 3034 0230   12–1C
28 Rivington Street, EC2   awaiting tel   13–1B
13 Philpot Lane, EC3   020 7998 7676   10–3D

"Still a legendary destination with consistently excellent meats, sides, drinks all far cheaper than at Hawksmoor" – these "dark and noisy" operations are "a go-to destination when you want some serious meat (perhaps more chophouse than steak house), with many good options that don't dent the wallet"; and widely seen as "a better bet than other big high-end steak chains". "They pack the punters in, so a good tip is to request a booth". "Steaks are cooked just right. Staff are happy and helpful. Why didn't I go here years ago?". Top Menu Tips – "Sunday lunch is legendary". And "try the 'All-In' for a variety of chops on excellent grilled flatbreads, and a couple of tasty sides between two. Also a (poorly promoted) option to BYO for £10 corkage at any time". / theblacklock.com; blacklockchops.

Blanchette W1 £88 3 2 2
9 D'Arblay St   020 7439 8100   4–1C

"Very 'French' in feel… and buzzing (maybe too buzzing, conversation can be difficult)" – this busy Soho bistro is named for the mother of the three brothers (Maxime, Malik and Yannis) who founded it. The short menu covers the bases with meat, fish and vegetarian sections, and for larger groups, sharing plates of charcuterie – or, more unusually, cheese and honey pairings – come into their own. / W1F 8DS; blanchettesoho.co.uk; blanchettelondon; Mon-Sat 11 pm.

Blandford Comptoir W1 £82 3 3 3
1 Blandford Street   020 7935 4626   2–1A

This "cosy and welcoming Marylebone" wine-bar/restaurant from sommelier Xavier Rousset is "perfect for an unrushed evening", combining "charming service" and a menu of "excellent Mediterranean (mostly Italian) dishes done really well" with a "specialist Rhone wine list that's a real treat". / W1U 3DA; blandford-comptoir.co.uk; blandfordcomptoir; Tue-Sat 10 pm.

Bleecker Burger £29 2 2 1
205 Victoria St, SW1   020 3384 4333   2–4B
The Balcony, Westfield White City, W12   020 3582 2930   1–3B
104 Tooley St, SE1   no tel   10–4D **NEW**
Unit B Pavilion Building, Spitalfields Mkt, E1   020 7427 6620   13–2B
Bloomberg Arcade, Queen Victoria St, EC4   020 7929 3785   10–3C

"No gimmicks and great flavours" is the recipe for a "semi-religious experience" at this small group (which also has three delivery-only outlets): for its many fans, "still the gold standard by which all burgers in the UK should be judged". "Gloriously juicy meat with just the right amount of extras" all "comes together in the most mouth-watering way". You "don't come for the experience" though: they are "very cramped when busy", if "still somehow cool". In August 2024 they opened a new site not far from London Bridge. / bleecker.co.uk; bleeckerburger.

Bleeding Heart Bistro EC1 £70 3 4 4
Bleeding Heart Yard   0207 2428238   10–2A

"It was very sad when the Bleeding Heart restaurant never reopened" – a victim of Covid-19 – "but the adjoining bistro" in a Dickensian yard "hidden around the back of Hatton Garden" is "still going strong" under its long-term *owners Robert & Robyn Wilson (who established the business in 1983). "In a convenient location between the City and the West End", the venue has always been popular amongst expense-accounters and "minimal intervention from the efficient service means it's a great choice for a business lunch" and always feels "busy and buzzy". The "reliable, classic French bistro cuisine provides something on the menu for all tastes" and "is consistently of a high standard"; and while the cellar is not quite as deep as when the restaurant was in full swing, there remains "a fairly comprehensive wine list". Top Tip – in summer, "the really lovely terrace is an oasis in this busy part of London".* / EC1N 8SJ; bleedingheart.co.uk; bleedingheartbistro; Mon-Sat 9 pm.

Blue Boar Pub SW1 £80 2 3 2
Conrad London St James, 22-28 Broadway 020 3301 1400 2–3C
"It's a lovely surprise that Sally Abé has moved to the Conrad St James and opened both a restaurant (The Pem, see also) and this pub, as the area has been a gastronomic desert for some time" and it's undoubtedly a boon to local politicos and lobbyists. But with its spacious layout and leather bucket chairs, it's rather plush by pub standards and prices are not those of your local boozer (cod 'n' chips is £24, a sausage roll £12). Fans say it's *"really enjoyable"* but there are also one or two 'off' reports. / SW1H 0BH; blueboarlondon.com; blueboarpub; Mon-Sat 11 pm, Sun 10 pm.

Bluebird SW3 £96 2 2 3
350 King's Road 020 7559 1000 6–3C
This *"Chelsea stalwart"* occupies an elegant, landmark King's Road site that was converted in 1997 by the late Sir Terence Conran, having been built in the 1920s as a car showroom. Nowadays part of D&D London, it has never really fired on all cylinders, providing *"decent-enough food in a trendy, relaxed space"* that offers many different options – from café and courtyard, to a bar, to the large modern upstairs restaurant (where steak or fruits de mer are amongst the top options; and which also serves brunch and afternoon tea). One day, someone will really make something of this site. / SW3 5UU; bluebird-restaurant.co.uk; bluebirdchelsea; Mon-Wed, Fri, Thu, Sat 10.30 pm, Sun 9.30 pm; SRA-3 stars.

Bob Bob Ricard £92 2 3 5
1 Upper James Street, W1 020 3145 1000 4–2C
Level 8, 122 Leadenhall Street, EC3 020 3145 1000 10–2D
"Tap the 'Press for Champagne' button, add a little caviar tasting plate to the low-level lighting and small booth seating, and you have an ideal formula for a romantic dinner!" or, indeed, for a casual business tête-a-tête at Leonid Shutov's willfully decadent retro-diners, styled in a kind of Art Deco steampunk. Both at the Soho original and in the newer City spin-off that occupies a floor of "The Cheesegrater", they provide *"an amazing setting"*; and *"somehow the totally OTT gaudiness of the place makes the overall experience a genuinely fun one"*. Fans also say *"the Beef Wellington is really very good"* and approve of its other luxurious comfort food like Lobster Mac 'n' Cheese, Chateaubriand for One, or Salmon en Croute. *"It's not cheap mind you"* and harsher critics say the food *"just doesn't cut it"* (*"the novelty of the fun Champagne button sadly wears off when the dishes arrive; and while the bling and the booths create an atmosphere of unrestrained wealth, I prefer restaurants where food is the prime objective"*). / bobbobricard.com.

Boca a boca W1 NEW £64 3 3 3
18 Charlotte Street 020 4580 1407 2–1C
"An interesting and tasty choice of tapas" and paellas plus *"good service"* win solid ratings for this new Hispanic arrival on Fitzrovia's foodie Charlotte Street, which took over the site of Ampéli (RIP), and is in fact Ukrainian-owned, as the London branch of a restaurant launched in war-torn Kyiv two years ago by entrepreneur Andrii Nokonov. / W1T 2LZ; bocaaboca.co.uk; Tue-Sat 11 pm.

F S A

Bocca di Lupo W1 £69 **4 4 3**
12 Archer St   020 7734 2223   4–3D
"Absolutely brilliant" – Jacob Kenedy's "go-to place in Soho" (in a backstreet near Piccadilly Circus) remains one of the most interesting Italian restaurants in the UK. "No stereotypical Cucina Italiana here": "the stellar menu is constantly changing" and the finest and freshest ingredients are treated with the utmost simplicity and respect in "regional small plates" that are "seasonal, well-judged and always memorable"; and which can be paired with "a very fine Italian cellar covering every price point". "Thoughtful and friendly staff" help "everything function like clockwork"; and while "the room is a little challenging" ("it can be NOISY") it "has a very good atmosphere". Top Menu Tips – "mince-stuffed olives Ascolani, Amberjack carpaccio with rosemary oil and orange zest, Sweetbreads with morels and Marsala, Sicilian cannoli with a light and tangy ricotta filling". "Heaven for olive oil and garlic lovers. Courgette flower with mozzarella and anchovies, Wild garlic pappardelle with duck are all to die for. Every dish packs a punch, down to the sweet Pig's Blood and Chocolate Paté". / W1D 7BB; boccadilupo.com; bocca_di_lupo; Mon-Sat 11 pm, Sun 9.30 pm.

Al Boccon di'vino TW9 £95 **4 5 4**
14 Red Lion Street   020 8940 9060   1–4A
"My favourite restaurant of all time!" say fans of this Richmond stalwart – "a unique and authentic Italian experience". Patron Riccardo Grigolo hosts a no-choice, multi-course Venetian wedding feast over three or four hours, that makes you "feel like you are a guest in an Italian home" and with "an outstanding quality of food, ambience and staff". Arrive hungry! / TW9 1RW; nonsolovinoltd.co.uk; al-boccon-di-vino; Tue-Sat 11 pm, Sun 5 pm.

Boisdale of Belgravia SW1 £116 **2 3 4**
13-15 Eccleston Street   020 7730 6922   2–4B
"Simply a great night every time" – "a wonderfully club-like, somewhat masculine environment" characterises Ranald Macdonald's red-walled Belgravian stalwart, which he started as a young man in 1986 shortly after a stint in the wine trade. The decorative theme is Scottish – the owner is after all the 24th chief and captain of Clanranald – and the menu features "top steaks" alongside haggis, lobster and burgers; plus a wide large variety of other, predominantly British dishes. Regular live music is a feature, as is "a great cocktail bar and lovely cigar terrace". "Okay, the food's nothing to write home about, but there's nothing wrong with it either". / SW1W 9LX; boisdale.co.uk; boisdale_restaurants; Mon, Sat, Tue-Fri 1 am, Sun 4 pm.

Bombay Brasserie SW7 £96 **3 4 2**
Courtfield Road   020 7370 4040   6–2B
A stalwart of more than 40 years' standing – this grand Indian near Gloucester Road tube station "always provides a top-notch meal with good service". Flying somewhat under the radar these days under the ownership of the luxury Taj Hotels group, it was particularly well known in its 1980s heyday. / SW7 4QH; bombayb.co.uk; bombaybrasseriesw7; Tue-Sat 10.30 pm, Sun 10 pm.

Bombay Bustle W1 £86 **4 3 4**
29 Maddox Street   020 7290 4470   3–2C
"Carefully spiced and beautifully cooked Indian food" takes centre-stage at the more casual little sister of Jamavar from Mayfair-based restaurateur Samyukta Nair. Everything on the menu is "interesting and tasty", and "the express menu is a bargain" for this part of town. / W1S 2PA; bombaybustle.com; bombaybustle; Mon-Sat 10.30 pm, Sun 9.30 pm.

Bombay Palace W2 £69 **4 4 2**
50 Connaught St   020 7723 8855   7–1D
"Back with a bang!" – this survivor from the 1990s near Edgware Road has served "gold-standard" Indian food in a comfortable setting for decades. One

regular opines that it has "improved considerably after a bit of a blip" during the pandemic – although there's still the occasional "variable" report. "Service is friendly but professional". / W2 2AA; bombay-palace.co.uk; bombaypalacelondon; Mon, Thu, Tue, Wed, Sun 10 pm, Fri & Sat 10.30 pm.

Bondi Green W2 £60 3 3 3
1-2 Canalside Walk   020 3325 1340   7–1C

"Aussies know how to do a breakfast", and this "always-friendly" outlet of the 'Daisy Green Collection' (big modern cafés generally in recent developments; of which there are about 15) is also well-located by the canal in Paddington ("every restaurant we've been to in the Green collection has been good but Bondi Green is in a lovely location as well"). "Try the Shakshouka or the Fancy Bacon Roll if you're a sinner or the Healthy Start if you're not. Either way, the coffee is excellent". / W2 1DG; daisygreenfood.com; daisygreencollection; Mon-Sat 10 pm, Sun 9 pm.

Bone Daddies £47 3 2 3
Victoria St, SW1   no tel   2–4B
30-31 Peter St, W1   020 7287 8581   4–2D
46-48 James St, W1   020 3019 7140   3–1A
1 Phillimore Gardens, W8   020 3668 5500   8–1D
24 Old Jamaica Road, SE16   020 7231 3211   10–4D
22 Putney High St, SW15   020 8246 4170   11–2B
211 Old Street, EC1   020 3019 6300   13–1A

"Deeply flavoured and satisfying" ramen noodles in an "addictive" 20-hour pork bone broth combine with a "noisy hustle and bustle" at this "rock 'n' roll ramen" chain established in 2012, now with seven venues across central London. Perhaps the "quick and easy" (and noisy) vibe does not translate as satisfyingly from its original Soho site to the suburbs: a branch in leafy Richmond closed down last year, as did a Putney branch before it. / bonedaddies.com; bonedaddies.

BONGA NW5 £25 4 3 2
8 Fortress Road   02033436788   9–2B

"A tiny, smart, very small Korean in Kentish Town which seems to get better as it goes along". "Takeaway is maybe the main business, but there are a few tables with a dozen covers by the kitchen" – "service is fast and you're in for some very reliable Korean staples (bibimbap is a favourite and kids like Yangnyeom fried chicken)". "Some people rave about New Malden for Korean cuisine, but in my experience this is a cut above". / NW5 2ES; Tue-Sun 10.30 pm.

Bonoo NW2 £64 3 3 3
675 Finchley Road   020 7794 8899   1–1B

"The food tastes fresh and is not heavy" at this "consistently great" Childs Hill operation, specialising in "Indian tapas-style street food". That TripAdvisor have ranked it #1 out of 15,000+ London restaurants may be over-egging it a bit, but they must be doing something right as a Muswell Hill spin-off is on the cards. / NW2 2JP; bonoo.co.uk; bonoolondon; Mon-Sun 10.30 pm.

Il Bordello E1 £62 3 3 4
Metropolitan Wharf, 70 Wapping Wall   020 7481 9950   12–1A

Stalwart Italian local in a converted Wapping warehouse, whose pizza and pasta dishes "never disappoint". It's been going since the late '90s and much of its appeal is as a lively local linchpin of the neighbourhood. / E1W 3SS; ilbordello.com; ilbordellorestaurant; Mon-Sat 11 pm, Sun 10.30 pm.

Borough Market Kitchen SE1 £72 3 3 2
Jubilee Place   020 7407 5777   10–4C

The old car park behind Borough Market is now a covered street-food zone with about 15 different stalls – "I know it's a bit of a tourist trap these days, but there's still something about walking around, grabbing something new to try, or just hitting your old favourite". / SE1 9AG; boroughmarket.org.uk; applebeesfishlondon; Mon-Thu 10 pm, Fri & Sat 11 pm, Sun 6 pm.

Bouchon Racine EC1 £96 5|5|3
66 Cowcross Street   020 7253 3368   10–1A

"Transporting you to a French bistro in Lyon" – Henry Harris's phenomenal, year-old sequel to his Knightsbridge Racine (which closed in 2015) just marches on and has quickly become one of the Top-10 most notable destinations in our annual diners' poll, thanks to its huge and "sophisticated foodie fan base". "It has an unpromising location – up a narrow staircase" above The Three Compasses pub near Farringdon – but once inside it's "always buzzing" and "such a fun place to eat". The "sublime" food from the blackboard menu here is "the stuff of dreams for lovers of traditional French cooking" ("no wonder so many chefs eat there!"): "proper French classics executed with skill and passion" ("just don't check your cholesterol!"); and all "in generous portions and at ungreedy prices". "It feels like it's been here for decades, with its very confident and focussed menu"; and there's "exemplary service from engaged and knowledgeable staff". Just one thing… "it's almost impossible to get a table…". Top Menu Tips – "the rabbit in mustard sauce with Alsace bacon is one of the best dishes ever"; "delicious tête de veau with Henry Harris's sauce ravigote"; "Escarole and Mimolette salad and Bayonne ham with Celeriac remoulade is generously portioned and very tasty". / EC1M 6BP; bouchonracine.com; bouchonracine; Tue-Sat 10 pm.

Boulevard WC2 £66 2|3|3
40 Wellington St   020 7240 2992   5–3D

"Convenient, if unexciting, medium-priced brasserie two minutes from the Royal Opera House" that's worth knowing about in the touristy 'minefield' it inhabits. The Gallic staples are "fairly priced" ("in particular, the set menus are good value") and "service is acceptable for such a busy, central establishment". Top Tip – "great pre-theatre". / WC2E 7BD; boulevardbrasserie.co.uk; boulevardbrasseriewc2; Mon-Thu 11 pm, Fri & Sat 11.30 pm, Sun 10 pm.

Brackenbury Wine Rooms W6 £64 2|4|4
111-115 Hammersmith Grove   020 3696 8240   8–1C

On a tranquil Hammersmith corner, with a good-sized pavement terrace for the summer months, this attractive and affordable destination makes a useful rendezvous and has the looks of a smart neighbourhood bistro rather than a wine bar. Its neighbouring café, 'La Cave', is a popular weekend breakfast spot: "it has the best pastries and head barista Justin is a character". / W6 0NQ; winerooms.london; wine_rooms; Mon-Sat 11 pm, Sun 9.30 pm.

Bradley's NW3 £82 2|2|2
25 Winchester Rd   020 7722 3457   9–2A

Simon & Jacinta Bradley's "reliable neighbourhood restaurant" near Swiss Cottage station is one of the capital's stalwart local champions, offering an unfailing combination of "well-presented dishes, friendly service and well chosen wines" for 32 years and counting. "Rarely busy at lunchtime", it's also a "very useful pre-theatre restaurant" for those heading to the Hampstead Theatre around the corner. Ratings, though, remain capped by those who view it as "a venue that's convenient but dull". / NW3 3NR; bradleysnw3.co.uk; /bradleysrestaurant/; Wed-Sat, Tue 9 pm, Sun 2.30 pm.

La Brasseria £89 2|2|2
42 Marylebone High Street, W1   020 7486 3753   2–1A
290 Westbourne Grove, W11   020 7052 3564   7–2B

In the fair number of reports on the Fraquelli brothers' Italian brasseries in Marylebone and Notting Hill, the range of opinion spans from "solid and reasonably priced" to "average and somewhat overpriced". No-one suggests they are either very good or particularly terrible – "spacious"… "very pleasant"… "perfectly decent" are the kind of descriptions people attach. Business-wise though, they are going great guns, with backing from industry heavyweight Simon Woodroffe (founder of Yo!) and in February 2024 they successfully crowdfunded £1.2m to open a third Brasseria in late 2024, taking over the former site of the confusingly similarly-named 'La Brasserie' in South Kensington – which operated there under that name for 30 years – and where they now aim to 'combine Italian flavour and style with New York service and a Parisian grand brasserie atmosphere'. / labrasseria.com; brasseria_nottinghill.

Brasserie Blanc £64 222
119 Chancery Lane, WC2   020 7405 0290   2–2D
Goldhurst House, Parr's Way, W6   020 8237 5566   8–2C
9 Belvedere Rd, SE1   020 7202 8470   2–3D
60 Threadneedle St, EC2   020 7710 9440   10–2C
"An impressive and speedy pre-theatre set meal at the SE1 branch…"; "Reliable for quick lunch, and always has a discount…"; "Great Sunday lunch and a warm welcome for the children…" – at its best, this classic Gallic group is "a decent chain serving popular brasserie fare to a fair standard and with a pleasing bustle". But there is a sharp disparity between its overall marks – which are average-to-low – and the celebrity of its backer; and one harsh diner's comment carries with it a ring of truth: "I cannot reconcile how Raymond Blanc can live with his continued, if hands-off, connection with this creation. The accountants rule, menus are static and unadventurous; and standards vary between branches and visits; but it is many years since a visit was truly satisfying". / brasserieblanc.com; SRA-3 stars.

**Brasserie of Light,
Selfridges W1** £84 234
400 Oxford Street   020 3940 9600   3–1A
"A top stop-off after you finish your shopping" – Richard Caring's spectacular venue on the second floor of Selfridges has plenty of pizzazz and is a destination in itself. The brasserie fare "is very similar to that at The Ivy" (no surprise, its essentially part of that group) "but Damain Hirst's flying Pegasus sculpture helps give the place the upper hand stylewise" – the famous and striking centrepiece to an AbFab chamber filled with light by its huge windows. / W1A 1AB; brasserie-of-light.co.uk; brasserieoflight; Mon-Sat midnight, Sun 11 pm.

Brasserie Zédel W1 £61 235
20 Sherwood St   020 7734 4888   4–3C
"If you're looking for glamour on a budget this is your place!". "A truly stunning fin-de-siècle style French brasserie, of a type which probably doesn't exist in Paris anymore!" – this "superb Beaux-Arts dining room" inhabits a dazzling Grade I listed basement just seconds from Piccadilly Circus, and although it looks like it's been around forever, actually only opened in 2015. One of London's Top-20 destinations in our annual diners' poll, it inspires a broad spectrum of opinions, but the overall conclusion is that it is "still firing (mostly) on all cylinders" and "more or less the same as before Jeremy King lost the boardroom battle to run it". In particular, it has a "terrific ambience" (regularly zhooshed up with live music) and "despite changes in management, it still offers outstanding value for such a prime location" ("Wonderful prices. How do they do it?"). True, as ever there are sceptics who feel it "cynically churns out substandard dishes flung from a kitchen conveyor belt". But, surely that's true in Paris too! Of course, catering on this scale means the vast, "something-for-everyone" menu of Gallic brasserie fare feels a bit "formulaic". Yet, "stick to the simpler dishes (the more expensive ones are more hit-and-miss) and the food is good", especially at "prices which won't frighten your father-in-law!". And the service – if not quite as sharp as when Jeremy bestrode the floor – is really pretty decent. "Get there early to treat yourself to a cocktail in the Bar Americain next door before your table is

ready". Top Menu Tips – "Still the best Andouillette in town"; "the Carrottes Rappés is delicious as is the bread and butter to go with it and the Steak Haché with delicious peppercorn sauce and skinny chips is just heaven"; "one of the only places in the West End with a good Île Flottante". / W1F 7ED; brasseriezedel.com; brasseriezedel; Mon-Sat 11 pm, Sun 10 pm.

Brat E1 £93 5 4 3
First Floor, 4 Redchurch Street no tel 13–1B
Tomos Parry's phenomenally successful haunt occupies the first floor of a converted Shoreditch pub (over the Smoking Goat, see also), but with its own separate entrance. Somehow, he brilliantly captured the zeitgeist with his Basque-influenced cooking over fire, producing food that's as "simple" as it is "outstanding". "Ingredients are carefully sourced, prepared with care and the flavours really come through". Many reports recommend you "order the turbot!" ('Brat' meaning Turbot in Parry's native Welsh), but it's a rather large dish if you are just a couple and the rest of the menu is just as worthy of exploration. "The room is casual and buzzy" and tightly packed, but "despite the cosy tables it still feels like you have your own space". Top Menu Tip – "Basque cheesecake is a highlight: great flavour and so light". / E1 6JJ; bratrestaurant.com; bratrestaurant; Mon-Sun 10 pm.

Brat at Climpson's Arch E8 £111 4 3 2
Climpson's Arch, 374 Helmsley Place 020 7254 7199 14–2B
"Truly outstanding all round"; star chef Tomos Parry's now-permanent wood-fire spin-off in a covered courtyard and adjoining railway arch in London Fields has "staff who care, food that's different and a great buzz without being so loud you can't have a conversation". It's worth it to "go as a crowd so you can get to taste all the fantastic dishes on offer": typical are Roasted Chicken Rice or Whole Crab with Hay Butter. / E8 3SB; bratrestaurant.co.uk; bratrestaurant; Wed-Sat 10 pm, Sun 9 pm.

Bravi Ragazzi SW16 £52 4 3 2
2a Sunnyhill Road 020 8769 4966 11–2D
This Streatham fixture punches way above its weight, having drawn pizza-hounds from across London for more than a decade. Neapolitan-born co-founder Andrea Asciuti is also behind Peckham Rye's 081 Pizzeria.
/ SW16 2UH; bravi-ragazzi.business.site; braviragazzipizzeria; Mon-Sun 10.30 pm.

Brawn E2 £82 5 4 4
49 Columbia Road 020 7729 5692 14–2A
"Simple… seasonal… superb" sums up chef-patron Ed Wilson's approach at this East London fixture, near Columbia Road flower market – and after 15 years, "the food is better than ever". "Despite the carnivorous name (and logo!)" the menu also incorporates "impressive and delicately cooked fish and seafood". Natural wines are a big theme – "uber cool, weird and wonderful bottles that taste better than they look" – "but there's lots for the traditional palate, too". Top Tip – "go on weekday lunchtimes to avoid booking".
/ E2 7RG; brawn.co; brawn49; Tue-Sat, Mon 10.15 pm.

Bread Street Kitchen EC4 £82 2 2 2
10 Bread Street 020 3030 4050 10–2B
Gordon Ramsay's comfortable, upscale brasserie chain continues to inspire feedback that's very mixed and surprisingly limited for the sizeable empire of an international megastar. Naysayers reckon: "What a disappointment! Average food is served in a cavernous space by staff who seemed unhappy to be there"; or that "they no longer seem like they care, just serving formulaic, bland food". This year's most positive comment? "It was actually much better than I expected, having no great hopes. Service and speed were pretty laid back, which suited us. The food was well-cooked and presented, even if menu choices (mains especially) struck me as a bit weird and perhaps trying to cover too many bases". / EC4M 9AJ; gordonramsayrestaurants.com; breadstreetkitchen; Mon-Sat 11 pm, Sun 9 pm.

F S A

Breakfast Club £46 3 3 2
Branches throughout London
"What is better than an amazing breakfast?..." and you are certainly spoilt for choice all day long at this greasy-spoon-esque chain, which is celebrating its 20th year in 2024 with the addition of a St Pancras branch to its empire of 16 caffs (11 of them in the capital) and 3 pubs. / thebreakfastclubcafes.com; thebrekkyclub.

Briciole W1 £70 3 3 2
20 Homer St   020 7723 0040   7–1D
This *"super-friendly local trattoria"* near Edgware Road tube station has built a big fan club with *"good, honest, unflashy"* food backed up by a *"beguiling wine list"*, and works equally well for *"a quick business lunch with colleagues or an informal evening meal with friends"* – *"if only it weren't so noisy!"*. Top Tip – *"Try the Wild Boar Ragu"*. / W1H 4NA; briciole.co.uk; briciolerestaurant; Mon-Sun 10.45 pm.

Brick Lane Beigel Bake E1 £9 5 2 1
159 Brick Ln   020 7729 0616   13–1C
This legendary 24/7 East End bakery is *"worth the hype, and the queue, for top salt beef bagel action"*. Ignore the *"grumpy service and horrible interior (please don't gentrify!)"* in the knowledge that *"one of life's great pleasures is noshing a fully loaded salt beef bagel outside the shop while it's still piping hot"*. Last summer, the operation made its first foray into pizzas with a residency at the Hoxton. It also endured a social media panic as news spread that its near neighbour the Beigel Shop (both businesses use the traditional European spelling) had closed due to a family dispute. / E1 6SB; beigelbake.co.uk; beigel_bake; Mon-Sun midnight.

Brigadiers EC2 £78 5 3 3
Bloomberg Arcade, Queen Victoria Street   020 3319 8140   10–3C
The cooking is awesome and *"the bar is mega!"* according to the many fans of this JKS outpost in the Bloomberg Arcade. Modelled on an Indian Army mess, *"it's always been a very masculine, 'City boys' type place (some evenings the male:female ratio is at gay-bar disparities!)"*. The quality of the *"inauthentic but deliciously tasty"* cooking is undisputed, but there's lively debate about what's best on the menu: *"the short rib curry is the stand-out here"*; no, *"the biryani in pie crust is the best Indian dish in town"*. / EC2R 8AR; brigadierslondon.com; brigadiersldn; Mon-Sat 10.30 pm.

The Bright Courtyard W1 £93 3 2 2
43-45 Baker St   020 7486 6998   2–1A
"Excellent dumplings" and other Cantonese and Shanghainese dishes are served in *"good portions"* at this London outpost of a Shanghai-based group. Harsher voices say the Marylebone office-block interior is *"miserable but spacious"*, but it's a popular destination nonetheless. / W1U 8EW; lifefashiongroup.com; BrightCourtyard; Mon-Sat 10.30 pm, Sun 9.30 pm.

Brinkley's SW10 £77 1 2 3
47 Hollywood Rd   020 7351 1683   6–3B
"The food is pretty basic, but that's not why people go" to wine merchant John Brinkley's Chelsea brasserie, a long-time hangout for a loyal 'Sloane Ranger' crowd who discovered the place in the '80s – *"the wine list is excellent and not greedily priced, and the atmosphere remains great"*. There are suggestions, though, that its *"buzz"* is on the wane (*"the place has been sliding for at least two or three years"*), but people have been saying this for over a decade now! / SW10 9HX; brinkleys.com; brinkleysrestaurant; Mon-Sun 11 pm.

Brinkley's Kitchen SW17 £78 2 3 3
35 Bellevue Rd   020 8672 5888   11–2C
Overlooking Wandsworth Common, John Brinkley's local venue offers "pleasant if unremarkable" cuisine and benefits from his knowledge of wine – "more quiet than the one at Hollywood Road but a great place to have a nice relaxed dinner". / SW17 7EF; brinkleys.com; brinkleyskitchen; Tue-Sat 11 pm, Sun 4 pm.

Brooklands SW1 £185 4 4 3
1 Grosvenor Place   020 8138 6888   2–3A
"Love Claude Bosi and there are superb views too!" – two highpoints at this September 2023 debut, which occupies the glam rooftop of the swanky Peninsular London: the newly opened outpost of HK's oldest hotel, just south of Hyde Park Corner. Gastronomically, Bosi is acclaimed in one or two reports for having created "the best of the new restaurants open this year" with "first-rate" modern cuisine that's "creative and flavoursome"; and with service to match. The "unusual" interior design generally gets the thumbs-up, but "is perhaps a touch corporate"; and "the layout of the room means some tables are unable to make the most of what is otherwise a fine outlook over Hyde Park". Top Menu Tip – "at £58 per person, the 'Concorde Lunch Menu' offers unsurpassed value (albeit no expensive ingredients)". / SW1X 7HJ; peninsula.com; peninsulahotels; Tue-Sat 9.45 pm.

Brookmill SE8 £57 3 3 2
65 Cranbrook Road   020 8333 0899   1–4D
"A very good find" in St John's, between Deptford and Lewisham, this pub-with-rooms boasts well-prepared food and "warm and efficient staff". Attractions include a "great Sunday lunch, with a full range of roasts served with great big Yorkshire puds and plenty of gravy". / SE8 4EJ; thebrookmill.co.uk; brookmillse8; Sun & Mon 8.45 pm, Tue-Sat 9.45 pm.

The Brown Dog SW13 £66 3 4 4
28 Cross Street   020 8392 2200   11–1A
Hard to discover by accident: this "community-owned eating pub, lost deep in the backstreets of Barnes" – in the charming 'Little Chelsea' Victorian conservation area – has some of the "best pub food in the area" and "great wines for a pub". There's a cosy back yard for al fresco meals in the summer. / SW13 0AP; thebrowndog.co.uk; browndogbarnes; Tue-Sat 10.30 pm, Sun 8.30 pm.

Brown's Hotel,
The Drawing Room W1 £110 3 4 4
Albemarle St   020 7493 6020   3–3C
For an "exquisite afternoon tea" in the archetypal English mould, the "relaxing" wood-panelled lounge of this elegant but unflashy Mayfair hotel is "just lovely" and perennially ranks alongside more famous names like the Ritz down the road in the eyes of its fanclub. The hotel dates from 1837 and counts Queen Victoria and Agatha Christie as former patrons. / W1S 4BP; roccofortehotels.com; browns_hotel; Mon-Sun 9 pm.

Brumus,
Haymarket Hotel SW1 £78 2 3 4
1 Suffolk Pl, Haymarket   020 7470 4000   2–2C
"A good spot in the West End if you want to guarantee a table in nice surroundings" – this all-day dining room in a boutique hotel has an "unassuming entrance on Haymarket but once inside, the unique decor, colourful artworks and African mud-cloth screens make quite an impact". It's not a foodie choice, but "the set menu is perfect for pre-theatre dining, with a good range of choices", while the "smart but relaxed" atmosphere also makes it "good for business lunches". / SW1Y 4BP; brumus.com; Tue-Sat midnight.

Bruno E9 NEW £37
211a Victoria Park Road   no tel   14–2B

In Hackney's Victoria Park Village, this January 2024 newcomer is the latest venture from Swiss-born wine specialist Michael Sager (of Sager + Wilde), who aims to deliver a 'very personal' selection of natural wines, accompanied by Swiss-style stuffed pretzels and other light nibbles. It doubles as a bottle shop by day. / E9 7JN; bruno-london.com; bruno___london; Mon-Sun 11 pm.

Brunswick House Café SW8 £70   4 4 5
30 Wandsworth Rd   020 7720 2926   11–1D

A "quirky" but "gorgeous restaurant in a listed building" surrounded by modern skyscrapers – this "Vauxhall institution" occupies a much-chandeliered showroom of architectural antiques (run by LASSCO), which adds a unique sense of occasion to chef Jackson Boxer's "assured" and "interesting" preparation of "modern British classics". "Quiet and serene, with a diverse and older crowd of a lunchtime – it's buzzing and vibrant with a younger clubbier crowd on a weekend". Top Tip – "the Dexter beef and bone marrow tartare with shallots is the best steak tartare in London". / SW8 2LG; brunswickhouse.london; brunswick_house; Wed-Sat, Tue 10 pm, Sun 4 pm.

Trattoria Brutto EC1 £63   3 4 5
35-37 Greenhill Rents   no tel   10–1A

"Shocking news when Russell Norman died" in November 2023 – his legacy remains this "buzzy, brilliant Italian trattoria in the City of London" that was his "homage to hearty Tuscan food" and which is now run by his widow Jules and son Ollie. Perhaps it's "a bit too cramped for comfort" and there's "loud, thumpy music", but most diners feel "it just gets everything right". "It's hard to get a table, but with Negronis at £5…who is surprised?". The food is "not stellar, but fine-to-good" and – importantly – also generous and comforting (as exemplified by its best known dishes the 'Bistecca alla Fiorentina' and its 'Coccoli' – cuddles – of deep fried dough with soft cheese and prosciutto). "Cosy, cute and very romantic, go there for any occasion… but with a date it's even better!" / EC1M 6BN; msha.ke; Brutto; Tue-Sat 10.30 pm.

Bubala £42   4 4 3
15 Poland Street, W1   no tel   4–1C
65 Commercial Street, E1   no tel   13–2C

"Don't worry you won't miss the meat!" – "Bubala really seems to tap into what modern dining and modern food is about"; "the depth of flavour is unbeatable" at these "fantastic Middle Eastern-inspired vegetarian restaurants" in Soho and Shoreditch. "You definitely feel you're in a hip part of town once the waiting staff arrive at your table and plentiful food arrives quickly". "An excellent choice if you want something plant-based and memorable" – "the only problem is that it's always crowded!" ("it's so hard to get a table, book well in advance"). Top Menu Tips – "The 'Bubala knows best' set menu has a great selection and is very filling"; "Oyster mushroom skewer and the sublime Halloumi with honey are real highlights"; "the smoky Baba ganoush is unforgettable". / bubala.co.uk; https://www.instagram.com/bubala_london/?hl=en.

The Bull N6 £75   3 3 3
13 North Hill   020 8341 0510   9–1B

In lovely Highgate, with a huge leafy terrace and historic interior – this "lively" gastropub is a top destination locally, praised for its high all-round standards. Pies of the day and Thursday steak nights enliven a familiar gastropub repertoire. / N6 4AB; thebullhighgate.co.uk; bull_highgate; Mon-Thu 11 pm, Fri & Sat midnight, Sun 10.30 pm.

Bull & Last NW5 £81   2 2 3
168 Highgate Rd   020 7267 3641   9–1B

"It just does everything right!" according to fans of Joe Swiers & Ollie Pudney's phenomenally successful destination, which for many years has *topped our survey as north London's top gastropub, thanks not least to its location near Parliament Hill and the ease of "a long walk over Hampstead Heath" to walk off lunch. Hmmmm. That's always been our annual diners' poll's conclusion hitherto anyway. But this year's feedback was much less settled, with numerous reports saying it's "not as good recently" and "despite the hype, produces decidedly underwhelming cooking". Hopefully just a rough patch?* / NW5 1QS; thebullandlast.co.uk; thebullandlast; Mon-Thu 11 pm, Fri & Sat midnight, Sun 10.30 pm.

Burger & Beyond £53 4 3 2
10 Old Compton St, W1 020 8017 1453 5–2A
Bank End, SE1 020 4580 1293 10–4C
147 Shoreditch High Street, E1 020 3848 8860 13–1B

Having graduated from food trucks and market stalls to permanent sites in Shoreditch, Soho and Borough Yards, this classy fast-food operation is on the rise – with improved ratings to match. "I don't even like burgers, but the vegan burger dripping with sweet Korean sauce – made especially without mayo for my fussy taste – was a total surprise, and drop-dead gorgeous". / burgerandbeyond.co.uk.

Burger & Lobster £84 3 3 2
109-125 Knightsbridge, SW1 020 7235 5000 6–1D
10 Wardour Street, W1 020 3205 8963 5–4A
26 Binney Street, W1 020 3637 5972 3–2A
29 Clarges Street, W1 020 7409 1699 3–4B
36 Dean Street, W1 020 7432 4800 5–2A
6 Little Portland Street, W1 020 7907 7760 3–1C
18 Hertsmere Road, E14 020 3637 6709 12–1C
52 Threadneedle Street, EC2 020 7256 9755 10–2C
Bow Bells Hs, 1 Bread St, EC4 020 7248 1789 10–2B

A "great concept, expertly delivered" – the two headline dishes are served up in posh, comfortable diner style at this nine-strong London group (with another dozen branches around the world). As a gimmick it doesn't generate the buzz it once did, but both of the main dishes receive a good rep in feedback, in particular the "excellent and good-sized lobster" (and "for lobster it's not that expensive"). / burgerandlobster.com; burgerandlobster.

Busaba £52 2 2 3
Branches throughout London

"Solid if far from spectacular" Thai-fusion cooking characterises this 10-venue group, whose overall performance has picked up in the last year without attracting much feedback. The concept was launched by restaurant magician Alan Yau in 1999 – the same year he created world-beater Hakkasan; he is no longer involved in either. / busaba.com; busabaeathai.

The Butcher's Tap and Grill SW3 NEW £84 2 2 2
27 Tryon Street 0203 958 4444 6–2D

TV chef Tom Kerridge relaunched the former Queen's Head pub between Sloane Avenue and the King's Road in November 2023 as the Chelsea branch of his Marlow-based concept. The name is reflected by its menu of "top steaks alongside other simple pub food" and fans applaud "superbly cooked steak from the butcher's counter that's a real treat". Even they, however, may note that it's also an "expensive" indulgence and a worrying number of reports are very indifferent, saying "it's fine for a quick burger", but that "food, service and ambience here in no way justifies the extraordinary prices". / SW3 3LG; thebutcherstapandgrill.co.uk; Mon-Sat 10 pm, Sun 9.30 pm.

Butler's Restaurant, The Chesterfield Mayfair W1 £92 3 3 3
35 Charles St 020 7958 7729 3–3B

Old-fashioned Mayfair dining room within a luxurious 94-bedroom hotel, whose retro offerings include Dover sole filleted at the table and a wide variety of afternoon teas. For a traditional British experience, it's recommended in all reports. / W1J 5EB; chesterfieldmayfair.com; chesterfieldmayfair; Mon-Sun 10 pm.

Byron £48 2 3 3
Branches throughout London
Boy, this chain has shrunk over the years: there are just nine nationally now, of which four are in London: Covent Garden, Tottenham Court Road, South Kensington and Westfield. Needless to say, there's nothing like the volume of feedback it once generated, but it's all good with no disasters and a number of "really top-class burgers" enjoyed this year. / byron.co.uk/about-us; ByronBurgersUK.

C&R Café W1 £37 3 3 2
3-4 Rupert Court   020 7434 1128   4–3D
"A terrific find" on the edge of Chinatown, where the owner Rosa's family recipes have – for over 20 years now – provided an "authentic" taste of Malay-Chinese cooking, "with some fiery dishes that are all magnificently spicy and well made". "Ask the staff what they recommend and some surprises will end up on your plate!" / W1D 6DY; cnrcaferestaurant.com; C&R; Tue-Fri 10 pm, Sat 11 pm.

Cabotte EC2 £94 3 5 4
48 Gresham St   020 7600 1616   10–2C
"In the culinary void that seems to exist in the City", Xavier Rousset & Gearoid Devaney's venue is one of the few places that "rarely fails to deliver" when it comes to a high-quality meal and – "especially for this location – provides a great blend of decent food, wine, and particularly service" ("amicable and timely without being overpowering"). "Excellent food in the French style" is overseen by executive head chef Edward Boardland and ownership by two master sommeliers results in a "superb, heavily Burgundy-facing wine list" that's also "reasonably priced". Top Tip – "very knowledgeable sommelier as you'd expect, but the team are equally accepting if you BYO" and "corkage is reasonable too!" / EC2V 7AY; cabotte.co.uk; cabotte_; Mon-Fri 10 pm.

The Cadogan Arms SW3 £82 3 2 4
298 King's Road   020 3148 2630   6–3C
In terms of delivering "really decent" food on the King's Road (a rarity) and "an amazing Sunday roast", the three-year-old revamp of this "beautiful" early Victorian Chelsea pub must be accounted a success, and it becomes "BUSY!". If the backers were not JKS Restaurants in partnership with Kitchen Table's James Knappett one would say 'job done', but by the standards of such megastar restaurateurs, the result is good – not outstanding. / SW3 5UG; thecadoganarms.london; cadoganarmspublichouse; Mon-Sat 10 pm.

Cafe Britaly SE15 NEW
191 Rye Lane   020 7358 0735   1–4D
"Lovely addition to the bustling Peckham gastro-scene" – a *"tiny café"* opened in late spring 2024 in the former Supa Ya Ramen site on Rye Lane. As the name hints, it doesn't take itself too seriously, providing a more-thoughtful-than-it-sounds take on classics from spaghetti carbonara to fish finger sandwiches. It opened too late for much survey feedback. But the result, according to one early report, is *"delicious Italian/British fusion food, great cocktails and lovely service"*. (It's the creation of a former Bocca di Lupo duo: chef Alex Purdie and ops director Richard Crampton-Platt: Alex was also part of the brigade at Bouchon Racine). / SE15 4TP; cafebritaly.com; Sun-Thu 10 pm, Fri & Sat 11 pm.

Cafe Cecilia E8 £67 3|3|3
Canal Place, 32 Andrews Road   0203 478 6726   14–2B
"Slightly off the beaten track but worth the trek" – Max Rocha's "joyous" if "minimalist" Hackney canalside spot is "a fantastic venue, and a slightly quirky one given the charming but industrial view". It inspires nothing but upbeat feedback for "French bistro food (e.g. Onglet & Chips) cooked to perfection"; and it does a "very good breakfast" too. "Busy, but they don't hurry you". / E8 4RL; cafececilia.com; cafececilialondon; Thu-Sat 8.30 pm, Wed 3 pm, Sun 3.30 pm.

Café Deco WC1 £75 3|2|2
43 Store Street   020 8091 2108   2–1C
"Really nice, and often outstanding dishes" are acclaimed by most reports on this former greasy spoon in Bloomsbury from ex-Rochelle Canteen chef Anna Tobias and the 40 Maltby Street team: and they say the simple, modern bistro dishes are backed up by a "very fair wine list" with a "good selection of natural wines". (A more sceptical, minority view is that "although the place hits the nerve of the Zeitgeist – with food suggesting honesty and simplicity, complete with an air of sophistication – its success is a pricey London phenomenon possibly explained by the decline in home cooking").
/ WC1E 7DB; cafe-deco.co.uk; cafe_deco_bloomsbury; Tue-Sat 9.30 pm.

Café du Marché EC1 £69 3|3|5
22 Charterhouse Sq   020 7608 1609   10–1B
Now in its 40th year, this "charming, family-run brasserie", "hidden away near Smithfield Market", is "about as close as you'll get to France" without leaving Blighty. With a "great atmosphere, but still quiet enough to be able to chat", it's "a great place to seal a business deal" – but equally "French is always best for romance!". In the evenings, "regular live music adds to the relaxed atmosphere". / EC1M 6DX; cafedumarche.co.uk; cafedumarche; Tue-Sat 9.30 pm.

Cafe François SE1 NEW
Borough Market   no tel   10–4C
From the team behind Maison François in St James's, this autumn 2024 newcomer in Borough Market promises a 'modern French canteen' with influences as diverse as Montreal and California. Features include rotisserie chicken and pâtisserie from the in-house bakery. / SE1 9AL; Tue-Sat 9 pm, Mon 7 pm.

Café in the Crypt,
St Martin in the Fields WC2 £37 2|2|5
Duncannon St   020 7766 1158   2–2C
"We always come here when in London, as it's such an atmospheric venue in a fantastic location" – St Martin-in-the-Fields has a superb, brick-vaulted crypt and its self-service cafeteria provides an unusually affordable option in this prime area. It's variable though – hit lucky and you can have "a good value, very casual meal, if from a limited menu"; but one or two reports this year noted "real disappointment with the food offering". / WC2N 4JJ; stmartin-in-the-fields.org; stmartininthefields; Mon-Sat 5 pm.

Café Japan NW11 £41 3|3|2
626 Finchley Rd   020 8455 6854   1–1B
This "consistently good local Japanese" near Golders Green station is nowadays owned by Japanese fish and seafood wholesaler T&S Enterprises (who run the Atariya brand), and serves "fantastic food at very reasonable prices". It remains a pretty functional little space which has "maintained high standards" for sushi and sashimi over more than two decades. / NW11 7RR; atariya.co.uk; cafejapanlondon; Wed-Sun 10.30 pm.

FSA

Café Kitsuné SW1 £49
19 Motcomb Street   020 7034 5425   6–1D
A Japanese accent to the pastries adds exoticism (and expense?) to a trip to this swish perch, in the beating bougie heart of Belgravia. It originally opened in the foyer of the stunning-looking Pantechnicon building next door, which – in summer 2024 – rebranded as '19 Motcomb Street' – leading (we understand from the press) to a relocation of the café to the 'Halkin Arcade'. / SW1X 8LB; pantechnicon.com; _pantechnicon; Mon-Sun 7 pm.

Café Maja W6 £32   **3** 2 2
238-246 King Street   020 8563 8550   8–2B
"Everyone loves this place" – the bustling "café within the Polish Cultural Centre (POSK)" near Ravenscourt Park is "slightly scruffy" but no-one cares given its super-cheap prices: you don't need fret about the cost-of-living crisis here. "Wonderful and relaxing", it's "a great place to talk for ages" with "lovely coffee and really good cakes (cheesecake is fabulous); and they also offer hearty really good Polish home cooking like soups and pancakes". / W6 0RF; Tue-Sun 10 pm.

Cafe Murano £78   **3** **3** **3**
33 St James's St, SW1   020 3371 5559   3–3C
36 Tavistock St, WC2   020 3371 5559   5–3D
Pastificio, 34 Tavistock Street, WC2   020 3535 7884   5–3D
184 Bermondsey Street, SE1   020 3985 1545   10–4D
"Classic, uncomplicated Italian dishes are done accurately and well-flavoured" at Angela Hartnett's trio of "deservedly popular" modern trattorias. "Consistently enjoyable, with a buzzy atmosphere and lovely staff", they are widely tipped as a "good standby" for many occasions, and the worst anyone had to say about them this year is that they can seem "unimaginative but competent". Top Tip – "the pasta is the thing here – especially the spicy rigatoni – but the menu is broad enough for kids and their parents (with a decent wine list); and staff are patient with families"; and "good-value set lunch". / cafemurano.co.uk; cafemurano.

Café Petiole WC2 NEW
South Wing, Somerset House, The Strand,   07842 797541   2–2D
For a healthy, budget bite in the environs of Somerset House, grab 'n' go or grab a perch at this May 2024 newcomer, whose gorgeous setting, high ceilings and cane chairs add to its genteel attractions. It's from Rishim Sachdeva, of the excellent Tendril in Mayfair, and the mostly vegan selection (sarnies, salads, etc) includes Tendril favourites including its tiramisu, alongside new dishes with an emphasis on baked goods. / WC2R 1LA; Sun-Wed 05, Thu-Sat 10 pm.

Café Spice Namaste E16 £69   **5** **4** **4**
1-2 Lower Dock Walk, Royal Dock   020 7488 9242   12–1D
"Shame it's now so out-of-the-way, but well worth a visit" – after 26 years on the fringe of the City, Cyrus & Pervin Todiwala relocated their famous Indian venue to this new unit on the Royal Docks in 2022. It's a "light and airy setting" (not far from London Excel and City Airport) with bright views over the water and docks. "Cyrus continues to evolve his dishes, for all occasions", and "the Todiwalas are excellent hosts too": "staff are so passionate and personal to all who come and dine" on the "wonderful Indian food with a Portuguese twist". / E16 2GT; cafespice.co.uk; cafespicenamasteldn; Tue-Sat 10 pm.

Cah Chi KT3 £60   **3** **3** 2
79-81 Kingston Road   020 8949 8880   1–4A
"A great surprise: very interesting food choices and truly helpful staff" – New Malden is known for its large Korean expat community, and this family-run Korean BBQ (relocated in 2023 from its former location) makes a good place to discover the cuisine. / KT3 3PB; cahchi.co.uk; cahchibbq; Tue-Sat 10.30 pm, Sun 10 pm.

FSA RATINGS: FROM **1** POOR — **5** EXCEPTIONAL

F S A

Caldesi £89 **3**|**3**|**2**
118 Marylebone Ln, W1   020 7487 0754   2–1A
29 Belsize Ln, NW3   020 3880 7474   9–2A **NEW**
"Classic Italian dishes are executed as well as one could hope for" at Giancarlo & Katie Caldesi's "long-established" Marylebone stalwart: "the food is always very good – ragu a case in point – and the specials and seasonals can be mouthwatering". That remains the majority view anyhow, although its critics feel results are "competent if unexciting". Still, it's proved a successful base for expansion, as the couple also run a restaurant in Bray (complete with cookery school) and in April 2024 added a new offshoot in Belsize Park: an initial report says the NW3 branch is "a welcome addition, well-designed with friendly staff; and serving a relatively short menu including pizza and pasta, if at West End prices". / caldesi.com.

The Camberwell Arms SE5 £68 **5**|**4**|**3**
65 Camberwell Church St   020 7358 4364   1–3C
"Still pumping out the big and loud flavour bombs with a simple style that suits the venue" ("technically well-cooked, robust dishes", which the "in-house butchery helps make even more special"): this 10-year-old "in the heart of Camberwell" is a sibling to Waterloo's Anchor & Hope, and has Mike Davis at the stoves, who learnt his trade at the A&H. That it still feels like an "unpretentious" boozer is key to its appeal ("its clients are hipsters who don't like posh restaurants"). Top Menu Tip – "incredible Steak and Guinness pie". / SE5 8TR; thecamberwellarms.co.uk; thecamberwellarms; Tue-Sat 11 pm, Sun, Mon 5 pm.

Cambio de Tercio SW5 £89 **4**|**3**|**3**
163 Old Brompton Rd   020 7244 8970   6–2B
"Unchanged over the years but still a Spanish star in west London with plenty of charm and a style all of its own" – Abel Lusa opened this high-quality Hispanic venture in South Kensington in 1995 and has maintained it as "a consistent performer" ever since. "If you love well-prepared Spanish food and wines, you'll find both here" alongside "excellent and friendly" service. "In June and July each year it's filled with tennis players" and both Nadal and Alcarez are well known to be major fans (eating here regularly with their families and ordering take-out during Wimbledon). As a result, Abel has developed pop-ups serving his food at major tennis championships around the globe. / SW5 0LJ; cambiodeterciogroup.co.uk; cambiodeterciogroup; Tue-Thu, Sun 11 pm, Fri & Sat 11.30 pm.

Camille SE1 **NEW** £41 **3**|**4**|**3**
2-3 Stoney Street   020 3794 8958   10–4C
"Bistro food at its best" is given a decidedly modern British retread at this classy new, but traditionally decorated bistro in Borough Market, which has been a fave rave of the press critics in 2024. It's from the team behind Soho's Ducksoup; and the menu and website says it 'leans into French regional cooking' from 'imagined jaunts' through La Patrie. But the ultimate culinary result appears more like a Gallic glaze over modern British nose-to-tail cooking (e.g. Calf Brains, Broad Beans & Mint; or Lamb Heart, Peas & Ewe's Curd). All of a fair number of reports rate the food good-to-exceptional. / SE1 9AA; camillerestaurant.co.uk; camille_se1; Mon-Sat 10.30 pm, Sun 9.30 pm.

The Campaner SW1 £95 **3**|**3**|**3**
1 Garrison Close, Chelsea Barracks   020 4580 1385   6–3D
Few postcodes are as stratospherically expensive as the shiny new developments of Chelsea Barracks, in which this open-all-day yearling – from a group based in Barcelona – resides. It does have its pluspoints, especially if you are lucky enough to be one of the plutocratic locals, including an airy, handsome space with vaulted brick walls (and massive lampshades). But when quiet it can appear "dreary"; and given that the Spanish cuisine is fully priced, even though it's "well-executed", diners (especially non-locals) can find

F S A

it "hard to think of a reason to return". Top Menu Tip – good rice dishes. / SW1W 8BP; thecampaner.com; thecampanerchelsea; Tue-Thu midnight, Fri & Sat 12.30 am, Sun 6 pm.

Cantinetta Antinori SW1
4 Harriet Street   020 4580 1354   6–1D

Florence, Vienna, Zurich, Monaco… and, since April 2023, Belgravia now boast outposts of this Tuscan wine dynasty's empire – run by the 26th generation of a family whose brand-extension into the restaurant trade started in 1957. Despite a relatively prominent location – a side street off Sloane Street – it has attracted no feedback in our annual diners' poll in its first year of operation. It's also been largely ignored by the press, although in April 2024, The Evening Standard's Joanna Taylor reported "excellent" food even if a meal here "may set you back more than flights to Pisa". / SW1X 9JR; cantinetta-antinori.com; cantinettaantinori_london.

Canton Arms SW8   £62   **3** **3** **4**
177 South Lambeth Rd   020 7582 8710   11–1D

This "gastropub of real standing" (est. 2010) a short walk from Vauxhall is just the place to "get your laughing gear on some excellent modern British fare". "It looks like a pub" and is a "proper South London boozer at the front, where you can have a quiet pint", but "you don't judge the book by the cover" – in the back is a "well thought-through carnivore's paradise" ("go hungry for big plates of usually rich food"), with a "good selection of wines by the glass". "Booking is obligatory", although not quite as difficult as its more famous stablemate the Anchor & Hope, close to Waterloo and the South Bank. Top Menu Tip – "offaly tasty options not easily found elsewhere". / SW8 1XP; cantonarms.com; Tue-Sat 9.45 pm, Sun 3.45 pm.

Canton Blue,
The Peninsula SW1 NEW   £134   **3** **4** **3**
1 Grosvenor Place   020 8138 6888   2–3A

This luxurious international hotel chain (whose 300-room original is the oldest hotel in Hong Kong) opened just south of trafficky Hyde Park Corner in September 2023. Its "extravagantly decorated" ground-floor Cantonese dining room has received a mixed rep in the newspapers (in his January 2024 review, Giles Coren in The Times said it "didn't pass muster") but our reports suggest a fair performance by the standards of posh hotel chains. Its advocates say it's "very expensive but faultless" with "amazing" and "perfectly served" cuisine (particularly classic dishes such as seafood dumplings, char sui and Peking Duck, which all receive a thumbs-up). And service is praised as "really helpful, accommodating and professional". Those who are less convinced don't damn it but say "it's overpriced for food that's only OK, and served in a windowless room". (There's also Brooklands at roof level, see also). / SW1X 7HJ; peninsula.com; /thepeninsulalondonhotel/; Mon-Sun 9.30 pm.

Capital Hotel,
The Restaurant at The Capital SW3   £102   **3** **3** **2**
22-24 Basil Street   020 7591 1202   6–1D

All shopped out at Harrods? Two minutes' walk from the back doors, this small boutique hotel dining room has gone informal in recent years, replacing its former haute cuisine offering with bare table-tops and an all-day menu. It was most recommended this year for its afternoon tea, which is served from noon so can double for lunch. The current theme is Alice in Wonderland's Mad Hatter's Tea Party. / SW3 1AT; therestaurantatthecapitallondon.com; thecapitalhotel; Mon-Sun 9.30 pm.

Caractère W11   £139   **3** **3** **3**
209 Westbourne Park Road   020 8181 3850   7–1B

"Combining the best of French and Italian gastronomy" – Emily Roux and her husband Diego Ferrari continue to put in an assured performance at their "lovely neighbourhood restaurant" in Notting Hill. The cuisine is of "excellent quality", yet not particularly striving for its own sake: aptly described in one report as "enjoyable fine dining, comfort dishes". You can either opt for à la carte – three courses for £92 per person – or go for a five-course 'Build Your Own Tasting Menu' option at £120 per person. "Simply divine: expensive but worth it!" / W11 1EA; caractererestaurant.com; caractererestaurant; Tue-Sat 9 pm.

Caraffini SW1 £80 3 4 3
61-63 Lower Sloane Street   020 7259 0235   6–2D

"They know their clientele" (most of whom are of a certain age), and "really look after them" at this "absolutely classic Italian" south of Sloane Square, founded 30 years ago by Paolo Caraffini. "The food feels like pure 1960s-style London/Italian and is very competently cooked". "There's always a great welcome (when they get to know you!), it's not over-expensive and has a warm and bubbly atmosphere". / SW1W 8DH; caraffini.co.uk; caraffinirestaurant; Mon-Sat 10.30 pm.

Caravaggio EC3 £66 2 3 2
107-112 Leadenhall St   020 7626 6206   10–2D

"Very dependable for a nice business lunch" in the heart of the City near Lloyd's – this upscale "steady" Italian occupies an august former banking hall where Luciano Pavarotti sang for his supper on the opening night in 1996. Top Menu Tip – "it's one of the few places where you should choose the grilled liver". / EC3A 4DP; caravaggiorestaurant.co.uk; caravaggio_ldn; Mon-Fri 10 pm.

Caravan £66 2 2 2
Yalding House, 152 Great Portland Street, W1   020 3963 8500   2–1B
30-35 Drury Lane, WC2   020 3955 8500   5–1D
1 Granary Sq, N1   020 7101 7661   9–3C
30 Great Guildford St, SE1   020 7101 1190   10–4B
Unit 2, Reuters Plaza, E14   020 3725 7600   12–1C
11-13 Exmouth Mkt, EC1   020 7833 8115   10–1A
Bloomberg Arcade, Queen Victoria St, EC4   020 3957 5555   10–3C

A particularly solid choice for brunch – this "buzzy" Kiwi-run chain (with seven branches) fits the bill well, with "interesting small plates" of pan-global fusion food and an emphasis on notably good coffee (which they roast in-house). On the downside, the food is often "passable and no more" and their "lively" interiors (Granary Square in particular) can become "hopelessly crowded", giving rise to incidents of "slapdash service". Still, they're "fun" and "reasonably priced". (See also Vardo.) / caravanonexmouth.co.uk.

Caravel N1 £53 3 4 4
172 Shepherdess Walk   020 7251 1155   14–2A

For a "romantic" evening, fans tip this permanently moored barge on the Regent's Canal about 15 minutes walk north of Old Street tube. It's consistently well-rated all round, including its modern bistro cuisine. / N1 7ED; thestudiokitchen.co.uk; caravel_restaurant; Thu-Sat, Tue, Wed 11 pm, Sun 4 pm.

Carlotta W1 £70 1 2 4
77-78 Marylebone High Street   no tel   2–1A

The "beautiful dining room" and "glitzy decoration" ensure this Italian-American-themed Marylebone yearling from the Big Mamma Group is "a great hit on Instagram". But "that doesn't compensate for some very average food and utterly ridiculous prices" – many reporters reckon it's "all show and no substance" – "and not particularly fun" either. / W1U 5JX; bigmammagroup.com; bigmamma.uk; Mon-Wed 09.45 pm, Thu-Sat 10.15 pm, Sun 9 pm.

Carmel £81 5 3 4
7-8 Market Place, W1   020 4546 8324   3–1C **NEW**
Lonsdale Road, NW6   020 3848 2090   1–2B

"I'm addicted to their hispi cabbage!" – Josh Katz's marvellous Queen's Park three-year-old sits in a mews at the "über-trendy end of Lonsdale Road"; and everything about it hits a surefooted note as a "high-quality" neighbourhood spot that actually draws fans from miles away. "Every dish is a winner" with "very interesting flavours" permeating the "excellent, small Middle Eastern plates": "such as aubergine, merguez sausages and beans, grilled chicken and wondrous za'atar-strewn bread and dips; and there's a wine list full of interesting bangers". Even fans can find it a bit "crowded" (with some of the seating at a communal table), but on most accounts it's a "great place for a leisurely meal of sharing plates". No reports as yet on its new spin-off in Fitzrovia, which opened in the middle of our annual diners' poll in April 2024.

Carousel W1 £73 5 4 3
19-23 Charlotte Street   020 7487 5564   2–1C

"Visits from chefs from around the world are a splendid way to try great food at ridiculously low prices", at this "always fabulous" operation, which has established itself as a fixture of London gastronomy over the past 10 years. They bring their A-game to showcase their best dishes, resulting in some truly "brilliant" and celebratory meals – so it's always worth taking a chance on something unfamiliar that might "blow you away". Initially operating in Marylebone, they moved to this new large Fitzrovia site in 2021. / W1T 1RL; carousel-london.com; carousel_ldn; Tue-Sat 11 pm.

Casa do Frango £57 3 3 4
Sir Simon Milton Square, SW1   020 3943 7777   2–4B
31-32 Heddon Street, W1   020 3535 5900   4–3A
32 Southwark Street, SE1   020 3972 2323   10–4C
3 King John Court, EC2   020 7654 3020   13–1B

"Simple and so good!" – MJMK's chain (they also own Kol and Lisboeta) of "posh Nandos" makes an outstanding choice for a "bustling if noisy" night out on the cheap. "Excellent piri piri chicken 'n' chips" is at the heart of the food offering, but there are also brilliant sides (such as "very good African rice and slaw") and some fab veggie options. The original SE1 branch remains the most commented-on, and has a "lovely" plant-filled upstairs. The other branches are perhaps a fraction less vibey, although the newly opened Victoria outlet wins praise as "a good airy space". / casadofrango.co.uk; casadofrango_london.

Casa Fofó E8 £90 5 4 3
158 Sandringham Road   020 8062 2489   14–1B

"Favourite restaurant of all time!" – "Stunning flavours and textures, offered by the fixed-price, no-choice, but ever-changing taster menu" inspire adulation for Adolfo de Cecco's "unpretentious" shop-conversion in Dalston. It may be one of East London's true culinary heavyweights, but the style is "totally informal and allows the food to be the star". "Service is impeccable and the food is brought to your table by the chefs themselves". And "how does he do it for the price?" – £122 for the eight courses plus wine pairing (a meal might run – roasted beetroot tart; bread and butter; monkfish with bergamot sauce; pig skin congee with XO sauce; Jerusalem artichoke with umeboshi sauce and tahini; cheese with onion ice cream; yuzu granita; dried mushroom and frozen tofu). One report in particular typifies the love the places generates: "we eat out in proper restaurants twice most weeks, so we don't stint ourselves, and from the receipts can count a full 50 visits to Casa Fofó since the beginning of 2023, and we never seem to be offered the same dish twice!" / E8 2HS; casafofolondon.co.uk; casafofolondon; Wed-Sun 9.30 pm.

Casa Pastór & Plaza Pastór N1 £73 2 2 3
Coal Drops Yard   020 7018 3335   9–3C

"The tacos are good, the margaritas even better", say fans of this 'little sister' to the Hart Bros' El Pastor Mexican brand. Much hyped when it opened six years ago, these days it generates limited feedback in our annual survey of diners, but all reports agree it's at least "serviceable" for a meal in fashionable Coal Drops Yard, near King's Cross. / N1C 4AB; tacoselpastor.co.uk; Tue, Wed 11 pm, Thu-Sat 11.30 pm, Sun 8 pm.

Casa Tua WC1 — £53 — 2 2 2
106 Cromer Street   020 7833 1483   9–4C

"A corner independent Italian in the underserved backstreets opposite King's Cross and St Pancras" and "a short walk from the stations". Perhaps it's too uneventful to make much of a trip, but fans say it's "well worth seeking out if you are in the area" for "fresh pasta and tasty, simple dishes at fair prices". (The original venture was actually a still-existing sibling of the same name in Camden Town, on which we receive much more limited feedback).
/ WC1H 8BZ; casatuacamden.com; casatualondon; Mon-Sun 10 pm.

Casse-Croute SE1 — £75 — 4 4 4
109 Bermondsey St   020 7407 2140   10–4D

"You could be in France" at this "fantastic, proper Gallic bistro" on foodie Bermondsey Street that's a "top culinary experience" – "its competitors are much more elegant, while this is cramped and scruffy, but there is a real homely welcome" and "wow! The food is so good!" / SE1 3XB; cassecroute.co.uk; cassecroute109; Mon-Sat 10.30 pm, Sun 4.30 pm.

Cavita W1 — £97 — 2 2 3
56-60 Wigmore Street   020 3928 1000   3–1A

"A really lovely atmosphere" is a high point for fans of Adriana Cavita's chilled two-year-old in Fitzrovia, in which the well-known chef from Mexico City presents tacos and street food alongside sharing dishes of grilled fish and steaks cooked in homemade Red Mole sauce over coals. Inconsistent feedback hits its ratings though: the odd dish doesn't work (maybe it's something about the London palate) and service is, on occasion, "VERY slow".
/ W1U 1PU; cavitarestaurant.com; cavita.restaurante; Tue-Sun 10 pm.

Cecconi's — £88 — 2 2 3
19-21 Old Compton Street, W1   020 7734 5656   5–2A
5a Burlington Gardens, W1   020 7434 1500   4–4A
58-60 Redchurch Street, E2   020 3841 7755   13–1C
27 Poultry, EC2   020 3828 2000   10–2C

"The energy is fab" at this "busy and buzzy" Mayfair haunt, whose large central bar, pavement tables and green leather stools import a sense of chic Italian glamour to this corner-site a minute from Bond Street. The Italian food (cicchetti, risotti, pastas, traditional mains) doesn't detract from the occasion, but is "highly priced for average quality", albeit "all decent"; and "service can suffer when it's over-busy". Nowadays part of Soho House, its branches spread from Berlin to West Hollywood, via the City of London (in The Ned). Comments on the latter aren't terrible, but less enthusiastic than those for W1. / cecconis.co.uk; cecconislondon.

Cedric Grolet, The Berkeley SW1 — £101 — 2 4 3
Wilton Place   020 7235 6000   6–1D

"OMG, out of this world... but very expensive". This renowned Parisian pâtissier's first outlet outside of Paris (opened in 2022) is a bright and rather gorgeous bakery space within the famous Knightsbridge five-star hotel. Its contribution to the luxe afternoon tea scene is 'Goutea' – a Frenchified take on afternoon tea at £85 which can be booked for breakfast, lunch or dinner! Or, for a mere £135 per person, you can sit at the counter for an even bigger blow-out of six sweet and two savoury courses. Notwithstanding that all the limited feedback we have on it this year is positive, anyone with a sharp sense of value for money should run a mile. / SW1X 8RL; the-berkeley.co.uk; cedricgrolettheberkeley; Mon-Sun 7 pm.

F S A

Cent Anni SW19 £60 2 3 3
33 High Street   020 3971 9781   11–2B

This "good, reliable Italian local" in Wimbledon Village majors in home-made pasta and thin-crust pizza, while "other items like calves' liver are lovely". "The midweek offers are not as good as they used to be", however, while "the menu rarely changes". / SW19 5BY; centanni.co.uk; centannirestaurant; Mon-Sat 11 pm, Sun 10.30 pm.

Cepages W2 £67 4 3 4
69 Westbourne Park Road   020 3602 8890   7–1B

This "hidden gem" of a wine bar, "tucked away in the stuccoed splendour of Westbourne Park", serves "sophisticated French food" in tapas-size portions and "good (if expensive) wines" in "stylish yet cosy" surroundings, with exposed brickwork and wooden tables . / W2 5QH; cepages.co.uk; cepages_london; Tue-Sat 11 pm.

Ceru £44 3 2 2
7-9 Bute St, SW7   020 3195 3001   6–2C
13 Queensway, W2   020 7221 2535   7–2C

"Interesting and tasty small plates" – "sort of evolved eastern Mediterranean" – is backed up by a "short and eclectic wine list" focused on the same region at Barry & Patricia Hamilton's Levantine duo in Queensway and South Kensington. With its "fast, efficient service", the latter is a "good place for pre-Albert Hall dining". Top Menu Tip – for brunch, "the Turkish breakfast (halloumi, merguez, baked eggs, spicy tomato crush, pitta bread)". / cerurestaurants.com; ceruLondon.

Chakana E8 NEW £54 3 3 3
41 Broadway Market   020 3649 7494   14–2B

Vibrant Andean dishes – including distinctive ceviche, tiradito and causa starters (and with lots for vegans and veggies) – win a thumbs-up (if on limited feedback) for this September 2023 newcomer in Hackney's hip Broadway Market, which marks the return to the capital of former Lima (Fitzrovia) head chef Robert Ortiz (who also launched the original Chakana in Birmingham four years ago). / E8 4PH; chakana-restaurant.co.uk; chakana.restaurant; Tue-Thu 10.30 pm, Fri & Sat 11.30 pm, Sun 9 pm.

Champor-Champor SE1 £69 3 2 2
62 Weston St   020 7403 4600   10–4C

"Such good Thai food hiding away" near Guy's Hospital in the shadow of the Shard – this funkily decorated venue mixes Malay influences into its unusual cuisine, with results that have stood the test of time since it opened 25 years ago. / SE1 3QJ; champor-champor.com; champorchamporldn; Mon-Sat 10 pm, Sun 9.30 pm.

Charlie's at Brown's W1 £118 3 5 5
Brown's Hotel, Albemarle Street   020 7493 6020   3–3C

"Gorgeous room… beautiful menu… classy crowd" – this "spacious and finely decorated" wood-panelled dining room is one of London's better traditional eating options, and sits at the heart of a Mayfair hotel originally founded in 1837 and nowadays owned by Rocco Forte (it is named for his father). Adam Byatt (of Trinity in Clapham, see also) oversees a "very well-executed safe menu of classic tasty dishes such as Chicken Milanese, Calves' liver with mash, or delicious Sirloin with chips and salad". And service remains "exceptional" even after the departure last year of star maître d', Jesus Adorno. / W1S 4BP; roccofortehotels.com; browns_hotel; Mon-Sun 10 pm.

Chateau W4 £54 3 4 2
213 Chiswick High Road   020 87422 344   8–2A

"Some of the best Lebanese food around W4", "miles away from the usual formula" can be enjoyed at this Chiswick High Road outfit with a "great

owner from Beirut". It's "also a fab cake/dessert shop during the day", which makes it "great for either brunch or dinner". / W4 2DW; chateau-chiswick.com; chateau_chiswick; Mon-Sat 10 pm, Sun 6 pm.

Chatora TW9 £65 4 3 3
100 Kew Road   020 8948 6786   1–4A
"In the lost part of Richmond" (on the way to Kew) – "a very good curry house" spread over three levels, whose staff are "always really friendly". Head Chef Sunil produces a menu that intersperses less familiar dishes and ingredients with tandoori classics: "it's much much better than so much of what's available locally, and well worth the extra short walk from the town centre". / TW9 2PQ; chatora.co.uk; Tue-Sun 10 pm.

Chayote E1 NEW £61   3 3 2
2 Tower Bridge House, St Katharine's Way,   020 3031 7601   10–3D
Innovative, family-run Latino newcomer that opened in October 2023 in St Katharine Docks (with views of Tower Bridge) that brings together Mexican-fusion dishes with Peruvian and Spanish influences, from former Barrafina head chef Tomasz Baranski. Fans say "it's the most interesting restaurant in the area, but it's not yet always well-patronised (which can sometimes dampen the ambience)". / E1W 1AA; chayote.co.uk; chayote_skd; Tue-Sat 10 pm.

The Cheese Barge W2 £59   3 3 3
Sheldon Square   07862 001418   7–1C
"Only for cheese lovers… and that's me!" – the clue is in the name at Mathew Carver's "fun and different" venue – a 96ft custom-built, double-decker barge permanently moored in Paddington Basin, which showcases "a great selection of British cheeses with interesting pairings". "Out-of-town visitors love it". Top Menu Tip – "The curried cheese curds are amazing". / W2 6HY; thecheesebar.com; thecheesebarldn; Mon-Sat 9 pm, Sun 7.15pm.

Cher Thai SW4 £48   4 4 3
22 North Street   020 3583 3702   11–1D
"Flavours with tingly freshness and a big punch" mean that this "tightly packed" (and "noisy") Clapham four-year-old is "the best Thai" for its fans – "it's definitely reservations only". "Service is friendly and efficient and the ambience is good but it's not for lingering these days as they turn the tables". ("I hate Harden's because it's now so popular that it's goodbye to the days of walking up to this local with any confidence"). / SW4 0HB; cherthailondon.co.uk; cherthailondon; Tue-Thu 10.30 pm, Fri & Sat 11 pm, Sun 10 pm.

Chet's W12 £47   2 3 4
Hoxton Hotel, 65 Shepherd's Bush Green   020 3540 3150   8–1C
Bringing a "welcome dash of glamour to Shepherd's Bush Green", the recently arrived Hoxton Hotel has a stylish and spacious diner featuring the cooking of LA chef Kris Yenbaroong, whose "Californian-Thai food is perfectly enjoyable (if no more than that)". Service is personable, and it's a fun place to linger for an "excellent post-meal G&T" in their rather swish bar/lounge. / W12 8QE; chetsrestaurant.co.uk; chets_ldn; Mon-Sun midnight.

Chettinad W1 £45   3 3 2
16 Percy St   020 3556 1229   2–1C
This "good-value" contemporary Indian in Bloomsbury offers "reliable" cooking from Tamil Nadu on India's southern tip. Like its neighbour Sagar, it offers a selection of dosas, but here the menu isn't vegetarian with many options 'From our butchers' or 'From our Fishermen's nets' and chicken 'From our Farm'. (If you're up Leicester way, they also have a branch not far from the De Montfort Hall). / W1T 1DT; chettinadrestaurant.com; chettinad_restaurant; Mon-Sun 10 pm.

F S A

Chez Antoinette £48 222
The Caxton, 22 Palmer Street, SW1   020 3990 5377   2–4C
Unit 30 The Market Building, WC2   020 7240 9072   5–3D
"Excellent for an informal French meal at very affordable prices" – this Gallic pair are the creation of Lyon-born Aurelia Noel-Delclos, who named them after her food-loving grandmother. With its "child-friendly menu" and "well-designed bistro-brasserie ambience", the newer Victoria branch has overtaken the site in the touristic heart of old Covent Garden market in popularity. Don't expect the earth – they serve "reasonable, bistro-type fare".
/ chezantoinette.co.uk.

Chez Bruce SW17 £112 554
2 Bellevue Rd   020 8672 0114   11–2C
"Just a fantastic highlight for South London" – for the 19th year running, Bruce Poole & Nigel Platts-Martin's "outstanding neighbourhood restaurant" (in "a lovely location by Wandsworth Common") is voted London's No.1 favourite destination in our annual diners' poll, drawing adulation from across the capital as well as adoration from the immediately adjacent postcodes. It's "a high-class restaurant but an unfussy one": chef Matt Christmas's modern British cooking is "imaginative" – "with lovely touches throughout" – but "not with silly complications"; and there's "no tasting menu or small plates, thank goodness!". When it comes to wine, "they really know what they are doing" and offer "one of the most varied and high-quality wine lists around, with lots of classics, and plenty of new options to try". "The regular presence of Bruce himself (more common since lockdown) is welcome" and it's a "very slick operation": "friendly, not too pretentious" and "seemingly effortlessly convivial". The room itself is slightly "cramped" to some tastes, but is buoyed along by the "seductive buzz of contented diners". "It's still the one to beat – the standards never drop… if anything, it gets better!" / SW17 7EG; chezbruce.co.uk; chez.bruce; Tue-Thu 9.15 pm, Fri & Sat 9.30 pm, Sun 9 pm.

Chez Elles E1 £65 333
45 Brick Ln   020 7247 9699   13–2C
You'll find "French dialled up to 11" at this fun 'bistrotheque' in the curry heartland of Brick Lane. Locals say it's "a great restaurant to have in the neighbourhood – the service is always friendly and the food reliable".
/ E1 6PU; chezellesbistroquet.co.uk; chezellesbistro; Tue-Sat 10.30 pm.

Chez Roux W1 NEW
The Langham, 1C Portland Place   020 7636 1000   2–1B
Following his closure of the iconic Le Gavroche, Michel Roux's first London foray under the family brand is this May 2024 debut in the hotel where he ran 'Roux at the Landau' for many years. This newcomer isn't in the old space for the Landau but is dinner-only in the hotel's Palm Court, where Michel already consults on lunch and afternoon tea (and he also helps run the adjoining Wigmore gastropub). The fact that it's under the 'Chez Roux' banner (also used by his consultancy at the Greywalls Hotel in Scotland) hints at a level of aspiration that's 'haute', but not at the dizziest of gastronomic heights. / W1B 1JA; palm-court.co.uk; Mon-Sat 11 pm, Sun 10.30 pm.

Chicama SW10 £99 322
383 King's Road   020 3874 2000   6–3C
This seafood specialist in Chelsea's King's Road gives a coastal Peruvian treatment to supplies from Cornish fishermen, with crudo and ceviche as warm-ups to dishes like half a Galician Octopus or Miso Black Cod. It's a spinoff from Pachamama in Marylebone (see also) and is likewise rated as "very enjoyable" in most (if not quite all) reports. / SW10 0LP; chicamalondon.com; chicamalondon; Mon-Sun 11 pm.

FSA RATINGS: FROM 1 POOR — 5 EXCEPTIONAL

Chick 'n' Sours £44 4 3 3
1 Earlham Street, WC2 020 3198 4814 5–2B
390 Kingsland Rd, E8 020 3620 8728 14–2A
"Excellent fried chicken with a Korean twist" and "good cocktails" earn a "hallelujah" for this upbeat duo, whose original Haggerston branch celebrates its tenth anniversary in 2025; the Covent Garden branch came later. Although their punchy cocktails are a big part of the attraction, it's also "great for kids, with a special offer every half term", and the "beef dripping chips" go down well. / chicknsours.co.uk; chicknsours.

The Chiltern Firehouse W1 £115 2 3 5
1 Chiltern St 020 7073 7676 2–1A
"Restaurants are part-theatre, part-food" and most reports dwell on the trade-off between the two at this famous scene in Marylebone. For fans, "it's easy to see why celebs love it": "there's always a frisson of excitement in the dining room" and "service and food don't disappoint as they do in other 'in-crowd' places". At the other end of the spectrum, there are one or two who see it as "crazily overpriced, yet decidedly average and full of absolute tossers". A fair middle view is that "the Chiltern Firehouse excels at the performance, especially if you sit in the huge outside with large open fire, majorly effective heaters, and awnings if it rains. The food is only OK, but the ambience and people-watching are stellar!" / W1U 7PA; chilternfirehouse.com; chilternfirehouse; Mon-Sun 10 pm.

China Tang,
Dorchester Hotel W1 £113 3 2 2
53 Park Ln 020 7319 7088 3–3A
This "atmospheric Cantonese restaurant in the Dorchester" was designed by the late Sir David Tang 20 years ago, and "whisks you to 1930s Shanghai when you walk in". "One of the finest Chinese restaurants in London", its menu lists "some mind-boggling but expensive dishes", such as Japanese size 18 abalone at £388 or Peking duck with 125 grams of Kristal caviar at £480. Dip your toe in the water with the dim sum menu (which is served in the evenings as well as at lunchtimes). Or, from late 2024, pop into the Harrods Food Halls, where there's a new 'China Tang' stall. / W1K 1QA; chinatanglondon.co.uk; ChinaTangLondon; Mon-Sun 11 pm.

Chinese Cricket Club EC4 £72 3 2 3
Crowne Plaza, 19 New Bridge Street 020 7438 8051 10–3A
For a Chinese meal in the City, a number of reporters recommend this venue at the Hyatt Regency hotel in Blackfriars (fka the Crowne Plaza, reopened post-refurb in summer 2023). The unusual name marks the debut of the Chinese national cricket team in 2009, the year the restaurant opened. Classic dishes range from dim sum and Peking duck to xiao long bao. / EC4V 6DB; chinesecricketclub.com; ChineseCricketClub;; Mon-Sun 9 pm.

La Chingada SE8 £26 3 3 2
206 Lower Road 020 7237 7448 12–2B
Don't run a mile from the plastic life-size Mexican guarding the door to this basic cantina in a grungy corner of Surrey Quays, if you want to discover its "top-notch, authentic Mexican dishes", and in particular "excellent tacos". The odd aficionado of Latino fare crosses town for this place. (There's also a branch near Euston at 160 Eversholt Street). / SE8 5DJ; lachingada.co.uk; lachingadalondon; Tue, Fri-Sun 10.30 pm, Wed & Thu 9.30 pm.

Chishuru W1 £102 4 3 2
3 Great Titchfield Street 07960 002150 3–1C
"A fascinating culinary experience" – Adejoké Bakare's 50-seat Chishuru vn2.0 opened in Fitzrovia in September 2023 and is a follow-up to the Brixton venture where she first made her name by channelling tastes she encountered in her Nigerian childhood into a culinary mashup suited to the capital. The result is "distinctive food that's boldly spiced and flavoured" and

"soooooo tasty" – to the extent it won many reporters' nominations as their best meal of this year. But while nearly all feedback says it's "deserving of its good reviews and its Michelin star", ratings here are not quite off-the-charts; and the slightly left-field award by the tyre men may unhelpfully distort some people's expectations, especially as the interior itself is no great shakes ("having been to the original, it was lovely to see the 'grown-up' version, but the room still has that 'pop-up' feeling… and not in a good way. Still, I hope it does well as there aren't many places like this. I'm sure the Michelin star will help its longevity"). / W1W 8AX; chishuru.com; chishuru; Mon-Fri 9.30 pm.

Chisou £98 5 4 2
22-23 Woodstock Street, W1   020 7629 3931   3–2B
31 Beauchamp Pl, SW3   020 3155 0005   6–1D
Fans say these straightforward Japanese operations "set a benchmark for quality sushi and sashimi", backed up by a "fabulous sake selection" and "charming service". The Mayfair branch is "something of an oasis off the bustle of Oxford Street", and like its Knightsbridge sibling is "very reasonably priced for the area and quality of food". Top Tip – "good omakase".
/ chisourestaurant.com; chisoulondon.

Chook Chook SW15 £48 4 4 2
137 Lower Richmond Road   020 8789 3100   11–1B
"A non-typical local Indian restaurant serving Putney with high-quality, authentic Indian food" – in "huge, freshly cooked, super-tasty portions and with interesting sundries". The "railway carriage theme is a bit of a stretch" for some, but "the food quality and quick service make it worth a detour".
/ SW15 1EZ; chookchook.uk; chookchooklondon_; Mon-Thu 10.30 pm, Fri & Sat 11 pm, Sun 10 pm.

Chop Chop at the Hippodrome WC2 NEW £62 3 3 2
Cranbourn Street   020 7769 8888   5–3B
Below the UK's biggest casino (so over-18s only), this new basement Chinese venue sits on the fringe of Chinatown. It's in partnership with Four Seasons, a veteran of the area known for excellent duck, which – in particular – is "spot on" here. In other respects, reports suggest the menu (quite short by the rambling standards of the area) is "well-executed if not overly exciting". "Those who mourn Y-ming [a nearby old-timer that closed two years ago] will love it here, as although the atmosphere is very different, it's so lovely to see William again!" (who was maître d' at Y-ming for over 25 years). Top Tip – "it is open late, which post-Brexit is a real plus given that most kitchens now are closing earlier". / WC2H 7JH; hippodromecasino.com; hippodromecasino; Mon-Sun 4 am.

Chotto Matte £74 3 4 3
11-13 Frith St, W1   020 7042 7171   5–2A
26 Paddington Street, W1   020 7058 4444   2–1A
These clubby Nikkei haunts from former Nobu exec Kurt Zdesar in Soho and Marylebone have spawned an international group with outlets in North America and the Middle East – with Manchester scheduled to follow this year. The food can be "excellent", and the joints are "buzzing" (so don't go if you want a quiet evening, or the "thumping and repetitive club music spoils the dining experience"). / chotto-matte.com; chottomatteldn.

Chourangi W1 £69 3 3 3
3 Old Quebec Street   020 3582 2710   2–2A
This three-year-old near Marble Arch is worth a visit for its "very interesting menu" of regional Bengali food, named after a district of Calcutta where an amalgam of Mogul, Chinese and European cuisines developed 300 years ago. "Order the signature tasting menu to try most of it" say fans of the project, from chef-restaurateur Anjan Chatterjee and airline entrepreneur Aditya Ghosh. / W1H 7DL; chourangi.co.uk; chourangildn; Sun-Thu 10 pm, Fri & Sat 10.30 pm.

FSA

Christopher's WC2 £103 2 3 4
18 Wellington St   020 7240 4222   5–3D
Opened in 1870 as London's first licensed casino, this impressive Covent Garden mansion is proof that it takes more than a fine space in a handy location to make a terrific eatery. Relaunched as a luxurious American restaurant in 1991 (by the son of a Tory grandee), it aims to import Manhattanite sophistication, top-quality surf 'n' turf and high-class brunch to the capital, alongside a popular Martini bar. But, while it does still receive the odd nomination as a place for a business lunch, it's largely ignored in our annual diners' poll nowadays. / WC2E 7DD; christophersgrill.com; christopherswc2; Tue-Thu midnight, Fri & Sat 1 am, Sun 5 pm.

Chucs £95 2 2 3
25 Eccleston Street, SW1   020 3827 3000   2–4B
65 Lower Sloane Street, SW1   020 3827 2999   6–2D
31 Dover St, W1   020 3763 2013   3–3C
97 Old Brompton Road, SW7   020 8037 4525   6–2B
The Mayfair original of this small group is celebrating its tenth year, with a Belgravia sibling and café-style offshoots in similarly chichi Chelsea and Kensington. It channels a retro 'dolce vita' vibe, with an Italian menu that "delivers on the brief if nothing more". The latest addition is an all-day café, which opened in December 2023 next door to the Dover Street flagship. / chucsrestaurants.com; chucsrestaurants.

Chuku's N15 £65 3 3 3
274 High Road   no tel   1–1D
"Tasty Nigerian food with a modern twist" has won an enthusiastic following for Emeka and Ifeyinwa Frederick's West African 'tapas' joint in Seven Sisters – a lively, "cheap 'n' cheerful" choice whose "fame deserves to be spread far and wide". / N15 5AJ; chukuslondon.co.uk; chukusldn; Tue-Sat 10.30 pm, Sun 8.30 pm.

Churchill Arms W8 £48 3 4 4
119 Kensington Church St   020 7792 1246   7–2B
This "always entertaining", flower-bedecked 1750 tavern near Notting Hill Gate "still scores bang for the buck" with the Thai menu it has served for more than 25 years in a buzzy conservatory to the back of the main pub. It's lost some of its renown for exceptional value in recent times, but it remains a somewhat eccentric one-off, whose popularity makes booking essential in the evening. (The pub was renamed to honour the wartime leader, whose grandparents apparently supped here). / W8 7LN; churchillarmskensington.co.uk; churchillarmsw8; Mon-Sat 9.30 pm, Sun 9 pm.

Chutney Mary SW1 £98 4 4 4
73 St James's Street   020 7629 6688   3–4D
"You get the whole deal" at this superb Indian all-rounder in St James's: the venture which – when it was first located in SW10 – formed the first link in the restaurant chain owned by Ranjit & Namita Mathrani and the latter's sister, Camellia Panjab (which nowadays, as MW Eats, also encompasses the Masala Zone chain, plus Veeraswamy and Amaya). The "amazing" cuisine features "a deliciously innovative mix of regional Indian dishes"; service is "impeccable (especially from the manager, Kanwal"); and the "glamorous dining room" is well-suited to any occasion. / SW1A 1PH; chutneymary.com; chutneymary.london; Mon-Sat 10.30 pm, Sun 10 pm.

Chutneys NW1 £27 3 3 2
124 Drummond St   020 7388 0604   9–4C
An "amazing lunchtime buffet" and a good choice of "reliable vegetarian dishes" pull in a regular crowd at this "stalwart" of the 'Little India' enclave behind Euston station. / NW1 2PA; chutneyseuston.uk; chutneysnw1; Mon-Sat 11 pm, Sun 10.30 pm.

FSA RATINGS: FROM 1 POOR — 5 EXCEPTIONAL

Ciao Bella WC1 £59 **3 4 5**
86-90 Lamb's Conduit St   020 7242 4119   2–1D

"What a joyful experience!" – "anyone who doesn't love Ciao Bella is mad". This buoyant Bloomsbury fixture serves "unpretentious authentic Italian home cooking in a really great atmosphere" that's "somewhat chaotic when busy" and "never changes". After retiring from her 20-year career as a critic last year, Marina O'Loughlin revealed that this is where she eats out when paying for herself. Foodie flourishes are entirely absent though – its prime selling point is offering "good value for money in such a high-cost city". / WC1N 3LZ; ciaobellarestaurant.co.uk; ciaobella_london; Mon-Sun 10.30 pm.

Cibo W14 £86 **3 5 3**
3 Russell Gdns   020 7371 6271   8–1D

"A wonderful quiet dining room", where "the staff are top-notch, the atmosphere too" – Gino Taddei & Sally Eidlitz's "lovely" restaurant between Kensington and Olympia "has been going for years" and "they have fed generations" with "top-quality Italian cuisine". Many describe it as "a favourite local" – a view shared by the late Michael Winner. / W14 8EZ; ciborestaurant.net; Mon-Sat 9.30 pm.

Cigalon WC2 £63 **3 4 4**
115 Chancery Lane   020 7242 8373   2–2D

"Consistently lovely for any occasion" – this unusually attractive venue occupies a graciously converted former Georgian auction house in Chancery Lane (dating from 1807), complete with period glass ceiling. It celebrates its 15th anniversary this year as part of Pascal Aussignac's Club Gascon group, and offers "good value Provence-inspired cuisine and unusual wines from South West France and Corsica". The basement cocktail bar, Baranis, boasts London's only indoor pétanque court. / WC2A 1PP; cigalon.co.uk; cigalon_london; Tue-Fri 9 pm.

Cilantro Putney SW15 £70 **3 2 2**
244 Upper Richmond Road   02033439317   11–2B

"A clear cut above your standard Curry House (without attempting anything Michelin-chasing)" – this first UK outpost of a family-owned Indian group occupies the simple Putney premises that were, for years, Ma Goa (RIP). It aims for a "delicious, healthy take on Indian cuisine". Everyone agrees the food is yummy. But while some reports say "their claims to be 'healthy' appear to play out with lovely dishes lacking an oily, ghee-laden feel to them"; others "totally don't understand its billing – it all tasted good-to-very good, but was not remotely advisable for my waistline or blood pressure!" / SW15 6TG; cilantro.london; cilantro_london; Tue-Sat 10.30 pm, Sun 9 pm.

Cinder £87 **3 3 3**
66 Belsize Lane, NW3   020 7435 8048   9–2A
5 St John's Wood High Street, NW8   0207 4358 048   9–3A

"Everything is flame-grilled – including the olives!" at this Belsize Park three-year-old from chef-patron Jake Finn (ex-LPM and The Ritz), whose second branch in St John's Wood is equally highly rated. They are "buzzy, sometimes noisy" places, "famous locally for their triple cooked potatoes". Top Menu Tip – "the standout chargrilled leek salad with ricotta and hazelnuts". / cinderrestaurant.co.uk.

Cinnamon Bazaar WC2 £65 **3 3 3**
28 Maiden Lane   020 7395 1400   5–4D

"A tasty offshoot of the great Cinnamon Club" – Vivek Singh's "prettily decorated" cafés ("resembling a tropical garden centre cafe!") offer a "good-value", "Indian-with-a-twist" menu: "hot curry staples" plus options "reminiscent of street food". Practically all comments refer to the original – "a go-to in Covent Garden" for its very many fans – but he also opened in Richmond this year, taking over the former Carluccio's venue diagonally opposite the station. One caution in reports – it looks time to pep up the decor in WC2 – it risks looking a bit "shabby". / WC2E 7NA; cinnamon-bazaar.com; thecinnamoncollection; Mon-Sat 10.30 pm, Sun 9 pm; SRA-3 stars.

The Cinnamon Club SW1   £91   4 3 5
Old Westminster Library, Great Smith St   020 7222 2555   2–4C
"In the memorable setting of Westminster Library" – "still with book-lined walls" – "few restaurants can beat the ambience of this old room" (one of the Top-40 most commented-on venues in our annual diners' poll). Opened in 2001, it can genuinely claim to have helped 'redefine expectations of Indian cooking' in the UK, thanks to Vivek Singh's "always-innovative cuisine using seasonal ingredients" ("calling it an Indian restaurant conjures up a misleading picture: this is fine cooking characterised by first-class ingredients and restrained spicing so that delicate flavours can still be enjoyed"). Staff are typically "courteously graceful" (though occasionally "unresponsive" this year) and "the unusual space makes for an atmosphere for calm enjoyment". "It is worth mentioning the wine list, which includes some fascinating Indian wines that are well worth investigating". / SW1P 3BU; cinnamonclub.com; thecinnamoncollection; Mon-Sat 11 pm; SRA-3 stars.

Cinnamon Kitchen   £61   4 3 2
4 Arches Lane, SW11   020 3955 5480   11–1C
9 Devonshire Sq, EC2   020 7626 5000   10–2D
"If you're in the mood for some delicious Indian cuisine", this duo from Vivek Singh make a more affordable alternative to his flagship Cinnamon Club, pleasing both vegetarians ("great-tasting paneer butter masala") and omnivores ("the chicken 65 is a particular favourite"). The cavernous City branch can get "incredibly noisy", but the newer Battersea Power Station branch earns a lot of positive feedback, and is seen as a "viable competitor to Dishoom", its near neighbour. / cinnamon-kitchen.com; cinnamonrestaurants; SRA-3 stars.

Cinquecento   £52   3 2 2
6 Greek Street, W1   020 7287 7705   5–2A
1 Cale Street, SW3   020 7351 9331   6–2C
233 Portobello Road, W11   020 3915 3797   7–2B
"Real quality pizza, good portion sizes and reasonable prices" have driven the rapid growth of this Chelsea-based group, launched five years ago by Carmelo Meli and Emanuele Tagliarini. A couple of reports also give a shout out to the "short but reasonably priced wine list". / cinquecentopizzeria.com; https://www.instagram.com/cinquecentopizzeria/?hl=en.

Circolo Popolare W1   £66   3 3 5
40-41 Rathbone Square   no tel   5–1A
"A top party place" – Paris-based Big Mamma Group's "huge and buzzing" omaggio to the Sicilian trattoria in Fitzrovia boasts an "amazing atmosphere" buoyed up by ongoing Insta-success which helps draw in an energetic crowd skewed to twenty- and thirty somethings. The food's not for the cognoscenti of Italian cucina, but it is "consistent" and low cost. / W1T 1HX; bigmammagroup.com; bigmamma.uk; Mon-Sat 10.30 pm, Sun 10 pm.

Ciro's (Pizza Pomodoro) SW3   £65   2 2 3
51 Beauchamp Pl   020 7589 1278   6–1C
"Despite his branches in Hollywood and Dubai having closed, the original staggers on" at Ciro Orisini's Knightsbridge veteran: an old-fashioned cellar, to which a visit has been a rite of passage for the gilded youth of Knightsbridge since 1978. "It's not really about the pizza and pasta, which is average in all but price – hit a good night, and with the live music and dancing, a visit to Ciro's can still hit the spot". / SW3 1NY; pomodoro.co.uk; Sun-Wed 11 pm, Thu-Sat midnight.

FSA

Citro N6 £63 3 4 2
15A Swain's Lane   07840 917586   9–1B
"Lovely Italian food, excellent small plates and delicious pastas or pizzas for kids" are the ingredients that make this *"good neighbourhood spot"* from brothers Nunzio & Salvatore a hit with Highgate locals. / N6 6QX; eatcitro.com; citro_restaurant; Tue-Sat 10 pm, Sun 3 pm.

City Barge W4 £68 2 2 4
27 Strand-on-the-Green   020 8994 2148   1–3A
A *"great riverside location and view"* at Strand-on-the-Green in Chiswick makes this *"lovely pub"* a *"perfect summer place"*. It's part of The Metropolitan Pub company, with their menu of pies plus other traditional dishes. / W4 3PH; citybargechiswick.com; CityBargeW4/; Sun-Thu 10.30 pm, Fri & Sat 11 pm.

City Social EC2 £123 3 3 4
Tower 42 25 Old Broad St   020 7877 7703   10–2C
"Great vibes and view of the city" are undisputed attractions of Jason Atherton's City eyrie on the 24th floor of Tower 42 (which old timers will remember was the highest building in the UK till 1990). Critics say *"the food here is a little bland and not as memorable as you would want given the standard and price"*, but more common is the view that it's all-round *"excellent"* and it remains a firm favourite for business entertaining. (It's now one of only two survivors of Atherton's 'Social' brand). / EC2N 1HQ; citysocial-london.com; citysocial_london; Mon-Fri 9.45 pm, Sat 9.30 pm.

Clap SW3 NEW £132
Sixth and seventh Floor, 12-14 Basil Street,   020 3988 0044   6–1D
Tucked away a short walk from the back doors of Harrods – a design-led Japanese venue from a Middle East-based group that came to London from Beirut via Dubai and Riyadh (and which also runs Sucre in Soho). Set over three glossy storeys, there's a ground-floor cafe and rooftop bar in addition to the main dining room with open kitchen. We're not sure about the name, but limited initial feedback on its food is mostly upbeat (*"good quality, albeit omakase was somewhat unimaginative"*). Top Menu Tip – you can try it out with their affordable three-course business lunch for £35 per person. / SW3 1AJ; claprestaurant.com; Mon-Sat 11 pm, Sun 10.30 pm.

The Clarence Tavern N16 £68 3 3 3
102 Stoke Newington Church Street   020 8712 1188   1–1C
"Decent hearty gastro food" that's *"great for sharing"* distinguishes this Grade II listed pub in Stoke Newington as a popular choice. But while it's *"a cut above most gastropubs"* – and its team even helps run the food for Kettners in Soho – it's yet to achieve the stellar ratings of some of its siblings in the Anchor & Hope stable. / N16 0LA; clarencetavern.com; theclarencetavern; Tue-Sat 10 pm, Sun 5 pm.

Clarette W1 £103 3 3 4
44 Blandford St   020 3019 7750   3–1A
Owner Alexandra Petit-Mentzelopoulos is a scion of the family who own Bordeaux's epic Château Margaux, which explains the unusually heavyweight wine list at this attractive and comfortably converted Tudorbethan pub in Marylebone. Over 50 vintages, including 14 Château Margaux wines, are available by the glass (using the Coravin system) from a list whose emphasis is on clarets and top Burgundian names. Its modern European cuisine has Francophile leanings and – though not the main event compared to the wine – plays a respectable supporting role. / W1U 7HS; clarettelondon.com; clarettelondon; Tue-Sat 11 pm, Sun 8 pm.

FSA

Claridge's Foyer & Reading Room W1 £127 3 4 4
49 Brook Street   020 7107 8886   3–2B
"Gorgeous Art Deco décor", "super-reliable professional service" and "endless refills of sandwiches and scones" are just the ingredients required for a "perfect, slow afternoon tea" that is one of the capital's top treats in that department. The Foyer is also a "superb venue" earlier in the day, "guaranteed not to sabotage your breakfast business pitch". Top Tip – "it's probably a good idea to dress up: it seems to affect where I'm seated!" / W1K 4HW; claridges.co.uk; claridgeshotel; Mon-Sun 10 pm.

Claridge's Restaurant, Claridge's Hotel W1 £105 3 4 4
49 Brook Street   020 7107 8848   3–2B
It's a total case of 'Back to the Future' in this Art Deco dining room. After a string of collabs with the likes of Gordon Ramsay, Simon Rogan and Daniel Humm, it reopened in late 2023 much as it was 20 years previously, before all the celeb nonsense set in. Some bemoan this lack of stardust, but it's hard not to find positives in the "delightful room" and "proper service". That the conventional, posh brasserie cuisine is no longer 'pushing the envelope' similarly makes it "boring and bland" to the excitement-seekers, but on balance the rating for food here is "better-than-average" and we're with those who say "the new format is an improvement on what it was before": if you're a very posh hotel dining room in Mayfair, don't fight it! Top Tip – "the set lunch is very good and fairly priced for such a special location", as is the pre-theatre deal. / W1K 4HW; claridges.co.uk; claridgeshotel; Mon-Sat 9.30 pm, Sun 5 pm.

Clarke's W8 £118 4 5 3
124 Kensington Church Street   020 7221 9225   7–2B
"Sally has triumphed in maintaining stands and a smile across the decades" and the "super-civilised institution" she opened in 1984, south of Notting Hill Gate, has shown rare staying power. That "there is always a really warm welcome" from the "effective and nurturing" staff goes down well, as does the way she has "maintained excellence with the finest seasonal produce perfectly cooked" (inspired by Alice Waters of Chez Panisse in California, her friend and mentor since the late 1970s). "Simple but elegant decor" and a strong wine list focused on North America complete a picture which still inspires practically zero criticism. / W8 4BH; sallyclarke.com; sallyclarkeltd; Tue-Sat 10 pm.

Clipstone W1 £91 3 3 2
5 Clipstone Street   020 7637 0871   2–1B
More than the sum of its parts, Will Lander & Daniel Morgenthau's highly regarded Fitzrovia corner-site looks uneventful but achieves a "convivial and relaxed atmosphere" ("similar in feel to a neighbourhood restaurant in New England") thanks to its "charming" staff. On the menu – "extremely well-constructed, flavoursome and unfussy food" from a "changing menu" matched by an "accessible wine list" ("very good by the glass"); and all at a "fair price". / W1W 6BB; clipstonerestaurant.co.uk; @clipstonerestaurant; Tue-Sat 9.45 pm, Sun 8.45.

Clos Maggiore WC2 £107 3 4 5
33 King St   020 7379 9696   5–3C
"The go-to place to celebrate a special anniversary" – this "enchanting" Covent Garden haunt is "magical for a special occasion or simply a treat"; and is yet again voted Londoner's No.1 choice for a hot date in our annual diners' poll. If possible, try to book a table in the "beautiful flower-filled conservatory", where there's an opening ceiling in summer and a log-fire in winter: "upstairs, the cosy and intimate dining rooms have a whiff of that atmosphere (e.g. similar white flowers across the ceiling) but are perhaps for more mature relationships!". While not its USP, its French cuisine is by no means incidental – "beautifully presented and bursting with flavour"; but it is

upstaged by the wine list, which is "a rival to 'War and Peace' in length". Service that's "extremely helpful and very welcoming" caps off an impressive all-round performance. Top Tip – "the weekday set lunch is astonishingly good value for such cooking, particularly as it also offers a small carafe of well chosen wine for a pretty modest supplement". / WC2E 8JD; closmaggiore.com; clos_maggiore; Mon-Sat 10.30 pm, Sun 10 pm.

Cloth EC1 NEW £40 4|4|4
44 Cloth Fair   0208 143 0345   10–2B

"Reminds me of Noble Rot… and I can give no higher praise" – one very enthusiastic report on this wine-led spring 2024 newcomer, which has a dead cute location down an alleyway by Smithfield Market, in a row of houses that escaped the Great Fire in 1666. (Premises some might still remember as Betjeman's Wine Bar, long RIP, named for the late poet laureate who used to live on the first floor). Backed by specialist wine importers, Joe Haynes and Ben Butterworth, its stoves are manned by Tom Hurst, former head chef at Lasdun and a graduate of some of London's best modern kitchens, and initial feedback is very promising. In a May 2024 review, The Financial Times's Tim Hayward found the creative small plates "mixed but fascinating… I loved the new place… I want creativity and experimentation, and if that's really happening, I expect as many near misses as palpable hits". / EC1A 7JQ; clothrestaurants.com; clothrestaurant; Mon-Fri 10 pm.

The Clove Club EC1 £224 3|3|2
Shoreditch Town Hall, 380 Old St   020 7729 6496   13–1B

Daniel Willis, Isaac McHale & Johnny Smith helped establish the East End as a credible culinary destination, with the launch over a decade ago of this trailblazing venue (est. 2013) in Shoreditch Town Hall. "It is one of those tasting menu restaurants" – a no-frills (fairly uneventful) chamber whose cuisine on launch seemed dazzlingly weird and wonderful, and which is nowadays a key pillar of London's foodie hall-of-fame, with two Michelin stars and – until this year – the UK's leading position on the World's 50 best ranking. However, the verdict of our annual diners' poll has for some years been more cautious than the general critical consensus, and this uneven pattern continues this year. The main event is an eight-course tasting menu for £195 (with wine pairing at £175), which is hailed as "faultlessly executed" in upbeat feedback but seen in sceptical commentary as merely tolerable-to-disappointing. But most striking this year was a general lack of interest full stop: feedback was notably scant compared with the venue's stratospheric media profile. Perhaps this good-but-no-longer-great view is beginning to become more widely held? The venue lost its World's 50 Best ranking this year (slipping to 80th position). / EC1V 9LT; thecloveclub.com; thecloveclub; Tue, Wed 1.30 pm, Thu-Sat 8.30 pm.

Club Gascon EC1 £174 4|3|3
57 West Smithfield   020 7600 6144   10–2B

"An unfailing choice, near Barts" – Pascal Aussignac's & Vincent Labeyrie's homage to gutsy Gascon cuisine and wine opened in 1998 in an idiosyncratic and grand marble-walled former Lyons Tea House near Smithfield Market. It's now one of London's longest established temples of French gastronomy, but chef Pascal has lightened and modernised his cuisine over the years (and foie gras – once omnipresent – only makes the odd appearance on menus nowadays). There is a six-course tasting menu for £120, but also a much cheaper three-course version; and you can also eat here à la carte. / EC1A 9DS; clubgascon.com; ClubGascon; Tue, Sat, Wed-Fri 9.30 pm.

Coal Office N1 £83 3|3|4
2 Bagley Walk   020 3848 6085   9–3C

"It's busy, it's buzzy, but the focus is on the high standard of cooking" at this brilliant collab between the Tom Dixon studio and famous Israeli chef Assaf Grannit, by hip Granary Square. "The good vibe and great decor are down to the design and accessories" (Dixon's London studio is in the adjacent building) but it's Assaf's "unique combinations of wonderful flavours" in the Tel Aviv-inspired small plates that have built its reputation: "enough to tickle the most jaded palate: lots of herbs, pomegranate, chilli, with brilliant bread and dips". That said, the food is "rather simple for the prices charged": "a bit overpriced if very delicious". Top Tip – the outdoor terrace comes into its own in summer. / N1C 4PQ; coaloffice.com; coaloffice; Mon-Wed, Sat & Sun, Thu & Fri 11 pm.

The Coal Shed SE1 £84   3 2 2
One Tower Bridge   020 3384 7272   10–4D

This "very accommodating" grill house occupies quite a stylish modern unit near Tower Bridge and is the "London copy" of an operation in Brighton. A good selection of fish, chicken and vegetable options is available alongside a wide array of steaks: "quality of the ingredients is excellent and presentation is special". Top Tip – a good pre-show dining option near the Bridge Theatre. / SE1 2SE; coalshed-restaurant.co.uk; thecoalshed; Tue-Sat, Mon 11 pm, Sun 6 pm.

The Cocochine W1 NEW £167
27 Bruton Place   020 3835 3957   3–3B

Tim Jefferies, who runs the photography gallery Hamiltons, and his business partner, Sri Lankan-born Larry Jayasekara – head chef at Pétrus until 2018 – opened this art-filled Mayfair passion project in March 2024. Money has been little object in the expense-be-damned fit-out of four floors, which incorporate a ground-level dining room (with 28 covers); seven-seat chef's table adjoining a huge kitchen; a 14-seat event space; and space to store over 1,500 wines on site (which also incorporates two adjoining buildings). Larry's £145 menu is – huge round of applause – à la carte, not tasting-based, and shows the originality one might hope for from pre-launch research which incorporated travel to 28 countries! The venture opened too late for survey feedback, but reviewers in the press and online have raved. The best restaurants are not run for money, and there's no sign that profit is the main motive here. Jefferies has signed a 20-year lease: this looks set to be a mainstay of Mayfair dining in the years to come. / W1J 6NQ; thecocochine.com; larry_jayasekara; Tue-Sat 9.45 pm.

Colbert SW1 £84   2 3 3
51 Sloane Sq   020 7730 2804   6–2D

"There's a real feeling of a French Brasserie in the centre of London" at this Wolseley Group operation, whose ideal situation – on a corner of Sloane Square – makes it an ideal meeting place. "There's always a great buzz, especially in the bar", the menu of brasserie staples "suits all spectrums of the age range" and it's "reasonably priced" too, especially for this glossy bit of town. There's been "no drop in standards since C&K's departure" from the group – indeed ratings here have strengthened across the board. / SW1W 8AX; colbertrestaurant.com; colbertchelsea; Mon-Sat 10.30 pm, Sun 10 pm.

Le Colombier SW3 £101   3 5 4
145 Dovehouse Street   020 7351 1155   6–2C

"Just like being in Paris" – this "classic French brasserie" in a Chelsea backstreet is "a perennial favourite", run by "a strong core team who have been here for ages", with patron "Didier Garnier keeping a close eye on things". It's "always full with many locals", and is also a "great place to dine with business colleagues – good food and service guarantee you can concentrate on the business at hand". A key feature is "possibly the best-value wine list in London, especially if you are a fan of Rhone and/or Claret" (and with "a good selection of half bottles"). / SW3 6LB; lecolombier.restaurant; Tue-Sat 10.30 pm.

Colonel Saab WC1 £70   4 4 4
Holborn Hall, 193-197 High Holborn   020 3004 0004   5–1D

Inspired by his parents' travels with the Indian army, Roop Partap Choudhary's extravagantly decorated restaurant has proved an unexpected hit in

Holborn's Victorian former town hall – a venue that has seen a succession of previous occupants fail. "The decor shows the owner's love for his family heritage; the food shows the passion for true Indian cooking; the service is spectacular". Its success has led to the late 2023 opening of a second, larger branch just off Trafalgar Square (in the former WC2 branch Jones Family Project, RIP). / WC1V 7BD; colonelsaab.co.uk; colonelsaab; Mon-Sat 10 pm.

Colony Grill Room,
Beaumont Hotel W1 £108 3 3 4
8 Balderton Street, Brown Hart Gardens   020 7499 9499   3–2A
"A private, discrete setting" with *"reasonably spaced tables and no music"*, together with *"no-nonsense good grills and fish"* win a fair number of recommendations – including for business meals – for this Art Deco hotel dining room, a short walk from Selfridges, which features striking murals above its plush banquettes and wood panelling. It consciously aims to import Manhattan style down to the slant on its menu of salads, crustacea and steaks. / W1K 6TF; colonygrillroom.com; thecolonygrillroom; Mon-Sat 9.45 pm, Sun 8.45 pm.

Coppa Club £66 2 2 3
29 Brewhouse Lane, SW15   020 3937 5354   11–2B
Three Quays Walk, Lower Thames St, EC3   020 7993 3827   10–3D
This comfortably decorated national chain feels akin to dining in a hotel, but minus the bedrooms; and its two London branches – near the Tower and in Putney – benefit from attractive Thames-side locations, where *"it's lovely to sit outside on a warm day by the river, or year-round in one of their igloo pods"*. *"There's a warm fire inside with cosy armchairs"*, too, which make the venues *"fine for coffee or snacks"*, although for more substantial meals *"the food is only OK"*. / coppaclub.co.uk; coppaclub.

Copper Chimney W12 £54 3 3 3
Westfield London, Ariel Way   020 8059 4439   1–3B
"Authentic cooking from the open kitchen" elevates this Indian venue, easily missed amidst the anonymous units around Westfield Shepherd Bush's Southern Terrace. It's the London representative of a chain founded in 1972 in Bombay by JK Kapur (with 15 locations in India) and specialises in North Indian cuisine. / W12 7GA; copperchimney.uk; copperchimney_uk; Sun-Thu 10 pm, Fri & Sat 11 pm.

Coq d'Argent EC2 £100 3 4 4
1 Poultry   020 7395 5000   10–2C
"Perfect for a slick business lunch" – *"if the weather permits get an outside table"* at this D&D London operation on the top floor of No 1 Poultry, where you eat just a minute's walk from the Bank of England amidst leafy roof terraces. Despite the upheavals at its owning group (sold to new private equity owners in October 2023) it put in a stronger-than-ever performance this year. True, *"it's best when the meal is not at your own expense"*, but perennial complaints were absent this year. Instead, *"nothing but praise for the lovely staff and excellent kitchen"*; and for the *"consistently good"* modern French cuisine: *"I've taken numerous guests – all very happy!"* / EC2R 8EJ; coqdargent.co.uk; coqdargent; Mon-Sat 10 pm, Sun 6 pm; SRA-3 stars.

Cora Pearl WC2 £87 3 3 3
30 Henrietta Street   020 7324 7722   5–3C
This *"super-cosy"*, *"chic and friendly restaurant is very welcome"* in Covent Garden, *"an area of chains and tourist traps"* – with a *"simple menu"* of 'elevated comfort food', it's *"hard to beat for an early pre-theatre meal"*. Named after a mid-Victorian courtesan who learned her trade nearby (although she made the big time in Paris), it is the younger sibling to Kitty Fisher's (see also). / WC2E 8NA; corapearl.co.uk; corapearlcg; Mon-Sat 9.30 pm, Sun 3.30 pm.

CORD EC4 — £96 — 3|3|3
85 Fleet Street   020 3143 6365   10–2A

Founded in 1895 in Paris, the famous 'Le Cordon Bleu' culinary institute hit London in 2012 in Bloomsbury; and then opened here in the Lutyens-designed former Reuters HQ in 2022. All reports agree this in-house restaurant is "a beautiful room" – "light and well spaced" – if occasionally "lacking a bit of spark". Service is "correct" and the modern European menu focuses on "seemingly simple dishes", whose "realisation ranges from exemplary refinement to the merely satisfactory". / EC4Y 1AE; cordrestaurant.co.uk; cordrestaurant; Mon-Fri 10 pm.

Core by Clare Smyth W11 — £231 — 5|5|4
92 Kensington Park Rd   020 3937 5086   7–2B

"Not just the best meal this year, but the best meal I've ever had!…" – "quite divine and out of this world…" – "my favourite three star!…" – "simply stunning…" – "wonderful and unforgettable…" – the superlatives just pile up in reports on Clare Smyth's "sublime" Notting Hill landmark, which is "exceptional on every level" (and a close-tie with nearby The Lebury in our annual diners' poll as our survey's No. 1 choice for culinary excellence in London). It could be called "a culinary theatre", but "the serene ambience is the opposite of that in the movie 'Boiling Point'". "The kitchen clearly supervises every dish", and "it's worth every penny to experience a master of her craft letting sheer quality ingredients shine in the simplest and most stunning of ways". The consistency of feedback here is also incredibly impressive, with little in the way of criticism made of the very many meals recorded in one of the Top-20 most mentioned restaurants in our annual diners' poll. Staff – "drilled with military precision" – "find the perfect balance between being friendly and welcoming and unstuffy, while still making it feel like a special experience". "They just get it absolutely spot on!" / W11 2PN; corebyclaresmyth.com; corebyclaresmyth; Thu-Sat, Tue, Wed 9.45 pm.

Cork & Bottle WC2 — £75 — 2|2|4
44-46 Cranbourn St   020 7734 7807   5–3B

"A wonderful old-school oasis below the hell that is Leicester Square" – this "fabulous throwback to a proper wine bar" is "remarkably unchanged" since Don Hewitson opened it in 1971 (and his successor Will Clayton sticks to the winning formula). "The famous ham-and-cheese pie is well worth its million-odd portions! and is the perfect accompaniment to a great wine list". / WC2H 7AN; thecorkandbottle.co.uk; thecorkandbottle; Mon-Sat 11.30 pm, Sun 10.30 pm.

Cornus SW1 NEW — £150
27 Eccleston Place   020 3468 8751   2–4B

Open in summer 2024 atop a new converted warehouse (the 'Ice Factory') bordering Belgravia's Eccleston Yard development near Victoria, this rooftop newcomer is a follow-up from Joe Mercer Nairne & David O'Connor, who are behind Medlar in distant Chelsea. The latter has long felt overlooked – especially by the large tyre manufacturer who runs a restaurant guide – perhaps here the duo will achieve the Michelin-esteem that has eluded them for so long. / SW1W 9NF; Mon-Sun 11 pm.

Corrigan's Mayfair W1 — £139 — 3|4|4
28 Upper Grosvenor St   020 7499 9943   3–3A

"Richard Corrigan's grown-up Mayfair flagship", just off Park Lane, is a favourite spot for enjoying top-quality British Isles cuisine, where the emphasis is on the best produce be it 'furred, foraged, finned or feathered'. Typical feedback applauds dishes such as "brilliant ox cheek" or "a great fish selection prepared with aplomb"… "mouth-watering". There's a "great value set menu", but "beware of straying too far from it, as otherwise racking up a hefty bill is very, very, very easy". / W1K 7EH; corrigansmayfair.com; Corrigans Bar & Restaurant; Tue-Sat 11 pm.

F S A

Côte £60   1 2 **3**
Branches throughout London

"Yes, it's a chain with an unadventurous menu and average cooking, but – judging by the buzzy tables of old friends catching up and office parties – this chain is getting it right": so say supporters of these ubiquitous Gallic brasseries, which are tipped by their legions of fans (including parents) as a *"cheap 'n' cheerful"* standby, charging *"good prices for proper French food"* – *"slightly formulaic but nevertheless a standard for an informal lunch"*. Its ratings continue to plummet, though, boosting those who feel that *"sadly, standards have really declined of late"*; and – with some incidents reported of *"shockingly average food"* – there are those who feel that *"what was once a fairly reliable and good value (if predictable and unexceptional) chain has become a tired lottery, with quality varying hugely between branches"*.
/ cote.co.uk; coteuk.

Cottura W4 £48   **3 3** 2
6-8 Elliott Road   020 8747 0100   8–2A

"Boasting handmade pasta every day" – this Chiswick yearling takes on the attractive if slightly cramped site off the high street that was formerly Michael Nadra (RIP) and offers *"an elevation of traditional pasta dishes"*. Fans say its *"homemade sauces and dishes are outstanding"* and the worst criticism it attracted is hardly damning: *"not bad, just not amazing; nice plating but it's still just a nice plate of pasta"*. Top Menu Tip – very affordable weekday set lunch (from one course for £12 to three for £20). / W4 1PE; cottura.co; Wed-Fri, Tue, Sat 10 pm, Sun 3 pm.

The Counter £65   **3** 2 **3**
15 Kingly Street, W1   07500 612914   4–2B **NEW**
108 Golborne Road, W10   07500 612914   7–1A **NEW**

"Fantastic Greek and Turkish dishes, including unusual items, create a memorable meal" (buoyed up by wine from Turkey, Greece Georgia and Armenia) at this *"very popular and buzzy (if also crowded and noisy)"* two-year-old ocakbasi near the top of the Portobello Road from chef Kemal Demirasal. In April 2024, he opened a sequel in Soho's Kingly Street (with an 'Under the Counter' basement bar), where a variety of cuisines from around the Eastern Mediterranean are the inspiration.

Counter 71 N1 £180   **4 5 3**
71 Nile Street   no tel   14–2A

"A wonderful curation of British produce and informative service" – Joe Laker's 16-seat two-year-old in Smithfield offers *"some of the best counter dining in London"* according to its small but passionate fan club. In the nondescript streets north of Old Street roundabout, an old corner pub has been transformed with a big open kitchen behind a marble counter. *"Faultless course after course are all served with the care and attention they deserve, with thoughtful wine pairings that further elevate the experience"* (the nine-course tasting menu is currently £120 per person). More than one reporter tips it as *"a restaurant to watch"* that's *"heading for a Michelin star"*.
/ N1 7RD; counter71.co.uk; counter_71; Tue-Sat midnight.

The Cow W2 £84   **3** 2 **4**
89 Westbourne Park Rd   020 7221 0021   7–1B

Tom Conran's lively Bayswater favourite celebrates its 30th anniversary this year, and remains *"a wonderful spot for a long lunch, starting with Guinness and oysters"*. There has been no need to update the Irish pub theme, which is as fashionable as ever (as witnessed in the recent launch of The Devonshire off Piccadilly Circus). The artless cooking is *"foodie"* but straightforward, with seafood (oysters, whelks, cockles, crab or a pint-of-prawns) the top pick. Top Tip – tiny, cute first-floor dining room, with a separate menu. / W2 5QH; thecowlondon.com; thecowlondon; Mon-Sat 11 pm, Sun 10.30 pm.

FSA RATINGS: FROM **1** POOR — **5** EXCEPTIONAL

Coya — £116 — 3|2|3
118 Piccadilly, W1   020 7042 7118   3–4B
Angel Court, 31-33 Throgmorton St, EC2   020 7042 7118   10–2C
"Excellent ceviche" and "amazing cocktails" take top billing at Arjun Waney's vibey Peruvian operation, which has branches in Mayfair and the City, as well Paris, Marbella, Mykonos and the Middle East. There remains an undercurrent of feeling that it's "over-priced", but the overall verdict is that "the food is great!" / coyarestaurant.com; coyamayfair.

Crate Brewery and Pizzeria E9 — £37 — 3|2|3
7, The White Building, Queens Yard   020 8533 3331   14–1C
Just across the canal (technically the River Lea) from the Olympic Park, this Hackney Wick mainstay exudes vibey East End cred, especially when you can pose in summer on the large, sunny terrace. On the menu: funky pizza and brews from the right-side-of-grungy in-house microbrewery, at good prices. Unsurprisingly, it can be utterly rammed at peak times. / E9 5EN; cratebrewery.com; cratebrewery; Sun-Thu 11 pm, Fri & Sat 1 am.

Crêpes à la carte NW1 — £33 — 3|3|2
112 Kentish Town Road   020 36 89 36 85   9–2A
"As good as any in France really!" – the clue is in the name at this Kentish Town café, which "may only be fair in appearance but makes genuine French crêpes from French ingredients and by French staff". "It's only a matter of feet between the kitchen and your table so your meal is crispy at the edges when you get it". "Simple and delicious!" Top Menu Tip – "the crêpes are good, but go for the galettes, which are the best – made with Breton buckwheat and not overdone in any way – and have a cup of cidre brut aussi!" / NW1 9PX; crepesalacarte.co.uk; Tue-Sun 10 pm.

Crisp Pizza W6 — £62 — 5|3|3
The Chancellors, 25 Crisp Road   07515 930582   8–2C
"The secret is well and truly out now" – "Carl (the owner) makes some of the best pizza in London", selling out daily from the unpromising-looking Hammersmith boozer he was born in (near the bridge, behind Riverside studios). His 'pies' are "insane", fully justifying "the hype about being the best" created by influencers including Dave Portnoy of America's Barstool Sports and rapper Action Bronson. A former semi-pro footballer, Carl McCluskey developed his own recipe for NYC-style crisp-base pizza when he took over the Chancellors pub in – yes – Crisp Road when his grandmother retired during the pandemic. He has talked of moving to Mayfair, but as of summer 2024 was still pumping out the pizzas on home turf. / W6 9RL; crisppizzaw6; Wed-Fri 9.30 pm, Sat & Sun 9 pm.

Crispin at Studio Voltaire SW4 NEW — £65 — 3|4|3
1A Nelsons Row   no tel   11–2D
"Only just opened and very popular" – Dom Hamdy (of Bistro Freddie fame) looks to have another winner on his hands with this spring 2024 newcomer, which occupies part of the lobby of a Clapham studio complex: "the space is the entrance, at night disguised by brown curtains". "Friendly staff" succeed in boosting the mood of what critics say "is not the best interior"; and they "serve small and large plates from a changing menu, which can sell out fast". (In his April 2024 review, The Evening Standard's Jimi Famurewa was reluctantly bowled over: "Hamdy and his team have done the unthinkable: brought cool, swagger and weapons-grade restaurant sexiness to an area that even locals are prone to decry as a culinary tundra"). / SW4 7JR; crispinlondon.com; Wed, Sun 3 pm, Thu-Sat 11 pm.

Crocker's Folly NW8 — £59 — 3|3|4
23-24 Aberdeen Place   020 7289 9898   9–4A
This "stunning and ornate pub" in St John's Wood with a "high-ceilinged, intricately decorated and chandeliered" dining room is the perhaps-unlikely setting for "delicious Lebanese food from the Maroush group" (who have

owned it for over a decade now). The monumental, late-Victorian Renaissance-style building was originally intended as a railway hotel for a mainline London terminus that ended up being built half a mile away (in Marylebone) – hence the 'folly' of the name. / NW8 8JR; maroush.com; maroush; Mon-Sun midnight.

The Crossing SW13 £81 3|3|3
73 White Hart Ln   020 8392 1617   11–1A

"The back garden is gorgeous in the summer and very family friendly" at this "lovely local" on the outskirts of Barnes as you head into Sheen. Restaurant investor, Christian Arden relaunched it in 2021 during the tough Covid times and the place has never perhaps attracted as much PR as it deserves for its steaks (cooked over open fire in the garden BBQ), pizza and other fare; and his "fabulous team always really look after the locals". / SW13 0PW; thecrossing-barnes.co.uk; thecrossingbarnes; Mon-Sun 11 pm.

Crudough £40 3|4|3
10 Navigator Square, Archway, N19   020 7272 1672   9–1C
360-362 Saint John Street, EC1   020 3691 8938   9–3D **NEW**

"There are plenty of pizza options but this is one of the very best" up North London way, with the five-year-old Archway original joined in 2023 by a branch in a pub near Angel. The "hand thrown" sourdough pizzas are "thin-crust and cooked super-fast, with a range of interesting toppings" washed down with "great craft beer". "The interior is a little basic but always busy and with good reason" – it helps that staff are "super-friendly".
/ crudough.com.

The Crystal Moon Lounge, Corinthia Hotel London SW1 £109 3|4|4
Whitehall Place   020 7321 3150   2–3C

"The lemon meringue eclair I still dream about…" – the swish lounge of this super-lux five-star near Embankment provides "a lovely setting and a very satisfying experience" when it comes to a celebratory afternoon tea. "Pastry chef Yago Doamo is always updating the offering with seasonal and luxury ingredients" and the setting – "with its massive central chandelier and abundant flower arrangements – is glorious". / SW1A 2BD; corinthia.com; corinthialondon; Mon-Sun midnight.

Cubé W1 £145 4|4|2
4 Blenheim Street   020 7165 9506   3–2B

"Fantastic, authentic traditional sushi and other Japanese food (sourcing the best fish)" alongside service that's always good' inspire high ratings for this sushi restaurant, near the top of Bond Street. There are now two counter spaces alongside table seating: in both locations you can order from the large à la carte, but there is also an omakase option, which – at £108 per head – is relatively affordable by Mayfair standards. There's also a carefully chosen drinks list to suit all budgets (including fine sakés at nearly £1,000 per bottle). / W1S 1LB; cubemayfair.com; cubemayfairuk; Mon-Sat 11 pm, Sun 10 pm.

The Culpeper E1 £62 3|2|4
40 Commercial Street   020 7247 5371   13–2C

A "great place for a casual meal", this 1846 boozer on a Spitalfields corner was smartly refurbed ten years ago into a pub (ground floor) with restaurant (first floor), plus bedrooms and a rooftop terrace – the latter incorporating "a high wall, so it's well sheltered from winds". "Execution is to a high standard" in the restaurant from a menu that's more 'modern-bistro' than it is 'gastropub' (you'll look in vain for a burger or fish 'n' chips). / E1 6LP; theculpeper.com; theculpeper; Mon-Sat midnight, Sun 9 pm.

Cycene E2 — £226 — 5|4|4
9 Chance Street   020 7739 9733   13–1C

"A wonderful experience, moving from room to room with service in the bar… then restaurant… and even the kitchen!" – This I'm-funky-and-I-know-it Shoreditch venue (which started out as Mãos under Nuno Mendes) is part of the 'Blue Mountain School', whose website reads like a parody of East London now-ness (it is "an environment dedicated to nurturing engagements and interactions between diverse practices", apparently). Fortunately reports continue to suggest that the intimate atmosphere avoids pretension; and that there's also plenty of real substance to the exceptional cuisine from a ten-course omakase-style offering, for which it's suggested you allow three hours. For most of the meal, you choose between the 'Dining Room' and the 'Hearth Room': in the latter, if you are fewer than four in your party seating may be communal. BREAKING NEWS – in August 2024, well known chef Theo Clench moved on to be replaced by Taz Sarhane, who had been with the team since January. No great changes have been headlined, and we've maintained its rating. / E2 7JB; bluemountain.school; bluemountainschool; Tue-Sat 11.30 pm.

Cyprus Mangal SW1 — £57 — 3|3|3
45 Warwick Way   020 7828 5940   2–4B

"Huge portions of fresh and wonderfully satisfying Turkish home cooking" are the order of the day at this Pimlico grill not far from Victoria station, which celebrates its 20th anniversary this year. "The lamb shish kebab has a wonderful seasoning and succulence, and arrives with plenty of rice and salad". / SW1V 1QS; cyprusmangal.co.uk; cyprusmangal; Mon-Sun 11 pm.

Da Mario SW7 — £54 — 3|3|4
15 Gloucester Rd   020 7584 9078   6–1B

Near the Albert Hall, on a quirky site built in the Venetian Gothic style to please Queen Victoria, this "typically bustling family-run Italian" opened in 1967, and offers a "standard menu, with properly cooked pasta" and dependable pizza. "Kids are really well looked after, just like being in Italy" – as Princess Diana found, when she used to take Wills and Harry out for a treat from nearby Kensington Palace. / SW7 4PP; damario.co.uk; da_mario_kensington; Mon-Sun 11.30 pm.

Da Mario WC2 — £79 — 2|3|2
63 Endell Street   020 7240 3632   5–1C

Regulars say this "proper, family-run trattoria in Covent Garden [unusual in itself, Ed] could be in any city in Italy, with a narrow dining room and cosy tables" – "genial host Andrea will recommend items on the menu and the food and wine are excellent". But its old-fashioned and personal appeal can pass some people by completely: "if you want to know what dining in a slightly run-down, cramped restaurant in the 1950s was like, this is your place…" / WC2H 9AJ; da-mario.co.uk; da_mario_covent_garden; Mon-Sat 11 pm.

Da Paolo W1 — £55 — 3|3|2
3 Charlotte Pl   020 7580 0021   2–1C

Celebrating its 35th anniversary this year, this traditional Italian in Fitzrovia is "chaotic and very small", so you're "packed like sardines" – but that's part of the appeal to fans, who reckon it's "great fun" and "worth returning to". / W1T 1SD; dapaolo.co.uk; Mon-Sat 10 pm, Sun 4 pm.

Da Terra, Town Hall Hotel E2 — £320 — 5|5|4
8 Patriot Square   020 7062 2052   14–2B

"Exquisite…", "Superbly inventive…" – few restaurants attract such consistently superlative feedback and ratings as Rafael Cagali's "worthy successor to Viajante and The Typing Room" in Bethnal Green's former town hall. Influenced by his Brazilian heritage, the dishes are "fantastic and unique" with "superb ingredients and precise execution" running through the *entire, three-hour tasting menu (which is £245 per person; £180 per person at lunch). "Knowledgeable and friendly staff and the lovely space combine to create an exceptional culinary experience". The only gripe is the obvious one – it's mightily pricey. On practically all accounts, though, it's "worth it" and "seems to get better every time". / E2 9NF; daterra.co.uk; daterrarestaurant; Wed-Sat 8 pm.*

Daddy Bao SW17 £37 433
113 Mitcham Road   020 3601 3232   11–2C
"Great value, great flavours" sums up the appeal of this fun Tooting venue, which serves a short menu of filled Taiwanese buns and cocktails, and is named in honour of owner Frank Leung's father, Joe (who ran a restaurant in Salisbury for 32 years). As of September 2024, it has a Taiwanese cocktail bar, Good Measure, in the basement. See also Mr Bao in Peckham. Top tip – "I loved the beef tataki". / SW17 9PE; daddybao.com; daddybao; Tue, Wed, Sun 09.45 pm, Sat, Fri 10.45 pm, Thu 9.45 pm.

Daddy Donkey EC1 £20 332
50b Leather Lane   020 7404 4173   10–2A
"Authentic burritos on Leather Lane" from Mexican food veteran Joel Henderson, who celebrates the 20th anniversary of his first London street-food stand this year. / EC1N 7TP; daddydonkey.co.uk; daddydonkeyburritos; Mon-Thu 7 pm, Fri 3 pm.

Daffodil Mulligan EC1 £85 443
70-74 City Road   020 7404 3000   13–1A
"Irish hospitality + imaginative food cooked over wood fire = success", according to all feedback on Richard Corrigan's stylish five-year-old venue by Silicon roundabout, where the open kitchen dominated by a fiery grill leads onto a stylish modern interior. Though the food is strongly rooted in the British Isles, it's very much a 21st-century menu: "the small plates allow for a range of excellent tasty dishes" (e.g. Sugar Pit Pork, Wood-fired Lobster, Sea Bass Ceviche). The location near Old Street tube perhaps feels a bit peripheral, but "once inside there's an energetic atmosphere in what's a big space. Downstairs in Gibney's Bar is even busier and the noise level even greater". / EC1Y 2BJ; daffodilmulligan.com; daffodilmulligan; Tue-Fri 11.30 pm, Sat midnight.

Dalla E9 NEW £49
120 Morning Lane   02030164179   14–1B
On the former site of wine bar Peg in Hackney's Morning Lane, this neighbourhood newcomer opened in late 2023 with a focus on relatively traditional Italian cooking from chef Mitchell Damota. Co-founder Gennaro Leone also runs a design gallery nearby, so the tiny interior is classily decked out. Reports please! / E9 6LH; dallarestaurant.com; dalla.restaurant; Wed-Sat 10 pm, Sun 5 am.

La Dame de Pic London,
Four Seasons Hotel EC3 £196 443
10 Trinity Square   020 7297 3799   10–3D
Evens Lopez has been at the stoves since June 2022 at this five-star hotel near the Tower of London. Run from afar by Anne-Sophie Pic – France's most decorated female chef – it has held two Michelin stars for many years, yet has a fairly low profile largely due to its City-fringe location, in the monumental former HQ of the Port of London Authority (which, apparently, also served as the venue for the inaugural meeting of the United Nations General Assembly in 1946!). A fair number in our annual diners poll who do make the trip say the dining room is a "wonderful" environment with modern French cuisine that's "just superb", from a selection of menus starting at £145 per person. What's encouraging is that criticism of the place is most notable by its absence. / EC3N 4AJ; ladamedepiclondon.co.uk; ladamedepiclondon; Tue-Thu, Sat 8.30 pm, Fri 9 pm.

F S A

Danclair's SW9 £47 4 3 2
67-68 Granville Arcade, Coldharbour Lane   020 7733 9800   11–2D
"Not a place for a posh dinner, but lip-smackingly good tucker and a fun night out" – that's the deal at Brian Danclair's vibrant small gaff "in the heart of Brixton Village Market", close to his Fish Wings & Tings. The menu is "super-tasty", often with a Jamaican twist; and "you get a very warm welcome from the boss". / SW9 3PR; danclairskitchen.co.uk; danclairskitchen; Tue-Sun 10.30 pm.

Daphne's SW3 £105 3 2 5
112 Draycott Ave   020 7589 4257   6–2C
The "real Chelsea set" meets up at this "buzzy" haunt near Brompton Cross, founded by Richard Burton's agent Daphne Rye. Now 60 years old and part of Richard Caring's empire, it has managed to retain its magic as "somewhere to be seen, not to eat" – whatever your view on the Italian victuals: "fantastic" or "overpriced and simple". "Start with a cocktail at the friendly bar and go from there – it's always fun watching the ladies who lunch" (as it was in the 1990s, when it was infamously full of folks hoping to rubber-neck Princess Di, whose favourite it was). / SW3 3AE; daphnes-restaurant.co.uk; daphneslondon; Mon-Sat 11 pm, Sun 10.30 pm.

Daquise SW7 £73 2 2 3
20 Thurloe St   020 7589 6117   6–2C
"Unchanged since it opened" in 1947, this Polish institution by South Ken tube station serves "very authentic", "reliably interesting" and "sometimes rather stodgy" East European home cooking to an adoring audience who wouldn't want to change a thing. "I love the ambience – bright daylight, serious lunch crowd; evenings the vodka kicks in more". / SW7 2LT; daquise.co.uk; daquise_london; Tue-Sun 11 pm.

Darby's SW11 £84 3 3 4
3 Viaduct Gardens Road, Embassy Gardens   020 7537 3111   11–1D
Overlooking the back of the US Embassy, Robin Gill's comfortable modern brasserie occupies a high-ceilinged unit on the ground floor of a block within the Nine Elms' forest of new developments. Attractions include an NYC-style oyster bar; chiller cabinets showcasing its steaks; regular live music; an on-site bakery; and an outside terrace in summer. It's still perhaps more of an amenity to the locals than it is a destination, but all reports rate it highly. / SW11 7AY; darbys-london.com; darbyslondon; Wed-Sat 10 pm.

Darjeeling Express W1 £88 3 3 2
Kingly Ct   020 7287 2828   4–2B
Back in Carnaby's Kingly Court, where it began in 2017, this former supper club wins praise for "excellent" Indian dishes cooked by an all-female brigade of 'housewives'. High-profile founder Asma Khan was one of Time magazine's '100 most influential people' of 2024, and "it's great to see her still walking the tables". The setting, though, can seem a bit "canteen-like"; and a disappointed minority are just not sold on its performance generally ("I simply do not understand the enduring hype around this utterly mediocre restaurant. The food is simplistic, basic and just not especially good"). / W1B 5PW; darjeeling-express.com; darjeelingexpress1; Mon-Sat 10 pm.

Darkhorse E20 £55 3 3 2
16-19 Victory Parade, East Village   020 8534 4579   14–1D
"Love this restaurant which we've been going to regularly since it opened!" – this large, modern brasserie has established itself over eight years as one of the best bets for a meal in Stratford's East Village, thanks to its "friendly service" and a selection of dishes majoring in steaks and roasts from the charcoal oven. "First time and the hard surfaces made the restaurant very noisy, but the food is very tasty!" / E20 1FS; thedarkhorserestaurant.com; Mon-Thu 11 pm, Fri & Sat 1 am, Sun 10.30 pm.

F S A

Daroco Soho W1
Ilona Rose House, Manette Street   0208 143 6370   5–2A
Tucked away in a new development near Tottenham Court Road tube (part of Ilona Rose House), this large and expensively designed October 2023 newcomer is the first London spin-off from a Parisian group. No survey feedback as yet, but in her November 2023 report The Guardian's Grace Dent gave cautious approval to its "fancy pizza, titivated pappardelle and hyped-up tiramisu": despite "expecting very little", she judged the food "more than decent" (particularly the "huge, sloppy, soft-based and floofy-edged" pizza) and the overall venture "a vast, daft restaurant in the heart of tourist land, but… also much better than it needs to be". Top Tip – it has a fair amount of outside seating on its terrace. / W1D 4AL; daroco.com; daroco_group; Mon-Sun 11 pm.

The Dartmouth Castle W6   £64   **3 3 3**
26 Glenthorne Rd   020 8748 3614   8–2C
Worth knowing about near Hammersmith Broadway, this well-appointed pub is "highly recommended" for its convenient location a few minutes' walk from the station, its characterful interior, cute outside terrace and – not least – its very decent Italian-leaning menu. "Dog-friendly" is another plus for some. / W6 0LS; thedartmouthcastle.co.uk; thedartmouthcastle; Mon, Sat, Tue-Fri 9.30 pm, Sun 8.30 pm.

Darwin Brasserie, Sky Garden EC3   £93   **2 2 4**
1 Sky Garden Walk   033 3772 0020   10–3D
London's highest rooftop brasserie is on the 36th floor of the Walkie Talkie – "booking a meal here is the easiest way to get the view as the free public tickets vanish very quickly when made available!". "The venue does not trade too rapaciously on the location and offers a pleasant if unambitious menu". ("The view is best appreciated from the 'Sky Garden' that surrounds the restaurant, so it is worth taking time before or after eating to explore that"). / EC3M 8AF; skygarden.london; sg_darwin; Sun-Thu 10 pm, Fri & Sat 10.30 pm.

Dastaan KT19   £50   **5 4 2**
447 Kingston Rd   020 8786 8999   1–4A
"Breathtakingly outstanding dishes" have put this "top-notch Indian" in the outer southwestern 'burbs firmly on every curry-hound's map over the past nine years – it justifies a "long drive", or "makes a bumpy ride on the 406 bus worthwhile". Ignore the modest Ewell shop front off the A3 Tolworth turn-off, you'll find cooking of "the highest standard" that rivals the best in the West End – and "at a truly affordable price". / KT19 0DB; dastaan.co.uk; dastaan447; Tue-Sun 10.30 pm.

Daylesford Organic   £74   **1 2 2**
44b Pimlico Rd, SW1   020 7881 8060   6–2D
6-8 Blandford Street, W1   020 3696 6500   2–1A
76-82 Sloane Avenue, SW3   020 3848 7100   6–2C
208-212 Westbourne Grove, W11   020 7313 8050   7–1B
Lady Bamford's quartet of deli-cafés are the London satellites of her organic Cotswolds estate, and – on the plus side – their careful design can give the impression that one has fallen into the pages of 'Country Living'. Not helped by inconsistent standards over many years, though, they continue to generate mixed feedback in our annual diners' poll. "A perfect location for a late breakfast" is at the positive end. Negatives include: "I had the impression some staff were in their first job" and "the food can be poor here: it comes from Daylesford Farm and in some cases should never have left it…" / daylesfordorganic.com; daylesfordfarm.

FSA RATINGS: FROM **1** POOR — **5** EXCEPTIONAL

FSA

Dean Street Townhouse W1 £80 2 2 3
69-71 Dean St   020 7434 1775   4–1D
"Clubby and crowded, but with an endearing Soho atmosphere nonetheless" – this retro all-day brasserie in a boutique hotel is "a go-to place" as a "fun" and stylish haunt… so long as you don't mind it being "full of annoying Soho House types (I would use a stronger word, but it probably includes me!)". It "won't win any awards for the food" – which is at the comfort end of the spectrum, with "mince and tatties always on". / W1D 3SE; deanstreettownhouse.com; deanstreettownhouse; Mon-Thu midnight, Fri & Sat 1 am, Sun 11 am.

Dear Jackie W1 NEW £113
20 Broadwick St   020 7047 4000   4–1C
Opulently decked out with old-fashioned decor incorporating acres of red fabric, this engagingly flamboyant new hotel basement provides a cosy Soho escape. No survey feedback as yet, but online reviews suggest that for those who are not particularly budget-conscious and seeking a comfortable rather than a foodie experience, it may find a niche; and in a January 2024 review the FT's Tim Hayward gave a thumbs-up to its traditional-ish, Italian-inspired cuisine. You can unwind pre- or post-meal in the hotel's rooftop bar. / W1F 8HT; broadwicksoho.com; broadwicksoho; Sun-Thu midnight, Fri & Sat 12.30 am.

Decimo WC1 £106 3 3 4
The Standard, 10 Argyle St   020 3981 8888   9–3C
"Everyone wanted to give the ambience a 6/5!" Few London eateries have as much drama as Peter Sanchez-Iglesias's double-height Mexican venue, atop King's Cross's so-hip Standard Hotel, where huge floor-to-ceiling windows provide dramatic vistas of London… and that's just from the toilets! You access via a red, pill-shaped lift creeping up the outside of the building to a gob-smacking view of the top of St Pancras Station opposite. Surprisingly, it doesn't inspire quite as many positive ratings as one might expect, perhaps because it's far-from-cheap. That said, its combination of tacos, Latino seafood and steaks (most of it grilled), all of them washed down with mezcal cocktails, was well rated this year. Top Tip – "visit before 6.30 pm Tue-Fri for the 'Menu del Dia' at £30 per person". / WC1H 9JE; decimo.london; decimo.london; Tue, Wed midnight, Fri & Sat 2 am, Thu 1 am.

Defune W1 £96 4 3 2
34 George St   020 7935 8311   3–1A
Claiming to be London's oldest Japanese restaurant (although originally it operated a couple of streets away), this Marylebone veteran just off Baker Street has always had its pros and cons. The main plus is its traditional sushi and other fare incorporating "super-fresh fish". On the downside, critics have perennially found it OTT pricewise; and even fans – who say it's "super-relaxed at the counter chatting with the friendly Itamae" – also note that "atmosphere can be a little lacking". / W1U 7DP; defune.com; defune_restaurant; Mon-Sat 10.45 pm.

Dehesa W1 £66 2 2 2
25 Ganton Street   020 7494 4170   4–2B
"Still a really good location and format" – this Soho 'tapas haven' is increasingly forgotten about nowadays, but can still merit a visit. Its Italian/Spanish dishes "aren't as good as they used to be" but are "solid, and better than many offerings in the area"; and there's an interesting selection of drinks. Also, "it has a really relaxed style, but with all the vibe of neighbouring Carnaby Street". / W1F 9BP; saltyardgroup.co.uk; dehesarestaurant; Wed-Sat 11 pm, Mon & Tue, Sun 10 pm.

F S A

Delamina £54 3 3 3
56-58 Marylebone Lane, W1   020 3026 6810   3–1A
151 Commercial Street, E1   020 7078 0770   13–2B

"Really enjoyable and imaginative Middle Eastern food" at "reasonable prices" wins very consistent praise for this modern duo in Marylebone and Shoreditch from Tel Aviv-born Limor Chen and her husband Amir. It's "family- and veggie-friendly" too, with very welcoming service. In late 2024, a new Delamina branch is planned for the periphery of Covent Garden. Top Menu Tips – "Charred Cauliflower; also the moist and tasty date cake". / delaminaeast.co.uk; delaminakitchen.

The Delaunay WC2 £76 2 3 4
55 Aldwych   020 7499 8558   2–2D

"Smoothly run and charming – the Wolseley's "grown-up" Theatreland cousin off Aldwych is "another Corbin & King former favourite that seems to be surviving pretty well under a change of management", a switch that "doesn't seem to have dented its consistent quality". The "lovely surroundings are reminiscent of a coffee house in Vienna" and its "well-spaced tables and professional service make it a particularly classy choice for a discreet business lunch". The Mittel European brasserie fare is "undemanding" and "won't excite" ("it's not about the food here"), but the menu provides "a wide choice" and "the overall package is pure quality and not too expensive for what it is". In particular, "they make breakfast into an occasion" with an excellent selection of choices and coffee. Top Menu Tips – "Fantastic schnitzels"; very pleasant Veal Bratwurst with sauerkraut; or reasonable Chicken soup with spätzle". At breakfast, "eggs royale is an indulgent choice"; and "you will never taste better kedgeree than theirs!" / WC2B 4BB; thedelaunay.com; thedelaunay; Mon-Sat 10.30 pm, Sun 9.45 pm.

Delfino W1 £81 3 2 2
121a Mount St   020 7499 1256   3–3B

"Delicious pizza and pasta" at remarkably sensible prices for the area draw a steady crowd to this recently refurbished family-run Italian (est. 1953) on a Mayfair corner site. / W1K 3NW; delfinomayfair.com; Delfinomayfair; Mon-Sat 10.30 pm.

Les 2 Garcons N8 £79 4 5 3
14 Middle Lane   020 8347 9834   9–1C

"A diamond gem of the neighbourhood!" – this "unique", if "tiny and cramped" traditional Gallic bistro in Crouch End is "always a joy", according to most of the many who comment on it. "Chef Robert and FOH Jean-Christophe are simply wonderful" ("two guys having fun on their own terms") and "the interaction with the owners and French retro-cooking served with real enthusiasm make for a really delightful experience" (and one that's "pretty good value considering the quality"). More cautions reporters like it, but say "it's fine if you treat it as a local bistro that's good but not exceptional all round" ("we ourselves do not visit for the quality of the cuisine, but it's the lovely and jolly service and the liveliness of the atmosphere that justify the 30-mile round trip from Theydon Bois!"). Fans, though, say it's sheer "perfection": "if I lived nearby I'd go every night!". Top Menu Tips – "perfect onion soup"; excellent rib-eye with peppercorn sauce; "beautifully rich Tarte Tatin". / N8 8PL; les2garconsbistro.com; les2garconsbistro; Tue-Sat 9.30 pm.

The Devonshire W1 £79 3 4 5
17 Denman Street   no tel   4–3C

"What an addition!" – Just north of Piccadilly Circus, a "dream team" including Flat Iron founder Charlie Carroll and Guinea Grill ex-manager Oisin Rogers have created the most commented-on debut of the year in our annual diners' poll, as well as London's new No. 1 gastropub. "Downstairs: it's a proper, bustling pub with excellent beer and creamy Guinness. Upstairs: it's more a set of pub 'dining rooms' than a restaurant" and with "the backdrop of a real, open-fire grill". When it comes to the "great quality food, simply

FSA RATINGS: FROM 1 POOR — 5 EXCEPTIONAL

cooked" it's "more a case of 'old time favourites' than 'cutting-edge' cuisine… less Instagram and more 'get it down you', leaving little to be criticised", albeit allowing for a certain amount of "hype". "Full of laughter and happy punters", "energetic" service is "brilliant from start to finish". "What a cracking place!!". Just one problem – "it's impossible to get a reservation!". Top Menu Tips – "steak, lobster, scallops, crab, soufflé are all brilliantly executed"; "Steak and Guinness suet pudding is gorgeously rich"; "particularly love the bread-and-butter pudding"; and "the fact there's a good-value set menu". / W1D 7HW; devonshiresoho.co.uk; devonshiresoho; Mon-Sat 10 pm, Sun 5.30 pm.

Dim Sum Duck WC1 £44 4 3 2
124 King's Cross Road 020 7278 6018 9–3D

"Just like a hole-in-the-wall in Hong Kong" – "if you can stand the long wait on grimy King's Cross Road" and "are prepared to eat sitting on someone else's lap because there's no space inside (all part of the charm!)" then you can enjoy some "excellent" dim sum at this cheap eat of contemporary urban legend – "we just wanted to keep ordering and eating everything on the menu!" / WC1X 9DS; dimsum-duck.business.site; dimsumandduck; Tue-Sun, Mon 10 pm.

Din Tai Fung £62 2 2 2
11 St Giles Square, WC2 awaiting tel 5–1A
5-6 Henrietta Street, WC2 020 3034 3888 5–3D

"You can't go past the xiao long bao" – "soup-filled dumplings hand-made onsite and steamed to order" – say fans of this Taiwanese-based global chain with three London outlets (in Covent Garden, CentrePoint and Selfridges). "All the other dishes are a bit hit and miss", though, while a well-travelled minority reckon they're "nothing like the original restaurants in Asia", with prices – by comparison to e.g. Singapore – that are "off the scale". But you must go: "cute robots help clear the plates!" / dintaifung-uk.com; dintaifunguk.

Dinings £104 5 3 3
22 Harcourt St, W1 020 7723 0666 9–4A
Walton House, Walton St, SW3 020 7723 0666 6–2C

"The food is always spectacular", say fans of these top-quality, low-profile Japanese restaurants, which we continue to list under their common brand even though the ownership of the business was split between the individual chefs who run them a few years ago. Reports remain almost indistinguishable between them, although SW3 under chef Masaki Sugisaki inspires more feedback and has more of a "neighbourhood gem" feeling than its W1 namesake, perhaps thanks to its "really cosy" setting off chichi Walton Street. / dinings.co.uk; https://www.instagram.com/dinings_sw3.

Dinner by Heston Blumenthal, Mandarin Oriental SW1 £171 2 2 3
Mandarin Oriental, 66 Knightsbridge 020 7201 3833 6–1D

"The theatrical elements are sometimes ridiculous, but it's very unlikely you would go away unhappy", according to fans of culinary boffin Heston Blumenthal's Knightsbridge dining room. Here the unique culinary approach is not his Fat Duck's 'molecular gastronomy', but to re-package recipes researched from Tudor and Georgian cookbooks for the modern era. Most famous is the "sublime meat fruit" (a kind of pâté made to look like a satsuma) but recent menus include the likes of "'Ragoo of Pigs Ear on Toast' (c.1727)" and other concoctions. At its best "it's a great and memorable experience" and one for which Michelin have awarded a coveted two stars. But there's perennially a huge disconnect between this accolade and its performance in our annual diners' poll. Even fans concede it's "hugely expensive"; and year in year out there's a very significant proportion who are "incredibly disappointed" with the food; or who feel "it's trading on one or two exceptional dishes at eye-watering prices that don't match what's on offer". By day in particular, this large chamber is a "beautiful" space, with Hyde Park *glimpses, particularly from the tables near the windows, while by night the ambience can be more "clinical", not helped by incidents of "charmless" or "inattentive" service. If Heston were not world famous, the tyre man might have taken away at least one star here a long time ago.* / SW1X 7LA; dinnerbyheston.com; dinnerbyhb; Mon-Sun 9 pm.

Dishoom £53 4 4 5
22 Kingly St, W1   020 7420 9322   4–2B
12 Upper St Martins Ln, WC2   020 7420 9320   5–3B
The Barkers Building, 4 Derry Street, W8   020 7420 9325   6–1A
Stable St, Granary Sq, N1   020 7420 9321   9–3C
Wood Wharf, 15 Water Street, E14   020 7420 9326   12–1C
7 Boundary St, E2   020 7420 9324   13–1B

"You nearly always have to queue for a table – often for at least an hour – but the atmosphere is amazing and the food is worth the wait" at Shamil & Kavi Thakrar's unbelievably successful chain: again, the most commented-on business in our annual diners' poll, which has stormed the capital since it first opened in Covent Garden in 2010. Outlets in Canary Wharf and Battersea Power Station opened in late 2024, bringing the total in London to seven, and each branch has its own intriguing character, with the unifying theme being a homage to the Irani cafés of post-war Bombay. "Very much a well-oiled machine, there is little sign of any drop-off in quality as the group expands", while "for such large places the brilliant service is remarkably friendly and efficient". Meanwhile, the "deeply flavoursome and satisfying" menu has introduced Londoners to "authentic and delicious dishes that aren't just another copycat Indian selection", with such "zingy and exciting flavours". And morning-time in London will never be the same again, since the advent of their "great Anglo-Indian breakfasts". All-in-all, "the whole approach is inclusive and exciting", "it's always buzzy and fun too"; and "overall and for the price point you can't go wrong!". Top Menu Tips: "the black dal is to die for!"; "superb okra fries"; "the roomali roti is sublime"; "the lamb chops are excellent"; "Chicken Ruby is dreamy". In the mornings, "the unfailing Bacon naan is a thing of poetry"; "chilli cheese toast hits the spot every time", and "drink the lemon ginger and honey chai". / dishoom.com; dishoom; SRA-2 stars.

Diwana Bhel-Poori House NW1 £36 3 2 1
121-123 Drummond St   020 7387 5556   9–4C

"It's virtually impossible to spend more than £15 a head" at this "old-school Indian restaurant serving very high-quality vegetarian snacks". Established in 1971 and "still going strong", it's a star of the Drummond Street enclave by Euston station known as 'Little India', and has shown major staying power over the decades (including "hanging on through HS2 works and the station redevelopment"). The dated interior is showing its age, but anyone interested in what the 1970s really looked like should pay it a visit. / NW1 2HL; diwanabph.com; diwanabhelpoorihouse; Mon-Sat 10.30 pm, Sun 9.30 pm.

The Don EC4 £95 3 4 3
The Courtyard, 20 St Swithin's Lane   020 76211148   10–3C

"It's back" under new ownership and management – tucked away in the former HQ of Sandeman's port dynasty, this City haunt was "much missed by locals in search of a good 'working' lunch, and is settling back into operation nicely" after a four-year interregnum. The modern European cuisine and service are consistently well rated, and "the experience is not too expensive" – while the 600-bottle wine list, appropriately strong on port, is "as good as they come". / EC4N 8AD; sandemanquarter.com; https://linktr.ee/thesandemanquarter; Tue-Thu 9.30 pm, Fri 2.30 pm.

Donia W1 NEW £75 4 3 3
Kingly Ct   no tel   4–2B

"Like nothing I have had before!" – this "great new opening" debuted in November 2023 "in a calming setting on the top floor of Kingly Court" ("a classier space than the rest of Kingly Court might lead you to imagine"). Its "very splendid modern Philippine cooking" includes "some truly interesting dishes" and it was immediately hailed by some as "the best Filipino" in town (FT critic, Tim Hayward gave it a rave review for changing his entire perception of East Asian food!). Top Menu Tip – "the liver-peppercorn sauce with the lechon pork is mind-bendingly good". / W1B 5PW; doniarestaurant.com; donia.restaurant; Tue-Sat 10 pm, Sun 9 pm.

Donostia W1 £102 3️⃣2️⃣3️⃣
10 Seymour Pl   020 3620 1845   2–2A

Twinned with Lurra across the road, this superior Marylebone bar/restaurant with an open kitchen serves "delicious" Basque-style tapas and pintxo dishes, including beef from both long-lived Rubia Gallega and Friesian cattle. The Spanish wine selection is carefully chosen with an emphasis on the Basque region – the whole idea for the venture came from their well-established wine import business. / W1H 7ND; donostia.co.uk; donostiaw1; Mon-Sat 10.30 pm, Sun 9 pm.

Doppo W1 £85 3️⃣4️⃣4️⃣
33 Dean Street   020 7183 2100   5–2A

Despite its heart-of-Soho location and an early review from The Standard's David Ellis, this "excellent new Italian" with an elegant interior and Tuscan-influenced menu has not stirred huge media or online attention in its first 18 months. A small but enthusiastic fan club hails "fabulous pasta" in particular, which slips down with "wonderful well-priced wines by the glass too". / W1D 4PW; dopposoho; Tue-Sat 11.30 pm.

Dorian W11 £125 3️⃣2️⃣3️⃣
105-107 Talbot Road   020 3089 9556   7–1B

"Justifiably winning its first Michelin star this year, this gem of a 'neighbourhood' restaurant is another sublime addition to the booming Notting Hill foodie scene" – that's still the most popular take on Chris D'Sylva's in-crowd sidestreet haunt. "The ambience is hectic as the restaurant is always full and the tables quite tight", but fans say "this only adds to the sensation that you are eating in a real destination". Overseen by chef Max Coen, "excellent fish and delicious roasts" are perhaps to be expected given D'Sylva's connection to the nearby Notting Hill Fish Shop and Supermarket of Dreams; and "sitting at the bar watching fire-grilled meats and sampling deliciously creative little bites" can be "one of the absolute gastronomic pleasures of the year". Even its supporters, though, acknowledge that "it's absolutely not a dinner that will be easy on the wallet" and – given the "crowded and loud" setting – sceptics increasingly conclude the place is "overhyped" and "far too much of a scene": "Well, it is in Notting Hill, a territory of the super-rich, but surely even they consider VFM?" / W11 2AT; dorianrestaurant.com; thedoriansf; Tue-Sat, Mon 11 pm, Sun 10 pm.

Dotori N4 £40 4️⃣3️⃣2️⃣
3a Stroud Green Rd   020 7263 3562   9–1D

This "tiny, unbookable but excellent" Finsbury Park stalwart has been a source of "great home-cooked Korean and Japanese food" for 15 years. It's good value, too, which means it gets "a little crowded". Cash only! / N4 2DQ; dotorirestaurant.wix.com; dotori_london; Tue-Sat 10.30 pm, Sun 9.30 pm.

Double Standard WC1 £68 2️⃣4️⃣5️⃣
The Standard, 10 Argyle St   020 3981 8888   9–3C

Handily placed for St Pancras (opposite), this funky bar makes a super-convenient rendezvous by King's Cross and attracts a funky crowd. A greater attraction than the dependable upscale diner fare is the superb, authentically 1970s decor bequeathed by its former incarnation as Camden Town Hall annexe; and there's a (deafening) soundtrack to match (from the same era). Top Tip – large rear garden terrace for the summer. / WC1H 8EG; standardhotels.com; isla.london; Sun-Wed midnight, Thu-Sat 1 am.

F S A

The Dove W6 £52 2 2 5
19 Upper Mall 020 8748 9474   8–2B
As riverside pubs go, few ooze the ancient charm of this cute, historic Hammersmith hostelry, where James Thompson penned 'Rule Britannia' back in 1740. In other respects, nothing about it is game-changing, but the appeal of its cosy log fires in winter and riverside terrace in summer underpin its ferocious popularity (you must book). / W6 9TA; dovehammersmith.co.uk; the_dove_hammersmith; Mon-Sat 11 pm, Sun 10.30 pm.

The Dover W1 NEW £93 3 3 5
33 Dover Street 020 3327 8883.   3–3C
"Brava! The candle-lit tables are so classy" at this New York-style Italian newcomer in a prime Mayfair address, which is one of the most romantic arrivals of recent times, and a perfect antidote to the vogue towards tedious minimalism with its panelling, tablecloths, velvet curtains and acres of space. It's the creation of well-connected ex-Soho House head honcho Martin Kuczmarski, and to say the press critics have raved breathlessly would be an understatement. But our reports say it deserves the acclaim. No culinary fireworks are attempted – the aim is classic Italian-American comfort food (Spaghetti Meatballs, Chicken Cordon Bleu, Filet Mignon & Fries…) – and it does what it does well. / W1S 4NF; thedoverrestaurant.com; thedoverrestaurant; Mon-Wed midnight, Thu-Sat 1 am, Sun 6 pm.

Dovetale by Tom Sellers W1 £100 2 1 3
1 Hotel Mayfair, 3 Berkeley Street   020 3137 4983   3–3C
Tom Sellers' magic seems to be most notable by its absence in this celeb-chef-branded venue: the dining room of a much-hyped new hotel, which opened in a prime site opposite The Ritz in summer 2023. That's not to say it's completely lacking fans, with one or two reports hailing "the best meal of the year" and cuisine that's "seasonal, playful and thoughtful" in an "amazing venue, with a beautiful terrace". And the "wide-ranging wine list" has some "really unusual offerings and sensible-but-exciting possibilities" that are "not crazily priced". Even so, a concerning proportion of reports here are of disappointment, noting OTT prices and "poor service": e.g. "a very basic meal that cost nearly £300!! Ouch! The room was nice but that's about it!". (And, oddly given Sellers' huge media profile, most of the major press critics have remained silent about the place despite having had a year to pop along). / W1J 8DJ; 1hotels.com; dovetalelondon; Mon-Sat 10.15 pm, Sun 8 pm.

Dragon Castle SE17 £61 3 2 2
100 Walworth Road   020 7277 3388   1–3C
"Huge emporium by the Elephant & Castle" that's "firing on all cylinders again" for "solidly decent dim sum at fair prices" and with "more regional dishes added to the menu" of late. "Big round tables with lazy susans make it ideal for big parties", although "service can be a bit chaotic". / SE17 1JL; dragoncastlelondon.com; dragoncastle100; Mon-Sun 11 pm.

The Drapers Arms N1 £55 3 2 3
44 Barnsbury Street   020 7619 0348   9–3D
Nick Gibson's famous Islington gastropub offers "British cuisine with a creative twist" that is "utterly delicious, generous, and most of all memorable". There's a "strong selection of craft beers and ales", and a "renowned wine list put together by Nick and priced ungreedily". This year's worst complaint – "just a bit too noisy and busy, which can affect the service". / N1 1ER; thedrapersarms.com; thedrapersarms; Mon-Sat 10.30 pm, Sun 8.30 pm.

Dream Xi'an EC3 NEW £32
Unit 2A, Tower Place   020 8143 3966   10–3D
Near the entrance to the Tower of London, this spring 2024 newcomer sits at the foot of a modern development and is the creation of Guirong Wei (of Master Wei and Xi'an Impression). It opened too late for survey feedback,

FSA RATINGS: FROM 1 POOR — 5 EXCEPTIONAL

but, given its heritage (and the dire options in the area – including the iffy provisions within the Tower itself), it sounds like a good bet, especially if The Guardian's Grace Dent is to be believed: despite an "ultra-touristy location" she has "yet to leave any of Wei's places not delightedly flecked with umami, sweet, hot and vinegary sauces… and this was no exception" thanks to its compulsive biang biang noodles, as well as a wider menu of steamed dim sum and fried bao. / EC3R 5BU; dreamxian.co.uk; dreamxianec3r; Mon-Sat 10 pm, Sun 9 pm.

Dropshot Coffee SW19 £28 2 3 4
281 Wimbledon Park Road   07445 673405   11–2B
Familiar to tennis fans arriving at Southfields tube for Wimbledon – Ed Savitt's independent coffee shop has queues even when the championships are not on. With serious coffee and a good selection of toasties and other light bites, it now has spinoffs near Wimbledon Town station and in Putney. / SW19 6NW; dropshotcoffee.co.uk; dropshotcoffeeldn; Mon-Sun 5 pm.

The Duck & Rice W1 £78 3 2 2
90 Berwick St   020 3327 7888   4–2C
"The signature duck and rice is delicious" at this Oriental gastropub on Berwick Street in Soho, which offers a broad range of options from dim sum and 'small chow' to Lobster Cantonese at £68. And the stylish interior works well too. But, despite consistently solid marks, this place (created by Hakkasan and Yauatcha impresario, Alan Yau) has never made huge waves. Indian-in-a-pub is finally starting to work as a concept – maybe Chinese-in-a-pub will have its day too… / W1F 0QB; theduckandrice.com; theduckandrice; Sun & Mon 10 pm, Tue-Sat 11 pm.

Duck & Waffle EC2 £100 2 2 3
110 Bishopsgate, Heron Tower   020 3640 7310   10–2D
"Dining on the 40th floor" ("you ride up a small glass-enclosed elevator") of the City's Heron Tower – with *"walls that are all glass, for an incredible view of London"* – is *"a great experience"* that's *"worth all the hype"*. The signature duck & waffle dish (2 million sold!) *"is normally OK"*, but really *"the food should be much better"*. The 24/7 opening hours make it ideal for a late-night date, while *"weekend brunch with views is lovely for a special occasion"*. / EC2N 4AY; duckandwaffle.com; duckandwaffle; Mon-Sun midnight.

Ducksoup W1 £85 4 4 3
41 Dean St   020 7287 4599   5–2A
"A tiny Soho wine bar", with an ever-changing array of biodynamic wines and selection of vinyl for you to choose from. Launched in 2011, it doesn't attract the volume of feedback it once did, but can still produce *"sensational small plates of seasonal European cuisine"*. / W1D 4PY; ducksoupsoho.co.uk; ducksoupsoho; Wed-Sat, Mon & Tue 10 pm, Sun 5 pm.

The Duke of Sussex W4 £68 2 3 3
75 South Pde   020 8742 8801   8–1A
With its airy dining room and cute garden, this popular old boozer – a spacious Victorian tavern overlooking Acton Green Common – might look an unlikely-seeming destination for *"a lovely tapas lunch"*. The idea of a Spanish-inflected menu has worked well for years, though, supplemented by some larger, more typical pub dishes, including Sunday roasts. The quality of the cooking can be variable, with the occasional complaint (*"terrible paella!"*) interspersed in reports of *"very good Spanish food"*. / W4 5LF; thedukeofsussex.co.uk; thedukew4; Mon-Thu 11 pm, Fri & Sat midnight, Sun 10 pm.

Dumplings' Legend W1 £44 3 2 2
16 Gerrard St   020 7494 1200   5–3A
"You can see the staff making the very fresh dumplings from scratch" as you enter this modern take on the traditional dim sum experience in Chinatown – they claim to make 8,000 a day! *"Clean-tasting and fast food"* is the result –

"expect big queues at the weekend". Top Menu Tip – "the BBQ meats are ace, too". / W1D 6JE; dumplingslegend.com; dumplingslegend; Mon-Thu 11 pm, Fri & Sat 3 am, Sun 10 pm.

The Dusty Knuckle £40 5 3 3
429 Green Lanes, N4   020 3903 7598   9–1D
Car Park, Abbot Street, E8   020 3903 7598   14–1A
Outstanding and creative sandwiches, "fresh pastries" and "delicious brews" make this social-enterprise (it supports at-risk young East Londoners) one of the capital's highest-rated café-bakeries. The "wonderful brunches" mean "it can get very busy round midday", both at HQ in Dalston Junction and at the Green Lanes, Harringay offshoot. At the former, its street cred is enhanced by a grungy location down a side street from off the main drag. The latter is more civilised, with evening service, pizza and wine. / thedustyknuckle.com; thedustyknuckle.

The Dysart Petersham TW10 £103 5 4 4
135 Petersham Road   020 8940 8005   1–4A
This "restrained and rather old-school" Richmond gem "was always good but has improved in the last few years" to become a major culinary destination. Kenneth Culhane's "refined" dishes are "cooked to perfection and beautifully presented" in the "lovely setting" of an Arts & Crafts house next to glorious Richmond Park. "Unobtrusive, efficient and friendly service" and an "interesting selection of wine" make every meal here "a very special experience". / TW10 7AA; thedysartpetersham.co.uk; thedysartpetersham; Wed, Sun, Thu-Sat 8.30 pm.

The Eagle EC1 £49 4 3 5
159 Farringdon Rd   020 7837 1353   10–1A
"The original gastropub and still streets ahead of the competition" – this enduring institution (est. 1991) continues to put in a remarkably enduring performance on Farringdon Road. Chef Ed Mottershaw rustles up a daily changing menu of "cleverly constructed, intelligently put together flavours… like the dishes you wish you cooked at home…"; "no faff, pretence or posturing, just honest fare packed with hearty flavour and devotion to the palate". / EC1R 3AL; theeaglefarringdon.co.uk; eaglefarringdon; Mon-Sat 10.30 pm.

East Pan Asian Restaurant HA0 £35 3 3 2
1 Glacier Way   020 8998 7105   1–2A
"Above a giant Chinese Cash & Carry, this restaurant serving excellent, freshly made dim sum and traditional Cantonese dishes" is Alperton's finest contribution to London gastronomy; and a "well-priced" one at that. "Plenty of options on the menu are not available on the English version" and include "affordable, great lobster" dishes. / HA0 1HQ; eastrestaurant.co.uk; Sun-Thu 9 pm, Sat 10 pm.

Eat Tokyo £41 3 2 2
16 Old Compton St, W1   020 7439 9887   5–2A
50 Red Lion St, WC1   020 7242 3490   2–1D
27 Catherine St, WC2   020 3489 1700   5–3D
17 Notting Hill Gate, W11   020 7792 9313   7–2B
169 King St, W6   020 8741 7916   8–2B
14 North End Rd, NW11   020 8209 0079   1–1B
628 Finchley Rd, NW11   020 3609 8886   1–1B
"A wide range of typical Japanese dishes that have not been anglicised, including sushi that's always fresh and well-prepared (with true tastes, unlike at the ubiquitous chains)", helps inspire a big fan club for this "homely" chain. They are "not the grandest of places" – with service that's "quick and efficient" rather than particularly charming – but it "always feels like you are eating in Japan" here; and "they get the job done with decent value for

money". They must be doing something right as they are "always packed" and there are "often queues out the door". Top Tip – "the bento boxes are particularly good and with generous portions". / eattokyo.co.uk; eattokyoldn.

Eataly EC2 £60 3|2|2
135 Bishopsgate   07966 544965   10–2D

"Big and loud" – this 42,000 sq ft behemoth is part of Oscar Farinetti's 40+ strong global chain showcasing Italian produce. Many folks "love wandering around and trying all the different snacks available (a great date activity!)" and there seems to be no doubt that "it provides well above-average food"; but there's also a widespread acceptance that for a lingering meal, it's "lacking in atmosphere". Top eat-in option? "Bloody good pizza" with "crisp base and good toppings… why do other places find this so hard?" / EC2M 3YD; eataly.co.uk; eatalylondon; Mon-Sat 9.30 pm, Sun 8.30 pm.

Edera W11 £66 3|4|3
148 Holland Park Ave   020 7221 6090   7–2A

"If you like fresh fish, pasta with truffles and a good choice of other Sardinian specials, this is the place for you" – is the enthusiastic verdict on this Holland Park fixture that has just celebrated its 20th anniversary. "Family-run" and "very popular with locals", it's perfect before opera in the park. / W11 4UE; edera.co.uk; Mon-Thu 10.30 pm, Fri & Sat 11 pm.

8 at The Londoner WC2
The Londoner, 38 Leicester Square   020 7451 0102   5–4A

A "fascinating interior" – with moody design; great rooftop views over London from some tables; and an adjacent Shima Garden that's open to the sky – adds to the lure of this eighth-floor izakaya, at the top of one of London's more recent five-star arrivals on Leicester Square. It's yet to make waves as a foodie hotspot, although the ambition is there with a minimum spend for bookings at £100 per person; and sakés and wines running to £10,000 per bottle. Such feedback as we have is too limited for a rating but mostly upbeat, particularly about the venue. / WC2H 7DX; thelondoner.com; thelondoner; Tue-Sun 6 pm.

The eight Restaurant W1 £39 4|2|2
68-70 Shaftesbury Avenue   020 3332 2313   4–3D

This two-year-old café on the edge of Chinatown won high praise this year as a "fantastic choice for modern Hong Kong-style cuisine", served in a "contemporary designer interior". There's a huge selection of dishes on the menu, and service is "very efficient". Top Menu Tip – "fabulous crispy pork with rice (better than a lot of local competition)". / W1D 6LZ; theeightrestaurant.co.uk; theeightlondon; Mon-Sun 10.30 pm.

Ekstedt at The Yard,
Great Scotland Yard Hotel SW1 £122 3|4|3
Great Scotland Yard   020 7925 4700   2–3C

"Mesmerising (even hypnotic) food and the live-fire kitchen meant I didn't notice anything much that was going on around me!" – Stockholm star-chef Niklas Ekstedt's dining room in Westminster's Hyatt hotel captivates many diners with its theatrical Scandi flourishes. His "enthusiastic team" delivers "engaging explanations of each dish" and creates a "very interesting menu" that can be "absolutely fabulous". Even those who say the food is "very good" however, can still feel it is "very overpriced". / SW1A 2HN; ekstedtattheyard.com; ekstedtldn; Tue-Sat 9 pm.

El Pastor £57 3|3|5
Brewer Street, W1   020 3092 4553   4–3C
7a Stoney Street, SE1   no tel   10–4C
Battersea Power Station, SW11   no tel   11–1C **NEW**

"The tacos are still loaded and delicious and the frozen margaritas are exceptional" at the Hart Bros' "lively" Latino haunts: particularly the original

SE1 branch – a "fabulous Mexican street food venue under the arches in Borough Market". (The newer Soho branch with its basement 'Mezcaleria Colmillo' bar inspires good marks but much less feedback). In April 2024, they launched a new, 90-cover site in Battersea Power Station, with adjoining 60-cover, open-all-year, outdoor riverside terrace. / tacoselpastor.co.uk; tacos_el_pastor.

Ela & Dhani SW13 £37 **3**|**4**|2
127 Church Road   020 8741 9583   11–1A
This smart little "neighbourhood Indian" with "better-than-average cooking" opened three years ago on the main drag in Barnes, from a trio of friends who grew up together in the Punjab – one of whom runs the nearby Barnes Pantry. ('Ela & Dhani' mean cardamom and coriander in Sanskrit). / SW13 9HR; eladhani.co.uk; ela_and_dhani; Tue-Sun 10 pm.

The Elder Press Café W6 £21 **3**|**3**|**3**
3 South Black Lion Lane   020 3887 4258   8–2B
"A lovely little cafe" near the river in Hammersmith whose serene interior is a surprise given a location barely 100m from the whizzing traffic of the A4. Chef Lindsay Elder and her "friendly" staff provide (somewhat pricey) fancy buns, "great salads" and other light fare to passers-by and West London ladies who either lunch or do coffee. / W6 9TJ; theelderpress.co.uk; theelderpress; Mon-Sun 5 pm.

Electric Diner W11 £26 2|**3**|**4**
191 Portobello Rd   020 7908 9696   7–1B
At the foot of Portobello's iconic Electric Cinema, this "fun" and "crowded" trustafarian favourite has always been "more about being seen than about the food". The ambience is successfully "rather like an American diner (but with the buzz of the Soho House crowd that it's part of)", and for "reliably simple food" of the "proper stodge" variety, the "quality is OK". / W11 2ED; electricdiner.com; Sun-Wed 11 pm, Thu-Sat 1 am.

Elis E2 £74 **4**|**4**|**3**
Town Hall Hotel, Patriot Square   020 7871 0460   14–2B
Chef Rafael Cagali's "casual option" – next door to his high-flying Da Terra in the old Bethnal Green Town Hall – "has rather flown under the radar" since opening two years ago; but it's a "most underrated restaurant", whose "fabulous" small plates reflect the founder's Italian-Brazilian background. There's also "great music": it takes its name from bossa nova singer Elis Regina. Top Menu Tip – "Palm Heart and Scamorza pastel – absolute heaven!" / E2 9NF; restaurantelis.co.uk; elis.ldn; Mon-Fri 9 pm, Sat 2.30 pm.

Elliot's £81 **3**|**3**|**3**
12 Stoney St, SE1   020 7403 7436   10–4C
121-123 Mare Street, E8   020 3302 5252   14–2B
"A buzzy place with great sharing plates", pizza and grills from the wood-fire oven plus a "really interesting and varied natural wine list, with many available by the glass": Brett Redman's bar/café is a staple of SE1, with an opening frontage that looks onto one of the entrances of Borough Market. Founded in 2011, it spawned a Hackney spin-off three years ago. While both remain well-supported, ratings here over the years are steadily heading into more middling territory. / elliots.london; elliotslondon.

Elystan Street SW3 £108 **4**|**4**|**4**
43 Elystan Street   020 7628 5005   6–2C
Phil Howard's stylish, but "relaxed and friendly" HQ sits in one of the side streets surrounding Brompton Cross and its straightforward excellence makes it "a go-to for a high-quality meal" (numerous diners reported their best meal of the year here). Phil "has a very sure instinct about sourcing and his approach to his modern European cuisine is informed by tradition (but not in any way old-fashioned) and delicious"; with a 'flexitarian' approach evident in

many dishes ("love what they do to a cauliflower"). Top Tip – "consistently the best lunch in town". / SW3 3NT; elystanstreet.com; elystanstreet; Mon-Thu 2100 pm, Fri 21 pm, Sat 9 pm, Sun 3.30 pm.

Emilia's Crafted Pasta £57 333
215 Baker St, NW1   0 203 340 0694   2–1A **NEW**
12 George Street, Wood Wharf, E14   020 8176 1100   12–1C
77 Alie Street, E1   020 3358 0317   10–2D
Unit C3 Ivory House, St Katharine Docks, E1   020 7481 2004   10–3D
"Simple pasta done very well" lives up to the billing at this straightforward chain, which added a branch on Baker Street complete with outside terrace to its other three locations at the start of 2024. They are "nothing amazing, but the food is good, the service friendly, and it is a very easy option" when out and about or "when cooking just feels like a chore". / emiliaspasta.com; emiliaspasta.

Empire Empire W11 £55 333
16 All Saints Road   no tel   7–1B
This "very enjoyable", "casual Indian" yearling in Notting Hill is decked out "based on a disco theme" – a nod from founder Harneet Baweja (behind Gunpowder, see also) to his dancing dad's '70s nightlife – and provides a "clean-tasting" and "interesting twist on traditional Punjabi Indian fare", including "awesome biryanis". / W11 1HH; empire-empire.restaurant; empirempire_london; Mon-Sat 10.30 pm, Sun 9 pm.

Endo at The Rotunda W12 £287 554
TV Centre, 101 Wood Lane   020 3972 9000   1–2B
"Wow! – How to describe the extraordinary gastronomic experience created by master sushi chef, Endo, and borne from his obsession with quality and refusal to compromise on even the tiniest detail?" Diners are blown away by Endo Kazutoshi's 16-seater on the eighth floor of the old BBC TV Centre in White City, where he presents over 20 courses at the cost of £250 per person. "Every dish is an experience and the theatre of chef Endo's entertaining presentation and explanations is a delight. It may seem like no bargain, especially if you take the (recommended) sake pairings, but it is nevertheless excellent value". It closed for a five-month refurb over summer 2024 – "Good luck getting in here after the reopening!" Since 2020 it has been recognised by Michelin, but "we have no clue as to how this has just a single star, while Alain Ducasse for example has three!" / W12 7FR; endoatrotunda.com; kazutoshi.endo; Tue-Fri 9 pm, Sat 2 pm.

Enoteca Turi SW1 £94 333
87 Pimlico Road   020 7730 3663   6–2D
"Despite the change of owners, still excellent" – under Dominic Ford & David Gleave, "Pam and Giuseppe's tradition of authentic Italian food and wine pairings continues" at this Pimlico stalwart (which they sold on retirement in 2023). Inevitably, "it has lost some of the family-run charm" after the switch, but even if the famous Italian wine list "is not quite in Guiseppe's league under the new owners, it's still awesome!". And overall, there is a feeling that the quality of the "refined", "seasonal" Italian cuisine has held up well, albeit that it's "quite pricey". Top Menu Tips – "Cuttlefish and Pea Puree; Guinea Fowl breast and Sausage". / SW1W 8PH; enotecaturi.com; enotecaturi; Mon-Sat 10 pm.

The Enterprise SW3 £73 234
35 Walton St   020 7584 3148   6–2C
Set on the ultra-bougie Chelsea/Knightsbridge borders, this charismatic haunt is "a pub to go to eat rather than drink", with white tablecloths and smart banquette seating; and "really buzzy". / SW3 2HU; theenterprise.co.uk; Mon-Sat 11 pm, Sun 10.30 pm.

FSA

L'Escargot W1   £101   3 4 4
48 Greek Street   020 7439 7474   5–2A

"A Soho favourite for decades" – this Gallic landmark (est. 1927 but ultimately dating back to 1896 and London's oldest French restaurant) is "a real treat" and the epitome of a classic Theatreland haunt. (It's named for the snail farm that once inhabited its cellar!). In living memory, it has had quite fancy culinary associations. Nowadays, though – while the kitchen is still accomplished – this "sophisticated" dining room presents modern French cuisine that's less ambitious than a few years ago, all in an "un-rushed" fashion that's well-suited to a "romantic" meal. Top Tip – "a great pre-theatre supper"… "we were completely wowed by the service and ambience; the food was standard – paté followed by a steak frites – but the service was at the level of a top-flight restaurant… a great experience that much exceeded expectations". / W1D 4EF; lescargot.co.uk; lescargotsoho; Tue-Sat 10.30 pm, Sun 5 pm.

Escocesa N16   £75   3 2 2
67 Stoke Newington Church Street   020 7812 9189   1–1C

"Just wonderful" Stoke Newington tapas bar "very popular locally" for its "great sharing plates" and "wide range of Spanish wines, many by the glass". Scottish seafood is the prime focus for dishes that put a Hispanic twist on Caledonian produce, all courtesy its Glasgow-born founder, ex-music producer Stephen Lironi. Top Tip – "we always eat early to take advantage of the half-price oysters before 7pm". / N16 0AR; escocesa.co.uk; escocesa_n16; Mon-Thu 10 pm, Fri & Sat 11 pm, Sun 9.30 pm.

Esters N16   £20   3 3 2
55 Kynaston Road   020 7254 0253   1–1C

"Worth the local hype (and the queue)", says fans of this small, bright and breezy modern café in Stoke Newington, which has become known over the years for its "twists on the classic brunch options" – "imaginative pairings that don't sound like they should work but really do". / N16 0EB; estersn16.com; Mon-Sun 5 pm.

Estiatorio Milos SW1   £140   3 2 4
1 Regent Street   020 7839 2080   4–4D

Hang with a "smart, interesting-looking set of diners" at Costas Spiladi's luxurious Greek venture in St James's – part of his international chain, whose 10 other branches include three in NYC, as well as outlets in Miami, Athens and Dubai. It aims to evoke the brilliant blue waters of the Med and showcases an "excellent" array of fish and seafood on glittering counters of ice, where you choose your catch and specify how it's to be prepared. On the downside, service can be "variable" and it is – predictably – "very expensive". / SW1Y 4NR; estiatoriomilos.com; estiatoriomilos; Mon-Sat 11 pm, Sun 10 pm.

Evelyn's Table at The Blue Posts W1   £163   4 3 3
28 Rupert Street   07921 336010   4–3D

"A really special experience for serious foodies" – Layo & Zoë Paskin's (also of Barbary and Palomar fame) intimate 12-seater is part of a period Chinatown pub, where they have created different venues on each level. Here in the former beer cellar, "the only option is the kitchen counter, so you are right in on the action" and the creation of "superbly executed cuisine" from a small team, which is now headed by Seamus Sam, former head chef at Tom Aiken's Muse, whose August 2024 arrival post-dated our diners' poll. Feedback volume and ratings have slipped marginally since Luke Selby left for Le Manoir at the end of 2022. The most critical report? "A perfectly competent meal, served in an appropriately reverential atmosphere, albeit a cramped and uncomfortable setting (but then places of worship often are) by suitably devout believers and not cheap". But perhaps there will now be an uptick under the new chef? Top Tip – a variety of drink pairings range from 'Firm Favourites' to 'No & Low' (a mixture of alcohol-free and low ABV wines). / W1D 6DJ; thebluepostsco.uk; evelynstable; Mon-Sat 11 pm.

FSA RATINGS: FROM **1** POOR — **5** EXCEPTIONAL

FSA

Everest Curry King SE13 £34 3 3 2
24 Loampit Hill   020 8691 2233   1–4D
"New and improved (they've expanded into the surprisingly spacious premises next door, leaving the original location for takeaways-only)" – the Sivarajah family's stalwart of over 20 years' standing is about 10 minutes' stroll from Lewisham station. It's renowned locally for "very good southern-Indian/Sri Lankan food" and there's been "no noticeable drop in standards, due to the big move". / SE13 7SW; Mon-Sun 11 pm.

Everest Inn SE3 £61 3 3 2
41 Montpelier Vale   020 8852 7872   1–4D
"The food never disappoints" at this better-than-standard Nepalese and Indian specialist on the edge of Blackheath Common. Notwithstanding the choices of artworks and wall hangings, the contemporary interior avoids the classic curry house look. / SE3 0TJ; everestinn.co.uk; everestinn; Tue-Thu 10.30 pm, Fri & Sat 11 pm, Sun 10 pm.

Evi's (fka Souvlaki Street) SE22 £40 3 4 2
18 North Cross Road   07598 932505   1–4D
"A really fun place (not fancy at all) – nice, simple Greek food, but done with panache and a smile": Evi Peroulaki and Conor Mills moved on from Pop Brixton (where they traded as Souvlaki Street) to this neighbourhood spot in East Dulwich. Our early feedback is upbeat, and in his September 2023 review, The Evening Standard's Jimi Famurewa praised "a special little place", where dishes "knock you over with their culinary acuity, gushing succulence and punching, vibrant freshness". / SE22 9EU; evisrestaurant.com; evislondon; Tue-Sat 9.30 pm, Sun 3 pm.

Faber W6 NEW £43 3 3 4
206 Hammersmith Rd   0208 161 9800   8–2C
"What a great restaurant to land in Hammersmith!" – this seafood newcomer has immediately won a big local fanclub. "Worth seeking out, even though it's in an odd spot just off the Broadway roundabout", it has a "smart" and surprisingly "glamorous" dining room and provides "excellent-quality fish and seafood". "Dishes are well-priced and everything is prepared to a good standard". It's from the team behind The Victoria seafood pub in Mile End, and they hope it's the first of a small chain across London. / W6 7DH; faberrestaurants.co.uk.

Fadiga W1 £41 3 4 2
71 Berwick Street   020 3609 5536   4–1C
"Real Bolognese starters and pastas made by real Bolognese" win praise for this "popular, authentic, family-run restaurant" in Soho. Michela makes the pasta every day, her husband Enrico cooks it and their daughter Carlotta serves it. It's tiny, so "booking is essential – but you may still have to wait if the previous occupants of your table can't bring themselves to leave!". Top Menu Tip – "tiramisu is a highlight". / W1F 8TB; fadiga.uk; fadiga_ristorantebolognese; Tue-Sat 11 pm.

Fair Shot Café W1
17 South Molton Street   no tel   3–2B
Need a light lunch or coffee and bite in Covent Garden? – You can have one in an elegant, high ceilinged space and boost the life chances of someone with learning difficulties or autism when you visit Bianca Tavella's excellent fixture, which every year gives 15 young people (aged 18-25 years) with special needs the opportunity for work experience. / W1K 5QT; fairshot.co.uk; fairshotcafe; Sun-Fri 6 pm, Sat 6.30 pm.

Fallow St James's SW1 £107 4 3 4
52 Haymarket   020 8017 1788.   4–3B
"Helping reclaim the West End with proper food!" – Jack Croft, Will Murray & James Robson's four-year-old venture progressed via pop-ups (including a

year on Heddon Street) to occupy this big site with an open kitchen at the south of the Haymarket. "It's a lovely, buzzing environment" in which to enjoy some "beautiful" modern British food: a mix of bold small plates and larger dishes with a focus on sustainability. "They've hit on a winning formula for breakfast" too. Top Menu Tip – "Braised Dairy Ribs are massive chunks of love and the crab with ponzu snapped crackled and popped as much as anything ever eaten". / SW1Y 4RP; fallowrestaurant.com; fallowrestaurant; Mon-Sat 11 pm, Sun 10 pm.

La Famiglia SW10 £87 2 2 5
7 Langton Street   020 7351 0761   6–3B

Regulars still adore this Chelsea haunt with origins in the Swinging Sixties – "not the best food in town" and "at Chelsea prices"; but "an old-established family-run Italian restaurant with a lovely atmosphere, an old-fashioned dessert trolley, spotlessly clean and full of character". In particular, local parents say it's "lovely for families for Sunday lunch". Founded by Tuscany-born Alvaro Maccione, who fed everyone from Frank Sinatra and Elizabeth Taylor to Michael Caine and Princess Margaret back in the day, it's still "very popular with loyal Chelsea supporters (and some players...)", while Simon Cowell was also spotted here last year. / SW10 0JL; lafamiglia.co.uk; lafamiglia.sw10; Tue-Sat 9.30 pm, Sun 8.30 pm.

Farang N5 £54 4 3 3
72 Highbury Park   020 7226 1609   9–1D

"Original and cleverly spiced new-wave Thai food" graces the "unusual menu" at this former pop-up in Highbury from chef Sebby Holmes – "brace yourself for a decent walk afterwards if you're tempted to eat rather too much of the very delectable food". Top Tip – "the cleverly done make-at-home range is almost as good as the restaurant". / N5 2XE; faranglondon.co.uk; farangldn; Wed-Sat 9 pm.

Fare EC1 £64 3 3 2
11 Old Street   020 3034 0736   10–1B

With a bright, modern interior lit by big floor-to-ceiling windows, this flexible neighbourhood amenity near Old Street is a canteen and bar that opens all day from breakfast. It's from the team behind well-known Hackney wine bar Sager + Wilde, hence an above-par drinks offering. But food is far from incidental: there's a "constantly changing, seasonal menu" of southern European small plates, some larger risotti, pasta and burgers and it majors in a big range of pizza. Top Tip – it "can handle large parties with ease". / EC1V 9HL; farelondon.com; farelondon.com; Mon-Sat 11 pm.

Fatt Pundit £60 3 3 2
77 Berwick Street, W1   020 7287 7900   4–1C
6 Maiden Lane, WC2   020 7836 8883   5–3D

An "interesting menu" – with "the spicing just right" – is offered at this "great concept", serving the cuisine developed by the historic Hakka Chinese community in Kolkata. The only complaint relates to the "very cramped tables" at its two venues, in Soho and Covent Garden. / facebook.com/fattpundit; fattpundit.

Fazenda,
Rodizio Bar & Grill EC2 £113
100 Bishopsgate   020 3370 7202   10–4D

This outpost of the all-you-can-eat, Brazilian-inspired national steakhouse group sits at the foot of the 100 Bishopsgate tower and opened in early autumn 2023. It has yet to spark a huge volume of survey feedback, but the Evening Standard's Jimi Famurewa gave it a mostly positive report card, particularly its cuts of meat wielded by "skewer-wielding passadors... characterised by luscious, high-grade flavour, careful seasoning, and adroitly applied char". Veggies and desserts were equally well received, although the 'salad bar' and à la carte section wasn't so successful. Overall he pronounced it "keenly run" and "occasionally fantastic". / EC2M 1GT; fazenda.co.uk; Fazenda.group; Mon-Sat 10 pm, Sun 8.30 pm.

Fenchurch Restaurant, Sky Garden EC3 — £111 — 2 3 4
20 Fenchurch St   033 3772 0020   10–3D

Still-limited and somewhat up-and-down feedback on the posher part of this foliage-filled space on the 37th floor of the 'Walkie Talkie' (your reservation gives you access to the surrounding 'Sky Garden', for which you otherwise need a ticket). Nowadays the stoves are overseen by Anguillan-raised Kerth Gumbs, who puts a Caribbean spin on some dishes, be it from the à la carte or the 9-course tasting menu for £95. The odd critic considers it "overpriced and mediocre", but fans say it's "exceptional and romantic". / EC3M 3BY; skygarden.london; sg_skygarden; Wed-Sun 9.30 pm, Tue 9 pm.

Fez Mangal W11 — £51 — 3 3 2
104 Ladbroke Grove   020 7229 3010   7–1A

"A go-to place for consistently good-quality kebabs" and "good Turkish food" in Ladbroke Grove. There's a "lively atmosphere" – "more civilised upstairs" – and the BYO policy keeps the bill under control. / W11 1PY; fezmangal.net; fezmangal; Mon-Sun 11 pm.

50 Kalò di Ciro Salvo WC2 — £53 — 4 2 2
7 Northumberland Avenue   020 7930 9955   2–3C

"The pizza is so good! – with lovely premium ingredients for the toppings too" – at this showcase just off Trafalgar Square for Ciro Salvo's Naples-based chain. The cavernous space is "very lively"… to the extent it can seem "a little bit too loud". Top Menu Tip – "great supplì" (Roman-style rice croquettes). / WC2N 5BY; xn–50kal-yta.it; 50kalolondon; Mon-Sun 11 pm.

Fischer's W1 — £72 — 3 4 4
50 Marylebone High Street   020 7466 5501   2–1A

"Ticking all the boxes whether for breakfast, lunch, Kaffee und Kuchen, or dinner" – this "handsome" Wolseley Group operation in Marylebone Village, inspired by the grand cafés of Vienna, put in a stronger all-round performance this year as a "reasonably priced" and "dependable" rendezvous in a pricey part of town. Its "Austrian-style menu in a lovely brasserie style" has "a good choice of food with something for everyone", helping to make it "a good place to meet friends and with no pressure to move on". / W1U 5HN; fischers.co.uk; fischerslondon; Tue-Sun 10 pm, Mon 9.30 pm.

Fish & Bubbles W11 NEW — £41
192 Kensington Park Road   no tel   7–1A

This spritzy new seafood café in Notting Hill was brought to us in February 2024 by the brothers behind its neighbour (one of West London's three-strong La Mia Mamma Italian chain). It presents an innovative mix of gourmet seafood panini and bruschetta, plus giant fritto misto sharing boards (sold 'al metro'), all washed down with negronis and bubbles a-go-go! (Restaurant anoraks will nostalgically remember the premises from their now-forgotten days as 192: a key haunt back in the day for the likes of David Hockney, Kate Moss, Mick Jagger etc, when Notting Hill was still thought of as edgy). / W11 2ES; fishandbubbles.uk; fishandbubbleslondon; Sun-Thu 10.30 pm, Fri & Sat 11.30 pm.

Fish Central EC1 — £47 — 4 4 3
149-155 Central St   020 7253 4970   13–1A

"Brilliant on every level" – this family-run Greek-Cypriot chippy in Clerkenwell has provided "great fresh fish at incredible prices" for more than five decades. "The staff are simply divine", providing "really fun service", and "the community work the restaurant carries out is unparalleled". / EC1V 8AP; fishcentral.co.uk; fishcentralrestaurant; Mon-Thu, Sat 10 pm, Fri 10.30 pm.

fish! SE1 £78 2 3 2
Cathedral St 020 7407 3803 10–4C

With "a varied and interesting menu of fish and seafood" – this "light and buzzy" glass-fronted modern fish restaurant satisfies most diners as "a good pitstop amidst the hum of Borough Market" – although there are persistent gripes that it's "just not imaginative enough for the prices, exploiting the tourist location". Top Tip – "nice for a team dinner (when the madding crowds have gone)". / SE1 9AL; fishkitchen.co.uk; fishboroughmarket; Sun-Wed 10 pm, Thu-Sat 11 pm.

Fishworks £84 3 2 2
7-9 Swallow St, W1 020 7734 5813 4–4C
89 Marylebone High St, W1 020 7935 9796 2–1A
2-4 Catherine Street, WC2 020 7240 4999 5–3D

"You know that you'll get a decent meal" at these "unpretentious" 'Fishmongers & Restaurants' in Covent Garden, Marylebone and off Piccadilly, where you can buy retail from the wet counter or proceed to eat in at the adjoining dining room. "A wide variety of fish and seafood can be cooked to your specification" and "it's the perfect place for some nice, simple cooking". Any drawbacks? The food is "good but rather unimaginative"; "ambience is a little lacking; and the service level is not as good as could be". / fishworks.co.uk; FishworksUK.

Fiume SW8 £78 2 2 3
Circus West Village, Sopwith Way 020 3904 9010 11–1C

With its "great terrace" by the Thames and prime position at the Battersea Power Station, this smart modern Italian from D&D London was one of the first openings in the development and certainly looks "elegant and modern". "Good, but a little expensive" summarises input on the traditional Italian menu, where even cheaper options like the small selection of 'Pinsa' (Roman-style pizza) will set you back £20. / SW8 5BN; fiume-restaurant.co.uk; Fiume.London; Mon-Thu, Sat 9.30 pm, Fri 9.45pm, Sun 8.30 pm; SRA-3 stars.

The Five Fields SW3 £221 5 4 3
8-9 Blacklands Ter 020 7838 1082 6–2D

"Hidden off the King's Road" in "an attractive townhouse" in a backstreet near Peter Jones – Taylor Bonnyman's "romantic" venue is "just lovely in every respect". Chef Marguerite Keogh's "exceptionally well thought-out" modern British cuisine is "incredibly well thought-out: dishes taste sublime and the presentation is a work of art in itself". "The wine pairings are really interesting" and "Nuno, the sommelier, gave comprehensive explanations of all the wines": part of a team delivering service that's "excellent and not cloying". "It's under the radar, but one of the best restaurants in town": "highly recommended". (It also deserves kudos for its "exceptional sustainability", with produce sourced from its own one-and-a-half-acre kitchen garden in Sussex). / SW3 2SP; fivefieldsrestaurant.com; the5fields; Tue-Sat 10 pm.

500 N19 £58 4 4 3
782 Holloway Rd 020 7272 3406 9–1C

This "neighbourhood gem" near Archway (named in tribute to the tiny Fiat 500) is a "truly brilliant family-run Italian" with an "ambience that takes you back in time". Opened in 2007 by chef Mario Magli, it's "still a go-to for a top-notch Italian meal", with "imaginative food and the feeling that the owner really cares". Its fan club is more-than-local, and numerous best meals of the year are reported here. / N19 3JH; 500restaurant.co.uk; 500restaurant; Wed-Sat 10 pm, Sun 9 pm.

FKABAM (Black Axe Mangal) N1 £59 3 3 4
156 Canonbury Road no tel 9–2D

"Totally uncompromising: it is what it is and therefore cooks from the heart while listening to loud music!" – ex-St John chef Lee Tiernan is celebrating 10 years at his "unique" heavy-metal BBQ on Highbury Corner (renamed a

couple of years ago with a nod to Prince). Renowned for its bad-ass spicy flatbreads, it's an address on every food tourist's list: "now that it's set menu only [published on Instagram], it's a bit more restricting, but it's always good fun". / N1 2UP; blackaxemangal.com; blackaxemangal; Wed-Sat 10.30 pm.

The Flask N6 — £59 — 2 3 4
77 Highgate West Hill   020 8348 7346   9–1B

Grade II listed pub in posh Highgate (whose former patrons include Dickens). Run by Young's, the gastropub fare is solidly rated, but the chief highpoints include its attractively updated period charms, big outside terrace and cosy dining conservatory with large skylight. / N6 6BU; theflaskhighgate.com; theflaskhighgate; Mon-Sat 11 pm, Sun 10.30 pm.

Flat Iron — £40 — 3 3 3
17 Beak St, W1   020 3019 2353   4–2B
42-44 James Street, W1   no tel   3–1A
17 Henrietta St, WC2   020 3019 4212   5–3C
9 Denmark St, WC2   no tel   5–1A
9 Young Street, W8   no tel   6–1A
47-51 Caledonian Rd, N1   no tel   9–3D
112-116 Tooley Street, SE1   no tel   10–4D
41-45 The Cut, SE1   no tel   10–4A
Soho Wharf, 11 Clink Street, SE1   no tel   10–3C
88-90 Commercial Street, E1   no tel   13–2C
77 Curtain Road, EC2   no tel   13–1B

"A limited-choice menu, but one that seems to work" underpins the success of this "no-frills" steakhouse chain created by Charlie Carroll in 2012 and now with just under a dozen London branches (with 2024 seeing its arrival in Victoria and just off Hammersmith Broadway). "You know just what you are going to get" and "the quality/value factor makes it a sound bet": "decent steaks and a few rustic sides"; and "don't forget the lovely (free) salted caramel ice cream on the way out!". "Not a place to linger", but "it never disappoints". / flatironsteak.co.uk; flatironsteak; SRA-3 stars.

Flesh and Buns — £72 — 3 2 2
32 Berners Street, W1   020 3019 3492   3–1D
41 Earlham Street, WC2   020 7632 9500   5–2C

Noisy izakayas in Fitzrovia and Covent Garden from the Bone Daddies group, "serving a good range from the stickier and more crowd-pleasing end of Japanese cuisine", along with "tasty pan-Asian small plates including their signature bao buns". Top Menu Tips – "great yakitori, lovely beef-fat chips". / fleshandbuns.com; fleshandbuns.

Florencio Pizza W1 NEW — £40 — 3 4 3
14 Seymour Place   020 8143 8232   2–2A

This newbie pizzeria in Seymour Place from Argentinian chef Diego Jacquet of nearby Zoilo attracted "quite a bit of hype" at its November 2023 launch. Its biggest fans say it's superb, and nobody rates it worse than good all-round. Apparently "it's all in the dough", fermented for 24 hours from an original blend of flours. / W1H 7NF; florenciopizza.com; florencio_pizza; Tue-Sun 10 pm.

Foley's W1 — £56 — 3 3 3
23 Foley Street   020 3137 1302   2–1B

"A jolly pan-Asian mish-mash that's good value for the West End" inspires ongoing interest in this Fitzrovia venue. Most of the action is on the ground floor, but there's also an outdoor bar and basement chef's counter. / W1W 6DU; foleysrestaurant.co.uk; foleysrestaurant; Mon-Thu 10 pm, Fri & Sat 10.30 pm, Sun 9 pm.

Fonda W1 NEW
12 Heddon St   no tel   4–3B
Open towards the second half of 2024 in Mayfair's foodie Heddon Street, chef Santiago Lastra's newcomer is a sequel to his smash-hit Kol, but is more accessible pricewise. It's inspired by the regional cuisines of Mexico, where 'fonda' means a family-owned restaurant; and a 'comal' (clay griddle for cooking the likes of corn masa) is a centrepiece. Hero dishes include Duo de Callo (confit whole scallops on a gooseberry, sesame and burnt jalapeno salsa). / W1B 4BZ; fondalondon.com; Mon-Sat 11 pm.

Fortnum & Mason,
The Diamond Jubilee Tea Salon W1   £92   3 3 4
181 Piccadilly   020 7734 8040   3–3D
"How can you ignore a proper English high tea at Fortnum's… the grandness of their fluffy (raisin and non-raisin) scones, the beautiful desserts, the soft but tasty sandwiches, with an all-you-can-eat provision… oh and the choice of 100+ tea leaves". Many reports hail this well-known, third-floor chamber (an "institution" that's actually a relatively modern creation, opened as it was by her late majesty, Queen Elizabeth II, a dozen years ago in 2012) as a "quintessential English experience"; and "celebrating with high tea and Champagne here is hard to beat". Criticism is notably absent in reports and fans claim this is "the pick of the capital's high-end tea rooms". "The cake trolley is great fun and while the whole experience is punishingly expensive, it does – just about – feel like good value". Top Tip – "The savoury afternoon here is every bit as beautifully presented as any of the sweet options, a blessing for those who enjoy the extravagance and ritual of afternoon tea but prefer to avoid too much sugar!" / W1A 1ER; fortnumandmason.com; fortnums; Mon-Sat 8 pm, Sun 7.30 pm.

Fortnum & Mason,
Field by Fortnum's W1 NEW   £70   2 2 2
181 Piccadilly   no tel   3–3D
The late queen's favourite grocer continues to mix it up when it comes to its food offering, recently opening this late 2023 newcomer: a casual-ish café above the food halls serving morning pastries and bacon sarnies, plus an all-day modern bistro menu (pork cutlet, chicken & mushroom pie…). Even fans note "this is not the cheapest restaurant in town… well it wouldn't be, would it?" But "enjoyable food with great flavours" makes it a worthy addition. Overall ratings are middling across the board, though, and critics say: "Fortnum's needs to do better than this". / W1A 1ER; fortnumandmason.com; Sun-Fri 6 pm, Sat 7 pm.

Fortnum & Mason,
The Parlour W1   £35   2 3 4
181 Piccadilly   0845 6025694   3–3D
"I love the idea of an ice cream parlour at F&M!" say most reporters who visit this "attractively decorated room with views of Piccadilly" on the first floor of this venerable grocer's shop (whose Royal Warrant was renewed by King Charles following the death of his late mother). For most reporters it's "just a total joy of nostalgic indulgence and great fun": "excellent for children who love ice cream and who can create their dream concoctions; and with very good Welsh rarebit for the adults". A small minority of reports are more sniffy ("a tacky experience, compounded by a huge bill!"). / W1A 1ER; fortnumandmason.com; Mon-Sat 8 pm, Sun 5 pm.

Fortune Cookie W2   £48   3 2 1
1 Queensway   020 7727 7260   7–2C
Almost everyone has walked past this 30-year fixture next-door to Queensway tube station at some point. Those who have dropped in for a meal have found "delicious and authentic Cantonese food", including roast

duck and seafood – "but don't expect friendly service". Top Menu Tip – "beef with black bean sauce and crispy noodles". / W2 4QJ; Tue-Sat 10.30 pm, Sun 9.30 pm.

45 Jermyn St SW1 £91 3️⃣3️⃣3️⃣
45 Jermyn Street   020 7205 4545   3–3D

"Whether for a cocktail or caviar at the bar or sequestered in one of the red leather booths", this 10-year-old venue in Fortnum & Mason's (with its own street entrance) "is made for romance" ("I can't imagine anyone not being seduced by a shared plate of lobster spaghetti, flambéed dramatically tableside"); and also has fans for business entertaining thanks to "staff who can't do enough for you". For many reporters, though, its top feature is the "brilliant breakfast" – "there's a reason this place is always busy in the mornings". (The food rating has recovered after a "terrible dive in 2023", with "the kitchen much improved from January 2024"). / SW1Y 6DN; 45jermynst.com; 45jermynst; Mon-Sat 10.15 pm, Sun 4.45 pm.

Forty Four SW14 £55 4️⃣4️⃣3️⃣
44 Sheen Lane   0208 8787 600   11–2A

Some "all-round superb" meals thanks to chef Leonard Kola win praise from fans of this "lovely" neighbourhood venue in East Sheen, a couple of whom had their best meal of the year here. The menu is quite eclectic, with some focus on steak and seafood grills, plus seafood and vegetarian curries. Top Tip – early evenings and daytimes at weekends there are set deals from £22 per person. / SW14 8LP; fortyfourrestaurant.co.uk; Tue-Sun 10 pm.

40 Maltby Street SE1 £63 4️⃣4️⃣3️⃣
40 Maltby St   020 7237 9247   10–4D

"Steve Williams is a skilled chef backed by an interesting natural wine list" and his canteen attached to a biodynamic wine warehouse in a railway arch behind London Bridge station has helped put the area on the culinary map. It's "a top example of natural wine + amazing food celebrating the ingredients"; and its no-frills environment belies its importance over the past decade in "the genesis of many great new arrivals on the London food scene". / SE1 3PA; 40maltbystreet.com; 40maltbystreet; Wed-Sat 9.30 pm.

Forty Three Sichuan Kitchen SW8 NEW £35 4️⃣3️⃣2️⃣
43 South Lambeth Road   0778 393 0696   11–1D

"An amazing combination of flavours and heat" is the reward for a visit to this Sichuan newcomer: a relatively simple-looking walk-in operation on two floors near Vauxhall Park. "Staff are knowledgeable and helpful" and the ingredients are high-quality (for example, only Iberico pork is used). Top Menu Tip – "anywhere that takes rabbit seriously is very good news!" / SW8 1RH; 43kitchen.com; Wed-Fri, Tue, Sat 10 pm, Sun 3 pm.

Forza Win SE5 £50 3️⃣3️⃣4️⃣
29-33 Camberwell Church Street   07454 898693   1–3C

Bash Redford and Michael Lavery started their project as a supper club a dozen years ago, cemented their reputation in Peckham, and moved to Camberwell in 2022, where they have raided the Whites & Neutrals section of the colour chart to create "a great vibe" in artfully decorated premises. The Italian menu is traditional in design: "delicious plates" matched with "a fantastic wine list". These days they also have branches at the National Theatre and in Peckham Rye. / SE5 8TR; forzawin.com; forzawin; Tue-Sat 10.30 pm, Sun 3.30 pm.

Forza Wine £65 3️⃣2️⃣4️⃣
Floor 5, Rye Lane, SE15   020 7732 7500   1–4D
Royal National Theatre, SE1   020 7452 3555   2–3D NEW

The top floor of the National Theatre has been through a number of incarnations and its latest is the autumn 2023 spin-off from Peckham Rye's hip roof-top bar that's long been a favoured spot for sundowners and nibbles

for fun-loving SE15 types. Most reports see this new branch as "a fabulous addition to the Forza family", saying: "at last, the National Theatre has a buzzy restaurant to be proud of – with its fab location, a table on the beautiful and spacious wrap- around terrace is unbeatable on a sunny day, serving lovely sharing plates of modern Italian-ish tapas and an excellent drinks list". On the downside, service can be "a bit chaotic" and "all over the place". Top Menu Tip – "memorable cauliflower fritti with aioli. Yum!"
/ forzawine.com; forzawine.

Four Regions TW9 £60 343
102-104 Kew Rd 020 8940 9044 1–4A
This stalwart family-run Chinese of over three decades' standing is "always enjoyable" and continues to attract a high volume of consistent praise for somewhere in a trafficky suburban location (just north of Richmond, on the way to Kew). / TW9 2PQ; fourregions.co.uk; Four Regions; Mon-Sat 11 pm, Sun 10.30 pm.

Four Seasons £69 411
11 Gerrard Street, W1 020 7287 0900 5–3A
12 Gerrard Street, W1 020 7494 0870 5–3A
23 Wardour Street, W1 020 7287 9995 5–3A
84 Queensway, W2 020 7229 4320 7–2C
"The best roast duck in the world? I have no idea, but it's certainly superb" at these Cantonese canteens… and "you definitely don't go for the ambience. No, You go for the duck… if you're really smart, the roast pork… or even better, the pork and the duck!". "But the service is comically, disastrously rude – and your arteries will probably thank you if you don't go too often". Launched 35 years ago in Queensway, the group now has outlets in Chinatown, Soho, the Hippodrome (Chop Chop), Colindale's Bang Bang Oriental food hall and Oxford. / fs-restaurants.co.uk; fourseasons_uk.

14 Hills EC3 £103 223
120 Fenchurch Street 020 3981 5222 10–3D
"A great view" is the undeniable plus point of this D&D London venue, on the 14th floor of the scraper at 120 Fenchurch Street. Other than the odd recommendation as a business lunching venue, however, it inspires strikingly few reports for a venue boasting 2,500 evergreen plants and – though harsh critiques are lacking – its luxe-brasserie menu incorporating oysters, sashimi, caviar, steaks and other grills goes uncommented-on. / EC3M 5BA; danddlondon.com; 14hillsldn; Mon-Sat midnight, Sun 10.30 pm; SRA-3 stars.

Fox & Grapes SW19 £63 343
9 Camp Rd 020 8619 1300 11–2A
"A favourite in the Wimbledon Village/Common area!" – this Georgian pub is co-owned by TV chef Paul Merrett and his Jolly Pubs group (which includes the Victoria in East Sheen). Aside from the odd nod to cheaper pub-grub dishes, most of the menu is somewhat more ambitious bistro-style fare.
/ SW19 4UN; foxandgrapeswimbledon.co.uk; foxandgrapeswimbledon; Wed-Sat 9.15 pm, Sun 8 pm.

The Fox & Hounds SW11 £73 343
66-68 Latchmere Road 020 7924 5483 11–1C
The attractions of this well-rated Battersea pub include "an excellent range of beer", a "fantastic" flower-filled beer garden and "brilliant Sunday roasts", alongside the Mediterranean-influenced menu that's served the rest of the week. / SW11 2JU; thefoxandhoundspub.co.uk; thefoxbattersea; Mon-Sat 10 pm, Sun 9 pm.

The Fox and Pheasant SW10 £67 344
1 Billing Road 020 7352 2943 6–3B
This "upmarket" and "traditional" pub tucked away on the edge of Chelsea near Stamford Bridge is owned by singer James Blunt and his wife Sofia, and

mimics a country local with a "cosy bar area and a lovely conservatory". The "delicious food" is at its best for Sunday lunch, when it's "the perfect place for a pint of beer and some roast pork". / SW10 9UJ; thefoxandpheasant.com; thefoxandpheasantpub; Sun & Mon 11 pm, Tue-Sat midnight.

Frame N4 NEW £48 3 3 3
7 Clifton Terrace   020 7209 2970   9–1D
"Opened in late 2023 in the trendy new cultural quarter around Finsbury Park tube", this indie caff is hailed by early fans as "a fantastic addition to the area thanks to its wide choice of breakfast/brunch and lunch dishes", plus "tasty" coffee and other brews. "The interior has a restrained Scandi-style aesthetic, but don't think IKEA! We're talking more upmarket". Top Menu Tip – "divine chocolate brownies". / N4 3JP; framefinsbury.co.uk; Mon-Sat 8 pm, Sun 6 pm.

Francatelli SW1 NEW
St. James's Hotel & Club, 7-8 Park Place   020 7316 1621   3–4C
Previously Seven Park Place (RIP), this St James's chamber was relaunched in mid 2024 under its same long-term chef William Drabble, but now branded for his predecessor at the stoves of the St James's Club, of which this dining room is part – one Charles Elmé Francatelli, who subsequently went on to cook for Queen Victoria. Francatelli was the author of 'The Modern Cook' published in 1854, which apparently provides inspiration for many of Drabble's dishes. The venue opened too late in the day for survey feedback, but in an early May 2024 review, it faced a 'hatchet job' from the first press critic to visit: The Telegraph's William Sitwell. But Drabble's record historically has been exemplary, so it's a little hard to believe that most meals here will be quite as awful as Sitwell's; in fact past form would suggest they could be rather good: reports please! / SW1A 1LS; /stjameshotelandclub/; Thu-Sat, Tue, Wed 9.30 pm.

Franco Manca £40 2 2 2
Branches throughout London
"Well-cooked, crisp-based sourdough pizzas with an emphasis on toppings" have helped this successful chain achieve a higher food score nowadays than its old rival PizzaExpress (which shares an almost-identical volume of feedback). With its high-growth days behind it, though, its middling ratings support those who feel it "used to be better"; and it risks slipping into a performance that's neither here nor there. Service in particular is a weakness – it "can be erratic with lots of waiting"; some diners complain of "under-seasoned" or "soggy" recent meals; and its branches have never had much in the way of pizzazz. Overall, it's still oft-cited as a "safe" and "decent-value" option that's "perfect for families", but as it becomes longer in the tooth some sense of reinvention would be welcome. Since 2023, it's been ultimately owned by Tokyo Stock Exchange-listed Toridoll Holdings, who also own Marugame Udon – hopefully they have some bright ideas on keeping the brand fresh. / francomanca.co.uk; francomancapizza.

Franco's SW1 £97 3 3 3
61 Jermyn St   020 7499 2211   3–3C
"It is not the cheapest option in town", but this "always-busy", "classic" Italian (founded in 1945) is very "well-situated" and "does deliver consistency"; hitting just the right note for a "Central Casting" crowd of St James's regulars, many of them clad in the expensive pin-striped suits sold in the local gents' outfitters. "The food is good without being exceptional"; "staff know their clientele and make them feel special" and although the question is raised – "do the tables have to be so close together?" – such "intimate" seating is perfect for the local property and art dealers to gossip over. "It's pricey for sure… but that's Jermyn St for you". / SW1Y 6LX; francoslondon.com; francoslondon; Mon-Sat 11 pm.

F S A

Franklins SE22 — £65 — 2 3 3
157 Lordship Ln   020 8299 9598   1–4D

This "real local favourite" in East Dulwich from Rod Franklin and Tim Sheehan has served seasonal British cooking for more than 25 years, and is "famed for its Sunday roasts for carnivores" (but there's more to it than meat, and "the varied menu always has an excellent selection of veggie/vegan dishes"). To the odd sceptic, it's "OK, but really no more than that".
/ SE22 8HX; franklinsrestaurant.com; franklinsse22; Mon-Sat midnight, Sun 10.30 pm.

Frantoio SW10 — £72 — 3 2 3
397 King's Rd   020 7352 4146   6–3B

Opposite the site of Vivienne Westwood & Malcom McLaren's once-famous 1970s boutique at World's End, this traditional neighbourhood trattoria has a small but enthusiastic fan club of locals, some of whom doubtless used to shop over the road, but who nowadays sport more conventional Chelsea attire. / SW10 0LR; frantoio.co.uk; Frantonio_london; Mon-Sun 11 pm.

The Freak Scene SW6 — £48 — 4 3 3
28 Parsons Green Lane   020 7610 9863   11–1B

"Next level!" – high-profile Aussie ex-Nobu head chef Scott Hallsworth now has two Freak Scenes: one in Parsons Green (with hot pots, buns, sashimi, grills…) and a newer one near his home in Balham (more focused on sushi, plus robata dishes). Both show his trademark culinary style of "fun, elevated izakaya food" – "exciting menus with bold flavours and combinations" – all served in a "buzzy and friendly" environment. / SW6 4HS; freakscenerestaurants.com; FREAKSCENESW6; Tue, Wed 10.30 pm, Thu-Sat 11 pm.

Frederick's N1 — £77 — 3 4 5
106 Camden Passage   020 7359 2888   9–3D

In a "brilliant setting" among the antique shops of Camden Passage, this "reliable, high-class stalwart has been going for over 50 years, and is never disappointing". "The food is unoriginal but good quality and excellently prepared, while the staff are unfailingly efficient and welcoming". There's a "super bar, and garden dining is especially lovely come summer-time". You wouldn't head here for a rave, though – having recruited an army of regulars over so many years, it's perhaps inevitable that "the restaurant vibe is large tables of posh pensioners having a jolly time". / N1 8EG; fredericks.co.uk; fredericks_n1; Tue-Sat 10 pm.

The French House W1 — £78 — 5 4 5
49 Dean Street   020 7437 2477   5–3A

"Tiny, but perfect in every other way" – "you couldn't ask for better bistro food" than that produced by Neil Borthwick (Angela Hartnett's husband) at this quirky dining room, where "simple dishes are realised with flair" and with "big, big flavours". "Downstairs is a throwback to Soho boozers of yesteryear, you head upstairs to eat" – the room where General de Gaulle composed some of his speeches during WWII. "With six or seven small tables, it's a rustic and cosy room, complete with very friendly and entertaining service, a humble and charming chef, and a feel of spit-and-sawdust, it's the perfect spot for a cosy Soho supper". Top Menu Tip – "the crisp bacon jowl will live long in the memory… and even longer on the hips!" / W1D 5BG; frenchhousesoho.com; frenchhousesoho; Tue-Sat 9 pm.

Frog by Adam Handling WC2 — £248 — 4 4 3
35 Southampton Street   020 7199 8370   5–3D

"The stories behind the dishes are so lovely" at Adam Handling's Covent Garden HQ, where diners face the open kitchen to enjoy an eight-course menu presented by the chef and his team for £195 per person. "The wow-factor of the beautiful presentation really adds to the overall pleasure of the meal" and "you will seldom see such intricately and delicately plated dishes". For most diners, "there's substance to match all the theatrics" too, with the resulting tastes on the plate being "absolutely superb". But there are also

those who – while acknowledging "flashes of brilliance" – still feel that "'we're-trying-so-hard' screams from every dish" to the extent of seeming "pointless" or "pretentious". "And then there's the bill…" which even fans concede is "daftly expensive". The main verdict though? "can't wait to return!". Top Tip – corkage free lunchtimes: BYO at no extra cost!
/ WC2E 7HG; frogbyadamhandling.com; Frogbyah; Wed-Sat, Mon & Tue 11 pm.

La Fromagerie £57 2 3 2
2-6 Moxon St, W1   020 7935 0341   3–1A
52 Lamb's Conduit St, WC1   020 7242 1044   2–1D
30 Highbury Park, N5   020 7359 7440   9–2D

"Perfect for cheese lovers": the "quirky and atmospheric" cafés adjoining these excellent retail cheese emporia – particularly the well-known branch in Marylebone – are particularly "good for lunch", offering cheese and charcuterie boards alongside simple dishes like pan-seared salmon or paté en croute. Top Tip – worth remembering for breakfast. / lafromagerie.co.uk; https://www.instagram.com/lafromagerieuk/?hl=en.

Fumo WC2 £59 2 3 4
37 St Martin's Lane   020 3778 0430   5–4C

The "really lively atmosphere and helpful, cheerful staff" make this Italian spot from the San Carlo group "a nice pre-theatre dining venue" a few minutes' walk from the Coliseum. One could argue that "there's nothing exceptional about the cicchetti on offer", but the place "doesn't feel like a chain" and is consistently well-rated in (practically) all reports. / WC2N 4JS; sancarlofumo.co.uk; sancarlorestaurants; Sun-Fri 11 pm, Sat midnight.

Gaia W1 NEW £124 3 3 3
1 Berkeley Street   020 3961 0000   3–3C

Across Piccadilly from The Ritz, this glorious-looking (and extremely pricey) newcomer – all high ceilings, marble and pale blue banquettes – rather jarringly markets itself as a 'refined Greek taverna'; and is the London outpost of a Russian-owned, Dubai-based brand which also has outlets in Doha and Monte Carlo. The 'refined taverna' styling, though, does more faithfully capture the relatively homespun menu, overseen by British-Nigerian chef Izu Ani: this includes classics like taramasalata, spanakopita and moussaka alongside a more glam ice-counter of fish and seafood, where you select your choice and specify how you want it prepared. "Nice… but not cheap", only go if your wallet doesn't mind an exhausting work-out. / W1J 8NE; gaia-restaurants.com; gaia__ldn.

Galata Pera TW8
1 Town Meadow   020 8560 1798   1–3A

At the foot of a block a short walk from downtown Brentford, in an attractive waterside location, this unexpectedly smart venue with large outside terrace is mostly a local amenity, but – once discovered – would make a useful destination for an 'away from it all' meal, especially in summer. It provides a competently prepared selection of Turkish dishes. / TW8 0BQ; Tue-Sat 9.30 pm, Sun 5 pm.

Galvin Bistrot & Bar E1 £68 2 2 2
35 Bishops Square   020 7299 0404   13–2B

"Galvin restaurants always deliver", say fans – but even so it is difficult to avoid a sense of missed opportunity with this bistro next door to the brothers' flagship, La Chapelle. All reports rate it acceptably well, and no disasters are reported, but amidst some "fabulous" accounts, there are also those with elements that are "average" or "slightly disappointing". / E1 6DY; galvinrestaurants.com; galvinbistrot; Mon-Sat 9.15 pm.

FSA

Galvin La Chapelle E1 £129 4 5 5
35 Spital Sq 020 7299 0400 13–2B

"A stunning venue with top-notch Gallic-inspired cuisine": the Galvin Bros' "beautiful" operation has all the elements for a "memorable experience" and – though its City-fringe location by Spitalfields Market makes it a huge hit for expense-accounters ("when you want to impress with a very elegant meal"), it's also a "romantic favourite for the most special occasions". Often mistaken for a converted chapel, the "dream location" of its ecclesiastical-style space was actually constructed to house a late-Victorian girls' school, and was superbly stylishly converted by the Galvins in 2009. "Despite the striking surroundings, the staff manage to make it feel relatively informal": "they are attentive but give you space and time". And the food? "first class", "precise French cuisine" that's fully priced of course, but few begrudged the bill this year. Top Menu Tip – "Always try the magnificent Crab Lasagne: to die for!" / E1 6DY; galvinlachapelle.com; galvinlachapelle; Mon-Wed 9.15 pm, Fri & Sat 9.30 pm, Thu 9.15 pm, Sun 9 pm.

La Gamba SE1 £63 2 1 2
Unit 3, Royal Festival Hall, 020 7183 0094 2–3D

"A step above the chains that proliferate on the South Bank" is how fans see this "nice tapas bar" in the South Bank Centre itself (with outside terrace): they say it serves "surprisingly good tapas in such a tourist area" – "a miracle considering the location". But "are they coasting on the basis of initial reviews in the press?". In aggregate, ratings in our annual diners' poll are very indifferent here this year, with too many reports of "rather confused service" and "uninspiring" cooking. / SE1 8XX; lagambalondon.com; lagamba.london; Mon-Sun 11 pm.

The Game Bird SW1 £124 3 4 4
16-18 St James's Place 020 7518 1234 3–4C

This "sumptuous" and "traditional" dining room hidden away in St James's is long on "elegance and friendly service" and remains something of an "unknown gem". The cuisine results from the collaboration of star chef Lisa Goodwin-Allen (from sister property up North near Blackburn, Northcote) with the executive chef here, Jozef Rogulski and – although some disappointments were registered this year – overall ratings remained high. Top Tips – in the afternoon, there's "an extensive range of teas and trolley service for both savoury and sweet choices"; and "the very elegant breakfast is a lovely experience". / SW1A 1NJ; thestaffordlondon.com; thestaffordlondon; Mon-Sun 9 pm.

Ganapati SE15 £48 3 3 2
38 Holly Grove 020 7277 2928 1–4D

After 20 years, Peckham pioneer Claire Fisher's "refectory-style" venue "keeps on delivering wonderful South Indian food", including "some cracking veg dishes, though it's not all vegan by any means". "We first went 16 years ago and it has remained consistent through all this time – the difference is that then it was a lone star in an area short of places to eat, now it's one of many". Top Menu Tip – "homemade paratha is a must". / SE15 5DF; ganapatirestaurant.com; ganapati.peckham; Tue-Sat 10.30 pm, Sun 10 pm.

Gandhi's SE11 £45 3 4 2
347 Kennington Rd 020 7735 9015 1–3C

This "enjoyable" if "typical local curry house" in Kennington was opened by Zalal Uddin in 1982 and is still family-owned. It makes the most of its proximity to the Oval – offering "very good service in trying, post-cricket, circumstances" – and to Parliament, which makes it a "good bet for MP-spotting". / SE11 4QE; gandhis.co.uk; Tue-Sat 10.30 pm, Sun 9.30 pm.

Ganymede SW1 £92 | 3 | 3 | 3 |
139 Ebury Street   020 3971 0761   2–4A

This "consistently reliable" venture (part of the small Lunar Pub Company group) took over the site of Belgravia's long-serving Ebury Wine Bar (long RIP) in 2021. The website terms it a 'Bar & Dining Room' and neither the brasserie-style menu nor the stylish contemporary decor are particularly pub-like. In any case, it works equally well "for a family get-together or business". Top Menu Tip – "it stands out for its pithiviers and its cocktails".
/ SW1W 9QU; ganymedelondon.co.uk; ganymedesw1; Mon-Sat 10 pm, Sun 9 pm.

The Garden Cafe, Garden Museum SE1 £67 | 3 | 3 | 3 |
5 Lambeth Palace Rd   020 7401 8865   2–4D

This quietly ambitious kitchen at Lambeth's Garden Museum is a real magnet for diners in-the-know ("I'd happily eat here once a week if I lived locally – it's always different!"). Former Noble Rot head chef Myles Donaldson delivers a daily changing lunch menu that's not vegetarian or even vegan, but strong on both camps and on delivering "good, healthy food". The interior is simple, but enhanced by floor-to-ceiling windows looking onto the street and into the garden. (There's also coffee, cakes, etc all day). / SE1 7LB; gardenmuseum.org.uk; gardenmuseum; Mon, Wed & Thu, Sat & Sun 3 pm, Tue, Fri 9 pm.

Le Garrick WC2 £68 | 2 | 3 | 3 |
10-12 Garrick Street   020 7240 7649   5–3C

Looking for that "great, little, traditional French bistro in the heart of theatreland"? For many in our annual diners' poll, this "family-run" venue where much of the seating is in an atmospheric brick-arched cellar is "a firm favourite", helped by its "reasonable prices": "we have been visiting for 20 years, celebrating birthdays and engagements as well as their Bastille day and Beaujolais special events – it feels like a home from home". Don't expect culinary fireworks, though – sometimes the food is "underwhelming" ("still, despite it being below par, because of the staff we enjoyed ourselves!)"
/ WC2E 9BH; legarrick.co.uk; le_garrick; Mon-Sat 11 pm.

The Garrison SE1 £84 | 3 | 3 | 3 |
99 Bermondsey Street   020 7089 9355   10–4D

"A great discovery, even though it's been there a long time" – this green-tiled gastropub helped put Bermondsey on the gastronomic map in the early noughties. The food is more bistro fare (e.g. Chicken Liver Parfait, Steak Frites, Chocolate Crémeux) than pub grub, and although you can eat cheaply here, you can also push the boat out on the more ambitious main dishes.
/ SE1 3XB; thegarrison.co.uk; thegarrisonse1; Mon-Thu 11 pm, Fri & Sat midnight, Sun 10 pm.

The Gate W6 £64 | 3 | 2 | 3 |
51 Queen Caroline St   020 8748 6932   8–2C

"High-end vegetarian cuisine" – with "such inventive recipes" – has carved a brilliant reputation amongst veggies and carnivores alike for Michael and Adrian Daniel's characterful stalwart, which "has been around forever" (well, since 1989). It occupies an attractively quirky space too, over a Hammersmith church near the Eventim Apollo, but – albeit a "really nice and friendly venue" – one or two reporters feel "the venue and service could do with refreshing" (and its two spin-off branches closed this year). Top Menu Tips – "dreamy aubergine dish" and "courgette flower and the red Thai curry and mushroom are both favourites". / W6 9QL; thegaterestaurants.com; Tue-Sat 10.30 pm, Sun 10 pm.

The Gatehouse N6 £66 | 2 | 2 | 2 |
1 North Road   020 8340 8054   9–1B

This imposing black-and-white pub in central Highgate offers enjoyable tapas, as well as "the usual pub menu", and a "great selection of beers". It's one of those places where the sum is greater than the parts, helped by the area –

and it also houses upstairs one of the capital's leading off-West End theatres. / N6 4BD; thegatehousen6.com; thegatehousen6; Mon-Thu 11 pm, Fri & Sat midnight, Sun 10.30 pm.

Il Gattopardo W1 NEW £125 3 4 4
27 Albemarle Street   020 3839 5000   3–3C

"Sexy, Amalfi-in-the-1960s decor and music" inspire early-days fans of this high-end Mayfair Italian from the group behind Zuma and Roka, where a key feature is a hidden courtyard terrace with fully retractable roof. With its "gorgeous home-cooked Italian classics and luscious desserts for sharing", fans say that "if your partner is not in love by the end of the meal, you need a new partner". Not everyone shares such enthusiasm though: a minority think "it seems to appeal to a smart set with good bank balances and easily impressed palates" (and this was somewhat the view of the FT's Tim Hayward in his December 2023 review who – notwithstanding "extremely competent" cuisine – discerned "style over substance" in an "undifferentiated international hi-luxe" setting). / W1S 4HZ; gattopardo.restaurant; gattopardorestaurant; Mon-Sat 8.30 pm, Sun 5 pm.

Gaucho £87 3 3 3
Branches throughout London

Credit is due to this upscale, Latino-inspired steakhouse chain, which has had its ups and downs in recent times as it's gone through numerous MBOs and behind-the-scenes financial deals; but which has significantly recovered its game since Martin Williams returned to the helm a couple of years ago. Criticism was most notable by its absence this year: "there may be better steak out there for less money, but there's nothing wrong with the food", indeed the "excellent steaks" (and the other fare as well) were widely acclaimed for being "reliable" this year, and a more lively atmosphere and better service have returned to their "lovely", funkily designed branches. The big South American wine list is a consistent draw too. (With 12 branches in London, it's been in the UK since 1994, but was actually originally founded on the Continent in 1976). Top Top – the Richmond branch has a particularly good waterside location. / gauchorestaurants.co.uk; gauchogroup; SRA-2 stars.

Gauthier Soho W1 £132 4 4 4
21 Romilly St   020 7494 3111   5–3A

"If all vegan restaurants were this good, I'd never eat meat" – Since Alexis Gauthier went fully meat-free in 2021, his "lovely old Soho townhouse" has put "a vegan twist on French classics, served with charm and style". It was an incredibly brave move for a conventional venue whose renown was built on classic Gallic cuisine: a beautiful and romantic old Georgian building on many levels, where you have to knock on the door to gain access. The result is an "exceptional foodie experience, with incredible flavours". Where there are complaints from diners, they often relate to the use of flesh or cheese substitutes ("Gauthier, you really don't need to make vegan food look like meat"). But for most diners, "the acid test of a vegan restaurant is whether the food is good enough to stop you thinking about veganism. And Gauthier wins this easily!" with "food of the highest quality, unusual at times and innovative, and never failing to impress". Service here is particularly strong too: "helpful and thoughtful, never pushy". Its ratings are still not quite back to the pre-2021 pinnacles here since he broke with meat and the audience is perhaps not quite as large as it was. Overall, though, it seems to be a decision that's working out increasingly well. / W1D 5AF; gauthiersoho.co.uk; gauthierinsoho; Tue-Sat 9.30 pm.

Gazette £67 2 2 2
79 Sherwood Ct, Chatfield Rd, SW11   020 7223 0999   11–1C
147 Upper Richmond Rd, SW15   020 8789 6996   11–2B
218 Trinity Road, SW17   020 8767 5810   11–2C
17-18 Took's Court, EC4   020 7831 6664   10–2A

"Correct Gallic fare where comfort rather than wow is the name of the game" sums up this "good-value French bistro" group, which has a flagship in Battersea and branches in Putney, Wandsworth Common, the City and at the Institut Français in South Kensington. Sceptics judge it "rather run-of-the-mill", but more commonly it's seen as a useful standby and continues to garner a voluminous amount of feedback. In particular, fans say, it's a "favourite place for steak & chips because they do it the French way". / gazettebrasserie.co.uk.

Gem N1 £51 3 3 2
265 Upper Street   020 7359 0405   9–2D
Offering a combination of Turkish, Kurdish and Greek dishes, this "cheap 'n' cheerful" grill on the Islington main drag has been "a mainstay in the neighbourhood for years, and with good reason". / N1 2UQ; gemrestaurant.org.uk; gemrestaurantuk; Mon-Sat midnight, Sun 5 pm.

German Gymnasium N1 £77 1 1 3
1 King's Boulevard   020 7287 8000   9–3C
This "beautiful venue", built in 1865 for the German Gymnastics Society, is let down by a restaurant from D&D London which "fails to deliver" on multiple fronts – it's "overpriced", "the food is meh", and "service is terrible from top to bottom". The "prime location" near King's Cross and St Pancras means it's busy, and on the plus side there can be a "lively atmosphere", "the German breakfast menu is good", and the selection of food is "mostly authentic" (wurst, schnitzel, spätzle und so weiter), if "heavy-handed" in execution. For the majority of reporters, though, it just doesn't cut the mustard – "if you like poor imitations of German pub food in a noisy barn, this is the place for you". / N1C 4BU; germangymnasium.com; thegermangym; Mon-Sat 10 pm; SRA-3 stars.

Gerry's Hot Subs EC1 NEW
50 Exmouth Market   0203 409 5511   10–1A
In Exmouth Market, a tribute to the North American deli sandwich tradition from Ottawa-born and Detroit-raised Andre Blais (ex-Belgo and Bodeans). The Observer's Jay Rayner gave it a rave review. / EC1R 4QE; gerryshotsubs.com; gerryshotsubs; Mon-Thu 10 pm, Fri & Sat 11 pm, Sun 9 pm.

Giacomo's NW2 £57 3 3 2
428 Finchley Rd   020 7794 3603   1–1B
This "great local no-frills and no-nonsense Italian" in Child's Hill is a family-run operation of four decades' standing, and a haven for home-cooked classics including 'pasta di casa'. / NW2 2HY; giacomos.co.uk; Tue-Sun 10.30 pm.

Ginger & White Hampstead NW3 £15 3 3 4
4a-5a Perrins Court   020 7431 9098   9–2A
This "cramped and often noisy eatery" is a day-time favourite in Hampstead, serving a superior range of light bites – well-suited to brunch in particular – alongside buns, cakes and "excellent coffee and herbal teas". / NW3 1QS; gingerandwhite.com; gingerandwhitelondon; Mon-Fri 5.30 pm, Sat & Sun 6 pm.

Ginza SW1 £105 3 3 3
15 Bury St   020 7839 1101   3–3D
"You can sit at the grill if you want added excitement" at this traditional basement Japanese in St James's, where there's the option of either a teppanyaki or sushi counter, as well as more conventional seating and a private room. All reports this year were of "superb" meals. / SW1Y 6AL; ginza-stjames.com; ginzastjames; Mon-Sun 10.30 pm.

Giovanni's WC2 £65 2 2 3
10 Goodwin's Court, 55 St Martin's Ln   020 7240 2877   5–3C
"Traditional Italian food served in one of the older restaurants in London" generally works out better than might be expected at this Theatreland stalwart in the tourist hell around Covent Garden. The Ragona family from Sicily launched the business in 1952, and their "cosy" premises in an ancient courtyard has a fair few fans (including The Observer's Jay Rayner, whose

September 2024 review harked back to his first childhood visit in 1972). It makes an "excellent pre-theatre choice", albeit that it's "very expensive even allowing for the location". / WC2N 4LL; Tue-Sat 9.30 pm.

Giulia W12 £66 4 3 3
77 Askew Rd   020 8743 0572   8–1B

"A reminder of how good Italian cooking can be" is to be found at Giulia Quaglia's neighbourhood two-year-old in ever-posher 'Askew Village', which offers a short menu of three-four options for each course (including 'primi'). "Even the bread is exceptional" and even those who consider it "expensive for Shepherd's Bush" say "you won't be disappointed". / W12 9AH; giuliarestaurant.co.uk; giulia.restaurant; Tue-Sat 10.30 pm, Sun 4.30 pm.

Gloria EC2 £70 2 4 5
54-56 Great Eastern Street   no tel   13–1B

"Slightly mad" but irresistible – "I've not known anyone leave unhappy", squeal fans of Paris-based Big Mamma Group's original London site, which is a "fun and partyish" slice of OTT, retro Italian pastiche on a Shoreditch corner-site filled with plants and nostalgic Amalfi-coast-inspired bric-a-brac. The rich food from a large, traditional Italian menu – with plenty of pizza and pasta alongside grills and salads – isn't at all 'foodie' but is certainly filling and good value. / EC2A 3QR; bigmammagroup.com; bigmamma.uk; Mon-Wed 10.45 pm, Thu-Sat 11 pm, Sun 10.30 pm.

Go-Viet SW7 £61 3 3 2
53 Old Brompton Rd   020 7589 6432   6–2C

This "enjoyable" South Kensington Vietnamese offers "tasty and original dishes" in a "clean-looking, functional" dining room that's very different from ex-Hakkasan chef Jeff Tan's first venture (the street food-style Viet Food in Chinatown). / SW7 3JS; vietnamfood.co.uk; govietnamese; Sun-Thu 10.30 pm, Fri & Sat 11 pm.

La Goccia WC2 £69 2 2 3
Floral Court, off Floral Street   020 7305 7676   5–3C

In Covent Garden's Floral Court, this "buzzy" and "cheerful" charmer is a central London offshoot of Richmond's famous Petersham Nurseries. Leading onto an attractive courtyard, it shares its parent venue's strength in being at its best in warmer months, when you can eat rather romantically al fresco. It offers "an interesting range of mostly small plates, not typically found on the menu of Italian restaurants in London", but "some are not well executed" and a meal can "end up being expensive". / WC2E 9DJ; petershamnurseries.com; petershamnurseries; Mon-Wed 10 pm, Thu-Sat 11 pm, Sun 4 pm.

Goddards At Greenwich SE10 £28 3 3 2
22 King William Walk   020 8305 9612   1–3D

"Lovely chilli beef pie 'n' mash and baked beans… and a fabulous crumble for dessert" – such are the culinary delights of this traditional pie shop from a family who've been in the business in the area since 1890. There's a vegan option, as well as pies with chicken, cheese & onion or eels. / SE10 9HU; goddardsatgreenwich.co.uk; Sun-Thu 7.30 pm, Fri & Sat 8 pm.

Gold W11 £77 2 2 4
95-97 Portobello Road   020 3146 0747   7–2B

This "atmospheric" Portobello Road haunt – a four-storey old boozer from nightclub entrepreneur Nick House (Mahiki and Whisky Mist) – is "full of people drinking cocktails and celebrity spotting". "The food is fine – the usual dukka-and-cauliflower Middle East of nowhere works" – but that hardly matters since you "go there to see and be seen, not to chat (too loud) or to eat ('rustic')". / W11 2QB; goldnottinghill.com; goldnottinghill; Mon-Thu 12.30 am, Fri & Sat 1 am, Sun 11.30 pm.

Gold Mine W2 £47 3 2 2
102 Queensway   020 7792 8331   7–2C

Some of "the best Chinese roast duck and excellent char siu" can be found at this no-frills Cantonese in Queensway (with a sibling in Chinatown) – "if you can put up with the surroundings". / W2 3RR; goldmine.bayswater; Sun-Thu 11 pm, Fri & Sat 11.15 pm.

Golden Dragon NW9 £45 3 2 2
399 Edgware Road   020 8205 8333   1–1A

"Very large Chinese restaurant" on the ground floor of Colindale's Bang Bang Oriental Food Hall (with a sister venue in Chinatown) that has an "extensive menu" focused mainly on Cantonese cuisine. It's "frequented by lots of Chinese diners" (always a good sign). Top Tip – it's an easy visit as the site has a "large underground free car park". / NW9 0FH; gdlondon.co.uk; bangbangoriental; Mon-Thu 10 pm, Fri & Sat 10.30 pm, Sun 9.30 pm.

Golden Dragon W1 £55 3 3 2
28-29 Gerrard St   020 7734 1073   5–3A

"Huge Cantonese restaurant" over two floors on Chinatown's main drag, praised for its "sensibly priced and fine-quality dim sum", along with "good crispy duck with pancakes". "Service is brisk but friendly", and its capacity makes it "good for walk-ins". / W1 6JW; gdlondon.co.uk; goldendragon_uk; Mon-Thu, Sat 11 pm, Fri 11.30 pm, Sun 10 pm.

Golden Hind W1 £52 3 2 2
73 Marylebone Ln   020 7486 3644   2–1A

"A throwback – but in a good way" – this veteran Marylebone chippy dates back to 1914, and still knows how to "keep it simple". "For a Northerner, it's hard to find good fish 'n' chips in London, but this is one of the few places that fits the bill. Go for the cod 'n' chips with mushy peas and lashings of malt vinegar, accompanied by bread and butter (white of course) and a pot of tea". / W1U 2PN; goldenhindrestaurant.com; Mon-Sat 10 pm.

Good Earth £80 3 4 3
233 Brompton Rd, SW3   020 7584 3658   6–2C
143-145 The Broadway, NW7   020 8959 7011   1–1B
11 Bellevue Rd, SW17   020 8682 9230   11–2C

"It might not be for a true aficionado of Asian food, but the welcome is genuine, the food is always meticulously cooked and presented, service standards are high, and it has pleased us for many years" – one report neatly encapsulates the strong virtues of this rather "glamorous", "good-but-pricey" Chinese group: a family-owned chain with branches in Knightsbridge, Mill Hill, Wandsworth Common and Esher. "Why not save yourself the trip to Chinatown and enjoy a meal without the crowds, bad service, and soulless dining rooms!" / goodearthgroup.co.uk.

Goodbye Horses N1 NEW
21 Halliford Street   no tel   14–2A

Open in July 2024 in De Beauvoir, on the border between Islington and Hackney, this wine bar and restaurant serves biodynamic and natural wines alongside seasonal and sustainable sharing plates. Also on-site, pour-over specialist coffee shop Day Trip and gelato bar the Dreamery. / N1 3HB; goodbyehorses.london; goodbyehorsesldn; Mon-Thu 10 pm, Fri & Sat 11 pm, Sun 9 pm.

Goodman £91 3 2 2
24-26 Maddox St, W1   020 7499 3776   3–2C
3 South Quay, E14   020 7531 0300   12–1C
11 Old Jewry, EC2   020 7600 8220   10–2C

Misha Zelman, Ilya Demichev & George Bukhov-Weinstein's trio of NYC-style steakhouses offer a straightforward combination of top cuts of steak with "an extensive selection of wines – from the affordable to the ridiculous – both from old and new world to accompany the many meats on offer"; and "the non-steak options are surprisingly tasty" too. Oft-compared in years gone by with Hawksmoor, it is somewhat eclipsed by the latter nowadays and reports this year included one or two disappointing accounts, particularly when it came to the lacklustre ambience. / goodmanrestaurants.com; goodman_london.

Gopal's of Soho W1 £48 4 3 2
12 Bateman St   020 7434 1621   5–2A

"A favourite curry house for many years" – this stalwart Soho venue opened in 1988 and is a well-preserved time capsule of what the curry experience looked like when nobody dreamt of an Indian restaurant ever winning a Michelin star. "Everything is always high-quality and really tasty and the price is super-competitive for the area; and the staff are lovely too". / W1D 4AH; gopalsofsoho.co.uk.

Gordon Ramsay SW3 £231 2 2 1
68-69 Royal Hospital Rd   020 7352 4441   6–3D

The 'f-word' is increasingly applied to the bills here, as well as the famous TV show that created the celebrity of the world's most famous chef, of which this "unassuming door in a quaint little Chelsea street" is the original flagship. "You might mistake the venue itself for a townhouse: the dining room is actually quite small and intimate": nitpickers would also say "the decor is a bit dull" and "looking a bit dated"; and with "an ambience bordering on stilted". Feedback on service likewise ran the whole gamut this year – from "impeccable"… to "perfect, but without displaying any personality"… to "ice-cold and robotic". Perceptions of the cooking are also very varied, and hard to isolate from both the expectations raised by three Michelin stars and the "eye-watering prices". Fans say it's "the treat of the year" with "fabulous" cuisine: be it from the three-course à la carte for £180 per person, the longer 'Menu Prestige' for £210 per person; or the 'Carte Blanche' surprise menu for £260 per person. But dishes can also seem "pretty but over-engineered"; and even some who think the food here is "enjoyable" sometimes acknowledge "it doesn't merit three Michelin stars". Real doomsters just find the restaurant's ongoing renown "baffling – if this was a new restaurant I don't think it would even get one star". And then there is the cost. Even diehard fans say "the pricing is the top end of the top end" (and that "you do get stung on the drinks"). And those who consider it "the most overrated place ever" just say: "don't waste your money!" / SW3 4HP; gordonramsayrestaurants.com; restaurantgordonramsay; Tue-Sat 9.15 pm.

Gordon's Wine Bar WC2 £48 2 2 4
47 Villiers Street   020 7930 1408   5–4D

Quirkiness in spades is the particular appeal of this Dickensian watering hole – London's oldest wine bar, whose best tables are in a superbly ancient candle-lit cellar which originally housed wine shipped to its front door by barges on the Thames. But in summer its outside comes into its own, boasting as it does a huge terrace adjoining leafy Victoria Embankment Gardens. "It has a very good wine list" – while the cold food is somewhat incidental: "a simple menu of quality ingredients" majoring in cold cuts and cheeses. Fun fact: it's owned by entrepreneur Simon Gordon (the place was already called 'Gordon's' when he bought it), who owns the increasingly ubiquitous Facewatch anti-shoplifting software, which was originally developed to stop thefts at the bar. / WC2N 6NE; gordonswinebar.com; gordonswinebar; Mon-Sat 11 pm, Sun 10 pm.

The Goring Hotel, Dining Room SW1 £136 2 3 5
15 Beeston Pl   020 7396 9000   2–4B

"A wonderful room that's very light and with well-spaced tables" – this "quintessential" traditional hotel dining room, just around the corner from Buckingham Palace, is well-suited to a special occasion and is popular for business, romance or "a pricey family treat". Opened in 1910 by Otto Goring, it is part of the only five star hotel in London still to be run by the family who opened it (Jeremy Goring is the current CEO), which has always lent the whole establishment a more personal style than its corporate competitors. Historically, the dining room's British fare has been more notable for its traditional values than its finesse, and diners in our survey acclaim it as "reliable" if rather "undemanding": perfect for traditionalists, but less 'haute' than its Michelin star might suggest. Breakfast, for example, is a big attraction here, as is one of the "best afternoon teas in the UK". When it comes to lunch and dinner service, dishes like "first class lobster" excel. The old school service is well-rated but "not what it was" a few years ago, in the opinion of some regular guests. In May 2024 the space reopened, complete with an opulent new interior, care of Russell Sage Studio and a new kitchen for Executive Chef Graham Squire: hopefully all the new kit for the kitchen will mean this year's food rating is on the cautious side. / SW1W 0JW; thegoring.com; thegoring; Mon-Sun 9.45 pm.

Gouqi SW1 £132 4 3 2
25-34 Cockspur Street   020 3771 8886   2–3C
This "really high-end Chinese" off Trafalgar Square is a "real treat", delivering "exceptionally delicious and elegantly presented cuisine" from Tong Chee Hwee, the masterchef behind Hakkasan, who began cooking professionally in Singapore an astonishing 62 years ago. There's no question that it's "expensive and a bit lacking in atmos", but the "cracking dishes" and "amazing dim sum" ensure that it's often "very busy and lively". / SW1Y 5BN; gouqi-restaurants.co.uk; gouqilondon; Sun-Thu 10 pm, Fri & Sat 10.30 pm.

Goya SW1 £98 3 3 2
34 Lupus St   020 7976 5309   2–4C
"Fantastic Spanish food" – including a wide range of "good-quality tapas" but also with an interesting variety of larger main dishes – has attracted a loyal local following for this Hispanic veteran in Pimlico over more than three decades – "great service adds to the fun". Not far from Victoria, it's a handily situated and affordable venue for larger groups. / SW1V 3EB; goyarestaurant.co.uk; Mon-Sat midnight.

Granary Square Brasserie N1 £57 2 3 4
1 Granary Square   020 3940 1000   9–3C
A "lovely setting at a very convenient location in King's Cross" – overlooking the fountains of Granary Square from its large and leafy outside terrace – is sometimes let down by "average and rather overpriced food" at this stylish brasserie – although for the most part it still "seems better than its Ivy Collection cousins" (minus the stained glass, it's really an Ivy in disguise). On the plus side, there's a "reasonable fixed-price lunch menu". / N1C 4AB; granarysquarebrasserie.com; granarysquarebrasserie; Mon-Sun midnight.

Granger & Co £69
237-239 Pavilion Rd, SW1   020 3848 1060   6–2D
105 Marylebone High Street, W1   020 8079 7120   2–1A
175 Westbourne Grove, W11   020 7229 9111   7–1B
Stanley Building, St Pancras Sq, N1   020 3058 2567   9–3C
50 Sekforde St, EC1   020 7251 9032   10–1A
Celeb chef Bill Granger passed away in December 2023, and although the group he founded is still oft-nominated as a brunch favourite it's perhaps no surprise that these "stylish" Aussie-inspired haunts inspired more mixed reports in this year's annual diners' poll. Rather than itemise this year's ups-and-downs, at this time of change it seems more appropriate to postpone a rating till next year. / grangerandco.com; grangerandco.

Grasso W1 NEW £61 2 3 3
81 Dean Street   020 3089 4374   4–1D
From a family with roots in Sicily-via-New York – on a big, 180 seat, ex-Wagamama site in Soho – this retro US newcomer serves classic Stateside Italian dishes such as spaghetti with meatballs, chicken parm, penne alla

vodka and Caesar salad. It's a big hit on social media, but our early feedback is more cautious: "one of the hot places of the moment, it was hard to book, loud and buzzy; but the food's no more than hearty comfort food".
/ W1D 3SW; grassosoho.com; grasso_soho; Tue-Thu 11 pm, Fri & Sat midnight.

The Grazing Goat W1 £92 2 2 3
6 New Quebec St   020 7724 7243   2–2A
True to the Cubitt Group's "comfortable" standards, this is a "lovely and above-average gastropub not far from Marble Arch" (with eight boutique hotel bedrooms). Foodwise, it's a "reliable" bet, with the group's menu ranging from small plates to poshed-up gastropub staples via oysters and steaks.
/ W1H 7RQ; thegrazinggoat.co.uk; thegrazinggoatw1; Mon-Sat 9 pm, Sun 8 pm; SRA-1 star.

Great Nepalese NW1 £47 3 2 2
48 Eversholt St   020 7388 6737   9–3C
By the side of Euston station, this "splendid, long-established" café – founded by Gopal and Renu Manandhar in 1982 and now run with their sons – is still "as good as ever", with a menu featuring Nepalese specialities including momo dumplings. / NW1 1DA; great-nepalese.co.uk; greatnepaleserestaurant; Mon-Sat 10.30 pm.

Green Cottage NW3 £60 3 2 2
9 New College Parade   020 7722 5305   9–2A
A Swiss Cottage institution for more than half a century, this local Chinese venue (est. 1972) is in the classic (for London) Cantonese mould and still dependably well-rated on the food front. / NW3 5EP; greencottage22.com; Mon-Sun 10.30 pm.

Greenberry Café NW1 £66 2 2 3
101 Regents Park Road   020 7483 3765   9–2B
This "vibrant and busy" hangout in Primrose Hill is "obviously very popular with locals", plying them with "huge salads offset with brownies and ice cream", along with decent coffee and cocktails. In particular, it's a big local favourite for a "released breakfast… if you can get a table". / NW1 8UR; greenberrycafe.co.uk; greenberrycafe; Sun & Mon 3 pm, Tue-Sat 10 pm.

The Grill by Tom Booton W1 £147 3 4 3
53 Park Lane   020 7629 8888   3–3A
Old farts lament the good old days at this historic space, ruthlessly rebranded last year (f.k.a. The Dorchester Grill) by the hotel to make it seem more hip and zeitgeisty (with the website proclaiming: 'From Essex roots to the future of The Dorchester, Tom Booton heralds the next kitchen generation, blazing into our lives with a brilliant new angle on modern British dining'. Wow!). Decor-wise this means a moody, back-lit bar; an absence of the soft furnishings that once characterised the place; and, of course, not a tablecloth in sight. The menu, meanwhile, puts a comfort-foodish spin on a wide-ranging selection that's more posh brasserie than it is haute cuisine, and which includes small and large plates: from 'Freddy's prawn tacos' to 'Ribeye for two on the bone'. Feedback is still quite sparse, but all accounts are upbeat and some report exceptional cooking that's remembered as the best meal of the year. Top Tip – fab lunch deal – three courses for £35 per person. / W1K 1QA; dorchestercollection.com; thedorchester; Mon-Sat 10.30 pm, Sun 4 pm.

Grumbles SW1 £70 3 4 3
35 Churton St   020 7834 0149   2–4B
"An institution that's been there forever" (well, since 1964) – this "fun, local bistro" is a "go-to in Pimlico for 'cheer-you-up' comfort food" from a menu that has barely changed over the decades (moules marinière, fish pie with piped potato, calves' liver and bacon, crème brûlée). The original wood panelling is unchanged, and "the very friendly team have also been there since the dawn of time!" / SW1V 2LT; grumblesrestaurant.co.uk; grumblesrestaurant; Mon-Sun 10.15 pm.

FSA

The Guildford Arms SE10 £65 3 3 3
55 Guildford Grove   020 8691 6293   1–3D
"Good all-round" feedback continues to win a thumbs-up for Guy Awford's Georgian tavern in Greenwich, where much of the menu comes from the robata grill. Summer is the best time to visit to enjoy the fab garden.
/ SE10 8JY; theguildfordarms.co.uk; guildfordarms; Tue-Sat 11 pm, Sun 8 pm.

The Guinea Grill W1 £122 3 3 4
30 Bruton Pl   020 7409 1728   3–3B
"Wonderful old school charm" oozes from this offbeat Young's pub, in a quiet Mayfair mews. The public bar at the front is characterful, but it's the charming and comfortable adjoining grill room (opened in 1952, and significantly extended over the years) that makes this place such a magnet for steak-lovers and business wheeler-dealers. As well as dishes like Chateaubriand, Côte de Boeuf and Sirloin – and sides like Haggis or Ox Heart – there's a wide variety of traditional dishes and some of "the best pies in town". After personnel changes last year, ratings took a dive, but it returned to a good all-round performance in this year's annual diners' poll and is "now on top form". Top Menu Tip – "best devilled kidneys ever".
/ W1J 6NL; theguinea.co.uk; guineagrill; Mon-Sun 11 pm.

The Gun E14 £85 2 2 4
27 Coldharbour   020 7515 5222   12–1C
"Love, love, love sitting outside on a summer's evening" – this Grade II listed Docklands tavern has a riverside location to die for (10 minutes walk from Canary Wharf and opposite The O2) and a cosy historic interior too. Its days as a foodie magnet are long gone nowadays though – expect OK scoff, but no better than at others in the Fullers chain. / E14 9NS; thegundocklands.com; thegundocklands; Mon & Tue 11 pm, Wed-Sat midnight, Sun 10.30 pm.

Gunpowder £64 3 3 2
20 Greek Street, W1   020 3813 7796   5–2A
One Tower Bridge, 4 Crown Square, SE1   awaiting tel   10–4D
11 Whites Row, E1   020 7426 0542   13–2C
"Novel dishes full of spice and intrigue" draw a "buzzy" crowd to this "refreshingly innovative" and hugely successful modern Indian trio: an "elevated street-food experience that's really good fun". The "tiny but perfectly formed" Spitalfields original is "still the best", say fans, but the food also hits the spot at "tapas-style" venues in Soho and Tower Bridge.
/ gunpowderlondon.com; gunpowder_london.

Gymkhana W1 £104 4 3 3
42 Albemarle St   020 3011 5900   3–3C
It was this "top-tier" Mayfair Indian – opened in 2013 – that started to show London that the Sethi family of all-conquering JKS Restaurants fame were not a one-hit wonder (having founded Trishna five years before). "Inventive and exciting, whilst ticking all the boxes that make Indian 'curry houses' so appealing", it inspires nothing but praise for its "consistently superb" culinary alchemy, which is served in a colonial-inspired wood-panelled interior decorated with prints and the odd stuffed animal head. If you follow Michelin's recommendations however, the elevation of chef Sid Ahuja's cuisine as London's first Indian restaurant to receive a second Michelin star is a bit puzzling. Diners express views for and against in our annual diners' poll, but most noticeably, despite its high ratings the destination doesn't inspire many nominations as diners' top meal of the year (as would be expected for such a luminary); there are other Indian restaurants in our poll that out-score it; and the contrast with the level of adulation received by A Wong (London's first Chinese two star), is stark. Perhaps we are just so spoilt for Indian cuisine in London that we don't always fully appreciate it? Top Menu Tips – "The muntjac biryani is fantastic"; "it is worth going for the lobster claw in scrambled duck egg alone"; and "the pork cheek vindaloo is a standout!"
/ W1S 4JH; gymkhanalondon.com; gymkhanalondon; Mon-Sun 10.45 pm.

F S A

Haché £61 3 3 2
95-97 High Holborn, WC1   020 7242 4580   2–1D
329-331 Fulham Rd, SW10   020 7823 3515   6–3B
24 Inverness St, NW1   020 7485 9100   9–3B
37 Bedford Hill, SW12   020 8772 9772   11–2C
147-149 Curtain Rd, EC2   020 7739 8396   13–1B

Burgers served à la française in a brioche bun still win a good level of support for this 20-year-old fast-food group. Having shrunk to just two branches – Balham and the Camden flagship, the latter said to be a favourite of Amy Winehouse back in the day – they are now part of Jamie Barber's Hush Mayfair operation, with former branches in Kingston, Holborn and Chelsea upgraded into brasseries. / hacheburgers.com.

Hainan House N1 NEW £18
88 Upper Street   no tel   9–3D

As well as specialties from the island of Hainan, Cantonese, Hakka, and Min dishes add interest to the Southern Chinese menu of this Islington yearling: a first bricks 'n' mortar project from restaurateur Sunny Wu. It's not attention-grabbing in looks – perhaps why reporters have yet to vote on it – but in a February 2024 press review, The Evening Standard's Jimi Famurewa was impressed, if "for no other reason than the fact that no one else is really doing it" (i.e. cuisine like this) – "flavours are both mellow and highly unexpected… embrace the experimental, tactile blur of slurped herbal broths and snaffled quail eggs, then Hainan House, to the uninitiated, can feel like learning a thrilling new culinary language". / N1 0NP; hainanhouse.co.uk; Mon-Sat 9.30 pm, Sun 8 pm.

Hakkasan £123 3 2 3
17 Bruton St, W1   020 7907 1888   3–2C
8 Hanway Pl, W1   020 7927 7000   5–1A

"Divine dim sum" served in a moody, nightclubby setting ("very dark basement lighting" at the original) has helped this slick pan-Asian chain go from an obscure basement near Tottenham Court Road tube (which opened in 2001) to become a glam, international chain with 11 locations from Miami to Mumbai. Prices have always seemed a bit "excruciating" and performance generally is "not as good as it once was", but this remains one of the Top-50 commented-on brands in our annual diners' poll; and there's still lots of praise for its "attractive" style, "fantastic" cooking (the dim sum in particular, as well as the duck) and "wonderful cocktails". Less so for the "perfunctory" or "artificially polite" service, which, over the years, is increasingly acknowledged as just part of the package. / hakkasan.com; hakkasanlondon.

Ham Yard Restaurant,
Ham Yard Hotel W1 £78 2 3 4
1 Ham Yd   020 3642 1007   4–3D

"Hidden away in Soho", this surprisingly "calm" hotel restaurant in a quiet courtyard just minutes from Piccadilly Circus is "a great place to take a visitor" to escape the hustle of the surrounding streets. "Efficient service" and a "high-ceilinged dining room" make it a decent option for a working lunch, pre-theatre dining or post-work drinks, although foodwise it's a question of "pleasant comfort food". Top Tip – recommended for afternoon tea.
/ W1D 7DT; firmdalehotels.com; firmdale_hotels; Mon-Sun 10.30 pm.

Hannah,
County Hall SE1 £246 4 4 3
Belvedere Rd   020 3802 0402   2–3D

Former UMU head chef, Daisuke Shimoyama's "high-end kaiseki" is winning ever-greater recognition for his solo Kyoto-style venture, and his "charming" service helps offset the slightly odd location, near the London Eye, in the rear of the gigantic former HQ of the long-defunct Greater London Council. Daisuke started his career as a teenager washing pots in Kanagawa, and here serves a wide variety of options ranging in price from £45 for a five-course lunch, up to £185 for a 12-course dinner (which comes with the option of a £115 sake pairing). Having been largely ignored for its first seven years of operation, the foodie world has finally woken up to the place and the plaudits are starting to flow in: in the first half of 2024, the Financial Times's Tim Hayward pronounced it "the best kaiseki in London" (and suggested everyone "go immediately"), a sentiment also echoed by well-known food-blogger Andy Hayler, who (while noting "it's not a cheap outing") visited twice in a similar period with the same conclusion. / SE1 7PB; hannahrestaurant.london; hannah_japanese_restaurant; Wed-Sun 9 pm.

Hare & Tortoise £45 **3**|**3**|**2**
11-13 The Brunswick, WC1   020 7278 9799   2–1D
373 Kensington High St, W14   020 7603 8887   8–1D
156 Chiswick High Rd, W4   020 8747 5966   8–2A
38 Haven Grn, W5   020 8810 7066   1–2A
296-298 Upper Richmond Rd, SW15   020 8394 7666   11–2B
90 New Bridge St, EC4   020 7651 0266   10–2A

"Where else can you get a range of Japanese, char kway teow, laksa and pad thai, all in one restaurant?" – Ding Chu's pioneering Pan-Asian canteens (first branch WC1 in Bloomsbury in 1996) continue to put in a consistent if low-key performance. "Busy, crowded and cheap", "you will find something to your taste", "service is friendly and efficient" and – for the likes of "a quick meal after going to the cinema" (either in WC1 or W4) – it's ideal.
/ hareandtortoise.co.uk; hare_tortoise.

Harrods Dining Hall SW1 £92
Harrods, 87-135 Brompton Road   020 7225 6800   6–1D
Evocative Edwardian tiling – dating from 1904 – and a sympathetic revamp from David Collins studio maintains this "bustling" gold-hued, Grade II period interior as one of London's traditional gems. It was relaunched in October 2023, with six outlets. None of them is for value-seekers, but such limited feedback as we have suggests that pushing the boat out for Sushi by Masa (from NYC celeb chef Masayoshi Takayama) is justified: "the exquisite delicacy of the sushi, hand-rolled at the counter in front of you, means Masa's three-star New York reputation is intact" (eat à la carte or there's an £80 fixed menu). It's a better bet than a trip to the adjacent Kerridge's Fish 'n' Chips (which can seem "shockingly expensive"). / SW1X 7XL; harrods.com; harrods; Mon-Sat 9 pm, Sun 6 pm.

Harrods, The Georgian SW1 **NEW**
87-135 Brompton Rd   020 7730 1234   6–1D
Quintessential British dining – including a bold attempt to become an archetypal destination for afternoon tea – is the aim of this major relaunch by Harrods, of its large 'grande dame' restaurant dining space on the fourth floor. Created in 1911 with a not-insubstantial 160 covers (and 25 chandeliers!), this 10,333 sq ft space always used to languish next to the toy department and to be rather forgotten about. No more! With a significant revamp by David Collins Studio, the store is again attempting to turn the place into a top destination, seemingly with more gusto than has marked its efforts in years gone by. Chef Calum Franklin (the 'pie king', who used to run the kitchen at Rosewood London's Holborn Dining Room) has been recruited to concoct a menu of retro luxurious British classics, incorporating: oysters and caviar; '1909 - Harrods Diamond Jubilee' Consommé; and Pâté en croûte 1960 with Cumberland sauce. Pies will include 'The Georgian Pie Experience' to share, as well as Beef & shin, Chicken penny, and Beef Wellington.
/ SW1X 7XL; harrods.com.

Harwood Arms SW6 £93 **4**|**4**|**3**
Walham Grove   020 7386 1847   6–3A
"The best British cooking, with an emphasis on the finest seasonal meat and ingredients" (particularly "the best game") has won renown for this "relaxed, well-spaced and dog-friendly" venue, owned by Ledbury supremo, Brett

F S A

Graham. You might argue it's "more of a restaurant than a pub" nowadays, but it would be splitting hairs as it still looks the part of a backstreet Fulham boozer; and – even if food is served throughout – you can still drink at the bar. (It's typically voted London best pub in our annual diners' poll, but was for the first time in years knocked off its perch this year by The Devonshire). Top Tip – "Sunday lunch really is as good as is claimed! And in itself very good value". / SW6 1QP; harwoodarms.com; theharwoodarms; Mon-Thu 9.15pm, Fri & Sat 9.15 pm, Sun 8.15 pm.

Hatched SW11 £86 3 3 3
189 Saint John's Hill   020 7738 0735   11–2C
This "excellent hidden Battersea gem" flies beneath the radar, showcasing the skills of chef Shane Marshall, who works from an open kitchen. Local fans recommend the "fabulous Sunday roast which you all share". / SW11 1TH; hatchedsw11.com; hatchedsw11; Wed-Sat 11 pm, Sun 1.30 pm.

The Havelock Tavern W14 £75 2 2 2
57 Masbro Rd   020 7603 5374   8–1C
This "comfortable and friendly gastropub" with a blue-tiled facade has been a staple foodie feature of the backstreets behind Olympia for three decades. Nowadays part of The Metropolitan Pub Company: "the menu doesn't change as much as it used to", but is very acceptable, with a focus on pies (e.g. confit duck or braised rabbit), alongside other deftly realised traditional classics (perhaps Steak Sandwich, or Chicken Kiev). / W14 0LS; havelocktavern.com; havelocktavern; Mon-Sat 11 pm, Sun 10 pm.

Haven Bistro N20 £55 3 4 3
1363 High Road   020 8445 7419   1–1B
"Excellent-quality food at a reasonable price" is behind the 24-year success of Austrian-born chef Julius Oberegger's Whetstone bistro. The cuisine is "mostly modern European but with an eye on pan-Asian flavours" – which makes it "an oasis" in a part of north London where the standard dining options are Greek, Turkish or pizza. / N20 9LN; haven-bistro.co.uk; /havenbistro_bar/; Mon-Sat 11 pm, Sun 10.30 pm.

Hawksmoor £96 3 3 3
5a Air St, W1   020 7406 3980   4–4C
11 Langley St, WC2   020 7420 9390   5–2C
3 Yeoman's Row, SW3   020 7590 9290   6–2C
16 Winchester Walk, SE1   020 7234 9940   10–4C
Wood Wharf, 1 Water Street, E14   020 3988 0510   12–1C
157 Commercial St, E1   020 7426 4850   13–2B
10-12 Basinghall St, EC2   020 7397 8120   10–2C
"Simply love Hawksmoor!". Founded by Will Beckett and Huw Gott, this phenomenal steakhouse chain remains one of the Top-5 most-mentioned restaurant groups in our annual diners' poll and also one of the most popular. At heart – despite expansion to the 10 UK sites, one in Ireland and two in the US (Chicago, launched in July 2024, is the latest) – the essentials of the brand haven't changed since they first opened near Spitalfields in 2006: "the steak and the sides are all thumping winners" ("chewy char on the all-grass-fed meat and perfect chips"); "cocktails are a standout attraction" ("those cherry Negronis are a bit too addictive!"); "service is smiley"; all the above is "unbelievably popular"; and consequently they are seemingly able to charge "silly prices", while not deterring their huge fan base. Opening in the City also helped establish the brand as a huge client-entertaining favourite: "if you're doing business with carnivores, the excellent steak, red wine, service, and professional ambience should help you seal the deal". Meanwhile, "good fish and veggie options" have been added to the menu in recent times, perhaps to help defuse the obvious criticism that beef farming is not that super for the planet. In July 2024 – three years after the business tried to float on the stock exchange – majority owners, Graphite Capital, put their 51% stake in

the business up for sale for a reported £100m valuation. Will and Huw will, it seems, retain their stake. Top Tip – "BYO is £5 on a Monday!"
/ thehawksmoor.com; hawksmoorrestaurants; SRA-3 stars.

Haz £69   3 2 2
9 Cutler St, E1   020 7929 7923   10–2D
14 Finsbury Square, EC2   020 7920 9944   13–2A
34 Foster Ln, EC2   020 7600 4172   10–2B
64 Bishopsgate, EC2   020 7628 4522   10–2D
6 Mincing Ln, EC3   020 7929 3173   10–3D

"Fresh food and an affordable set menu for lunch" are prime attractions of this cheap 'n' cheerful Turkish chain – a fixture after more than two decades in the City, where there are now five branches, plus a more recent pan-Mediterranean spinoff in Covent Garden, Olea Social. / hazrestaurant.co.uk; hazrestaurantofficia.

Hélène Darroze,
The Connaught Hotel W1 £283   2 2 2
Carlos Place   020 3147 7200   3–3B

A "magical place with extraordinary food", is how fans view the Mayfair operation of this celebrated French chef (holder of the Legion d'Honneur no less), which for about a quarter of diners in our annual poll lives up to its Michelin billing as one of London's premier dining rooms (they awarded it three stars in 2021). Her occupation of the main dining room of this blue-blooded hotel has always been somewhat controversial, however, and its ratings continue to plummet ever since its elevation to the Tyre Co's top award. It doesn't help that a dreadful recent makeover has turned this gorgeous, period chamber into something "very corporate feeling" ("and as for the colour scheme, what were they thinking?"). Most problematic, though, is the fact that the cost of a meal has become "holy cow expensive!". Even those who consider her cuisine "flawless" think the final bill is "insane" and more than a third of reporters nominate this as their most overpriced meal of the year ("it was very disappointing, smacking of chef not present and outrageous charging, particularly the criminal charges for wine pairings"). / W1K 2AL; the-connaught.co.uk; theconnaught; Tue-Sat 9 pm.

Heliot Steak House,
The Hippodrome Casino WC2 £83   3 3 3
Cranbourn Street   020 7769 8844   5–3B

Irish Wexford Tomahawk… Hereford Fillet Chateaubriand… Argentinian Ribeye… USDA prime fillet – the high quality of the steaks are a point of pride for Simon Thomas who owns London's biggest and busiest casino, where the restaurant occupies an interesting space converted from the old circle of the former Hippodrome Theatre. NB under 25s must have ID. Top Tip – superb pre-theatre deal at £24 for two courses. / WC2H 7AJ; hippodromecasino.com; hippodromecasino; Sun-Thu 10 pm, Fri & Sat 11 pm.

Helix,
The Gherkin EC3 £91   2 3 5
30 St Mary Axe   0330 1070816   10–2D

Book in advance to enjoy a meal on the 40th floor of a London icon – Norman Foster's famous 'Gherkin' – whose glass-walled (and roofed!) brasserie is run by well-known caterers, Searcy's. There's a fair-value, something-for-everyone set menu on offer, but it's not aiming for culinary fireworks: the best bet here is to book yourself in for a splurgy afternoon tea, complete with fizz. / EC3A 8EP; searcysatthegherkin.co.uk; searcysgherkin.

Henri WC2 NEW
14-15 Henrietta Street   020 3794 5313   5–3C

Open in June 2024, in Covent Garden's Henrietta Hotel, an Art Nouveau-styled bistro from hot chef Jackson Boxer (of Brunswick House and Orasay) in concert with the Paris-based Experimental Group, with whom he opened a restaurant at Cowley Manor in the Cotswolds last year. Here, he's inspired by his jaunts to Paris as a young chef, with classics such as Fried Pied de Cochon, Grilled Snails and Globe Artichoke, and Steak-Frites, alongside a 'charcoal grill' section with celeriac; a half or whole Roast Chicken and a hefty 1 kg Côte de Boeuf: to finish, the likes of Lemon Sorbet or Riz au Lait. / WC2E 8QH; henriettahotel.com; Mon-Sun 11 pm.

Heritage SE21 £57 3 3 3
101 Rosendale Road   020 8761 4665   1–4D
"A real winner" – "fine, inventive dishes" make it worth knowing about Dayashakar Sharmer's Indian in the 'burbs of West Dulwich: a cut-above, both for its location and by the standards of modern local curry houses. / SE21 8EZ; heritagedulwich.co.uk; Tue-Sat 10.30 pm, Sun 9 pm.

The Hero of Maida Vale W9
55 Shirland Rd   02034321514   9–1A
On a corner of civilised Maida Vale, this sizeable gentrified boozer has been through a number of foodie incarnations in recent times. With the departure of Henry Harris to Bouchon Racine, it has fallen to the team behind Notting Hill's Pelican (see also) to take up the mantle here. You'll find stripped-down interiors and 'nostalgic British food' in the main bar, plus a smarter Grill Room upstairs. In his May 2024 review, the Evening Standard's David Ellis had one excellent trip food wise – one less so – but said the old place was looking terrific (what he actually said was that it's a "Dezeen wet dream of stripped wood and plaster walls, of barley leg stools and candle-topped tables"). Reports please! / W9 2JD; theherow9.com; thehero_w9; Mon-Sat 11 pm, Sun 9 pm.

Hide W1 £195 3 3 3
85 Piccadilly   020 3146 8666   3–4C
A striking location on Piccadilly overlooking Green Park – particularly from the elegant first-floor – makes this luxurious two-floor operation something of a Mayfair landmark (old-timers may remember the site as Fakhreldine, long RIP). Entirely relaunched in 2018 after a super-luxurious, multi-gazillion pound makeover, its nowadays under the same ownership as Hedonism Wines and not only boasts a "huge and superbly crafted wine list" but with notice you can order any of the 9,000 vintages stocked by HW. Originally launched as two restaurants – 'Hide Above' and 'Hide Below' – the culinary operations merged in 2022 and on either of its elegant two floors you can now choose either the luxurious à la carte (with caviar, wood-grilled fish, steaks and seafood) or the nine-course menu conceived by acclaimed chef Ollie Dabbous for £160 per person. "The food is actually better than the smart location would indicate, if not cheap"; and if you go the whole hog with the nine-courser you get "exquisite taste combinations, with beautiful preparation" that – for some diners – is "a highlight of the year" ("so much so I took out another mortgage and visited again!"). Caveats? "Notwithstanding some amazing dishes, they don't always hit the top notes you expect at the price". And, despite the luxurious glamour of the setting, the odd reporter "doesn't love the atmosphere", which can seem "a bit sterile". Harsh critiques, though, are notable by their absence. Top Tip – "breakfast is a work of art, with a warm welcome and very Mayfair clientele (a mix of hedge funders and Arabs!)" / W1J 8JB; hide.co.uk; hide_restaurant; Sun-Thu 10 pm, Fri & Sat 10.30 pm.

Hiden N4 NEW £23
53 Stroud Green Road   no tel   9–1D
On Finsbury Park's Stroud Green Road, this Japanese-style curry specialist is a new (October 2023), slightly larger sibling to an older, more 'hole-in-the-wall' style sister operation at Coal Drops Yard in King's Cross. No survey feedback as yet on its choice of three sauces (beef, mild chicken and lentils) to accompany its signature breaded chicken katsu, but when Hideaki Yoshiyama's original branch opened, it attracted the interest of The Financial

Times's Tim Hayward who found its "stretched and battered foodway, reconstructed with the kind of rigour I find irresistible". / N4 3EF; hidencurry.com; hidencurry; Tue-Sat 8 pm, Sun 5 pm.

High Road Brasserie W4 — £75 — 2 3 4
162-166 Chiswick High Road   020 8742 7474   8–2A
Shopping in Chiswick of a weekend? The large outside deck of this prominently situated brasserie on the high street remains "a top place for brunch" and – as one of Soho House's earlier outposts – is a magnet for local media moguls and C-suite types out with their lovely families. / W4 1PR; highroadbrasserie.co.uk; highroadbrasserie; Sun-Thu 11 pm, Fri & Sat midnight.

High Timber EC4 — £73 — 3 3 2
8 High Timber Street   020 7248 1777   10–3B
Easily missed, "near the Millennium (wobbly) Bridge" directly opposite Tate Modern, Neleen Strauss's "sparse" riverside venture is worth investigating. The focus is simple: "great steaks (from Yorkshire) with everything else – including passionate rugby support – from South Africa". Star of the show is, some would say, the "Saffer wine list – a reasonably priced one, too". / EC4V 3PA; hightimber.com; hightimberrestaurant; Mon-Fri 10 pm.

Hispania EC3 — £94 — 3 2 4
72-74 Lombard Street   020 7621 0338   10–2C
"High-quality" Hispanic dishes, all delivered in "a fine setting" – across two floors of the former Lloyds Bank HQ near the Bank of England – help create an "amazing atmosphere" at this "bustling restaurant": not just one of the most attractive dining options in the City but also one of London's better Spanish restaurants. It's occasionally let down by "rather glacial and not very attentive service". / EC3V 9AY; hispanialondon.com; hispanialondon; Mon-Fri 10 pm.

Holborn Dining Room, Rosewood London WC1 — £97 — 2 2 3
252 High Holborn   020 3747 8633   2–1D
"Stylish surroundings, well-executed classics and pies that are still amazing" win tips – especially for a business meal – for this British brasserie in a grand hotel, whose prominent "Midtown" location on Holborn and in the heart of Legal Land is well served by its high-ceilinged space lined with plush leather banquettes. It continues to inspire the odd 'off' report though, largely relating to high prices and the occasional incident of poor service. Top Menu Tips – though pies are the main menu feature, charcuterie and seafood also feature. / WC1V 7EN; holborndiningroom.com; holborndiningroom; Mon-Sun 10 pm.

The Holland W8 — £55 — 3 3 3
25 Earls Court Road   020 4599 1369   8–1D
A short walk south from the Kensington entrance to Holland Park, this corner gastropub was converted a couple of years ago and makes an "atmospheric" choice. The menu is "short and not cheap for what you get", with a focus on high-quality dishes like rib of beef to share or wild sea bass. / W8 6EB; thehollandkensington.co.uk; thehollandkensington; Wed-Sat 11 pm, Mon & Tue 10 pm, Sun 6 pm.

Holy Carrot Portobello W11 NEW — £60
156 Portobello Rd   no tel   7–1B
'Sustainable dining that's both flavoursome and fashionable' is the aim of ex-fashionista, Irina Linovich's sequel to her successful Knightsbridge tenancy, which opened in mid 2024. Plant-first cooking – through ferments, open-fire cooking and sustainably sourced seasonal produce – is overseen by exec chef Daniel Watkins (founder of Dalston's iconic ACME Fire Cult). Dishes will include 'Sexy Tofu', Asparagus, citrus & coconut butter and Matcha 'tiramisu'. Expect also natural and biodynamic wines and low-waste cocktails. / W11 2EB; Mon & Tue 11 pm, Wed-Sat 12.30 am.

Home TW11 £33 | 4 | 2 | 4 |
10 Church Lane 020 8977 3077 1–4A

"Can't beat this local favourite" – "a husband-and-wife-run Chinese" out in the boonies of Teddington, which provides an appropriately "homely" setting in a row of shops; and where fans say the food is "superb and freshly cooked". "Even better that it is BYO". Service was solidly rated this year, but the odd blip is not unknown. / TW11 8PB; Tue-Sat 10 pm.

Home £55 | 3 | 4 | 3 |
94 Church Road, SW13 awaiting tel 11–1A **NEW**
146 Upper Richmond Road, SW15 020 8780 0592 11–2B

This "lovely Putney spot" is "the best neighbourhood restaurant ever", according to its local fanclub – in particular, "Craig and his team have customer service down to a fine art". It's set amidst the pick 'n' mix of restaurants near East Putney Tube, and a pavement terrace with awning leads onto rather a stylish interior, with eye-catching tiled floor, brick walls and a long bar; and they serve a jazzy modern bistro menu. In September 2024 they opened a second branch, Home SW13, in next-door Barnes (taking over from Church Road, RIP). Top Tip – "love the scrap-eat Mondays where they use up all the weekend excess on a surprise great-value set menu"; "and those cauliflower croquettes are divine!"

Homeslice £66 | 3 | 2 | 3 |
50 James Street, W1 020 3034 0621 3–1A
13 Neal's Yd, WC2 020 7836 4604 5–2C
374-378 Old Street, EC1 020 3151 1121 13–1B
69-71 Queen Street, EC4 020 3034 0381 10–3C

"Fantastic pizza that's good value" continues to win praise for Alan & Mark Wogan's (the sons of the late Sir Terry) three-strong chain in Neal's Yard (the original), Marylebone and the City. The 20-inch pizzas are enough to feed 2-3 people and flavours can be split 50/50. / homeslicepizza.co.uk; homesliceldn.

Homies on Donkeys E11 £24 | 4 | 3 | 3 |
686 High Road Leytonstone 07729 368896 14–1D

Energetic outside signage, a no-less-colourful graffitied interior, and a soundtrack of pumping hip hop help set up an impactful experience at this year-old taqueria in the middle of Leytonstone, brought to us all by owner and head chef, 'Smokey'. There's no cutlery for the excellent tacos, which come in about 10 different varieties – you are invited to 'get messy'! / E11 3AA; homiesondonkeys.com; homiesondonkeys; Tue, Thu 10 pm, Fri & Sat 11 pm.

Honest Burgers £52 | 3 | 2 | 2 |
Branches throughout London

"Can't go wrong with Honest Burger!" – This well-established chain's ratings may be in the middle ground nowadays, but it induces little in the way of criticism and inspires a large and extremely loyal fan club for whom it remains "by far the best of the burger chains". "The menu choice is fairly limited, but the really tasty burgers are cooked well and the rosemary fries are brilliant!". "Better still, they will serve your burger rare or medium rare if you wish, which many places refuse to do!" Top Tip – "each branch has its own special". / honestburgers.co.uk; honestburgers.

Honey & Co WC1 £73 | 4 | 3 | 3 |
54 Lamb's Conduit Street 020 7388 6175 2–1D

"Flavours that transport you to the Middle East" inspire adoration for fans of Sarit Packer and Itamar Srulovich's "interesting" café, which moved to Bloomsbury (to the former site of Cigala, RIP) in 2022 having been a major media sensation when it first touched down near Warren Street 10 years earlier. The "brilliant range of eastern Med tapas" is "fresh and delightful" and acclaimed by many for their best meal of the year: an impressive achievement for a relatively humble operation. If there's a criticism, it's that some reporters feel the raves are overdone, judging the performance *"enjoyable but not exceptional". Top Menu Tips – "The Falafel starter is magic (and I am comparing it with a number of experiences in the Middle East)". "Slow- cooked lamb is smooth, tender and tasty, and the stuffed aubergines are a flavour and texture sensation"; "finally onto cheesecake… unlike any previously experienced!" / WC1N 3LW; honeyandco.co.uk; honeyandcobloomsbury; Mon-Sat 10.30 pm.*

Honey & Smoke W1 £78 3 3 2
216 Great Portland Street   020 7388 6175   2–1B

"Delicious Middle Eastern dishes" emerge from the grill at this venture near Great Portland Street from 'Honey & Co' (see also) foodie power-couple, Sarit Packer and Itamar Srulovich. *"The combination of flavours is exceptional"*, and *"the portions always go further than you'd expect"*. True to its Levantine origins, it's not a grand place: *"the dining room feels like a parish hall"*. / W1W 5QW; honeyandco.co.uk; honeyandsmokerestaurant; Tue-Sat, Mon 10.30 pm.

Hoppers £50 3 3 2
49 Frith St, W1   no tel   5–2A
77 Wigmore Street, W1   020 3319 8110   3–1A
Unit 3, Building 4, Pancras Square, N1   020 3319 8125   9–3C

"Absolutely delicious Sri Lankan dishes" attract a *"noisy, buzzy"* crowd to this *"squashed"* Soho spot, which celebrates its 10th anniversary this year (and whose owners, JKS Restaurants, have now opened spinoff branches in King's Cross and Marylebone). *"Staff work their socks off to get everyone fed"* and the grub – *"bone marrow vadhuvai + roti chennai, cabbage, aubergine, hopper etc"* – is *"tasty, and not shy on spice"* (it's also *"particularly good for people on gluten-free or lactose-free diets as they supply separate menu cards"*). All this said, the cooking no longer excites the adulation of the early days, with a suspicion in some quarters that it's now *"only slightly different to a 'normal' curry"*. / hopperslondon.com; hopperslondon.

Hot Stone N1 £91 2 2 2
9 Chapel Market   020 3302 8226   9–3D

"Fresh, innovative sushi and sashimi" share billing with *"fantastic wagyu beef cooked on stones"*, according to fans of this *"buzzy dining room"*, which has moved from Islington to Fitzrovia in a reshuffle of ex-Zuma chef Padam Raj Rai's restaurant portfolio. Even supporters feel *"the voucher system – and the upsell when using the vouchers – can be annoying"* though, while critics reckon *"the food doesn't live up to the hype, hence the constant discounted offers"*. / N1 9EZ; hotstonelondon.com; hotstonelondon; Mon & Tue, Fri & Sat 9.30 pm, Wed & Thu 9 pm, Sun 8.45 pm.

Hotel Dalhousie W11 NEW
226 Westbourne Grove   no tel   7–1B

Open in summer 2024 in Westbourne Grove: this retro-feel Indian named after a Raj-era hill station is the follow-up to Trafalgar Square's Tandoor Chop House. The culinary focus is on North Indian tandoor cooking, with weekday breakfast morphing into thali feast brunches at the weekend. / W11 2RH; Mon-Sun 9 pm.

The Hound W4 NEW
210 Chiswick High Road   020 3872 5533   8–2A

On the site of The Crown (RIP) – and before that Carvosso's (long RIP) – Chiswick's former police station has been through a number of incarnations as a would-be pub, with none sticking despite it having a characterful site. This latest is from the mighty JKS Restaurants so hopes are high, although the JKS track-record pub-wise is ever-so slightly 'meh' so far, so who knows? It's a big site, featuring a pub floor, reception room, two private dining rooms, a big, covered outdoor courtyard, and a south-facing front terrace, with a menu inspired by British pub classics. / W4 1PD; thehound.london; Sun-Wed 10 pm, Thu-Sat 11 pm.

Humble Chicken W1 — £210 — 5 4 3
54 Frith Street 020 7434 2782 5–2A

"'Fusion' may be a dirty word but it works a treat" at this "really good multi-course omakase" from Tokyo-born Angelo Sato, who trained under Clare Smyth and was head chef at Restaurant Story. Originally focused on chicken skewers, it has morphed into a more ambitious outfit, serving a set 16-course dinner that is "full or surprises" and "one of the most exciting options in Soho nowadays". / W1D 4SJ; humblechickenuk.com; humblechicken_uk; Tue-Thu 10 pm, Fri & Sat 11 pm.

Humble Grape — £73 — 2 3 3
11-13 Theberton Street, N1 020 3887 9287 9–3D
2 Battersea Rise, SW11 020 3620 2202 11–2C
18-20 Mackenzie Walk, E14 020 3985 1330 12–1C
8 Devonshire Row, EC2 020 3887 9287 10–2D
1 Saint Bride's Passage, EC4 020 7583 0688 10–2A

It's "all about the wine, as you might expect" at James Dawson's "relaxed" wine-bar group, whose branches boast a "splendid list" of "high-quality and well-sourced" bottles. The food is very much "second fiddle", though "unobjectionable", while the most interesting venue is the original one, off Fleet Street, "hidden in the vaults of St Bride's Church". Top Tip – "go on a Monday night for wine at shop rather than restaurant prices". / humblegrape.co.uk; humblegrape.

Humo W1 — £98 — 4 5 4
12 St George Street 020 3327 3690 3–2C

"Superb meals cooked over wood" on a four-metre grill have established well-travelled Colombian-born Miller Prada as one of London's rising star chefs at this Mayfair yearling, with influences from his Japanese mentor, Endo Kazutoshi. Fashion-wise it's 'very now', which divides diners: fans say, "fire and smoke is becoming a fad, but it's beautifully executed at Humo – getting it right takes a lot of skill and Miller and team have that in spades". There is some push-back, however, against "cult worship at the feet of the Gods of Indoor BBQ to paid-up acolytes: even though my wife thought it 'really rather good', I came away musing on how little we ate for so much money…" / W1S 2FB; humolondon.com; humolondon; Mon-Sat midnight.

Hunan SW1 — £127 — 4 3 2
51 Pimlico Road 020 7730 5712 6–2D

"The dishes just keep coming and not one of them disappoints" at the Peng family's Pimlico veteran – "an unusual Chinese restaurant that asks what you like and produces a banquet of what suits you until you say you've had enough". "They've been doing it for a long time" (since 1982) "and they do it well" – it remains one of London's better Chinese restaurants in a "rather agreeable retro way". "The team try hard to make every visit special" and – though it is quite "pricey" – it's excellent "for a treat". / SW1W 8NE; hunanlondon.com; hunanlondon; Mon-Sat 11 pm.

The Hunan Man W1 NEW — £38 — 3 2 3
45 Grafton Way 020 7387 8599 9–4C

From veteran Hunanese chef JianRen Zhoul, this new arrival on Goodge Street brings an unfamiliar regional Chinese cuisine to London. Some "love it, and visit often" for "the range of flavours" on offer – a view shared by Observer critic Jay Rayner, who in his January 2024 review acclaimed "the best version of Chongqing chicken I have ever had the good fortune to try". The riposte from some reporters? "Good, but not as good as some of the reviews had led me to expect!" / W1T 5DQ; Mon-Sat 10 pm, Sun 9.30 pm.

Hutong, The Shard SE1 — £137 — 2 2 5
31 St Thomas St 020 3011 1257 10–4C

"Being situated so high up in the Shard", this glossy Asian venue (part of the

HK-based Aqua group) on the 33rd floor of the UK's highest building has "one of, if not THE best outlook in London", making it "perfect for any celebration, with atmospheric lighting to boot in the evening". The stratospheric expense of a meal here, though, dampens its ratings. Fans say, "yes, you pay a premium, but the food is amazing" and "beautifully presented". But even such supporters can still leave "feeling totally fleeced", or that it's "insanely reliant on the outlook" given a bill that "arrives like a dragon's fire in the face". This is particularly keenly felt by those who encountered incidents of "haphazard" service. / SE1 9RY; hutong.co.uk; hutongshard; Mon-Thu 10 pm, Fri 3.30 pm, Sun 10 pm.

Ibai EC1 NEW
92 Bartholomew Close   awaiting tel   10–2B

A smart new modern Basque steakhouse near Smithfield Market that debuted in summer 2024 to universal press acclaim. At the stoves is ex-Chiltern Firehouse chef Richard Foster, who is backed by Nemanja Borjanovic and William Sheard – the duo behind the lauded meat supplier Txuleta. One of Borjanovic's projects is to bring a Galician Blond herd to the UK, whose meat will be featured in the restaurant (he also co-owns Lurra and Donostia – both Basque-influenced restaurants in Marylebone). Top Menu Tip – the croque monsieur is possibly the cult-hit dish of the year. / EC1A 7BN; Wed-Sat 11 pm, Sun 5 pm.

Ibérica   £70   2 2 3
70 Victoria St, SW1   020 7636 8650   2–4B
195 Great Portland St, W1   020 7636 8650   2–1B
12 Cabot Sq, E14   020 7636 8650   12–1C
89 Turnmill St, EC1   020 7636 8650   10–1A

"Decent tapas for the price" – with "all the usual suspects (patatas bravas, padron peppers, tortilla, croquettas)" – win praise for this Hispanic quartet, now well into their second decade. These days the cooking is reckoned "competent", if "not up to the earlier standards" – perhaps a reflection of improved competition. Top Menu Tip – "it's worth checking out the vegetable dishes" ("with some left-field options for the adventurous; the beetroot with coffee was great!") / ibericarestaurants.com; ibericarestaurants.

Ikoyi WC2   £352   3 2 2
180 The Strand   020 3583 4660   4–4D

"Quite unique!" – Jeremy Chan and Iré Hassan-Odukale have won renown (including two Michelin stars and the 2nd highest score in the UK on World's 50 best 2024) for their transformation of West African culinary traditions into an "incredible" and groundbreaking haute-fusion mashup; and a meal at this copper-shaded and minimalist venue (relocated a couple of years ago from St James's) is acclaimed in a majority of reports as an "exceptional" and "creative" all-round experience. Even fans, however, often note that it's also become a "very, very expensive" one, while for a significant minority it's a "disappointing" or even "joyless" one too. Chief concerns are cooking that can seem "too complicated" or "unmemorable (and I was longing to try it!)"; "robotic" staff "not engaging with customers and barely explaining dishes" is another repeat complaint. / WC2C 1EA; ikoyilondon.com; ikoyi_london; Mon-Fri 8 pm.

Imad's Syrian Kitchen W1   £42   4 5 4
Kingly Ct   07473 333631   4–2B

"You've read the cookbook, now try the restaurant!" – Chef Imad Alarnab lost everything when he was forced to flee from war-torn Damascus 10 years ago, taking to the road and cooking for fellow refugees. In a heartwarming and much-told tale of triumph over adversity, he has rebuilt his life and business, and is now in his second, bigger premises in Soho's Kingly Court, universally acclaimed in many reports as a "fun, flavoursome joint, rammed with folk relaxing and having a good convivial experience"…; "a special place. The *atmosphere. The story. The simplicity but tastiness of the food". / W1B 5PW; imadssyriankitchen.co.uk; imadssyriankitchen; Mon-Wed 9.30 pm, Thu-Sat 10 pm, Sun 4.30 pm.*

Imperial Treasure SW1 £161 4 3 3
9-10 Waterloo Place   020 3011 1328   4–4D
"Our Hong Kong and Singaporean friends rate this as the best in London!" – this "top-drawer" West End venture is now over five years old and the first European outpost of a 20-strong Singapore-based group with spin-offs in HK, Shanghai, Beijing and also one in Tokyo. It occupies a swish, converted banking hall in the West End, where the styling is "modern and chic while still being comfortable". "The Peking Duck (which must be ordered in advance) is delicious, but the other menu choices are also terrific". The catch is obvious – notwithstanding its excellence, "it feels expensive for the experience". / SW1Y 4BE; imperialtreasure.com; imperialtreasureuk; Mon-Sat 10.30 pm, Sun 10 pm.

In Horto SE1 £80 3 3 4
53b Southwark Street   020 3179 2909   10–4B
A "lively covered but somewhat-open-air restaurant" ('In Horto' being Latin for 'in the garden') arranged around a wood-fired oven, whose leafy calm provides a welcome refuge in the busy area around London Bridge. "It's great for groups as it serves interesting sharing food" (mostly high-quality meat or fish from the aforementioned oven). / SE1 1RU; inhorto.co.uk; in.horto; Tue-Sat 11.30 pm.

Inamo £65 2 2 3
134-136 Wardour Street, W1   020 7851 7051   4–1D
11-14 Hanover Place, WC2   020 7484 0500   5–2D
"The table games will keep you busy throughout!" at these gimmicky and heavily marketed venues in Soho and Covent Garden, where kids love the interactive table-tops, and funky sushi in the shape of a caterpillar. Sceptics say "everything is a bit bland and the rooms feel quite dated", but in the right mindset – especially with younger kids in tow – it can be a fun outing and the pan-Asian menu has something for everyone. / inamo-restaurant.com; inamorestaurant.

Indian Ocean SW17 £34 3 3 3
214 Trinity Rd   020 8672 7740   11–2C
"Very popular locally" for its "well-priced, high-quality food", this old-school family-run curry house near Wandsworth Common has stood the test of time. / SW17 7HP; indianoceanrestaurant.com; Mon-Sun 10.30 pm.

Indian Zing W6 £66 4 4 3
236 King St   020 8748 5959   8–2B
Chef patron Manoj Vasaikar's "bustling" venue near the entrance to Ravenscourt Park celebrates its 20th anniversary this year and diners remain "thoroughly impressed" by this superior neighbourhood venue – the cooking is "varied and interesting" and its most ardent fans say that "for all the Michelin stars dolled out to fancier Indian restaurants in London, I think this place does things better!" / W6 0RS; indian-zing.co.uk; indianzinguk; Mon-Sun 10 pm.

Indigo,
One Aldwych WC2 £75 3 2 3
1 Aldwych   020 7300 0400   2–2D
"A very good pre-theatre meal" makes this mezzanine spot in a luxury hotel near Covent Garden a particularly useful option for eating around a show. It's also "great for those who are gluten or dairy free", and "the children's chocolate-themed afternoon tea themed on Charlie & The Chocolate Factory is absolutely great". Any downsides? It's "a bit noisy". / WC2B 4BZ; onealdwych.com; onealdwychhotel; Mon-Sat 9.30 pm, Sun 11.

INÉ NW3 NEW £180 3|4|3
16 Hampstead High Street   020 7794 2828   9–2A
"A great new japanese restaurant in Hampstead" from the team behind Taku Mayfair, where patron Takuya Watanabe has installed his protégé Law Kwok Meng as head chef ('Iné' is Japanese for rice). *"Let's hope it survives in this notoriously difficult suburb"* – all reports say the food is *"very good"* and *"service is particularly attentive"* – you either eat à la carte (prepared by chef Andrew Lim), or go for the full blow-out of a 17-course omakase served personally by chef Meng. However the *"high culinary ambitions here have prices to match"* and even some fans *"can't help feeling it may be overpriced for NW3"*. (You can also now just drop in for a drink here too, at their newly opened 'Upstairs at INÉ', serving specialty sakes and showcasing emerging artists). / NW3 1PX; takumayfair.com; inebytaku; Tue-Sun 10 pm.

Inis Café E3 NEW
13 Rookwood Way   no tel   14–2C
Part of a hip project for London's fashionistas on 'Fish Island' beside the Hertford Union canal in Hackney Wick – this newly opened (May 2024) café sits at the foot of a converted block by the water that's part of a campus with studios, manufacturing, co-working and venue spaces. One of the founders was a former high-up at The Ginger Pig whose meat features on the wide, easygoing and brunch-friendly menu presided over by chef Craig Johnson (formerly of Arbutus and The Corner Room). Coffee is from local roastery Bad Coffee. / E3 2XT; Tue-Thu 11 pm, Fri & Sat midnight, Sun 10 pm.

INO W1 £62 4|4|3
4 Newburgh Street   020 3701 6618   4–2B
"Taking Greek tapas to another level" – this *"intimate"* Soho 'gastrobar' is named for 'wine' in ancient Greek, and part of the 'Funky Gourmet' group who own Opso (see also) as well as a Michelin two-star operation in Athens. Even some fans who find the cooking exceptional can caution that *"the small and trendy location boosts costs, while multiple dishes also help tot up the bill"*. / W1F 7RF; inorestaurant.com; ino.restaurant; Mon-Sat 11 pm.

Ishtar W1 £72 3|2|3
10-12 Crawford St   020 7224 2446   2–1A
Established in 2004, this upmarket Turkish spot in Marylebone *"has maintained a high level of quality for many years"*, and is *"always worth a visit"* for its *"attentive staff and good food"* – most notably mezze and charcoal-grilled meat. / W1U 6AZ; ishtarrestaurant.com; ishtarlondon; Sun-Thu 11 pm, Fri & Sat midnight.

Isla WC1 £67 2|4|4
The Standard Hotel, 10 Argyle Street   020 3981 8888   9–3C
"Outdoors is excellent on a fine day" on the foliage-filled terrace of the lounge dining room of this hip hotel – all the more remarkable as it's just seconds away from St Pancras station over the road. *"Indoors is not as much of an attraction"*, unless you are a fan of 1970s decor in which case it's a must-visit given its former life as Camden Council Library (with many of the books still on hand to add to the vibe). On the menu: *"light and fresh"* if not particularly ground-breaking modern European dishes; all delivered by particularly can-do staff. See also The Double Standard and Decimo. / WC1H 8EG; islalondon.com; Isla.London; Mon-Sun 11 pm.

Isola by San Carlo W1 £53 3|3|3
3-5 Barratt Street, St Christopher's Place   020 7846 8604   3–1A
"Good food in generous portions, excellent service and a lively ambience" tick all the boxes at this Italian brasserie – an outpost of the Birmingham-based San Carlo group, which took over this sizeable site – a former Carluccio's in St Christopher's Place, near Selfridges – three years ago. Its large outside terrace

with 50 covers takes advantage of this pedestrianised enclave, which feels surprisingly tranquil for somewhere just off Oxford Street. / W1U 1BF; sancarloisola.co.uk; isola_bysancarlo; Mon-Sun midnight.

It's Bagels NW1 NEW £46 4|2|2
65 Regent's Park Road   020 3340 0073   9–3B
"The best bagels in London"! Self-taught baker Dan Martensen and Caravan head baker Jack Ponting worked on perfecting a New York bagel recipe and opened this bricks-and-mortar place in September 2023 in Primrose Hill. There's the odd table, but it's primarily take out. / NW1 8XD; itsbagels.com; its__bagels; Mon-Sun 5 pm.

Italian Greyhound W1 £64 3|2|2
62 Seymour Street   020 3826 7940   7–1D
The "sturdy" but "delicious Italian food" wins solid ratings for this smart-casual three-year-old on a corner near Marble Arch. The "pleasant surroundings" include a modern wood-panelled dining room and an agreeable 20-seat outside terrace. / W1 5BN; theitaliangreyhound.co.uk; greyhoundmarylebone; Mon-Sat 11 pm, Sun 10.30 pm.

The Ivy WC2 £97 2|3|3
1-5 West Street   020 7836 4751   5–3B
"The magic has gone" for many critics of this Theatreland icon whose 'chainification' under Richard Caring (who put the Ivy group he created up for sale for £1bn in January 2024) has reduced this original site to "living on its past celebrity status": "everything is slightly better than at the café and brasserie spin-offs found in humdrum regional shopping centres and other backwaters… but not much". It's certainly "a lot easier to book than it used to be" – the A-listers are long gone and "the clientele seems less highbrow, with more sportswear and baseball caps". But – to be fair – its ratings are middling, not terrible; and many diners feel that "while not as special as it once was, we still enjoy it". Though more "corporate" in atmosphere, it still has a "beautiful interior"; service is "a little bit patchy" at times, but mostly gets it right; and the menu of "British classics with a smattering of Continental and Asian dishes" – never the prime attraction – is "acceptable". Top Tip – "Can't go wrong for a business lunch" that's "reliable if nothing special". / WC2H 9NQ; the-ivy.co.uk; the_ivy_collection; Mon-Sat 11 pm, Sun 10.30 pm.

The Ivy Asia £87 3|2|3
8-10 North Audley Street, W1   020 3751 4990   3–2A
201-203a King's Road, SW3   020 7486 6154   6–3C
20 New Change Passage, EC4   020 3971 2600   10–2B
"Stunning food in a stunning setting with St Paul's as a to-die-for backdrop…" (in EC4); "the superb atmosphere of the very colourful room sets the mood…" (in SW3): – Praise isn't short on the ground for these maximalist pan-Asian venues. They are easy to diss, but most reporters actually feel that, OK, they're "a bit pricey" for their hotch-potch of pan-Asian "classical dishes"; seem "slightly tasteless"; are "very noisy"; but, for all that, overall are "still a lot of fun". There is also though, a minority of diners that loathe them for a variety of reasons; and feel that "the prostitution of the Ivy brand continues apace". ("The western siblings are fine, but this faux-Asian set-up is a travesty – the worst sort of western cultural appropriation and arrogant corruption…"; "opulent surroundings and extravagant presentation cannot disguise overpriced and underwhelming food…"; "it's all flashing lights and selfies. We will not be going back!") / theivyasia.com; theivyasia.

The Ivy Café £93 1|1|2
96 Marylebone Ln, W1   020 3301 0400   2–1A
120 St John's Wood High St, NW8   020 3096 9444   9–3A
75 High St, SW19   020 3096 9333   11–2B
9 Hill Street, TW9   020 3146 7733   1–4A

"The dangers of overextending the brand are writ large at these places" – the sub-sub-brand derivatives from the Theatreland classic, which haven't taken off like the slightly posher 'Ivy Brasserie' spin-offs (perhaps because "they do this better at Côte"). They are not without supporters, who say they have fab locations and "look great" (SW19 is particularly "delightful"); or that although "supper is terribly disappointing, for breakfast they are an absolute joy enhanced by the refined surroundings". Too often, though, they are dismissed as a "so-so brasserie chain that's only really aiming for gullible out-of-towners" nowadays. / ivycollection.com/our-restaurants.

The Ivy Grills & Brasseries £93 1 1 3
66 Victoria Street, SW1   020 3971 2404   2–4B
26-28 Broadwick St, W1   020 3301 1166   4–1C
1 Henrietta St, WC2   020 3301 0200   5–3D
197 King's Rd, SW3   020 3301 0300   6–3C
96 Kensington High St, W8   020 3301 0500   6–1A
1 Tower Bridge, SE1   020 3146 7722   10–4D
50 Canada Square, E14   020 3971 7111   12–1C
Dashwood House, 69 Old Broad St, EC2   020 3146 7744   10–2D

What does it say about the culinary tastes of the British middle classes that this spin-off chain, with about 40 locations based on the original Theatreland icon, has been such a rip-roaring success? True, there's some "great people-watching" at the "always buzzing" Chelsea Garden venue (which has one of SW3's best gardens). And, without doubt, those branches in Kensington, Tower Bridge and Kingston also particularly stand out amongst the rest for their "super atmosphere". In general though, the knock-off look of their locations "isn't a patch on the original on West Street, yet pretends to be exactly the same". And when it comes to their brasserie dishes: although its many followers tout them as "acceptable, albeit nothing special", their rating-average identifies them as "underwhelming tick-box fare"; all offered by service that's very "indifferent". And yet they are "always busy"! In June 2024, it was announced that billionaire Richard Caring had successfully sold his entire Ivy restaurants stake. Now that he is laughing all the way to the bank, it will be interesting to see if ratings reverse, continue or deepen their southward trend. / theivymarketgrill.com.

Ixchel SW3 NEW £72 4 3 4
33 Kings Road   020 7251 3871   6–2D

"Delicious and interesting Mexican-fusion cuisine" and "lovely", funky, bright decor combine to make this "fun" November 2023 newcomer a "fantastic addition to the King's Road" in Chelsea. Chef Ximena Gayosso highlights the flavours of the Yucatan Peninsula with a mix of tacos, tostadas and ceviches leading onto mains with plenty of fish and seafood, all washed down by one of the biggest tequila and mezcal collections in Europe. / SW3 4LX; ixchellondon.com; ixchel.london; Thu-Sat midnight, Sun-Wed 11 pm.

J M Oriental NW9 £48 4 4 4
28 Heritage Ave   020 8912 6215   1–1A

"It's worth the trek to Colindale for the superior dim sum on offer" at Andrew Hung's "high-end Chinese" three-year-old. Andrew gave up a career in architectural engineering to pursue the project and the commitment shows through: "the interior is beautifully designed, and the service is slick, friendly and engaging. Top-class and highly recommended!" / NW9 5GE; jmoriental.co.uk; jm_oriental; Tue-Fri 10.30 pm, Sat 11 pm, Sun 10.15 pm.

Jacuzzi W8 £72 3 3 5
94 Kensington High Street   no tel   6–1A

"A stunning space that's great for a fun night out" – Big Mamma group's "exotic" Kensington mega-trattoria is "definitely a place to impress" (especially if you are relatively young-at-heart). With four floors, 4,000 sq ft and 170 seats, it would be amazing if its pizza, pasta and other Italian fare

FSA

was totally consistent, but the poor reports from last year have subsided and it received a much better rep this year. / W8 4SH; bigmammagroup.com; bigmamma.uk; Mon-Sat 10.15 pm, Sun 9.45 pm.

Jam Delish N1 £55 343
1 Tolpuddle Street   07957 439777   9–3D

"Super-creative and super-tasty Caribbean food is served in a cool and buzzy setting" at siblings Jordan & Chyna Johnson's neighbourhood restaurant and cocktail bar north of Islington's Chapel Market. The surprise is that it's vegan! with intriguing plant-based substitutes in dishes such as 'saltfish' sushi; Bajan fried 'fish' tacos; and 'Oxtail' chow mein. / N1 0XT; jamdelish.co.uk; jam.delish; Tue-Sat 10.30 pm, Sun 7 pm.

Jamavar W1 £91 322
8 Mount Street   020 7499 1800   3–3B

"A high class of Indian food and a smart interior" has helped propel Samyukta & Dinesh Nair's grand venue in the heart of Mayfair into the top rank of London's subcontinental restaurants. Many of our reports agree that the food here can be "exceptional", but even some fans feel its reputation, accolades and prices are overblown. Even more sceptical souls just have "no idea why this has a Michelin star". / W1K 3NF; jamavarrestaurants.com; jamavarlondon; Mon-Sat 10.30 pm, Sun 9.30 pm.

Jamie Oliver Catherine Street WC2 NEW £87 223
6 Catherine Street   020 3084 7565   5–3D

"Lovely jubbly!" – The 'Naked Chef' made his return to the national restaurant scene in November 2023 with this "rustic" venue inside the Theatre Royal, Drury Lane, serving a miscellaneous menu mixing pasta, steaks and quite interesting sharing dishes (Lobster Thermidor say, or Chicken & Rabbit Pie) with the likes of burgers and Chicken Caesar. It inspired no particular criticisms, but it's hard to get too thrilled: "a nice venue but the food's average…"; "a good choice, but pricey for Covent Garden". / WC2B 5JY; jamieolivercatherinest.com; jamieolivercatherinest; Sun-Wed 10.30 pm, Thu-Sat 11 pm.

Jang EC3 NEW £86
The Mezzanine, First Floor, Royal Exchange   020 8187 2209   10–2C

Open in June 2024 in the City's august Royal Exchange (alongside a sibling cocktail bar called Engel) – a modern Korean restaurant from former D&D London CEO Des Gunewardena. It aims to be the flagship of his ambitious new company D3 Collective, with ex-Seoul Bird chef, Dana Choi running the kitchen. / EC3V 3LQ; jangrestaurant.co.uk; jang.london; Mon-Fri 9.30 pm.

Jeru W1 £110 443
11 Berkeley Street   020 3988 0054   3–3C

Aussie celeb chef Roy Ner's "excellent" 'reimagined Mediterranean food' at his three-floor Mayfair showcase elicits ecstatic outbursts from fans, whether for "the bread, the bread, I dream of that bread!" (there is an in-house bakery); or his signature dish from the open kitchen – the "amazing chocolate-fed wagyu and black garlic ketchup". But even amongst converts, there's still the odd fret about the prices – in particular, "it's hard to find any bargains on the wine list". / W1J 8DS; jeru.co.uk; jerulondon; Sun-Thu 10.30 pm, Fri & Sat 12.30 am.

Jikoni W1 £86 324
21 Blandford Street   020 7034 1988   2–1A

A 'no-borders kitchen' philosophy informs the "funky mixture of Middle Eastern, Indian and African food" at chef and food-writer Ravinder Bhogul's "busy and buzzing" Marylebone venue: it serves "combinations of ingredients you might think won't work but really do", and these "are matched by the equally unusual spice cocktails". Top Tip – "the set lunch is a steal and the caramelised aubergine is amazing". / W1U 3DJ; jikonilondon.com; jikonilondon; Tue, Sat, Wed-Fri 10 pm, Sun 9 pm.

FSA RATINGS: FROM 1 POOR — 5 EXCEPTIONAL

Jin Kichi NW3 £63 **4**|**4**|**3**
73 Heath St   020 7794 6158   9–1A

This "top-value Japanese for its quality, now happily doubled in size", has drawn aficionados from across London to its Hampstead premises for decades, to sample sushi, yakitori and other delicacies. Guests can perch at sushi or grill bars where "you can watch the genuine article being prepared under your nose" – or sit at tables where "we were allowed to drink tea all afternoon when lunch just wasn't long enough". / NW3 6UG; jinkichi.com; Jinkichi_Restaurant; Tue-Sun 10.30 pm.

JinCheng Alley WC1 **NEW**
43 New Oxford Street   07376 666 858   5–1C

In New Oxford Street, Holborn, an authentic Sichuan newcomer aimed at well-heeled Chinese tourists. It inspired a couple of promising initial reports, and Times critic Giles Coren was also impressed by 'exquisite' cooking to thrill adventurous diners, while scaring others. / WC1A 1BH; Mon-Sun 10.30 pm.

Joe Allen WC2 £63 **1**|**3**|**4**
2 Burleigh St   020 7836 0651   5–3D

This Theatreland relic retains much of its 1970s Manhattan charm – it's the long-established sibling to a famous NYC brasserie by Times Square, and moved five years ago to a new Covent Garden site just around the corner from the old one (though you'd never know: it looks just the same). As a destination for "great cocktails" it's superb, but as a restaurant its retro American brasserie fare and steaks (with famous off-menu burger) is decidedly "tired and past its sell-by date"… as it has so often been over the decades. / WC2E 7PX; joeallen.co.uk; joeallenlondon; Tue, Thu-Sun 11 pm, Wed .

JOIA SW11 £114 **3**|**3**|**4**
Battersea Power Station, Circus Road West   020 3833 8333   11–1C

"A beautiful room overlooking the Power Station" – the 16th-floor flagship restaurant at Battersea's new art'otel showcases "classic Portuguese dishes" from chef Henrique Sá Pessoa of Lisbon hotspot Alma. A year on from its opening, there is the odd doubter who feels "they charge too much money… the best part is the view"; but most reports say it "truly delivers on both taste and ambience". / SW11 8BJ; joiabattersea.co.uk; joiabattersea; Tue-Thu, Sat 10.30 pm, Fri, Sun 3 pm.

Jolene N7 £30 **3**|**3**|**5**
318-326 Hornsey Road   020 3915 6760   9–1D

"Buzzy, hipstery joint" by Newington Green that's "similar to the related Westerns Laundry": "shared tables add to the fun" and it provides "very good casual dining" – "a mix of small and large plates", and "with the same preference for natural wines (perhaps not universally successful, but they serve a decent range)". The output from the in-house bakery is a feature and it only uses grains grown without chemicals. The odd report discerns a "slight tendency to 'bistromathics', where the bill surprises" and the charge for some small plates is a mite "cheeky". Top Menu Tips – "excellent pizzetta, fab roasted leeks in sauce gribiche". / N7 7HE; bigjobakery.com; bigjobakery; Mon-Sun 4 pm.

Jones & Sons £69 **3**|**3**|**3**
98-106 High Road, E18   020 3336 7579   1–1D **NEW**
Stamford Works, 3 Gillett Street, N16   020 7241 1211   14–1A

"Busy at times, but still with a great vibe" – this converted Victorian factory in Dalston (opened in 2013) will be familiar to some as the location for the 2021 hit film 'Boiling Point'; and wins acclaim for its grills and other modern British dishes. In June 2024, they launched a new two-floor spin-off in South Woodford: this time in a fine-looking Georgian building – a large site with 150 covers and a 50-seat outside terrace. It has a similarly flexible menu, with options for snacks, brunch, and Sunday lunch.

FSA

The Jones Family Kitchen SW1 £91 **3**|**3**|**4**
7-8 Eccleston Yard   020 3929 6000   2–4B

"Good grills" ("great steak" in particular) are the centrepiece of the menu at this popular indie spot in Pimlico's stylish Eccleston Yards development. The overall experience is boosted by its chic ex-warehouse interior, "friendly staff" and the "very pleasant outdoor space". / SW1W 9AZ; jonesfamilykitchen.co.uk; jonesfamilyrestaurants; Tue-Sat, Mon 11.30 pm, Sun 10 pm.

José SE1 £62 **5**|**3**|**4**
104 Bermondsey St   020 7403 4902   10–4D

"Just about edges Barrafina" – José Pizarro's tiny tapas bar is a mainstay of Bermondsey Street, and is renowned for his "excellent tapas, with old favourite dishes joined by an array of changing specials" – "no wonder there's always a queue". "It's cramped, but always relaxed and friendly". José was honoured by King Felipe VI this year with The Cross of the Order of Isabella the Catholic (loosely equivalent to a knighthood) for his contribution to popularising Spanish cuisine outside Spain… and it all began here! Top Menu Tips – "smoked sardine salad with frisé is delicious, as is fried goat's cheese with honey". / SE1 3UB; josepizarro.com; jose_pizarro; Mon-Sat 10.30 pm, Sun 10 pm.

José Pizarro EC2 £71 **3**|**2**|**2**
Broadgate Circle   020 7256 5333   13–2B

If you've seen José P on telly and want to try one of his restaurants, maybe head south to Bermondsey rather than opt for this more anonymous unit in the City's Broadgate Circle. By the standards of the Square Mile though, its mix of tapas, sherries and Spanish vino is fab and "always popular". Top Tip – all day on Mon & Sat, choose three tapas for £20 per person. / EC2M 2QS; josepizarro.com; josepizarrorestaurants; Tue-Sun 6 pm.

José Pizarro at the RA W1 £65 **3**|**3**|**4**
Royal Academy, Burlington Gardens, Piccadilly   020 7300 5912   3–3D

"Way above average for a gallery" – "authentic, high-quality Spanish cuisine" from the Bermondsey-based tapas supremo "always impresses" at this august venue, which is highly commented-on nowadays. The "gracious" ("almost stately") Royal Academy surroundings "add to the pleasure", so "match lunch with an exhibition for a perfect day out" (although given the central location, it's "worth coming even if you are not visiting for the art"). Top Tip – "you need to book if you want to sit in the lovely room with well-spaced tables, otherwise they may put you out in the corridor!" / W1J 0BD; josepizarro.com; jose_pizarro; Tue-Thu, Sat & Sun 6 pm, Fri 9 pm.

Josephine SW10 NEW £85 **4**|**4**|**4**
315 Fulham Road   no tel   6–3B

"No wonder it's packed every day, when the food is this good" – chef Claude Bosi's Chelsea newcomer is off to a flying start and one of the most talked-about debuts in our annual diners' poll, as well as amongst the fooderati in-crowd. It's his and his wife Lucy's tribute to the 'bouchons' of his native Lyons (named in memory of his grandmother) and the "rustic hearty fare from Bosi's homeland" is "exceptionally well-executed". With swathes of cream, eggs, pastry, butter or cheese in most dishes, the "wonderful Lyonnais food" is "not for the calorie-conscious but there is a reason why these recipes are such a part of our food heritage", and succeeds in making it "very much the bistro it's trying to be". In set-up, "it's like being transported to France, with jammed-in tables" ("you will be part of the next table's conversation whether you like it or not!") and retro decor. Top Menu Tips – "special mention has to go to the utterly superb sweetbread in morel sauce and do leave space for the Rum Baba to finish, lethally laced with enough booze to float a battleship". / SW10 9QH; josephinebouchon.com; josephinebouchon; Sun-Thu 9 pm, Fri & Sat 9.30 pm.

FSA RATINGS: FROM **1** POOR — **5** EXCEPTIONAL

The Jugged Hare EC1 £80 3 2 3
49 Chiswell Street   020 7614 0134   13–2A

"Proper British food" of the "sort that isn't fashionable any more" is the USP of this pub near the entrance to the Barbican arts centre. The "seasonal fare with some wonderful dishes you rarely see in other restaurants" is "filling and tasty", and the Sunday roast is particularly recommended. Top Menu Tip – "try the cod's head: absolutely amazing, but not for the faint-hearted!" / EC1Y 4SA; thejuggedhare.com; thejuggedhare; Mon-Sun 11 pm.

Juno W8 NEW £180 4 4 3
2-4 Farmer Street   020 7243 6436   7–2B

"Los Mochis' new omakase experience" – this separately branded, super-ambitious tiny counter has opened above the Mexican/Japanese Notting Hill bar/restaurant, to excellent initial feedback. "It seats only 6 people and food is prepared by Los Mochis executive chef, Leonard Tanyag, and sous chef, Han. Leonard seems to genuinely enjoy the guest interaction and is very happy to talk about his processes and thinking behind food that's innovative but accessible, with every course different to the others but harmonious with them; and with ingredients of exceptional quality". Top Menu Tips – "Standout dishes were the three-day beetroot-cured cuttlefish nigiri with smoked salt and yuzu kosho and the snow crab taco with cedar-charred spring onion and spicy aioli, served in rice paper". / W8 7SN; losmochis.co.uk; Mon-Sat 10.30 pm.

Junsei W1 £76 3 3 2
132 Seymour Place   020 7723 4058   7–1D

Traditional yakitori from a grill using charcoal created from Japanese oak is the speciality at this three-year-old restaurant towards the very north of Seymour Place, just before it hits the Marylebone Road. They know their way around a chicken here, with skewers from the thigh, neck, gizzard, heart, liver… Order à la carte, or there's an omakase for £70 per person (and drinks pairings from £55 per person). / W1H 1NS; junsei.co.uk; junsei_uk; Mon-Sat 10 pm, Sun 9 pm.

Kachori SE17 NEW £50 3 4 3
12 Ash Avenue, Elephant Park   020 7358 6955   1–3C

"Wow, what a start for this big, bustling, comfortable modern Indian restaurant", which is celebrating its first year in the new Elephant & Castle development. With former Benares and Gymkhana exec chef Brinder Nerula running the kitchen, it's "an unexpectedly good find at very reasonable prices". / SE17 1GQ; kachorirestaurant.com; kachori_london; Tue, Thu 10 pm, Fri & Sat 11 pm.

Kadiri's NW10 £35 5 4 2
26 High Rd   020 8459 0936   1–1A

"It looks exceptionally unlikely from the outside", but it's worth discovering this stalwart Indian which has been "nestled away in Willesden Green" for over 40 years now. Fans say it does the "best biryani in London" – for which it's particularly known – but "all the dishes are excellent". The family arrived in the UK from the coastal town of Rajpur via East Africa and describe the cuisine as 'Kokni soul food'; the results are "rich, tasty and fresh". / NW10 2QD; kadiris.com; Mon-Sun 10 pm.

Kaffeine £17 3 5 3
15 Eastcastle Street, W1   020 7580 6755   3–1D
66 Great Titchfield Street, W1   020 7580 6755   3–1C

"Superb coffee" is the name of the game at "one of the original Aussie coffee shops in London" – still providing "exemplary service and high standards" after 15 years under its Melburnian founder, Peter Dore-Smith, and now with two branches in Fitzrovia. There's also a pretty extensive menu of snacks and light bites to get you through the day. Top Tip – "try the great peanut butter made in-house". / kaffeine.co.uk; kaffeinelondon.

FSA

Kahani SW1 £87 3 4 2
1 Wilbraham Place   020 7730 7634   6–2D
"Impressive cooking with subtle flavours" from an ex-Tamarind head chef, Chennai-born Peter Joseph, makes this "basement venue" near Sloane Square "perfect for a meal before a Cadogan Hall event". Service is "considerate and courteous", and "the prices aren't crazy despite the location". / SW1X 9AE; kahanilondon.com; kahani_london; Mon-Sat 10.30 pm, Sun 8.45 pm.

Kai Mayfair W1 £145 4 4 3
65 South Audley St   020 7493 8988   3–3A
Billed by Malaysian-born founder Bernard Yeoh as 'liberated Nanyang [ie South Seas Chinese] cooking', the well-accoladed cuisine at this Mayfair fixture has impressed diners for more than 30 years, with Adele one of the more recent celebs to sing its praises. High-quality hit dishes include a "definitive wasabi prawns and slow-cooked pork"; and there's no compromise on the quality of the drinks offering, with a comprehensive selection of teas, cocktails and wines. But… "the prices! £23 for a plate of broccollini tells me the trick is to get someone to take you there!" (and, you can spend over £10,000 per bottle on the wine). / W1K 2QU; kaimayfair.co.uk; kaimayfair; Mon-Sun 11 pm.

Kaifeng NW4 £80 3 4 3
51 Church Road   020 8203 7888   1–1B
"Well-supported and popular for its high quality" – this offbeat kosher Chinese has long been Hendon's main contribution to London gastronomy. It's always had a reputation for pushing the envelope pricewise, which it justifies with its consistent standards and relatively plush interior (panelled, paintings, table cloths). / NW4 4DU; kaifeng.co.uk; Sun-Thu, Sat 10.30 pm.

Kanada-Ya £43 4 3 2
3 Panton St, SW1   020 7930 3511   5–4A
28 Foubert's Place, W1   020 3435 8155   4–1B
64 St Giles High St, WC2   020 7240 0232   5–1B
3B Filmworks Walk, W5   020 3375 2340   1–3A
35 Upper Street, N1   020 7288 2787   9–3D
"Proper Kyushu-style ramen with a thick, silky broth" is the secret behind this small London noodle chain from former pro cyclist Kazuhiro Kanada. "Especially great on a typical cold, rainy London day", it's "a go-to for a quick, cheap and (relatively) healthy supper in town" ("I've stopped for ramen at all the main chains and a few indies, and for my money this is the very best bowl at a great price"). The sixth branch opened in summer 2024 at Westfield Shepherd's Bush. / kanada-ya.com; kanada_ya_ldn.

Kanchana @ The King's Arms SE1 £35 3 2 3
25 Roupell St   020 7207 0784   10–4A
"Hearty Thai fayre in a glorious boozer" – that's the deal at this "amazing family-run restaurant" which is "tucked away at the back of a pub near Waterloo". Top Tip – if you like beer, the pub markets itself as a 'real ale pub', with eight on tap at any one time. (NB. There is actually more than one King's Arms in SE1 so make sure you get the right one). / SE1 8TB; Thu-Sat, Wed 9.30 pm.

Kanishka W1 £111 3 3 2
17-19 Maddox Street   020 3978 0978   4–2A
"Great-tasting food with perfect flavours means Kanishka is a place to return", according to the many fans of Atul Kochhar's Mayfair venture, not far from Regent's Street. Pan-Indian in its culinary approach, his chef Ashok Kumar caters to a wide variety of budgets with menus that range from brunch and set deals, through a wide à la carte selection, to a tasting menu at £105 per person. On the downside, some reporters said their meal was "not bad, but not as good as hoped for at the prices charged". / W1S 2QH; kanishkarestaurant.co.uk; kanishkamayfair; Tue-Sat 10 pm, Sun 9 pm.

Kaosarn £43 3️⃣3️⃣2️⃣
110 St Johns Hill, SW11   020 7223 7888   11–2C
181 Tooting High Street, SW17   020 8672 8811   11–2C
Brixton Village, Coldharbour Ln, SW9   020 7095 8922   11–2D
"Consistent and authentic Thai food" earns a shout-out for this low-key, family-run trio, in Brixton, Battersea and Tooting. Prices are reasonable and the ability to BYO in each location is a further boost to the value of a meal. / kaosarnlondon.co.uk; kaosarntooting.

Kapara by Bala Baya W1 £65 4️⃣3️⃣2️⃣
James Court, Manette Street   020 8079 7467   5–2A
"Brilliant Middle Eastern/Israeli food" and a "very interesting wine list" earn a thumbs-up for this Soho yearling from chef Eran Tibi. It's "not a vegan or vegetarian restaurant, but delivers plenty of dishes that tick those boxes", with food "as flavour-packed as anything you're ever likely to eat". / W1D 4AL; kapara.co.uk; kapara; Mon-Sat 1 am, Sun 5 pm.

Kappacasein SE1 £12 5️⃣3️⃣2️⃣
1 Stoney Street   no tel   10–4C
"There are only two things on the menu at this Borough Market hole in the wall, but who cares when one of them is the most incredible three-cheese, onion and leek toastie you've ever had?". (The other is raclette, melted over baby new potatoes.) Cheesemaker Bill Oglethorpe's stall has been a market fixture since 2008, and is "definitely worth the queue!". / SE1 9AA; kappacasein.com; kappacasein; Thu, Sat, Fri 5 pm.

Kashmir SW15 £54 3️⃣3️⃣2️⃣
18-20 Lacy Road   07477 533888   11–2B
The Kashmiri cuisine is "deliciously different and always most enjoyable", say fans of this interesting "modern Indian restaurant" in Putney. It was opened in 2016 by Kashmiri-born chef-patron Rohit Razdan and his wife Shweta, who arrived in London via New Delhi and Singapore. / SW15 1NL; kashmirrestaurants.co.uk; kashmirrestuk; Sun-Thu 10.30 pm, Fri & Sat 11 pm.

Kazan SW1 £66 3️⃣3️⃣2️⃣
93-94 Wilton Rd   020 7233 7100   2–4B
"A Pimlico gem", say fans of this "informal local Turkish" fixture behind Victoria station, whose "very welcoming service team" have helped earn it a loyal following over two decades. You could make a meal of the mezze, but the best reviews are of dishes from the 'Fire Grill' (e.g. "delicious Chicken Pirzola and Ottoman grill of mixed meats"). / SW1V 1DW; kazan-restaurant.com; Kazan_Restaurant_London; Mon-Sat 10 pm, Sun 9.30 pm.

Kebab Queen WC2 £131
4 Mercer Walk   020 7439 9222   5–2C
Pamir Zeydan and his team spoon indulgent, vaguely kebab-inspired creations (eight courses of them for £95 per person) onto a custom-designed, heated countertop at this hidden 10-seater: Le Bab's zany, once-secret flagship in the basement of their Covent Garden branch. The idea is for you to scoop the courses up in your fingers as part of a zeitgeistily offbeat foodie adventure. But while it has proved an enduring pitstop for those seeking something out-of-the-ordinary – and won excellent ratings last year – it generated little feedback this year either in our survey or the press. It's still well-followed by the Insta-crowd though, with dishes, menu-changes and chef holidays regularly updated. / WC2H 9FA; eatlebab.com; eatlebab; Wed-Sat 11 pm.

Kennington Tandoori SE11 £58 3️⃣4️⃣3️⃣
313 Kennington Rd   020 7735 9247   1–3C
Celebrating its 40th anniversary in 2025, this well-established fixture serves "decent food that's just a little smarter than average". It has attracted plenty of useful publicity over the years thanks to high-profile patronage by politicians from both sides of nearby Parliament (Brown, Prescott, Cameron,

BoJo), who refer to it as 'the KT'. Keen Westminster-watchers will be interested to note how many newbie MPs beat a path to its door this year... / SE11 4QE; kenningtontandoori.com; Kennington tandoori; Mon-Sun midnight.

Kerridge's Bar & Grill, Corinthia Hotel WC2 £120 2 2 2
10 Northumberland Avenue   020 7321 3244   2–3C
"Brasserie food has been jazzed up to fit into the style of the Corinthia" by TV-star Tom Kerridge, and it's an approach that has proved enduring at this cavernous and moodily decorated bar/restaurant on Northumberland Avenue, which he runs in partnership with the adjoining, deluxe five-star hotel. Even those who say the cooking is "well done", however, say it's "not a choice for the budget-conscious" and an increasing number of reporters experience "rushed service" and feel it's a case of "a lot of hype for ordinary food at escalated prices". / WC2N 5AE; kerridgesbarandgrill.co.uk; kerridgesbandg; Mon-Sat 10.30 pm, Sun 9 pm.

Kettners W1 £68 2 2 4
29 Romilly St   020 7734 6112   5–2A
Despite its cosy and historic charm, it's tempting to omit this cosy Soho landmark which dates from 1867. It once was a major West End destination, and still has a gorgeous Champagne bar, but Soho House (owners since 2016) seem to have been mostly interested in converting its upstairs event spaces into 33 bedrooms, leaving the downstairs dining room run to be run in partnership with a North London pub (The Clarence Tavern x Kettner's): "the food is average but it has a nice setting". / W1D 5HP; kettners.com; kettnerssoho; Mon-Wed midnight, Thu-Sat 1 am, Sun 11 pm.

Kibou London SW11 £63 2 2 3
175-177 Northcote Road   020 7223 8551   11–2C
This "handy local" in Battersea's 'Nappy Valley' (from a Cheltenham-based group) has "interesting and fun decor" and offers a range of modern Japanese dishes that includes "reasonably priced sushi". Marks remain capped by those who say the food is "good but a bit variable". / SW11 6QF; kibou.co.uk; kiboucheltenham; Mon-Fri 3.30 pm, Sun 3 pm.

Kiku W1 £74 3 4 2
17 Half Moon St   020 7499 4208   3–4B
A "super-reliable" Mayfair veteran, which (having opened in 1978) claims to be the "oldest family-run Japanese" in London, and serves "well executed, unpretentious Japanese food at reasonable prices". "It's my local canteen!" says one reporter… a sentiment shared by many staff from the nearby Japanese embassy, which makes "booking essential at lunchtimes!" / W1J 7BE; kikurestaurant.co.uk; kikumayfair; Mon-Sat 10.15 pm.

Kiln W1 £55 5 4 4
58 Brewer Street   no tel   4–3C
"Addictive! Watching the chefs fire the meat whets the appetite" at Ben Chapman's "boundary-pushing classic" in Soho: a "unique and amazing" Thai BBQ whose "visceral cooking over flames provides a sensory experience, with food that's also exceptional". "And it's such a cool place", if "crowded" – "lovely sitting at the bar, enjoying the ordered chaos of the kitchen, having a drink and sampling all the different dishes; and the committed front of house team make this a very special meal". Food quality is "holding up well: they don't seem to have downgraded their offerings to make them more 'accessible'"; although they are "able to satisfy a chilli-phobe as well as a spice seeker". Top Menu Tips – "their pork chop haunts me with its fatty char and savoury flesh"; and "the Chicken & Soy is still an all-time favourite". / W1F 9TL; kilnsoho.com; kilnsoho; Mon-Sat 11 pm, Sun 9 pm.

Kima W1 £110 4 4 3
57 Paddington Street   07745 205136   2–1A
This yearling in Marylebone from the team behind nearby Opso provides an "amazing Greek fish experience" with a "great fin-to-gill ethos" – "choose one of the lovely fresh fish and it comes as a carpaccio, chargrilled head and gills (yes please!) and a fillet, again chargrilled". In his February 2024 review, The Telegraph's restaurant critic William Sitwell was smitten, hailing it as "a game-changer, offering some of the finest Greek food I have ever tasted". / W1U 4JA; kimarestaurant.com; kima.restaurant.london; Tue-Sat 11.30 pm, Sun 11 pm.

Kindred W6 £57 3 3 3
Bradmore House, Queen Caroline Street   020 3146 1370   8–2C
"A calm retreat" that comes as a "pleasant surprise", just one minute's walk from the tube gates of Hammersmith: this cosy cellar bar is found in the middle of the Broadway at the foot of Bradmore House: a grade II listed eighteenth-century property rebuilt as part of the area's redevelopment. The basement forms the in-house eatery for the co-working space occupying the building and anyone else who knows about it, with a short and affordable menu: "I wasn't expecting much, but this was great!" / W6 9YE; wearekindred.com; londonkindred; Tue, Wed 11 pm, Thu-Sat midnight, Mon 6 pm.

Kinkally W1 NEW £64
43 Charlotte Street   07934 609152   2–1C
Slickly designed venue in Fitzrovia's foodie Charlotte Street that opened in autumn 2023 and which is named for its traditional Georgian khinkali dumplings. Initial survey feedback (too limited for a rating) says it can appear pricey – maybe try it out first by going for cocktails in the techno-pumping 'Bar Kinky'. / W1T 1RS; kinkally.co.uk; kinkally.restaurant; Tue-Thu 11 pm, Fri & Sat 11.30 pm, Mon 10.30 pm.

Kioku at the OWO SW1
Whitehall   020 3907 7500   2–3C
Atop the Old War Office (OWO) in Whitehall, this summer 2024 arrival is a second rooftop venue in a London landmark to be under the direction of sushi master Endo Kazutoshi (the other being at the former HQ of the Beeb, see Endo at the Rotunda). Especially for this mega-luxe hotel, the launch pricing is perhaps surprisingly (and sensibly) approachable: it is not a tasting-only format, with an à la carte menu featuring mains from £25-£25, a lunchtime three-course menu for £55 per person and a tasting menu at £130 per person. It is also very much NOT solely dedicated to the sushi for which Endo is renowned, but includes many modern European dishes: for example Pork Ravioli or Turbot with Smoked Sabayon. So the spin is very different from his W12 HQ. Planning a special meal? The venue includes a private dining room set in one of the OWO's historic turrets! / SW1A 2EU; Sun-Wed 10.30 pm, Thu-Sat 11 pm.

Kipferl N1 £60 3 3 2
20 Camden Passage   020 77041 555   9–3D
This "very Austrian" café-restaurant in Islington's atmospheric Camden Passage is "a bit different from the usual" for London, with a menu of "schnitzel, noodles, Tyrolean breakfast, daily soups and various sausages" – plus of course "great coffee and exceptional cakes". It's "not a place for dieters... but the layered torte is worth the calories!" / N1 8ED; kipferl.co.uk; kipferl_london; Mon-Thu 10 pm, Fri & Sat 11 pm, Sun 7 pm.

Kitchen Table W1 £330 4 4 4
70 Charlotte Street   020 7637 7770   2–1C
"An exceptional meal all round, with fantastic, seasonal cuisine" is how all the numerous reports we receive describe James Knappett & Sandia Chang's 18-seat chef's table experience in Fitzrovia, which has one of the highest reputations amongst the capital's most renowned tasting experiences. Even

F S A

so, its "eye-watering prices" are of concern to both fans and foes alike. A rare critic says that "everything about the place misses the mark for me, apart from the food. I am in a minority, but just not a fan". More representative is the following enthusiasm: "somehow I have managed to justify to myself spending this much on a meal four times now. That's how good I think it is!" / W1T 4QG; kitchentablelondon.co.uk; kitchentable1; Tue-Sat 11 pm; SRA-1 star.

Kitchen W8 W8 £100 3 3 2
11-13 Abingdon Road   020 7937 0120   6–1A

"Feeling like a neighbourhood restaurant but with the Michelin-standard cooking you would expect from Phil Howard (a partner in the management)": this "charming venue" – "tucked down a side street away from Kensington's main drag" – remains something of a "hidden star". But even those who feel it continues to "excel quietly" can feel that the "low-key" setting, though "comfy", "needs an injection of energy". Top Tip – "the £34 fixed-price lunch is a steal". / W8 6AH; kitchenw8.com; KitchenW8; Mon-Sat 9 pm, Sun 8 pm.

Kitty Fisher's W1 £82 2 3 3
10 Shepherd's Market   020 3302 1661   3–4B

This "great little bistro" in Mayfair no longer excites as it did at launch 10 years ago (when former prime minister David Cameron and his wife Sam Cam were regulars). Fans reckon it's "still a top dining option in Shepherd Market" thanks to its menu of sophisticated "comfort food"; but increasingly it "doesn't quite live up to expectations" ("all a bit crowded and the food was just about OK"). / W1J 7QF; kittyfishers.com; kittyfishers; Mon-Sat 9.30 pm.

Knife SW4 £84 4 4 3
160 Clapham Park Road   020 7627 6505   11–2D

"The staff are so lovely and accommodating" and help underpin the strong all-round support for this long-running steakhouse, on the fringes of Clapham and Brixton. It serves a curt menu with the focus on steak supported by a few options for non-meat-eaters. Look out for the black-tiled exterior – complete with large red neon signage: by contrast the interior is quite low key. / SW4 7DE; kniferestaurant.co.uk; kniferestaurant/; Wed-Sat 10 pm, Sun 4.30 pm.

KöD
2 St Anne's Ct, W1   020 4600 0432   4–1D
9a Devonshire Square, EC2   0204 586 5729   10–2D **NEW**

This brick-lined City steakhouse yearling in Devonshire Square – part of a Scandi chain with branches in Copenhagen, Oslo, Aarhus and Stavanger – so far has generated limited feedback (so no rating as yet), but all positive: "tried this for a family lunch and although the menu is limited it was excellent". Hungry? For £69, you can indulge in an 'All you can eat' meat-fest, with bottomless booze for 1 1/2 hours. In summer 2024, they opened their second branch in Soho, in the Kingly Court space that was formerly Block Soho (RIP).

Koji SW6 £94 3 3 3
58 New King's Rd   020 7731 2520   11–1B

"By far my favourite in South West London and beyond!" – Robert & Pat Barnett's "very buzzy" pan-Asian in Parsons Green took over where its former incarnation Mao Tai left off as a place for a big night out for Fulhamites not wishing to schlep into the West End. "The food is always super-fresh; there's a diverse wine list and the cocktails are as good as you'll get anywhere… it's always my eating place of choice even if it can be a bit heavy on the wallet…" / SW6 4LS; koji.restaurant; kojirestaurant; Mon-Sun 10 pm.

Kokum SE22 £45 4 4 2
58 East Dulwich Road   020 3551 1883   1–4D

"Definitely better than your average Indian" – this East Dulwich yearling opened in August 2023 and is the work of Sanjay Gour and Simereon Lily Patel, who have other outlying hits in the form of Ewell's Dastaan and Sheen's

Black Salt (see also). According to one SE22 resident "it's certainly the best (and most lauded, rightfully) suburban launch we can think of in the SE postcodes" and generated a large volume of feedback in our annual diners' poll. "If you're looking for a bland korma you won't find it here" – Chef Manmeet Singh Bali's food is "unusual, if not necessarily hugely authentic, and deliciously spicy. Meanwhile the cocktails are phenomenal for Zone 2!" / SE22 9AX; kokumlondon.com; kokumlondon; Tue-Sat 11 pm, Sun 9 pm.

Kol W1 — £126 — 4 4 4
9 Seymour Street   020 3829 6888   2–2A

'Mexican soul, British ingredients' is the mantra at Santiago Lastra's and MJMK's "high-end" Latino venue off Portman Square, which has acquired a formidable reputation for its "wonderful" cooking – "their way of handling chillies is a masterclass" and contributes to a "fantastic" nine-course menu for £175 per person, all served in a "casual" and stylish setting. It's "maybe a little overhyped claiming its the 17th best restaurant in the world" – and the UK's best restaurant – according to World's 50 Best listing: it certainly isn't the highest scoring restaurant in our annual diners' poll and for its deepest critics "the phrase Emperor's New Clothes comes to mind". But that's not a widespread feeling of scepticism: the general impression is of an excellent venue that deserves most, just not quite all, of the accolades that have come its way. / W1H 7BA; kolrestaurant.com; kol.restaurant; Tue-Sat 1 am.

Kolae SE1 NEW — £50 — 5 3 4
6 Park Street   no tel   10–4C

"A fantastic new addition to London's Thai food scene, and to the serious places around Borough Market" – this "achingly cool" newcomer ("stripped back to the naked brick") is "well-located towards the end of the market". A spin-off from Som Saa (see also), "it puts the emphasis on BBQ dishes" and results are "spot-on: full of flavour, with a good balance across the menu in terms of heat and flavour-profile". But some dishes (e.g. Pepper Curry) are "hot enough to immobilise your central nervous system, so ask! Sitting at the bar watching these guys work and having the chance to chat to them is also a great treat". Top Menu Tip – "The mussel skewers are definitely the standout dish. The chef explained that they steam the mussels before marinating them in curry paste, hot smoking them, and finally finishing them over coals with a second sauce. The care and time that goes into the dish really shows in the deep, smokey flavour, which was bursting with vibrancy and all of the delicacy and aromatic spicing that you would expect of a top-class Thai". / SE1 9AB; kolae.com; kolae_london; Mon-Sat 10 pm.

Kolamba — £51 — 3 2 2
21 Kingly Street, W1   020 3815 4201   4–2B
12 Blossom Street, E1   ?020 3435 7174   13–2B NEW

"Robust Sri Lankan dishes" ("could be challenging if you don't like hot food") feature on the "interesting menu" at this Soho five-year-old, which "considering the dead central London location is a good-value option". Husband-and-wife founders Aushi & Eroshan Meewalla opened a second branch near Liverpool Street last year. Top Menu Tip – "slow-cooked beef curry, full of earthy spices and sugary sweetness".

Koya — £47 — 3 2 2
50 Frith St, W1   020 7434 4463   5–2A
10-12 Broadway Market Mews, E8   07342 236933   14–2B
Bloomberg Arcade, Queen Victoria Street, EC2   no tel   10–3C

These noodle bars are "great if you need a quick and satisfying lunch" – either in the original Soho branch, which celebrates its 15th anniversary this year, or its offshoots in the City's Bloomberg Arcade and Hackney. They specialise in udon noodles, which are fatter than ramen and served in a more refined and traditional Japanese dashi stock. koya.co.uk; koyalondon.

Koyn W1 — £103 — 3 4 4
38 Grosvenor Street   020 3376 0000   3–2B

"A new contemporary izakaya in Mayfair" set over two floors, which was opened a couple of years ago by Samyukta Nair and her family: "yes it's pricey, but the atmosphere is banging and the food is varied and fun". In June 2024, they decided to shake things up, rebranding the existing upstairs 'Koyn Japanese' and relaunching the newly refurbished downstairs space as 'Koyn Thai', with Bangkok-born chef Rose Chalalai Singh overseeing the existing Kiwi chef, Rhys Cattermoul. / W1K 4QA; koynrestaurants.com; koynlondon; Mon-Sun 10.45 pm.

Kricket — £57 — 4 5 4
12 Denman Street, W1   020 7734 5612   4–3C
2 Television Centre, 101 Wood Lane, W12   020 7734 5612   1–2B
41-43 Atlantic Road, SW9   020 3826 4090   11–1D
6 Frobisher Pas, E14   020 3835 8800   12–1C **NEW**

"Brilliant, innovative and constantly changing" – Will Bowlby & Rik Campbell's "unfailingly interesting" street-food cafés provide "real Indian food… cooked by Brits" and inspire a large army of fans for this small group, which added a fourth Canary Wharf outlet in early 2024 (and has announced a fifth branch will be coming to Shoreditch at the end of the year). They have achieved an all-round success story: "super-friendly service" scores incredibly highly as does the "buzzy environment". And in Soho, "the restaurant is now supplemented by the Soma Bar next door" with an array of funky cocktails.

Kudu SE15 — £65 — 4 4 3
119 Queen's Rd   020 3950 0226   1–4D

This "wonderful little local restaurant" is now the flagship of a Peckham-based 'Collective' (Little Kudu, Curious Kudu, Kudu Grill) from second-generation restaurateur Amy Corbin (daughter of Corbin & King's Chris) and her South African-born partner Patrick Williams, who infuses some dishes on the "quite unusual" menu with a light Saffa spin: "engaging and fun" with food that's "spot-on". Top Tip – gorgeous cute garden. / SE15 2EZ; kuducollective.com; kudu_restaurant; Thu-Sun 10 pm.

Kudu Grill SE15 — £58 — 3 4 3
57 Nunhead Lane   020 3172 2450   1–4D

The braai is central to the cooking of many South African-inspired dishes at Amy Corbin & Patrick Williams's open-fire restaurant, which occupies a trendily converted former Truman's pub in Nunhead. On the plus side, fans say it's "so good!", but on the minus side, feedback is surprisingly limited given the coverage it has been accorded by its famous associations (Amy's father, Chris Corbin, being restaurant royalty). / SE15 3TR; kuducollective.com; kudugrill; Wed-Sat 10 pm, Sun 2.30 pm.

Kung Fu Noodle W1 — £29 — 3 2 2
64 Shaftesbury Avenue   020 7287 4261   5–3A

Tipped for "cheap 'n' cheerful" chow in the borders of Theatreland, Alex Xu's two-year-old Chinese pitstop on the borders of Chinatown specialises in hand-pulled noodles and dishes from Gansu province in the North West of China; and in an October 2023 review, The Times's Giles Coren described its soupy dishes as "vast and authentic". / W1D 6LU; chinatown.co.uk; kungfunoodleuk; Sun-Thu 9.30 pm, Fri & Sat 10.30 pm.

Kutir SW3 — £75 — 4 4 4
10 Lincoln Street   020 7581 1144   6–2D

"Excellent high-end Indian cooking" from chef-patron Rohit Ghai makes this "Chelsea gem, with a lovely ambience spread across rooms in a beautifully decorated townhouse" a real contender for "the best Indian in London" – "expensive, but worth every penny". Top Tip – cute first-floor roof terrace for either a meal or cocktails. / SW3 2TS; kutir.co.uk; kutirchelsea; Tue-Sun 10 pm.

The Ladbroke Arms W11 £73 3|2|4
54 Ladbroke Road   020 7727 6648   7–2B

"Such a charming pub in Notting Hill, with a lovely garden at the front" – "perfect for a long, lazy, lingering Sunday afternoon" – "and excellent gastropub food"; it's "always buzzing and friendly". / W11 3NW; ladbrokearms.com; ladbrokearms; Mon-Sat 11 pm, Sun 10.30 pm.

Lahore Kebab House E1 £39 4|2|2
2-10 Umberston St   020 7481 9737   12–1A

"For over 30 years I've been turning up here and it always delivers!" – This legendary, ultra-no-frills Pakistani canteen in the East End is "always fun, authentic and consistent" and fans say it provides "the best curry in town… if you are prepared to forgive the service and ambiance". And "with free BYO, it's as cheap as it gets". Top Menu Tips – renowned for its lamb chops, "tandoori chicken is to die for" and "mango lassi is made with Alphonso mangoes so a much better taste and a much less sweet drink than you find elsewhere". / E1 1PY; lahore-kebabhouse.com; lahorekebab; Mon-Fri 1 am.

Lahpet £60 4|3|2
21 Slingsby Place, WC2   020 3883 5629   5–3C
39-45 Bermondsey St, SE1   020 4580 1424   10–4D **NEW**
58 Bethnal Green Road, E1   020 3883 5629   13–1C

"Most interesting and different Burmese cuisine" is thriving in London with the arrival of this "revelatory" trio in Covent Garden, Shoreditch and most recently Bermondsey, from founders Dan Anton and chef Zaw Mahesh – "service can be somewhat surly but the dishes inspire". Top Menu Tip – "don't miss the sensational tea-leaf salad" (from which the restaurant takes its name). / lahpet.co.uk; lahpet.

Laksamania W1 £53 2|2|2
92 Newman Street   020 7637 9888   3–1D

This well-discovered Malaysian destination off Oxford Street "does much more than laksa", with a lineup of hawker-style street-food favourites. Reports on the cooking this year noted hits and misses: "satay was outstanding… but noodles fell apart and had no wok flavour…"; "great laksa!"; "the vegan variety lacked the authentic taste…" / W1T 3EZ; laksamania.co.uk; laksamania; Mon, Wed & Thu 9 pm, Fri & Sat 9.30 pm, Sun 8 pm.

The Landmark, Winter Garden NW1 £95 3|3|5
222 Marylebone Rd   020 7631 8000   9–4A

"A wonderful glass ceiling over palm trees" within a soaring, eight-storey atrium creates one of London's loveliest (and most Instagrammed) spaces: the heart of a plush hotel near Marylebone station (which is currently celebrating its 125th anniversary). "All afternoon teas in London have extortionately doubled in price in the last few years, but this one sort-of deserves it, as all dishes are high quality, they refill unlike at some others" and "there's no rush to be out for the next sitting to come in". You can also breakfast and lunch here, but these occasions inspire little feedback. / NW1 6JQ; landmarklondon.co.uk; the_landmark_london; Mon-Sun 10 pm.

The Lanesborough Grill SW1 £100 3|3|4
The Lanesborough, Hyde Park Corner   020 7259 5599   2–3A

"Chef Shay Cooper has upped the ante here", in the "magnificent" dining room (with "large, well-spaced tables") of this extremely plush hotel on Hyde Park Corner: a gracious space, with a domed glass ceiling (lit naturally). His modern British cuisine won the venue much more consistent praise this year, including for a "wonderful – and surprisingly reasonably priced – Sunday lunch". Top Tip – the £40 menu du jour is a steal here – but you must book online. / SW1X 7TA; oetkercollection.com; thelanesboroughgrill; Mon-Sun 10 pm.

Langan's Brasserie W1 £78 2 3 2
Stratton Street   020 7491 8822   3–3C
This large and famous "Mayfair institution" – site of 1970s and '80s revels under late founder Peter Langan and once co-owned by actor Michael Caine – fell from fashion decades ago, but was significantly relaunched in late 2021. "The food was never that special even when Langan was in charge so that hasn't changed, but the price has moved up substantially" since its rebirth, making it more than ever a case of "average everything, dressed up as chic". There's still the occasional report of "a great time over a long lunch" from its loyal band of client entertainers, but the majority view is that even its bubby conviviality is increasingly called into question: "this is nothing like the original: it's Langan's gone hedge fund". / W1J 8LB; langansrestaurants.co.uk; langansbrasserie; Mon-Sat 10.30 pm, Sun 9.30 pm.

Palm Court, The Langham W1 £105 3 3 3
1c Portland Place   020 7636 1000   2–1B
"Michel Roux does the afternoon tea menus here" (it operates as Chez Roux in the evening) and his input "adds a little extra individuality in the London High Tea Hotel market, which can seem quite overcrowded". It's a gracious chamber too, in the centre of an imposing five-star hotel opposite Broadcasting House, and claims that on its opening in 1865, it was the first major venue to offer the ceremony of Afternoon Tea. / W1B 1JA; palm-court.co.uk; langham_london/; Mon-Sun 11 pm.

Lasdun SE1 £78 2 2 2
National Theatre, Upper Ground   020 7452 3600   2–3D
"Finally! A restaurant worthy of the NT" is how many reporters greet this new all-day venue from the well-connected team who run The Marksman pub, lauding its "British cooking with a focus on ingredients and seasonality". For an arts venue establishment, the level of feedback it generates is through the roof! Even fans, though, can find it "a little overpriced for what is on offer"; and, given the concrete-heavy aesthetic of the surroundings, "the ambience scores higher the more you like Brutalism!". Then there are those who visited on the back of gushing hype in the press, who say that "the reviewers must have eaten somewhere else" and "led us to expect much better". They say "the revamp of the difficult space still doesn't quite work; the food is OK but not inspiring and pricey for what it is"; and that service is very "hit 'n' miss": "the best thing I can say is that it's convenient for the National!" / SE1 9PP; lasdunrestaurant.com; lasdunrestaurant; Mon-Sat 11 pm.

Launceston Place W8 £112
1a Launceston Place   020 7937 6912   6–1B
If Hollywood was going to film a cutesome Kensington scene, it might well choose the picturesque sidestreet location of this "ideally romantic" townhouse, where it's "always a pleasure to have a meal" and which, under various owners, "has been satisfying diners for a few decades now". The "quiet and cosy" interior is "conducive to conversation" and sets the scene for Ben Murphy's "classy" modern European cuisine from an "impressive menu that's excellently presented". At least, it did before August 2024, when Murphy resigned – presumably demoralised by Michelin's stoic (pig-headed?) refusal to recognise this place with a star despite it being so clearly merited. His final services are in October 2024, and given the uncertainty surrounding this D&D London venue we've removed its excellent ratings for the time being. At dinner choose a three-course à la carte for £75 per person, or a seven-course tasting option for £105 per person. Top Tip – lunch is a relatively cheap £42 per person for three courses. / W8 5RL; launcestonplace-restaurant.co.uk; launcestonplace; Wed-Sun 9.30 pm; SRA-3 stars.

FSA

The Laundry SW9   £70   3 3 3
374 Coldharbour Lane   020 8103 9384   11–2D
Converted from a Victorian laundry by Brixton Market – this "friendly local with tasty small plates, an appropriate wine list and the bustle of Brixton life" has a distinctly Antipodean flavour – owner Melanie Brown founded the New Zealand and Australian Cellars, while exec chef Samantha Harvey hails from Sydney. It has a "great outdoor space for lunch", too. / SW9 8PL; thelaundrybrixton.com; brixtonlaundry; Mon-Thu 11 pm, Fri & Sat 11.30 pm, Sun 8 pm.

Lavo W1   £100   3 3 4
30 Marylebone Lane   020 8158 7588   3–1A
"There's a fun, party atmosphere with loud music (that might not be to everyone's taste)" at this Italian yearling in a swish boutique hotel: part of the US Tao Group, who also own Hakkasan and Yauatcha; and who run Lavo siblings in LA, NYC, Singapore and Mexico City. It's a kind of rich man's Gloria – you go more for the colour-changing ceiling light feature and to channel ersatz Italian Hollywood glamour than you do to mull over the authenticity of its comfort foodish menu, which takes in pizza, pasta and the likes of chicken parmigiana on the way to the climax of its signature 'indulgent 20-Layer Chocolate Cake'. Even so, most reports insist it's "a great addition to Marylebone". / W1U 2DR; taogroup.com; lavolondon; Sun & Mon 9.45 pm, Tue-Sat 10.45 pm.

Laxsa W1   £35   4 2 2
37 Old Compton Street   020 7734 6361   5–3A
"Excellent, cheap 'n' cheerful" spot in the heart of Soho with a first-floor dining room above a small pavement-level café. "This place does the best Malaysian noodles – I have been there at least ten times and (despite the name of the place) I haven't ordered the laksa yet because I keep getting distracted by their Wat Tan Hor and Hokkien Mee, which are as good as the best to be found in Kuala Lumpur!" / W1D 5JY; Mon-Thu 11 pm, Fri & Sat midnight, Sun 10 pm.

Layla W10   £15   3 3 3
332 Portobello Road   no tel   7–1A
"Great coffee and artisanal bakery" again win high ratings from a small but enthusiastic fan club for this bright haunt in a unit at the foot of a newish block, at the north end of the Portobello Road. / W10 5PQ; laylabakery.com; layla_w10; Mon-Sun 4 pm.

Le Bab   £64   3 3 2
Kingly Ct, W1   020 7439 9222   4–2B
4 Mercer Walk, WC2   020 7240 9781   5–2C
Battersea Power Station, SW11   07944 242329   11–1C
408 Coldharbour Lane, SW9   CLOSED   11–2D
130 Kingsland High Street, E8   020 3877 0865   14–1A
231 Old Street, EC1   020 3456 7890   13–1A
This 10-year-old group with six sites offers a "good-value and tasty" take on the Middle Eastern kebab, served with a "modern twist" alongside "noteworthy cocktails". "A seat at the counter is fun" at the original Kingly Court branch in Carnaby Street, which has a 'fine dining' option downstairs, Kebab Queen (see also). / eatlebab.com; eatlebab.

The Ledbury W11   £249   5 4 4
127 Ledbury Rd   020 7792 9090   7–1B
"One of the greats and absolutely deserving its three stars" – chef Brett Graham and his backer Nigel Platts-Martin closed this Notting Hill icon during the Covid-19 pandemic, only to triumphally reopen it in 2022, pitching it even more ambitiously (and expensively) than it was before. Support from the annual diners' poll was unprecedented this year, with over 80% of diners acclaiming it as their best meal of the year – "I didn't think it was possible to surpass its previous performance, but somehow it did!..."; "a favourite

restaurant of anywhere in the world" where "attention to detail is apparent throughout", not least in the superlative tasting menu for £225 per person. The latter encompasses eight courses and 'goes for it' more than it once did in terms of recherché ingredients. Mushrooms are also a feature from a post-refit cabinet; as is the venison for which Brett's pub the Harwood (see also) is also known. "The refurb has helped the atmosphere" and service too is "flawless, but keeps things relaxed". "It's all too good for the health of my future bank balance, I fear…" / W11 2AQ; theledbury.com; theledbury; Tue-Sat 9.15 pm.

Legare SE1 £57 3 4 3
Cardamom Building, 31g Shad Thames 020 8063 7667 10–4D
This "little gem" near Tower Bridge in Shad Thames serves a "concise but well put-together menu" of Italian-inspired plates, accompanied by "good natural wines". It was founded five years ago by Jay Patel, a former Barrafina manager, with thoughtful ex-Trullo chef Matt Beardmore running the kitchen. / SE1 2YB; legarelondon.com; legarelondon; Wed-Sat, Tue 10 pm, Sun 4 pm.

Lemonia NW1 £70 2 2 2
89 Regent's Park Rd 020 7586 7454 9–3B
"Still going strong" after 45 years, this big, "family-friendly, community-spirited" taverna on Primrose Hill boasts a "reliable Greek-Cypriot menu that suits all tastes". "Visit for the ambience rather than the food and you won't be disappointed" – it's the sort of place where "many of the waiters have served for decades; and once-young guests can often be seen tucking in with now grown-up children as well as grandchildren in tow". / NW1 8UY; lemonia.co.uk; lemonia_primrose_hill; Mon-Thu 10 pm, Fri & Sat 10.30 pm, Sun 4 pm.

Leo's E5
59 Chatsworth Road 020 4599 8598 14–1B
A menu of Italianate breakfast dishes segues into lunches of café staples and subsequently more ambitious evening fare including homemade pasta and antipasti (alongside low-intervention Italian wines) at this Clapton hotspot, atmospherically shoe-horned into a gentrified former greasy spoon. Over its first year of operation it attracted too limited feedback for a full rating, but such feedback as we have is all positive. / E5 0LH; leosrestaurant.bar; leos.london; Wed-Sat 10 pm, Sun 3 pm.

Leroy EC2 £100 4 3 3
18 Phipp Street 020 7739 4443 13–1B
Hip Shoreditch corner venue, serving interesting small plates matched by a wide-ranging wine list from founder, sommelier Ed Thaw. In February 2024, it lost the Michelin star that always jarred with its vibey, casual style – to the concern of absolutely none of our reporters, who still feel it's an affordable and accomplished favourite. / EC2A 4NP; leroyshoreditch.com; leroyshoreditch; Mon-Sat 9.45 pm.

Levan SE15 £69 3 2 2
3-4 Blenheim Grove 020 7732 2256 1–4D
This contemporary European venue behind Peckham Rye station is still one of the most interesting restaurants in Peckham ("absurd-sounding, I know, to our parents' generation, but that makes it very cool!"). That said, it no longer attracts the superlative ratings of five years ago, and one school of thought finds it "overrated and expensive". Inspired by the 'bistronomy' movement of Paris, it serves appropriately "interesting" low-intervention and natural wines. / SE15 4QL; levanlondon.co.uk; levanlondon; Tue-Sat 11.30 pm, Sun 3 pm.

Levante SE13 £27 4 3 2
11 Lewis Grove 020 8355 3522 1–4D
"Run by Suleiman the friendly owner – for a long time this Turkish Grill House was literally the ONLY good place to eat in central Lewisham!" and is tipped in our poll as an excellent "cheap 'n' cheerful" choice. "Kebabs are

taken seriously here, properly charred over coals, and good stews are offered as the set meal of the day". (In his February 2024 review, The Observer's Jay Rayner also declared himself a fan: a "happy find. I left invigorated, fed and very grateful"). / SE13 6BG; levantelewisham.uk; Mon-Sat 11 pm, Sun 10 pm.

The Light House SW19 £69   3 3 3
75-77 Ridgway   020 8944 6338   11–2B
This "great local restaurant" has notched up 25 years in Wimbledon Village, and "turns out far better food than you might expect from a local spot". An "interesting menu" of Mediterranean-influenced dishes means it is frequently packed. / SW19 4ST; lighthousewimbledon.com; lighthousewimbledon; Mon-Sat 10 pm, Sun 3 pm.

Light On The Common SW19 £60   3 3 3
48 High St   020 8946 3031   11–2B
"After extensive renovations, it's finally reopened… it was worth the wait!" – this "great local" in Wimbledon (inevitably not quite on the Common – a sibling to the Light House) has "reopened after a makeover" complete with an attractive, light-filled rear conservatory. The "delicious" modern cooking is "simple and fresh" – "it's perfect for a night out with friends or family". / SW19 5AX; lightwimbledon.co.uk; Mon, Wed & Thu, Sun 10 pm, Fri & Sat 11 pm.

Lilienblum EC1 £85   3 2 3
80 City Road   020 8138 2847   13–1A
The menu "reads like some crazy dream" (e.g. '6 spicy instruments that will swirl your soul') at this yearling from Israeli celeb chef Eyal Shani near Old Street roundabout. "When it arrives, the results can be more sedate than they sound", but generally deliver "fresh Mediterranean flavours". The setting – a large contemporary space at the foot of a new block – can seem "soulless" but mostly receives a thumbs-up in reports. / EC1Y 2BJ; lilienblum.co.uk; lilienblumlondon; Tue-Sat 11.30 pm.

Lina Stores £51   2 2 3
13 Marylebone Lane, W1   020 3148 7503   3–1A
51 Greek Street, W1   020 3929 0068   5–2A
20 Stable Street, N1   awaiting tel   9–3C
22 The Pavement, SW4   020 3326 5548   11–2D
19 Bloomberg Arcade, EC4   020 3002 6034   10–3C
"We love the pistachio decor and the spacious seating", say fans of this expanding chain, which had operated as a treasured old deli in Soho for over 75 years before starting to branch out as a pasta-chain in 2018. Impressions of it are something of a mixed bag though. To fans, its stylised outlets are "very convenient" and "can be trusted for a good-value and enjoyable experience with excellent food" (mostly pasta) in "sensible portions". On the downside, though, are a fair number of diners to whom it's a good concept whose execution is "perfectly fine but unexciting" ("starters good, pasta average-to-good, but compared with folk who had raved to me about other branches, I was left with a sense of 'meh?'"). Still, their backers are enthusiastic and this year they added new locations in Greek Street and South Kensington. / linastores.co.uk; linastores.

Lisboeta WC1 £80   3 2 2
30 Charlotte Street   020 3830 9888   2–1C
"On the money in almost every sense": innovative chef Nuno Medes opened this three-storey Fitzrovia haunt (in partnership with MJMK Restaurants) in 2022 and it continues to inspire fans with its "fabulous and interesting Portuguese cooking" – "a bit hit 'n' miss, with some odd combinations, but the quality is undeniably good". Ratings have slipped a bit, though, from its heady debut: service is not always super-organised and "the music needs to be a bit less loud!" (although apparently Nuno likes it that way). Top Menu Tip – "scallops with black pudding is especially good". / WC1B 4AF; lisboeta.co.uk; lisboeta.london; Mon-Sat 11 pm.

F S A

Lita W1 NEW £237 2 2 3
7-9 Paddington Street   02081912928   2–1A

"Fine food but spectacularly expensive" is a fair summary of views on this Marylebone newcomer, whose level of sophistication is somewhat at odds with its attractive but deceptively casual style. Co-founder Luke Ahearne is a former head chef at Corrigan's in Mayfair, and cooks over wood on a dramatic grill, with simple, ingredient-led dishes inspired by the southern Mediterranean. But its 'bistro' billing is belied by prices that mount vertiginously (particularly on the wine list); and even though many reporters do see it as a "class act", too many feel "the high cost matches the area, not the food or drink on offer". "A meal for two with a decent bottle of wine was £630!! Hello!??" / W1U 5QE; litamarylebone.com; litamarylebone; Mon-Sat 9.45 pm, Sun 4 pm.

Little Social W1 £80 2 2 3
5 Pollen Street   020 7870 3730   3–2C

With the closure of Pollen Street Social opposite (as Mary's, see also), Jason Atherton's elegant small Mayfair venue is now one of his two remaining 'Socials'. It still wins praise for its "delicious, bistro-style offer" (e.g. "superb succulent pork chop with mash") and "lovely booths and dining at the bar". But its ratings slipped this year: service has seemed more up-and-down of late; and there is a view that it's "a competent bistro with sound cooking but otherwise unexciting". Perhaps as the dust settles on the reshaping of the Atherton empire, it will regain its va-va-voom? / W1S 1NE; littlesocial.co.uk; _littlesocial; Tue-Sat 9.45pm.

Little Taperia SW17 £59 3 3 3
143 Tooting High St   020 8682 3303   11–2C

"Delicious tapas" ensure a very loyal local crowd keeps returning to this lively little fixture near Tooting Broadway tube station – it's "always loud and cheery. The food is mostly a hit and the occasional slight miss goes unnoticed in the good time had by all" – "I often take three generations there, and they all enjoy it". Former food journalist Madeleine Lim linked up with local restaurateur Hikmat Antippa to launch it in 2015. / SW17 0SY; thelittletaperia.co.uk; littletaperiatooting; Sun-Thu 11 pm, Fri & Sat midnight.

Liu Xiaomian W1 £17 3 2 2
Kingly Ct   no tel   4–2B

"High-quality noodles with spicy toppings from nuclear-grade down to wimp" is the draw to this first floor canteen in Kingly Court, Carnaby – the first permanent venue for Chongqing natives Liu Qian & Charlene Liu, whose noodles in hot broth and other specialities from central-western China have been a big hit on the supperclub circuit. "Do a couple of things really well seems to be the ethos here" and the "basic menu is delicious and filling". All this plus "speedy service and simple decor make for a satisfying time". (In March 2024, The Times's Charlotte Ivers confessed her new-found addiction to the mouth-numbing flavours here: "it is no exaggeration to say I have thought of these dumplings every day since…"). / W1B 5PW; liu-xiaomian.com; liu_xiaomian; Tue-Sat 9 pm.

Llama Inn, The Hoxton EC2 £80 2 4 4
1 Willow Street   020 7550 1071   13–1B

Hip import from Booklyn, which is the latest incumbent on the gorgeously decorated rooftop of Shoreditch's 'Hoxton Hotel', where the city-fringe viewscape is of The Barbican and Square Mile. The press have by-and-large raved since it touched down in autumn 2023, with The Evening Standard's Jimi Famurewa hailing the "thrilling new context" given to its Peruvian dishes, and The Telegraph's William Sitwell branding it "the best thing to come out of Peru since Paddington". But our annual survey is less impressed, noting that – especially at the price – its Nikkei/Latino dishes can seem "disappointing":

FSA RATINGS: FROM 1 POOR — 5 EXCEPTIONAL   149

"a great social media campaign doesn't make a great restaurant!"
/ EC2A 4BH; llamainnlondon.com; llamainnldn; Sun & Mon 10 pm, Tue, Wed 11 pm, Thu-Sat midnight.

Llewelyn's SE24 £75 3 4 3
293-295 Railton Rd 020 7733 6676 11–2D

This classy venue opposite Herne Hill station is a *"favourite local"* – there's a *"superb buzz"* about the place (although for some reporters that translates as *"a heavy decibel level"*) thanks to its *"consistently good"*, contemporary cuisine and *"charming service"*. An *"interesting and reasonably priced wine list"* seals the deal. / SE24 0JP; llewelyns-restaurant.co.uk; llewelynslondon; Tue-Thu 9 pm, Fri & Sat 9.30 pm, Sun 3.15 pm.

La Lluna N10 £59 3 2 2
462 Muswell Hill Broadway 020 8442 2662 1–1B

A *"very good choice of tasty tapas"* wins praise for this Hispanic fixture on Muswell Hill Broadway as *"a great neighbourhood spot"* (including for breakfast, which is quite a feature). Also with a spin-off in Whetstone.
/ N10 1BS; lalluna.co.uk; lallunalondon; Mon-Thu, Sat & Sun 11 pm, Fri midnight.

Locanda Locatelli,
Hyatt Regency W1 £113 3 3 3
8 Seymour St 020 7935 9088 2–2A

"Classy and sophisticated Italian food" in *"a buzzy environment"* with a *"posh clientele"* still inspires a lot of love for Giorgio & Plaxy Locatelli's well-known destination off Portman Square. *"You certainly aren't transported to the streets of Florence or Milan with the hotel's sleek decor"*, but its moody style is often recommended for a romantic dinner. On the downside, though, resistance to its price-level grew significantly this year, with almost one third of nominations in our annual diners' poll as the most overpriced meal of the year. / W1H 7JZ; locandalocatelli.com; locandalocatelli; Thu-Sat, Tue, Wed 11 pm, Sun 10.30 pm.

Lolo SE1 NEW
102 Bermondsey Street 07494 181903 10–4D

Jose Pizarrro celebrates his 25th year in London – and recent high honours from the King of Spain for his services to Spanish cuisine – with this third venture in Bermondsey Street (and his seventh in the capital overall), which launches in summer 2024. It's open all day, and his first operation to serve breakfast. / SE1 3UB.

London Shell Co £110 3 4 4
The Grand Duchess, Sheldon Sq, W2 07818 666005 7–1C
The Prince Regent, Sheldon Sq, W2 07553 033636 7–1C
Unit 4, Sonny Heights, Swains Lane, N6 020 4568 8586 9–1B

"Very good seafood and the unusual setting of travelling along the canal as the swans glide by" is a winning formula, which has helped siblings Leah & Harry Lobek grow this business from a narrow boat ('The Prince Regent') on the Grand Union Canal to include a permanently docked barge in Paddington basin ('The Grand Duchess') and – since last year – a *"local restaurant in lovely Swains Lane just by Hampstead Heath"*, which is *"also a very good fishmonger"*. The odd meal includes *"mixed results"* – and seating on the boats can be *"cramped"* – but *"prices are reasonable"* and the best reports are of *"delicious and simple roasted fish"* and *"amazing platters of cold dishes, from oysters to crab"*. *"Delightful staff"* boost the vibe in all locations. Top Tip – in N6, there's also a *"huge choice of wines"*.

The Lore of the Land W1 £86 3 4 4
4 Conway Street 020 3927 4480 2–1B

Under the ownership of film director Guy Ritchie (pals David and Cruz Beckham have been spotted here), this *"first-class"* pre-Victorian Fitzrovia boozer is thriving. Everything is *"done well"*: and at heart, the food is *"simple,* and well-sourced" (although this description possibly under-sells a menu featuring such dishes as Wiltshire Venison Tartare with Togarashi Mayonnaise and South Coast Brown Crab Risotto with Coriander and Cherry Harissa dressing). / W1T 6BB; gritchiepubs.com; loreofthelandpub; Mon-Thu, Sat 11 pm, Fri midnight, Sun 7 pm.

Lorne SW1 £77 5 5 3
76 Wilton Road   020 3327 0210   2–4B

"Katie Exton and her team continue to shine" at her "lovely, cosy Pimlico neighbourhood restaurant" which "punches well above its price point". "It's not super luxe by any means, but its focus is put onto things that matter most" with "an intimate vibe" and "a quality of cuisine that's far higher than the venue would suggest" ("interesting dishes and flavours without being too crazy"). She is a wine expert by training, and it shows in the "brilliantly curated and sensibly priced wine list with an incredible choice for a restaurant of its small size". "A useful place in this area: particularly good for meeting people getting into Victoria". Top Menu Tips – "the lamb and game are unbeatable". / SW1V 1DE; lornerestaurant.co.uk; lorne_restaurant; Tue-Sat 9 pm.

Los Mochis £57 4 3 4
2 Farmer St, W8   020 7727 7528   7–2B
100 Liverpool Street, EC2   020 7243 6436   10–2D

"Excellent, innovative and delicious food" – a surprising Mexican/Japanese fusion dubbed 'Baja-Nihon cuisine' by its founder, restaurant entrepreneur Markus Thesleff – has made quite an impact at this "amazing" Notting Hill three-year-old (on the former site of famous chippy Geale's, RIP), leading to the launch last year of a City branch with a huge rooftop terrace next to Liverpool Street station. Top Tip – "everything in this restaurant is gluten-free and suitable for coeliacs" (it's also nut- and celery-free).

LPM (fka La Petite Maison) W1 £127 4 3 3
54 Brook's Mews   020 7495 4774   3–2B

"A splash of Mediterranean sunshine in Mayfair" – the "food tastes of its ingredients" at this Nice-comes-to-Mayfair fixture, whose "loud music" and energetic crowd only add to the vibe. True to its Côte d'Azur impression, it's also "nose-bleedingly expensive", a factor acknowledged by both fans and the odd foe alike. The latter says it "thinks it's better than it is" and is just "chock-full of hedge fund types having business lunches with a shocking bill to match". But to boosters, "it's brilliant and the best" – "sure, prices are high, but when even the table-display tomato tastes like one of the best you have ever had, it has to be worth it!". "Service is spot-on and there's always some fun to be had people watching. It's only ever a good experience!" / W1K 4EG; lpmlondon.co.uk; lpmlondon; Mon-Sat 10.30 pm, Sun 9.30 pm.

Luc's Brasserie EC3 £80 3 3 3
17-22 Leadenhall Mkt   020 7621 0666   10–2D

"A City Institution!" – Looking down onto Leadenhall Market from the eves of the old Victorian structure (which it has inhabited since the 1980s), this traditional brasserie is an excellent all-rounder by the standards of Square Mile lunch spots. The classic French fare is not going to distract from your lunch, but prices are sufficiently reasonable as to make this a bill that can be paid, if necessary, from your 'personal account'. / EC3V 1LR; lucsbrasserie.com; Wed-Sun 10 pm.

Luca EC1 £100 4 3 4
88 St John St   020 3859 3000   10–1A

"A tiny nondescript frontage" north of Smithfield Market hides this "deceptively large" and "classy" Italian – a sibling (though you would never know it) of The Clove Club (see also). You enter through the "very convivial" bar (where they serve "a stunning set business lunch") to enter "a spacious environment" including "a romantic hidden back terrace". The cuisine is "sensational old school Italian cooking": "classic dishes are elevated by the clever use of subtle flavours" and there's "a beautifully-put together wine list (a not cheap, but interesting selection)". Top Menu Tip – "worth it for the Parmesan churros, or the homemade Limoncello". / EC1M 4EH; luca.restaurant; luca.restaurant; Wed-Sat, Tue 10 pm.

Luciano's SE12 £60 3 4 3
131 Burnt Ash Road   020 8852 3186   1–4D

"A fabulous neighbourhood restaurant"… even more so given that the neighbourhood in question is Lee. "Kitchen competence far outweighs the modest location", delivering high quality home-made pasta and wood-fired pizza. The Luciano in question is owner Enzo Masiello's father. / SE12 8RA; lucianoslondon.co.uk; lucianoslondon; Tue-Thu 10.30 pm, Fri & Sat 11.30 pm, Mon 10 pm, Sun 9.15 pm.

Lucio SW3 £102 3 3 3
257 Fulham Rd   020 7823 3007   6–3B

"You are always made welcome by the family at this well-established Italian restaurant" in Chelsea. "I was searching for an Italian nearby and was guided here by Harden's – a delight! with an attractive setting and delicious and well-presented cooking". (It's nowadays run by the sons of the founder Lucio Altana, who spent many years as maître d' of Princess Di's old favourite, San Lorenzo in Knightsbridge). / SW3 6HY; lucirestaurant.com; luciorestaurant; Tue-Sat 10.30 pm, Sun 3 pm.

Lucky & Joy E5 £52 4 3 2
95 Lower Clapton Road   07488 965966   14–1B

"Exciting, innovative, interesting Asian-fusion dishes at great value prices" mean you should keep an eye out for this easily-missed venue amidst busy Clapton high street. The food is primarily Chinese, but flavour and fun, not foodie purity, is first priority (Sichuan Negronis anyone?). It's not super-plush, but fans say "the ambience has improved recently with a refurb". / E5 0NP; luckyandjoy.co.uk; luckyandjoyldn; Tue-Sat 10.30 pm.

Lucky Cat £91 2 3 2
10-13 Grosvenor Square, W1   020 7107 0000   3–2A
Level 60, 22 Bishopsgate, EC2   020 7107 0000   10–2D **NEW**

Gordon Ramsay's pan-Asian brand is now a group, with the Mayfair original followed by branches in Manchester and (scheduled for an early 2025 opening) on the 22nd storey of the City's tallest tower, 22 Bishopsgate. Habitual poor ratings have risen a notch this year, amid praise for "a great atmosphere, with service and food to match" – so perhaps standards have risen. But even broadly positive reporters point out that "the food is underwhelming for the price" – "the problem is that there are better Asian-inspired restaurants in central London at better prices".

Lulu's SE24 £45 3 3 3
291 Railton Road   no tel   11–2D

"An offshoot of Llewelyn's" (just next door) – this cute Herne Hill yearling is a "very buzzy" deli/bakery/bar serving "interesting food choices and a wide range of drinks and tipples". "The emphasis is on small plates (some would say very small!)" / SE24 0JP; lulus.london; Tue, Sun 4 pm, Wed & Thu 9 pm, Fri & Sat 9.30 pm.

Lupins SE1 £58 4 4 3
66 Union St   020 3908 5888   10–4B

"Handy for the local South Bank theatres", this "small, unassuming place" close to Tate Modern from Lucy Pedder and Natasha Cooke has won a strong following over seven years thanks to "an interesting and well-executed menu" of small and larger plates, all "in a friendly atmosphere and at a reasonable price". Top Menu Tip – "The enormous and delicious Cheddar fritters are a must!… Roasted Pigeon in a stout sauce along with Confit rabbit, ribollita & cavolo nero is a highlight… definitely save space for dessert". / SE1 1TD; lupinslondon.com; lupinslondon; Tue-Sat 9.30 pm.

Lurra W1 £79 4 4 3
9 Seymour Place   020 7724 4545   2–2A
"Top-notch" Basque cooking – "always of the highest quality" – again wins plaudits for this Seymour Village venture that celebrates its 10th anniversary this year. Whole turbot and large cuts of mature beef grilled over charcoal are the standouts on a very focused menu, while "the staff are amazing, friendly and flexible". Sister venue Donostia (see also) nearby is a good bet for a lighter meal. / W1H 5BA; lurra.co.uk; lurraw1; Mon-Sat 10.30 pm, Sun 3.30 pm.

Lussmann's N6 NEW
2 Highgate High St   020 4603 4888   9–1B
Andrei Lussmann has another go at a London opening 20 years after his first, with this summer 2024 arrival in Highgate: the sixth in his Hertfordshire-focused chain. Opposite Waterlow Park, with 130 covers, it incorporates a café, bar and walled garden seating 30. The 'Lussmann's locals' set menu, available from 12pm-6.30pm daily, is £20.95 for two courses and £23.95 for three. / N6 5JL; Tue-Sat 10 pm.

Lutyens Grill, The Ned EC2 £115 3 3 4
27 Poultry   020 3828 2000   10–2C
"Well-spaced tables are comfortable to the point of luxury" in this club-like, wood-panelled chamber – the highpoint of the food offerings within Soho House's gargantuan hotel: the conversion of the opulent former Midland Bank HQ just next to the Bank of England. Its "pricey" caviar, oysters, "top Dover Sole", wide selection of steaks and Beef Wellington carved from the trolley all provide excellent sustenance for the local power brokers ("I have won more business here than in any other restaurant"). / EC2R 8AJ; thened.com; thenedlondon; Mon-Sat midnight.

Lyle's E1 £106 5 3 2
The Tea Building, 56 Shoreditch High Street   020 3011 5911   13–1B
At the foot of the 'Tea Building' in Shoreditch and launched by James Lowe a decade ago, "Lyles has remained at the top of its game for many years" and is "a restaurant that works for romance, lunch with friends, client dinners and all points in between". Notwithstanding holding a position on the World's 50 ranking till 2023 – it has gradually "faded from the media glare since its launch", but has lost none of its culinary fizz, and a visit can still be "an eye-opener" as amongst "the best sharing-plates restaurants in London". "Seasonally rotating menus" produce "well-rounded and fresh-tasting" British dishes, "with high-quality ingredients pushed to the foreground"; and with "daring paired wines". "The bare, utilitarian setting with an open kitchen makes for a loud and buzzing experience, but creates a relaxed vibe", which is boosted by the "consistently friendly and knowledgeable service" ("staff give you as much information as you want and have a clear love of the place – you do not think they are temps!"). Top Menu Tip – "the menu changes but the bread and the brown butter madeleines thankfully never leave". / E1 6JJ; lyleslondon.com; lyleslondon; Tue-Sat 9 pm; SRA-3 stars.

Lyon's N8 £61 3 3 3
1 Park Road   020 8350 8983   1–1C
First-time guests are "massively surprised" to find "really inventive and tasty cooking" – especially "seafood with a twist" – at this family-run Crouch End local. It's a "lovely, romantic spot", too – although "it can feel cramped and noisy when busy". / N8 8TE; lyons-restaurant.com; lyonsseafood; Tue-Sat 10 pm.

M Restaurant EC2 £100
60 Threadneedle St   020 3327 7770   10–2C

Martin Williams's 'gastro playground' at the heart of the City is now the sole survivor of what was once a four-strong group operation (the Canary Wharf outlet having shut up shop in the last 12 months). Feedback has dwindled, but if its determinedly deluxe, carnivorous formula is to thrive anywhere, it is here in the Square Mile. Amidst glossy, Miami-esque interiors, it offers fine steaks alongside an extensive wine list (with over 100 choices by the glass) priced for the local expense-accounters. As well as numerous event spaces, there is also a private members' club, and The Players' Lounge sports bar (a showcase for Bang & Olufsen's desirable audio-visual range). / EC2R 8HP; mrestaurants.co.uk; Tue, Wed, Sun 5 pm, Thu-Sat 11 pm.

Ma La Sichuan SW1 £51   4 3 3
37 Monck Street   020 7222 2218   2–4C

"High-quality and sometimes very punchy Sichuan food" is the order of the day at this understated-looking spot on a Westminster corner. Chef Zhang Xiaozhong presides over a "huge menu" which takes in some unusual dishes "including offal", while the proximity of Parliament brings a "changing cast of MPs, lords and sundry politicos, which makes people-watching fun". / SW1P 2BL; malasichuan.co.uk; malasichuan; Tue-Sat 10.30 pm, Sun 10 pm.

Macellaio RC £74   2 2 3
39-45 Shaftesbury Avenue, W1   020 3727 6161   5–3A
6 Store Street, WC1   020 3848 7230   2–1C
84 Old Brompton Rd, SW7   020 7589 5834   6–2B
Arch 24, 229 Union St, SE1   07467 307682   10–4B
124 Northcote Rd, SW11   020 3848 4800   11–2C
38-40 Exmouth Market, EC1   020 3696 8220   10–1A

You walk past "chiller meat displays" as you enter Roberto Costa's Italian group. Macellaio means 'butcher', and the focus is on quality steaks, particularly the Piemontese Fassona breed, but also including cuts from the UK (from Herefordshire) and with tomahawk and Halal options; all matched with an "extensive wine list". "For a great and reasonable dinner (including pre-theatre) and excellent steaks" it does still have fans. But its support has waned in both quality and quantity in recent years, and the group has halved in size since the last edition, shedding branches in Bloomsbury, Borough and Clapham (all RIP) to focus on Theatreland/Soho, Exmouth Market and the South Kensington original. All of the (relatively few) reports say the food is still mostly good but increasingly there are caveats: "Hmmm, the steaks are getting pretty… not bad, but no longer as good value". Top Menu Tip – the "dessert theatre of tiramisu created at the table". / macellaiorc.com.

Made in Italy £58   3 2 2
249 King's Rd, SW3   020 7352 1880   6–3C
59 Northcote Rd, SW11   020 7978 7711   11–2C

"A great pit-stop on a night out" – these "busy, buzzy" rustic spots in Chelsea's King's Road and Battersea's 'Nappy Valley' major in a wide selection of sourdough pizzas, although the exact offering is slightly different at the two sites (for example pasta in SW3 but not SW11). Attractive lunch deals too. Top Tip – the 'La Terrazza' heated rooftop terrace in Chelsea is worth discovering but walk-ins only and has its own menu. / madeinitalygroup.co.uk; madeinitalylondon.

Maggie Jones's W8 £70
6 Old Court Pl   020 7937 6462   6–1A

Named for the booking pseudonym of the late Princess Margaret (who lived for many years at nearby Kensington Palace), this stalwart bistro is perennially popular for its superbly welcoming, quirky style (a kind of quaint, old-farmhouse, rustic chic) rather than its 1970s Anglo-French cuisine. A fire closed it in early 2024 – a reopening in 2025 is suggested by its website. / W8 4PL; maggie-jones.co.uk; maggiejonesrestaurant; Wed-Sat 9.30 pm.

F S A

The Maine Mayfair W1 — £116 — 3̄ 3̄ 4̄
6 Medici Court, 20 Hanover Square   020 3432 2192   3–2C
Montreal-born 'tastemaker' Joey Ghazal's no-expense-spared transformation of a 1720 Hanover Square townhouse into a sleek 350-cover American brasserie still does not generate a huge number of reports three years on from its late 2021 launch. But they are all upbeat – fans say its "NY 1960s-meets-London 1920s vibe" is a winner, with live entertainment from jazz to burlesque, a basement bar for cocktails, and a straightforward menu that takes in brunch classics, steaks, Italian-American favourites and New England-style seafood – "all done well, if at a price…" / W1S 1JY; themainemayfair.com; themainemayfair; Mon-Sun 1 am.

La Maison Ani SW1 NEW
1 Cadogan Place   0 20 7858 7250   6–1D
In the Carlton Tower Jumeirah hotel, off Sloane Street, a French-inspired all-day venue from Dubai-based British-Nigerian chef Izu Ani. The menu is built around French classics, with a burger, pizza and pasta selection to suit the international hotel clientele. / SW1X 9PY; lamaisonanilondon.com; Mon-Thu 10.30 pm, Fri & Sat 11 pm, Sun 10 pm.

Maison Bertaux W1 — £16 — 3̄ 4̄ 5̄
28 Greek St   020 7437 6007   5–2A
This "magical place" – "the best patisserie in town, magnifique!" – is a living monument to old Soho, having been founded in 1871 by a Communard exile from Paris. "Great scones, proper clotted cream, and the best cream cakes in London – still cooked on the premises" – reward visitors (but it "gets busy, and is very popular with tourists"). / W1D 5DQ; maisonbertaux.com; maison_bertaux; Mon-Sun 6 pm.

Maison François SW1 — £95 — 2̄ 3̄ 4̄
34 Duke Street St James's   020 3988 5777   3–3D
For a quick 'hit' of Parisian chic in St James's, this "comfortable" and "nicely buzzing" brasserie – with its white leather seating and artfully muted design – is just the job. Its "reliably delivered, French bistro-style dishes" are particularly recommended for an "excellent if pricey light lunch"; and especially liked for a business meal ("it's bustling, but the reasonably spaced tables and corner tables allow for an uninterrupted discussion; service is always professional and a solid wine list is managed by the knowledgeable team"). On the downside, it can also seem like a place for those who "like burning money". Top Tips – "I love every time of day at Maison François, but especially breakfast!"; "the dessert trolley is out of this world!" with "the various drawers revealing pastries of top quality". And "Frank's Bar downstairs is louche and great fun too". / SW1Y 6DF; maisonfrancois.london; maisonfrancoislondon; Mon-Sun midnight.

Makoto Sushi Bar W4 — £48 — 3̄ 3̄ 1̄
57 Turnham Green Terrace   020 8987 3180   8–2A
This "excellent small sushi bar with no frills" near Turnham Green tube may look unprepossessing, but is above par for a local Japanese café. / W4 1RP; sushi_makoto; Mon-Sat 10 pm, Sun 9 pm.

Mali Vegan Thai SW5 — £35 — 4̄ 3̄ 2̄
5 Hogarth Road   02038193507   6–2A
"Wonderful Thai food that just happens to be vegan" (claiming to offer the only such menu in the UK!) has won a strong fanclub from surrounding postcodes for this "bustling and busy" venue, in the restaurant enclave near Earl's Court tube. "Meat is not missed" even by carnivores thanks to the "interesting and really tasty selection of dishes". Top Tip – "they have an attractive outside area making it a good choice in summer". / SW5 0QT; malivegan.co.uk; Tue-Sun 08.30 pm.

F S A

Mallow £61 3️⃣2️⃣4️⃣
1 Cathedral Street, SE1   020 7846 8785   10–4C
12 Park Drive, Wood Wharf, E14   020 8050 8704   12–1C

"Light… surprising… confounding vegan food" wins little but praise for the original branch of this spin-off brand from the long-established Mildreds group: a large and "lovely space by Borough Market" that's won renown for its "innovative and delicious plant-based cuisine, served in a lively atmosphere and feeling like decent value for money too". The principal drawback is service that's "not always on the ball" ("expect to wait a long, long time at busy periods"). In June 2023, they opened in Woods Wharf too – "a welcome addition to the Mallow family, where the regular menu is reliably great and the brunch is fun too". Top Tip – the cooking is "at its best when not trying to mimic meat and fish, when it can veer off course. Small plates are the best of it and therefore it's best to approach a meal mezze style". / mallowlondon.com.

Mambow E5 NEW £60 5️⃣3️⃣2️⃣
78 Lower Clapton Road   no tel   14–1B

Singapore-born Abby Lee made this "lively" bricks-and-mortar debut in Clapton in November 2023, having established a glowing reputation for her Chinese-Malaysian cooking at pop-ups and a stint in Peckham Market. You may have to queue and "it's a laid-back setting with service likewise". But her food is the biz: "a riot of colours and great fiery flavours on your plate", with many dishes seldom seen elsewhere (which channel her Peranakan heritage and Nyonya cuisine). The signature dish is Sambal served with Calamansi Kerabu (a kind of citrus-fruit salad). / E5 0RN; mambow.co.uk; mambow_ldn; Tue-Sat 9.30 pm, Sun 2.30 pm.

Mandarin Kitchen W2 £71 3️⃣2️⃣1️⃣
14-16 Queensway   020 7727 9012   7–2C

"Just love this authentic busy Chinese!" – Since 1978, this "bustling" linchpin of Queensway has won a huge following and is a "favourite Chinese" for many Londoners. Despite its grungy, '70s-tastic interior and brusque service, it's actually known for high-quality seafood: in particular, lobster and noodles with ginger. That said, its ratings were more middling this year, on the back of some who say "the positivity this resto attracts continues to puzzle me"; or who find dishes "solid but uninspiring". Top Menu Tip – "We always eat exactly the same things: salt and pepper asparagus, lobster with ginger and spring onions, Peking duck, chicken with dry chilli and ginger… because they're so damned delicious; and fantastic value!" / W2 3RX; mandarin.kitchen; mandarinkitchenlondon; Mon-Sat 11.15 pm, Sun 23.

Mangal 1 E8 £40 5️⃣3️⃣2️⃣
10 Arcola St   020 7275 8981   14–1A

"An all-time favourite…the original Dalston Turkish grill has still got it!" – "Hungry locals, TV chefs, cash-strapped diners and famous artists all cram in and loyally dine" at this celebrated grill-house: "one of the forest of old-school Turkish joints on the Dalston/Stoke Newington strip". "It's a bright, clattering room with meats grilled to smoky perfection": "succulent, delicious and very reasonably priced, especially as you can BYO". "There's no booking: just queue up to get into this fairly cramped, jolly, caff-like place". "Despite legions of copycat establishments that have sprung up in recent years it still leads the field!" / E8 2DJ; mangal1.com; mangal_ocakbasi; Mon-Sun midnight.

Mangal 2 N16 £89 3️⃣2️⃣2️⃣
4 Stoke Newington Rd   020 7254 7888   14–1A

"Exceptionally curated, mouthwatering Turkish cuisine" – "I DREAM of the food!" – has won fooderati fame for this 30-year-old Dalston fixture, which Ferhat and Sertaç Dirik took over from their father Ali in 2020 to relaunch in a contemporary idiom. Their efforts were recognised by the publication of their first cookbook by prestige publisher Phaidon in October 2024.
/ N16 8BH; mangal2.com; mangal2restaurant; Wed-Fri, Mon & Tue, Sat 11 pm.

FSA

Manicomio £93 2|2|2
85 Duke of York Square, SW3   020 7730 3366   6–2D
6 Gutter Lane, EC2   020 7726 5010   10–2B

"While I do go to this place and enjoy it, I question whether it is good value for what it is: it's safe and reliable but couldn't be said to be top-notch" – the verdict we deliver pretty much every year on these civilised Italians in Chelsea and the City, which, so long as you are fairly cost-insensitive, provide a "smart and buzzy" environment for meeting a pal or holding an informal business lunch, with Italian cooking that's "generally well done if a little uninspired". Top Tip – cute, heated outside terrace in SW3. / manicomio.co.uk; manicomiorestaurant.

Manteca EC2 £53 3|4|4
49-51 Curtain Road   020 7033 6642   13–1B

Chris Leach and David Carter's "of-the-moment hot-spot is still packing 'em in" to this "Shoreditch icon", where "some lovely Italian dishes propel it above your ordinary Italian place": "small plates of interesting pastas, salads and exceptional meats" (the latter often "cured on the premises"). "The utilitarian seating and the too-small tables are not designed for lingering, but they are still failing to put off the hordes heading to its unlovely location in trendy old Shoreditch. Book ahead". Top Menu Tip – "the brown crab Cacio e Pepe remains one of those legendary dishes that you have to try". / EC2A 3PT; mantecarestaurant.co.uk; manteca_london; Mon-Sun 11 pm.

Manthan W1 £64 3|3|2
49 Maddox Street   020 7491 9191   3–2C

Prolific chef Rohit Ghai's Mayfair three-year-old offers dishes inspired by the home cooking he grew up with in Madhya Pradesh. There's a "very small menu" by Indian standards, but that is no bad thing. Top Menu Tip – "best ever lamb chops". / W1S 2PQ; manthanmayfair.co.uk; manthanmayfair; Tue-Sun 10 pm.

Manuel's SE19 £66 3|4|4
129 Gipsy Hill   020 86701 843   1–4D

This "local Italian" independent is a Gipsy Hill staple, excelling for "well-cooked and presented traditional dishes and interesting specials" – "everything is freshly prepared" and "good value for money". It offers regular live music nights (plus also catering, custom cakes and Sicilian olive oil). / SE19 1QS; manuelsrestaurantandbar.com; manuelsrestaurantgipsyhill; Wed-Sat, Tue 10.30 pm, Sun 9 pm.

Manzi's W1 £68 2|2|2
1 Bateman's Buildings   020 35404 546   5–2A

"Down a dodgy alleyway in Soho", this "spectacularly camp new seafood emporium is presided over by a sculpture of Poseidon with mermaids perched at the corners of the bar". Named for a "venerable" post-war fish and seafood institution that for decades operated just north of Leicester Square (to close in 2006), this "massive investment" is not a relaunch as such, but a homage to its former namesake by restaurant impresarios Jeremy King and Chris Corbin, who ironically ended up parting company with owners, The Wolseley Group, before the project's ultimate debut in June 2023. After its first year in operation, it still feels like a work in progress. To fans it's "OTT… in a good way" thanks to the "amazing decor" and a menu of "seafood heaven" ("Monkfish Wellington is an instant classic"). The verdict is split though by critics who think it's just "ludicrously opulent", "soulless" and "formulaic" ("as charming as a motorway service station, with decor that Bet Lynch would have been proud of; and overpriced food that's more 'Tesco Finest' than catch of the day"). It doesn't help that service can still be "a bit rough around the edges"; but with work it feels like this still has the potential to be a worthwhile institution in the making. / W1D 3EN; manzis.co.uk; manzissoho.

FSA RATINGS: FROM 1 POOR — 5 EXCEPTIONAL

F S A

Marceline E14 NEW
10 Water Street   020 7554 3344   12–1C

Open in late summer 2024: another huge floating pavilion at the Wood Wharf development near Canary Wharf, with a Manhattan-style French bistro from chef Robert Aikens: the identical twin of Muse's Tom, now back in London after 30 years in the US. Classic French dishes, plus a terrace and bar with a 'two-sip martini' costing £6. / E14 5GX; marceline.london; marceline.london; Thu, Sun 4.30 pm, Fri & Sat 8.30 pm.

Marcella SE8   £51   3 3 3
165a Deptford High Street   020 3903 6561   1–3D

One of Deptford's few culinary hotspots worth remembering – this white-walled café on the high street "remains an excellent option for elevated Italian dining" (certainly by local standards). The menu is short but interesting: typically a couple of pasta options and two or three main dishes with a meat, fish and veggie option. / SE8 3NU; marcella.london; marcelladeptford; Wed & Thu, Tue 9.30 pm, Fri & Sat 10 pm, Sun 4 pm.

Maremma SW2   £68   3 3 3
36 Brixton Water Lane   020 3186 4011   11–2D

An "honest and unpretentious Tuscan-focused menu" is the specialty at this "delightful Italian restaurant with a local neighbourhood vibe" near Brockwell Park (which is named after Tuscany's Maremma marshes). Its sizable fan club is more than local ("I love this place, it's always buzzing…"; "if in doubt, fall back on this cute little local for romance"). / SW2 1PE; maremmarestaurant.com; maremma_restaurant; Wed-Sat 10 pm.

Maresco W1   £81   3 3 3
45 Berwick Street   020 7439 8483   4–1C

"Heavenly seafood" adds to the appeal of this "cosy restaurant" in Soho serving "lovely tapas" (with an emphasis on fish). It's the third venue specialising in Scottish seafood presented Spanish-style (after Bar Esteban in Crouch End and Escosesa in Stoke Newington) from Glasgow-born Stephen Lironi, who switched careers after starting out as a musician in Scottish post-punk band Altered Images, alongside his wife Clare Grogan. / W1F 8SF; maresco.co.uk; maresco_soho; Mon-Sat 11 pm, Sun 4 pm.

Margot WC2   £92   3 3 4
45 Great Queen Street   020 3409 4777   5–2D

"A proper first-date venue" – this "very sophisticated" and "inviting" eight-year-old brasserie in Covent Garden "delivers on all aspects of an excellent restaurant", including highly competent cooking, professional standards and an elegant interior. Top Tip – the pre-theatre set menu is more ambitious than most. / WC2B 5AA; margotrestaurant.com; margotldn_; Tue-Sat 9.30 pm.

Mari Deli & Dining W6   £65   4 4 4
1A Eyot Gardens   020 7041 9251   8–2B

"Quirky" little Neapolitan deli on a dead cute corner near the Thames, whose tented pavement tables are a magnet for passers-by at weekends. "Okay, it's not hugely comfortable and a little crowded (it's really just a little corner shop) but who cares?" – its "traditional dishes to eat in or takeaway" (think filling pasta and creamy cakes) are very highly rated by its fans and add to its "memorable" appeal. And "they really seem to take pleasure in looking after you in just the way you want to be looked after". / W6 9TN; maridelidining.com; Mon-Sun 11 pm.

Maroush   £68   3 2 1
5 McNicol Drive, NW10   020 3941 3221   1–2A
38 Beauchamp Pl, SW3   020 7581 5434   6–1C
56 Edgware Rd, W2   020 7224 9339   7–1D

Covid-19 was not kind to Marouf & Houda Abouzaki's long-established Lebanese chain, and none of its Maroush-branded branches now survive in its original Edgware Road heartland (not counting their Ranoush and Beirut Express branches which do still operate there). Of its longstanding outlets, only Maroush II – the seasoned Beauchamp Place café/restaurant a short walk from Harrods – now remains with its dated, once-glam interior; and it's still "always consistent with the quality of the food" (although rather than the full restaurant menu, some feel "the best option is to grab a shawarma" from the sandwich selection in the café). The Abouzakis have far from given up, though, with the 2021 opening of "a very modern canteen, located in the middle of the Park Royal industrial estate", which is well-rated by those who've made the trip. / maroush.com; maroush.

Maru W1 £271 543
18 Shepherd Market   020 3637 7677   3–4B
New arrival Yasuhiro Ochiai is more present nowadays overseeing the preparation at this elegant but tiny Shepherd Market venue, founded in 2021 by chef and owner Taiji Maruyama, who himself designed many elements of the experience, down to personally making the crockery! The main event is an omakase menu that can run to 20 courses, priced at £210 per person (there's a lunch alternative at £160 per person). During the period of the handover, feedback – though more limited than we would like – has remained "exceptional all-round", and we have maintained its rating on this basis.
/ W1J 7QH; marulondon.com; maru__london; Tue-Sat 11 pm.

Marugame Udon £18 332
Branches throughout London
"High-quality udon" – Japanese wheat noodles served with a wide choice of extras, including tempura, katsu curry and various soups; plus the option of rice-based dishes – are the USP of this Kobe-based global chain which arrived in the UK three years ago and now has nine branches across London (plus one in Reading) to add to its 800+ back in Japan and further 250 globally. Be prepared to specify what you want at the counter as you enter – then you collect your cooked-to-order dish, add garnishes and find a table.
/ marugame.co.uk; marugameuk; SRA-2 stars.

Mary's W1 NEW £99
8-10 Pollen St   020 7290 7600   3–2C
In August 2024, this grill-led venue took over the Mayfair premises of Pollen Street Social (RIP) – where Jason Atherton launched his entrepreneurial career after quitting Gordon Ramsay 15 years ago. Mary's will consist of a main restaurant, with the Blind Pig cocktail bar from Soho's Social (also RIP) transferring to take over the former bar at PSS. Meanwhile, the old chef's counter will serve smash burgers to walk-ins. In an added twist, the whole operation is scheduled to close down completely from January to April 2025 for a major refurb that will see the burger bar moving downstairs into a new 'speakeasy-style' basement. / W1S INQ; Mon-Fri 7.30 pm, Sat & Sun 10 pm.

Masala Zone £65 334
244 Piccadilly, W1   020 7930 6622   4–4C
9 Marshall St, W1   020 7287 9966   4–2B
48 Floral St, WC2   020 7379 0101   5–2D
147 Earl's Court Rd, SW5   020 7373 0220   6–2A
"What a stunning location!" – the year-old operation on the huge, historical site of 'The Criterion' (built in 1873) has brought new prominence to this long-established, budget Indian street-food chain (part of the formidable MW Eats business). It dominates feedback on the group, which has soared into the Top-40 brands mentioned in our annual diners' poll: "they have created an intoxicating venue using the wonderful 19th-century decor to great effect". "All their branches are well decorated but the new restaurant is spectacular, with the gold ceiling of the old Criterion Brasserie and lots of mirrors lightening the room". "And considering its location (right on Piccadilly Circus) the price is very reasonable" ("perfect for a pre-theatre meal"). At all locations, the menu "is almost completely unlike your standard suburban

curry house and invites experimentation"; "there are many and varied street-food choices"; and "thalis are especially delicious and extremely filling". That said, diners reported a few "ordinary" meals at the chain this year – the pressure of incorporating such a demanding new site? Top Tip – "They now do breakfast! My new favourite for visitors and treating the family!"
/ masalazone.com; masalazone.

Master Wei WC1   £34   4 3 2
13 Cosmo Place   020 7209 6888   2–1D
"Gloriously textured noodles and flavoursome sauces" draw a wide-ranging crowd (including plenty of Chinese students studying nearby) to Wei Guirong's "friendly" Shaanxi canteen near Russell Square. It's a sibling to Xi'an Impression near the Emirates Stadium and the new Dream Xi'an at Tower Bridge. Top Menu Tip – "for the price you pay, the cold chicken in sesame sauce and the biang biang noodles are amazing". / WC1N 3AP; master-wei.com; @master.wei.3150; Mon-Sat 9.45 pm, Sun 9 pm.

Mauro Colagreco SW1   £155   3 4 3
The Old War Office, Whitehall   020 3907 7510   2–3C
A "very glamorous location" in Whitehall's mega-grand new OWO hotel has become home to the London outpost of French Riviera chef, Mauro Colagreco. In his October 2023 review The Evening Standard's Jimi Famurewa was mightily unimpressed at the "vertiginous madness of its prices", dubbing it "high on cost, low on laughs, you'll leave bored or broke". But our feedback – if relatively limited – is very much more upbeat with a couple of reporters' best meals of the year provided by its modern French cuisine. The setting is very restrained: all corniced ceilings, beige sofas and white table cloths. There's a three-course à la carte for £110 per person, or a five-course tasting menu at £165 per person. / SW1A 2EU; theowo.london; raffleslondon.theowo; Tue-Sat 10 pm.

Max's Sandwich Shop N4   £30   3 4 3
19 Crouch Hill   no tel   9–1D
"Is it an expensive sarnie, or cheap fine dining?!" – Either way, fans tip pundit 'sandwicher' Max Halley's Crouch Hill café for its "inventive, premium sandwiches". And it's also a "great little place that's relaxing and a bit different". / N4 4AP; maxssandwichshop.com; @lunchluncheon; Wed & Thu, Sat 11 pm, Fri midnight, Sun 6 pm.

Mayha W1   £270   3 4 4
43 Chiltern Street   020 3161 9493   2–1A
"Every dish is divine and it's so interesting sitting at the 11-seat counter watching your food being prepared" if you visit this Marylebone two-year-old focused on omakase. An offshoot of a Beirut-based group – and with a basement cocktail bar – it is unusually vibey for this genre of venture. "There are all the expected ingredients: caviar, wagyu beef, lobster and all are just exquisite; with sushi that's a work of art". One or two reports consider it "overpriced" and it's not perhaps as 'pure' as those venues run by the Japanese masters. But more representative is the view that "while you may not think the cost is a bargain, the fact that Michelin have yet to award it a star means it's not yet as expensive as other omakase restaurants that do have Michelin stars". Top Tip – you can walk in for lunch, when there's a lower-priced omakase option, or you can eat from relatively inexpensive bento boxes served in the bar. / W1U 6LS; mayhalondon.com; mayhalondon; Tue-Sat midnight.

Mazi W8   £79   4 4 4
12-14 Hillgate St   020 7229 3794   7–2B
"It feels like you're in Greece" at this "buzzy modern Greek with delicious sharing plates" in Hillgate Village off Notting Hill Gate. A huge favourite for a strong local fanclub, who hail the food as "consistently excellent… even

sophisticated". It's "small and cramped" and "can be quite noisy when very busy", but "friendly and happy service completes the holiday vibe". / W8 7SR; mazi.co.uk; mazilondon; Mon-Sun midnight.

MEATLiquor £51 3 2 2

37-38 Margaret Street, W1 020 7224 4239 3–1C
15-17 Brunswick Centre, WC1 020 3034 2136 2–1D
17 Queensway, W2 020 7229 0172 7–2C
133b Upper St, N1 020 3711 0104 9–3D
14-15 Hoxton Market, N1 020 7739 8212 13–1B
37 Lordship Lane, SE22 020 3066 0008 1–4D
7 Dartmouth Rd, SE23 020 3026 1331 1–4D
74 Northcote Road, SW11 020 7228 4777 11–2C

"Ambience is not key when you just want to stuff your face!" – you "just get a great dirty burger" at these tongue-in-cheek diners, whose signature offering is the 'Dead Hippie'. Founded 16 years ago from the back of a truck by Scott Collins and Yianni Papoutsis, at the time a technician with the English National Ballet, it now has 15 London outlets and a national delivery operation. / meatliquor.com; meatgram.

Med Salleh Kopitiam W2 £40 3 2 2

35 Inverness Terrace 020 7792 2140 7–2C

"Great Malaysian cooking at very low prices" has won a fair following for Med Pang and Koi Lee's street-food operation in the ground-floor restaurant of a hotel just off Queensway. "Although not a meat-free restaurant, there is an extensive veggie selection of Malaysian street food", plus "very good satay and roti chennai, good laksa" all "clean-tasting". "It can get very busy and a little chaotic (part of its charm?)". / W2 3JS; medsalleh.london; Mon-Thu 9.30 pm, Fri 10 pm, Sun 9 pm.

Med Salleh Viet W2 £40 3 2 2

108 Chepstow Road 020 7221 8031 7–1B

On the Bayswater/Notting Hill borders – from the Malaysian team behind nearby Med Saleh Kopitiam (see also) – a bright, no-frills Vietnamese yearling specialising in pho and grills. In The Times's March 2024 review, Giles Coren gives it the thumbs-up, but our reporters are a little more circumspect, with good-to-middling ratings and some 'off' dishes reported. For a "cheap 'n' cheerful" meal, however, it looks worth a whirl. (And in mid 2024 they added a new branch in Earl's Court in the Dreamtel Kensington). / W2 5QS; medsalleh.co.uk; Tue-Thu 9 pm, Fri & Sat 9.30 pm, Sun 3.30 pm.

Mediterraneo W11 £72 3 2 2

37 Kensington Park Rd 020 7792 3131 7–1A

Well into its third decade as a Notting Hill stalwart, this "buzzy neighbourhood Italian" provides "a friendly welcome" and "reliably consistent" if pretty "standard" cooking from a wide menu that incorporates a broad selection of pasta dishes as well as more substantial meaty and fishy options. It has two stablemates on the same street, Essenza and Osteria Basilico. / W11 2EU; mediterraneo-restaurant.co.uk; mediterraneo_nottinghill; Mon-Sun 10.30 pm.

Medlar SW10 £115 4 5 3

438 King's Rd 020 7349 1900 6–3B

"A very classy restaurant that never seems to get the praise it deserves" – David O'Connor & Joe Mercer-Nairne's "understated" feature in deepest Chelsea is nevertheless one of the Top-20 most commented-on destinations this year in our annual diners' poll. The Insta crowd are entirely absent – this is one for seasoned foodies and wine trade types and "while of more-than-local interest there is no pretension or fussiness". "There's always something of real interest on the menu" and the "terrific modern British/European dishes are served at very fair prices", in a "a quietly elegant setting" by a team that "hits all the right notes". There's "an interesting wine list to suit all *budgets, with a sommelier who looks after you"*, but *"those in-the-know take advantage of the reasonable corkage charge at both lunch and dinner"*. *"Why it doesn't have a Michelin star is incomprehensible!"* – the tyre company gave the place one after it opened in 2011, bafflingly took it away, and then seemingly have never quite been able to get over themselves to give it back. Perhaps with the opening of Cornus (see also) in Eccleston Yards (Belgravia), the tyre man will finally return the accolades this team so clearly deserves. Top Menu Tips – *"The warm chocolate mousse tart is on my last ever meal wish list"*; *"the cheese board is one of the best in London"*. The three-course lunch for £47.50, married to £15 corkage: *"what's not to like?"* / SW10 0LJ; medlarrestaurant.co.uk; medlarchelsea; Mon-Sat 10.30 pm, Sun 9.30 pm.

Megan's   £51   2 2 3
Branches throughout London
A *"buzzy"* atmosphere and *"welcoming service"* are the strong suits of this *"expanding group"*, with 16 branches in London and another handful nearby. While nobody disputes that they're *"lovely to sit in"* and offer *"value for money"*, the *"Middle-Eastern-inspired cooking"* divides opinion, with some reporters *"pleasantly surprised by the tasty food"* and others bemoaning *"underwhelming"* dishes that *"sound better than they taste"*. / megans.co.uk; megansrestaurants.

Mei Ume,
Four Seasons Hotel EC3   £170   3 3 2
10 Trinity Square   020 3297 3799   10–3D
"Well-executed Chinese and Japanese fare (if at strictly expense account-only prices)" from Singapore-born chef Peter Ho, wins consistent praise this year at this plush dining room. Part of the Four Seasons hotel in the extremely imposing former headquarters of the Port of London Authority (built in 1922), near Tower Hill, this august chamber *"very much feels like the high-end hotel restaurant that it is"*. / EC3N 4AJ; meiume.com; meiumelondon; Tue-Sat 9.30 pm.

Mele e Pere W1   £55   3 4 4
46 Brewer Street   020 7096 2096   4–3C
This *"lively family Italian restaurant in Soho"* has a *"lovely vibe"*, *"very authentic food"* and a *"brilliant vermouth bar"* ('vermuteria') serving their own, home-distilled creations. It's a modern place, founded by three brothers from northern Italy. Top Tip – *"head down to the basement for the best atmosphere"*. / W1F 9TF; meleepere.co.uk; meleeperesoho; Mon-Wed 10 pm, Thu-Sat 11 pm, Sun 9 pm.

The Melody Restaurant W14   £89   3 3 3
153 Hammersmith Road   020 8846 9119   8–2C
Something of an unexpected find on the Hammersmith Road – part of the Victorian former premises of St Paul's Boys School were converted into a hotel some years ago and incorporate this smart dining room looking onto a small park. A variety of relatively affordable menus – Sunday Lunch, Afternoon Tea, and, more recently, a steak and whisky pairing – make it a flexible venue, particularly suited to a family occasion. / W14 0QL; themelodyrestaurant.co.uk; themelodyrestaurant; Tue-Sun 11.30 pm.

The Melusine E1   £74   3 3 2
Unit K, Ivory House, St. Katharine Dock   02077022976   10–3D
This *"relaxed"* and *"rather good"* seafood specialist is *"one of the best offerings in St Katharine Dock"*, offering a *"delightful menu"* – *"we had cod cheeks and ravioli, oysters, brill and octopus followed by different and interesting ice creams"* – alongside a *"decent selection of Greek white wine"*. Co-founder Theodore Kyriakou was behind Livebait and The Real Greek in the '90s. / E1W 1AT; themelusine.co.uk; themelusine_skd; Mon-Sat 10.30 pm, Sun 9.30 pm.

Meraki W1 £92 3 3 3
80-82 Gt Titchfield St 020 7305 7686 3–1C

"Fun, vibey atmosphere and slick service" are key to the success of this upscale Greek outfit in Fitzrovia (with sister venues in Mykonos and Riyadh), which gets "loud" at busy times – perhaps "too loud". Owned by Peter Waney, brother of Arjun (Zuma, Roka), it's "not cheap, but the food is better than you'd think" – "fresh, light and modern", with "imaginative twists on every dish". / W1W 7QT; meraki-restaurant.com; merakilondon; Tue, Wed, Mon 10.30 pm, Thu-Sat 11 pm, Sun 9.30 pm.

Mercato Metropolitano SE1 £47 3 3 4
42 Newington Causeway 020 7403 0930 1–3C

"Take your pick and follow your street-food taste buds" at these "vibrant and buzzy food halls, with a huge variety of pop-up vendors". Launched 10 years ago at Milan's World Expo, the concept reached London in 2016 with the opening of the first MM in an old paper factory near Elephant & Castle; a deconsecrated Mayfair church came next, followed by Wood Wharf in Canary Wharf and then Ilford in summer 2024 – in each case fostering a "great community spirit". / SE1 6DR; mercatometropolitano.com; mercatometropolitano; Mon-Wed 11 pm, Fri & Sat 1 am, Thu midnight, Sun 10 pm.

The Mercer EC2 £84 2 3 2
34 Threadneedle St 020 7628 0001 10–2C

This "City classic" in a former banking hall near the Bank of England makes a "safe if unexciting choice for dining with 'colleagues'" or clients. "Nothing hits a high note but neither is it tuneless" – which suits its besuited business clientele just fine. There's a wide range of traditional-ish brasserie fare, with daily specials, pies, steak and British Cheeses each something of a menu feature. / EC2R 8AY; themercer.co.uk; themercerrestaurant; Mon-Fri 9.30 pm.

Le Mercury N1 £42 2 2 2
140a Upper St 020 7354 4088 9–2D

"I simply don't grasp how they keep their prices so low!" – this "insanely cheap bistro" has provided "decent" Gallic fare in a prime Islington location opposite the Almeida Theatre for 40 years. It hardly matters that the cooking is "pretty run-of-the-mill, "but you can't argue with the highly quaffable French plonk, amiable staff, and dishes that are very pleasant". / N1 1QY; lemercury.co.uk; @lemercury; Mon-Thu 11 pm, Fri & Sat 11.30 pm, Sun 10 pm.

Meson don Felipe SE1 £56 2 2 3
53 The Cut 020 7928 3237 10–4A

"Fancy? No. Value? Yes" – this bustling tapas bar directly opposite the Young Vic theatre offers "tasty, simple, quickly prepared dishes, delivered with energy and charm at a fair price". Launched in 1987, well before London's tapas boom, "it has survived for so long, it must be doing something right". ("The real joy? Absolutely packed and not a single photo being taken!"). / SE1 8LF; mesondonfelipe.com; mesondonfelipe; Mon-Sat 11 pm.

Meza Trinity Road SW17 £49 4 4 3
34 Trinity Rd 07722 111299 11–2C

"Lovely, reassuringly fresh Lebanese food" is the straightforward explanation for the popularity of this "good-value" Tooting café. / SW17 7RE; mezarestaurant.com; meza_res; Sun-Thu 11 pm, Fri & Sat 11.30 pm.

Michael Nadra NW1 £84 3 3 2
42 Gloucester Ave 020 7722 2800 9–3B

"In beautiful Primrose Hill", just by the Regent's Canal, this quirkily situated 'Restaurant, Martini Bar & Garden' showcases Michael Nadra's "really lovely" modern European food, and attracts very consistent praise from fans across north London. (His original W4 venue shut down a couple of years ago). / NW1 8JD; restaurant-michaelnadra.co.uk; michaelnadra; Wed-Sat 9.30 pm, Sun 9 pm.

F S A

Midland Grand Dining Room NW1   **£85**   2 2 4
St. Pancras Renaissance Hotel, Euston Road   020 7341 3000   9–3C
"The impressive dining room steals the show" at this "high-ceilinged" chamber – part of the vast Gothic Revival St Pancras Renaissance Hotel, but with its own separate entrance off the busy Euston Road (and "in an area full of informal and very noisy restaurants, this carpeted dining room offers a sufficiently quiet ambience for business dining"). It was well-known when Marcus Wareing ran it as The Gilbert Scott (RIP), but since he left, its pros and cons are little changed – the chief drawback is British Cuisine that "is at best assured but sometimes falls some way short of the ambition of the prices". In July 2024, after our annual diners' poll had concluded, chef Patrick Powell left the venue in the hands of Charlie Crote. / NW1 2AR; midlandgranddiningroom.com; midlandgrand; Tue-Sat, Mon 9.45 pm, Sun 4 pm.

Mignonette TW9 NEW
109 Kew Rd   020 8240 1215   1–4A
Chef John McClements, who ran the local Ma Cuisine group for three decades (and also founded the highly regarded restaurant McClements in Twickenham), has come out of retirement to launch this modern French bistro with a focus on affordability, just five minutes' walk from Richmond station on the Kew Road. On the menu – affordable meat options rather than prime cuts (such as steak tartare, stuffed pig's trotter and ox cheek bordelaise), plus daily fish specials and also vegetarian/vegan options. / TW9 2PN; Mon, Wed & Thu, Sun 10 pm, Fri & Sat 11 pm.

Mildreds   **£58**   3 3 3
128 Wilton Rd, SW1   020 8050 0164   2–4B NEW
45 Lexington St, W1   020 7494 1634   4–2C
79 St Martin's Lane, WC2   020 8066 8393   5–3B
200 Pentonville Rd, N1   020 7278 9422   9–3D
9 Jamestown Rd, NW1   020 7482 4200   9–3B
1 Dalston Square, E8   020 8017 1815   14–1A
"They succeed in making vegan food interesting!" at this successful chain, founded in Soho in 1988 and which is no longer merely veggie but since 2021 fully plant-based. "While packed and buzzy in set-up, it's nevertheless a good destination for a healthy stopover" according to the many who commented on it in this year's annual diners' poll: "as a meat-eater, I was taken under sufferance but impressed!". In May 2024, they added a new branch near Victoria coach station. / mildreds.co.uk; mildredsrestaurants.

Milk SW12   **£27**   3 2 3
20 Bedford Hill   020 8772 9085   11–2C
Fans still cross the neighbouring postcodes to brunch at this Antipodean-inspired brunch favourite, in deepest Balham (which has been a trendy local hotspot for over 10 years now). Have your phone ready to look up all the never-before-seen Asian flourishes to the dishes. Top Menu Tip – fish sando. / SW12 9RG; milk.london; milkcoffeeldn; Mon-Fri 3.30 pm, Sat & Sun 4 pm.

Milk Beach Soho W1   **£92**   3 4 3
Ilona Rose House, Manette Street   020 4599 4271   5–2A
"Aussies know how to do brekkie, that's for sure"; and this two-year-old, all-day Antipodean in Soho (the follow-up to an earlier Queen's Park venture) proves it once again. At other times of the day, the food is "not haute cuisine, but good and reasonably priced" ("I'm not a fan of sharing plates but these were well prepared"). "And full marks to maître d' Dale, who works the room like a charm!" / W1D 4AL; milkbeach.com; milkbeachlondon; Mon-Wed 11 pm, Thu-Sat midnight, Sun 4 pm.

MiMi Mei Fair W1   **£104**   3 4 4
55 Curzon Street   020 3989 7777   3–3B
Empress MiMi – keeper of the most revered Chinese culinary secrets – is the fictional inspiration for Samyukta Nair's chic, Shanghai-inspired three-year-old:

"an old converted Mayfair townhouse turned into a really charming three-storey restaurant". Feedback on its luxurious Chinese cuisine is relatively limited, but says that "every dish is spot-on". It is fully priced though, especially if you start straying into the 'signature' parts of the menu featuring lobster, caviar and Peking duck. / W1J 8PG; mimimeifair.com; mimimeifair; Mon-Sat 10.30 pm, Sun 10 pm.

Min Jiang, The Royal Garden Hotel W8 — £106 — 5 4 5
2-24 Kensington High St   020 7361 1988   6–1A

"As good as anywhere in town, never mind the views" – "amazing!"; this deluxe Chinese dining room at the top of a five-star hotel in Kensington remains an unusually impressive all-rounder. It's "best to go in daylight, because of the panoramic view of Kensington Gardens and Hyde Park" and offers "a most professional and delightful experience from start to finish". Thankfully, this includes the exceptional Chinese cuisine. "The Peking Duck, ordered in advance, is the best ever" and "dim sum is special" too: "cannot be beaten for quality or presentation!". Top Menu Tip – "you could pass over the pre-order duck and concentrate instead on working your way through other options, such as the Gong Bao king prawns with cashew nuts and chilli (brilliant) and the beef with black pepper sauce. Not to forget the delicious range of teas, which is topped up regularly". / W8 4PT; minjiang.co.uk; minjianglondon; Mon-Sun 10.30 pm.

Mistress SW1 NEW
48-49 Saint James's Street   020 3727 6997   3–3C

In the basement below Caviar House on Piccadilly, this restaurant and members' bar opened in February 2024. The mood board for the design was 'Parisian decadence' (with straplines on the website like 'The Mistress will see you now'). Decorwise, this translates into acres of plush dark-red fabrics set against white tablecloths. No survey reports yet on the Gallic-inspired sharing plates of lobster, caviar and truffle with – as the website puts it – 'a supporting cast of French fries, and oysters'. That gold leaf is felt necessary to gild some of the puddings, though, may hint at priorities that don't always put flavour first. / SW1A 1JT; Mon-Thu 11 pm, Fri & Sat midnight.

Miznon — £59 — 4 3 3
8-12 Broadwick Street, W1   no tel   4–1C
14 Elgin Crescent, W11   no tel   7–1B

"A fast, fun and casual concept, with delicious, tasty Israeli food" – Eyal Shani's outlets in Soho and Notting Hill are part of his international chain based out of Tel Aviv and serve a huge array of "top pitas" with most conceivable kinds of filling (including fish 'n' chips!) washed down with a fair drinks selection. Book for dinner, but walk-in only at lunch. / miznon.co.uk.

Mon Plaisir Restaurant WC2 — £78 — 2 2 3
19-21 Monmouth Street   020 7836 7243   5–2B

Fabio Lauro and his family – the new owners since 2022 – still have work to do in reinjecting life into this "very French" and "old-fashioned bistro", near Covent Garden, which started small after WWII and has grown into various neighbouring buildings over many years. Fans still applaud its "Gallic bistro staples served in a cosy romantic space" and claim it has "perked up on the last couple of visits" (having been in decline up to the prior owner's retirement). But while reports of "disappointing" or "less-than-mediocre" meals are in a minority, they remain too commonplace and its ratings in our annual diners' poll remain well off their past best – "such a pity, the place still has potential". / WC2H 9DD; monplaisir.co.uk; monplaisiragram; Mon-Sat 9.30 pm.

Monkey & Me W1 £45 3 2 2
114 Crawford St   020 7486 0400   2–1A
This well-regarded Thai has established itself as a stalwart local in Marylebone since it opened in 2007. "The lunch menu is particularly good value" at under £15 for two courses. / W1H 2JQ; Mon-Sun 11 pm.

Monmouth Coffee Company £7 3 4 3
27 Monmouth St, WC2   020 7232 3010   5–2B
Spa Terminus, Unit 4 Discovery Estate, SE16   020 7232 3010   12–2A
2 Park St, SE1   020 7232 3010   10–4C
"The aroma is breathtaking and you will want to linger longer than one cup", especially at the original WC2 branch of this renowned coffee chain: "a tiny, friendly place where you always share a table with someone interesting"; and with "an exceptional array of coffees from around the world". "Yes, you will likely have to queue; and no, it is not somewhere to linger with friends. But for the best coffee served by supremely knowledgeable staff in special surroundings, this is still the benchmark, with outstanding pastries too". / monmouthcoffee.co.uk; monmouthcoffee.

Morchella EC1 NEW £88 4 4 4
84 Rosebery Avenue   0207 916 0492   10–1A
"I can see what the hype is all about…"; "I just love this…"; "my new fave and can't wait to go back…"; "it's going to be huge!" – This Med-inspired Exmouth Market newcomer (on the site of Firebrand Pizza, RIP) is one of the year's better launches, and the raves in the press are matched by those in our annual diners' poll. Chef Daniel Fletcher's bold Med-inspired small plates are "extremely interesting and made with thought and care" and delivered by "friendly and efficient staff" in a "lovely high-ceilinged venue" that's been "beautifully designed". "It's worth sitting at the counter and watching the ridiculously busy pass!" Top Menu Tips – "best pudding I have eaten all year (the orange and olive pudding)". / EC1R 4QY; morchelladining.co.uk; morchelladining; Tue-Sat 10 pm, Sun 9 pm.

Morito £60 3 2 2
195 Hackney Road, E2   020 7613 0754   14–2A
32 Exmouth Mkt, EC1   020 7278 7007   10–1A
This "buzzy and enjoyable location" for "very well-executed Mediterranean small dishes" is the more casual offspring of Sam & Sam Clark's Moro next door in Exmouth Market – and now has its own spin-off in Hackney Road. The original Spanish/Moorish fusion has taken on additional influences from further afield, including Crete and the Middle East. Top Menu Tip – "good cheese fritters with Cretan honey and Cretan sausage and yoghurt with first rate flatbread". / morito.co.uk; moritotapas.

Moro EC1 £83 4 3 2
34-36 Exmouth Mkt   020 7833 8336   10–1A
"Still great even after all these years" and "still an absolute favourite" – Sam & Sam Clark's inspired stalwart helped put Exmouth Market on London's foodie map when it opened in 1997, with its "super-flavoursome" Spanish/North African food from an "ever-changing menu", all "washed down with wonderful wines" (predominantly Spanish, but also from Portugal and Lebanon) and fine selection of sherries. Fans say there's "a lovely buzz" too, but the room can be horribly "noisy"… "is it getting worse?" / EC1R 4QE; moro.co.uk; restaurantmoro; Mon-Sat 10.30 pm, Sun 3 pm.

Morso NW8 £79 3 3 2
130 Boundary Road   020 7624 7412   9–3A
In the underserved environs of Abbey Road, this modern Italian bar/café is worth remembering for its "really tasty Italian tapas-type dishes and some excellent Grappa!" / NW8 0RH; morsolondon.co.uk; morsolondon; Wed-Sun 10 pm.

Motcombs SW1 £73　223
26 Motcomb St　020 7235 6382　6–1D

"Now that the once-legendary host-patron Philip Lawless has passed, it isn't quite the same" at this old-fashioned bar/brasserie (est. 1982) in ever-posher SW1, which once epitomised 'Sloane Ranger' territory. Some of its older denizens still exude a certain "Belgravia bonkers" energy, but fans still like its "hearty" fare, best enjoyed in summer when the large pavement terrace comes into its own. / SW1X 8JU; motcombsbelgravia.com; motcombsofbelgravia; Mon-Sun 11 pm.

Mount Street Restaurant W1 £116　234
The Audley, 41-43 Mount Street　020 38409860　3–3A

This "extravagantly fabulous" two-year-old is the flagship Mayfair restaurant from Artfarm – the hospitality arm of international Swiss art dealership Hauser + Wirth – "an unusual dining room with $50 million-worth of art on the walls!". To be fair, some diners do report their meal of the year here, but the consensus view is that the rather classical cuisine (lobster pie, beef Wellington, Dover sole…) is "merely decent" – "mediocre fare for the (extremely high) price", with "little or no innovation". If you just want to ogle the art, and the cruet set inspired by American artist Paul McCarthy's 'butt-plug Christmas tree', an affordable option would be to breakfast on porridge with Durslade Farm honey for under £10. / W1K 3AH; mountstrestaurant.com; mountstrestaurant; Mon-Sat 10 pm, Sun 4.45pm.

Mountain W1 £98　434
16-18 Beak Street　020 7437 6138　4–2B

"Uniquely fabulous" is how diners describe Brat-founder Tomos Parry's Soho yearling: "an open-grill-dominated casual eatery" near the foot of Carnaby Street that its biggest fans hail as "an instant classic that's perhaps the opening of the year". The "refreshingly original menu – spider crab omelette and mutton chops anybody?" – "lives up to the hype"; there's an "especially good wine list"; and the overall vibe is "trendy but not overly so" ("huge fun, it feels like being at a great party"). Drawbacks? "Upstairs can be a bit noisy when it gets busy" and the "low-key and charming" service can sometimes be "curiously erratic". And it's really "not cheap" or, if you prefer, "so expensive!" (but very arguably "that reflects the quality and creativity of the dishes"). Top Menu Tip – mixed views on the signature Anglesey lobster: "Giles Coren made it sound amazing!" but critics say "what apparently serves up to five is lovely, but we found it barely enough for two!" / W1 9RD; mountainbeakstreet.com; mountain.restaurant; Mon-Sat 9.45 pm, Sun 8 pm.

Mr Bao SE15 £41　443
293 Rye Lane　020 7635 0325　1–4D

"Great Taiwanese bao buns", "lovely service and good cocktails" have brought success to this welcoming Peckham local (est. 2016 – now with spinoffs Daddy Bao in Tooting and Master Bao in both Stratford and Shepherd's Bush Westfields). "The menu can look a tiny bit samey, but that's a bit misleading". Top Menu Tip – "weekend brunch is superb: don't miss Taiwanese sausage with Cantonese scrambled eggs, mapo beans and hash browns on the side". / SE15 4UA; mrbao.co.uk; mrbaouk; Mon-Fri 10.45 pm, Sat 11 pm, Sun 9.45 pm.

Mr Falafel W12 £9　521
15 Uxbridge Road　07307 635548　8–1C

"All falafels are definitely not created equal", agree fans of this 25-year-old family-run spot that's "well worth seeking out in marvellous Shepherd's Bush Market" – "the freshly fried falafels and all the trimmings are eyebrow-wagglingly good!". Motto 'We Speak Falafel Fluently' – you can order the dish in various styles from around the Arab World, including the owners' native Palestine. "Arrive early to grab a table and avoid the queue". / W12 8LH; mrfalafel.co.uk; mr_falafel_london; Mon-Sat 6 pm.

F S A

Murano W1 — £138 — 4 4 5
20-22 Queen St   020 7495 1127   3–3B

"Excellent on every count!" – Angela Hartnett's elegant Mayfair HQ is strong on "understated luxury" and yet is a case of "unfussy fine dining" without the striving and pretentiousness that can go with this level of cuisine. Under chef George Ormond (in place since autumn 2023), the menu is "inventive but unmistakably Italian" and his "refined" dishes are "beautifully prepared" and all delivered by the "professional yet unfussy" staff. Perhaps because of its personable approach, it's seldom recommended by expense accounters; certainly, when it comes to the bill, it's viewed as being relatively affordable: "not cheap obviously, but quite good value for this class of place". / W1J 5PP; muranolondon.com; muranolondon; Mon-Sat 10 pm.

Muse SW1 — £220 — 3 4 4
38 Groom Place   020 3301 2903   6–1D

Tom Aikens's "intimate townhouse restaurant in Belgravia" has a "pleasant location away from the busy streets" where you eat on two floors, with some of the seating perched counter-style and with other diners sat at tables. "The concept of the menu is that it is based on Tom's upbringing" and the result of the multi-course offering is "truly world-class cuisine" with "amazing depth of flavour" all provided with "exceptional service". There is a trade-off that was more evident in feedback this year, however: it's "great… but very expensive!" / SW1X 7BA; musebytomaikens.co.uk; musebytomaikens; Tue-Sat 8 pm.

Myrtle SW10 — £90 — 4 2 2
1a Langton Street   020 7352 2411   6–3B

Anna Hough's "Chelsea gem", in a quiet backstreet near World's End, features a "carefully chosen menu highlighting counties of Ireland" that reflects her Dublin upbringing, and "her modern interpretation of traditional Irish dishes" helps "bring real character and innovation" to a small townhouse setting. Its ratings, though, slipped palpably this year on gripes about staffing and the ambience: "the service felt a little awkward and the seating is quite cramped – still, it's a nice concept and the food generally is lovely". / SW10 0JL; myrtlerestaurant.com; myrtlerestaurant; Tue-Sat 10 pm.

Napoli on the Road W4 — £40 — 3 3 3
9A Devonshire Road   020 7062 5723   8–2A

"Evolving the humble pizza into something that's much more": Michele Pascarella opened five years ago in Chiswick just off the high street in this "small, rather cramped and noisy" spot. Fans say that pizza "doesn't get better than this" and they are "imaginative" in style, with a selection that's "seasonally changing, plus classics". / W4 2EU; napoliontheroad.co.uk; Tue-Sun 10 pm.

Naughty Piglets SW2 — £58 — 4 4 3
28 Brixton Water Ln   020 7274 7796   11–2D

Celebrating its 10th anniversary this year, Margaux Aubry's "exceptional" Brixton wine bar always "does a great job in making you feel welcome" in a "tiny space". Co-founder Joe Sharratt is no longer involved, so Margaux's "great wine list" is now accompanied by cooking from a succession of guest chefs – which means "the only complaint, that the menu rarely changes", no longer holds, so now it can be more of a "regular haunt". / SW2 1PE; naughtypiglets.co.uk; naughtypiglets; Tue-Sat 9.30 pm.

Nautilus NW6 — £39 — 5 4 1
27-29 Fortune Green Rd   020 7435 2532   1–1B

Perennially one of the highest-rated chippies in our survey, this family-run shop in West Hampstead serves "the most incredible, consistent fish 'n' chips" – using "wonderful fresh fish that can be grilled" or fried in "matzo meal batter that's just lighter than other batters and tastes so good". It's a

FSA RATINGS: FROM 1 POOR — 5 EXCEPTIONAL

friendly place, too: "been eating there for many years – clients feel like a large family and regulars often meet up there". "The surroundings are much less notable than the food…" / NW6 1DU; nautilusfishandchip; Mon-Sun 10 pm.

Nessa W1 £75 3 3 2
1 Warwick Street   020 7337 7404   4–3B

"Enjoyable if not 'set-the-world-alight' food, decent service and a nice environment" sums up feedback on this two-year-old bistro-style venue, open to the public on the ground floor of stylish Soho members' club 1 Warwick. It wins most praise for a "fantastic brunch", but one or two reporters expected more from ex-Duck & Waffle chef Tom Cenci – "it's nice enough, but is in a competitive area and could be even better (and maybe it will get better)". / W1B 5LR; nessasoho.com; nessasoho; Mon-Wed midnight, Thu-Sat 1 am, Sun 6 pm.

Nest EC1 £108 4 4 3
374-378 Old Street   07769 196972   13–1B

"Creative, seasonal menus focusing on one core ingredient at a time make Nest a unique proposition" – and there's been "no let-up in quality" following the 2023 move from Hackney to "an improved and more spacious location" by Shoreditch Town Hall. "Execution and warm personal service are still bang-on" and there's an "improved wine list with some real rarities (fairly marked-up too!)" – all of which makes this "a place to return to again and again". / EC1V 9LT; nest_food/; Tue-Sat 8.30 pm.

New Loon Fung W1 £60 3 2 1
42-44 Gerrard St   020 7287 9026   5–3A

This "very buzzy and long established" Chinatown operation serves "excellent fresh classic dim sum and Cantonese favourites" in a "large" space with "traditional decor" (that more harsh reports characterise as "awful"). Despite the "sterile surroundings and matter-of-fact service, it's full of Chinese diners, which suggests the food is what it's all about". / W1D 5QG; Tue-Fri 11 pm, Sat 10.30 pm, Sun 10 pm.

Newens: The Original Maids of Honour TW9 £44 3 4 3
288 Kew Road   020 8940 2752   1–3A

"I've been coming here for at least 50 years and it's always excellent!" – these "unique and historical" 1940s tea rooms opposite Kew Gardens are a well-conserved capsule of WWII-era style that's "very touristy of course, but also very atmospheric" and "homely in feel". "It's a tradition well worth keeping up for the delicious Maids of Honour tarts" (said to derive from a recipe from the Tudor period) and other calorific treats. Top Tip – "the afternoon teas are best known, but the lunch is quite good" and "they serve great breakfasts". / TW9 3DU; theoriginalmaidsofhonour.co.uk; theoriginalmaidsofhonour; Mon-Sun 6 pm.

1905 W1 £75 3 3 4
40 Mortimer Street   020 7436 8090   3–1C

"Interesting Cretan regional dishes, enthusiastic waiting staff and a good vibe" are the salient features of this Fitzrovia two-year-old, named after the island's 1905 revolution and claiming to be the first Cretan restaurant outside Greece. There's also a "fairly priced" list of Cretan wines, many of them natural. / W1W 7RQ; 1905.london; 1905.london; Sun-Thu 11 pm, Fri & Sat 11.45 pm.

The Ninth London W1 £116 4 3 3
22 Charlotte Street   020 3019 0880   2–1C

"Lovely combinations of flavours are expertly executed" at Jun Tanaka's inviting and "buzzy" Fitzrovia restaurant, where his cuisine is consistently praised by a big fan club as "really fresh and seasonal, and very satisfying". And, especially given the high quality, a visit "doesn't break the bank" either.

F S A

Top Tip – "the incredible value set lunch is a joy for a Michelin star restaurant – please go!" / W1T 2NB; theninthlondon.com; theninthlondon; Mon-Wed 9 pm, Thu-Sat 9.30 pm.

No. Fifty Cheyne SW3 £116 3 3 5
50 Cheyne Walk   020 7376 8787   6–3C

"The prettiest of restaurants" – this atmospheric haunt off Chelsea Embankment is perfect for a "romantic evening experience", which can kick off in the cute 'Ruby Bar'; and which has beautiful river views from the upstairs 'Drawing Room'. Its owner, impresario Sally Greene, spent a reported £3 million upgrading the Georgian property from the former Cheyne Walk Brasserie five years ago, and hired Jason Atherton protégé Iain Smith to put together a grill menu of luxurious surf 'n' turf using prime British ingredients. / SW3 5LR; fiftycheyne.com; 50cheyne; Wed-Sat midnight, Sun 5.30 pm.

Noble Rot WC1 £85 3 3 3
51 Lamb's Conduit Street   020 7242 8963   2–1D

"The wine is – as always – the star attraction" at Mark Andrew & Dan Keeling's original venue, which will celebrate its 10th anniversary in 2025, and which is once again one of the Top-10 most commented-on entries in our annual diners' poll. "Wonderful passionate staff really know the wines": "the list is so long!" with select vintages listed on the "terrific blackboard, where there's always something new to explore". And the "intimate" ("slightly cramped") environment is perfectly suited to tippling – an "old school" wine bar in Bloomsbury that (previously trading for decades as 'Vats', RIP) had been completely forgotten-about before they took it over. Fans say the "robustly delicious and bold" bistro food "nearly matches up, with some really good dishes kicking around here and there". But "the bill can add up" ("those 125ml glasses don't last long"); and while there were no specific criticisms this year, ratings here in general are more middling than once they were: perhaps the strains of now running three rather than just two sites? / WC1N 3NB; noblerot.co.uk; noblerotbar; Mon-Sat 9.30 pm.

Noble Rot Mayfair W1 £63 3 4 4
5 Trebeck Street   020 7101 6770   3–4B

"Retaining its legendary predecessor's character" from when it was Boudin Blanc (RIP), Dan Keeling & Mark Andrew's latest 'Noble Rot' (opened in April 2023) continues to slot well into quaint Shepherd Market ("such a very interesting part of London"): "the interior has a lot of charm and leans into an 'old London' vibe", while still seeming "buzzy, relaxed and fun". "Wine choices take precedence over food selections: the list is well-crafted and varied, and is also well-priced (and the highly knowledgeable team know the list, and help you navigate it with excellent suggestions)". There's "a very wide choice of interesting wines by the glass too". A few diners are "disappointed, to be honest" by bistro cooking they say is "pretty unremarkable and not cheap". Most diners, though, are more upbeat, praising its "quite traditional" fare as "unfussy, but superbly executed". / W1J 7LT; noblerot.co.uk; noblerotmayfair; Mon-Sat 9.30 pm.

Noble Rot Soho W1 £79 4 5 4
2 Greek Street   020 7183 8190   5–2A

"On the site of the old Gay Hussar in Soho", Dan Keeling & Mark Andrew's "tightly spaced" drinking den has recreated the "wonderful raffish atmosphere" of its famous predecessor. In combination with the attractions of its "fabulous wine list" – "always with something new to try"; with the huge draw of "outstanding vintages by the glass"; and "presided over by knowledgeable and really friendly staff" – it "makes you nostalgic for the days of the long long lunch", especially "if a cheeky afternoon away from work can be arranged". A few critics view its culinary performance as "indifferent" to the point of being "vastly overrated", but most diners hail its "unfailingly good Anglo-French classics" as "superb food, where they manage to elevate the simple into something special". Nowadays one of the Top-40 most-mentioned locations in our annual diners' poll, its most ardent fans claim "there's no better place to eat in London", especially if you go for the "amazing value set meal". Top Menu Tips – "The Liver Pâté Choux bun nibbles are addictive"; "the roast chicken with rice and Jura vin jaune sauce is pretty good too". / W1D 4NB; noblerot.co.uk; noblerotsoho; Mon-Sat 9.30 pm.

Nobu, Metropolitan Hotel W1 £135 4 3 2
19 Old Park Lane   020 7447 4747   3–4A

"An oldie but a goodie" – Nobu Matsuhisa's first restaurant in Europe when it opened in 1997 on the first floor of a Park Lane hotel remains "a truly special place" that still offers "the same excellence after all these years". It's "expensive" (always has been), "doesn't have the best decor" (a long-running complaint), "but it hands-down serves some of the best Japanese food in London", from a menu of Nikkei-fusion dishes including the signature miso black cod that spawned a thousand imitators. / W1K 1LB; noburestaurants.com; nobuoldparklane; Mon-Fri 9.30 pm, Sat 10.30 pm, Sun 10 pm.

Nobu Portman Square W1 £125 4 4 3
22 Portman Square   020 3988 5888   2–1A

With its wizard sushi and Nikkei dishes, this Marylebone four-year-old from Nobu Matsuhisa still earns impressive ratings – a strong performance for a global restaurateur who was at the height of fashion 25 years ago, and still works 9am-11pm at the age of 75. "The specials menu in addition to the classics sets them apart from the Roka/Zuma scene" – although even fans complain about "OTT prices". The restaurant is attached to a hotel launched under the Nobu Hotel brand spun out successfully around the world in the past decade. / W1H 7BG; london-portman.nobuhotels.com; nobulondonportman; Sun-Thu 10 pm, Fri & Sat 10.30 pm.

Nobu Shoreditch EC2 £132 4 3 3
10-50 Willow St   020 3818 3790   13–1B

"Food, vibes and service are impeccable… the price is ludicrous" – situation normal then that this Shoreditch-fringe boutique hotel, whose surprisingly big subterranean Nikkei restaurant looks onto a large sunken garden. With the brand's signature sensational sushi and sashimi, plus more substantial fish and fusion dishes, it is finally emerging as some reporters' "favourite Nobu" after a slow start, which was hit by the pandemic and subsequent WFH. / EC2A 4BH; london-shoreditch.nobuhotels.com; nobulondonshoreditch; Mon-Wed 10 pm, Thu-Sat 10.30 pm.

Noci £46 3 2 3
4-6 Islington Green, N1   020 3937 5343   9–3D
Circus Road West, SW11   020 3540 8252   11–1C **NEW**
15-17 Hill Rise, TW10   020 3910 4933   1–4A **NEW**
The Bower, 211 Old Street, EC1   020 3780 0750   13–1A **NEW**

This "relatively new addition" to the capital's Italian restaurant scene "doesn't disappoint", serving "delicious homemade pasta and a good variety of starters" at the four sites it has opened in two years (Islington, Battersea Power Station, Shoreditch and, most recently, Richmond). It's the brainchild of Andy Bassadone – one of the UK's most successful restaurateurs who, for example, rolled out Côte; and it is part of the Various Eateries group owned by Hugh Osmond (of PizzaExpress and Punch Taverns fame). / nocirestaurant.co.uk.

Noizé W1 £110 4 5 4
39 Whitfield St   020 7323 1310   2–1C

"Brilliantly-executed-but-unfussy food paired with exceptional-and-well-priced wines" is winning ever-higher acclaim for master-sommelier Mathieu Germond's low-key Fitzrovian… and people already thought it was pretty cracking to start off with. Founded in 2017 after Mathieu quit Pied a Terre, it's named for the village in the Loire Valley where his grandparents ran a *farm and "for the true Francophile, it's a real find". "Mathieu is the don when it comes to affordable vintages: he will often recommend a cheaper bottle than a 'known' producer: the mark of a great somm'"; and service generally is exceptional: "delightful, knowledgeable and gracious", which contributes to the "delightfully buzzy" atmosphere. Chef George Farrugia (installed in 2021) is "cooking up a storm" at present, and numerous dishes are enthusiastically mentioned in reports: "the 'Sole Fritter' snack is probably the finest two-bite snack ever"; "the duck meatball starter which sounds a bit ordinary, is unbelievable"; "the Muscat broth will almost have you licking the bowl". "Ask Mathieu to choose a glass to go with your choices: you'll appreciate the incredible knowledge as you get a description of each one with terroir, flavours and why it matches your food. You learn so much… and get fabulous glasses of wine!" / W1T 2SF; noize-restaurant.co.uk; noize_restaurant; Wed-Fri, Tue, Sat 9.45 pm.*

NoMad London WC2 — £134 — 2 3 5
28 Bow Street 020 3906 1600 5–2D

The Atrium – a "beautiful" glass-ceilinged space in a New York-style boutique hotel carved out of the former Bow Street Magistrates' Court – is undoubtedly one of the most spectacular and "atmospheric" settings for a meal in Covent Garden. But one or two reporters feel that "they need a better menu" as the current one is "underwhelming" ("food was average with a few honourable exceptions"). / WC2E 7AH; thenomadhotel.com; thenomadhotel; Mon-Thu midnight, Fri & Sat 1 am, Sun 11 pm.

Noor Jahan — £53 — 3 4 3
2a Bina Gardens, SW5 020 7373 6522 6–2B
26 Sussex Place, W2 020 7402 2332 7–1D

"A Classic for South Ken and after all this time still the best curry house there is!" – this family-run "local favourite" has lasted over six decades and is "always jammed and lively". Service has mellowed over the years – it's quite "amusing" and "friendly" nowadays. The cooking? "Pretty standard stuff, but perfectly good and consistent". / noorjahansw5.co.uk.

Nopi W1 — £99 — 3 2 3
21-22 Warwick St 020 7494 9584 4–3B

The cuisine at influential food writer Yotam Ottolenghi's Soho flagship is – like that at his deli-diners – rooted in the flavours of the Middle East, backed up by other influences from further afield. Many guests say they "loved every minute of the experience", but so-so service helped take the gloss off a couple of meals here this year. Top Menu Tip – "the crispy mushrooms are amazing". / W1B 5NE; ottolenghi.co.uk; nopi_restaurant; Mon-Sat 10.30 pm, Sun 4 pm; SRA-2 stars.

The Norfolk Arms WC1 — £55 — 3 3 2
28 Leigh St 020 7388 3937 9–4C

"Reliable and fun" gastropub serving an "interesting range of Spanish tapas", that belies its appearance as a standard Victorian boozer in the backstreets between King's Cross and Russell Square – a useful option "in an area with limited choice at reasonable prices". / WC1H 9EP; norfolkarms.co.uk; Tue-Sat, Mon 11 pm, Sun 1 am.

Norma W1 — £94 — 3 3 3
8 Charlotte Street 0203 995 6224 2–1C

"Meals just flow from gorgeous dish to gorgeous dish" at this "comfortable" Sicillian restaurant in a Fitzrovia townhouse, which inspires nothing but praise this year. The menu is a good mix between "creative" and more familiar dishes ("excellent parmigiana and pasta for example"); and it's all washed down with "beautiful wines". The golden-hued Moorish-inspired decor verges on "lavish", with tiled floors and "nice booths", plus "outside tables that are worth it on a sunny day". / W1T 2LS; normalondon.com; norma_ldn; Mon-Sat 10.30 pm, Sun 5 pm.

Normah's W2 — £29 — 3 3 1
23-25 Queensway Market   07771 630828   7–2C

"Don't be put off by the venue!" – a very basic pitstop inside Queensway Market (itself, a bright, tacky, rambling mass of stalls on this touristy street, between the two tube stops). Run by Normah Abd Hamid, who "can usually be found in the cramped kitchen cooking your meal with love – her very special ingredient!" – and the Malaysian food at this tiny cafe is very good indeed". / W2 4QP; normahs.co.uk; normahs_place; Tue-Sat 9 pm.

Normans Cafe N19 — £29 — 3 4 3
167 Junction Road   no tel   9–1C

"Best bubble 'n' squeak in town" – this tiny, faux-traditional caff in Tufnell Park (est. 2020 as it says on the website) is the kind of greasy spoon where beans on toast comes with Red Leicester; the coffee is filter; and you can view the playlist online #caff. / N19 5PZ; normanscafe.co.uk; Normanscafelondon; Wed-Sun 3 pm.

North China W3 — £48 — 3 3 2
305 Uxbridge Rd   020 8992 9183   8–1A

The Lou family's stalwart fixture is approaching its half a century in Acton (it opened in 1976). What's sustained it over all these years? – a "consistently high standard of cooking, which combines with friendly service in a well-decorated dining room that's usually nicely buzzing". Top Menu Tip – "I've yet to have better spare ribs anywhere – including China!" / W3 9QU; northchina.co.uk; northchinafood; Tue-Sun 10.30 pm.

North Sea Fish WC1 — £53 — 4 3 2
7-8 Leigh St   020 7387 5892   9–4C

Backstreet Bloomsbury chippy known for its "very reliable battered fish 'n' chips", while the "fresh grilled fish is always superb, particularly the halibut". Run for almost half a century by two generations of the Beauchamp family, its traditional style makes this "a great place to take visitors to London". / WC1H 9EW; northseafishrestaurant.co.uk; thenorthseafish; Mon-Sat 9.30 pm.

The Northall, Corinthia London WC2 — £147 — 3 4 4
10a Northumberland Ave   020 7321 3100   2–3C

As 'plain vanilla' posh hotel brasseries go, this elegant and airy chamber near Embankment station puts in a polished performance, yet arguably flies under the radar in terms of media profile (and inspires only limited feedback in our annual diners' poll). André Garrett's cuisine is "very good" and staff are "professional and friendly". Top Tip – "excellent lunch menu" at £39 for two courses. / WC2N 5AE; corinthia.com; corinthialondon.

Notto — £63 — 3 2 2
198-200 Piccadilly, W1   020 3034 2190   3–3D
4 Henrietta Street, WC2   020 3034 2191   5–3D

"Really good pasta in the unexpected location of tourist-central Piccadilly" – and at "pretty good value for this quality" – has won numerous fans for this post-lockdown venture, which now has a second branch in equally touristy Covent Garden. Given the well PR'd involvement of Phil Howard, the kitchen genius behind The Square (long RIP) and Elystan Street, it's perhaps short on magic, but nearly all reports rate it as a good "cheap 'n' cheerful" all-rounder. / nottopastabars.com.

Novikov (Asian restaurant) W1 — £140 — 2 2 4
50a Berkeley Street   020 7399 4330   3–3C

'Blini Baron', Arkady Novikov's London outpost remains a magnet for glossy Mayfair eurotrash types, with its luxe pan-Asian menu of sushi, sushi rolls, robata, wok and hot pot dishes (there is also a completely separate Lake-Como-comes-to-London back room, serving Italian cuisine, that's never as highly commented on). It's never been a choice for anyone remotely *concerned about value. (PS. Next time you hop over to the Balearics, you can drop in on his newish spin-off at Ibiza Gran Hotel).* / W1J 8HA; novikovrestaurant.co.uk; novikovrestaurant; Mon-Sun midnight.

Numero Uno SW11 £71 2 3 2
139 Northcote Road   020 7978 5837   11–2C
A "great old-school Italian" that has provided "engaging" and stalwart service in Clapham's 'Nappy Valley' for decades, with "more than adequate food and a jolly relaxed atmosphere". / SW11 6PX; numerounorestaurant.co.uk; numerounoclapham; Mon-Sun 11 pm.

Nuovi Sapori SW6 £57 3 3 3
295 New King's Rd   020 7736 3363   11–1B
Near Parsons Green, this small and family-owned Italian, in an updated traditional style, delivers just what you'd want from a high-quality local restaurant: "better-than-average food is cooked to a high standard; staff are friendly; and it's always busy". / SW6 4RE; nuovisaporilondon.co.uk; Mon-Sat 11 pm.

Nusr-Et Steakhouse SW1 £200 1 1 1
101 Knightsbridge   01821 687738   6–1D
"Extremely disappointing all around, especially considering the price"… and that's the most favourable feedback this year! – the infamous Knightsbridge outpost of Nusret Gökçe's (Salt Bae) global empire (at the foot of a hotel near Harrods), whose famously pricey menu for prime cuts (including a Giant Tomahawk steak for £630 or baklava coated in 24-carat gold for £50) continues to inspire limited and poor feedback in our annual diners' poll. But, it still dishes up easy meat for the tabloids, with numerous 2024 stories (e.g. June 2024 in The Daily Mail: "I flew to Turkey to eat at Salt Bae's restaurant – because the flight and meal was less than the cheapest steak at his London venue"). To grab your own selfie, drop in for the relatively affordable set lunch, which prior to drinks and extras is £39 per person. / SW1X 7RN; nusr-et.com.tr; wearenusret; Mon-Sun midnight.

O'ver £73 3 4 3
1 Norris Street, St James's Market, SW1   020 7930 9664   4–4D
44-46 Southwark Street, SE1   020 7378 9933   10–4B
Forget sourdough: the magic ingredient at this Neapolitan duo in Borough and St James's is apparently pure Mediterranean seawater – whatever the formula, it results in notably tasty pizza, with a choice of Neapolitan and 'Gourmet' varieties (and there's also a short selection of other main dishes, including pasta). "Service is very good", too, and the ambience "enjoyable". / overuk.com; over_uk.

Oak £69 3 2 4
243 Goldhawk Rd, W12   020 8741 7700   8–1B
137 Westbourne Park Rd, W2   020 7221 3355   7–1B
"Thin and crispy pizza with coarse semolina in the base" is the main focus at this smart Notting Hill pub conversion, where "the tapas-style starters and excellent pizzas are rather more interesting than the main-course choices". The Oak W12 near Ravenscourt Park and the Bird in Hand at Brook Green operate on similar lines. / theoaklondon.com; theoaklondon.

Oak & Poppy NW3 £70 3 3 3
48 Rosslyn Hill   020 3479 4888   9–1A
"Very pleasing decor" adds to the vibe of this upscale, casual neighbourhood haunt, which occupies a former pub (fka The Rosslyn Arms) as you head down the hill out of Hampstead village – brunch on smashed avocado or burgers surrounded by well-healed locals under a retractable glass ceiling. / NW3 1NH; oakandpoppy.co.uk; oakandpoppyhampstead; Tue-Sat 11 pm, Sun 10.30 pm, Mon 10 pm.

FSA

Obicà Mozzarella Bar,
Pizza e Cucina £67 2|2|3
19-20 Poland St, W1   020 3327 7070   4–1C
1 West Wintergarden, 35 Bank St, E14   020 7719 1532   12–1C
Unit 4 5-7 Limeburners Lane,, EC4   020 3146 2261   10–2A
"Surprisingly decent Italian fare… proper (and huge) pizza and pasta and, if you have room, pleasing puddings" carves an ongoing niche for these smartly decorated outposts of an international Italian chain (started in 2004), where – as the name hints – many dishes feature Mozzarella di Bufala. / obica.com; obicamozzarellabar.

Oblix,
The Shard SE1 £123
31 St. Thomas Street   020 7268 6700   10–4C
Breathtaking views are a surefire attraction at Rainer Becker's 32nd-floor venue – the first to open in The Shard over 10 years ago now. There are two dining areas – 'Oblix East' for bar snacks, afternoon tea, cocktails and a short three-course menu; or 'Oblix West' for a more substantial à la carte, with steak, fish and rôtisserie chicken for sharing. We need more reports though – such feedback as we have is positive, but too limited to make for a safe recommendation. / SE1 9RY; oblixrestaurant.com; oblixrestaurant; Mon-Sun 10 pm.

Ochre WC2 £67 2|3|3
The National Gallery, Trafalgar Square   020 7747 2525   2–2C
Establishing itself in the National Gallery's "classy" – but previously habitually mediocre – dining room, off Trafalgar Square, this two-year-old is a "stylish, light and airy" spot, serving "reliably good brasserie-style fare" ("we stayed for hours and never felt pressured to leave, which is a bonus in London"). Top Tip – "the evening openings (Thursday-Saturday) are an excellent pre-theatre option in an area dominated by indifferent chains"; a single course with a glass of wine costs under £20. / WC2N 5DN; nationalgallery.org.uk; nationalgallery; Sun-Wed 6 pm, Thu-Sat 11 pm.

Ognisko Restaurant SW7 £64 3|4|5
55 Prince's Gate, Exhibition Road   020 7589 0101   6–1C
"A favourite stylish, civilised option" that's surprisingly affordable for somewhere so close to South Kensington's museums and the Royal Albert Hall – this stunning, "romantic" chamber in an émigrés club (founded in 1940) can still seem like "something of a hidden gem" although it has been extremely well-discovered for decades now (more so since Jan Woroniecki took over its management in 2015) and is "always busy and buzzing". There's "a characterful bar for aperitifs of all descriptions" and "a table outside on a summer's day is perfect" when they open a huge rear terrace adjacent to Prince's Gardens at the back. On the menu: "hearty and original Polish fare" that will not win prizes for finesse, but will for value, alongside "a brilliant selection of vodkas" and other tipples. / SW7 2PG; ogniskorestaurant.co.uk; ogniskorestaurant; Mon-Thu 11.30 pm, Fri & Sat midnight, Sun 10.30 pm.

OITA Wood Green N22 £50 4|4|3
13-27 Station Road   020 8888 0300   1–1C
"Top-notch sushi at very affordable prices" proves there is culinary life in N22 at (Chinese) chef Fan Yi's four-year-old venture – the dining option at Wood Green's 'Green Rooms' hotel. It is named for the Kyushu island prefecture of Oita: the origin of the restaurant's signature dish of chicken karaage. "This is a place you can visit frequently without breaking the bank". (There is also an – uncommented on – offshoot in Chinatown at 47 Gerrard St). / N22 6UW; oitarestaurant.com; oitarestaurant; Mon-Sun 11 pm.

FSA RATINGS: FROM 1 POOR — 5 EXCEPTIONAL

F S A

Oka £58 3 4 3
19 New Cavendish Street, W1 020 7486 4388 3–1A
Kingly Ct, W1 020 7734 3556 4–2B
251 King's Road, SW3 020 7349 8725 6–3C
11 Elgin Crescent, W11 020 7792 9064 7–1B **NEW**
71 Regents Park Rd, NW1 020 7483 2072 9–3B
88 Church Road, SW13 020 8741 8577 11–1A
"A favourite for midweek sushi" – this 12-year-old pan-Asian group from Israeli-born Ohad Kastro started in Primrose Hill and has expanded to six outlets in a series of well-heeled locations, with Barnes and Chelsea particularly commented-on. Perhaps not a choice for foodie purists, they provide a convivial setting for "an interesting and varied menu of Asian-inspired" dishes prepared to an admirably consistent standard. (One gripe – the "astonishing number of takeaway food packages collected by delivery drivers" was an irritant in a couple of reports this year). / okarestaurant.co.uk; okarestaurant.

Okan,
County Hall SE1 £45 4 3 3
Belvedere Rd 07746 025394 2–3D
"A great discovery! – Brilliant budget Japanese food is served right in the tourist hell of County Hall" at this "small and off-beat" canteen, which is "hard to find but worth searching for (just like such places in Japan)". It offers "a little slice of Osaka on London's South Bank" down to its "authentic" tastes ('Okan' apparently means Mum in Osakan dialect) and – with its "great onigiri and okonomiyaki" is a "perfect place to try Japanese food that is not sushi or the ubiquitous ramen". There are two more branches in Brixton (not listed). / SE1 7PB; okanlondon.com; Mon, Wed & Thu, Sun 10 pm, Fri & Sat 11 pm.

The Old Bull & Bush NW3 £62 2 2 4
North End Rd 020 8905 5456 9–1A
Yes, the boozer from the distantly-remembered song – a music-hall hit for Edwardian chanteuse Florrie Forde. It nowadays pitches itself as a 'country pub in the city', thanks to its leafy location, between Golders Hill Park and Hampstead Heath West: so no real change from Florrie's era, when Cockneys would visit on a day trip. The renovated tavern certainly remains an attractive destination – the menu is not particularly 'gastro' but a bit too fancy to be described as 'pub grub' (think steak or sea bass rather than burger or fish 'n' chips). / NW3 7HE; thebullandbush.co.uk; oldbullandbush; Mon-Sat 11 pm, Sun 10.30 pm.

Oliveto SW1 £81 3 2 2
61 Elizabeth Street 020 7730 0074 2–4A
"Inspirational Sardinian food" and "wonderful pizza" (with 21 different toppings) are on the menu at Mauro Sanna's smart Belgravia haunt (formerly occupied by its stablemate Olivocarne), which has a distinctive and chic (chilly?) monochrome design. There's an all-Italian wine list showcasing small producers from Sardinia. / SW1W 9PP; olivorestaurants.com; olivorestaurants; Sun-Fri 10 pm, Sat 10.30 pm.

Olivo SW1 £90 3 3 3
21 Eccleston Street 020 7730 2505 2–4B
After 35 years, Mauro Sanna's "buzzy local haunt" in Belgravia "continues to deliver excellent traditional Italian/Sardinian cuisine" to an often "packed house". For all the "high gastronomic standards and buzzy atmosphere" though, even some of its most ardent fans recognise that "it is rather expensive" (even allowing for the well-heeled nature of the locality).
/ SW1W 9LX; olivorestaurants.com; olivorestaurants; Mon-Fri 10 pm, Sat 10.30 pm.

FSA

Olivomare SW1 £95 4 3 2
10 Lower Belgrave Street   020 7730 9022   2–4B
"Superb" cooking from a "precise seafood menu" means Mauro Sanno's "busy" Sardinian spot is, to its many fans, "just perfect" – "you can go for business and pleasure". "My favourite affordable Italian restaurant" may be the claim of a regular used to Belgravia prices, but "the house wine can't be faulted at £25 a bottle". "People criticise the decor, the table spacing and noise levels but I like the vibe, and it's always busy!" / SW1W 0LJ; olivorestaurants.com; olivorestaurants; Mon-Sun 10.30 pm.

Olympic Studios SW13 £60 2 2 3
117-123 Church Road   020 8912 5170   11–1A
If you're a fan of '70s 'Dad Rock' then chances are your vinyl collection includes disks recorded at this legendary Barnes studios – nowadays converted into an indie cinema, restaurant and funky (for Barnes) members club. Foodwise, it's a "useful" all-day operation, benefiting from its prime position on the main drag of Barnes, and a wide pavement terrace that catches the summer sun. Perhaps that makes it complacent: the brasserie fare is too often mightily ordinary. / SW13 9HL; olympiccinema.co.uk; olympicstudios; Mon-Sat 9 pm, Sun 7 pm.

Olympus Fish N3 £48 3 4 2
140-144 Ballards Ln   020 8371 8666   1–1B
This family-run chippy in Finchley Central is known for its "reliable food" and is "very busy at weekends". Founded in 1998, its menu features Turkish small plates alongside a choice of fish delivered fresh from Grimsby. / N3 2PA; olympusrestaurant.co.uk; olympusfish; Mon-Sun 9.45 pm.

Oma SE1 NEW
2-4 Bedale Street   0 2081296760   10–4C
On the top floor of the Borough Market site that was Rabot 1745 (RIP), David Carter's late-spring 2024 newcomer (see also Agora) opened just in time to inspire one early report rating it very highly. The press meanwhile have gone into full-on meltdown over what The Times's Giles Coren hails as the "hands down, pants off run around screaming, slam-dunk best-of-the-year-so-far joint in central London". The carefully researched dishes from Colombian chef Jorge Paredes are, according to The Evening Standard's Jimi Famurewa "gently heretical… rather than authentic" – or as Giles puts it "Greek in spirit but Turkish, Yemeni, Italian, Lebanese, not fusion, not parodic, not taking the piss" – leading to results he hails as "genius". Top Menu Tip – the spanakopita, which leaves Coren riffing on W.H. Auden ("Cut off the telephone. Stop the dog from barking with a juicy bone") and which The Guardian's Grace Dent terms "frankly obscene". / SE1 9AL; oma.london; oma.london; Tue-Sat 10.30 pm.

Ombra E2 £64 3 4 4
1 Vyner St   020 8981 5150   14–2B
"Basic in decor and set-up, but given the delicious food and solid buzz, who cares?" – this "busy" Hackney Italian gets its swing from "staff who clearly want to be at work and have a good time"; not to mention, in summer, its superb location on Regent's Canal complete with heated terrace. The Italian food is also far from an afterthought and can be "fabulous" ("a wild mushroom squid and lardo dish was sweet, mushrooms intense with the seafood playing its part; sardine pasta and pheasant were both excellent – well-cooked, well-balanced, well-seasoned and with great little touches").
/ E2 9DG; ombrabar.restaurant; ombrabar.restaurant; Mon, Thu-Sat 10 pm, Sun 3 pm.

Omni SE15 £65 3 4 3
24a, Peckham Rye   020 7450 6347   1–4D
"No omni-shambles here!" – "just creative vegan tasting menus at a staggeringly affordable price". This three-year-old in Peckham Rye offers an "ever-changing, seasonal small-plates menu at prices representing amazing

value" – "some dishes are a hit, others a bit meh, but there's no faulting the ambition, the intent or the general likeability of the place". / SE15 4JR; theomnicollective.com; theomnicollective; Tue-Sat 11 pm.

108 Brasserie W1 £82 2 3 2
108 Marylebone Lane   020 7969 3900   2–1A

"They know what they are doing" at this comfortable hotel brasserie, well-located with a covered terrace on Marylebone Lane. Even its harshest critic – who finds the menu "pretty standard if uninteresting" – says that it suits "a functional business lunch". But most reports are more upbeat – "there's nothing to 'frighten the horses' but what they do, they do well. A place to come and please everyone and be able to have a proper conversation. Hooray!" / W1U 2QE; 108brasserie.com; 108marylebonelane; Mon-Sat midnight, Sun 9.30 pm.

104 Restaurant W2 £190 5 4 4
104 Chepstow Road   020 3417 4744   7–1B

"Food with outstanding provenance and in generous portions" delivered with service that's "friendly and professional" wins ongoing praise from a small but dedicated fan club of Richard Wilkins's small corner-restaurant on the border between Notting Hill and Bayswater (which seats 16 at maximum capacity). The restaurant's website recommends that you allow three hours for its 'carte blanche tasting menu'. / W2 5QS; 104restaurant.com; 104restaurant; Wed-Sun 9.30 pm.

1 Lombard Street EC3 £96 2 4 4
1 Lombard St   020 7929 6611   10–3C

"The original of the City's high-quality restaurants" – ex-Goldman banker, Soren Jessen's venture in a converted banking hall near the Bank of England "is still going strong" and recently celebrated its 25th anniversary. A linchpin of business entertaining in the Square Mile, "the large dining room is well-equipped for both discreet business meetings or more lively get-togethers" and "very good front-of-house staff recognise when deals are being done": "they can get you in and out in an hour". "The menu is broad but appropriate for the besuited clientele, with a mix of traditional British dishes and a hint of European cuisines". "It is not going to be a gastronomic knockout, but that's not what you go for: it's decent high- quality food at decent-but-not-astronomical prices". Top Tip – also a "great venue for breakfast". / EC3V 9AA; 1lombardstreet.com; 1lombardstreet; Mon-Fri 11 pm.

123V W1 £65 3 3 2
39 Brook St   020 7494 3111   3–2B

"The vegan sushi is wonderful, fresh and inventive" at this Mayfair outlet, which is a spin-off brand for plant-based evangelist chef Alex Gauthier, who runs the celebrated Gauthier (see also) in Soho. Following the closure of Fenwick's department store – he has moved it to the tucked-away nearby site vacated by Native at Browns (which itself has moved out of London, to Worcestershire). 123V's menu used to be wider than just sushi, but has narrowed its focus to the Japanese-inspired plates that were everybody's fave – even among omnivores. Top Tip – the new site has a gorgeous courtyard, which comes into its own in the summer months. / W1K 4JE; 123vegan.co.uk; 123vegan_w1; Tue-Sat 11 pm, Mon 6 pm.

Les 110 de Taillevent W1 £99 3 4 3
16 Cavendish Square   020 3141 6016   3–1B

"A truly epic wine list" (almost 2,000 bins), "with virtually all options available by the glass" – and including some "lovely, mature vintages" – is the special appeal of this Parisian import, which occupies a traditionally smart corner-site in Fitzrovia, across the square from the back of John Lewis. The modern French cuisine that provides a foil to the wine is in a fairly conventional mould but consistently well-rated. / W1G 9DD; les-110-taillevent-london.com; 110london; Mon-Sat 10.30 pm.

F S A

Opera Tavern WC2   £66   3 2 3
23 Catherine Street   020 7836 3680   5–3D

"Keeping up its standards" – this "sweet" and stylish converted pub near the Royal Opera House operates over two floors. It's part of the Salt Yard chain, and serves the Spanish and Italian tapas for which the group is known: "good food", but some feel it's "expensive" for what it is. / WC2B 5JS; saltyardgroup.co.uk; operatavernldn; Mon & Tue 10 pm, Wed-Sat 11 pm, Sun 8 pm.

Opso W1   £109   3 3 2
10 Paddington St   020 7487 5088   2–1A

"Modern Greek cuisine with a twist" earns consistently strong ratings for this 10-year-old in Marylebone, which is "definitely a cut above the traditional taverna". Sibling to the more casual INO in Soho, it's from the accomplished team behind well-known Funky Gourmet in Athens. / W1U 5QL; opso.co.uk; opso_london; Mon-Fri 11.30 pm, Sat 10.30 pm, Sun 10 pm.

Orange Pekoe SW13   £41   3 3 3
3 White Hart Ln   020 8876 6070   11–1A

"More than a café" – although it functions as a "great local coffee spot" – this Barnes institution is "a delightful sanctuary for tea lovers, with a superb variety of teas from around the globe". "Treat yourself to their classic afternoon tea, complete with delicate sandwiches, scones and a selection of teas. It's a quintessentially British experience" without the expense of a West End hotel (but you will still have to book). / SW13 0PX; orangepekoeteas.com; orangepekoeteas; Mon-Sun 5 pm.

The Orange Tree N20   £68   2 2 3
7 Totteridge Village   020 8343 7031   1–1B

This "large, well-decorated gastropub" overlooking the village pond in Totteridge, on London's northern fringe, serves a broad menu that majors in steaks, burgers, seafood and pizza. The odd blip is noted in reports foodwise, but it's nominated by a number of locals as their top pub. / N20 8NX; theorangetreetotteridge.co.uk; Mon-Sat 11 pm, Sun 10 pm.

ORANJ E1   £55   3 2 4
14 Bacon Street   no tel   13–1C

Just around the corner from Brick Lane, this "buzzy Shoreditch dining room" in a 2000 sq ft Victorian warehouse is "always showcasing a fab chef" (from the UK, but also further afield) with "residencies of one-week to two-months duration". "It's usually packed with yoof enjoying themselves and one of the new wave of food and natural wine places that the press are always writing about". / E1 6LF; oranj.co.uk; Tue-Sat 11.30 pm.

Orasay W11   £64   4 3 4
31 Kensington Park Road   020 7043 1400   7–1A

"Jackson Boxer's superlative Notting Hill bolthole continues to stun" its fans with an "ever-evolving menu" of "delicious", seafood-inspired dishes "evoking the rugged spirit of the Hebrides". Now five years old, it's a thoughtfully designed space, with a mixture of surfaces creating an urbane ambience that suits the neighbourhood. But while most reports say "there's never a dud dish to be seen", its ratings slipped a fraction this year on the odd surprisingly dire experience. Perhaps just a blip? Top Menu Tip – "the scallop with vin jaune, if you're lucky enough to find it on the menu, is absolutely not to be missed!" / W11 2EU; orasay.london; orasay.london; Tue, Wed, Fri & Sat, Thu 10 pm.

Oren E8   £77   4 3 2
89 Shacklewell Lane   020 7916 6114   14–1A

"An interesting menu with excellent cooking" wins fans for Oden Oren's small Eastern Mediterranean bistro in Dalston, although some reports argue that "he needs to do something about the acoustics". Since 2023, he's also run a deli near London Fields. / E8 2EB; orenlondon.com; orenlondon; Tue-Sat 11 pm, Sun 7 pm.

FSA

Orient London W1 £60 4 3 2
15 Wardour Street   020 7989 8880   5–3A
"Great dim sum" backed up by more substantial Cantonese and Sichuan dishes have established this unshowy venue as one of the area's best bets. It's easy to find: it's right by the archway at the entrance to Chinatown! / W1D 6PH; orientlondon.com; orientlondon; Sun-Thu 11 pm, Fri & Sat 11.30 pm.

Origin City EC1 £110 4 3 3
12 West Smithfield   020 4568 6240   10–2A
"Sourcing from their 600-acre estate in Argyll and fish farm in Loch Fyne", the Landsberg family have – with this "traditional-in-a-good-way" Smithfield yearling – "created a restaurant that serves a Best of British menu that is, generally, a roaring success". "Sustainably sourced food is expertly cooked" and "while it emphasises nose-to-tail cooking, it does so in a much more restrained manner than nearby St John". "There's an interesting short wine list (including from their own vineyard in Provence) at quite modest mark-ups, particularly for the City". "Coupled with friendly service, the result is awesome!". Top Menu Tips – "Black Pig, Rabbit, Duck and Foie Gras terrine, which draw together its various meat components into one delightful whole"; also "a very good Clam & Mussel Chowder, quite a refined Morteau Sausage with well-flavoured Puy lentils; and first-rate faggots in an intense jus". / EC1A 9JR; origincity.co.uk; origincity.co.uk; Mon-Sun 9 pm.

**Ormer Mayfair by Sofian,
Flemings Mayfair Hotel W1** £152 4 4 4
7-12 Half Moon Street   020 7016 5601   3–4B
"Well worth a visit" – this "sympathetically restored" Mayfair hotel is originally Victorian (from the 1850s), although the wood panelling and square cornices of this basement dining room owe their looks to the 1930s. It continues to perform extremely consistently under chef Sofian Mstefi, who provides a seven-course menu for £122 per person (and there's also a five-course option for £85 per person served Tuesday-Friday). We received nothing but all-round praise this year, with it winning nominations as both a business and romantic venue; and with many reporters enjoying their best meals of the year here. / W1J 7BH; flemings-mayfair.co.uk; flemingsmayfair; Tue-Sat 9 pm, Sun 12 pm.

Oro Di Napoli W5 £45 4 3 3
6 The Quadrant, Little Ealing Lane   020 3632 5580   1–3A
"Worth a detour" – "some of the best pizza outside Italy" is found at this "excellent Neapolitan pizzeria", "run by an Italian family in an unlikely suburban location" in Ealing. "The barman makes a mean negroni to get the evening off to a great start". / W5 4EE; lorodinapoli-ealing.com; lorodinapoliealing; Mon-Sun 10.15 pm.

Orrery W1 £104 3 3 4
55 Marylebone High St   020 7616 8000   2–1A
"I love it!" say fans of this stalwart of Marylebone dining, set on the first floor of a former stables overlooking St Marylebone churchyard; and with a "lovely rooftop terrace for hot weather". Opened in 1997 by the late Terence Conran and now part of D&D London, its accomplished modern French cuisine delivered a couple of best meals of the year in our current annual diners' poll, and is generally judged as very "reliable" (especially by the standards of the group). / W1U 5RB; orrery-restaurant.co.uk; the_orrery; Sun-Wed 9 pm, Thu & Fri 10 pm, Sat 2.30 pm; SRA-3 stars.

Oscar Wilde Lounge at Café Royal W1 £104 3 3 5
68 Regent St   020 7406 3333   4–4C
"London at its most decadent" – this is one of the capital's top afternoon teas in the Café Royal's stunning rococo grill room (dating from 1865): "an opulent chamber packed with history, as well as mirrors so you can see everyone else!" (not to mention endless nymphs and cherubs painted all over

F S A

the ceilings). It's *"a traditional afternoon tea and all the better for it – a great selection of really fresh sandwiches, followed by scones (with the best strawberry jam ever) and, if you still have room, the patisserie options (and if you don't have room, don't worry as they will pack it up beautifully for you to take home). And to wash it all down, there is a tea menu and you can choose as many different teas as you would like to try. And you are helped through it all by charming and knowledgeable staff. A delight"*. / W1B 4DY; hotelcaferoyal.com; hotelcaferoyal; Wed-Sun 5.30 pm.

Oslo Court NW8 £80 3 4 4
Charlbert Street   020 7722 8795   9–3A

"Oslo Court is one of a kind" and *"still going strong after 40 years"* at the foot of an apartment block north of Regent's Park. *"Old School in the extreme"*, it's a *"classic that never goes out of fashion"*… at least if your idea of 'classic' is drawn from the era of the mid-1970s. *"From the peach tablecloths to the generous servings of melba toast, butter curls and crudités, it's like going back in time… in a good way. Staff make you feel very special, the whole experience is warm and fun and the classic cooking is great"*, so long as you are looking for the antithesis of modern food fashion. *"The menu is incredibly large and there's a long list of specials too"* (remember Avocado & Prawns? Or Melon with Parma Ham? Dover Sole Véronique?). *"Bring an appetite"* as *"portions are excellent"*. Also, go in festive mood: seemingly everyone over the age of 80 in north London is there to celebrate an occasion (*"I lost count of how many times Happy Birthday was sung at lunch last Saturday."*). Top Tip – *"the waiter who has been there years still serves the best desserts"*. / NW8 7EN; oslocourtrestaurant.co.uk; oslocourt; Mon-Sat 11 pm.

Osteria Antica Bologna SW11 £69 3 3 2
23 Northcote Rd   020 7978 4771   11–2C

This *"long-standing local"* is a fixture of Clapham's 'Nappy Valley', serving rustic Italian dishes for more than 30 years. A typical report: *"recently returned for the first time in decades. Why did we wait so long? Food is excellent, service friendly and efficient, and prices very reasonable by London standards. My wife's veal cutlet was the largest, tenderest and tastiest I have ever tried and my pasta with wild boar ragu was superb. We won't be waiting nearly so long again!"* / SW11 1NG; osteria.co.uk; osteriaanticabologna; Tue-Fri 21.45 pm, Sat 10 pm, Sun 3.30 pm.

Osteria Basilico W11 £79 3 4 3
29 Kensington Park Rd   020 7727 9957   7–1A

This *"old-school"* Notting Hill Italian has been *"a great crowd-pleaser for the whole family"* for more than 30 years. According to one local: *"you will not have a great meal but on the other hand I've never had a bad one"* – as a result it can be *"extremely busy, but the service is great"* and keeps on top of things. Essenza and Mediterraneo in the same street (see also) are its younger stablemates. / W11 2EU; osteriabasilico.co.uk; osteriabasilico; Mon-Sun 10.30 pm.

Osteria Tufo N4 £66 3 3 3
67 Fonthill Rd   020 7272 2911   9–1D

This *"amazing little neighbourhood gem"* is a Finsbury Park fixture, serving *"100% authentic southern Italian cooking"*. *"The surroundings may not be glamorous but the food is very well prepared and authentic"*, and service under owner Paola is *"always friendly"*. / N4 3HZ; osteriatufo.co.uk; osteriatufo; Tue, Thu-Sat, Wed 10.30 pm, Sun 9 pm, Mon 10 pm.

Otto's WC1 £107 5 5 4
182 Gray's Inn Road   020 7713 0107   2–1D

"Old-fashioned? Yes. Expensive? Yes. But Gorgeous!" – Otto Tepasse's *"charming and theatrical"* bastion of classical cuisine near Gray's Inn showcases *"fabulous French food"*, most famously its signature duck or lobster pressed at your table. The cuisine is *"very rich"* by today's standards,

and "not at all your everyday haute cuisine" – but "melt-in-the-mouth gorgeous" and the venue's "great retro feel with its own character" means a visit is always special. Although the restaurant has been open since 2011 (and featured in this guide for years), a recent flurry of critical attention has brought Giles Coren from The Times and a gaggle from the Evening Standard to test themselves against the 'Grande Bouffe' blowout menu. Top Menu Tips – as well as the famous à la presse dishes, "Duck Pie – so ducky!" / WC1X 8EW; ottos-restaurant.com; ottos_restaurant; Wed-Fri, Tue, Sat 10 pm.

Ottolenghi £71 3|3|3
28 Pavilion Road, SW1   020 3824 2818   6–2D
63 Marylebone Lane, W1   020 3148 1040   2–1A
63 Ledbury Rd, W11   020 7727 1121   7–1B
287 Upper St, N1   020 7288 1454   9–2D
32-34 Rosslyn Hill, NW3   020 3761 6960   9–2A **NEW**
50 Artillery Pas, E1   020 7247 1999   10–2D

"Go mad for further adventures in veg" at Yotam Ottolenghi's famous deli-cafés, whose Middle Eastern inspired menus are best known for their "creative" salads and meat-free dishes (bread and pastries are also "fabulous") but there are also some meat and fish options. They are far from cheap, but "the spicing is interesting", "the flavours are immense" and "the small-plates format allows you to try a number of options". "A great spot for brunch" or "to drop in for cake and tea". The Islington branch is most commented-on, and in December 2023 its newest sibling (also in north London) opened on Rosslyn Hill, Hampstead, while a branch in Richmond, in the leafy southwest, is scheduled for late 2024. / ottolenghi.co.uk; ottolenghi; SRA-2 stars.

Oxo Tower, Restaurant SE1 £113 1|1|2
Barge House St   020 7803 3888   10–3A

"OK, but I have always thought it too expensive" is sadly one of the more enthusiastic reports we received this year on this South Bank landmark, whose "great views" over the Thames and St Paul's are less of a rarity than when it first launched in 1996 with the opening of so many rooftops nowadays. Over three-quarters of feedback here are nominations for either 'most overpriced' or 'most disappointing' meal of the year in our annual diners' poll. The modern British menu is too often judged "expensive and tasteless", which it shouldn't be when a bowl of chips costs £9. "It's so disappointing because its great views and location should make it a fantastic restaurant". "A tourist trap if ever I've seen one". / SE1 9PH; oxotowerrestaurant.com; oxo_tower; Mon-Sun 9.30 pm; SRA-3 stars.

Oxo Tower, Brasserie SE1 £96 1|2|3
Barge House St   020 7803 3888   10–3A

"A most enjoyable meal in an attractive setting" is reported by just over half of reporters visiting the cheaper section of this rooftop landmark on the South Bank. The remainder, though, "expect much, much better at these prices": "it has a great view but very disappointing food and service – trading off its location!" / SE1 9PH; oxotowerrestaurant.co.uk; oxo_tower; Mon-Sun 9.30 pm; SRA-3 stars.

The Oystermen Seafood Kitchen & Bar WC2 £80 4|3|2
32 Henrietta St   020 7240 4417   5–3D

"Our favourite seafood place in central London", chorus the many fans of this appropriately named outfit "in the touristic area of Covent Garden" – "I love this place for the location, the energy and the super-fresh dishes" ("there's no greater fun than wrestling with a crab" here or the oysters and lobster!). "Attentive staff" and a "lively, unpretentious atmosphere" are part of the appeal, and the "quick service helps if you're on the way to the theatre". Any negatives? It "may be a bit cramped", with an "interior that's a bit stark for some". / WC2E 8NA; oystermen.co.uk; theoystermen; Tue-Sat, Mon 10 pm, Sun 9 pm.

Pachamama £78 3 4 3
18 Thayer Street, W1   020 7935 9393   3–1A
73 Great Eastern Street, EC2   020 7846 9595   13–1B
This 10-year-old Marylebone spot (with an offshoot in Shoreditch) provides a "great introduction to delicious Peruvian food" – ceviches, plus mains from 'land', 'sea' or 'soil' – with "attentive and friendly staff" on hand to advise. Top Menu Tip – "the sticky aubergine is incredible". / pachamamalondon.com; pachamamalondon.

Padella £45 5 3 4
6 Southwark St, SE1   no tel   10–4C
1 Phipp Street, EC2   no tel
"No-one, and I mean no-one who I've taken here, has ever said a bad word; and moreover, many have returned separately. It's my No. 1 'go-to' for casual dining with friends, whose subsequent advocacy says it all!" – Tim Siadatan and Jordan Frieda struck gold with this "constantly busy" duo of superior pasta pitstops, which are rightly famous on social media and one of London's ultimate cheap eats. They offer "the best fresh pasta" (which you can watch being made through the windows from early morning on) "at great value prices, which is why they are sooo popular: why you must book well in advance in EC2" or expect to queue in SE1 ("which operates an effective virtual queuing system"). / /padella_pasta.

Pahli Hill Bandra Bhai W1 £86 4 3 3
79-81 Mortimer Street   020 8130 0101   3–1C
"It needs to be talked about way more", say fans of this high-quality Indian venture near Selfridges – the first London outpost of New Delhi's Azure Hospitality (and named for one of Mumbai's posher 'burbs). Head chef, Avinash Shashidhara "spent 10 years at the River Café and the quality of cooking shows through with some of the tastiest Indian food you can imagine": "mind-blowing" flavours and "spot-on spicing that's perfectly balanced and in no way overpowering". Top Menu Tip – "food from the tandoor is a highlight". / W1W 7SJ; pahlihillbandrabhai.com; pahlihillbandrabhaiuk; Mon-Sat 10 pm.

Paladar SE1 £71 3 4 4
4-5 London Road   020 7186 5555   10–4A
"It's like a big party!", say fans of this "fun" Latino haunt – a hidden gem off the beaten track near Elephant & Castle (on St George's Circus). "I never expected such a lively place to have such high-quality cuisine, superb cocktails and an extraordinary South American wine list": chef Jose Rubio-Guevara's menus 'mix-and-match' culinary ideas from Colombia, Ecuador, Mexico and Peru. / SE1 6JZ; paladarlondon.com; paladarlondon; Tue-Fri 9.45 pm, Mon 9 pm, Sat 10 pm, Sun 8 pm.

Palm Court Brasserie WC2 £65 2 2 3
39 King St   020 7240 2939   5–3C
"Busy… touristy… but capable, in a neighbourhood where most restaurants (including for a pre-theatre meal) are well underperforming": this "long-established brasserie next to the Covent Garden piazza" is decorated in an engaging, traditional Parisian style and won a strong thumbs-up this year as one of the best bets in the surrounding tourist hell. "The food is reliable and fairly priced, especially if you can get a deal (which is not difficult)". "Always use this place for coffee. Love it, and seriously good snacks". / WC2E 8JS; palmcourtbrasserie.co.uk; Mon-Sun 10 pm.

FSA

The Palomar W1 — £82 — 4 3 3
34 Rupert Street   020 7439 8777   4–3D

"Simple and yet so exciting" – Zoë & Layo Paskin's "friendly" Tel Aviv-inspired grill on the edge of Chinatown is celebrating a decade in business, and fans say it's "still good after all these years". The "consistently excellent" Middle Eastern plates "look straightforward but are prepared with real care and finesse"; and there's a "great atmosphere, especially if you sit at the bar (I love everything about this place!)". However, even fans sometimes note that "prices have risen" over the years; and there are a few reporters who are "worried it might be becoming a victim of its own success: the food is still delicious but it's so busy it can feel a bit stressful". / W1D 6DN; thepalomar.co.uk; palomarsoho; Mon-Wed 10 pm, Thu-Sat 10.30 pm, Sun 9 pm.

La Palombe W8 NEW — £78
267 Kensington High Street   0207 602 6777   8–1D

James Chiavarini, owner of long-established Italian Il Portico a few doors along, keeps relaunching this Kensington-fringe site: it was Pizzicotto, then Pino… now this Basque- inspired bistro, incorporating game and funghi cooked over a wood-fire grill. It's up for debate as to whether this latest incarnation has cracked it: on the plus side, Charlotte Ivers in The Sunday Times found "a joyful mix" of food and wine; but on the minuses, initial feedback in our annual diners' poll includes a couple of "poor all round" reports: "nothing to tempt us on the menu". / W8 6NA; lapalombe.co.uk; Tue-Sat 10.30 pm, Sun 4 pm.

Paper Moon, The OWO SW1 — £125 — 2 3 4
Whitehall   020 3907 7500   2–3C

A chamber in the vast new Raffles Hotel provides an elegant and stately home to this offshoot of a luxe Italian chain (with siblings as far flung as Hong Kong, Bodrum and Doha). It's rated on limited and mixed feedback – fans say it's "a great addition to London's dining scene: a wonderful concept with a mix of fine dining, relaxed atmosphere and very good service". Others, though that – notwithstanding "very good service and ambience" – it's notably "overpriced" in terms of what arrives on the plate. / SW1A 2EU; papermoonrestaurants.com; Sun-Wed 10.30 pm, Thu-Sat 11 pm.

Papi E8 — £61 — 4 3 3
1f Mentmore Terrace   07405099952   14–2B

"Nobody else is serving food like this in London" ("it's very different – that's why I've eaten there six times…"), say fans of this hip yearling in London Fields from 'Hot 4 You' delivery service chef Matthew Scott, whose forte is "innovative dishes you think won't work… but they do!".. Charlie Carr's natural wine list incorporates arguably "London's best selection of orange wines". / E8 3PN; papirestaurant.com; papi.restaurant; Wed & Thu, Sun 10 pm, Fri & Sat 10.30 pm.

Paradise W1 — £70 — 3 3 2
61 Rupert Street   no tel   4–2D

"The powerful flavours of Sri Lankan cuisine" are "tweaked and twisted by an inventive kitchen" at London-born Dom Fernando's Soho venture, combining British ingredients with flavours from his family heritage. "Last visit they seem to have departed even further from Sri Lankan classics with their creations, but still never taking their foot off the flavour pedal". / W1D 7PW; paradisesoho.com; paradisesoho; Tue-Sat 11 pm.

Paradise Hampstead NW3 — £40 — 3 4 2
49 South End Rd   020 7794 6314   9–2A

"We keep going back for more!" – this "lovely local Indian" has pleased the Hampstead crowd for more than 50 years with its "food to suit all tastes",

FSA

"good value" and "charismatic owner (the son of the founder) who carries the service". No wonder it's "often packed". / NW3 2QB; paradisehampstead.co.uk; Mon-Sat 10 pm.

The Parakeet NW5 £73 4 4 4
256 Kentish Town Road   020 4599 6302   9–2C

"A fantastic new opening" in Kentish Town – "very noisy pub at the front, but as soon as you're through the curtains it feels like a secret and rather louche party, with epic food". It might "look like a gastropub" (it was previously a Victorian boozer, The Oxford Tavern), "but the cooking is high-class restaurant level, albeit you have to be a fan of fire-and-flame cuisine" – from ex-Brat chefs Ben Allen and Ed Jennings. All in all "a winner" – "always busy, permanently buzzing, with great staff who keep things moving well". Top Menu Tips – "Spider crab croquettes, grilled prawns in brown butter, melting pork chop, gamey rabbit chou farci". / NW5 2EN; theparakeetpub.com; Mon-Sat midnight, Sun 10.30 pm.

The Park W2 £79 3 4 5
123 Bayswater Road   020 3959 9000   7–2C

The sophistication of Manhattan's Midtown and Upper East Side was the style-guide for Jeremy King's fit-out of this prominent new Bayswater site: on the corner of Queensway facing Kensington Gardens. With its big windows, wood-lined walls, ever-so-flattering lighting and maroon leather banquettes, it's a very handsome space that could certainly hold its head up high on Park Avenue. It opened in mid 2024 soon after his re-launch of Arlington (see also), and was already into a majorly impressive stride on a first-week visit by your editor (with Jeremy himself, immaculately tailored as always, taking personal care that the service ticks along). As at all King's places, the food underpins the occasion: it's not, itself, the occasion. Here a long all-day menu (with another dedicated to breakfast) jumbles up comfort food treats with a vaguely US spin – pastas, salads, sandwiches… even hot dogs and ice cream sundaes – alongside (slightly) more crafted dishes such as Chicken Milanese or Ham Hock Pie. Yummy… but won't distract you too much from your conversation. (Rated on editor's visit, not our annual diners' poll.) / W2 3JH; theparkrestaurant.com; Mon-Sun 1 am.

Park Chinois W1 £171 2 2 3
17 Berkeley Street   020 3327 8888   3–3C

This glossy Mayfair venue modelled on 'the supper clubs of 1930s Shanghai' "has a real buzz" with "wonderful singers and a band to add to a great night". But while some diners feel the food is outstanding, ratings are undercut by the view that it's "middle-of-the-road Chinese that's well executed but nothing special and soured by the bill". / W1S 4NF; parkchinois.com; parkchinois; Tue-Thu, Sun midnight, Fri & Sat 2 am.

Parlour Kensal NW10 £71 4 4 4
5 Regent St   020 8969 2184   1–2B

Run by chef-patron, Jesse Dunford Wood for over 12 years now: "the menu is consistently interesting, beautifully prepared and delicious at this family-run gastropub" in Kensal Rise. Top Tip – "one of the best Sunday lunches in London, but don't just visit on Sundays…" / NW10 5LG; parlourkensal.com; parlouruk; Mon-Sun 10 pm.

Parrillan £124 2 2 4
Coal Drops Yard, N1   020 7018 3339   9–3C
Borough Yards, 4 Dirty Lane, SE1   no tel   10–4C

"A fun way to share and eat for a small group" – you BBQ your own meal at your table at the Hart Bros' duo of Hispanic haunts in Borough Yards and Coal Drops Yard, which take their inspiration from the Spanish 'parrilla' or grill. You can also eat more conventionally in SE1, allowing the chefs to do the work for you, and since it opened in 2022 this has become the more highly rated branch. In N1, there's the benefit of a large outside terrace "set under *cover outside, but with overhead heaters and heated cushions so you don't feel cold". You might feel the chill when the bill arrives though, especially at the N1 original ("the menu looked good and the food was fine, but all I could think of was how expensive it was. £8.40 for two mini croquettes just overshadowed how tasty they were"). / parrillan.co.uk; https://www.instagram.com/parrillanlondon.*

Parsons WC2 £72 4 3 3
39 Endell Street   020 3422 0221   5–2C

"I was blown away by the quality of the fish on my first visit" – this "tiny tiled fish restaurant" in Covent Garden "punches well above its weight" and is one of the most popular bets in our annual diners' poll in the area. It also boasts a "great wine list" (it shares ownership with nearby wine bar 10 Cases). Despite all its virtues, though, it's "very tight for space" – "some tables are bar tops with stools, although there are a few tables with chairs/banquettes (and on the pavement if it's not too cold)". / WC2H 9BA; parsonslondon.co.uk; parsons_london; Mon-Sat 10 pm.

Pastaio W1 £58 3 2 3
19 Ganton Street   020 3019 8680   4–2B

"Does one thing and does it well" – pasta is made fresh on site each day at Stevie Parle's "busy" Soho venue, and the resulting "great dishes are served quickly with a smile". It's "great value too", so "a good go-to with a few friends for a quick bite". Top Tip – "shows you don't need burgers and chicken nuggets to make a good kids' menu". / W1F 7BU; pastaio.london; pastaiolondon; Mon-Thu 10.30 pm, Fri & Sat 11 pm, Sun 10 pm.

Patara £78 3 3 3
15 Greek St, W1   020 7437 1071   5–2A
7 Maddox St, W1   020 7499 6008   4–2A
181 Fulham Rd, SW3   020 7351 5692   6–2C
9 Beauchamp Pl, SW3   020 7581 8820   6–1C
82 Hampstead High St, NW3   020 7431 5902   9–2A
18 High St, SW19   020 3931 6157   11–2B

For "a more upmarket Thai experience", head to the branches of Khun Patara Sila-On's "very pleasant" group (which is over 30 years old, with branches from Asia to Europe). "Well-presented flavoursome dishes" from "good-quality ingredients" are provided by staff who "always seem happy to see you". / pataralondon.com; pataralondon.

Paternoster Chop House EC4 £79 2 2 2
1 Warwick Court   020 7029 9400   10–2B

Now moved to Ludgate Hill from the Paternoster Square perch that originally provided its name, this D&D London restaurant is a "decent and safe option" – although a more upbeat description has it "doing what the City enjoys, with high levels of testosterone and impressive steaks". "Swarming with suits" – it's a natural for business entertaining. / EC4M 7DX; paternosterchophouse.co.uk; paternosterchophouse; Mon-Sat 9 pm; SRA-3 stars.

Patri £50 3 3 2
139 Northfield Avenue, W13   020 3981 3388   1–3A
103 Hammersmith Grove, W6   020 8741 1088   8–1C

"The food is different and good" – inspired by the street food sold on Indian railways – at these funkily decorated canteens, in a nondescript Ealing parade of shops and a somewhat cuter one on Hammersmith Grove. Top Menu Tip – "sharing Thalis are a must, with great flavour combinations and excellent value". / patri.co.uk.

Patty and Bun £45 3 3 2
18 Old Compton St, W1   020 7287 1818   5–2A
26 Kingly Street, W1   020 7287 9632   4–2A
54 James St, W1   020 7487 3188   3–1A

19 Borough High Street, SE1   020 7407 7994   10–4C
12 Northcote Road, SW11   020 7223 0900   11–2C
15 Park Drive, E14   020 3951 9715   12–1C
2 Arthaus Building, 205 Richmond Road, E8   020 8525 8250   14–1B
22-23 Liverpool St, EC2   020 7621 1331   10–2D

"You just cannot beat" the "brilliantly cooked, juicy/sloppy burgers", say fans of this indie group – "they're worth the dirty fingers afterwards". Founded by Joe Grossman in 2012, it now has seven outlets (plus two concessions) in London and another in Brighton, and after negotiating a tricky patch on home turf opened its first international branch in Dubai last year. / pattyandbun.co.uk; pattyandbun.

Pavyllon,
The Four Seasons Hotel W1   £146   3 3 3
Hamilton Place   020 7319 5200   3–4A

On the ground floor of a luxurious Park Lane five star – complete with its own pavement entrance – this year-old newcomer is a showcase for Parisian chef Yannick Alléno (who holds 15 Michelin stars worldwide and whose empire globally includes two other 'Pavyllons'). The interior is stylish – if in a slightly anodyne kind of way – and "the tables are a good size and reasonably spaced so it's particularly good for business". The "well-executed" menu has its fair share of luxury ingredients, but is not particularly 'foodie'; and you can eat à la carte or choose the four-course (£85 per person) or six-course (£110 per person) 'Immersive Mayfair' menu. Top Tip – "there is an excellent set lunch deal (at the reasonable price of £55.50 per person)". / W1J 7DR; pavyllonlondon.com; pavyllon_london; Mon-Sun 10.30 pm.

Peachy Goat SE24   £49   3 3 4
16 Half Moon Lane   020 7967 7386   1–4C

"A funky little place" – this "excellent local" in Herne Hill is run by brothers Luca and Ollie Sechi, whose culinary aim is plant-based Italian cuisine ('just like Mama used to make' – only without the meat, dairy or egg!'). "Astonishingly popular with a loyal crowd, the ambience is always lively". "I went with two reluctant carnivores who proclaimed it top-notch!" / SE24 9HU; peachygoat.com; peachygoatldn; Tue-Sat 10.30 pm, Sun 4 pm.

Pearl Liang W2   £54   3 3 3
8 Sheldon Square   020 7289 7000   7–1C

"Good-to-very-good dim sum", "excellent seafood" and "good duck" are the hallmarks of this "wonderful Cantonese" venue in a modern basement setting in Paddington Basin – although it has yet to recover the stellar ratings it achieved before the pandemic. Top Tip – it's often recommended for a family meal with kids in tow. / W2 6EZ; pearlliang.co.uk; pearl_liang_restaurant; Mon-Sun 10.30 pm.

Pearly Queen E1 NEW   £100   5 3 3
44 Commercial Street   020 8161 0399   13–2C

With the closure of Cornerstone (RIP), chef Tom Brown's main showcase for his "absolutely stunning" fish and seafood cuisine shifts to this "very cool" new venue near Spitalfields: one of the more commented-on newcomers in our annual diners' poll. "As you enter, there's a bar with seating and behind are a row of seats that look out the street – downstairs are tables as well as a small open kitchen". "The menu is similar to what he produced at Cornerstone (RIP)": there are oysters, crustacea and 'sea-cuterie' alongside "large plates, sides and desserts all designed for sharing". "Brilliant… and it has a great soundtrack too". Top Menu Tip – "Buffalo oysters with Ranch dressing 'to die for'!" / E1 6LT; thepearlyqueen.com; pearlyqueenshoreditch; Mon-Sat 10 pm.

F S A

Peckham Cellars SE15 — £68 — 3 3 2
125 Queens Road   020 7207 0124   1–4D

This "great sharing-plates restaurant with very accommodating staff" – and a "good wine selection", its primary focus – has been a linchpin in the emergence of Peckham's going-out scene ("I've never had a bad meal here: in principle I'm not a fan of small plates but here it all works"). / SE15 2ND; peckhamcellars.co.uk; peckhamcellars; Tue-Sat 11 pm.

The Pelican W11 — £71 — 4 4 4
45 All Saints Rd   020 4537 2880   7–1B

"A pretty perfect gastropub" in Notting Hill not far from Portobello Road, which was converted by James Gummer in 2022 and remains one of the biggest ongoing hits in the area. Chef Owen Kenworthy's "straightforward British food" is "interesting", "made with top-class ingredients" and "expertly cooked"; service is "charming"; and the artfully distressed decor sets up a "wonderful, very buzzy and trendy" atmosphere. Top Menu Tip – "the lobster pie makes it worth crossing town for". / W11 1HE; thepelicanw11.com; thepelican_w11; Mon-Sat midnight, Sun 10.30 pm.

E Pellicci E2 — £24 — 3 5 2
332 Bethnal Green Rd   020 7739 4873   13–1D

For the ultimate Full English, this superbly atmospheric greasy joe in Bethnal Green is justifiably renowned. It's arguably most notable for its Grade II listed Art Deco interior, but vital to its appeal is the "truly friendly service from the owners" (it has been run by four generations of the Pellicci family since 1900). / E2 0AG; epellicci.has.restaurant; pelliccicafe; Mon, Wed-Fri 3.30 pm, Sat 3 pm.

The Pem SW1 — £103 — 4 3 2
Conrad London St. James, 22-28 Broadway   020 3301 8080   2–3C

'Good in parts' is perhaps the fairest description of this comfy dining room in a five-star hotel near St James's Park tube, which continues to put in a 'Curate's Egg' performance. Recruiting ace chef, Sally Abé, a couple of years ago helped boost the profile of what was hitherto seen merely as a business venue convenient for parliamentarians from nearby Westminster. Nowadays, she presents "an interesting menu" championing British produce and recipes, resulting in "fabulous food, beautifully presented". On the downside, service can be "variable" and "while the decor is nice, the ambience is rather soulless as the restaurant is situated in the rather cavernous bowels of a hotel". / SW1H 0BH; thepemrestaurant.com; thepemrestaurant; Tue, Sat, Wed-Fri 9.30 pm.

Pentolina W14 — £68 — 4 5 3
71 Blythe Road   020 3010 0091   8–1C

"Always a warm welcome from the lovely husband-and-wife team" at this "perfect neighbourhood gem" lost in the backstreets near Brook Green, where "Michele is in the kitchen and Heidi front of house". For what it is, it would be hard to improve, with its "homely atmosphere"; and "hearty and well-seasoned Italian home cooking" from "a limited menu of crowd-pleasing dishes"; all at "reasonable prices". "Interesting" wine list too with "some good value for money rarities". / W14 0HP; pentolinarestaurant.co.uk; pentolina_london; Tue-Sat 11 pm.

Perilla N16 — £88 — 4 4 3
1-3 Green Lanes   020 7359 0779   1–1C

"Innovative casual dining" from acclaimed chef Ben Marks is served by "welcoming and knowledgeable staff" at this easygoing Newington Green spot – "lucky local residents!". It's "healthy modern British" fare, "always with a good selection of vegetarian dishes". Ratings have edged higher – a major achievement in a year during which the team opened a second venue with great success (Morchella in Exmouth Market, see also). / N16 9BS; perilladining.co.uk; perilladining; Tue-Sat 11.30 pm, Sun 9 pm.

FSA

Persian Palace W13 £34 3 2 2
143-145 Uxbridge Road   020 8840 4233   1–3A
"Not a lot has changed for years, fortunately" at this Ealing institution – the "authentic dishes" are served in "generous portions so large the plates overflow" – no wonder it's "always busy, and sometimes very noisy". / W13 9AU; persianpalace.co.uk; persianppalace; Mon-Sun 11 pm.

The Petersham WC2 £105 2 2 3
1 Floral Court, off Floral St   020 7305 7676   5–3C
This "absolutely beautiful" venue in Covent Garden's pretty Floral Court development is the central London satellite of the famous garden centre-turned-restaurant on the edge of Richmond Park and Ham Common. You pay a high price, though, for cooking that ranges from "delicious" to "overpriced" and no more than acceptable – the latter view shared by too many reporters to ignore. / WC2E 9DJ; petershamnurseries.com; petershamnurseries; Mon-Sat 9.30 pm, Sun 4 pm.

Petersham Nurseries Cafe TW10 £134 2 2 5
Church Lane, off Petersham Road   020 8940 5230   1–4A
"The plant-filled terrace was magical… it could be the wine, but I can't remember anything standing out foodwise…" – this garden centre café just outside Richmond Park became an unlikely hit under chef Skye Gyngell 20 years ago, and – with its shabby-chic greenhouse setting remains "a lovely place for a meal on a nice day", even if the food is nowadays undistinguished and "the prices definitely on the high side". In summer 2024 it finally prevailed after an astonishing 18-year standoff with Richmond council over evening opening, which had threatened its survival as a restaurant. / TW10 7AB; petershamnurseries.com; petershamnurseries; Tue, Wed, Sun 5 pm, Thu-Sat 11 pm.

Le Petit Citron W6 £63 2 3 3
98-100 Shepherds Bush Road   020 3019 1175   8–1C
"A decent attempt to reproduce Provençal cooking in Shepherd's Bush": Lawrence & Emily Hartley's "nice local bistro" north of Brook Green – "a successor to a spot that was Café Rouge for many years" (and briefly Mustard, RIP) – provides "French classics" with "friendly service". Critics feel that at times, "the food, though fairly authentic, can be just a bit underwhelming"; but the majority see "much to recommend the place" and feel it's a "welcome venture" in this underserved neck of the woods. Top Tip – "good set menu". / W6 7PD; lepetitcitron.co.uk; lepetitcitronw6; Mon-Sat 10 pm, Sun 4 pm.

Petit Ma Cuisine TW9 £63 3 3 3
8 Station Approach   020 8332 1923   1–3A
"Authentically Gallic bistro" near Kew station that's built a strong following over 16 years for its competitively priced "French classics". The retro 1950s styling – all gingham tablecloths and Impressionist posters – is part of the appeal. Top Tip – "good-value set lunch". / TW9 3QB; macuisinebistrot.co.uk; Tue-Sun 10 pm.

La Petite Auberge N1 £60 2 2 2
283 Upper St   020 7359 1046   9–2D
This "friendly French bistro on Islington's busiest street has all the predictable Gallic offerings – onion soup, escargots, crepes – and a decent wine list". It inspires few criticisms and is "pleasant enough" to be a useful address "well-placed for the Almeida theatre". / N1 2TZ; petiteauberge.co.uk; lapetiteauberge_n1; Mon-Fri 10 pm, Sat 10.30 pm, Sun 9 pm.

Pétrus SW1 £171 3 3 3
1 Kinnerton St   020 7592 1609   6–1D
"It always takes hours to decide on the wine!!" for fans of the grape at Gordon Ramsay's mutedly luxurious Belgravia haunt, which is built around a

wine cage and, of course, named for the famous Bordeaux appellation whose vintages contribute to its list. Though primarily nominated in our annual diners' poll in the category for 'Best Wine List', its modern French cuisine under head chef Orson Vergnaud (at the helm since 2022) returned to stronger form this year and in a quiet way this is again one of the better restaurants in Gordon Ramsay's stable. / SW1X 8EA; gordonramsayrestaurants.com; petrusbygordonramsay; Tue-Thu 9.15 pm, Fri & Sat 9.45 pm.

Pham Sushi EC2 £54 2 3 3
The Heron, 5 Moor Ln   020 7251 6336   13–2A
The original (Whitecross Street) branch has become take-away only, but this simple Japanese business has a new sit-down venue five minutes away. Having always been one of the few dining options near the Barbican, it's now practically in it – occupying a unit in a 31 storey building (Heron House) on nearby Moor Lane. Some reports rate it as very good, others only average, but it justifies its ongoing inclusion by the paucity of other decent options nearby. / EC2Y 9AP; phamsushi.com; phamsushi.

Phat Phuc SW3 £44 3 3 2
Chelsea Courtyard, 151 Sydney Street   020 7351 3843   6–3C
"Buzzing, busy, delicious, rushed, noisy, crowded…" – this noodle bar is everything you might expect from a Vietnamese street-food outlet; and is notably "good value for the area", situated as it is in a posh courtyard off Chelsea's King's Road. You could be forgiven for not realising that the name apparently means 'happy Buddha'. / SW3 6NT; phatphucnoodlebar.co.uk; phat_phuc_noodle_bar; Mon-Sun 6 pm.

Phoenix Palace NW1 £70 3 2 3
5-9 Glentworth St   020 7486 3515   2–1A
A "great traditional Chinese restaurant" seating 250, with "striking décor" near Baker Street tube that boasts "a huge menu", listing more than 300 dishes, including dim sum. Of its type, it's one of London's best and draws fans in our annual diners' poll from all points of the compass. Top Menu Tip – "the crispy noodles are the best in town". / NW1 5PG; phoenixpalace.co.uk; thephoenixpalace; Mon-Sat 11.30 pm, Sun 10.30 pm.

Piazza Italiana EC2 £81 3 3 3
38 Threadneedle Street   020 7256 7223   10–2C
Near the Bank of England, this Italian three-year-old occupies a particularly fine Edwardian banking hall (built in 1902). Had it not opened around the time of the pandemic, it might be better known – "it's not too noisy for a City restaurant and with good service and a reasonably priced lunch deal". / EC2R 8AY; piazzaitaliana.co.uk; piazzaitalianauk; Mon-Wed 10 pm, Thu-Sat 11 pm.

Pied à Terre W1 £155 4 3 3
34 Charlotte St   020 7636 1178   2–1C
"A new chef has arrived but standards are maintained" at David Moore's hallowed Fitzrovia townhouse, which has remained in London's top culinary ranks ever since it first launched in 1991 despite numerous changes of personnel, the latest incumbent at the stoves being chef Phil Kearsey, appointed in May 2024. With the option of a forward-looking plant-based menu, it provides a "great experience for all types of diner" ("we had a mix of omnivores, pescatarians, vegetarians and vegans and the tasting menu catered for us all"). "Service is attentive and the sommelier always happy to chat". Over the years, the limited space has been carefully refitted and designed, and it suits most occasions: "if you need a restaurant to perform for you, try Pied à Terre". / W1T 2NH; pied-a-terre.co.uk; PiedaTerreRestaurant; Thu-Sat 11.30 pm.

Pierre Victoire W1 — £57 — 2 2 3
5 Dean St 020 7287 4582 3–1D

This "fun, little traditional Gallic place in Soho" is "just what sixty-somethings picture when you say 'French restaurant'". "Very similar" to stablemate Prix Fixe, it's "still pretty good value" – although food-wise there are "far better choices in the area". / W1D 3RQ; pierrevictoire.com; @pierrevictoiresoho; Sun-Wed 11 pm, Thu-Sat 11.30 pm.

Pig & Butcher N1 — £71 — 3 2 3
80 Liverpool Road 020 7226 8304 9–3D

We're "very lucky to have it as our local", say regulars at this Islington gastropub with the unusual facility of an in-house butchery to ensure high-quality meat. "I've been dozens of times, and never had a bum meal". / N1 0QD; thepigandbutcher.co.uk; pigandbutcher; Sun-Wed 11 pm, Thu-Sat midnight.

The Pig's Ear SW3
35 Old Church St 020 3026 0466 6–3C

In Old Church Street, Chelsea, the first pub from the Gladwin brothers opened in mid 2024 – the latest addition to their 'Local & Wild' stable of restaurants supplied by the family farm in West Sussex (which includes Rabbit just up the King's Road). The grand late-Victorian tavern on a corner site was lavishly renovated as recently as 2021, when it was known as 'The Chelsea Pig'. / SW3 5BS; pigsearpub.com; Wed-Sat 9 pm, Sun 4 pm.

The Pig's Head SW4 — £82 — 3 3 3
87 Rectory Grove 020 4568 5830 11–1D

With its "top-notch, meat-focused food, warm and friendly service" and "great rustic dining room", this "magnificent old boozer in Clapham Old Town" is "lovely to have as a local but also worth a trip to visit"; even if there is the odd concern that "it doesn't know whether it wants to be a restaurant or a pub". It's from the team behind Islington's Smokehouse and the Princess of Shoreditch, who took over three years ago. / SW4 0DR; thepigshead.com; thepigshead; Mon-Fri 10 pm, Sat 10.30 pm, Sun 9 pm.

Pique Nique SE1 — £83 — 3 3 3
32 Tanner Street 020 7403 9549 10–4D

This southeast London fixture (sibling to nearby Casse-Croute) is said to "divide opinion" by some of its regulars. "It's in a random tennis clubhouse with an apparently Alpine theme in a park off Bermondsey Street" – a setting that some see as characterful and others "strange". As for the traditional cooking: "some dishes are decidedly average, but others are impressive"; and "while the food is meant to be shared, the portion sizes can be haphazard". The overall culinary verdict? "fairly authentically French and enjoyable". / SE1 3LD; pique-nique.co.uk; piquenique32; Mon-Sat 11 pm, Sun 5 pm.

PIRAÑA London SW1 NEW
7-9 Saint James's Street 020 3150 0079 3–4D

On quite a prominent site near St James's Palace that used to be Avenue (RIP), this new entertainment-led venue is part of a nightlife group with operations in London and Mykonos. Here, we are promised Nikkei cuisine, with 'hero' dishes such as Butter Roasted Chilean Sea Bass with Coriander Shiso Ponzu and Lamb Chops Anticucho with Aubergine Purée, Aji and Amarillo Yoghurt. / SW1A 1EE; pirana_london; Mon & Tue 11 pm, Wed-Sat 12.30 am.

El Pirata W1 — £58 — 2 4 4
5-6 Down St 020 7491 3810 3–4B

This "bustling" spot, tucked away in a Mayfair side street near Piccadilly and Green Park, is a "perennial favourite" ("great for a gossipy catch-up!") on account of its "fun, welcoming" atmosphere and prices that are notably kind for the area. Over its three decades it has attracted a long list of swashbuckling guests, ranging from Johnny Depp to Fred Sirieix. / W1J 7AQ; elpirata.co.uk; elpiratamayfair; Tue-Sat 10.45 pm.

Pita NW11 £25 3 2 2
102 Golders Green Road   020 8381 4080   1–1B

"A buzzy, kosher falafel bar in the middle of Golders Green always full of people spilling out into the street"; and with a large outside seated terrace. "Excellent falafel (freshly made) is served in pitas or wraps, with a really large choice of accompaniments". Top Menu Tip – "nice falafel, terrible fries". / NW11 8HB; pita.london; Wed-Sat 10.30 pm, Mon 10 pm.

Pivot by Mark Greenaway WC2 £99 2 3 3
3 Henrietta Street   020 3325 5275   5–3D

Overlooking Covent Garden's piazza from the first floor of a Georgian townhouse, this modern British bistro is overseen by well-known chef Mark Greenaway. That it provides "decent value for WC2" makes it a useful amenity for feeding the family or pre-theatre. Critics find the menu "too pared back" or "somewhat pedestrian", but all reports acknowledge that its fare is "all well-cooked". / WC2E 8LU; 3henrietta.com; pivotbarandbistro; Mon-Sat 11 pm, Sun 9 pm.

Pizarro SE1 £72 4 3 3
194 Bermondsey St   020 7256 5333   10–4D

"More formal than older sibling José up the road, but still relaxed and good fun" – José P's "splendid" and "buzzing" Bermondsey restaurant provides "wonderful Spanish flavours" from a menu focused on tapas and sharing dishes; alongside "a wine list which encourages you to explore lesser known Spanish varieties". "José Pizarro himself often eats here: what more endorsement do you need?!". One issue – it's a "noisy" room so a "great place for a rowdy lunch with friends" but it "could be a touch quieter". Top Menu Tips – "the jamon was as good as you'd expect"; "suckling leg of lamb, which was succulent and truly memorable"; "the croquetas and the fideua are cracking bursts of umami punch". / SE1 3TQ; josepizarro.com; josepizarrorestaurants; Mon-Sat 10.45 pm, Sun 8.45 pm.

Pizza da Valter SW17 £54 4 3 3
7 Bellevue Road   020 8355 7032   11–2C

This seven-year-old independent a couple of doors along from Chez Bruce on the edge of Wandsworth Common is reckoned by fans to offer among the "best pizza in town". "I only discovered it recently but it has become a favourite". / SW17 7EG; pizzadavalter.co.uk; pizzeriadavalter; Mon-Sun 11 pm.

Pizza East E1 £59 3 2 4
56 Shoreditch High St   020 7729 1888   13–1B

"Fun and easy-going" pizza haunt on the ground floor of Shoreditch's iconic Tea Building with a "great atmosphere" alongside "good-quality pizza that satisfies the tastes of adults and children alike". Opened by Soho House 15 years ago, it is now owned by Gordon Ramsay, who has opened a bar in the basement. / E1 6JJ; pizzaeast.com; pizzaeast; Mon-Wed 10 pm, Thu-Sat midnight, Sun 9 pm.

Pizza Metro SW11 £65 3 2 2
64 Battersea Rise   020 7228 3812   11–2C

Pizza sold by the metre ('al metro') was a novelty in 1993 when this simple Neapolitan pizzeria on Battersea Rise first opened its doors. It's not the fave rave that once it was, but remains a "good local" and one that the odd fan still crosses town for. / SW11 1EQ; pizzametropizza.com; pizzametropizza; Sun-Thu 10 pm, Fri & Sat 11 pm.

Pizza Pilgrims £42 3|3|3
Branches throughout London

"More hit 'n' miss than they used to be, but still a go-to chain" – the Elliot brothers' successful group is heading towards 20 branches in the capital, but *"still producing quality dishes despite becoming quite a brand"*: *"lovely scorched, pillowy-based pizzas with plenty of power in the ingredients"* and *"reasonably priced for the quality!"* Latest to launch, in June 2024, was a branch by Euston. / pizzapilgrims.co.uk; pizzapilgrims.

PizzaExpress £58 2|3|3
Branches throughout London

A huge fan club do try to suggest that it *"still serves the best pizza"*, but when you look at the mediocre overall food score for this venerable high street chain (est. 1965), one has to conclude that it's *"sad but true that this once market-leading pioneer is now well past its sell-by date"*: *"the pizzas have been so dumbed down"* that it *"now totally fails to compete with the rash of more modern pizzerias with much better and more genuine dishes"*. Owned by its creditors since 2021, service remains *"very pleasant"* (if *"now well-versed in up- and cross-selling"*) and the *"comfortable"* branches still help make it *"an excellent place for families"*. One particular gripe emerged this year – *"I am fed up of dining at a table, only for their takeaway delivery drivers to be coming in and out wearing their bike helmets"*.
/ pizzaexpress.co.uk; pizzaexpress.

Pizzeria Mozza W1 £51 4|3|3
Treehouse Hotel, 14-15 Langham Place   020 3988 4273   3–1C

"Delicious and different pizza" from star LA baker-chef Nancy Silverton – founder of La Brea Bakery and a James Beard Award winner – is *"worth undergoing the hotel ambience for"* at this café, adjacent to Treehouse Hotel London, which is opposite Broadcasting House. It opened a few months after Covid lockdowns ended in 2001, and has never perhaps inspired the buzz it deserves. / W1B 2QS; treehousehotels.com; pizzeriamozzalondon; Tue-Sat 10 pm.

Pizzeria Pappagone N4 £39 3|4|4
131 Stroud Green Rd   020 7263 2114   9–1D

This *"brilliant neighbourhood restaurant"* in Finsbury Park has plied regulars and blow-ins alike with *"great pizza, pasta and cocktails"* for more than a quarter of a century – *"we're always welcomed back like long-lost family members!"*. *"North London has no shortage of excellent pizza places, but this one wins by a crispy crust"*. / N4 3PX; pizzeriapappagone.co.uk; Mon-Sun midnight.

Planque E8 £86 4|5|4
322 Acton Mews   020 7254 3414   14–2A

This *"beautifully designed wine drinkers' hangout"* (both a restaurant and a wine store) in a pair of Haggerston railway arches has *"a cellar full of real rarities, super-knowledgeable and hospitable owner and staff. It's the creation of a Franco-Australian duo, founder Jonathan Alphandery and ex-P Franco chef Seb Myers, and its stimulating menu is made with the wine in mind"*: *"dishes presenting elegant and fresh modern twists on French and Nordic cookery"*. Club members get priority booking and can store their wine in the cellars, but members of the public can eat in the restaurant and one or two enjoyed their *"meal of the year"* here. / E8 4EA; planque.co.uk; _planque_; Mon-Fri 9.30 pm.

Plaquemine Lock N1 £53 4|3|4
139 Graham St   020 7688 1488   9–3D

"Cajun and Creole dishes served pub-style" – including *"delicious jambalaya"* – share top billing with live jazz at this *"really unusual and lively spot"* – a colourfully converted tavern across the road from the Regent's Canal in Islington, where restaurateur Jacob Kenedy (of Bocca di Lupo) channels his Louisiana roots. / N1 8LB; plaqlock.com; plaqueminelock; Mon-Thu 11 pm, Fri & Sat midnight, Sun 10 pm.

Plates EC1 NEW
320 Old Street   020 7096 1307   13–1B
Open on July 3 on Old Street in Shoreditch (well after our annual diners' poll had concluded), a high-end vegan restaurant from Great British Menu 2024 winner Kirk Haworth and his sister Keeley, offering a tasting menu format at £75 per person, plus drinks. Bookings may be hard to secure: the first batch sold out within hours of becoming available, three months ahead of launch! (As of July 2024, they are now fully booked until 16th February 2025 for tables of 2 or more…) / EC1V 9DR.

Plaza Khao Gaeng WC1   £37   5 4 3
Arcade Food Hall, 103-105 Oxford Street   no tel   5–1A
"Slightly frenetic, great fun, always packed and rightly so" – this "kick-ass" two-year-old from chef Luke Farrell (the flagship of JKS Restaurants' Arcade Food Hall in Centrepoint) is for fans "the one and only Thai in London", whose "elevated street food" "takes you back to Thailand" and whose "hot and cramped atmosphere fits the vibe". / WC1A 1DB; plazakhaogaeng.com; plazakhaogaeng; Mon-Sat 10 pm, Sun 8.30 pm.

The Plimsoll N4   £62   4 3 4
52 St Thomas's Road   020 3034 1099   9–1D
This "grotty Arsenal pub" near the old Highbury stadium in Finsbury Park has won wide acclaim for its "elevated pub food", with "small plates of tasty British classics" and a "banging Dexter burger" ("I dream about those burgers, they're that good"). There's a "nice old-school pub atmosphere too", with a "lively bar" and "great beer selection". Chef duo Jamie Allan & Ed McIlroy (aka Four Legs) have now opened their second transformation project, the former chippy Tollingtons (see also). Top Sartorial Tip – "baseball caps and trainers are ubiquitous". / N4 2QW; theplimsoll.com; the.plimsoll; Mon-Fri 11 pm, Sat & Sun midnight.

The Plough SW14   £62   2 2 3
42 Christ Church Rd   020 8755 7444   11–2A
Proximity to Richmond Park – a large terrace for sunny days – and a comfortable, attractive interior help justify the ongoing inclusion of this eighteenth-century Fuller's pub, near Sheen Gate. In other respects, its ratings remain resolutely ordinary. / SW14 7AF; plougheastsheen.co.uk; PloughSheen; Mon-Sat 11 pm, Sun 10.30 pm.

Ploussard SW11   £41   3 3 3
97 Saint John's Road   020 7738 1965   11–2C
"Every neighbourhood should have its Ploussard!" – a "cosy" little local that, over its first year, has proved a "more-than-welcome addition to Battersea Rise". Chef Matt Harris and Tommy Kempson of Brixton's Other Side Fried provide "vigorously flavoured" modern French "tapas-style dishes", backed up by a short selection of low-intervention wines. / SW11 1QY; ploussardlondon.co.uk; ploussardlondon/; Mon-Wed 10 pm, Fri & Sat 11 pm, Thu 10.30 pm.

Plum Valley W1   £53   3 2 2
20 Gerrard St   020 7494 4366   5–3A
"Fantastic dim sum with good-quality ingredients" make this family-run Cantonese "a good Gerrard Street standby". Now entering its fifth decade, the decor is "slightly cooler than in your average Chinatown restaurant". / W1D 6JQ; plumvalley.co.uk; plumvalleyrestaurant; Mon-Sun 10 pm.

Pollini W10 NEW   £95   3 4 3
79 Barlby Road   020 8962 8690   1–2B
A bold arrival in the featureless tracts of North Kensington, near the top end of Ladbroke Grove – this conversion of a huge (43,000 sq ft) and graceful Beaux-Arts former car factory (the Sunbeam Talbot Motor Company built in 1903) creates a new showcase for renowned art dealers, Carpenters

Workshop Gallery. They moved here from Mayfair in a £30m refurbishment creating a huge arts space, as well as a concert venue, event space… and restaurant! This latter occupies the vast marbled lobby: a "great space" says one early report, but an interior the Daily Mail's man, Tom Parker Bowles, found so monumental as to be "cold". On the menu: a chic contemporary take on Italian cuisine by well-travelled chef, Emanuele Pollini (voted Italian chef of the year by Gambero Rosso magazine in 2020). We have rated the venue on initial feedback of "top-notch Italian cuisine" – a view supported by favourable feedback from Tom PB and also (mostly) from William Sitwell in the Telegraph (who found a "classic menu to satisfy the purist Italophile", if one he felt needed a little more "guts"). Top Tip – check out the space without paying a fortune by eating from the simpler brunch or all-day menu (of panini and salads). / W10 6AZ; ladbrokehall.com; pollini_ladbrokehall; Tue-Sat midnight.

Le Pont de la Tour SE1   £96   3 4 4
36d Shad Thames   020 7403 8403   10–4D

"A table on the terrace with the beautiful view of Tower Bridge is a fabulous experience" at this veteran riverside restaurant – one of the late Sir Terence Conran's restaurant and design masterpieces when it opened as part of his 'gastrodome' development in 1991. It's fallen into obscurity since the days when the Blairs entertained the Clintons here, but a jump in ratings this year, backed up by reports of "improved" and "surprisingly good" meals, suggests that – just possibly – it's starting to get its mojo back after years of mediocrity in the D&D London stable. On the menu: a wide array of modern French dishes with plenty of steak and seafood, all backed up by a broad, high-quality wine list. / SE1 2YE; lepontdelatour.co.uk; lepontdelatourldn; Mon-Sat 9.30 pm, Sun 9 pm; SRA-3 stars.

Popolo EC2   £63   4 4 4
26 Rivington Street   020 7729 4299   13–1B

"Delicious tiny plates of interesting and seasonal Italian dishes" plus low-intervention wines delight diners at Jon Lawson's "casual and vibey small Shoreditch place", which – post Covid – is re-establishing its very impressive all-round ratings. "It's just a really great place to go: grab a seat at the kitchen bar and watch lovely food being expertly prepared". / EC2A 3DU; popoloshoreditch.com; popoloshoreditch; Tue, Wed 10 pm, Thu-Sat 11 pm.

Poppy's   £37   3 2 3
129-131 Brackenbury Road, W6   020 8741 4928   8–1C
270 King Street, W6   020 8741 3282   8–2C
30 Greyhound Road, W6   020 7385 9264   8–2C
78 Glenthorne Road, W6   020 8748 2351   8–2C

"Somewhat weird interiors" packed with chandeliers, stuffed animals and other antique-shop paraphernalia mean it's easy to be "transfixed by the decor" at these four neighbourhood cafés in Hammersmith (which added a new branch near Ravenscourt Park this year). The decor boosts what's essentially a cheap 'n' cheerful Thai caff experience: "a lot of the food is deep-fried but always fresh" and it's "staggeringly good value… and it's BYO!"

Porte Noire N1   £64   3 3 4
Unit A Gasholder 10, 1 Lewis Cubitt Square   020 7930 6211   9–3C

"Tucked away" near the canal at the foot of an old, repurposed gas-holder near King's Cross, this "lovely wine bar and restaurant" showcases Champagnes and wines from movie icon and co-owner Idris Elba's 'Porte Noire' brand. The food menu is "rather limited", but it's "nicely realised"; and "the wine list is exceptional". Service is professional, and it's a "sleek" looking and "buzzy" venue too (incorporating a handful of nice outside tables in summer). / N1C 4BY; portenoire.co.uk; portenoirekx; Mon-Sat 11.30 pm, Sun 5.30 pm.

F S A

Il Portico W8 £75 3 3 4
277 Kensington High St   020 7602 6262   8–1D
"One never tires of Il Portico", say fans of this *"lovely local Italian"* with *"an authentic feel"* opposite the Design Museum, which has been run by the Chiavarini family for more than 50 years. *"Everything is served with enthusiasm"* and *"if prices are a bit on the high side, it's because of the proximity of some very classy residential areas"*. / W8 6NA; ilportico.co.uk; ilportico.kensington; Mon-Sat 11 pm.

Portland W1 £98 3 4 2
113 Great Portland Street   020 7436 3261   2–1B
The *"outstanding quality and consistency"* of Will Lander and Daniel Morgenthau's Fitzrovia fixture, has helped celebrate its 10th anniversary this year and for such a central venue, it's unusual in feeling *"genuinely local in its approach and feel"*. The sophisticated cuisine is *"expertly prepared and carefully judged"* and manages to be *"complex without being overthought"*. *"Friendly, knowledgeable and professional service"* is a key strength and *"helps to jolly a slightly dull space"*. / W1W 6QQ; portlandrestaurant.co.uk; portlandrestaurant; Tue-Sat 9.30 pm.

Portobello Ristorante Pizzeria W11 £82 3 2 3
7 Ladbroke Road   020 7221 1373   7–2B
"Very good pizzas" are the pick of the broad Italian menu (also with seafood on display) at this Notting Hill Gate fixture, where the best seats in summer are on the large outside terrace. With a *"great family atmosphere"*, it's *"very much a local restaurant, and all the better for that!"*. / W11 3PA; portobellolondon.co.uk; portobello_ristorante_pizzeria; Sun-Thu 11 pm, Fri & Sat 11.30 pm.

The Portrait by Richard Corrigan WC2 £78 3 3 3
National Portrait Gallery, St Martin's Place   020 7306 0055   5–4B
"The fine rooftop setting" with *"charming views over to Trafalgar Square"* (and Big Ben off in the distance) help lend a *"special"* sense of occasion to this well-known destination that can otherwise seem a tad *"Spartan"* and *"echoey"*. *"After the National Portrait Gallery's stunning makeover, it reopened"*, overseen by Richard Corrigan in July 2023. Chef Corrigan's involvement keeps the menu focused on the British Isles and *"though the food isn't wildly ambitious, you can taste everything: it's a masterclass in the clarity of its flavours"*. At least, that's what its biggest fans think – a number of sceptics say it's *"not cheap"* and *"nothing memorable, but pleasant nonetheless"*. Top Menu Tips – *"Oysters, Sea bass in hollandaise with greens and the creamiest mash imaginable; finally, Chocolate fondant plated prettily with raspberries and teeny madeleines. Yom!"* / WC2H 0HE; npg.org.uk; theportraitrestaurant; Mon & Tue, Sun 5.30 pm, Wed-Sat 10.30 pm.

Potli W6 £55 3 3 3
319-321 King St   020 8741 4328   8–2B
"The food, from all corners of India, is packed with so much flavour" at this popular restaurant on the strip of eateries near the entrance to Ravenscourt Park. Welcoming service and a cosy, comfy and colourful interior rounds off an experience that remains well-rated all-round. / W6 9NH; potli.co.uk; potlirestaurant; Mon-Thu 10 pm, Fri & Sat 10.30 pm, Sun 9.30 pm.

La Poule au Pot SW1 £76 3 4 5
231 Ebury St   020 7730 7763   6–2D
"Nothing changes, and it doesn't need to" – at this *"old-fashioned"* French *"hideaway"* in Pimlico: *"always a delightful experience"* thanks to its *"rustic"* and *"quirky"* candle-lit setting (*"you may need your phone torch to read the menu"*), which every year ranks near the top of our annual diners' poll as one of London's top choices for a smoochy 'dîner à deux'. Its *"comforting, homely cooking"* is *"unashamedly French"*, and essentially unchanged since circa 1964 (which is when it opened); service, similarly, is very Gallic and, for the

most part, "utterly charming". Top Tip – "particularly lovely in the summer: sitting outside, one could be in La Belle France". / SW1W 8UT; pouleaupot.co.uk; lapouleaupotrestaurant; Mon-Sun 11 pm.

Pravaas SW7 NEW £44
3 Glendower Place   0203 161 7641   6–2C

Chef-owner Shilpa Dandekar (ex-Quilon and Raymond Blanc) opened this contemporary Indian close to South Ken tube station in early 2024 with 30 covers (plus a 20-seater private dining room in the basement). It's her first follow-up to the highly rated Pure Indian Cooking in Fulham High Street – reports please! / SW7 3DU; pravaas.com; pravaas.london; Mon-Sun 10.30 pm.

Prawn on the Lawn N1 £84   4|2|2
292-294 St Paul's Rd   020 3302 8668   9–2D

"Exceptional" fish and seafood is served at this "cool" fishmonger-turned-restaurant near Highbury Corner, which is "different every time you go as they decide what and how to cook each dish according to what is fresh". There's a perennial complaint that it's "quite expensive for a cramped space" that's "a bit too crowded for comfort" – which is why those lucky enough to have been to the Cornish offshoot in Padstow say they prefer it. / N1 2LH; prawnonthelawn.com; prawnonthelawn; Wed-Sat, Tue 10 pm.

Primeur N5 £70   3|4|4
116 Petherton Rd   020 7226 5271   1–1C

"It's so cute!" – this hipster hotspot in Newington Green still carries the 'Barnes Motors' signage of its origins as a 1940s car showroom, with a large glass frontage (which opens in summer). It's "a wonderful place to while away a sunny afternoon, and very pretty for a candlelit evening too". Choose from the blackboard menu of numerous, well-realised small plates, plus wines, beers and other tipples. / N5 2RT; primeurN5.co.uk; primeur_restaurant; Mon-Sat 11 pm, Sun 9 pm.

Princess of Shoreditch EC2
76 Paul St   020 7729 9270   13–1B

Just off Great Eastern Street, this characterful boozer has been a waxing and waning star of the Shoreditch culinary scene since the get-go; with a mezzanine dining room – up a spiral staircase from the main bar area – that's been a springboard for numerous well-known chefs. Though only inspiring middling praise in recent times, in August 2024, one of only two female winners of MasterChef: The Professionals – Nikita Pathakji – arrived at the stoves, promising an uptick in performance, with dishes such as cured sea bream with coal-smoked aubergine, harissa and preserved lemon. / EC2A 4NE; theprincessofshoreditch.com; princessofshoreditch; Wed-Sat 9 pm, Mon & Tue 10.30 pm, Sun 7 pm.

The Princess Royal W2 £91   3|3|3
7 Hereford Road   020 3096 6996   7–1B

"Made over several times, now in good hands with a restaurant-level menu executed well" – this smart Victorian tavern on the Bayswater/Notting Hill borders is part of the Cubitt House group, who sunk a packet into its renovation a couple of years ago. With its raw bar, oysters, seasonal salads and grills, it's the perfect pub for folks who aren't that mad about pubs. / W2 5AH; cubitthouse.co.uk; princessroyalnottinghill; Mon-Sat 10 pm, Sun 9 pm; SRA-1 star.

Prix Fixe W1 £53   3|3|3
39 Dean St   020 7734 5976   5–2A

This "fun" brasserie in Soho with an "old-style ambience" and a "good variety of French and less French food" is "brilliant value" for the West End – "and the quality is fine". "The staff make a real effort to please", and it really comes into its own with its set-price lunch and early evening meals (available before 4pm and 6.30pm respectively; at other times it's à la carte). / W1D 4PU; prixfixe.net; prixfixesoho; Mon-Sun 11.30 pm.

Provender E11 £60 3|2|2
17 High St 020 8530 3050 1–1D

This "local French venue in Wanstead" has been a reliable bastion of classic Gallic bistro cooking for 14 years. Its founder, veteran restaurateur Max Renzland, stepped down during the pandemic, since when the odd regular complains that the "the menu has been dumbed down", but its food ratings remain generally sound. / E11 2AA; provenderlondon.co.uk; provenderwanstead; Tue-Thu 11 pm, Fri & Sat midnight, Sun 10 pm.

Punjab WC2 £53 3|3|3
80 Neal St 020 7836 9787 5–2C

"A Covent Garden institution, this much-loved and invariably busy Indian restaurant has been a landmark in the area since 1951". A pioneer curry house that started out five years earlier in Aldgate, it is now run by the great-grandson of the founder and "prides itself on its original old-school" North Indian cooking ("I took a Punjabi friend for dinner, he reckoned it was almost as good as his grandmother's"). / WC2H 9PA; punjab.co.uk; punjabcoventgarden; Mon-Sat 11.15 pm, Sun 10.15 pm.

Pure Indian Cooking SW6 £56 4|3|3
67 Fulham High Street 020 7736 2521 11–1B

"Focusing on the food alone, this is right up there with the best" agree fans of chef-patronne Shilpa Dandekar's low-key Indian seven-year-old – on the trafficky segment of Fulham High Street leading up to Putney Bridge. It's "really worth a visit" to sample her "unusual but delicious" cooking. Shilpa's training combined Indian and European culinary traditions (Taj Group and Le Manoir aux Quat' Saisons). Her husband and co-founder, Faheem Vanoo, runs the front of house. / SW6 3JJ; pureindiancooking.com; pureindiancooking; Mon-Wed, Sat, Thu & Fri 11 pm, Sun 10.30 pm.

Qima Cafe W1 £15 4|3|4
Warren Street 02072098200 9–4C

"Poshest café with terrific (if rather pricey) pastries" – this "beautifully appointed" Yemeni spot on Warren Street with amazing coffee and Yemeni-inspired patisserie (e.g. their honey croissant) makes for an excellent caffeine-fueled pitstop. / W1T 5LT; qimacafe.com; Mon-Sat 7 pm, Sun 5 pm.

Quaglino's SW1 £96
16 Bury St 020 7930 6767 3–3D

Like a submarine, this famous St James's basement – a colossal 1929 ballroom rescued and revamped by the late Sir Terence Conran in 1993 – now lurks out of sight and out of mind for most savvy Londoner diners: remarkably, it inspired zero feedback in our annual diners' poll this year, a sure sign that the smart crowd moved on from its Q-bar, 'grand-entrance' staircase and designer-interior well over a decade ago. But, for a glam (if very pricey) night out, tourists and out-of-towners still seek it buoyant, attracted by its regular programme of entertainment fueled by posh brasserie nosh. Top Tip – especially if you hit the steak or caviar sections, à la carte prices here are pretty splashy. Maybe visit for brunch, Sunday Lunch or Mon-Thu pre-theatre, where there are prix-fixe menus for £40-£50 per head. / SW1Y 6AJ; quaglinos-restaurant.co.uk; quaglinos; Mon-Thu midnight, Fri & Sat 1 am, Sun 7 pm.

The Quality Chop House EC1 £114 3|4|3
88-94 Farringdon Rd 020 7278 1452 10–1A

"The great meat cookery never disappoints at this a quirky venue" – a Clerkenwell institution opened in 1869 as a 'Progressive Working Class Caterer' and nowadays part of Will Lander & Daniel Morgenthau's group. "Top quality cuts are cooked to a T" – "imaginative fare" that's full of "meaty goodness". The "uncomfortable pews" annoy some customers, but won't be replaced because they're Grade II listed – the private dining room upstairs is a good alternative if there are seven or more in your party. Top Menu Tip – the "confit potatoes always get 'wow' responses from first-timers". / EC1R 3EA; thequalitychophouse.com; qualitychop; Tue-Sat 10 pm, Sun 3.30 pm.

Quality Wines EC1 £65 3|3|4
90-94 Farringdon Road   020 3602 8115   10–1A

There's "a real buzz" around Quality Chop House's "little sibling next door", where chef Nick Bramham, working solo, knocks out a "short but enticing menu that changes every week" – "how he does it in the tiny kitchen is baffling!". "You might need to perch but it's great food and fun to visit". / EC1R 3EA; qualitywinesfarringdon.com; qualitywinesfarringdon; Tue-Sat 10 pm.

Quilon SW1 £94 5|4|2
41 Buckingham Gate   020 7821 1899   2–4B

In a plush hotel near Buckingham Palace, this "very classy" dining room "focuses on dishes from southern India's coastal areas, especially seafood" ("they also go out of their way to feed vegans in style"), all delivered with a "subtle" touch. Running the kitchen since 1999, Sriram Aylur has earned the right to be regarded as one of the capital's elite subcontinental chefs. A recurring gripe, though, concerns the uneventful decor and "stuffy atmosphere". / SW1E 6AF; quilon.co.uk; thequilon; Mon-Sat 11 pm, Sun 10.30 pm.

Quo Vadis W1 £91 3|3|5
26-29 Dean St   020 7437 9585   4–1D

"It always feels special" to visit the Hart Bros' 'Grande Dame of Dean Street' (est. 1926 in a historic building, where Karl Marx started to pen 'Das Kapital') – a cosseting haven of "warm and friendly" hospitality with "lovely decor"; and "for somewhere this clubby-feeling in the centre of town, it doesn't break the bank". Jeremy Lee's "monthly changing seasonal menu is a delight" – contemporary but with a slightly retro British vibe (and "it's always exciting to see what the pie of the day is"); thoughtful wine selection too – "some fair-priced reds" in particular. (At least that's the story painted in the vast majority of reports: ratings would be even higher were they not capped by a small but noticeable minority who found the performance this year "disappointing on a couple of occasions"; or "tired"). Top Menu Tips – "the smoked eel sandwich is so good it manages to live up to its reputation!". And "pie of the day is unmissable", "with wonderfully thin, crisp, buttery pastry". / W1D 3LL; quovadissoho.co.uk; quovadissoho; Mon-Sat 10 pm; SRA-2 stars.

Rabbit SW3 £72 2|3|3
172 King's Rd   020 3750 0172   6–3C

This "fun place" on the King's Road with "happy, smiling staff" and an "eclectic" faux-rustic interior is, for most diners, an enjoyable spot for a meal – even if the cooking doesn't always do full justice to the Gladwin Bros' 'Local & Wild' ethos (of food farmed and foraged by their family). We do have reports of "delicious light lunches" with "glorious comfort food", but it's patchy: for instance, one would-be fan opines – "having visited the family vineyard in Nutbourne on several occasions, we came with high hopes. The food was surprisingly mediocre, the game pie dry and unappetising. What should be a real gem was disappointing". / SW3 4UP; rabbit-restaurant.com; rabbit_resto; Mon-Sat 10.30 pm, Sun 8 pm.

Ragam W1 £39 4|3|1
57 Cleveland St   020 7636 9098   2–1B

It's "always a pleasure to eat the tasty, well-spiced and reliably classy Keralan food" at this "very good value" veteran in a basement near the Telecom Tower. There's "friendly service in the compact dining area", although the interior is not going to win design awards any time soon. Top Menu Tips – "love the fritters!"; dosas here are a perennial favourite too. / W1T 4JN; ragamindian.co.uk; Mon-Sat 11 pm.

RAI WC1 — £109
11-13 Bayley Street   020 8149 6248   2–1C
Re-launched in February 2024 at a new address in Bayley Street, Bloomsbury, this sushi and omakase specialist (from the team behind Islington's Hot Stone) had a brief run in Fitzrovia before closing down last year. With just 10 seats at tables and another eight at a sushi counter, it is a tiny space, but is big in culinary ambition. Too little feedback for a rating, but one report applauds "fantastic food with excellent service, in a beautiful venue". / WC1B 3HD; rairestaurant.com; rai.restaurant; Tue-Thu 11 pm, Fri & Sat 11.30 pm, Sun 10.30 pm.

Rambutan SE1 — £42   4 3 3
10 Stoney Street   no tel   10–4C
"Sooooo good Sri Lankan cooking!" – "spicy" with "fantastic ingredients and authentic flavours" – has won a major following for Cythia Shanmugalingham's Borough Market two-year-old. "Frequented by a hip crowd", it's a lively place too and "watching the chefs at work in the open kitchen is a joy", with much of the cooking over an open grill. "You need to order a lot to come out full though, which can make it a pricey pitstop". Top Menu Tip – "top rotis". / SE1 9AD; rambutanlondon.com; rambutan_ldn; Mon-Wed 10.15 pm, Thu-Sat 10.15pm, Sun 9 pm.

Randall & Aubin W1 — £86   4 3 4
14-16 Brewer St   020 7287 4447   4–2D
"Brilliant seafood and the best vibe" fuel the festivities at this upbeat venue – "still one of the most fun restaurants in London", where "watching Soho life go by is just brilliant!". The premises was converted almost 30 years ago from an Edwardian butcher's, famous for supplying The Ritz, the Savoy and Winston Churchill – hence the name and wonderful interior. Grab a high stool, a glass of fizz and a simple plate of something fishy and it's a great antidote to life's challenges. / W1F 0SG; randallandaubin.com; randallandaubin; Mon-Thu 10.30 pm, Fri & Sat 11.30 pm, Sun 9.30 pm.

Rasa N16 — £50   4 3 2
55 Stoke Newington Church St   020 7249 0344   1–1C
Das Sreedharan's famous bright pink Stoke Newington Keralan has won a legion of fans over the decades – "it was the first veggie restaurant I ever went to about 30 years ago and I didn't miss meat one bit". Various spin-offs have opened and closed in that time, most recently Rasa Street across the road. No longer with the rarity value it once enjoyed, its ratings remain very respectable all-round. Top Menu Tip – "lovely masala dosa". / N16 0AR; rasarestaurants.com; Mon-Sun 10.30 pm.

Rasa Sayang W1 — £54   3 3 2
5 Macclesfield Street   020 7734 1382   5–3A
"Authentic southeast Asian hawker cooking" draws "well-deserved queues" to this "noisy" Chinatown spot from Ellen Chew, who began her working life hawking Chinese-Malay street food in Singapore. "Yes, there are many more Asian super-expensive venues in and around London, but the sheer excellence and predictability of this well-known eatery can't be beaten". Top Menu Tip – "lovely, fluffy roti". / W1D 6AY; rasasayangfood.com; rasasayang_london; Mon-Sat 10 pm, Sun 9 pm.

Ravel's Bistro NW3 — £45   2 3 3
4 Fleet Road   02074853615   9–2B
Complete with a purple facade and awning billing itself as 'London's Best Kept Secret' – this dated-looking French bistro behind the Royal Free has been a feature of Gospel Oak for the last 25 years. For a "cheap 'n' cheerful" meal free of foodie pretensions it wins numerous recommendations as "a very pleasant and reasonable local". / NW3 2QS; ravelsbistro.com; Mon-Sat 10.30 pm, Sun 8.30 pm.

F S A

Ravi Shankar NW1 £38 **3** 2 2
133-135 Drummond St   020 7388 6458   9–4C
This "good and very cheap" vegetarian in a "great location" is a 42-year fixture of the 'Little India' zone behind Euston station, serving a wide range of bhel puri, thali set meals and south Indian dosas. There's also a "great buffet at weekends". / NW1 2HL; ravishankarbhelpoori.com; Mon-Sun 11 pm.

Rayuela W5 £72 **3** **4** **3**
9 Dickens Yard   020 4568 6659   1–4A
"A beacon of originality in a slightly characterless property development in Ealing Broadway" – this Hispanic venture with South American influences from a Colombian chef is, say fans, "a perfect blend of neighbourhood restaurant and Spanish fine dining". It was already a hot ticket locally before a rave January 2024 review from Giles Coren in The Times brought it to wider attention and perhaps inevitably one or two sceptics fear hype: "it is enjoyable but I feel that its reputation now creates excessive expectations". / W5 2TD; rayuela.co.uk; rayuela_uk; Wed-Sat 10.30 pm, Tue 10 pm, Sun 5 pm.

The Red Lion & Sun N6 £66 **3** **3** **3**
25 North Road   020 8340 1780   9–1B
One of north London's best known pub-destinations nowadays – this "popular, owner-run gastropub" in Highgate offers a "varied menu of lovely food at reasonable prices", including "highly rated Sunday roasts and a good selection of fresh seafood". It's a "very relaxing" place, "especially lovely on a summer's day in the garden", and is "perfect after a long walk on the heath". / N6 4BE; theredlionandsun.com; theredlionandsun; Mon-Sun 11 pm.

Regency Cafe SW1 £16 **3** **4** **5**
17-19 Regency Street   020 7821 6596   2–4C
A post-War gem in Westminster, this "bright, Formica-tabled institution serves old-fashioned greasy-spoon fare" and is a place of retro pilgrimage nowadays. Don't be put off by the "intimidating queue, which moves reasonably quickly – and there's always a table miraculously free in the end". "We returned for the first time in six years and it's still as great as it ever was…" – in fact, it's barely changed since opening in 1946. / SW1P 4BY; regencycafe.co.uk; _theregencycafe_; Mon-Fri 7.15 pm, Sat 12 pm.

Le Relais de Venise L'Entrecôte £58 **3** 2 **3**
120 Marylebone Ln, W1   020 7486 0878   2–1A
5 Throgmorton St, EC2   020 7638 6325   10–2C
"Still the best cheap steak in London" for fans, despite growing competition – these "bustling" and "tightly packed" Paris-based ventures thrive on an "unchanged formula (steak + salad + frites + secret sauce + French staff outfits + bustle)" with branches in Marylebone and the City, whose permanent queues testify to their winning style. "A bit bish, bash, bosh but great fun", they "do what it says on the tin, without grandstanding or ludicrous pricing (are you watching Hawksmoor?)". / relaisdevenise.com; lerelaisdeveniseofficial.

Restaurant 1890 by Gordon Ramsay WC2 £211 **3** **4** **4**
Strand   020 7499 0124   5–3D
"A true special-occasion destination" – Gordon Ramsay's bijou first-floor dining room in the Savoy has been one of his best openings of recent times and provided one reporter's "best meal in the last couple of years". James Sharp oversees a "fabulous" tasting menu that deals excellently with the constraints of the main kitchen being at a distance from the dining room. There's a thoughtful selection of wines by the glass – if you really want to push the boat out, you can even order 50 ml of 1779 Madeira for £750. The small space best suits it to an intimate diner à deux (easy conversation is provided by your bird's-eye view of the comings and goings at the Savoy's

main entrance); although there are a couple of tables for larger parties. "Expensive but can't fault it". / WC2R 0EZ; gordonramsayrestaurants.com; restaurant1890gordonramsay; Fri & Sat, Tue-Thu 9.30 pm.

Restaurant St. Barts EC1 £183 4 3 4
63 Bartholomew Close   020 4547 7985   10–2B

"Every course of the tasting menu is a revelation", say fans of Johnnie Crowe, Luke Wasserman & Toby Neill's "calm" and "imaginatively decorated" two-year-old, which enjoys fine views of St Bartholomew the Great and its cloisters through its floor-to-ceiling windows. The cuisine is strongly rooted in the British Isles and results can be "stunning" – "well deserving of the star" the tyre men awarded swiftly after it opened. Perhaps reflecting increasing prices (now £160 per person for a six-course menu), it didn't quite achieve the top ratings this year that it did in last year's annual diners' poll, and the odd critic feels it risks becoming "too cool, up itself and expensive". / EC1A 7BG; restaurant-stbarts.co.uk; restaurantstbarts; Tue-Thu 7.30 pm, Fri & Sat 8 pm.

Reubens W1 £63 3 2 3
79 Baker St   020 7486 0035   2–1A

Having suffered a fire in February 2024, Britain's longest-running kosher restaurant (est. 1973 on a different site) aims to relaunch by the end of the summer. (Its rating has been maintained on the principle that it is likely to emerge essentially unchanged from its former guise). Just the job when you have cravings for "good value salt beef and a high standard of meatballs": such needs can also be answered at Lee Landau's new Reubens-branded bakery on the other side of Baker Street. / W1U 6RG; reubensrestaurant.co.uk; reubens_restaurant; Sun-Thu 10 pm, Fri 6 pm.

Rhythm & Brews W4 £25 2 3 4
22 Walpole Gardens   020 7998 3873   8–2A

"Wonderful breakfasts, tasty coffee and cakes… and with a proper vinyl music background – what's not to love?". This pitch-perfect "indie coffee shop" near Turnham Green church "also sells records" and morphs into a mini music venue in the evenings, with live gigs and a licensed bar. / W4 4HA; rhythmandbrews.co.uk; rhythmandbrewscafe; Sun-Fri 5 pm, Sat 5pm.

The Rib Man E1 £11 5 4 -
Brick Lane, Brick Lane Market   no tel   13–2C

The Rib Man – aka Mark Gevaux – is a landmark feature of Brick Lane's Sunday market, with folks queueing for his BBQ ribs and pork rolls from pigs reared outdoors in Norfolk and Suffolk. Actually, you don't need to queue: nowadays you can order his meat and trademark 'Holy Fuck' and other colourfully named hot sauces online. / E1 6HR; theribman.co.uk; theribman; Sun 2 pm.

Riccardo's SW3 £59 3 4 3
126 Fulham Rd   020 7370 6656   6–3B

This "fantastically reliable spot for homemade pasta and Tuscan staples" on a Chelsea corner celebrates its 30th anniversary this year, and is arguably "either a relic or a classic… or maybe just a restaurant that knows what it is good at". "Relaxed and informal", with "friendly staff under the command of the wonderful Paz" – "it's an easy place to dine on your own". "Another plus is that practically the whole menu is also available as tapas/small dishes". / SW3 6HU; riccardos.it; riccardoslondon; Mon-Sat 11 pm, Sun 10.30 pm.

Rick Stein SW14 £92 2 2 3
Tideway Yard, 125 Mortlake High St   020 8878 9462   11–1A

A "brilliant location on the Thames" near Barnes Bridge can't mask the reality that this venue from the high-profile TV chef "doesn't live up to his reputation". Some reporters do hail it as a "go-to" for "imaginative" fish cooking, but for far too many diners it's "living on the Stein name" with "overpriced" food that "lacks edge" and whose "relatively high score for *ambience only truly applies if you get one of the tables by the floor-to-ceiling windows overlooking the river (fabulous on a nice day)".* In summer 2024, it was announced that the family are seeking a central London site for the brand – to cut the mustard in the West End it will need to be a step up from this one. / SW14 8SN; rickstein.com; ricksteinrestaurants; Mon-Sun 9 pm; SRA-1 star.

Riding House £64 2 3 3
43-51 Great Titchfield St, W1   020 7927 0840   3–1C
The Brunswick Centre, Bernard Street, WC1   020 3829 8333   2–1D
With its mix of grown-up comfort food and fashionable styling, Adam White's Fitzrovia fixture has long been a key destination for *"all-day brunch on Saturdays"*, and in recent times has added an attractive new sibling at the brutalist Brunswick Centre in Bloomsbury (there's also a related 'Railhouse' at Nova at Victoria). Top Menu Tip – *"kedgeree to die for"*. / ridinghousecafe.co.uk.

The Rising Sun NW7 £75 3 4 3
137 Marsh Ln   020 8959 1357   1–1B
A real *"neighbourhood gem"*, this *"fun"* and *"quirky"* 16th-century pub in Mill Hill serves *"what must be some of the best pub food in North London"*. It's presided over in fine style by brothers Luca and Matteo Delnevo, presenting a modern, British-Italian menu. / NW7 4EY; therisingsunhill.com; therisingsunmillhill; Tue-Sat 9.30 pm, Sun 8 pm.

Ristorante Frescobaldi W1 £97 2 2 2
15 New Burlington Place   020 3693 3435   4–2A
"Typical Italian fare" comes with a moneyed gloss at this 10-year-old venture off Savile Row from a Florentine banking family with a 700-year-old sideline in wine-making. There is a *"warm Mayfair buzz if you're into hedge fund types"*, and *"if you calm yourself with a couple of drinks before you see the prices on the menu, lunch here can be a very enjoyable experience"*. / W1S 5HX; frescobaldi.london; frescobaldi_london; Mon-Sat 11 pm, Sun 10 pm.

The Ritz,
Palm Court W1 £143 3 4 5
150 Piccadilly   020 7493 8181   3–4C
"The benchmark to which all others aspire" – this hallowed institution is a *"well-oiled operation"* and *"there's no better place for afternoon tea"*. Dud reports are practically unknown, and by nearly all accounts *"everything is flawless"*: *"you will never leave hungry"* as the cake and sarnies just keep on coming; service is *"exceptional"*; and *"the spectacular decor"* contributes to *"one of the best experiences ever"*. *"My mother always says a visit here 'suits me a treat'!"* / W1J 9BR; theritzlondon.com; theritzlondon; Mon-Sun 7.30 pm; SRA-3 stars.

The Ritz W1 £196 4 4 5
150 Piccadilly   020 7300 2370   3–4C
"The interior is so magnificent, it feels like eating in Versailles!" at this *"beautiful"* chamber, which many cognoscenti consider to be *"the most attractive dining room in London"*. If you are a natural traditionalist and have money to burn, *"this is the restaurant in London for that special meal"* because *"every time you go it feels like a perfect, memorable occasion"* (and *"thankfully a dress code is still in force!"*). Under John Williams and his team, *"absolutely stellar ingredients are superbly cooked with sensible updating of classic dishes; all combined with immaculate, polished silver service"*. It's *"undeniably expensive, yes"*, although fans feel it's *"worth every penny"*. In fact, some of the fooderati feel that *"surely two Michelin stars are warranted"*: *"I just can't see why the Guide only gives it one star, as it's so much better than some of the Gallic three stars not that far away!!"*. Top Menu Tips – *"The langoustines à la nage are perfectly cooked with magic flavours. The foie gras is perfection. The pigeon de Bresse utterly amazing – so hard to cook immaculately as it is. Don't start me on the truffle jus!"*. And *"there is usually some theatre when someone has ordered the Crêpes*

Suzette, cooked at the table, apparently with a healthy slug of booze, and with flames shooting up every so often around the room!" / W1J 9BR; theritzlondon.com; theritzlondon; Mon-Sun 9 pm; SRA-3 stars.

Riva SW13 £88 3 4 2
169 Church Rd   020 8748 0434   11–1A

"Serious, and seriously delicious food, served in a simple space that helps to focus attention on what matters" has made Andreas Riva's Barnes veteran a "staple of Italian food lovers", oft-cited by top food writers like Nigella Lawson as their favourite destination. It's boosted by "exceptionally long-serving, loyal staff" who provide regulars in particular with service they acclaim as "delightful, efficient, warm and friendly". A typical account of a meal might run as follows: "Specials of puntarelle, gnocchi and suckling pig, and the calves' liver and red onions from the menu, together with a dessert of tiramisu, were all faultless. Wines by the glass – a Pinot Bianco and a Tuscan Sangiovese – matched beautifully and were modestly priced". As often is the case here though, there is a contrarian viewpoint and it gained ground this year: "We hadn't been impressed with Riva when we had eaten there many years ago, but thought we'd try it again, after reading several very positive reviews. Our recent visit, however, confirmed our earlier verdict. The menu choice was uninspiring, service indifferent and the venue was run-down and in need of attention. Prices were high and the elderly man who seemed to be in charge ignored diners and sat at a table doing paperwork. We definitely won't be returning!" / SW13 9HR; riva.restaurant; Tue-Sat 10 pm, Sun 9 pm.

The River Café W6 £150 2 1 2
Thames Wharf, Rainville Rd   020 7386 4200   8–2C

"Things have gone crazy, price-wise, but it's still magic" – that's the perennial and worsening trade-off at Ruth Rogers' world-famous, Thames-side icon, tucked away between the Thames and a Hammersmith backstreet. Started in 1987 in the canteen of her late-hubbie's architectural practice (in partnership with Rose Gray), it's still faithful to its mission of "brilliant, simple, modern Italian food, from top-quality ingredients, superbly executed". And while "the food is uncomplicated in the sense that it is not fussy, there is nevertheless a sure-footed sophistication in its preparation". So far, so good, and pretty much everyone agrees that if money were no object a visit here (especially outside by the river in summer) is "just perfect". But verdicts on the ever-fraught juggle here between price, quality and value are increasingly going haywire. To its most loyal habitués (often arriving by chauffered car from posher postcodes): "is it expensive, yes, but worth it? Absolutely. I've never had a disappointing meal and have been going since 1990". To those who 'know the price of milk' however, it's "monumentally overpriced" and increasingly risks "spiralling to the clip-joint level" ("It's actually beyond a joke now, financially. Gone beyond very expensive into 'you don't actually want normal people here at all, do you?' territory"). "It would also help if they could get their staff organised". The "casual" service from posh public school girls on their 'gap y'ar' has always been of the love-it-or-hate-it variety, but can plain jar at such a premium price. / W6 9HA; rivercafe.co.uk; therivercafelondon; Mon-Sat 9 pm, Sun 3 pm.

River Café Café W6 NEW
Rainville Rd   020 7386 4200   8–2C

Next door to its world famous parent, this summer 2024 debut – an unused part of the former architect's practice with outside tables right by the Thames towpath – is an everyday spin-off from the mothership, aimed at capturing passers-by and foodie-anoraks who want to say they've had the Chocolate Nemesis without forking out for the whole shebang. Alongside coffee, it serves an all-day menu of filled brioche and bruschetta, salumi, cheeses and light bites, desserts and gelati. / W6 9HA; Mon, Wed & Thu, Sun 10 pm, Fri & Sat 11 pm.

F S A

Riviera SW1
23 St James's Street   020 8050 6932   3–4D

As with its glossy forerunners, Arian & Alberto Zandi's year-old attempt to import Côte d'Azur style to St James's seems yet to have unlocked the potential of this striking site (formerly Sake no Hana, RIP), which boasts 120 covers complete with open kitchen and ground-floor bar. Such feedback as we have is upbeat, but too limited for a reliable rating and in its first 12 months, despite its prominent location, it's been largely ignored by other reviewers too. / SW1 1HA; riviera-london.co.uk; rivieralondon; Mon-Sat 1.30 am, Sun 11.30 pm.

Roast SE1   £85   2 2 3
Stoney St   0845 034 7300   10–4C

Celebrating its 10th anniversary this year, this attractive operation makes the most of its spectacular setting overlooking Borough Market from a dramatic wrought-iron and glass structure (that once formed part of Covent Garden's Royal Opera House). Flying the flag for traditional British cuisine – in particular steaks and Beef Wellington – it is most popular for business entertaining, and particularly well-established as a "reliable and enjoyable" destination for work breakfasts, with "decent food, professional service and strong coffee" ("just what you need when entertaining clients at 8am"). In terms of value for money, though, it loses out to numerous neighbours in and around the market. / SE1 1TL; roast-restaurant.com; roast_restaurant; Tue-Fri, Mon, Sat 10 pm, Sun 6.30 pm.

Rocca   £52   2 3 3
73 Old Brompton Rd, SW7   020 7225 3413   6–2B
75-79 Dulwich Village, SE21   020 8299 6333   1–4D

There's "a lot to like and not much to dislike" at this duo of "basic neighbourhood Italians" in South Ken and Dulwich Village – even harsher critics (who say the food is "generic" or "just about passable") find them "pleasant"; and they're often "full of families" because the "excellent staff make kids very welcome". / roccarestaurants.com.

Rochelle Canteen E2   £75   3 3 4
16 Playground Gardens   020 7729 5677   13–1C

"Hidden away by a walled garden, with simple food from a tiny open-plan kitchen" – Melanie Arnold & Margot Henderson's (wife of St John's Fergus) well-known venue near Spitalfields occupies the converted bike sheds of a former school. "Surprisingly tranquil for this part of London", "on a summer's day the garden room is the perfect place to eat" (there's also an indoor space). "Simple , well-chosen food comes from a tiny open-plan kitchen" – "not flash but always interesting" with "fresh flavours". There was still the odd duff report this year, but inconsistency was much-reduced on last year's feedback. / E2 7ES; arnoldandhenderson.com; rochellecanteen; Mon & Tue, Sun 2.45 pm, Wed-Sat 7.30 pm.

Rock & Rose   £67   2 3 3
270-272 Chiswick High Road, W4   020 4537 4566   8–2A
106-108 Kew Road, TW9   020 8948 8008   1–4A

"For a jolly night out with the girls", these "warm and luxurious" west London haunts are just the job. An "extensive list of cocktails" is key to their allure – "the food is not the main attraction although it's perfectly acceptable". Lorraine Angliss (who also owns Annie's and Little Bird) opened the Richmond original in 2009; its Chiswick sibling followed in 2022.

Rock & Sole Plaice WC2   £64   3 3 2
47 Endell St   020 7836 3785   5–1C

"Perhaps it's not exactly exceptional, but who wants to spend a fortune on fish 'n' chips when this place hits the spot just as well?" This grungily cosy, no-frills veteran is on a Covent Garden site that's hosted a chippie since 1871 and its relatively mild pricing and handy location makes it a brilliant choice for

dependably feeding a big group in the West End on a budget. "Yes, it is full of tourists, but that shouldn't bother you". / WC2H 9AJ; rockandsoleplaice.com; rockandsolelondon; Mon-Sat 10 pm, Sun 9 pm.

Roe E14 NEW
Five Park Drive, Wood Wharf   020 7078 8808   12–1C

Jack Croft and Will Murray's majorly ambitious follow-up to their smash hit Fallow – this huge 500-seater opened in late Spring 2024 in Canary Wharf (next door to the floating Hawksmoor in Wood Wharf). It carries forward their sustainable ethos, with a nose-to-tail menu that includes a mixed grill of venison (it is, after all, named after a native breed of deer); along with vegetables grown on-site using an 'aeroponic' green wall. It opened too late for any feedback in our annual diners' poll, but on his May 2024 visit, The Evening Standard's Jimi Famurewa hailed it as "one of the defining, gravity-defying openings of the year" due to its "Ferrari on the driveway" styling and "triumphant" cooking including lamb "so succulent and yielding [it] fell off the bone under nothing but a hard stare". / E14 9GG; roerestaurant.co.uk; roerestaurant; Mon-Sun 10.30 pm.

Roger's Kitchen NW1   £65   4 3 3
71 Camden Road   020 8066 0747   9–2C

"Delicious Jamaican food from the original Mango Room chef" makes it worth discovering Roger Shakes's "favourite Caribbean". It's in a nondescript stretch of shops as you head out of Camden Town, but stylishly and comfortably appointed (e.g. tablecloths!). "Brilliant atmosphere at the weekend in particular". / NW1 9EU; rogerskitchen.co.uk; Mon-Sun 11 pm.

Rogues E2   £75   4 4 3
460 Hackney Road   020 3737 3690   14–2B

"Having started as a pop-up these guys are going from strength to strength" – Freddie Sheen & Zac Whittle opened their first permanent home in Cambridge Heath in March 2022. "It's one of the better options amongst the plethora of small-plates-and-wine joints to have opened all over east London (seemingly avoiding PR hype but nevertheless constantly packed, mainly from word of mouth)". There is a tasting option (for £50-60 per person), but most meals are à la carte featuring "imaginative flavour combinations done to a consistent standard and at comparatively friendly prices". Service is "friendly" and there's a good "buzz" (although not everyone is sold on its recent expansion). / E2 9EG; rogueslondon.com; Tue-Fri midnight, Sat 1.30 am, Sun 11.30 pm.

Roka   £99   3 2 3
30 North Audley St, W1   020 7305 5644   3–2A
37 Charlotte St, W1   020 7580 6464   2–1C
71-91 Aldwych, WC2   020 7294 7636   2–2D
Unit 4, Park Pavilion, 40 Canada Sq, E14   020 7636 5228   12–1C

"I keep going back to Roka, and have never had a bad meal there" – so say fans of Arjun Waney & Rainer Becker's slick Japanese-inspired venues, which are celebrating their 20th year in 2024. "Despite increasing competition, it remains a good choice, with sound cooking and good-value sushi, sashimi and robata dishes"; and despite perennial complaints that they are "way overpriced for tiny portions", quality has held up well. All that said, service is more often "amateurish" and "erratic" than it once was; and long-term fans have a point when they say the general performance is "not as good as it used to be" – the 2024 openings will be in Bahrain, Germany and Greece and there is growing impression of 'the same old, same old' in its original home market. / rokarestaurant.com; rokarestaurant.

Roketsu W1   £294   5 3 3
12 New Quebec Street   020 3149 1227   2–2A

"Everything is exceptional" at this "wonderful" three-year-old in Marylebone, where Kyoto-trained chef-patron Daisuke Hayashi presents "a delicious kaiseki set menu that changes with the seasons". The interior was created

from 100-year-old hinoki wood and shipped over from Japan, so "you are literally taken away to a small Japanese inn where all your five senses are immersed into a complete Japanese experience", and "everything is made and served with immense care". At the 10-seat counter you can also eat 'kappo'-style (where guest and chef design the menu together); or you can sit in the lounge, where an à la carte menu (consideraby cheaper) is served with a choice of 500 drinks. Whichever option you choose, you're in for a "wonderful treat", "with absolutely fantastic food". / W1H 7RW; roketsu.co.uk; roketsulondon; Tue, Wed, Sat, Thu & Fri 10 pm.

Roots TW11 £45 4 4 3
78 Teddington High Street   02089772322   1–4A

"A great local Indian" in leafy Teddington "where the cooking has a modern twist" – Mayur Nagarale opened this contemporary spot enlivened by a large, colourful mural in mid 2023 and it quickly won a more-than-local reputation, with fans crossing numerous postcodes for a meal. / TW11 8JD; rootsteddington.co.uk; Tue-Thu 9.30 pm, Fri & Sat 10.30 pm, Sun 9 pm.

Rosmarino SW17 £48 3 3 3
23 Trinity Road   020 8244 0336   11–2C

A "neighbourhood gem" near Tooting Bec station – this "buzzy" five-year-old from husband-and-wife team Daria Serra and Giovanni Renna's serves "really decent Italian cooking and good wines" in a "friendly" atmosphere – "what's not to like?". / SW17 7SD; rosmarinorestaurant.co.uk; rosmarinorestaurant; Tue-Sat 10.30 pm, Sun 10 pm.

Rosslyn Coffee EC4 £8 4 4 3
78 Queen Victoria Street   no tel   10–3B

"Unbeatable tastes and friendly staff" are the key attributes of this trio of intensely focused and internationally respected coffee shops, within walking distance of each other in the City. Founders James Hennebry and Mat Russell import from the world's best roasteries, and model their shops on the best in Melbourne (where Rosslyn Street is found). / EC4N 4SJ; Mon-Sun 11 pm.

Roti Chai W1 £49 3 2 2
3 Portman Mews South   020 7408 0101   3–1A

"Delicious Indian street food" is served on the ground floor of this fixture in a side alley off Oxford Street, near Selfridges, where "service is fast and friendly" too. Downstairs in the basement, it's a more formal and traditional restaurant set-up. "Tried both floors as they have different menus – both great, but definitely favour the upstairs". / W1H 6AY; rotichai.com; rotichai; Mon-Sat 10 pm, Sun 9 pm.

Roti King £15 5 3 1
40 Doric Way, NW1   020 7387 2518   9–3C
97 Lower Marsh, SE1   no tel   10–4A **NEW**
Battersea Power Station, SW8   020 4580 1282   11–1C
6 Artillery Ln, E1   no tel   10–2B **NEW**

"God those rotis are heaven!" – they make it "worth joining the inevitable queue" (including "lots of Malaysian students and Asian visitors enjoying a taste of home") for this "small Malaysian street-food cafe" in a packed little basement near Euston station. "A lot of patience is required lining up outside": the queue here is such a regular fixture that the council have allowed the installation of a long decked area in the parking bays on the street to accommodate it. "The fluffy roti canai itself is amazing: you watch chef swirling and stretching paper thin dough". But the "rich and aromatic" noodles and curries also on the menu can be just as rewarding. Don't expect a long foodie religious experience. The "functional" service will get you in and out in no time. There are also now a growing number of spin-offs, of which the most high-profile is in Battersea Power Station, whose shiny vibe could not be more at odds with the grungy original; and where there's "more of a feeling of a fast-food joint". Even so, it comes "highly recommended for *anyone looking to try some authentic and tasty Malaysian cuisine"; "it's good to find such a reasonable place near Battersea Power Station. You can sit outside if weather permits. But it's very popular and no booking, so go early to get a table". Also in Waterloo and – since this year – in Spitalfields. Top Tip in NW1 – takeaway lunch is easier than queueing and amazing value too.* / rotikinguk.

Rotunda Bar & Restaurant, Kings Place N1 £68 2 2 3
90 York Way   020 7014 2840   9–3C
A "lovely canalside location" at the foot of the Kings Place concert hall (and with a large outside terrace in summer) is the strong suit of this contemporary fixture, which is very well-appointed for an arts centre venue. "Excellent meat" is the top culinary attraction, supplied by the owners' farm in Matfen, Northumberland. / N1 9AG; rotundabarandrestaurant.co.uk; rotundalondon; Tue-Sat midnight, Mon 11 pm, Sun 5 pm.

ROVI W1 £95 4 3 3
59-65 Wells Street   020 3963 8270   3–1D
"The celeriac shawarma is to die for": all part of the "fabulous" mélange of Middle Eastern tastes – often "with a focus on vegetables" ('from root to tip, with a fresh focus on fermentation') – to be found in the "wonderful sharing plates" served at Yotam Ottolenghi's Fitzrovia flagship; and it provides "terrific, unusual cocktails" too. As is typical of his restaurant DNA, "you do pay a lot for these tastes" – to the extent that a small but notable minority find it "overrated and quite disappointing" – but most diners consider it "fabulous all-round". / W1A 3AE; ottolenghi.co.uk; rovi_restaurant; Mon-Sat 10.30 pm; SRA-2 stars.

Rowley's SW1 £94 3 2 3
113 Jermyn St   020 7930 2707   4–4D
"It's all about steak and chips at the heart of matters" (although there are a smattering of other dishes) at this "central, no-fuss steakhouse", whose "old-fashioned ambience" befits its near half-century in St James's (on the site of the original Walls meat business). "Discreet service" and a "quiet dining room" make it "ideal for those business discussions"; as does the "good wine list". It can seem pricey, but – by way of compensation – if you are hungry, you can have as many chips as you like! / SW1Y 6HJ; rowleys.co.uk; rowleys_restaurant; Tue-Sat 11 pm.

Royal China £71 3 2 2
24-26 Baker St, W1   020 7487 4688   2–1A
805 Fulham Rd, SW6   020 7731 0081   11–1B
30 Westferry Circus, E14   020 7719 0888   12–1B
This "always reliable" and "slightly upmarket" Cantonese group "remains the standard that all other dim sum places should be judged against – exemplary is an overused term here but is very much justified". But a somewhat dark cloud has hung over the operation since its prominent Baker Street branch was stripped of its licence to sell alcohol and fined £360,000 after a series of Home Office raids over six years discovered multiple cases of illegal immigrants working, in one case for 66 hours a week at almost half the minimum wage. As of August 2024, the Fulham Road branch is 'Temporarily Closed'. / royalchinagroup.co.uk.

Royal China Club W1 £81 3 2 2
38-42 Baker Street   020 7486 3898   2–1A
"The food is always good" at the Marylebone flagship of the Royal China group, while the "well-spaced tables, attractive presentation and attentive service" contribute to a somewhat more stately atmosphere than at other branches. It is, though, "pricey": "it feels like the same food as Royal China but costing 30% more". / W1U 7AJ; royalchinagroup.co.uk; Sun-Thu 11 pm, Fri & Sat 11.30 pm.

Royal Opera House,
Amphitheatre WC2 £79 233
Covent Garden   020 7304 4000   5–3D

"Great views" make it worth finding the lovely outside terrace of ROH's 'piazza' restaurant ("inside feels a bit like an airport lounge"). The food "isn't bad either" – with "special themed menus to fit the opera" – and it's a useful option even if you're not on audience duty. We don't normally list it, but it attracted quite a number of recommendations this year. / WC2E 9DD; rbo.org.uk; Mon-Sun 9 pm.

Royal Opera House,
Piazza Cafe WC2 £79 223
Covent Garden   020 7304 4000   5–2D

"Located on the fifth floor of the Royal Opera House" – this amenity for opera-goers is also open to the public throughout the week, and for the heart of Covent Garden its appeal for many probably lies in the general absence of hoi polloi from these cultured environs. Its top feature is a bright, glazed terrace with fine views over the area, which comes into its own in summer. Fans rave over its brasserie fare too (for example "excellent steak"), although they generally opt for the "well-priced set lunch menu"; critics say you get "rather small portions of OK food at high prices". / WC2E 8RA; rbo.org.uk; Mon & Tue, Sun 10 pm, Wed-Sat 10.45 pm.

Royal Opera House,
Floral Hall WC2 £79 234
Covent Garden   020 7304 4000   5–3D

After the revamp of the Royal Opera House at the turn of the 21st century, this "lovely", light-filled space was one of the highlights of its reopening. A "good choice for something to eat before a performance" – it's certainly "not cheap" but of decent quality for an arts-venue restaurant, and it's always a "great place to people-watch". / WC2E 9DD; rbo.org.uk; Tue-Sat 9.15 pm.

Rucola at The Conduit WC2 £73
6 Langley Street   020 3912 8400   5–2C

On the top (sixth) floor of a socially conscious club/community/workspace, in Covent Garden development The Yards, this rooftop space is now open to the public. There's a 'plant-forward' menu of northern Italian dishes as interpreted by a team originating in Brooklyn – so no beef on the outdoor terrace BBQ! / WC2H 9JA; theconduit.com; theconduitlondon; Mon-Sat 10 pm, Sun 4 pm.

Rudy's W1 £36 343
80-82 Wardour St   020 7734 0195   4–2D

"Reliably fresh pizza with Mancunian roots" – "so cheap yet utterly delicious" – is now available at seven locations across the capital (the majority of which have opened in the last 12 months) from this fast-expanding chain from Manchester's all-conquering Mission Mars – "how can Pizza Express et al still serve the old stuff?". Stablemate Albert's Schloss bierkeller also arrived in London in summer 2024 – all 18,000 sq ft of it – just off Piccadilly Circus. / W1 0TG; rudyspizza.co.uk; @wearerudyspizza; Sun-Thu 9.30 pm, Fri & Sat 10.30 pm.

Rules WC2 £85 335
35 Maiden Ln   020 7836 5314   5–3D

"Step back in time at London's oldest restaurant" – on this site, in Covent Garden, since 1798 – "where the best of British resounds in its decor, menu and ambience". "Sometimes derided for being outdated or a tourist trap" ("fellow guests were either Yanks or elderly Brexiteers"), it actually remains remarkably "popular with the locals" and its large fan club says "a visit should be on everyone's bucket list". Hollywood would be proud of the decor ("it looks like the kind of place you dine in before deciding to conquer a remote land in the name of the crown") and – though some of its antique

furnishings are vaguely "preposterous" – the "special time warp" that's created is "enchanting". The "classic" menu has a fair share of "old-school-boy favourites" featuring a good amount of meat and game; and although it is "expensive" and "won't blow you away", it is "done well". "The wine list is OK if not great (sort of gentlemen's club level) but at least the mark-ups are reasonable". "Don't forget to visit the hidden gem of an upstairs cocktail bar to get the full experience". Top Menu Tip – "the old fashioned steak and kidney suet pudding with rich extra gravy in a silver boat. Crisp on the outside, meltingly soft on the inside with gloriously tender pieces of meat". / WC2E 7LB; rules.co.uk; rules_restaurant; Mon-Fri 10 pm, Sat & Sun 11.30 pm.

Sabor W1 £71 5 5 5
35 Heddon St   020 3319 8130   4–3A

"The best Spain has to offer in the UK" – Nieves Barragan's "genius" dishes are "packed with so much flavour" at her and José Etura's incredibly "buzzy and popular" destination, off Regent Street. "The tapas counter is one of London's top places to eat (the only problem is getting a seat) to enjoy stunningly fresh fare, straight from the chef". "Service is fantastic and the buzz in the room is palpable": this is one of the vanishingly small number of restaurants ever to have been awarded a 5,5,5. Note: whereas the counter, bar, and revamped outdoor terrace are saved for walk-ins, you can book upstairs for El Asador dining room and also for parties up to 10 at the large 'La Mesa' table on the ground floor. Top Menu Tips – lots of dishes come highly recommended in reports: "the immaculate Suckling Pig always stands out"; "The Cuttlefish Pappardelle & Manchego Pesto is wonderful"; "Monkfish tempura is exceptional"; and the "Goat's Cheese Ice Cream & Liquorice Sauce" also rates mention. / W1B 4BP; saborrestaurants.co.uk; sabor_ldn; Tue-Sat 10.30 pm; SRA-1 star.

Sachi at 19 Motcomb Street (fka 'Pantechnicon') SW1 £92
19 Motcomb Street   020 7034 5425   6–1D

Feelgood vibes abound on the lovely rooftop (complete with retractable glass ceiling) of this swanky Belgravian site atop the building formerly known as 'Pantechnicon', whose crowd seems to be jetting in for the day from St Tropez (with pricing to match). It's closed as we go to press as it undergoes a major reformatting, but we're betting that on re-opening in late 2024 much of its original DNA will survive. The menu – on relaunch – will be Japanese (under the brand of what used to be the basement restaurant); and it will also be served in the space immediately below (previously Eldr). / SW1X 8LB; pantechnicon.com; _pantechnicon; Mon-Sat midnight, Sun 11 pm.

Le Sacré-Coeur N1 £53 3 4 3
18 Theberton St   020 7354 2618   9–3D

This "well-established and reliable French bistro" with a "faux-rural dining room" in Islington is "good value, friendly and welcoming", while the "simple and traditional cooking packs plenty of flavour in quite generous servings". Top Tip – "go for the set lunch" (three courses for under £20). / N1 0QX; lesacrecoeurbistro.co.uk; lesacrecoeurfrenchbistro; Sun-Thu 10 pm, Fri & Sat 10.30 pm.

Sael SW1 NEW
1 Carlton Street   020 7993 3251   4–4D

Hot on the heels of reformatting Pollen Street Social (into Mary's, see also), this new opening (debut late autumn 2024) in St James's Market may become Jason Atherton's West End flagship. It's on the grand and spacious, 115-cover site that was formerly Aquavit (RIP), made over with low lighting and dark hues; and incorporating a separate bar. The aim is accessible, best-of-British cuisine that's less 'haute' than at Pollen Street (though from its relocated chef, Dale Bainbridge). / SW1Y 4QQ; saellondon.com; Thu & Fri, Wed, Sat 11 pm.

FSA

Sagar £46 3 2 2
37 Panton Street, SW1   020 3093 8463   5–4A
17a Percy St, W1   020 7631 3319   3–1D
31 Catherine St, WC2   020 7836 6377   5–3D
157 King St, W6   020 8741 8563   8–2C

"If you like dosas, idlis and uttapams", these "cheap and cheerful" but "spotless and well-run" canteens in the West End (plus Hammersmith and Harrow) are "an excellent choice for very good South Indian vegetarian food" – they're also "a top option to take a crowd because they're not fazed by large tables", and "even carnivores don't complain" when they try the "tasty food". / sagarrestaurant.co.uk.

Saint Jacques SW1 £88 3 4 3
5 St James's St   020 7930 2030   3–4D

This "very trad' French" operation in St James's – on the former site of Boulestin and L'Oranger – is led by sommelier Richard Weiss and features a superior (if perhaps rather "safe") "bistro-style menu". "Equally good for business and social gatherings", it's "particularly pleasant when the courtyard is open". / SW1 1EF; saintjacquesrestaurant.com; saintjacquesrestaurant; Mon-Fri 22, Sat 10 pm.

St John Bread & Wine E1 £77 3 3 2
94-96 Commercial St   020 7251 0848   13–2C

"All the dishes are a wonderful hit to the taste buds" at this Spitalfields canteen. Despite its utilitarian decor, fans say "it just feels so relaxed" and is "a great but more accessible way to access the mighty St John cooking" with Fergus Henderson's trademark 'nose-to-tail' approach (snails, faggots, pig's ear soup etc). That said, one or two long-term regulars do feel it's "gone off the boil" a little recently – "still good, but it does seem to have slipped a little"; perhaps just a blip? Top Menu Tip – "save room for the madeleines!".
/ E1 6LZ; stjohnrestaurant.com; st.john.restaurant; Mon-Sun 9.30 pm.

St John Smithfield EC1 £89 4 4 3
26 St John St   020 7251 0848   10–1B

"The OG" of 'nose-to-tail' British cuisine and recherché offal-related dishes – Trevor Gulliver and Fergus Henderson's Smithfield icon is "as brilliant as ever" after all these years (it opened in 1994). Occasionally reports accuse it of "complacency", but for the most part they pay awed homage to its "top cooking and fine ingredients" delivered by "superb, genuinely engaging and caring staff". There's an "excellent wine list" too. "The matching stark white dining room" of this converted smokehouse "still has that Scandi-chic feel, but is oh-so-loud – perhaps the worst acoustic of any restaurant ever!". Top Menu Tip – "Worth it for the roast bone marrow alone"; suckling pig is a favourite for a group celebration; and "it's one place you must never pass on pudding!" ("amazing Marmalade Bakewell, Rhubarb Trifle, Steamed Sponge… all excellent"). / EC1M 4AY; stjohnrestaurant.com; st.john.restaurant; Mon-Sun 9 pm.

St Johns N19 £69 2 3 4
91 Junction Rd   020 7272 1587   9–1C

This well-known Archway pub (George Michael's favourite back in the day, apparently) benefits from a beautiful, high-ceilinged dining annex (originally a ballroom) and serves "what you might call traditional food with an international twist (particularly Spanish with some tapas evenings)".
/ N19 5QU; stjohnstavern.com; stjohnstavern; Tue-Sat 10 pm, Sun 6 pm.

St Moritz W1 £72 2 2 3
161 Wardour Street   020 7734 3324   4–1C

"Just like a little piece of Switzerland in London", Armin Loetscher's unchanging central Soho stalwart looks a little long in the tooth nowadays (est. 1974), but is just the job when you crave fondue, bratwurst and rosti (or veal, if you're feeling more fancy). No-one makes huge claims for its culinary

level, but as a rule its "traditional Swiss fare is done to a good standard".
/ W1F 8WJ; stmoritz-restaurant.co.uk; st.moritzsoho; Mon-Sat 11.30 pm, Sun
10.30 pm.

Sakonis £35 3 2 2
127-129 Ealing Rd, HA0   020 8903 9601   1–1A
330 Uxbridge Road, HA5   020 8903 9601   1–1A
This Wembley fixture (with spinoffs in Hatch End and Kingsbury) is best known for its all-you-can-eat Indian vegetarian buffet with a choice of 45 items, including an Indo-Chinese selection with dishes such as chilli paneer. The family-owned business started out 40 years ago as a market stall.
/ sakonis.co.uk; sakonis_uk.

Sale e Pepe SW1 £85 2 2 2
9-15 Pavilion Road   020 7235 0098   6–1D
Changing the guard was always going to be a challenge at this Knightsbridge trattoria – an "institution" established in 1974 – where long-established staff sustained a madcap vibe for decades. Since it was taken over and refurbished in early 2023, some still applaud an "unchanging, noisy and crowded Italian", but other old fans feel let down, saying: "what a disappointment! It's deadly dull compared with when it was family-owned"; and with the odd incident of "pushy" service. New owners the Thesleff Group have other high-performing properties, so hopefully feedback will settle with time. / SW1X 0HD;
saleepepe.co.uk; saleepepelondon; Fri & Sat 11 pm, Mon-Thu 10.30 pm, Sun 10 pm.

Le Salon Privé TW1 £75 3 3 3
43 Crown Rd   020 8892 0602   1–4A
Quaint, old-fashioned decor lends a "special" atmosphere to this "small neighbourhood restaurant" in St Margaret's. It's resolutely French in style, providing "good portions of excellent food" from a traditional menu, whose top features are a Plat de Fruits de Mer and 28-day aged Châteaubriand, both for £80. Be warned, though, "it gets extremely busy around rugby matches at Twickenham". / TW1 3EJ; lesalonprive.net; lesalon_prive; Tue-Sat
21.30 pm, Sun 4 pm.

Salt Yard £66 3 2 2
54 Goodge St, W1   020 7637 0657   2–1B
Westfield London, Ariel Way, W12   020 8161 1118   1–3B
New Hibernia House, Winchester Walk, SE1   020 8161 0171   10–4C
"Despite now being part of a rolled-out chain, they have managed to maintain good quality" at these tapas-haunts, whose original branch off Goodge Street was an early pioneer of the capital's trend to small plates. A minor gripe is of "packed" seating, but most feedback focuses on their "delicious food and well-thought-out wine list". / saltyardgroup.co.uk;
saltyardgroup.

Saltine N5 NEW £83 2 3 4
11 Highbury Park   020 7916 0949   9–2D
This cool-looking, new Highbury haunt is the latest from Mat Appleton & Jess Blackstone, who have opened a trio of cafés under the Fink's name in the area over the past dozen years. There's coffee, pastries and grab-and-go bites by day, with a short, seasonal dinner menu from chef Phil Wood (ex-St John and Spring) in the evening, along with cocktails and low-intervention wines. In his November 2023 review, The Evening Standard's Jimi Famurewa hailed "a wonderfully-composed, sneak-attack of a neighbourhood hit". Our reporters are a bit more cautious: "recently opened to a wave of social media posts, Saltine is trying hard but still finding its feet", with "food that's good but possibly not quite up to the hype around its opening? One or two dishes were exceptional but others were just 'nice'". / N5 1QJ; saltine.co.uk; Wed-Sat 11 pm,
Sun 9.30 pm.

FSA

Salut N1 £86 3 4 3
412 Essex Road   020 3441 8808   9–3D
"A little off the beaten track" at the far end of Islington, but "definitely a gem for this corner of London" – brothers Martin & Christoph Lange's "cracking neighbourhood restaurant" is "consistently good" ("I've never had a bad dish"). There's a fixed-price multi-choice menu to ensure "reasonable" bills. / N1 3PJ; salut-london.co.uk; salut.restaurant; Mon-Thu 9.15 pm, Fri & Sat 9.30 pm, Sun 9 pm.

Sam's Kitchen £45 3 4 4
59-61 Turnham Green Terrace, W4   020 3906 1020   8–2A
17 Crisp Road, W6   020 8237 1023   8–2C
Sam Harrison's "cute café just off the river in Hammersmith" is tucked away in a backstreet across the road from Riverside Studios (home to his mothership 'Sam's Riverside'). "It's often difficult to create an original breakfast menu but Sam's Kitchen manages it" with "an interesting and well executed-range of options". "On a sunny day, an outside table eating crab crumpets with poached eggs is so good!!" And it already has a welcoming sibling in a similar vein in Chiswick, in the parade of shops near Turnham Green tube: "some innovative dishes here for both breakfast and brunch from chef Abbey Hendren: especially the lemon and ricotta hotcakes... a local café with class!" Top Tip – look out for the regular smashburger nights.

Sam's Riverside W6 £82 3 4 5
1 Crisp Walk   020 8237 1020   8–2C
"Sam's absolutely nails it, as indeed does Sam Harrison himself when he's front of house" at this brilliantly successful venue, whose "fabulous" Riverside location – "with ideal views of Hammersmith Bridge" – invites many comparisons with the River Café just down the towpath. In fairness, "culinary comparisons with The River Caff are rather overblown": "Sam's is much better value, but it's different": the posh brasserie fare is "not aiming to be in the same league" and rates somewhere between "well-presented-and-delicious" and "tasty-if-unspectacular". The food is really "part of an overall package" which combines unusually "glamorous, sophisticated and comfortable" decor in a "bright and light interior" with "excellent, friendly and very efficient service", to create a supremely "convivial" experience that's "not cheap, but excellent value": "I always feel happy when I leave". (See also Sam's Waterside and Sam's Kitchen). Top Tip – "the cocktails here are a massive stand-out". / W6 9DN; samsriverside.co.uk; samsriversidew6; Mon-Sat 9.45 pm, Sun 4 pm.

Sam's Waterside TW8 £68 3 4 4
Catherine Wheel Road   020 8150 1020   1–3A
"Just what the local area needed!" – Sam Harrison's "newly opened outpost of Sam's Riverside makes the most of a relaxing waterside setting as part of the substantial new residential developments" in downtown Brentford. But it's "sufficiently separate to have its own identity and atmosphere", and is "really buzzing" as "there's nothing in the area serving food of this quality": a selection of approachable but interesting brasserie fare. Top Tip – "good-value set lunch menu". / TW8 8BD; samswaterside.co.uk; Tue-Sat 9.30 pm, Sun 4 pm.

Sambal Shiok N7 £51 3 3 2
171 Holloway Road   020 7619 9888   9–2D
"Oh my word, great laksa – the 'hot' will blow your socks off" at Mandy Lim's "simple Malaysian place" on the Holloway Road. Fans reckon it's "the best local restaurant you could ever want", with a "lovely buzzy atmosphere" and "friendly service" – "it's a bit cramped, but it's only a cafe really, so don't expect too much". / N7 8LX; sambalshiok.co.uk; sambalshiok; Tue-Thu, Sun 9 pm, Fri & Sat 9.30 pm.

San Carlo SW1 £90 3/2/3
2 Regent Street Saint James's 020 3778 0768 4–4D
"You never feel cramped or too close to other tables" in the gracious West End flagship branch of Carlo Distefano's national group of old-school, comfortable Italian restaurants (London was one of the last destinations of a chain nowadays numbering about 20). Culinary results are *"consistent"* from the *"very comprehensive menu"* – if there was a gripe this year, it was over the odd let-down on the service front. / SW1Y 4AU; sancarlo.co.uk; sancarlorestaurants; Mon-Sun 11.30 pm.

San Carlo Cicchetti £59 3/2/3
215 Piccadilly, W1 020 7494 9435 4–4C
30 Wellington St, WC2 020 7240 6339 5–3D
6 Hans Road, SW3 020 7846 7145 6–1D
"For a quick bite" in touristy parts of town, all with a bit of affordable glam thrown in, these *"closely packed"* Italians with their wide range of Venetian-style Cicchetti have carved a sizeable following: fans say *"the small-plates formula works well"* and *"the whole place buzzes"*. Ratings came under more pressure this year, though, with service – generally *"swift and charming"* – sometimes found *"rushed"* or *"rather random"*. / sancarlocicchetti.co.uk; sancarlorestaurants.

Santa Maria £48 5/4/3
160 New Cavendish St, W1 020 7436 9963 2–1B
92-94 Waterford Road, SW6 020 7384 2844 6–4A
11 Bond Street, W5 020 8579 1462 1–3A
189 Upper Street, N1 020 7288 7400 9–2D
"The pizza is second to none", combining *"top-quality ingredients and fabulous bases"* at this quartet of *"bustling"* pizzerias founded 15 years ago by Neapolitan-born Angelo and Pasquale. Since launching in Ealing, they have expanded slowly to Fulham, Islington and Fitzrovia – and the extent to which they've maintained their ratings is an achievement for an expanding group. / santamariapizzeria.com; https://www.instagram.com/santamariapizza.

Santa Maria del Sur SW8 £63 3/3/3
129 Queenstown Road 020 7622 2088 11–1C
With nearly two decades in Battersea under its belt, this Argentinian steakhouse continues to win all-round praise for its mix of affordable cuts and Latino wines. At lunch, there's a limited menu mixing empanadas, sandwiches and a simple steak 'n' chips. / SW8 3RH; santamariadelsur.co.uk; Mon-Sun 10 pm.

Santini SW1 £121 2/2/2
29 Ebury St 020 7730 4094 2–4B
This chic Belgravia Italian hosted the likes of Frank Sinatra and Bill Clinton in its 20th-century heyday under founder Gino Santini, and is now run by his daughter Laura. Ratings have been up-and-down over many years, though, and these days a common reaction is that *"it's fine, but..."* *"pretty unexciting"*, while the prices are steep – *"hard to believe people are paying for themselves: feels like the expense account is taking the pain"*. / SW1W 0NZ; santinirestaurant.com; santinirestaurant; Mon-Sat 11.30 pm.

Santo Mare W1 £99 3/3/3
87-89 George Street 020 7486 0377 2–1A
Fish is shipped directly from Italy to fill the plates of Andrea Reitano's upscale Marylebone six-year-old, north of Portman Square. The odd gripe that it's *"extremely expensive"* recurs this year, but no report rates it as anything less than *"very good all-round"*. / W1U 8AQ; santomare.com; santomare; Mon-Sun 11 pm.

Santo Remedio £72 3 3 2
152 Tooley Street, SE1 020 7403 3021 10–4D
55 Great Eastern Street, EC2 020 7403 3021 13–1B
A "very good Mexican near Tower Bridge", which has a more café-style spin-off in Shoreditch. Both serve a selection of tacos, tostadas and quesadillas and both make a feature of bottomless brunch, but at the original there's also regional dishes, like sea bass cooked over a wood-fire grill and Beef Short Rib with Oaxacan Mole. / santoremedio.co.uk.

Saravanaa Bhavan HA0 £54 3 3 2
531-533 High Rd 020 8900 8526 1–1A
"Great-value dosas" and other south Indian vegetarian dishes are a big draw at this outpost of an international chain which bills itself as the 'World's No.1 Indian Vegetarian Restaurant' and which reporters say is "just the job for a quick, satisfying bite to eat". There are actually seven in and around London (including in Leicester Square), but this is the one on which we receive most reports. The chain was founded in Madras (now Chennai) in the late 1970s by P Rajagopal, known in the Indian press as 'the dosa king'. He was convicted of the 2001 murder of a man whose wife he wanted to marry, and died five years ago. / HA0 2DJ; saravanabhavanlondon.co.uk; Saravanaa Bhavan London; Mon-Sun 10.30 pm.

Sartoria W1 £99 2 3 3
20 Savile Row 020 7534 7000 4–3A
D&D London's well-tailored venue on Savile Row "remains a firm favourite" to fans, who applaud its "beautifully cooked" Italian cuisine and elegant standards generally. But high-profile chef Francesco Mazzei left a couple of years ago and our current annual diners' poll inspired limited and mixed feedback: chief concerns are incidents of "mediocre food" and the fact that it's "not cheap". / W1S 3PR; sartoria-restaurant.co.uk; sartoriarestaurant; Mon-Sat 10 pm; SRA-3 stars.

The Savoy Hotel, The River Restaurant WC2 £110 2 2 2
The Savoy, 91 The Strand 020 7499 0122 5–3D
Three years on from a relaunch under its original name by Gordon Ramsay (it was formerly Kaspar's), this elegant chamber with Thames views from the window tables has yet to regain the lustre it enjoyed before the hotel relaunched in the noughties. It's not devoid of fans, but too often its cooking (of mainly fish and seafood) is critiqued for being "overpriced (and in some cases overcooked or over-sauced)". Sceptics say Big Sweary's name above the door is a saving grace – "if it wasn't a Ramsay restaurant they'd struggle". Top Tip – a good choice for a posh brek. / WC2R 0EU; gordonramsayrestaurants.com; riverrestaurantbygordonramsay; Mon-Sat midnight, Sun 11 pm.

The Savoy Hotel, Savoy Grill WC2 £156 1 1 3
Strand 020 7592 1600 5–3D
"Always a place to impress your business guest" – this famous chamber (one of Lady Thatcher's favourites back in the day) has "sufficiently widely spaced tables to encourage discreet conversation" and the Art Deco elegance of its surroundings has, by and large, survived its recent 'Gatsby' makeover. It's had its ups and downs under the Gordon Ramsay group's long (20+ years) tenure here and is not in a purple period currently. Much of the problem is "ludicrous prices". Those on expenses do acclaim "the iconic Arnold Bennett soufflé, the deeply satisfying Cote de Boeuf to share (if your guest is a meat eater: if not point him/her in the direction of the steamed turbot) and the magnificent Beef Wellington" but even they acknowledge "the bill is serious". Those paying their own way are more inclined to feel: "it used to be a favourite, especially for that special occasion, but the mark-up on the wines in particular have become a rip-off". / WC2R 0EU; gordonramsayrestaurants.com; savoygrillgordonramsay; Mon-Thu midnight, Fri-Sun 11.30 pm.

The Savoy Hotel, Savoy Lounge WC2 £116
The Strand   020 7420 2111   5–3D

"A special location for afternoon tea!" – the "beautiful" foyer of this celebrated hotel serves one of "the best teas in London", which fans say is "as good as it gets": "not too formal", with "service that's up-to-standard but not too stuffy" and "limitless sandwiches" amongst the "lovely and plentiful food, with no problems replenishing". In August 2024, the site closed to relaunch in November 2024 – renamed from its former 'Thames Foyer' branding to this new moniker, with a new look and a new menu of 'traditional recipes with a modern twist' (which will maintain the 'legendary afternoon tea'). Though likely a case of 'plus ça change', we've removed ratings for the time being. / WC2R 0ER; thesavoylondon.com; thesavoylondon; Mon-Sun 7 pm.

Scalini SW3 £96   3|3|3
1-3 Walton St   020 7225 2301   6–2C

"Friendly staff" and "very good" cooking draw an ever-appreciative crowd to this lively and very attractive Knightsbridge trattoria, which has notched up 35 years catering to a glam international crowd, for whom this is their idea of grabbing an informal bowl of pasta. Outposts in Cannes and the Middle East show the direction of travel in recent years. / SW3 2JD; scalinilondon.co.uk; scaliniuk; Mon-Sat 10.45 pm, Sun 10 pm.

Scandinavian Kitchen W1 £16   4|3|3
61 Great Titchfield St   020 7580 7161   2–1B

"Excellent smørrebrød" (open sandwiches) are on display at this Fitzrovia café, "but a lot of people go for the Swedish meatballs" – "this is where I head when homesick", says an expat reporter. "There also is a little shop downstairs selling Scandi goodies". / W1W 7PP; scandikitchen.co.uk; scandikitchen/; Mon-Fri 7 pm, Sat 6 pm, Sun 4 pm.

The Scarsdale W8 £60   2|2|4
23a Edwardes Sq   020 7937 1811   8–1D

This well-known pub makes the most of its stunning location in a Regency square in Kensington, with a "lovely terrace at the front for summer evenings" – and (if you can bag one) "the tables at the back are not too noisy even when the place is packed" (ie. always). Apparently it is Piers Morgan's favourite pub, where he has invited everyone from Meghan Markle to the celeb cronies he entertains at his annual Christmas drinks. / W8 6HE; scarsdaletavern.co.uk; scarsdalew8; Mon-Sat 11 pm, Sun 10.30 pm.

Scott's W1 £115   4|4|4
20 Mount St   020 7495 7309   3–3A

"It does rather ooze money and privilege, but the food is very good indeed" at Richard Caring's "chic" Mayfair A-lister: "a classic with crowd-pleasing glitz" where (in Ian Fleming's novels) commander Bond is a regular. "One of the grand seafood palaces of central London with a vast seafood bar", its cuisine is "not in the grand gourmet mould" – "high-quality" fish and seafood "prepared with flair" from an "evolving menu, such that old favourites are regularly joined by creative new dishes". "Service is always polished and efficient, and the room retains its glamour and buzz year in, year out": "a go-to for any significant celebration… or just for a treat". Top Tip – "perfect for business, with the best grilled Dover Sole". / W1K 2HE; scotts-restaurant.com; scottsmayfair; Mon-Wed 9.45 pm, Thu-Sat 10.30 pm, Sun 9.30 pm.

Scott's Richmond TW9 £114   3|2|4
4 Whittaker Avenue   020 3700 2660   1–4A

"A long-missing top-class option in Richmond" – one can quibble about whether or not Richard Caring's yearling fully lives up to its long-established Mayfair sibling, but no-one denies its "very special setting" with "elegant decor and beautiful riverside location"; and as it entered its second year of operation, it put in a much more rounded all-round performance in general.

OK, service in particular can still dip, and on occasion results are "ordinary", but its ratings improved palpably this year and acclaim for fish and seafood that's "simply presented but perfectly cooked" was much closer to the level one might hope for. The overall verdict – a little "overpriced", "but as a treat, it's worth it". / TW9 1EH; scotts-richmond.com; scottsrichmond; Mon-Sat 12.30 am, Sun midnight.

Scully SW1 £100 343
4 St James's Market   020 3911 6840   4–4D

"Absolutely fantastic flavours" are on the "great tasting menu" at Malaysia-born and Sydney-raised, Ramuel Scully's idiosyncratic venue in St James's Market, whose cuisine is flavoured by unusual ferments – some of them as much as a year old. It no longer generates the massive excitement of its early days, but still inspires lots of supportive feedback. / SW1Y 4QU; scullyrestaurant.com; scullyrestaurant; Wed & Thu, Tue, Fri & Sat 11 pm.

Sea Containers, Mondrian London SE1 £88 224
20 Upper Ground   020 3747 1000   10–3A

"This beautiful space by the river" – the stylish dining room of a South Bank hotel, designed by Tom Dixon – has "a wonderful view if you get a table by the window" and "plenty of space between the tables, so conversation is easy". Standards in other respects, though, have been up-and-down over many years. / SE1 9PD; seacontainerslondon.com; seacontainersldn; Mon-Sun 10 pm.

The Sea, The Sea SW3 £180 333
174 Pavilion Road   020 7824 8090   6–2D

"Lots of the fish is aged in-house and the flavours are second to none" at this chic fishmongers and seafood bar in a bougie backstreet off Sloane Street; and "sitting at the counter being served by the chef feels special". Sadly, though, its dazzlingly brilliant Haggerston sibling closed in March, leaving this Chelsea branch, which is primarily an amenity for the local ladies-who-lunch rather than a major magnet for serious foodies (as was the case in the East End, where the ambition was off the charts). / SW3 2TJ; theseathesea.net; theseathesea_; Tue-Sat 10 pm.

Seabird at The Hoxton, Southwark SE1 £97 324
The Hoxton, 40 Blackfriars Road   020 7903 3000   10–4A

Swish rooftop Iberian seafood specialist on the 14th floor of a modern Southwark hotel. It remains solidly rated for its luxe seafood – including nine varieties of oyster, alongside lobster and caviar – with scores that stack up respectably against fashionable restaurants with a view. Pick carefully, and you could make an affordable meal here, but the more luxurious options are very punchily priced. / SE1 8NY; thehoxton.com; thehoxtonhotel; Sun-Thu midnight, Fri & Sat 1 am.

The Seafood Bar W1 £87 332
77 Dean Street   020 4525 0733   4–1D

"Extravagantly sized platters" of "hot and cold seafood at good prices" are the winning proposition at this Soho venture from Amsterdam's De Visscher family. It's a "bright, clean and open space", whose atmosphere can seem "a bit prosaic, but who cares when you can get stuck into a tower of fishy treats?" / W1D 3SH; theseafoodbar.com; theseafoodbar; Sun-Thu 10 pm, Fri & Sat 10.30 pm.

Seafresh SW1 £64 332
80-81 Wilton Rd   020 7828 0747   2–4B

"Where every visitor to this country might usefully try our traditional national dish" – this 60-year-old Pimlico veteran a short stroll from Victoria station serves "excellent fish, good chips and mushy peas", and service is "pleasant"

F S A

too. Not compulsory, but you can stray beyond cod 'n' chips if you want to: be it with fritto misto, lobster thermidor, sea bass cooked on the bone…
/ SW1V 1DL; sfdining.co.uk; seafreshrestaurant; Mon-Sun 10.30 pm.

Searcys St Pancras Grand NW1 £80 2 2 3
Upper Concourse   020 7870 9900   9–3C
This "beautiful space" combines a large and unusually attractive Art Deco-style brasserie, with – outside its front door – what is claimed to be the 'longest Champagne bar in Europe', overlooking the Eurostar tracks (where afternoon tea with fizz is offered). It's certainly "convenient for business and meeting people" and some – perhaps fans of 'Brief Encounter' – also find it "romantic". The brasserie fare won't distract you from your liaison – a fair mid view is that it's "nice enough, but nothing very special for the price".
/ NW1 2QP; stpancrasbysearcys.co.uk; searcystpancras; Mon-Sat 9 pm, Sun 5 pm.

The Sea Shell NW1 £63 4 4 3
49-51 Lisson Grove   020 7224 9000   9–4A
This "institution" of a chippy on Lisson Grove is one of London's most venerable for the national dish (with original origins dating back to WWI). It's "always busy" with locals, tourists and taxi-drivers ("I envy the reduced prices they get!") and – though it's had its ups and downs over the decades – is currently riding high as a "top location for classy fish 'n' chips". / NW1 6UH; seashellrestaurant.co.uk; seashellrestaurant; Mon-Sat 10 pm, Sun 7 pm.

Sessions Arts Club EC1 £64 3 3 5
24 Clerkenwell Green   020 3793 4025   10–1A
"This Clerkenwell bolt-hole remains a genuine experience, accessed through a nondescript black door and a rickety brass lift before coming round a curtain into the expansive two-tier dining room". It's part of a large, Grade II listed courthouse which features in Dickens's 'Oliver Twist'. "From the moment you enter and take the lift to the wow factor of discovering the room itself onto the excellent food (up to the point where the staff gently encourage you to leave) it's a wonderful experience". The room itself is "like nowhere else": so "beautiful" and "glamorous". But while it's one of London's most atmospheric dining locations, the rest of the experience holds up well, with an "eccentric but good" small plates menu which "contains all manner of interesting morsels" and "a great wine list with interesting and eclectic choices". Top Tip – "A glass of champagne on the roof terrace in the sunshine is a wonderful prelude to a yummy lunch of sharing plates". / EC1R 0NA; sessionsartsclub.com; sessionsartsclub; Tue-Sat 10 pm.

Sesta E8 NEW
52 Wilton Way   020 7254 8311   14–1B
As Pidgin, these well-known Hackney premises sometimes struggled to inspire a level of diner excitement to match the level of hype generated by the fooderati, perhaps explaining the decision to close in summer 2024. It's a case of 'plus ça change', though, with an immediate re-opening by the current head chef Drew Snaith in partnership with former manager Hannah Kowalski. Initial reports on the menu speak of main dishes (so despite being in E8 it won't just be small plates), and some emphasis on meat and live-fire cooking. / E8 1BG; sesta.co.uk; pidginlondon; Tue, Wed 10 pm, Thu-Sat 11 pm, Sun 8 pm.

Sexy Fish W1 £108 1 1 1
1-4 Berkeley Square   020 3764 2000   3–3B
"A horror-fest of crassness" bringing "Essex-on-Berkeley" to Mayfair – Richard Caring's famous and glitzy seafood scene is "just not my type of restaurant" for most of the number who comment on it in our annual diners' poll. "With the accent on glossy surroundings, flamboyant menus of sushi, fish and seafood all backed up by that wretched waterfall", "it's

basically a night-club with food" and "absurdly expensive for what it is": an impressive 2/3 of those who rated it did so as their most overpriced meal of the year. / W1J 6BR; sexyfish.com; sexyfishlondon; Sun-Wed 1 am, Thu-Sat 2 am.

Shahi Pakwaan N2 £38   3 2 3
25 Aylmer Parade, Aylmer Road   020 8341 1111   1–1B

This "enjoyable and good-value" family-run operation in an East Finchley shopping parade specialises in the regional cuisine of Hyderabad, and is one of the best bets for a decent cuzza in this part of north London. / N2 0PE; shahipakwaan.co.uk; shahi_pakwaan009; Mon-Sat 11 pm, Sun 10 pm.

Shanghai Noir SW1 NEW £54   3 4 3
4 Greycoat Place   020 4549 1906   2–4C

"A new addition to the Old Westminster Fire Station in London" – this recent newcomer is found below Yaatra (see also) and is run by the same team as upstairs. "Interesting Indo-Chinese cuisine" – including many small plates – offsets a large menu of cocktails and teas, while the decor is themed in the mould of a "1930s Shanghai-style basement". / SW1P 1SB; shanghainoir.com; /shanghai_noir; Mon-Sat midnight.

Shayona NW10 £31   3 3 2
12 Pramukh Swami Rd   020 8965 3365   1–1A

"Brilliant large veggie Indian with a huge Indian supermarket attached", opposite Neasden's Hindu temple. Offering "superb snacks and veggie food in a real Indian environment", it's one of London's few restaurants to promise 'an air of spirituality and serenity' along with a 'yogic diet' to foster inner purity. Top Tip – combine a meal with a "visit to the fabulous temple for a special trip". / NW10 8HW; shayonarestaurants.com; Mon, Wed & Thu, Sun 10 pm, Fri & Sat 11 pm.

The Shed W8 £86   3 3 4
122 Palace Gardens Ter   020 7229 4024   7–2B

"Cute" and "fun" small operation, off Notting Hill Gate, which launched the Gladwin Bros' now five-strong group in London 13 years ago, and retains the "chaotic" feel that was always part of its shabby-chic charm. The 'Local & Wild' food, much of it sourced from or foraged near the family farm in Sussex, is an "interesting" proposition, and – notwithstanding the odd 'off' report – was generally well-rated this year. / W8 4RT; theshed-restaurant.com; theshed_resto; Tue-Sat, Mon 11.30 pm.

J Sheekey WC2 £98   3 3 4
28-34 St Martin's Ct   020 7240 2565   5–3B

"A wonderful oasis of civilisation in the middle of tatty, tourist London" – Richard Caring's "confident", "old-school" Theatreland "icon" (est. 1896) hides behind intriguing etched-glass windows in an unpromising alleyway between St Martin's Lane and the Charing Cross Road. A "seafood lovers' mecca": it's yet again voted as London's No. 1 destination for fish in our survey, and also – for the umpteenth year – the most commented-on restaurant in our annual diners' poll. "If you want gourmet preparations, you need to go elsewhere" – the straightforward cooking includes "no bells and whistles" and the focus is on "really well-executed traditional dishes" (such as their celebrated fish pie; "excellent Dover Sole off the bone"; or "perfectly pan-fried King scallops"). It occupies a series of "old world, cosy, crowded dining rooms with photos of celebrity guests adorning the wood-panelled walls" and it's "always a civilised pleasure to eat here". "Patchy service" has sometimes been a concern post-Covid, but its rating rebounded noticeably this year and, all said, it's judged as being "first-class". / WC2N 4AL; j-sheekey.co.uk; jsheekeyldn; Mon-Sat 11 pm, Sun 10 pm.

Sheesh W1
1 Dover Street   020 8559 1155   3–3C

Tabloid updates on its TOWIE-tastic happenings ("New Love Island romance confirmed as Lucinda Strafford packs on the PDA with beau Zac Nunns in London…") and a prominent Piccadilly location win an entry for Dylan Hunt's large Mayfair yearling. For some reason, no-one thinks to mention it in our annual diners' poll – if you're not wanting to hang with Chigwell royalty, its menu of 'Main Events' (e.g. Chicken Sheesh for £44), 'A Bit on the Side' (Black Truffle Cheesy Chips for £29) and 'After Party' classics (Baklava, £14) may not be your bag… / W1S 4LD; sheeshrestaurant.co.uk; sheesh_uk; Mon-Fri 1 am, Sat & Sun midnight.

Shikumen, Dorsett Hotel W12   £74   3 2 2
58 Shepherd's Bush Green   020 8749 9978   8–1C

At the foot of a large, Hong Kong-owned hotel beside Shepherd's Bush gyratory, this modern (rather anodyne) dining room has built a reputation, since it opened nearly ten years ago, for "absolutely wonderful" dim sum and superior roast duck from a wide-ranging menu. The food rating dropped a notch this year on the back of one or two reports of "average" results. / W12 5AA; shikumen.co.uk; shikumen.w12; Mon-Sun 11 pm.

Shilpa W6   £40   4 2 2
206 King St   020 8741 3127   8–2B

This basic-looking Keralan in Hammersmith is known locally for its "excellent" value – and in particular, "the breadth of its vegetarian options and fish dishes". Top Menu Tip – "outstanding masala dosa". / W6 0RA; shilpahammersmith.co.uk; Mon-Sun 10.30 pm.

The Shoap EC1   £25   4 2 2
406 Saint John Street   no tel   9–3D

"Empire Biscuits, school cake, and butteries the best you'll have anywhere in Scotland let alone London" win raves for this "excellent new Scottish deli" south of Angel: the first bricks and mortar outlet for 'Auld Hag' ('The Purveyors of Scottish Scran', who started up in 2021 during lockdown). If you're not a calorie-counter, rush now for the "morning rolls with square sausage and haggis". / EC1V 4ND; auldhag.co.uk; auldhag_; Sun-Wed 5 pm, Thu-Sat 11 pm.

Shoryu Ramen   £60   3 2 2
9 Regent St, SW1   no tel   4–4D
3 Denman St, W1   no tel   4–3C
5 Kingly Ct, W1   no tel   4–2B
35 Great Queen Street, WC2   no tel   5–1D
190 Kensington High Street, W8   no tel   8–1D
45 Great Eastern Street, EC2   no tel   13–1B
Broadgate Circle, EC2   no tel   13–2B

"You can't go wrong if you order tonkotsu" at this ramen group from Tak Tokumine of the Japan Centre – the noodles and 12-hour pork bone broth are "authentic" and some of the "best in town". The venues can be "cramped", and "the constant banging of a drum to indicate dishes being ready can grate". / shoryuramen.com; shoryu_ramen.

Sichuan Popo W8   £50   4 3 2
35 Earls Court Road   020 7937 6235   8–1D

"Delicious and authentic Sichuan cooking", with a focus on biang biang noodles, mini hotpots and dim sum, wins applause for this brightly-lit three-year-old café in Earls Court (with a sibling on Fulham Broadway). "Knowledgeable and helpful service" helps offset the few-frills interior. / W8 6ED; sichuanpopo.co.uk; sichuanpopo; Mon-Sat 11 pm, Sun 10 pm.

Silk Road SE5 £28 5 3 2
49 Camberwell Church St 020 7703 4832 1–3C

"Praise be to the gods of southeast London for the resurrection of Silk Road" following a six-month closure that had its legion of fans worried last winter. And "Christ the food is still great" – spicy Uigur fare from Xinjiang in northwest China, full of "lip-burning/numbing brilliance". (One regular, though, feels the "refurb is a bit mad – it's gone from 'crap canteen' to 'airport lounge in random Mediterranean resort!") / SE5 8TR; silkroadlondon.has.restaurant; thesilkroadbn; Mon-Sun 11 pm.

Silo E9 £68 4 4 4
Queens Yard, White Post Lane 020 8533 3331 14–1C

"Wow! Every dish has a story to tell and some of them are especially yummy!" at Douglas McMaster's groundbreaking 'zero waste' project, in Hackney Wick's 'White Building' (above the Crate brewery) in a high-ceilinged, white-walled post-industrial space. Considering its hipster credentials and admirable ethos, it has made surprisingly few waves here in the capital since the move from Brighton in 2019. Covid-19 didn't help, but it now seems to be gaining more recognition. "Sitting at the bar you get an excellent view of the kitchen mechanics creating the delicious dishes. The whole dining experience from source to fork is explained by friendly and knowledgeable staff. A unique dining experience that's extremely enjoyable". / E9 5EN; silolondon.com; silolondon; Wed-Sat 11 pm.

The Silver Birch W4 £94 4 4 2
142 Chiswick High Road 020 8159 7176 8–2A

"Delicious amuse bouche and melt-in-the-mouth guinea fowl!" – Nathan Cornwell's "exciting" cooking provided numerous reporters with their best meal of the year at this Chiswick venue, which owner Kimberley Hernandez is working hard to put on London's culinary map. One challenge is the anonymous location: a very pleasant but slightly uneventful space, easily missed amidst the jumble of chain-restaurants and furniture stores on Chiswick's high street. / W4 1PU; silverbirchchiswick.co.uk; silverbirchchiswick; Tue-Sat 9 pm.

Simpson's in the Strand WC2 £103
100 Strand 020 7420 2111 5–3D

Could it be a dream team? Restaurant supremo Jeremy King has partnered with Savoy owners Fairmont to mastermind the autumn 2024 relaunch of this celebrated temple to roast beef on the Strand (est. 1828) which backs onto The Savoy. King has described Simpson's as "the last of the 'grande dame' restaurants that still retains its original décor and features" and few relaunches carry such expectations and potential. The astonishing mediocrity of its traditional fare over recent decades has – notwithstanding its period charms; ongoing fame; large size; half-hearted relaunch after half-hearted relaunch; the huge surge in interest in dining out; and rising esteem for British cuisine – become an ever-more-obscure anachronism. King has said he envisions "a big-theatre brasserie", but one that would "very much hark on its tradition" ("I want people to walk in there and say, 'Oh good, they haven't changed it', although it will have changed"). Even if they have auctioned off the famous beef trolleys, if anyone can do it, it will be King… it could be so good. / WC2R 0EW; simpsonsinthestrand.co.uk; simpsons1828.

Singapore Garden NW6 £64 3 4 3
83a Fairfax Rd 020 7624 8233 9–2A

"So consistent after all these years" – this "old-school local Malaysian-Chinese" in Swiss Cottage has "been going for ages", but "you never tire of dining here" because "you know what you're going to get and you enjoy it immensely". Giles Coren, restaurant critic for The Times, was born in the next street and is a long-term regular, returning again and again for the "superb Singaporean laksa". But while it's "a cut above" and one of north London's most popular destinations, don't go expecting the earth ("everything is done well but it's not amazing"). / NW6 4DY; singaporegarden.co.uk; singapore_garden; Mon-Thu 10.30 pm, Fri & Sat 11 pm, Sun 10 pm.

Singapulah W1 NEW £46 3 3 2
53 Shaftesbury Avenue   020 3583 5815   5–3A

In prime Theatreland – on the corner of Shaftesbury Avenue and Wardour Street – Ellen Chew's February 2024 newcomer (she also owns Rasa Sayang in nearby Chinatown) aims to showcase specialist ingredients from Singapore (also available to buy retail). It's rated on limited but highly positive initial feedback: "the food is authentic from a shortish menu with the usual hawker favourites – it was good, even if like everywhere else in London, they still can't get the fish balls right!". / W1D 6LB; singapulah_london; Sun-Wed 9 pm, Thu-Sat 10 pm.

Singburi Royal Thai Café E11 £28 4 3 2
593 Leytonstone High Rd   020 8281 4801   1–1D

This cash-only BYO Thai in Leytonstone "never fails on the food front": "you can tell the owners have passion", and it's "great value for money". "The fast service can take some people aback, but it's all part of the charm!". There's a catch, though: "it's almost impossible to get a reservation". / E11 4PA; singburi_e11; Wed-Sat 10.30 pm, Sun 9.30 pm.

Six by Nico £77 3 3 3
33-41 Charlotte Street, W1   020 7580 8143   2–1C
6 Chancellor Passage, E14   020 3912 3334   12–1C

"A six-course themed taster menu, that changes every six weeks!" is the "playful idea" at Nico Simeone's national chain, whose two London branches (in Fitzrovia and Canary Wharf) are "great for special occasions, but also affordable for a regular monthly meal out to experience the different cuisines". At such keen prices, it's unreasonable to expect perfection and most diners acknowledge this: it's "a clever, and obviously very popular, concept, albeit one where the experience can seem a bit manufactured"; "although it doesn't always live up to expectations, when you get the right menu everything clicks into place"; so while inevitably it's "hit and miss, it's also great value", and "for a fun evening it does the job well". / sixbynico.co.uk; sixbynico.

Six Portland Road W11 £86 3 4 3
6 Portland Road   020 7229 3130   7–2A

"A gem of a local" – this "quite small" modern bistro in Holland Park is nowadays owned by Jesse Dunford Wood. "The menu changes regularly and there is always an interesting selection of dishes; while staff are welcoming, knowledgeable and helpful". One quibble – "it's lovely and with super food, but is it becoming a tad pricey?" / W11 4LA; sixportlandroad.com; sixportlandroad; Mon-Sun 10 pm.

64 Goodge Street W1 £92 4 5 4
64 Goodge Street   020 3747 6364   2–1C

"Another delicately balanced triumph from the clever people who bought you Clipstone, the Quality Chop House and Portland" – William Lander & Daniel Morgenthau's "great addition to the London restaurant scene" in Fitzrovia has instantly become one of the Top-50 most commented-on restaurants in our annual diners' poll; and is also one of the best. As with its siblings, the whole approach is all quite "restrained" and "grown-up". "Simply pitch-perfect seasonal French food" from chef Stuart Andrew ("akin to a slightly lighter version of traditional Lyon dishes, beautifully executed for the London/international clientele who might find the original a bit heavy going") is offered alongside a "strong wine list", with "enough variety and novelty to keep everyone interested". "All this is overlaid with superb staff who are casual but on-point, with the cheerful enthusiasm of happy, knowledgeable people serving happy, knowledgeable customers". There's the odd query as to whether the room is a little too crowded, but most diners feel it's a "very

classy and clubby space that's excellent for a romantic dinner, a business meeting, or a night out with friends". Top Menu Tip – "the snail bon bons are a superb pre-starter – they melt in the mouth"; "excellent duck – perfectly pink and very tender". / W1T 4NF; 64goodgestreet.co.uk; 64goodgestreet; Mon-Sat 10 pm.

Sketch,
The Lecture Room and Library W1 £248   3 4 5
9 Conduit St   020 7659 4500   4–2A

"Stunning food in the most unusual and exotic environment" has won renown for this "gorgeous" shimmering chamber on the top floor of the well-known Mayfair palazzo, which is much more lighthearted in style than most temples of gastronomy, yet has won the highest culinary accolades (not least three Michelin stars) for its creators: Parisian restaurateur Mourad Mazouz in collaboration with celebrated chef Pierre Gagnaire. Day-to-day, the head chef is Daniel Stucki, who presents "a variety of textures and flavours and unexpected combinations" in the "imaginative menus", and results are "exceptional" ("we ate here four times over the year; each meal was superlative and a fun experience"). Not everyone has always thought the place lives up to its stellar reputation however, and doubts were again in evidence this year with a significant number of reporters registering very disappointing meals. / W1S 2XG; sketch.london; lrl.sketchlondon; Thu-Sat, Wed 9 pm.

Sketch,
Gallery W1 £102   2 2 4
9 Conduit St   020 7659 4500   4–2A

"Whimsical" decor – including artworks from Yinka Shonibare on the walls and famous egg-shaped WC cubicles – creates the "quirky and distinctive ambience" of this fashionista favourite, which enjoys a spectacular location inside a Grade II-listed Palladian mansion in Mayfair. Despite the odd highpoint in reports though, the relatively straightforward cooking "doesn't live up to the hype" or "justify the prices" (in contrast to its genuinely good sibling upstairs in the 'Lecture Room & Library', see also). / W1S 2XG; sketch.london; sketchlondon; Sun-Thu 10 pm, Fri & Sat 11 pm.

Skewd Kitchen EN4 £76   4 4 3
12 Cockfosters Parade   020 8449 7771   1–1C

This "trendy Turkish restaurant in Cockfosters" has given the Anatolian grill a smart makeover over the past decade, and now "has the vibe of a West End restaurant, with a DJ at the weekend" and "faultless service". According to its biggest fans, "Cockfosters is becoming a destination thanks to restaurants like Skewd!" / EN4 0BX; skewd.com; skewdkitchen; Mon-Sun midnight.

Skylon,
Southbank Centre SE1 £81   2 2 2
Belvedere Road   020 7654 7800   2–3D

"The location and setting are the stars" at this spectacular venue – the flagship restaurant of the Brutalist Southbank arts centre, with plate-glass windows offering "wonderful views" over the Thames. Part of D&D London, the restaurant has long struggled to do its surroundings justice, with an often-"mediocre" offering that leaves even supporters regretting the "well done, if rather unimaginative menu". / SE1 8XX; skylon-restaurant.co.uk; skylonrestaurant; Mon & Tue 9 pm, Wed-Sat 10 pm, Sun 8.45 pm; SRA-3 stars.

SlowBurn London E17 £57   3 3 5
114b Blackhorse Lane   07541365064   1–1D

"Verging on peak-hipster (but don't let that put you off!)" – this jeans factory in Walthamstow is a "high-end denim garment manufacturer by day (they have a shop in Coal Drops Yard), but by night they clear down the working tables and have a fully functioning bar and à la carte dog-friendly restaurant!". "It's very surreal – tables are positioned up against the machines and there are bins full of denim waiting to be dyed". "Luckily, the food – while it won't win any Michelin stars, is interesting and well-executed". "The modern European menu is designed for sharing, with limited but hearty and delicious meat choices; and there's a lot of choice for veggies" ("with a bit of a focus on health and sustainability"). / E17 6AA; slowburn.london; Wed-Sat 10.30 pm, Mon 10 pm.

Smith & Wollensky WC2 £112 2|2|2
The Adelphi Building, 1-11 John Adam St   020 7321 6007   5–4D
"Amazing grass-fed" USDA prime steaks (hand-cut and dry-aged for 28 days) are the USP of this NYC-based brand, whose London outpost has a Manhattan-esque location, on the ground floor of the landmark Adelphi Building, just off the Strand. No-one doubts the quality of the offering, and the odd reporter had their best meal of the year here ("amazing!"). But the level of value is a perennial issue and even a fan who rated their visit as "outstanding" noted: "the price is high… everyone seems to be either on holiday or on expenses!" / WC2N 6HT; smithandwollensky.co.uk; smithwollensky; Mon-Thu 11.30 pm, Fri & Sat midnight, Sun 10 pm.

Smith's Wapping E1 £85 4|4|4
22 Wapping High St   020 7488 3456   12–1A
"The quality and simplicity of the fish dishes" – "superbly fresh ingredients served in generous portions" – "speak for themselves" at this classic Thames-bank venue in Wapping (sibling to Essex institution Smith's of Ongar): a "go-to" for its big fan club, where "the lovely views of the Thames and vibe further add to the great experience". Top Tip – "the set menu is good value, but if nothing takes your fancy then the à la carte is also reasonably priced". / E1W 1NJ; smithsrestaurants.com; smithswapping; Mon-Thu 11.30 pm, Fri & Sat midnight, Sun 11 pm.

Smiths of Smithfield, Dining Room EC1 £105 3|2|3
67-77 Charterhouse St   020 7251 7950   10–1A
Now branded as 'No.3 Rooftop Restaurant' (formerly, it was just ambiguously referred to as the top floor) – Smiths' flagship venue was once a top spot for business wining and dining thanks to its wide outside terrace and striking views over to the City and St Paul's. Ups and downs over many years have lowered its profile, but no-one rates the food badly nowadays, even if some think elements of the experience are "overpriced" or "disappointing". With the rebrand has come less emphasis on steak, and a sign-of-the-times refocus on fish and seafood (including a raw selection), but still alongside cuts of dry-aged, grass-fed British beef. / EC1M 6HJ; smithsofsmithfield.co.uk; thisissmiths; Mon-Wed 11 pm, Thu & Fri midnight, Sat 10 pm, Sun 5 pm.

Smoke & Salt SW17 £54 5|4|3
115 Tooting High St   no tel   11–2C
"Worth the rattling ride down on the Northern line!", says a fan from E18 of this neighbourhood spot, "tucked away in the relatively unlikely environs of Tooting". The "clever food" centres on brined half-chicken portions (with crispy battered cauliflower as the veggie alternative) plus a supporting cast of starters, small plates and puddings – results are "outstanding". / SW17 0SY; smokeandsalt.com; smokeandsaltlnd; Tue-Sun 9 pm, Fri & Sat 9.30 pm.

Smokestak E1 £56 4|3|3
35 Sclater Street   020 3873 1733   13–1C
"Buzzing, noisy, hot and smoky" – this "incredibly popular" and "unembellished" tribute to the BBQ traditions of the American South started out as a market stall before moving into "darkish, modern-industrial" premises in Brick Lane eight years ago. On the menu: "some of the best roasted meats – the beef brisket is amazing as are a number of the side dishes". (Founder David Carter has emerged as a hot-shot restaurant

FSA

creative, following up with Italian nose-to-tail joint Manteca and, most recently, Greek-inspired double act Agora and Oma in Borough Market). / E1 6LB; smokestak.co.uk; smokestakuk; Mon-Thu, Sat, Fri 11 pm, Sun 10 pm.

Smoking Goat E1 £67 5 4 3
64 Shoreditch High Street   no tel   13–1B

"Authentic… fiery… zingy" – Ben Chapman's Thai BBQ in a converted Shoreditch pub provides "creative dishes that are balanced, well-priced, and most importantly just bloody tasty!". "Great drinks" too which help fuel the happy, crowded vibe. Top Menu Tips – Fish Sauce Chilli Wings and Tom Yum Mama, Sausage & Mussels. / E1 6JJ; smokinggoatbar.com; smokinggoatbar; Mon-Sat 11 pm, Sun 10 pm.

Smokoloko E1 £19 4 3 3
Old Spitalfields Market, Bethnal Green Road   07508 675363   13–2B

"Still top street food IMO" – this oven shaped like an old steam locomotive is an eye-catching fixture in Spitalfield Market and delivers "amazing meats that melt in the mouth". / E1 6EW; smokoloko.uk; smokolokobbq; Mon-Sun 8 pm.

Socca W1 £116 2 3 3
41a South Audley Street   020 3376 0000   3–3A

This gracious and "well-spaced" two-year-old in the epicentre of posh Mayfair is a tribute to the cuisine of Provence and owes its existence to an unlikely partnership of prolific restaurateur Samyukta Nair (Jamavar, Koyn, MiMi Mei Fair) and star Lyonnais-born chef, Claude Bosi (Bibendum, Brooklands, Josephine). A fan would say the menu of modern French dishes is appealingly simple and luxurious – sceptics say it's "somewhat underwhelming, maybe due to silly pricing". Top Tip – "don't get put in the back room". / W1K 2PS; soccabistro.com; soccabistro; Mon-Sat 10.30 pm.

Sofalino N20 £45 3 4 2
1390 High Road   020 8445 9888   1–1B

There's something engagingly "old-fashioned" in approach at Adriano Bernabei and his family's "lovely local" Italian restaurant in Whetstone (although it's relatively youthful, having only been founded in 2011). The food is "always well-prepared and always tastes great". Top Menu Tip – "veal escalope with pasta comes recommended". / N20 9BH; sofalino.co.uk; Wed-Sat 10.30 pm, Mon 10 pm.

Soif SW11 £71 3 2 2
27 Battersea Rise   020 7223 1112   11–2C

With its "consistent no-frills French cooking" – charcuterie; "characterful small plates" and sharing dishes; plus a handful of modern French main plates – this rustic Battersea Rise fixture is always a "good bet" for an interesting meal and glass of wine. Founded by the team behind Les Caves de Pyrène, it drew attention for its small plate and natural wines formula a decade ago, although this is less of a stand-out combo now than it was back in the day. / SW11 1HG; soif.co; soif_sw11; Wed-Sat, Tue 11 pm, Sun 5 pm, Mon 9 pm.

SOLA W1 £211 4 3 2
64 Dean Street   020 7734 8428   5–2A

"THE place to go for top-class Californian cooking in London" – Victor Garvey's Soho five-year-old may be "eye-wateringly expensive" ("the price, ooh la la!") but serves "top-notch cooking well deserving of its Michelin star". "SoLa is that rare place that sources genuinely top-class ingredients and cooks them to perfection": presenting them in either a 10-course tasting menu for £139 per person, or 17-course tasting menu for £229 per person. There are also drinks pairings to the above (at £170 and £230 per person) and a "fabulous" wine list drawn mostly from the US (and primarily, but not exclusively, from the West Coast). Despite refurbishment two years ago, the café-style ambience is the weakest link in the experience. / W1D 4QQ; solasoho.com; solasoho; Wed-Fri, Tue, Sat 9.30 pm.

Sollip SE1 £136 5 4 2
8 Melior Street   020 7378 1742   10–4C
"Amazing fine dining with Korean flavours running through each dish creates a real joy for the taste buds" at Woongchul Park & Bomee Ki's passion project in a street in the shadow of The Shard. For foodies, it's a must-visit, with a "restrained, unshowy and a pleasing menu" mixing classic French culinary techniques with inspirations from their home country; and all "at a reasonable price for this level of cooking and quality of ingredients". Quality wines come from Keeling Andrew (associated with Noble Rot) although "more cheaper labels might encourage the topers amongst us to a bigger spend". Service is "amazing"; and the neutral, 28-cover space is super-tasteful (but maybe not one for thrill seekers). / SE1 3QQ; sollip.co.uk; sollip_restaurant; Wed & Thu 11 pm, Fri & Sat 11.30 pm.

Som Saa E1 £55 5 3 4
43a Commercial Street   020 7324 7790   13–2C
"Zingy, fiery" flavours ("so good we liked the food better than in Bangkok!") inspire raves for this "funky Thai restaurant" near Spitalfields Market – "well worth searching out for its authentically spicy (too spicy for some, note) food", and also "great for veggies and vegans (ingredients are so varied you can get your '30 plants a week' all in one lunch!)". After eight years, the team has opened a sibling, Kolae in Borough Market. Top Menu Tip – "stand-out whole deep-fried sea bass". / E1 6BD; somsaa.com; somsaa_london; Mon-Wed 10 pm, Thu-Sat 10.30 pm, Sun 9 pm.

Sông Quê E2 £43 3 3 2
134 Kingsland Rd   020 7613 3222   14–2A
"In Little Vietnam in Shoreditch", this brisk and busting canteen is an "institution" and, if nothing else, "scores well in its hygiene score by the standards of the area!" Service "if a little chaotic, is friendly" and its "home-style cooking, while not amazingly delicate, has plenty of choice, including very tasty pho". / E2 8DY; songque.co.uk; songquecafe; Mon-Sat 11 pm, Sun 10.30 pm.

Sorella SW4 £69 4 2 3
148 Clapham Manor Street   020 7720 4662   11–1D
"A short menu of high quality" continues to win acclaim for this "great little Italian off Clapham High Street", where the "delicious sharing plates" are inspired by renowned chef-patron Robin Gill's time working on the Amalfi coast. He first made his name here in Clapham with The Dairy, which opened 12 years ago and closed down in 2020. / SW4 6BX; sorellarestaurant.co.uk; sorellaclapham; Tue-Sat 10 pm, Sun 3 pm.

Soutine NW8 £71 2 2 3
60 St John's Wood High Street   020 3926 8448   9–3A
"Just a lovely space to be in" – the Wolseley Group's St John's Wood brasserie has "a very French feel" that takes its inspiration from 'the great boulevard cafés of Paris' and has been a boon to the area since it launched in 2019. The "unashamedly French" menu perhaps seldom hits the heights, but is awarded consistently good ratings by diners, and it's a particular breakfast favourite. / NW8 7SH; soutine.co.uk; soutinestjohn; Mon-Sat 10 pm, Sun 9 pm.

Spagnoletti NW1 £53 3 4 3
23 Euston Road   020 7843 2221   9–3C
"For a quick meal before boarding a train at King's Cross or St Pancras" across the road, this inviting café is worth remembering for "well-prepared" pasta in generous portions provided by "very attentive" staff. In summer 2024, after our annual diners' poll had closed, top chef Adam Simmons (ex-Ynyshir Hall and Danesfield House) joined as consultant, creating a new

menu of 'reimagined Italian classics' for Spagnoletti (named after an Anglo-Italian engineer who developed railway signalling in the 19th century).
/ NW1 2SD; spagnoletti.co.uk; spagnoletti_; Mon-Sun 9.30 pm.

The Spaniard's Inn NW3 £64 2 3 4
Spaniards Rd, Hampstead Heath   020 8731 8406   9–1A
This "crowd-pleasing destination" – dating from 1585 and "perfect after a walk on Hampstead Heath" – is a place of literary pilgrimage, frequented by Byron and Dickens, while Keats wrote his famous ode after listening to a nightingale sing in its garden. These days you'll find a menu of "well-cooked and presented pub classics". / NW3 7JJ; thespaniardshampstead.co.uk; thespaniardsinn; Mon-Sat 11 pm, Sun 10.30 pm.

Speedboat Bar W1 £59 4 3 4
30 Rupert Street   no tel   4–3D
"Chaotic" and "a bit mad", but "actually brilliant" – JKS Restaurants's genius if gaudy Chinatown two-year-old is inspired by Bangkok sports bars and hits the spot with a vibrant menu of "really good-value" morsels plus funky cocktails that go down a treat. It's like being in Bangkok… it "just needs to be about 20 degrees warmer outside!" / W1D 6DL; speedboatbar.co.uk; speedboatbar; Mon-Thu midnight, Fri & Sat 1 am, Sun 11 pm.

Spring Restaurant, Somerset House WC2 £133 3 3 4
New Wing, Lancaster Place   020 3011 0115   2–2D
With "light streaming through the windows", this "big, airy space in Somerset House" is "such a beautiful dining room": "not cosy" but "very elegant" and with "luxuriously spaced" tables, it's a really "great choice for an intimate conversation". Skye Gyngell's cuisine "is not in-yer-face gastro, but simply thoughtful, beautiful and heartwarming"; and together with the "personal" service it adds up to a "delightful" overall package. Top Tip – "the set lunch and early bird 'scratch' menus are good value" (utilising food that would otherwise be wasted). / WC2R 1LA; springrestaurant.co.uk; spring_ldn; Tue-Sat 9.30 pm.

St John Marylebone W1 £71 4 4 2
98 Marylebone Lane   020 7251 0848   3–1A
"Spot-on sea bream and lemon posset…"; "no bone marrow, but very good deep-fried rarebit, crispy pig cheek and the legendary Eccles cake and Lancashire cheese…" – this rare expansion from Fergus Henderson and Trevor Gulliver is still improving in its second year in Marylebone, offering a daily changing menu of the "simple and excellent" nose-to-tail dishes using "highly seasonal ingredients, perfectly cooked" that have won its stablemates such renown. It shares their low-comfort, utilitarian design, which at its best seems "charming if slightly quirky". / W1U 2JE; stjohnrestaurant.com; st.john.restaurant; Mon-Sun 9.45 pm.

Stem + Stem EC4 NEW £85 3 4 4
12 Bow Lane   020 8050 7532   10–2B
"What could be more romantic than a lovely meal and a bouquet of flowers from the in-house florist?" Ed & Dee Reid are striking a good tone with this City yearling on a picturesque alley north of Mansion House tube. Oysters and steaks to share and a selection of cheeses are featured on the focused menu of dishes sourced in the British Isles. End result: "relaxed ambience with good food" and there's also "a varied and interesting selection of wines".
/ EC4M 9AL; stemandstem.com; Mon-Fri 11 pm, Sat 1 pm.

Stick & Bowl W8 £25 4 2 2
31 Kensington High Street   020 7937 2778   6–1A
"Fresh-cooked, cheap Chinese food in good portions – and in an area of overpriced restaurants" – means fans are "so glad we have Stick & Bowl": a no-frills canteen that's been a landmark of Kensington High Street for over

30 years now; and where a curry with rice or noodle dish will set you back well under a tenner. Top Menu Tip – "the pork belly is to die for". / W8 5NP; stickandbowl.has.restaurant; stickandbowl; Tue-Sat 9.30 pm, Sun 9 pm.

Sticks'n'Sushi £79 3 2 3
Branches throughout London

"LOVE this chain and would happily eat there any day!" – These "always buzzy" Nordic operations (originating in Copenhagen 30 years ago) provide a "tasty mix of sushi and grilled yakitori kebabs" in Scandi-minimalist dining spaces. One or two reporters hesitate at the prices for these luscious morsels – "not sure you can justify the cost of leaving full up" – but the overall satisfaction-level is high. They added a branch in Richmond's former House of Fraser in May 2024 followed by another on Islington Green in September. / sticksnsushi.com; sticksnsushi.

Sticky Mango £66 3 2 2
33 Coin Street, SE1   020 7928 4554   10–4A
Butler's Wharf Building, 36c Shad Thames, SE1   020 7928 4554   10–4D

"Handy for the South Bank arts venues" – chef-patron Peter Lloyd took over the much-loved RSJ eight years ago with enough success to add another south Thames site near Tower Bridge to the brand (although a third site, in Islington, lasted just months in late 2023). "Soft shell crab, Roti canai, Singapore chilli lobster; Lamb Shank Massaman" have all been enjoyed – if there's a gripe, it's that the food is "good, but nothing exceptional" ("we enjoyed it, but my friend who is Singaporean by origin was disappointed that the menu was not more authentic"). Top Tip – "the pre-theatre menu of 3 courses for under £30 is excellent value". / stickymango.co.uk.

Story SE1 £281 3 5 3
199 Tooley St   020 7183 2117   10–4D

Tom Sellers established himself as one of the UK's top chefs at his singular foodie temple near Tower Bridge, which emerged from a major revamp in January 2024 complete with a second floor, outside terrace and new bar: a "delightful setting" glazed floor-to-ceiling. "He seems to be clearly targeting a third Michelin star, as prices seem to have shot up" and the current dinner offering is a nine-course tasting menu, with snacks and treats priced at £250 per person; with a classic drinks pairing at £125 per person. Opinions on its performance differ somewhat in our annual diners' poll; although, to be fair, this was also often the case here pre-refurb. One former fan was "disappointed after so many memorable meals", feeling results are now more "mundane"; and another repeat visitor considers the place "overpriced". But most accounts say it's still "top-quality" and a diner who has visited twice since the relaunch opines: "it's not quite three-star, but it's very close: with the right tweaks I'm sure they can get there!" / SE1 2UE; restaurantstory.co.uk; rest_story; Tue 9 pm, Wed 1 am, Thu 2 pm, Sat 10 pm.

Story Cellar WC2 £89 3 4 4
17 Neal's Yard   020 7183 0021   5–2C

Star chef Tom Sellers is responsible for this "great little bistro near the theatres" – an upscale, Parisian-style space on two floors with marble counters and leather seating, tucked away in Covent Garden and overlooking Neal's Yard (the "seating upstairs is great for watching the world go by"). "Simple, tasty food" is the watchword, with a good selection of seafood and fish and meat grills to counterpoint the headline event, which is rôtisserie chicken and fries (a whole bird costs £57). / WC2H 9DP; storycellar.co.uk; story_cellar; Tue-Sat 11 pm.

Straker's W10 £92 3 4 3
91 Golborne Road   020 3540 8727   7–1A

Insta-star (3M followers!) chef Thomas Straker's "packed" two-year-old off Portobello Road wins praise for its "convivial" style and "excellent" Med-inflected menu, including signature flatbreads that are "the best ever"; plus

F S A

starters like burrata, carpaccio or pasta followed by seafood and steaks ordered by the 100g. Launched on the back of social-media success under lockdown, there's a minority criticism that it's "oh so trendy (so I'm told) – but frothy, superficial and ultimately boring and expensive". Top Menu Tip – "knockout duck gnocchi". / W10 5NL; strakers.london; strakers__; Mon-Sun 11 pm.

Strand Café W4 £25 4 5 3
109 Strand-on-the-Green   020 8995 1012   1–3A
"Your classic local gem" – this family-run café in Strand-on-the-Green serves English breakfast and snacks by day and "some top Thai food" in the evening. "Friendly and efficient service" makes it a "lovely spot for a meal after a walk along a beautiful stretch of the Thames" – and it's "great value", too. / W4 3NQ; Mon, Wed & Thu, Sun 10 pm, Fri & Sat 11 pm.

Street Burger £52 2 2 3
13-14 Maiden Lane, WC2   020 7592 1214   5–3D
24 Charing Cross Road, WC2   020 7592 1361   5–4B
222 Kensington High Street, W8   020 7592 1612   8–1D
341 Upper Street, N1   020 7592 1355   9–3D
Entertainment District, The O2, SE10   020 7352 2512   11–1D
26 Cowcross Street, EC1   020 7592 1376   10–1A
One New Change, EC4   020 7592 1217   10–2B
Gordon Ramsay's four-year-old fast-food chain – one of several diffusion brands from the TV chef – has half a dozen sites across the capital. Views on it have always been somewhat mixed and became even more polarised this year: between those who consider it "a great new discovery" and those who feel it's "disappointing for an upmarket burger".
/ gordonramsayrestaurants.com/street-burger; gordonramsaystreetburger.

Studio Frantzén SW1 £169 4 4 3
Harrods, 87-135 Brompton Road   020 7225 6800   6–1D
A headline act in Harrods' pitch to be a gastronomic destination – this Nordic two-year-old is overseen from afar by a three-Michelin-star chef from Stockholm and occupies a striking, purpose-built, double-height space on the fifth floor. All reports agree its wide-ranging menu provides a "terrific blend of Scandinavian and Asian food" and the extensive array of wine-coolers at the edge of the room showcase a heavyweight wine selection. One or two reporters find the lower dining space "a bit moribund", but you can always head upstairs to the "lovely rooftop, with terrace" (which is covered and heated even in the winter months). / SW1X 7XL; harrods.com; harrods; Mon-Sat 9 pm, Sun 6 pm.

Studio Gauthier W1 £69 3 2 3
21 Stephen Street   020 8132 9088   5–1A
"Experimental vegan food" will justify the trip for plant-eaters to star chef Alexis Gauthier's year-old venture – a spin-off from his famous Soho restaurant which forms part of the British Film Institute Building off Tottenham Court Road. While The Telegraph's William Sitwell was not impressed in his October 2023 review (a "weird glimpse into the future of PC dishes mimicking those old shameful dinosaurs") our reports were uniformly upbeat, although one reporter didn't like the set-up (feeling "ambience is a bit lacking, as it is obviously a very casual café by day and then trying to be a fancier restaurant by night, and just ends up feeling a bit confused").
/ W1T 1LN; studiogauthier.co.uk; gauthierinsoho; Tue-Sat 11 pm, Mon 5 pm.

Sucre London W1 £89 2 2 3
47b Great Marlborough Street   020 3988 3329   4–1B
When it opened in 2021, Fernando Trocca's Soho reboot of his famous Buenos Aires 'asado' restaurant was hailed for its "delicious Argentinian food and suitably 'wow' dining room": a large, chandeliered space. A majority of reports do still say "the food is very special" here, but there are also some

diners who feel it's "not up to the reviews"; or even that it's "gone completely down the pan". / W1F 7HS; sucrerestaurant.com; sucre.london; Mon-Sat 1 am, Sun midnight.

SUDU NW6 — £35 — 3 3 3
30 Salusbury Road   020 7624 3829   1–2B

This "tasty and lively" Malaysian 'kopitiam' makes a "fantastic local restaurant" and has been a "good addition to Queen's Park" since opening two years ago. It's a 'second-gen' operation from siblings Fatizah and Irqam Shawal, whose parents opened Satay House in Paddington more than 50 years ago. / NW6 6NL; sudu.ldn; Sun-Thu 9.30 pm, Fri & Sat 10 pm.

Sukho Fine Thai Cuisine SW6 — £56 — 4 4 2
855 Fulham Rd   020 7371 7600   11–1B

This "high-quality" Fulham fixture serves some of the "best Thai food in West London" – attracting diners from across the capital to its modest-looking premises in a parade of shops: "We just wish it was closer to home". / SW6 5HJ; sukhogroups.com; sukho_fulham_london; Mon-Sat 10.30 pm, Sun 9.30pm.

Sumak N8 — £44 — 3 4 2
141 Tottenham Lane   020 8341 6261   1–1C

"A favourite neighbourhood spot over many years", say fans of this Crouch End Turk, for whom it "continues to outshine its competitors on Harringay's Green Lanes". The ambience has improved of late with "stylish but comfortable new chairs, slick marble-topped tables and trendy ceramic plateware and cutlery" but not everyone's wild about the "traditional murals depicting global tourist hotspots". / N8 9BJ; sumakrestaurants.com; sumakrestaurant; Mon-Sun 11 pm.

Sumi W11 — £104 — 4 3 3
157 Westbourne Grove   020 4524 0880   7–1B

"Lovely Japanese dishes in a charming minimalist room" win ongoing acclaim for Endo Kazutoshi's Notting Hill venue (named for his Mum!), which is much more laid-back than his famous Endo at the Rotunda. Sushi is the mainstay of the menu produced by chef Christian Onia, but there are also a smattering of robata and gohan (rice) options. It has a mutedly stylish, café-like interior and an outside sunny-days terrace. / W11 2RS; sushisumi.com; sumilondon; Tue-Sat 10 pm, Sun 9 pm.

The Summerhouse W9 — £84 — 3 3 5
60 Blomfield Rd   020 7286 6752   9–4A

"Watch the barges and ducks slip by as you eat a decent dinner" at this "lovely location on the canal" in Little Venice. It's a "romantic choice" without doubt, especially in the summer, and a reasonably gourmet one too, praised in particular for its "well-prepared fish". / W9 2PA; thesummerhouse.co; the_summerhouse; Mon-Sat 11 pm, Sun 10.30 pm.

The Sun Inn SW13 — £49 — 2 3 4
7 Church Road   020 8876 5256   11–1A

Overlooking Barnes Pond, this "great and gimmick-free" Grade II listed pub has a prime location in this chichi enclave. It's not a foodie hotspot, but "service is really helpful and cheerful" and "there's always good pub food" to be found. Top Tip – in summer, "sit on the terrace in front of the pub" or in the very large, tented area out back. / SW13 9HE; thesuninnbarnes.co.uk; Mon-Sat 11 pm, Sun 10 pm.

Sunday in Brooklyn — £80 — 2 2 3
10-12 James St, W1   awaiting tel   3–1A **NEW**
98 Westbourne Grove, W2   020 7630 1060   7–1B

Evoking the tao of lazy weekends in NYC – well, over the East River in Williamsburg in any case, which is where its Brooklyn namesake is actually located – this imported "brunch favourite" wins votes as a chilled haunt for burgers, maple praline pancakes and other tasty treats by day; and funkier, more ambitious dishes in the evenings. They must be doing something right, as in summer 2024 a sibling opened a short walk from Selfridges in St Christopher's Place.

Sune E2 NEW £76 4 5 4
129a Pritchard's Road 020 4568 6675 14–2B

"Brilliant combination of flavours" – from a menu of modern European small plates from chef Michael Robins – twinned with "interesting low-intervention wine from superstar sommelier and co-owner Honey Spencer" (who contributes to "some of the best service in town"), have won instant acclaim for this "lovely, relaxed Scandi-vibes" newcomer near Hackney's hip Broadway Market. Press critics have raved and reports in our annual diners' poll likewise view it as an "all-round knockout": "a place to visit regularly" if you live out East, and if not "a bit out-of-the-way, but worth the trip!". / E2 9AP; sune.restaurant; restosune; Wed-Sat 9.45 pm, Sun 3.30 pm.

Supawan N1 £60 4 3 3
38 Caledonian Road 020 7278 2888 9–3D

In the "quirky" surroundings of a shop that's a florist by day, this "vibrant and interesting Thai" is to be found in the no-man's-land around King's Cross ("the best place to sit is the section where they sell flowers – it's beautiful"). "It's a very busy and bustling restaurant and the food makes it clear why": chef Wichet Khongphoon's cooking is "true Thai (not the western version)" and the "good-value" dishes are "authentic, exceptionally tasty and worth continually revisiting". Top Menu Tip – "the waiter surprisingly suggested pairing the main course of sea bass fillet and tamarind sauce with beef cheek in Massaman curry. I was very glad that I took his advice because the blend was delicious". / N1 9DT; supawan.co.uk; supawan_thaifood; Tue-Fri 10 pm, Sat 10.30 pm, Sun 9.30 pm.

The Surprise SW3 £82 2 2 4
6 Christchurch Terrace 020 7351 6954 6–3D

This elegant 1853 tavern near Chelsea Physic Garden makes "an excellent local, if with prices befitting its location" and a menu of quite ambitious pub grub, following its transformation by Jack Greenall (of the Lancashire brewing dynasty). He now owns a select trio of west London pubs having acquired the Walmer Castle in Notting Hill and The Carpenter's Arms in Hammersmith last year. / SW3 4AJ; thesurprise-chelsea.co.uk; thesurprisechelsea; Mon-Sat 9.30 pm, Sun 8.30 pm.

Sushi Atelier W1 £75 4 3 2
114 Great Portland Street 020 7636 4455 2–1B

"Excellent, artful sushi", plus carpaccios, steamed dumplings, salads and ceviches – all washed down with a good selection of sake and Japanese draft beer – are the draw at this modern spot near Oxford Circus from the high-quality Chisou group. The interior, dominated by a long sushi counter, is "somewhat drab" for those with more exuberant tastes. / W1W 6PH; sushiatelier.co.uk; sushiatelierlondon; Tue-Sat 10 pm.

Sushi Kanesaka W1 £655 3 4 2
45 Park Lane 020 7319 7466 3–3A

"Fantastic sushi is delivered with epic flair and care… but the cost is mind-blowing and straying from value for money" at this Dorchester Collection yearling, which opened in July 2023 to easy headlines for offering the UK's most expensive menu (£420 per person… before the 15% service charge). It's a spin-off from Shinji Kanesaka's original in Tokyo with two Michelin stars and head chef Hirotaka Wada quickly won a star from the tyre men in the UK 2024 awards. Whether that justifies taking one of the nine seats at the counter (a single piece of 300-year-old cedar wood – there are also four in a private room) almost certainly depends on how deep your pockets are. Rice and Kobe beef imported from Japan, together with fish and seafood from

Cornwall, Canada and beyond all help to create an 18-course omakase experience that all feedback suggests is true to the website's claim of a 'true embodiment of Japanese fine dining'; and one that ranks favourably alongside London's other top Japanese counters. Whether your allotted two hours in a not-particularly-vibey room for such an experience is a worthwhile investment is down to whether you have the necessary disposable and that's your 'bag'. / W1K 1PN; dorchestercollection.com; 45parklane; Tue-Sun 08.30 pm.

Sushi Masa NW2 £47 3 3 2
33b Walm Lane   020 8459 2971   1–1A
Willesden Green locals rejoice at "such delicious cooking on the doorstep" – continuing the tradition established by its predecessor Sushi Say over 30 years of Japanese cuisine that would be "good enough for the city centre". Service is "very attentive and friendly", offering "careful and patient explanation of the menu". / NW2 5SH; sushimasa_id; Mon-Sun 10 pm.

Sushi Monster E4 £45 3 2 2
1st floor, 134-138 Station Road   020 3515 0678?   14–1D
"A mini Shinkansen Japanese bullet train that brings your sushi orders" is a UK first at this bright, first-floor Japanese café in Chingford: a fun cheap 'n' cheerful experience. "Downstairs is a proper pub (the 'Rusty Bike') complete with TVs showing sport and a selection of board games: you can order Thai and sushi on both floors. Yum!" (It goes without saying: this is not first choice for culinary purists). / E4 6AN; sushimonster.co.uk; Tue-Sun 10 pm.

Sushi Murasaki W9 £59 3 3 2
12 Lauderdale Road   020 3417 8130   7–1C
This low-key but authentic Maida Vale outfit is "a local favourite for a reason": "wonderful sushi, sashimi and other Japanese delicacies, expertly prepared and served by friendly staff who are always delighted to see you". It sits in a quiet parade of shops, complete with a sizable covered terrace at the front. Top Tip – "the weekday bento set lunch is particularly good value".
/ W9 1LU; sushi-murasaki.co.uk; sushimurasakiuk; Mon-Sat 22.15 pm, Sun 21.45 pm.

Sushi Revolution £41 3 4 2
240 Ferndale Road, SW9   020 4537 4331   11–1D
2-4 Stage Plaza, Curtain Rd, EC2   020 4537 4331   13–2B **NEW**
'Rebel against the establishment and join the sushi revolution!' – purists should steer clear of this small Brixton pitstop, where various funky meat, vegan and veggie options sit alongside more traditional Japanese sushi combos. Feedback was limited this year, but continues to rate it positively all-round. And they must be doing something right, as a new Shoreditch branch opened in June 2024. / sushirevolution.co.uk.

Sushi Tetsu EC1 £187 5 5 3
12 Jerusalem Passage   020 3217 0090   10–1A
"Pure craft" – Toru Takahashi's tiny 7-seat venue in a cute Clerkenwell alley does not go out of its way to advertise itself, with almost zero online presence, and bookings released weekly each Monday via a form on one of the booking platforms. He doesn't need to plug himself, though, as this is "hands-down some of the best sushi in London" (although, because it doesn't fit into a jelly mould, it goes without saying that Michelin have failed to recognise it, although those less cynical about how it operates have "no idea why they have yet to recognise this place"). For one reporter: "a recent trip to Japan and then a revisit here after confirms the standard at which this charming little shop is operating – on a par with some of the higher-end Tokyo spots. Delicious, imaginative sushi and the warmest of welcomes… the only issue is actually getting a seat!". The full menu is £187 per person, for 17-20 courses for which you should allow four hours. Or there's a somewhat cut-down Saturday lunch experience for £167 per person. Top Tip – email info@sushitetsu.co.uk for all the details. / EC1V 4JP; Mon-Sun 10 pm.

F S A

Sushisamba £126 2 2 4
Opera Terrace, 35 The Market, WC2   020 3053 0000   5–3D
Heron Tower, 110 Bishopsgate, EC2   020 3640 7330   10–2D
"Horribly overpriced but love the atmosphere" – to cut to the chase, that's the key take-away on this duo of Japanese/South American fusion outfits: part of a slick US-chain originating in NYC 25 years ago, and now with branches from Singapore to Las Vegas, via the Middle East. The WC2 branch sits on top of Covent Garden with exceptional views over to the Royal Opera House, although (for our money) it's the City original – up fast lifts on the 38th floor of the Heron Tower with fancy cocktail lounges and stunning views – that really stands out. The food – an eclectic Nikkei mashup incorporating tempura, crispy taquitos, samba rolls, sushi, robata dishes and large plates – is delicious but ultimately "nothing to write home about" when you consider the gargantuan cost. / sushisamba.com; SUSHISAMBA.

Sussex W1 £88 2 2 3
63-64 Frith Street   020 3923 7770   5–2A
"This farm-to-table bistro" from the Gladwin Brothers is celebrating five years in Soho and mostly receives a good rep, for its "delicious and local" cuisine and "friendly" approach. It's not entirely consistent though – even those who laud "admirable sustainable credentials and well-intended cuisine" can say "it does not quite hit a notable standard". / W1D 3JW; sussex-restaurant.com; sussex_resto; Tue-Fri, Mon, Sat 10.30 pm, Sun 8 pm.

The Swan W4 £71 3 3 4
1 Evershed Walk,119 Acton Ln   020 8994 8262   8–1A
This longstanding "local favourite", tucked away on the Chiswick-Acton border, benefits from a characterful Art Deco interior and "amazing secret garden" out back. The "efficient and friendly staff" serve a Mediterranean-influenced menu that "changes frequently to reflect seasonal ingredients". / W4 5HH; theswanchiswick.co.uk; theswanchiswick; Mon-Sat 10 pm, Sun 9 pm.

The Swan at the Globe SE1 £74 3 3 4
21 New Globe Walk   020 7928 9444   10–3B
"A wonderful location overlooking St Paul's and the river" – complete with "fantastic view of the Thames" – creates a "gorgeous", if unavoidably touristy, setting for this South Bank pub, which is incorporated into Shakespeare's Globe theatre. Locals support it too though: in particular it's "a lovely spot for afternoon tea" and "even if the teas are Shakespeare-themed, they aren't over-tacky". The contemporary British food is also well-rated at other times. / SE1 9DT; swanlondon.co.uk; swanglobe; Mon-Sat 9 pm, Sun 5 pm.

Sweetings EC4 £94 3 3 4
39 Queen Victoria St   020 7248 3062   10–3B
"'Unchanged by time' defines Sweetings" – in a quiet way, "one of London's iconic restaurants", although its clientele is almost exclusively made up of City brokers who have sustained it on its current site by Mansion House tube since the 1920s (it was founded elsewhere in the 1830s). "Unchanged service (efficient and friendly); unchanged team (some of whom – like the loyal customer base – are unchanged from the last century); unchanged atmosphere in the last 50 years" at least. Arrive by noon if you want to beat the traders to a seat at the small counter or sit in the dining room. "Superb fish" is "cooked simply and well in the English grilled style". "Kick off with the modestly priced pint of Black Velvet served in a pewter tankard. Try a half-dozen really fresh oysters with a lovely red onion and red vinegar dressing (you can almost hear the sea!). Follow with the fried plaice, homemade tartar sauce and new potatoes in butter". "Perfect". "It's not cheap" but "thank goodness it's still there". / EC4N 4SA; sweetingsrestaurant.co.uk; sweetingslondon; Mon-Fri 3 pm.

FSA RATINGS: FROM 1 POOR — 5 EXCEPTIONAL

Ta Ke Sushi W5 £47 4 4 3
3-4 Grosvenor Parade   020 8075 8877   1–3A
"Fantastic, authentic Japanese food at reasonable prices" (including "really good and varied sushi") means this four-year-old is "favoured by both locals and Ealing's Japanese expat community" – there's "always a few lone diners, a reliable indicator of a warm and welcoming place". Top Tip – "Friday is the best day to visit, for the special sushi offer". / W5 3NN; take-sushi.co.uk; takesushiealing; Mon-Sat 10.30 pm, Sun 10.30pm.

Tab X Tab W2 £39 3 4 3
Westbourne House, 14-16 Westbourne Grove   020 7792 3445   7–1B
Mathew & Charmaine Tabatabai's chic little Bayswater 'brunch café' ticks the boxes for tasty (and healthy) daytime treats with specialty coffee, and is a "lovely place to sit and people-watch" as the denizens of Westbourne Grove pass by. / W2 4UJ; tabxtab.com; tabxtablondon; Mon-Sun 4 pm.

Tabisca SW1 NEW £95
18-22 Holbein Place   07507 959728   6–2D
Conveniently tucked away in a backstreet near Sloane Square in Chelsea, this London offshoot of a restaurant in the Puglian city of Lecce opened without a PR blitz towards the start of 2024 and has yet to attract much in the way of press attention (nor feedback in our annual diners' poll). If you're a Chelsea carnivore though, it's worth considering as it specialises in steaks from around the world, backed up by cold meats, cheeses, and more standard Italian dishes. BREAKING NEWS: as of September 2024 the business is marked 'temporarily closed' on Google with no information on Instagram or the restaurant's website concerning a reopening. / SW1W 8NL; tabisca.com; @tabisca; Sun-Thu 11 pm, Fri & Sat 11.30 pm.

Table Du Marche N2 £65 3 3 3
111 High Road   020 8883 5750   1–1B
East Finchley is "so lucky to have this hidden high-street gem" – one of north London's more popular and "welcoming" local restaurants "serving delicious, well cooked food" from a resolutely French menu. Top Tip – "the three-course set lunch is a wonderful bargain". / N2 8AG; tabledumarchelondon.co.uk; tabledumarche; Mon-Sat 11 pm, Sun 9 pm.

Tacos Padre SE1 £42 4 3 2
Winchester Walk   07582 636186   10–4C
Well-travelled chef Nick Fitzgerald has worked in Mexico City restaurant Pujol, and his street-food stand in Borough Market serves some of the "best tacos in London". Now daytimes-only, following the closure of the evening restaurant. / SE1 5AG; tacospadre.com; tacospadre; Sun-Wed 3 pm, Thu & Fri 4 pm, Sat 5 pm.

Taka Marylebone W1 £110 3 3 3
109 Marylebone High Street   020 3637 4466   2–1A
Limited but good-all-round feedback again on this Japanese bar/restaurant in the heart of 'Marylebone Village'. It's not as expensive as some – as well as the à la carte menu, the 'signature set' is £65 per head, or there's omakase for two to share at £95 per person. / W1U 4RX; takalondon.com; takarestaurants; Fri & Sat, Tue-Thu 10 pm.

Takahashi SW19 £63 5 4 3
228 Merton Road   020 8540 3041   11–2B
"Peerless food and gentle, elegant service" again wins adulation for this "hidden gem" in an anonymous parade of shops near South Wimbledon tube. Ex-Nobu chef Taka and his wife Yuko have run this 12-seater for over 10 years now, where they deliver an "outstanding omakase" for such an affordable price – "absolutely exquisite" sushi; and "service that's very sympathetic". / SW19 1EQ; takahashi-restaurant.co.uk; takahashi_wimbledon; Wed-Sat 10.30 pm, Sun 7.30 pm.

F S A

TAKU W1 £380 5 3 2
36 Albemarle Street   no tel   3–3C
"Incredible to watch a master sushi chef at work close-up" and a perch at Takuya Watanbe's Mayfair 12-seater is one of the best vantage points in town at which to do so: with the counter in London presided over by head chef, Long Ng, and head sushi chef John Park. Those who've made the investment say it's "expensive but definitely worth a visit at least once", with the 'Signature Omakase' being £300 per person over 20 courses; or if you make it £400 per person the 'Prestige Omakase' includes more luxurious ingredients and extra courses. No-one suggests the culinary results are anything short of "brilliant… but there's not much engagement or ambience" beyond what's put on the plate. Top Top – Wednesday to Saturday lunch the 'budget' option is a 17-course 'Tasting Omakase' for £160 per person. / W1S 4JE; takumayfair.com; takumayfair; Wed-Sat 8.30 pm.

Tamarind W1 £87 4 3 2
20 Queen St   020 7629 3561   3–3B
Famous more than 20 years ago as the first Indian restaurant in London to bag a Michelin star, this Mayfair stalwart still wins fans with "brilliantly cooked and presented" cuisine that plays second fiddle to few places in the capital. "A table upstairs is the more pleasant choice" than in the basement. Top Menu Tips – "signature char-grilled lamb chops with crispy pistachio nut crumb – so tender and flavourful – and the Hyderabadi Lamb Biryani served in a pot with pastry crust… definitely melt-in-the-mouth". / W1J 5PR; tamarindrestaurant.com; tamarindofmayfair; Mon-Sat 10.15 pm, Sun 9.15 pm.

Tamarind Kitchen W1 £81 3 3 2
167-169 Wardour St   020 7287 4243   4–1C
This Soho outpost from the upscale Tamarind group serves some "lovely" Indian food in a simpler mould than its famous namesake: kebabs, curries and dishes from the tandoor. For the interior, they've gone for a funky café-style space, although at night the room can be "rather dark". / W1F 8WR; tamarindkitchen.co.uk; tamarindkitchenlondon; Mon-Thu 10 pm, Fri & Sat 10.30 pm, Sun 9.30 pm.

The Tamil Crown N1 NEW £53 3 4 3
16 Ella Street   020 3342 0709   9–3D
"Your local boozer… but with excellent sharing plates of fab Indian food!" – this repurposed pub near Angel tube operates over two floors and is "an offshoot of the ever-busy Tamil Prince" (see also) and opened in late 2023. "It offers delicious small plates and large plates with options for vegetarians and meat-eaters, but it's a smaller and less adventurous menu than the Tamil Prince". Results can be "absolutely fantastic", although "the small portions can make the prices seem rather high". Top Menu Tips – "Beef Uttapam recommended"; "roti are legendary"; "Coconut Prawn Moilee was a particular standout". / N1 8DE; thetamilcrown.com; the_tamil_crown; Mon, Thu-Sat 10 pm, Sun 9 pm.

The Tamil Prince N1 £51 4 3 3
115 Hemingford Road   020 7062 7846   9–2D
"Is it actually a pub? Who cares when the food is remarkable?" – this "refreshingly different" converted corner-tavern in Barnsbury "takes you by surprise" with its "superb, punchy Indian food, served to you perched on a bar stool, amidst a crowded boozer vibe". Opened in 2022, it's quickly become one of the Top-100 most talked-about restaurants in our annual diners' poll and lives up to the hype for most customers, even if "the elongated bar can feel a bit cramped and the interior becomes too noisy" ("on a balmy night, it's great to sit outside"). "Delicious cocktails and a mean Bloody Mary too". Top Menu Tip – "the lamb chops, the Lollipop chicken and the huge Bhatura will make you go back again and again". / N1 1BZ; thetamilprince.com; the_tamil_prince; Tue-Sat, Mon 10 pm, Sun 9 pm.

FSA

Tamp Coffee W4 £29 3 4 3
1 Devonshire Road   no tel   8–2A
This "vibey" independent coffee shop off the Chiswick High Road roasts its coffee and bakes its pasteis de nata in-house. With its menu of simple bakes, sarnies and smoothies, it's a natural choice for a quick bite of brunch. (From their website, you can also stock up on T shirts and baseball caps as they also run an apparel range under the Tamp brand). / W4 2EU; tampcoffee.co.uk; tampcoffee; Mon-Fri 3.30 pm, Sat & Sun 4 pm.

Tandoor Chop House WC2 £65 3 3 3
8 Adelaide Street   020 3096 0359   5–4C
Handily tucked away off Trafalgar Square, this popular venture presents an Indian restaurant in the style of a wood-panelled London chophouse. Rated well all-round, fans say it's "worth the journey just for the crispy lamb chops" (and "the chicken is a highlight, too"). / WC2N 4HW; tandoorchophouse.com; tandoorchop; Mon-Thu 11 pm, Fri & Sat 11.30 pm, Sun 10 pm.

Tao Tao Ju WC2 £50 3 3 2
15 Lisle St   020 7734 1122   5–3A
"Excellent dim sum and roast pork" are the mainstays of the extensive menu at this large, accomplished Cantonese fixture – one of the better bets for a traditional Chinatown experience. / WC2H 7BE; Mon, Wed & Thu, Sun 10 pm, Fri & Sat 11 pm.

Tapas Brindisa £70 2 2 3
46 Broadwick St, W1   020 7534 1690   4–2B
7-9 Exhibition Rd, SW7   020 7590 0008   6–2C
18-20 Southwark St, SE1   020 7357 8880   10–4C
25 Circus Road West, SW11   020 8016 8888   11–1C
Hotham House, 1 Heron Square, TW9   020 8103 8888   1–4A
This quintet of tapas bars from the well-known Iberian food importer attracts most attention for its locations – in particular its "lively and popular" original bar at the entrance to Borough Market; and most recent addition: a "lovely riverside spot overlooking the Thames at Richmond". Despite its renown – and some praise for its "small plates but big flavours" – ratings are held down by prices many reporters consider "high" for what's widely seen as "pretty standard tapas fare". / brindisakitchens.com; brindisaspanishfoods.

Taqueria £46 3 3 3
141-145 Westbourne Grove, W11   020 7229 4734   7–1B
8-10 Exmouth Market, EC1   020 3897 9609   10–1A
This Notting Hill taco stalwart "really feels like Mexico". Having operated from a stall on Portobello Road before opening on Westbourne Grove 20 years ago, it is one of London's longest-running taco specialists, and now has an offshoot in Exmouth Market. It's "great value", too, and the imported Mexican beers, mescals and tequilas go down a treat ("it's a good choice for lunch, especially if you have nothing else planned that day!") / taqueria.co.uk; taqueriauk.

Taro £40 2 2 2
1 Churton Street, SW1   020 7802 9776   2–4B
61 Brewer Street, W1   020 7734 5826   4–3C
356 Regents Park Road, N3   020 3544 1065   1–1B
414 Kennington Road, SE11   020 7735 7772   1–3C
193 Balham High Road, SW12   020 8675 5187   11–2C
76 High Street, E17   020 8520 2855   1–1D
"A bit of a dive to be honest, but the food is still so good!" – no-one claims Mr Taro's group is particularly stylish, but for "very generous portions of the classic Japanese dishes (including decent sushi, teriyaki and katsu curry)" these functional canteens hit the spot, and at a very good price. The latest (summer 2024) additions to its roster of eight venues are Catford in southeast London and Brentwood in Essex. / tarorestaurants.uk; tarorestaurants.

tashas SW11 NEW £41 3|2|2
3 Prospect Way   020 3011 1989   11–1C

Near the entrance to Battersea Power Station in an attractive, spacious new unit, this South African all-day cafe beamed down at the very end of 2023. Specials include a pork schnitzel fried in corn flakes, healthy salads and in-house twists on familiar cocktails. The Evening Standard's Jimi Famurewa was very impressed by brunch here in his February 2024 review ("I cannot see a universe where most of us will not be charmed by the gloss, rigour and sun-warmed generosity of Tashas"). Some of our initial feedback agrees saying it's "hit the ground running and very good in every respect". Not everyone's impressed, though, with the odd report of "disappointing" food and service that's "unconcerned". / SW11 8BH; tashascafe.com; tashascafeuk; Sun-Wed 10 pm, Thu-Sat 11 pm.

Tattu London WC2 £132 2|3|4
The Now Building Rooftop, Denmark Street   020 3778 1985   5–1A

Insta-friendly backdrops of interior trees festooned with blossom and desserts served with smoking dry ice help characterise the eventful experience at this "fantastic"-looking three-year-old in Oxford Street's 'Now Building'. Inevitably the pan-Asian food is not always centre-stage, but it is rated consistently solidly in our reports and no concerns are noted this year. Top Tip – you can dip your toe in the water, pre-theatre, Saturday lunchtime and all day Sunday with the 'Taste of Tattu' menu from £33.50 per person for two courses. / WC2H 8LH; tattu.co.uk; tattulondon; Tue-Sun 1 am, Mon midnight.

Tavernaki W11 £31 3|3|3
222 Portobello Road   07510 627752   7–1A

This family-run taverna in the heart of Portobello is "always a winner" for its classic Greek dishes served in a warm atmosphere – sometimes with live Greek music on the side. / W11 1LJ; tavernakiportobello.co.uk; tavernaki.portobello; Mon-Sun 11 pm.

Tavolino SE1 £72 2|2|3
Unit 1, 2 More London Place   020 8194 1037   10–4D

An incredible (if, nowadays, rather touristy) South Bank location – with a big outside terrace in summer – is the reason to discover this modern Italian with magnificent views of Tower Bridge and HMS Belfast from a new development next to the former City Hall. The Italian food can be good too, but is not the main driver for a visit. / SE1 2JP; tavolino.co.uk; tavolinokitchen; Sun-Wed 10 pm, Thu-Sat 10.30 pm.

Tayyabs E1 £37 4|2|2
83 Fieldgate St   020 7247 6400   10–2D

"Heaving and occasionally rowdy" Punjabi "institution" in Whitechapel that provides "outstanding food year after year" and is a "must-go" even "in spite of the packed lobby to get in and lines out the door". "It's not fine dining, but you get the same tastes and authentic flavours here that you might pay double or triple the price for in the West End" – "amazing food that's really worth it". "All the favourites are served at reasonable prices, helped along by the fact that it's BYO". "It's large and looks nicer than it did a few years ago (as it has had a 'glow-up' over the years)". "At busy times, you feel a bit like you're on the conveyor on the service front", which can feel "brusque" but can also be "extremely friendly". Top Menu Tips – "you come for the lamb chops and stay for the spectacular lentils and baby aubergine (or many other) dishes". / E1 1JU; tayyabs.co.uk; 1tayyabs; Mon-Sun 11.30 pm.

The Telegraph SW15 £56 2|3|4
Telegraph Road, Putney Heath   020 8194 2808   11–2A

With its "great location on Putney Heath", this well-known and spacious tavern is "ideal for families with dogs" – especially in summer in the big front garden – even if the food is "nothing special at all" ("fish 'n' chips is always a safe option"). It is now run by Brunning & Price of Chester, who are good on "small details like the basket of reading glasses next to the daily newspapers!". (The hill-top setting was the site of a link in the visual telegraph connecting the Admiralty with Portsmouth in the era before electricity – hence the name). / SW15 3TU; brunningandprice.co.uk; telegraphputneyheath; Mon-Thu 11 pm, Fri & Sat midnight, Sun 10.30 pm; SRA-3 stars.

temper £59 2 2 3
25 Broadwick Street, W1   020 3879 3834   4–1C
5 Mercers Walk, WC2   020 3004 6669   5–2C
Unit 53 5 Merchant Sq, W2   020 3967 7578   7–1D **NEW**
78 Great Eastern Street, EC2   020 3758 6889   13–1B
Angel Court, EC2   020 3004 6984   10–2C

"Fire-cooked" steaks, supplied from North Yorkshire, aged in-house and supplemented by "inventive" side dishes (tacos, parathas and more), are what put Neil Rankin's BBQ group on the map, with its fifth site opening in Paddington Basin last winter followed by a smashburger spinoff in White City. But even fans can note that what "was once a firm favourite has declined" – service is often "a bit all over the place" and dishes can arrive "lacking genuine flavour". / temperrestaurant.com; temperlondon.

The 10 Cases WC2 £84 3 3 3
16 Endell St   020 7836 6801   5–2C

"They order 10 cases of wines on a rotating basis so the wines change regularly" at this *"cosy, bustling little venue (recommended by a sommelier friend)"*, with *"simple French bistro food that's really well-cooked"* and *"sunny service to match"*. The result is *"never a bad meal or a boring glass of wine"* – *"how they manage to have such a good wine list with such favourable markups in Covent Garden is a puzzle"*. And *"it's in the perfect location for the theatre or opera"*. / WC2H 9BD; 10cases.co.uk; 10cases; Mon-Sat 10 pm.

10 Greek Street W1 £73 4 3 4
10 Greek St   020 7734 4677   5–2A

"Scrumptious food, Soho ambience: a winner!" – Cameron Emirali and Luke Wilson's *"intimate"* fixture has won renown above its size and inspires feedback from diners living all over London. The food from the open kitchen *"is amazing and interesting"* and *"it's a place to come back to"* (*"I've eaten at 10 Greek 20+ times, I've never had one bad mouthful of food"*). Top Tip – ask for their 'Little Black Book' of 'rarer wine gems'. / W1D 4DH; 10greekstreet.com; 10greekstreet; Tue-Thu 10 pm, Fri & Sat 10.30 pm.

Tendido Cero SW5 £78 4 4 3
174 Old Brompton Road   020 7370 3685   6–2B

"Fabulous tapas" as usual wins praise from this *"stalwart of South Kensington"* from Abel Lusa – one of his high-octane trio grouped together around Cambio de Tercio (see also) on the Old Brompton Road. Now in its 24th year, one or two regulars opine that it's firing on all cylinders again after a *"down patch"*, with *"new ideas"* and a return to *"the high standards they had before"*. / SW5 0BA; tendidocerortve; Tue-Sat 11.30 pm, Mon 11 pm.

Tendril W1 £63 4 3 2
5 Princes Street   07842 797541   4–1A

"Rishim Sachdeva's 'mostly' vegan food is consistently thrilling in its creativity, ingenuity and presentation" and long-time supporters welcome his graduation from a pop-up to this permanent site in July 2023 near Oxford Circus. Rishim *"magically roams the globe drawing from many cuisines which somehow harmonise"*. The *"smart (for a vegan restaurant)"* interior mostly pleases, but *"can perhaps seem a little hard-edged at times"*, but fans say *"I would enjoy Rishim's food on a bed of nails – it is brilliant!"* / W1B 2LQ; tendrilkitchen.co.uk; tendril_kitchen; Mon-Thu 11 pm, Fri 11.30 pm, Sat midnight, Sun 5 pm.

Terra Moderna NW3 £65 3 4 3
2b Englands Lane   020 4568 8525   9–2A

"A well-conceived shortish menu of varied and interesting food" has won a warm reception for coffee entrepreneur Jeffrey Young's 'Antipodean-inspired Modern Italian in the heart of Belsize Park'. A visit is buoyed along by "a warm welcome and efficient but unobtrusive service (everyone in our – not always easy to please – party said they'd like to go again soon!"). / NW3 4TH; terramodernalondon.com; terramodernaldn; Tue-Sat 11 pm.

Terra Rossa £69 2 3 3
139 Upper Street, N1   020 7226 2244   9–3D
62 Carter Lane, EC4   020 7248 6600   10–2A

"You can practise your Italian language skills" at this "genuine, quirky Puglian restaurant in busy Islington, with great service from real Italians who know the region". Even some fans concede that culinary results can be "mixed", with hits and misses reported in a single meal. Nevertheless, it's "always buzzing" and "might benefit from some sound absorbers as it can get very noisy". They also have a lesser-known spin-off near St Paul's.
/ terrarossa-restaurant.co.uk.

Terry's SE1 £49 2 4 4
158 Great Suffolk Street   020 7407 9358   10–4B

The idea that Borough would be achingly cool (or that you might need to book here!) would have seemed bizarre back in 1982 when former Smithfield trader Terry opened his traditional red-check-tablecloth caff. Nowadays if you want to grab your hipster full English before a day's Instagramming in the local food markets, you may need to join the virtual queue. / SE1 1PQ; terryscafe.co.uk; terryscafelondon; Mon-Sun 3 pm.

Testi N16 £35 4 2 2
38 Stoke Newington High St   020 7249 7151   1–1C

"A great, traditional Turkish outlet on the grimier stretch of Stoke Newington High Street" – this "Stokey stalwart" is "a favourite for a diverse crowd" and approaching its 25th year. "They show a fine hand on the grill and churn out some of the most addictive Turkish bread anywhere – streaked with meat juices (be careful not to fill yourself up before the actual food arrives!)". The upshot is "fresh salads, fluffy flatbreads, tasty kebabs and hearty portions". "It's comparatively comfortable and friendly, too". / N16 7PL; Mon-Sun 11.30 pm.

Thai Tho SW19 £27 3 4 3
20 High St   020 8946 1542   11–2B

This "good-quality local Thai favourite" is "no more expensive than an average takeaway" and fans claim "you won't find better quality for the money anywhere in Wimbledon". "Staff, predominantly family, are amazing and welcoming, with time for everyone"; and "during the tennis, this place comes alive with fans, players, pundits, coaches… all packed in". (A sister restaurant in Soho inspires no feedback). / SW19 5DX; thaitho.co.uk; @thaitho_ldn; Mon-Sun 3 pm.

Theo Randall, InterContinental Park Lane W1 £93 4 4 2
1 Hamilton Place   020 7318 8747   3–4A

"Brilliant" Italian dishes "cooked to perfection" inspire rave reviews for chef Theo Randall's well-known HQ, by Hyde Park Corner. For many diners, "the fact that it's a large, bare, windowless hotel restaurant is completely irrelevant" – "there is good space between the tables"; "the kind staff all try really hard"; and "it always feels like a treat (that's not as expensive as some other places)". The odd meal doesn't go well, at which time the "soulless" space seems more significant, but bad trips here are quite rare. Top Menu Tips – "at weekend lunchtime, Theo Randall does an excellent buffet antipasti followed by a set lunch with bottomless prosecco or Aperol spritz.

The restaurant always has a buzz when these meals are on with lots of large families. And the business three-course set lunch at £33 is amazing value!"
/ W1J 7QY; theorandall.com; theo.randall; Tue-Sat 10 pm, Mon 10.30 am, Sun 11 am.

Theo's SE5 £43 4|3|3
2 Grove Lane   020 3026 4224   1–3C
"Lovely, charred, soft-based pizza with reliably interesting (but not OTT) toppings and very tasty!" wins consistently high ratings from a strong local fan club for this duo of pizzerias in Camberwell and Elephant & Castle.
/ SE5 8SY; theospizzeria.com; theospizzeria; Mon-Sun midnight.

34 Mayfair W1 £144 2|3|2
34 Grosvenor Sq   020 3350 3434   3–3A
This "very professional", American-style grill near the former US Embassy in Mayfair is unusually restrained and low-profile for a Richard Caring venue. It does have its cheerleaders, who think it provides an all-round "wonderful" experience. Others, though, find it hard to look beyond the final price tag ("little is much above average except the horrendous prices!"). / W1K 2HD; 34-restaurant.co.uk; 34mayfair; Mon-Sat 11 pm, Sun 10 pm.

thirty7 WC2 NEW
37 Bedford Street   020 3951 1365   5–4C
"New opening from the people behind the Oystermen" (and Bedford Street Wines) that launched in late March 2024, also in Covent Garden – a minimalist, all-day operation that is not all about seafood this time round; and with meat sourced from the West Country. The menu is modern brasserie fare: one early experience was *"good all-round if hit and miss: some dishes were less impressive but some excellent"*. / WC2E 9EN; thirty7bedfordstreet.co.uk; Mon-Sat 10 pm, Sun 5 pm.

The Thomas Cubitt SW1 £81 2|3|3
44 Elizabeth St   020 7730 6060   2–4A
This smart and fashionable (sometimes "extremely loud") Belgravia gastropub is the original flagship of the upmarket Cubitt House group and named after the Georgian developer who built the area. Given the address, no surprise that its posh gastropub menu – which stretches to oysters, plus steak and chops – can seem "expensive" for what it is. / SW1W 9PA; thethomascubitt.co.uk; Cubitt House London; Mon-Sat 11 pm, Sun 10.30 pm; SRA-1 star.

Three Darlings SW1 NEW
241 Pavilion Road   awaiting tel   6–2D
The darlings in question are Jason Atherton's daughters and this autumn 2024 debut is the second in West London to carry the name of the new brand: the first being a hot dog dispensary within Harrods. Irha Atherton, Jason's wife is also active in the business which aims to be a neighbourhood bistro for a well-heeled local crowd. / SW1X 0BP; Tue-Fri, Sun 10.30 pm, Sat 11 pm.

Three Falcons NW8 £50 3|2|2
1 Orchardson Street   020 7724 8928   7–1C
"It can be noisy if there's football on" at this slightly quirky venue, which bills itself as 'Central London's First Indian Gastropub & Hotel' (this is true only if your conception of 'central London' incorporates the thin area north of the A40 and Edgware Road tube as you head out of town). Sky Sports vies for attention with a menu mixing breaded brie and fish 'n' chips with Indian cooking of some quality. / NW8 8NG; threefalcons.com; threefalcons; Mon-Sun 11 pm.

Three Uncles £38 4|2|2
Unit 3A Filmworks Walk, W5   awaiting tel   1–3A NEW
Hawley Wharf, 2nd Floor Foodhall, NW1   07597 602281   9–2B
Unit 19&20, Brixton Village, SW9   020 3592 5374   11–2D

12 Devonshire Row, EC2   020 7375 3573   10–2D
"A takeaway hole in the wall with some seating" characterises the branches of Pui Sing, Cheong Yew & Mo Kwok's HK-inspired group, which specialises in Siu Mei ("authentic roasted Chinese meats") served in "generous portions" plus noodles – "top Hong Kong food, affordable and better than at 'normal' sit-down restaurants". Towards the end of 2024, they will open their largest site to-date: a 50-cover restaurant in Ealing's Filmworks development. / https://www.instagram.com/three.uncles.

TING,
Shangri-La Hotel at the Shard SE1 £97 3 3 4
Level 35, 31 St Thomas St   020 7234 8108   10–4C
"The views are fantastic, especially if you get a window seat" at this 35th-floor venue at the top of the Shard. It's open from breakfast (Asian or Western) onwards, via lunch and afternoon tea to dinner, where there's an Asian-inflected menu where items like Glazed Cauliflower "Steak" with Couscous, Coconut & Lime Foam rub shoulders with more wholeheartedly Oriental dishes such as Bo Xao Luc Lac Five Spices Beef. Especially by the standards of the venues in the Shard, moans about prices are most notable by their absence. / SE1 9RY; ting-shangri-la.com; tinglondon; Mon-Sun 10.15 pm.

Tish NW3 £99 3 3 3
196 Haverstock Hill   020 7431 3828   9–2A
David Levin's elegant-looking brasserie near Belsize Park tube scores well for its "consistent quality" and "great location". And by the dire standards of London's kosher restaurant scene, it's one of the best all-rounders in town. / NW3 2AG; tish.london; tish_london; Mon-Thu 10 pm, Sun 22 am.

Toba SW1 £60 4 3 2
1 St James's Market, London SW1Y 4AH   020 3583 4660   2–2C
"Very good Indonesian food" makes it worth braving the lifeless environs of the St James's Market development for Pino Edward Sinaga's yearling, on the site that was the former location for Ikoyi (since relocated, see also). It's a follow-up to his Camden Market street-food operation inspired by his family's recipes and offers a vibrant selection with a good amount of choice. "For its location, it's great value too". / SW1Y 4AH; tobalondon.co.uk; toba.london; Tue-Fri 9.30 pm, Sat 10 pm, Sun 3 pm.

Toff's N10 £56 3 4 2
38 Muswell Hill Broadway   020 8883 8656   1–1B
A photo of Ronnie O'Sullivan's visit is "proudly displayed on the wall" of this Muswell Hill institution, and fans say "the best player ever to pick up a snooker cue is bang-on with his choice of North London fish restaurant!", acclaiming "fish 'n chips that goes down a treat", and has done for more than half a century. It was sold by its family owners in March 2024 to a national group with plans to spin it out as a brand – fingers crossed its appeal survives! / N10 3RT; toffsfish.co.uk; toffsfish; Mon-Sat 10 pm.

Tofu Vegan £23 4 2 2
105 Upper Street, N1   020 7916 3304   9–3D
28 North End Road, NW11   020 8922 0739   1–1B
54 Commercial Street, E1   020 7998 6640   13–2C
"Fantastic vegan Sichuan food" – "bursting with spices and tastes" – makes any one of this "deservedly popular" trio in Islington, Golders Green and Spitalfields Market (from the team behind omnivore Xi'an Impression) "a go-to place if you want to eat vegan with an Asian twist". "Don't go because it's vegan, but because the food is just so good!" / https://www.instagram.com/tofuveganlondon.

F S A

Toklas WC2 — £85 — 4 3 4
1 Surrey Street   020 3930 8592   2–2D
"Restaurants that open to a fanfare of plaudits from critics often go off the boil after the first year. Not so Toklas!" which is going from strength to strength in our annual diners' poll since it was launched just off The Strand in 2021 by the founders of Frieze art fair. It's a "large" and "relatively unadorned" space with a "great buzz that's not too loud", and whose "well-spaced tables allow enough room to talk". And in summer, the best choice is the large outside terrace which is "delightful" ("despite the view of rather decrepit buildings opposite!"). Chef Yohei Furuhashi presides over a "really interesting and ever-changing" menu that's "mostly Spanish or Italian-influenced", with "added little twists to make it different". There is also a "lovely in-house bakery" which contributes "creative but not wacky desserts and very good bread". "One to watch!" / WC2R 2ND; toklaslondon.com; toklas_london; Mon-Sat 11 pm.

Tokova Restaurant SW17 — £45 — 4 3 2
Broadway Market, Tooting High Street   0208 672 5246   11–2C
"Tucked away at one end of buzzy Tooting market", this "small" outlet promises 'A taste of the Basque Country' and is the work of owner and artist Cristina Ruiz and chef Jorge López. "It makes a real effort with simple but competent cooking" and "the authentic recipes are served on small plates so you can sample a range of the full-flavoured dishes". / SW17 0RJ; tokovarestaurant.co.uk; Tue-Sat 10 pm.

Tollington's N4 NEW
172 Tollington Park   no tel   9–1D
Open in June 2024 (after our annual diners' poll had concluded) in the former, family-run Finsbury Park chippy that provides its name: a Spanish-inspired seafood spot from Four Legs, the team behind The Plimsoll nearby. Expect casual drinks and standing bites at the front bar and restaurant seating at the back. / N4 3AJ; tollingtons.fishbar; Mon & Tue, Fri, Wed & Thu midnight.

Tommi's Burger Joint W1 — £37 — 3 2 2
30 Thayer St   020 7224 3828   3–1A
Veteran Icelandic fast-food moghul-turned-politician Tómas Tómasson – now 75, and a member of his country's parliament, the Althing, since 2021 – has won solid ratings for the "cheap 'n' cheerful" UK outlets of his small, international chain. Its London presence has dwindled to a single branch, however, and the business (up for sale in 2023) entered administration in summer 2024. For the time being, though, they are still cranking out the burgers on Thayer Street… / W1U 2QP; burgerjoint.co.uk; Mon-Fri 11.30 pm, Sat & Sun midnight.

Tomoe SW15 — £47 — 4 4 2
292 Upper Richmond Road   020 3730 7884   11–2B
This "remarkably good local Japanese" is "the real deal": the whole approach is "extremely authentic" (that includes the uneventful interior) and its "ultra-fresh sushi and sashimi plus hot dishes" help it stake a reasonable claim as "Putney's best restaurant". Top Tip – "sit at the bar for the best experience". / SW15 6TH; tomoelondon.co.uk; tomoe.london; Wed-Sat 9 pm.

Tongue & Brisket W1 — £15 — 3 2 1
23 Goodge Street   020 7637 7277   2–1C
"Wonderful salt beef sandwiches" and "other options in a bun" plus "great latkes and Reubens" justify a trip to this Soho pitstop (cousins to Pinner and Edgware's B&K Salt Beef Bars and with spin-offs in Goodge Street and Holborn). "You can eat in, but facilities are basic (or take away and find a bench). It's a great option when you are hungry but want to avoid the high-cost options in this area". / W1T 2PL; tonguebrisket.com; Mon, Sat 6 pm, Tue-Fri 7 pm.

F S A

Tonkotsu £51 2 3 3
Branches throughout London
This 15-strong London noodle chain (now with branches in Brighton, Birmingham and Bristol) is "a good stand-by" – perhaps it's "not as good as some of its competitors", but it is widely seen as "good value": in particular "the lunch-time meal deal" is a winner. / tonkotsu.co.uk; tonkotsulondon.

Tosa W6 £43 3 2 2
332 King St   020 8748 0002   8–2B
This "great little yakitori restaurant" near Stamford Brook station specialises in grilled Japanese skewers "cooked to order" as you watch, ideally from a perch at the counter. It's a "simple local" spot, scoring well for authenticity. / W6 0RR; tosa.uk; tosa_hammersmith; Wed-Sun 10.30 pm.

Toulouse Lautrec SE11 £73 3 3 4
140 Newington Butts   020 7582 6800   1–3C
Inspired by Art Deco Paris, this wood-panelled Gallic brasserie south of Elephant & Castle provides a "wonderful atmosphere", a menu of "food you want to eat" and "Meteor à la pression" – better still, there's a jazz club upstairs. Les patrons, brothers Noland & Florent Regent, grew up next door in the Lobster Pot – another Francophile's delight, run by their parents for 25 years until 2016. / SE11 4RN; toulouselautrec.co.uk; tlvenue; Mon-Thu, Sat 10 pm, Fri 11 pm, Sun 9.30 pm.

Tozi £66 2 1 3
8 Gillingham St, SW1   020 7769 9771   2–4B
3a Electric Boulevard, SW11   020 38 338 200   11–1D
The "buzzy" original in a Victoria hotel occupies "a great space" (modelled on Continental grand cafés); while its younger sibling in the new Battersea art'otel is agreeably modernistic in style. Both can provide "a decent dining experience", but even fans sometimes noted "service issues" this year, which holds back a more wholehearted recommendation.

The Trafalgar Tavern SE10 £68 2 3 5
28 Park Row   020 8858 2909   1–3D
This spectacular tavern, which opened in Queen Victoria's coronation year next to Greenwich's Royal Naval College, has "a great setting beside the Thames" complete with a historic interior, and is not surprisingly "a favourite with tourists". It can provide a good trip, but it can also "be let down by its typical pub grub". / SE10 9NW; trafalgartavern.co.uk; trafalgartaverngreenwich; Sun-Thu 11 pm, Fri & Sat midnight.

Trevi N5 £45 3 2 2
16-18 Highbury Crescent   020 7700 7161   9–2D
"You feel as if you've been teleported back to the '80s" (or maybe even earlier) at this "very old-school" Italian relic – a basic café/ristorante by Highbury & Islington tube. "Even if the food isn't hugely fashionable, it tastes really good and is pretty good value – I bet they make their carbonara with cream!" / N5 1RD; Mon-Sat 9 pm.

Trinco SE22 £45 3 2 3
20 Lordship Lane   020 8638 7812   1–4D
"A good addition to the very variable Lordship Lane food offerings" – Vibushan Thirukumar and Paul Hepworth Nelmes's year-old venture provides "a thali-style menu that allows you to sample interesting vegetarian cuisine of Sri Lanka (including hoppers and curries)". It is part of their Oru Space co-working and wellbeing hub (which has a sibling in Sutton) and won recent recognition with the Best Café award at the Good Food Awards 2024. Top menu tip – "masala crème brûlée was very good". / SE22 8HN; trinco.restaurant; trincobynight; Mon-Sun 4 pm.

FSA

Trinity SW4 £158 5 5 4
4 The Polygon   020 7622 1199   11–2D

"The place to be south of the river!" – Adam Byatt's renowned destination by Clapham Common slugs it out in our annual diners' poll with Chez Bruce 10 minutes away as the top culinary destination in these parts and comes strongly "recommended to South Londoners who don't want to go into the centre of town" to find a "memorable" meal. "Adam Byatt frequently stops by for a chat" and under chef Harry Kirkpatrick (who joined in July 2023) there's little but hymns of praise to the "excellent and technically accomplished cooking", which is matched by "some exceptional wines". Front of house staff "balance the formality expected with a Michelin star with easygoing friendly service and there's a really relaxed feel to the place", particularly now there are more "casual" options to eat here either at Trinity Upstairs (see also) or on the relatively newly added outdoor terrace.
/ SW4 0JG; trinityrestaurant.co.uk; Trinityclapham; Mon-Sun 8.30 pm.

Trinity Upstairs SW4 £75 4 4 4
4 The Polygon   020 3745 7227   11–2D

Set in a "light-filled room" above Trinity restaurant, overlooking Clapham Common, chef-patron Adam Byatt's "very casual" everyday option provides an affordable taste of his "reliably delicious" cooking, served at high tables. The 'Sunday Lunch Club' is the stuff of local legend – "essentially it's a Sunday roast but the 3-course menu is different every week and the roast main is always beautifully cooked. The portions are massive and they often come round offering seconds, which are hard to decline…" / SW4 0JG; trinity-upstairs.co.uk; trinityclapham; Fri & Sat, Tue-Thu 8.45 pm, Sun .

Trishna W1 £86 4 3 2
15-17 Blandford St   020 7935 5624   2–1A

Inspired by its famous namesake in Mumbai, this Marylebone venture was the initial launchpad from which JKS Restaurants started to take the capital by storm. Occupying quirky, U-shaped premises, it's quite "small and packed" and how "atmospheric" it appears slightly depends on where you are sat. Billing itself as 'Indian coastal cuisine', the menu is strong on fish and seafood, but by no means dominated by it: "classy" dishes with "knock-out" flavours.
/ W1U 3DG; trishnalondon.com; trishnalondon; Mon-Sat 10.15 pm, Sun 9.45 pm.

Trivet SE1 £150 3 3 2
36 Snowsfields   020 3141 8670   10–4C

"A restaurant for foodies" – this low-key venue in the streets south of London Bridge station results from a partnership between two ex-Fat Duck alumni and has acquired a stellar reputation as it approaches its fifth year. Chef Jonny Lake delivers "exquisite", "imaginative (and sometimes challenging)" dishes – "it's amazing to have food of this quality and no tasting menu, which is a testament to their confidence". And it's matched by "stunning" wine from a 450-bin list "beautifully curated and expertly managed" by sommelier Isa Bal – "the team happily talk you through options" and "it's worth trying the more unusual grapes they recommend for their complexity and variety". That said, not all meals here escape criticism, which – compounded by the "bland" setting and bills that can be "a bit breath-taking" – leads one or two reporters to query: "how, how, how does this place have two, not one, but two (just upgraded this year) Michelin stars!". Top Tip – on Monday nights, they open the space as 'Labombe Wine Bar', a new concept in which the restaurant's bar space offers wine to try by the glass recommended by Isa alongside a blackboard menu of more casual bites from Jonny. / SE1 3SU; trivetrestaurant.co.uk; trivetrestaurant; Wed-Sat, Tue 11 pm.

La Trompette W4 £118 4 4 4
3-7 Devonshire Rd   020 8747 1836   8–2A

"The culinary jewel in Chiswick's crown" – this cousin to Chez Bruce "located in a side street off Chiswick High Road" is many diners' idea of the "perfect neighbourhood restaurant". Having "survived the enlarging of the space" and a "change of staff a couple of years ago, things have now completely settled in as has chef Greg Wellman"; and its performance this year in our annual diners' poll was incredibly consistent. The modern French cuisine "is a bit cheffier and more refined than before", with "lots of interesting Asian/Japanese touches": "interesting, but not too cutting edge" and "most importantly full of flavour". There's also a "fascinating" wine list to match ("the commitment to wine, as opposed to just seeing it as a profit centre, is noteworthy" with "an outstanding sommelier who will suggest perfect accompaniment for the dishes but also provide answers to far-fetched requests!"). "It's all combined with seamlessly efficient service… not as easy to do as they make it look, I suspect!". "Sit outside on a warm day". Top Menu Tips – "excellent pasta/ravioli plates add to excellent versions of more classic dishes, and a recent rabbit terrine was world class". / W4 2EU; latrompette.co.uk; latrompettechiswick; Wed & Thu 9 pm, Fri & Sat 10 pm, Sun 3 pm.

Trullo N1 £84 4 3 3
300-302 St Paul's Rd   020 7226 2733   9–2D

"Perfection for simple high quality" – Tim Siadatan and Jordan Frieda's "lovely neighbourhood Italian" in Islington draws a big fan club from across town and provided many best-meals-of-the-year in our annual diners' poll thanks to its "exceptional pasta", "excellent grilled meats and fish" and "fairly priced Italian wine list". "Always busy and noisy", it's also rather "romantic". / N1 2LH; trullorestaurant.com; Mon-Sat 10.30 pm, Sun 9.30 pm.

Tsiakkos & Charcoal W9 £75 3 4 3
5 Marylands Road   020 7286 7896   7–1B

A lively local, just off the Harrow Road in Maida Vale, which "never disappoints". It's nothing fancy: "the mezze are a treat and really good ingredients are cooked very well indeed" (mostly from the charcoal grill). "There's always a friendly and relaxed atmosphere and service is excellent". / W9 2DU; tsiakkos.co.uk; tsiakkos; Tue-Sat 11 pm.

Tsunami SW4 £60 3 2 2
5-7 Voltaire Rd   020 7978 1610   11–1D

This "longstanding Clapham local fave" – run by three "Nobu refugee" chefs – "keeps knocking out very good-to-exceptional sushi and sashimi" after almost 25 years (although some of the cooked dishes are less successful). "Service is local, friendly and charming but can seem overrun", and the "ambience is Nobu-meets-nightclub". / SW4 6DQ; tsunamirestaurant.co.uk; tsunami_restaurants; Mon-Thu 11 pm, Fri & Sat 11.30 pm, Sun 10.30 pm.

TT E2 £58
17b Kingsland Road   020 7183 9503   14–2A

This good-looking Shoreditch rooftop has traded for a while as just a bar (called TT Liquor), but dropped the 'Liquor' part in summer 2024 to highlight the arrival of chef Sam Lone, who oversees the wood-fired oven that's the kitchen's main event. On the easygoing menu, seasonal sharing plates BBQ'd, baked and smoked over the coals; and some of them pickled for good measure. / E2 8AA; Tue-Thu midnight, Fri & Sat 1 am.

28 Church Row NW3 £64 3 4 3
28 Church Row   020 7993 2062   9–2A

"So much more than just a tapas bar" – this basement hideaway at the foot of a handsome Georgian terrace, near picturesquely located St John-in-Hampstead church, boasts a serious and eclectic wine list and a focused menu of Spanish and Italian small and sharing plates. / NW3 6UP; 28churchrow.com; 28churchrow; Mon-Sat 10.15 pm, Sun 9.15 pm.

28-50 £91 2 2 3
15-17 Marylebone Lane, W1   020 7486 7922   3–1A
4 Great Portland Street, W1   020 7420 0630   3–1C
300 King's Road, SW3   020 7349 9818   6–3C

This wine bar/restaurant group has a steady fanbase on the strength of its vinous offerings, although its "bistro fare" is perhaps not much better than "acceptable". The best of its four venues is probably the "cosy" Marylebone flagship with live jazz and late opening at '28-50 By Night', and there's a "very convenient" branch a minute's walk from Oxford Circus. / 2850.co.uk; 2850marylebone.

24 The Oval SW9   £65   3 4 3
24 Clapham Road   020 7735 6111   11–1D
In the underprovided area around Oval, it's well worth discovering this "nice neighbourhood spot near the cricket ground". Steak is a speciality (it's a sibling to Clapham's Knife, see also), but meat doesn't over-dominate the wide menu, and results remain consistently well-rated. Top Tip – 'secret' outdoor garden out back. / SW9 0JG; 24theoval.co.uk; 24theoval; Wed-Sat 9.30 pm, Sun 4.30 pm.

The Twenty Two W1   £135
22 Grosvenor Square   020 3988 5022   3–2A
A "beautiful room, by day or by night" makes this restaurant in a hip-by-the-standards-of Mayfair hotel and members' club (opened 2022) "great for a date", according to its fans. The modern British/Mediterranean food from chef Alan Christie is uniformly well reviewed in feedback. But it's also "priced accordingly" for this wealthy part of town; and wines below £100 per bottle are significantly in the minority on the list. Given relatively limited feedback, we've held off on a full judgement of its level of value for the time being. / W1K 6LF; the22.london; the22.london; Mon-Sun 9.30 pm.

Twist Connubio W1   £71   3 3 3
42 Crawford Street   020 7723 3377   2–1A
Charcuterie, sharing plates and dishes from the Josper grill provide a "delicious Italian/ Spanish mix" at this "lovely and buzzy" small outfit: worth discovering in a backstreet just around the corner from St Mary's Church, Marylebone. / W1H 1JW; twistconnubio.com; twistconnubio; Mon-Sat 11 pm.

222 Veggie Vegan W14   £47   3 3 2
222 North End Road   020 7381 2322   8–2D
Chef Ben Asamani's "lovely" long-running vegan café on busy North End Road in Fulham (by the crossroads with Lillie Road) celebrates its 21st anniversary this year – and nobody has a bad word to say about the place. Top Tip – the weekend lunch all-you-can-eat buffet is a steal at £18 a head. / W14 9NU; 222vegan.com; 222veganbowlfood; Mon-Sun 10 pm.

2 Veneti W1   £70   2 3 2
10 Wigmore Street   020 7637 0789   3–1B
This "pleasant Italian restaurant near the Royal Society of Medicine and Wigmore Hall" serves "quality food" with Venetian touches at a price that is "very reasonable for Marylebone". It also offers a "surprisingly good lunch deal". / W1U 2RD; 2veneti.com; 2veneti; Mon-Fri 9.45 pm, Sat 10 pm.

UBA EC2 **NEW**
61-67 Great Eastern Street   020 3995 3622   13–1B
Open in April 2024, this vibey pan-Asian spot is from the same Middle Eastern-based stable as Sucre and Clap and promises to 'seamlessly blend East London's dynamic spirit with the exotic allure of Pan-Asian flavours'. A couple of early reports say it's doing a pretty good job, but feedback is too limited for a definitive rating. / EC2A 3HU; Tue-Sat 9 pm, Sun 3 pm.

Uli   £80   3 3 3
15 Seymour Place, W1   020 3141 5877   2–2A
5 Ladbroke Road, W11   020 3141 5878   7–2B
"This unusual Asian-fusion restaurant" from Michael Lim "delivers extremely high-quality, fresh-tasting dishes almost uniformly across the board" from its

variety of cuisines – and "Michael always takes care of the customers". After almost three decades in Notting Hill, it now has a spinoff in Seymour Place, Marylebone, where it's "a very welcome addition". / ulilondon.com.

Umu W1 £168 444
14-16 Bruton Pl   020 7499 8881   3–2C

"Just simply heaven" – this discreet Japanese venue brought Kyoto-style, kaiseki dining to London when it first opened in 2004 and – despite having lost other parts of his once-extensive restaurant empire – founder Marlon Abela still owns it. Perhaps reflecting Abela's non-Japanese heritage, it's one of the more vibey top-end Japanese locations in town: it sits in a bijou Mayfair mews with svelte, elegant decor. As one of the first places to introduce Londoners to the vertiginous price-points of Japanese dining, it has always been seen as costly, but fans say it's "the most misunderstood restaurant: anyone who really knows Japanese food would praise this restaurant to heaven and back" on account of chef Ryo Kamatsu's "ever-changing, seasonal Japanese cuisine". The kaiseki menu is £250 per person, but you don't have to opt for it: there's a wide à la carte and they make a feature of using the 'Ikejime' method of killing fish designed to bring 'unparalleled flavour and texture when preparing sashimi'. All reports agree this place is "not cheap but does a sound job" – indeed most reports regard it as "exceptional" in all respects. / W1J 6LX; umurestaurant.com; umurestaurant; Tue-Sat 10 pm.

Undercroft W1 NEW
St George's Church, 2A Mill Street   no tel   3–2C

The London debut of top Brummie chef Brad Carter (of Carter's of Moseley, RIP) has helped put the spotlight on the autumn 2024 launch of the new restaurant space underneath the august St George's in Hanover Square, Mayfair. The Grade I listed building itself is full of history (Theodore Roosevelt was married here!) and this new conversion will incorporate an open kitchen, wine room and some outside tables. Expect smart revivals of forgotten dishes, such as sea tripe and seaweed soup or Tamworth pork with creamed snails. / W1S 1FX; undercroftldn; Mon-Sat 11 pm, Sun 7 pm.

Upstairs at The George W1 £87 223
55 Great Portland Street   020 3307 8136   2–1B

This "beautifully turned out" 18th-century tavern aims "at the upper end for pub food" (although the cooking "never strays into fussy fine-dining fare"). But while it mostly receives a good rep in reports – and its location near Oxford Circus makes it "handy when carpet shopping at John Lewis becomes all too much" – its performance is very modest for somewhere backed by the mighty JKS Restaurants and with a menu designed by chef James Knappett of Kitchen Table fame. / W1W 7LQ; thegeorge.london; thegeorgepublichouse; Mon-Sat 11 pm, Sun 8 pm.

Le Vacherin W4 £83 333
76-77 South Parade   020 8742 2121   8–1A

You could be in 'La France profonde' at this "great neighbourhood restaurant" by distant Acton Green. Foodwise, it's "more than a bistro – this is seriously good classical French cooking, more than worth the detour". There's "no greedy pricing, even on the wine", and "if it feels a bit old-fashioned, that's attractive in this era of chef worship and cult-like trends!". Top Menu Tip – "the cheese soufflé is a must every visit". / W4 5LF; levacherin.com; le_vacherin; Mon-Sat 10.30 pm, Sun 9 pm.

Vardo SW3 £79 334
9 Duke of York Square   020 7101 1199   6–2D

In a dramatic modern pavilion in Chelsea's Duke of York Square, this "buzzy and fun" venue (named after the Romany travelling wagon) boasts "plenty of outside seating" and is a particular summer favourite. Food-wise, it takes its cue from the Caravan group it is part of, delivering a global menu of *"innovative" sharing plates ("interesting choices for most palettes and to suit those with food intolerances"). / SW3 4LY; vardorestaurant.co.uk; vardorestaurant; Tue-Thu, Sun 10 pm, Fri & Sat 10.30 pm, Mon 9.30 pm.*

Vasco & Piero's Pavilion W1 £78 3 4 3
11 D'Arblay Street   020 7437 8774   4–1C

"Staff could not be nicer" at this veteran Soho Italian, which originally opened in 1971 but has shifted site twice in its lifetime (most recently in 2021, from nearby Poland Street). "The new venue is in the old style and it's as good as ever". Fans value "having a reliable, independent Italian in this part of London" and its "delightful", personal approach particularly underpins its appeal. It also helps that the cooking is "very authentic" and "reliable" too: "standard dishes from a sensibly short menu but nicely done". / W1F 8DT; vascosfood.com; Tue-Sat, Mon 11 pm.

Veeraswamy W1 £109 4 4 4
Victory House, 99-101 Regent Street   020 7734 1401   4–4B

"It may be the oldest Indian restaurant in London" (est. 1926), but this first-floor operation, "looking down on Regent Street", has "definitely kept up with the times" and its "attractive" verging on "funky" interior is thoroughly contemporary. Nowadays part of the excellent MW Eats group (with siblings including Chutney Mary and Amaya), its "colourful food is beautifully presented" and "well spiced"; "meat is succulent and tender" and there are "superior and delicate curries". "The cocktails are good too". / W1B 4RS; veeraswamy.com; veeraswamy.london; Mon-Sat 10 pm, Sun 10.15 pm.

Vero Caffe N12 £20 3 2 3
16 Sussex Ring   020 8445 2212   1–1B

Where the action is when in Woodside Park – this "friendly and popular local café with good coffee, inside and outside dining and friendly and efficient staff" came to attention in the survey this year. It's a modern and stylish shop-conversion on the high street, with a brunch-friendly menu and range of 'gourmet' burgers. / N12 7HX; verocaffe.co.uk; Mon-Sun 5 pm.

Via Emilia £49 3 2 2
10 Charlotte Place, W1   020 8127 4277   2–1C
37a Hoxton Square, N1   020 7613 0508   13–1B

The food of Emilia-Romagna is the inspiration for this Italian duo in Shoreditch and Fitzrovia. They major in pasta, with sliced meats, cheeses and wines from the region as back-up, and all reports say the food is of a good standard. / via–emilia.com.

Il Vicolo SW1 £73 2 4 2
3-4 Crown Passage   020 7839 3960   3–4D

"Good to see it's open again!" – this "charming and efficient" Italian has built a loyal following over the years, with "caring" service and "a real family feel" that's a welcome find in stuffy St James's. The new site is doors away from the old in quirky Crown Passage: "a welcoming space with clean lines and tables not overly close together". To the uninitiated, the traditional fare – Insalata Caprese; Calamari alla Brace; Ravioli del Buongustaio; Scaloppine al Limone – can seem a little "average", which undercuts its rating. Most reporters, though, applaud its "well-priced", traditional cuisine and consider it "a real surprise jewel in this neck of the woods". / SW1Y 6PP; ilvicolorestaurant.co.uk; Mon-Fri 10 pm.

The Victoria SW14 £69 3 3 4
10 West Temple Sheen   020 8876 4238   11–2A

This "long-time favourite gastropub near Richmond Park" in East Sheen has been owned by TV chef Paul Merrett for more than 15 years, and serves "great food and wine", including in the spacious rear conservatory and garden. "Never had a bad meal here", agree regulars – many of whom meet up in the bar for a "pre-Twickenham lunch". / SW14 7RT; victoriasheen.co.uk; thevictoriasheen; Wed-Sat 11 pm, Sun 10 pm.

Viet Food W1 £47 **4** 3 2
34-36 Wardour Street   020 7494 4555   5–3A
"Delicious and authentic Vietnamese food" is "served fast and functionally" to a packed house at ex-Hakkasan chef Jeff Tan's "fun and buzzy" warehouse-style Chinatown diner. Service is "very quick (too quick sometimes?)", which makes it "perfect for pre- or post-theatre", and "the small portions mean you can try more different dishes". Fans say it's "outstanding for the price you pay". / W1D 6QT; vietnamfood.co.uk; vietfoodlondon; Sun-Thu 10.30 pm, Fri & Sat 11 pm.

Viet Ngon N4 £35 **4** 3 2
145 Stroud Green Road   020 8054 4661   9–1D
"It's always busy" at this welcoming Vietnamese restaurant, north of Finsbury Park as you head towards Crouch End, thanks to its "friendly staff and authentic cooking" (including a good number of options for veggies and vegans). Top Menu Tips – pho noodle soups and the bun cha (grilled pork with vermicelli noodles). / N4 3PZ; vietyumyum.com; Mon-Sun 10 pm.

Vijay NW6 £45 3 **4** 2
49 Willesden Ln   020 7328 1087   1–1B
This "great local Indian" in Kilburn, now 60 years old, was a pioneer of Keralan cooking in the UK (and has fed celebs as diverse as Diana Ross and Harrison Ford over the years); and still serves "lovely dosas and appetisers" as well as "good vegetarian dishes". The odd report says "the dining room is looking really tired"… but they've been saying that for decades now and most diners warm to its unaffected style. / NW6 7RF; vijayrestaurant.co.uk; vijayindiauk; Sun-Thu 10.45 pm, Fri & Sat 11.45 pm.

Villa Bianca NW3 £82 3 2 3
1 Perrins Ct   020 7435 3131   9–2A
With its starched white tablecloths, this "comfortable" stalwart Italian, down a picturesque alley, has been a feature of central Hampstead since the 1980s. It has the strengths and weaknesses that can come with such territory, which includes "a real old-school Mediterranean menu" and professional service (which "can be a bit snotty"). But by and large it's "maintained its quality". / NW3 1QS; villabiancagroup.com; villabiancanw3; Tue-Sat 11 pm, Sun 10 pm.

Villa Di Geggiano W4 £93 3 **4 4**
66-68 Chiswick High Road   020 3384 9442   8–2B
It's the large leafy courtyard out front that catches the eye at the Bianchi Bandinelli family's slightly quirky venue. Drawing on five centuries of tradition from an estate near Siena, the aim to import a slice of Tuscan living to London would not seem out of place in, say, Chelsea, but seems a little offbeat on this rather trafficky stretch of the Chiswick High Road (although having the famous Metropolis recording studios next door doubtless helps provide custom). Fans say it's a "special" place – "quite expensive, but some of the best Italian around". / W4 1SY; villadigeggiano.co.uk; villa_di_geggiano_london; Tue-Sat 10.30 pm, Sun 9 pm.

The Vincent Rooms,
Westminster Kingsway College SW1 £48 **4** 3 3
76 Vincent Square   020 7802 8391   2–4C
"Beautifully prepared and served" by hospitality students, a meal at Westminster Kingsway College in Vincent Square is "always a pleasure (and I've never had a bad experience)" – it's "excellent value, too (don't tell everybody)". And while it can be "a bit funny" at times being a 'crash test dummy' for its student servers, "there's no need to be patronising – the kids

achieve a high level across the board". Meals are served on weekdays during term time in the Escoffier Room and more casual Brasserie, with wine pairings available. / SW1P 2PD; thevincentrooms.co.uk; thevincentrooms; Mon, Fri 3 pm, Tue-Thu 9 pm.

Vinoteca £63 222
18 Devonshire Rd, W4   020 3701 8822   8–2A
Borough Yards, Stoney Street, SE1   020 3376 3000   10–4C
7 St John St, EC1   020 7253 8786   10–1B
Bloomberg Arcade, Queen Victoria Street, EC4   awaiting tel   10–3C
"A great wine list from all corners of the globe" has helped underpin the ongoing popularity of this modern wine bar chain, despite a year that saw it sold out of administration and the closure of its popular King's Cross branch. Although this period inspired iffy marks and the odd report of "totally disorganised" service, the four remaining outlets still inspire tons of, albeit slightly lukewarm nominations as a handy option "for a simple meal": "don't expect any sort of culinary fireworks" from the "straightforward" dishes "but there are some very nice, reasonably priced wines" and the interiors are "definitely pleasant". Top Menu Tips – "lovely cheese croquettes and steak 'n' chips". / vinoteca.co.uk; vinotecawinefood.

Vivat Bacchus £74 222
4 Hay's Lane, SE1   020 7234 0891   10–4C
47 Farringdon Street, EC4   020 7353 2648   10–2A
'A taste of South Africa' is the promise of this City-fringe duo in Farringdon and London Bridge, which combine "an excellent choice of steaks" and dishes from the braai with a wide selection of South African wines. There's also the prospect of a trip to the (very un-African) walk-in cheese room to end off a meal. But even those who acknowledge "decent Saffa-inspired grills" can say "the overall feel of the place is a little tired" or "functional". And that it's "not cheap for what it is" was also a repeat-complaint this year. / vivatbacchus.co.uk; vivatbacchus.

Volta do Mar SW3 £67 333
100 Draycott Avenue   +44 203 051 2352   5–3D
"Excellent fish dishes and a very good selection of Portuguese wines" mean it's worth discovering this South Kensington venture, which can be "a find" to the uninitiated. The creation of Salt Yard founder Simon Mullins and his wife Isabel Almeida Da Silva, it "showcases food from Portugal and its diaspora" (South America, Africa and Asia) and moved to this new location in 2023 after four years in Covent Garden. / SW3 3AD; voltadomar.co.uk; voltadomar_ldn; Tue-Sat 10 pm, Sun 6 pm.

Vori W11 £96 333
120 Holland Park Avenue   020 3308 4271   7–2A
Markos Tsimkalis is celebrating his second year at this upbeat modern taverna near Holland Park station, where fish is a particular highpoint of a sunny Greek menu made from excellent ingredients (e.g. meat from nearby Lidgates), and with many dishes from the charcoal grill. High-quality Greek wines are a particular feature of an interesting drinks list, with a number of 'special pours' by the glass. / W11 4UA; vorigreekkitchen.co.uk; vorilondon; Tue-Sun 10 pm.

VQ £66
111a Great Russell Street, WC1   020 7636 5888   5–1A
325 Fulham Rd, SW10   020 7376 7224   6–3B
Wanting to eat in the wee hours? This stalwart chain has fed tolerable diner food 24/7 (VQ = Vingt Quatre, geddit?) to the denizens of the Fulham Road for so long as anyone can remember (before 1995 it was called 'Up all Night'); and has a more recent outlet (unusually, licensed till 4am, though you must be eating) that's more convenient if you are clubbing in the West End on the ground floor of a Bloomsbury hotel. / vqrestaurants.com; vqrestaurants.

F S A

Wagamama £59 2 2 2
Branches throughout London

"You know exactly what you are going to get, and it's fine for what it is" – that's the overall verdict this year on these enduring Japanese-inspired (but not especially authentic) ramen canteens. As always, there are those who say it "seems to have gone downhill", but its ratings for a cheap 'n' cheerful refuelling stop were actually pretty decent in the last poll – way ahead of many mass-market chains. Top Top – "a firm family favourite" that's "a hit with younger members of the family: service is quick and efficient and the food is always predictable". / wagamama.com; wagamama_uk; SRA-3 stars.

Wahaca £54 2 2 3
Branches throughout London

"For a large chain, they still do pretty much unbeatable Mexican fusion fare", say fans of these "busy and atmospheric" street-food cafés, now with 11 London branches and three others around the UK. That said, there are also some niggles in feedback; and the sentiment is widespread that – though "still enjoyable" – the food can seem "a little mass-produced". Even so, practically all diners still consider them "dependable for a quick, cheap 'n' cheerful bite". Top Tip – the new, 150-cover Paddington branch is their first opening in six years and puts a focus on sustainability and a menu including some larger sharing plates (e.g. grilled Achiote Seabass, Lamb Barbacoa and Chimichurri Cauliflower). / wahaca.com; wahaca; SRA-3 stars.

The Wallace,
The Wallace Collection W1 £52 1 2 5
Hertford House, Manchester Square   020 7563 9505   3–1A

"The location is the star" at this museum café – "a charming and very civilised glass-covered courtyard", which inspires a high level of feedback. It is most recommended for "a not-OTT afternoon tea". For other occasions, "the food is pleasant enough but the place wouldn't warrant inclusion were it not for the setting". / W1U 3BN; heritageportfolio.co.uk; wallacerestaurant; Mon-Sun 5 pm.

The Walmer Castle W11 £50 2 3 4
58 Ledbury Rd   020 4580 1196   7–1B

Notting Hillbillies are "thrilled that the Walmer Castle is back and thriving" under new owners Jack & Poppy Greenall (of The Surprise in Chelsea), following in the footsteps of David Beckham, Guy Ritchie and Piers Adam, who failed in two attempts to make a success of the grand mid-Victorian tavern. It's certainly a "great pub and dining room", and "the faux William Morris decoration is well done", but ratings are capped by the odd dissenter who feels "it's OK, but – at the price – should do better". / W11 2AJ; walmercastlenottinghill.co.uk; walmercastle_nottinghill; Tue-Thu 11.30 pm, Fri & Sat midnight, Sun 10.30 pm.

Watan SW17 NEW £39 3 3 3
180 Upper Tooting Road   020 3649 0062   11–2C

"A wonderful new entrant to the Tooting scene" – this August 2023 debut is from a group with operations in Southall and Ilford. It occupies a big, sheenily designed unit: "cavernous, stylish, neo nightclub in feel with table and banquette seating". "Afghan/Pakistani grills and curries are cooked in the glassed-off but visible kitchen": "curries are authentically spicy and good across all proteins". "It's already packed with a vibrant crowd of young adults and families at all hours: especially after prayers on Friday". "NB. it is a dry restaurant: not even BYO". / SW17 7EW; watanrestaurant.co.uk; Mon-Sun midnight.

The Water House Project E2 £140 5 4 4
1 Corbridge Crescent   07841 804119   14–2B

"A real event, with very complex and often-experimental food" – Gabriel & Patricia Waterhouse's "temple of high cuisine" started out in his flat and, since 2021, has occupied this Scandi-esque, high-ceilinged, light-filled space

near Regent's Canal. Bookings are available for 1-6 diners and much of the seating is at communal tables, to which the 'Long Form Menu' at £155 per person is served at peak times (with cheaper options at quieter times). "There's practically no choice on wine: either you have the wines provided or you have the non-alcoholic versions (same price)". All reports agree this is "amazing" cooking – "you might not love it all, but you will certainly find it interesting!" – and there's a general feeling that it is also "very good value for a great gastronomic experience". As to the overall set-up, while the odd report says the seating is "a bit rag tag", most say "don't be put off by the supperclub set-up or shared tables". / E2 9DS; thewaterhouseproject.com; thewaterhouseproject; Wed-Fri 11 pm, Sat 11.30 pm.

The Waterman's Arms SW13 £65 3 2 4
375 Lonsdale Road   020 4529 8970   11–1A

"Love this new spot on the river off Barnes High Street" with riparian views from its upstairs dining room windows and "really good food". It's a passion project from local boy Joe Grossman, founder of Patty & Bun, that is "several cuts above regular pub standard" – "the waiting staff are friendly, and able to recognise exactly which glass of wine has been requested without having to point at the menu!". On second thoughts, it "calls itself a pub, but is really a restaurant". / SW13 9PY; watermansarms.co.uk; thewatermans.arms; Tue-Sat 9.30 pm, Sun 4.30 pm.

The Wells Tavern NW3 £74 3 3 4
30 Well Walk   020 7794 3785   9–1A

"Consistently good food and a lovely atmosphere" backed up by "intelligently engaged and well-informed service" deliver everything you could reasonably expect from this handsome Georgian tavern in Hampstead, run for more than 20 years by Beth Coventry (sister of Fay Maschler, the doyenne of London restaurant critics). "The pub's keenness to welcome dogs (with their own menu) may divide opinion" – but also wins many friends. Top Menu Tip – "save room for dessert; it's sometimes the star of the show". / NW3 1BX; thewellshampstead.london; thewellshampstead; Mon-Sat 11 pm, Sun 10.30 pm.

Westerns Laundry N5 £76 3 3 4
34 Drayton Park   020 7700 3700   9–2D

This "super-cool local" off the Holloway Road near the Emirates stadium has been a kingpin of the hip sharing-plates dining scene since it opened seven years ago, making stylish use of a post-industrial space where diners are "packed in like sardines... which are delicious here!". The "healthy modern British" small plates menu always has "quite a few vegetarian dishes" and low intervention wines are a big feature. / N5 1PB; westernslaundry.com; westernslaundry; Tue-Sat 10.30 pm, Sun 9 pm.

The Wet Fish Café NW6 £59 3 3 3
242 West End Lane   020 7443 9222   1–1B

"A gem in West Hampstead" – "for a simple, well-executed fish dish, there's nowhere better to go", say fans of this atmospheric conversion of a 1930s fishmonger (and you can still buy fresh fish to cook at home). It's "great any time of day, but especially for a romantic dinner", while the "live music evenings are exceptional". / NW6 1LG; thewetfishcafe.co.uk; thewetfishcafe; Mon-Sun 10.30 pm.

Whyte's E8 NEW
Unit 3, 143 Mare Street   no tel   14–2B

Underground, guerrilla, pop-up chef Whyte Rushen opened this hipster Hackney haunt at the end of 2023 near London Fields – a small, modern bistro, with bare bulbs, open kitchen and not a tablecloth in sight. Oysters topped with pickled onion Monster Mash are an oft-cited dish in reviews, but much of the menu is a modern take on French bistro classics. But whereas the press have raved (Grace Dent, "pretty wonderful"; Charlotte Ivers in The Sunday Times, "too clever by half [but] nobody could claim this isn't just really

The Wigmore, The Langham W1 £66 3 4 4
15 Langham Place, Regent Street 020 7965 0198 2–1B
A "gem in the West End" – The Langham Hotel and Michel Roux Jr partnered in 2017 to create this reimagined British boozer north of Oxford Circus, and the result has proved to be one of Londoners' favourite gastropubs, not least thanks to its menu of "great refined pub classics" at "fair prices for the location". Casual enough for post-works drinks, it's also smart enough for an informal business meal. Top Menu Tip – "the best cheese toastie this side of the Alps". / W1B 3DE; the-wigmore.co.uk; wigmorelondon; Mon-Sat 11 pm, Sun 12 pm.

Wild W11 NEW £110 2 3 4
202—204 Westbourne Grove 0208 191 2407 7–1B
A spin-off from Chelsea's Wild Tavern, the DNA of owners George Bukhov-Weinstein & Ilya Demichev (who run the Goodman and Burger & Lobster chains) is evident at this late 2023 newcomer on one of Notting Hill's main drags, on a site that was previously 202 (RIP). "Buzzy", with a "sort of happening vibe", it "looks amazing" but most reports consider the mix of raw bar, pasta and grilled surf 'n' turf "overpriced" and "sounding better than it tastes"… "lovely to sit in, but wouldn't hurry back". / W11 2RH; wildnottinghill.com; Mon-Sat 10.30 pm, Sun 9.30 pm.

Wild by Tart SW1 £85 3 4 4
3-4 Eccleston Yard 020 7627 2176 2–4B
"A hidden gem in the heart of Pimlico" – this "fun and buzzy" space is part of the "super-cute" Eccleston Yards development, and is very stylishly housed in a 9,000 sq ft former power station (combining a restaurant, bar, retail store and events space). There's a "small but good menu" with eastern Med influences and "lots of vegetarian options" (although the "wine prices can be hard to swallow"). / SW1W 9AZ; tart-london.com; tart_london; Mon-Fri 6 pm.

Wild Honey St James SW1 £125 3 3 3
Sofitel, 8 Pall Mall 020 7389 7820 2–3C
"Stylish, friendly and with inspired cooking" – that's the most favourable take on Anthony Demetre's rather grand hotel dining room off Trafalgar Square, with its parquet floor and banquettes running down each wall. (It's not to be confused with the 'Wild Honey' he ran in Mayfair for many years). The cooking is modern British in style and even more reserved reports acknowledge it's "perfectly sound". It's also to be found in an area where value is thin on the ground: "in fairness, where else are you going to get such a good meal at this price in SW1 for goodness sake?" / SW1Y 5NG; wildhoneystjames.co.uk; wildhoneystjames; Wed-Sat 9.30 pm, Tue 2.30 pm.

Wild Tavern SW3 £133 2 2 3
2 Elystan Street 020 8191 9885 6–2C
With its alpine-themed interior, this Italian-ish Chelsea haunt from the team behind Goodman and Burger & Lobster opened to rave reviews just before lockdown. This year, though, its offering – combining a raw bar, with prime cuts of steak or fish from the grill and a selection of pasta – received little but opprobrium in our diners' poll for "ridiculously overpriced and average meals" ("you don't have a value-for-money category. If you did, this would score 0/10!"). / SW3 3NS; wildtavern.co.uk; wildtavern; Mon-Sat 10 pm, Sun 9.30 pm.

Wilson's SE13 NEW £65 3 4 4
77 Ladywell Road 020 3649 5585 1–4D
"A brilliant addition to southeast London" – this spring 2024 newcomer on Ladywell High Street is next door to organic food stockist Plenty and opposite

coffee shop Oscar's, both from the same founders (Alina & Joel Falconer). Chef Henry Freestone has worked in some of the hippest kitchens around town, including nearby Peckham Cellars and east London's Crispin and Bambi. Here he delivers a no-nonsense, modern British menu with three-four options at each course. / SE13 7JA; wilsonslondon.co.uk.

Wiltons SW1 £118   4 4 5
55 Jermyn St   020 7629 9955   3–3C

"Nowhere else like it!" – for "sheer class, history and pedigree" it is hard to match London's oldest restaurant in St James's (est. 1742, on this site since the 1980s). If you are a traditionalist, it is "perfect, perfect, perfect" – "a quintessentially British restaurant specialising in premium-quality fish and seafood – plus also game and meats" – whose discreet and comfortable old-world surroundings are typical of nearby clubland, complete with booths and well-spaced tables; and all orchestrated by "impeccable staff". It's best enjoyed if your Wealth Manager is treating you, obviously, although complaints about its notoriously terrifying prices were quite muted this year. Top Menu Tip – "Start with a dozen wonderful, plump oysters and a sharp red onion and red wine vinegar sauce. Then call over the carving trolley for several slices of perfectly rare meat from the large roast sirloin of beef". Or take your pick of the caviar, lobster or twice baked Stilton soufflé and "it's a case of lunchtime heaven". / SW1Y 6LX; wiltons.co.uk; wiltons1742; Mon-Sat 10.30 pm.

The Windmill W1 £69   2 2 2
6-8 Mill St   020 7491 8050   4–2A

"If you like pies, beer and wine", this Young's pub is – say fans – "a good choice", especially when you need relatively affordable sustenance in Mayfair. But despite serious investment in recent times – with the addition of an upstairs restaurant and roof terrace – ratings slipped this year (with a couple of reports such as: "not sure what's happened, but it's really gone downhill"; or "far too noisy and cramped, and the pies we had read so much about were not as good as M&S!"). / W1S 2AZ; windmillmayfair.co.uk; windmill_pub; Mon-Sun 9 pm.

The Wine Library EC3 £55   3 3 5
43 Trinity Sq   020 7481 0415   10–3D

"Recovering nicely from the Covid effect" – this "perennial favourite for lunch" near Tower Hill is a classic bolt hole for professional buddies conspiring to kill off an afternoon over a decent bottle. Run by an independent wine merchant in a superbly characterful Victorian cellar, it provides "basic platters" of cheese or charcuterie (with veggie/vegan options) to help absorb the "very good wine at accessible prices, with good advice from the owner". A flat £12 corkage fee makes it a good place to explore more expensive vintages, and it hosts regular events – "did a Chinese wine tasting... who knew?" / EC3N 4DJ; winelibrary.co.uk; thewinelibrary; Tue-Fri 8 pm, Mon 6 pm, Sat 5.30 pm.

The Wolseley W1 £89   2 3 4
160 Piccadilly   020 7499 6996   3–3C

"A people-watching heaven" – this epic Grand Café near the Ritz is renowned for the "busy" and "buzzy" clatter of its "beautiful", "high ceilinged" dining room and remains many a sophisticated Londoner's "gold standard for business"; particularly early morning over one of its "legendary breakfasts" (it's "a perfect way to start the day, with a client, a friend, or quietly in the corner with a newspaper"). However, its gigantic popularity has been won despite it being "nothing fancy in the food department"; and its broad menu of "traditional comfort food" has always been "tasty and well-presented… but formulaic". Drama ensued in 2022, when its founders Corbin & King were ousted in a boardroom battle. But even those who feel the place has perhaps "lost a bit of sparkle since the management shake-up" acknowledge that "on the ground, very little has changed". Top Tip – also good for "a classic afternoon tea. Delicious finger sandwiches and plain

The Wolseley City EC4 — £89 — 2 2 3
68 King William Street   020 3772 0600   10–3C

"A welcome and stylish addition to the City" – this vast newcomer has a Manhattan-esque exterior at the foot of a huge 1920s block facing onto London Bridge (the ground floor of the old House of Fraser building). Inside, it's "a mimic of the original" near the Ritz, with its high ceilings, monochrome tiled floor, and cream and chestnut colour scheme: "it may not have quite the same buzz as Piccadilly", but looks-wise "does the job well". It serves a similar "brasserie-plus" menu, and although results can be "mediocre", then firstly, this is also true of the original; and secondly, "as you would expect, the trade is mostly business lunchers" whose expectations tend to be modest. In fact, many reports rate it as "almost identical to its namesake" and often compliment its service too. Overall, though, ratings are dragged down by too many middling and poor reviews. No particular themes emerge as to where the main faults lie, but with a venue this big consistency is key and still seems to need work. Top Tip – as at the original, "breakfast is superb" and already popular with the local suits, with "duck egg and haggis particularly recommended". / EC4N 7HR; thewolseleyhospitalitygroup.com; thewolseley; Mon-Sat 11 pm, Sun 10 pm.

Wong Kei W1 — £37 — 3 2 2
41-43 Wardour St   020 7437 8408   5–3A

Many long-in-the-tooth Londoners regard this "no-nonsense", multi-floor Chinatown veteran as their "go-to Chinese restaurant in the West End". "The legend of Wong Kei was the sheer rudeness of the staff. Nowadays they are just casually brusque but still provide a wide range of well-priced Chinese dishes" – "where else to have a complete meal in the West End under a tenner? Wonton Soup with noodles is ordered even before the menu gets slapped on the table". Top Tip – "all dishes come with free green tea". / W1D 6PY; Mon-Sat 11.30 pm, Sun 10.30 pm.

Wright Brothers — £73 — 3 3 3
56 Old Brompton Rd, SW7   020 7581 0131   6–2B
11 Stoney St, SE1   020 7403 9554   10–4C
26 Circus Road West, SW8   020 7324 7734   11–1C

"A very good fish selection with great daily offerings" and "excellent seafood" win very many nominations for these ever-popular fish-and-seafood bistros in Borough Market, Battersea Power Station and South Kensington. All offer a "pleasant experience", with an appealing "casual" ambience, "friendly" staff and very "reliable" standards. In particular, SW8 has a "terrific location – right by the Power Station and the boat landing! – Step off and step straight inside!" / thewrightbrothers.co.uk; WrightBrosLTD.

Wulf & Lamb — £58 — 3 2 3
243 Pavilion Road, SW1   020 3948 5999   6–2D
66 Chiltern Street, W1   020 8194 0000   2–1A

A "very impressive all-plant-based menu" explains why this fashionable veggie pair in Chelsea and Marylebone are "always a bit too crowded and noisy" for some reporters. Their signature vegan burgers and mac'n'cheese make it "easy to forget the absence of meat". / wulfandlamb.com.

Xi'an Biang Biang E1 — £30 — 4 3 3
62 Wentworth Street   020 8617 1470   13–2C

"Great hand-pulled noodles" – "and the best cold starters" – are the highlights of a meal at this Spitalfields canteen featuring "spicy pot-stickers" from Shaanxi province in northwest China. ('Biang' is apparently an *onomatopoeia, said to resemble the sound of noodle dough hitting a work surface). / E1 7AL; xianbiangbiangnoodles.com; xiangbiangbiangnoodles; Mon-Thu 10.30 pm, Fri & Sat 11 pm, Sun 10 pm.*

Xi'an Impression N7 £47 5️⃣2️⃣1️⃣
117 Benwell Rd   020 3441 0191   9–2D

"The Biang Biang noodles are sensational" at this "brilliant and friendly BYO" opposite Arsenal's Emirates stadium ("I'm actually addicted to the food here!"); and "for the price, you're unlikely to find better in London". Its opening 10 years ago launched founder Guirong Wei as the standard-bearer for Shaanxi cuisine in London, and she has followed up with bigger, equally acclaimed venues in more central locations, Master Wei and Dream Xi'an (see also). Top Menu Tip – "the Biang Biang noodles are the headline dish, but the cold Liangpi noodles, the Qishan pork and the rich Paomo are also must-tries". / N7 7BW; xianimpression.co.uk; Xianimpression; Mon-Sun 10 pm.

Yaatra SW1 £85 4️⃣3️⃣3️⃣
4 Greycoat Place   020 4549 1906   2–4C

In the Old Westminster Fire Station, this "high-quality" two-year-old offers "interesting takes on Indian food", "nicely positioned on the spectrum of refined but not too refined, with punchy flavours but not to the point of aggression". The hardworking marketing team (so many emails!) is strong on offers which can deliver "really good value for such a top-class restaurant". Top Menu Tip – "the superb kebab platter and Keralan turbot". / SW1P 1SB; yaatrarestaurant.com; yaatrawestminster; Mon-Sat 10 pm.

Yama Momo SE22 £67 3️⃣2️⃣2️⃣
72 Lordship Ln   020 8299 1007   1–4D

"Reliable sushi and excellent cocktails" remain hallmarks of this East Dulwich neighbourhood spot – a spinoff from Clapham's Tsunami. / SE22 8HF; yamamomo.co.uk; yamamomo_eastdulwich; Mon-Thu 11 pm, Fri & Sat 11.30 pm, Sun 10.30 pm.

Yard Sale Pizza £44 3️⃣3️⃣2️⃣
54 Blackstock Road, N4   020 7226 2651   9–1D
46 Westow Hill, SE19   020 8670 6386   1–4D
39 Lordship Lane, SE22   020 8693 5215   1–4D
393 Brockley Road, SE4   020 8692 8800   1–4D
63 Bedford Hill, SW12   020 8772 1100   11–2C
622 High Road Leytonstone, E11   020 8539 5333   1–1D
15 Hoe Street, E17   020 8509 0888   1–1D
184 Hackney Road, E2   020 7739 1095   14–2A
105 Lower Clapton Rd, E5   020 3602 9090   14–1B

"Reliably excellent pizza" – "better than the other high street chains" – is what you'll find at this growing Clapton-based operation, now with 12 sites from Balham and Crystal Palace in the south to Tufnell Park (which, as of summer 2024, is the latest to open). They're perhaps "not smart as places to eat", but that hardly matters – and the "toppings are interesting without being off-puttingly un-pizza-ish". / yardsalepizza.com; yardsalepizza.

Yashin £115 4️⃣3️⃣2️⃣
117-119 Old Brompton Rd, SW7   020 7373 3990   6–2B
1a Argyll Rd, W8   020 7938 1536   6–1A

One of London's original beacons of "modern Japanese sushi dining" to those in-the-know, Yasuhiro Minemo & Shinya Ikeda's surprisingly under-the-radar venture has lit up a Kensington backstreet for 14 years – it can be "hard to find as it doesn't look like a restaurant and the only sign is a blackboard, but it's well worth it". "Focused on quality ingredients and an authentic approach" – it's far from inexpensive but consistently inspires "outstanding" feedback from its fans. It has spawned two offshoots: Ocean House in the old Brompton Library near South Kensington tube; and Sushi Kamon in Arcade Food Hall on Oxford Street. / yashinsushi.com.

F S A

Yasmin W1 NEW
1 Warwick Street   no tel   4–3B

Glam new rooftop terrace, bar and restaurant – part of the swish One Warwick members' club just off Piccadilly Circus (where Nessa, see also, is on the ground floor) – that opened in early summer 2024 (too late for survey feedback). It sounds like the 'killer cocktails' may be as much of a draw as the Istanbul-inspired sharing plates from chef Tom Cenci, but with this location that may not be a prime concern. / W1B 5LR; yasminsoho.com.

Yauatcha   £113   5 4 3
15-17 Broadwick St, W1   020 7494 8888   4–1C
Broadgate Circle, EC2   020 3817 9888   13–2B

"Consistently excellent dim sum" served in a vibey setting that "even after so many years is still a fun, cool place to be" ensures continuing plaudits for these sleek venues (founded by Alan Yau in 2004 and nowadays an international brand owned by Tao Group Hospitality with three siblings in India and one in Saudi Arabia). Food aside, its two London branches are very different – the original, intimate ground floor and basement in Soho contrasting with the more "spectacular", large, "light-filled" modern unit in the City's Broadgate development. Both scored highly this year – "service appears to have become a bit less standoffish"; and "the only drawback is eating too much!". Top Menu Tips – "Cheung fun, Venison Puff, Sichuan pork wonton and Wagyu beef puff are some of the tastiest things you can eat". / yauatcha.com.

The Yellow House SE16   £53   3 4 3
126 Lower Rd   020 7231 8777   12–2A

"Every year I struggle to come up with new ways of saying just how wonderful this extremely underrated spot is", say fans of this cherished local – a bright spark in the culinary void near Surrey Quays station. "They've been in situ for ages (thank goodness) yet the menu is always changing and continues to impress": "sourdough pizzas are the main event – the pear and gorgonzola and the tiger prawn with chorizo are particular favourites – and it also has a modern European and grill menu". / SE16 2UE; theyellowhouse.eu; theyellowhouserestaurant; Tue-Thu 9 pm, Fri & Sat 9.30 pm, Sun 5.30 pm.

Yeni W1   £65   3 3 3
55 Beak Street   020 3475 1903   4–2C

Following success in Istanbul, London-trained chef, Civan Er opened this stylish if fairly straightforward Soho operation in 2019. The focus is using British produce to create Turkish-influenced dishes cooked over open fire: "super-tasty food at a very reasonable price". Many dishes are to share, and 'Manti' (a type of filled dumpling) are a menu feature. / W1F 9SH; yeni.london; Tue-Sat 10 pm.

YeYe London E1   £20   3 2 2
14 Artillery Passage   02072479747   10–2B

"Not quite street food per se, but certainly fast, cheap and very specialised" – this simple canteen in a cute alley near Spitalfields Market is a "most superior noodle bar". Take care, "it could be addictive": "the various types of hand-pulled noodles are excellent" ("rich and spicy broth with giant meatballs and fall-apart ribs of pork"). "The nearby branch in Middlesex Street only does walk-ins but ALWAYS has a queue". / E1 7LJ; yeyelondon.co.uk; Mon, Sat 6 pm, Tue-Fri 7 pm.

YGF Malatang W6 NEW
Iberia House, 8 Hammersmith Broadway   020 3340 0513   8–2C

The first UK branch of one of China's largest chains (with more than 6,000 branches around the world) opened without fanfare in early 2024, just off Hammersmith Broadway. You can eat anything you like, so long as it's Malatang (hotpot): choose your own custom ingredients from the chiller cabinets lining the wall, place your order and you are called up when your broth has been prepared. A big TikTok hit with Asian students, it also got a thumbs-up from Daily Mail critic Tom Parker Bowles in his April 2024 review. / W6 7AL; Mon-Fri 5.30 pm, Sat 6 pm, Sun 4.30 pm.

YiQi WC2 NEW £58
14 Lisle Street   020 7287 2751   5–3A

In Chinatown, this modern Pan-Asian debut launched in early 2024 and features a wide range of intriguing dishes: including rice roasted in bamboo tubes; a wide range of noodles; meat cooked sous vide and seafood specials featuring crab, pomfret fish, skate and sea bass. Chef Lum Wah Cheok is a veteran of upmarket kitchens including Hakkasan and Yauatcha so it sounds promising; and while it has yet to attract any survey feedback, social media buzz about the place suggest it's excellent value, and Giles Coren of the Times in a July 2024 review declared, "it rocks and I'm going back". / WC2H 7BE; yiqipanasia.co.uk; yiqipanasia; Mon-Sat 11 pm, Sun 10.30 pm.

Yum Bug N4 NEW £39   4 4 2
110 Fonthill Road   no tel   9–1D

'The Bugs are here Baby' – that's the message at this funky, no-frills Finsbury Park newcomer, created by an entomologist and a designer seeking to demonstrate that insects are delicious and good for the planet. A pop-up in Shoreditch in late 2023 proved that the proposition had legs… now it has wings to fly! Most folks seem to love it, and one early survey report praises "a high variety of small-plate dishes with high protein content and friendly service". / N4 3HT; yumbug.com; _yumbug; Thu-Sat 10.30 pm.

The Yurt Cafe E14 £20   3 3 4
2 Butcher Row   0300 111 1147   12–1B

"A wonderful café tucked away in the grounds of The Royal Foundation of St Katharine in Limehouse" – London's 'first yurt café' (opened in 2016) provides "an oasis of calm" in the East End. Motto: 'Community, Creativity, Connection' – "it's open for breakfast, lunch and afternoon tea and does a small but lovely range of freshly cooked food". "In summer, there are tables outside under canopies where you can watch the butterflies in the community garden; in winter it is toasty, warm and cosy". Top Menu Tip – "amazing full English for breakfast". / E14 8DS; rfsk.org.uk; Sun-Wed 5 pm, Thu-Sat 10 pm.

Zafferano SW1 £119   4 4 3
15 Lowndes St   020 7235 5800   6–1D

This "old reliable favourite" in Belgravia celebrates its 30th anniversary this year, as ever serving "beautiful (if very expensive) Italian food" in a "fantastic ambience". A dazzling gastronomic phenomenon in its early days under founding chef Giorgio Locatelli, it's "not as busy as it used to be, but still worth a visit". / SW1X 9EY; zafferanorestaurant.com; zafferanorestaurant; Mon-Sun 10 pm.

Zahter W1 £99   3 3 3
30-32 Foubert's Place   07775 156768   4–1B

"Middle Eastern (Istanbul) dishes that are a little different" and can be "very good" win fans for this ambitious Soho three-year-old, which had to cope with the passing in August 2023 of co-founder and chef Esra Muslu. It has the same downsides that it has always had though – for some reporters "value just isn't there and while it may be delicious it's far too expensive". Top Tip – go as a couple and sit in the "stunning, central tiled bar downstairs" ("groups often sit upstairs and/or in a dull mezzanine area"). / W1F 7PS; zahter.co.uk; zahterlondon; Mon-Sat 10.30 pm.

Zaika of Kensington W8 £84   3 4 4
1 Kensington High Street   020 7795 6533   6–1A

"Exquisite, very subtle spicing, generous portions and extremely attentive and good-humoured service" all help retain a very loyal following for this high-quality Indian, which has occupied this grand, converted banking hall near

Kensington Gardens for 25 years now. "Although not cheap, its cost/quality ratio is one of the best in central London". / W8 5NP; zaikaofkensington.com; zaikaofkensington; Tue-Sat 10.15 pm, Sun 9.15 pm.

Zapote EC2 £44   4 4 2
70 Leonard Street   020 7613 5346   13–1B

"Superb elevated Mexican food" – "verging on fine dining" – is served at chef Yahir Gonzalez and former Sketch manager Tony Geary's Shoreditch yearling that "deserves more recognition". The Latino fare is "not the usual stuff", with "interesting dishes" showcasing "sensational flavours, often gently spiced but some more so for those who want it hot". "Knowledgeable and approachable staff" ensure a "very well-paced meal, with plates brought out in a thoughtful order (not whenever they're ready, like so many other supposedly top small-plates places)". Any sniping is generally reserved for the "industrial vibe" dining room, which some see as "far too noisy": "they could do with creating some nooks and a bit more privacy for some of the tables". / EC2A 4QX; zapote.co.uk; zapoteshoreditch; Mon-Thu 10 pm, Fri & Sat 10.30 pm.

Zayna W1 £58   4 3 3
25 New Quebec St   020 7723 2229   2–2A

A fixture near Marble Arch for 15 years, this smart operation is "more than a local curry house". Punjab-born founder Riz Dar spent many years working in California, and has bagged testimonials from the late Paul Allen of Microsoft and Shahid Khan, owner of the Jacksonville Jaguars and Fulham FC. / W1H 7SF; zaynarestaurant.co.uk; Mon-Sun 11 pm.

Zest SE13 NEW
Unit 1 Exchange Point, Loampit Vale   no tel   1–4D

"A much-needed new local in Lewisham" – this 'Brunch & Bar' operation at the foot of one of the area's shiny recent developments changes its offer over the day: from the obvious in the morning, to burger, soup and sarnies at lunch and a more brasserie-style offer in the evening. / SE13 7NX; zestbrunchandbar.co.uk; Tue-Sat 10 pm, Mon 5 pm.

Zheng SW3 £82   3 3 2
4 Sydney St   020 7352 9890   6–2C

Just off the King's Road, this Chelsea Malaysian endures on a site that's prominent if you are local, and out-of-the-way if you are not. It owes its longevity to a menu of "really good Malay/Chinese combinations". / SW3 6PP; zhengchelsea.co.uk; Mon, Wed-Sun 11 pm.

Zia Lucia £54   4 4 4
61 Blythe Road, W14   020 7371 4096   8–1C
Boxpark Wembley, 18 Olympic Way, HA9   020 3744 4427   1–1A
61 Stoke Newington High Street, N16   020 8616 8690   1–1C
157 Holloway Road, N7   020 7700 3708   9–2D
65 Balham High Road, SW12   020 3093 0946   11–2C
356 Old York Road, SW18   020 3971 0829   11–2B
49 Fulham Broadway, SW6   020 3822 0229   6–4A NEW
South Quay Plaza, 75 Hampton Tower, E14   020 4503 8859   12–1C
12a Piazza Walk, E1   020 7702 2525   10–2D

"Lush pizza" that's reliably "top-quality" has driven the expansion of this Islington-based group that has developed four different 48-hour ferment bases – including gluten-free and 'black vegetable charcoal' versions to reduce stomach gas; so "everyone's happy". The eight-year-old group now has nine sites in the capital (including a new one labelled as 'Chelsea' but on Fulham Broadway) and one in Reading. / zialucia.com; zialuciapizza.

Ziani's SW3 £68   3 3 2
45 Radnor Walk   020 7351 5297   6–3C

"If you want a traditional Italian restaurant in Chelsea, this is the place", say regulars at this tiny, "tucked away" trat "in a Chelsea side street off the

King's Road" – a quirky site they've been going to for yonks (mostly since before the founder, Roberto Colussi, died a few years ago). It can seem a bit "disorganised", but "even on a quiet Tuesday lunchtime, it's pretty much full and for a good reason: it's excellent value for money" by the standards of the area. / SW3 4BP; ziani.co.uk; Mon-Sat 10 pm, Sun 9.30 pm.

Zoilo W1 £91 3 4 3
9 Duke St   020 7486 9699   3–1A

"My 'go-to' lunch restaurant in the West End" – "the moment they pull back the curtains you enter a cosy, dimly lit part of Buenos Aires" at this Argentinian spot near the Wallace Collection, from well-travelled chef-patron Diego Jacquet (ex-El Bulli and Aquavit New York). "Lovely calm service adds to the romantic atmosphere". Top Menu Tip – "the Bife de Ancho (ribeye) is simply sensational: not to be missed". / W1U 3EG; zoilo.co.uk; Tue-Sat midnight.

Zuma SW7 £125 4 3 5
5 Raphael St   020 7584 1010   6–1C

"Still going strong" – the "electric, buzzy atmosphere makes for great people-watching" at Rainer Becker & Arjun Waney's charismatic Knightsbridge scene, whose cocktail bar is a 'Beauty & The Beast' bearpit of expensively clad Eurotrash-types. "It's expensive, but even knowing that it's still a great experience": "service tries hard without being terribly fast or particularly friendly" and delivers superb "precision cooking" from a bewildering Japanese-inspired array of luxurious robata dishes, sushi and sashimi, wagyu, lobster and seafood. / SW7 1DL; zumarestaurant.com; zumalondonofficial; Mon-Sat 11 pm.

AREA OVERVIEWS

AREA OVERVIEWS | CENTRAL

CENTRAL

Soho, Covent Garden & Bloomsbury
(Parts of W1, all WC2 and WC1)

£240+	Frog by Adam Handling	*British, Modern*	4 4 3
£230+	Aulis London	*British, Modern*	5 4 3
£210+	SOLA	*American*	4 3 2
	Alex Dilling Café Royal	*British, Modern*	2 2 2
	Restaurant 1890	*French*	3 4 4
	Humble Chicken	*Japanese*	5 4 3
£160+	Evelyn's Table	*British, Modern*	4 3 3
£150+	Savoy, Savoy Grill	*British, Traditional*	1 1 3
£140+	Northall, Corinthia	*International*	3 4 4
£130+	Gauthier Soho	*Vegan*	4 4 4
	NoMad London	*American*	2 3 5
	Spring Restaurant	*British, Modern*	3 3 4
	Kebab Queen	*Turkish*	– – –
	Tattu London	*Chinese*	2 3 4
£120+	Kerridge's	*British, Modern*	2 2 2
	Sushisamba	*Fusion*	2 2 4
£110+	Savoy, River Restaurant	*Fish & seafood*	2 2 2
	Dear Jackie	*Italian*	– – –
	Smith & Wollensky	*Steaks & grills*	2 2 2
	Savoy, Savoy Lounge	*Afternoon tea*	– – –
	Yauatcha	*Chinese*	5 4 3
£100+	Christopher's	*American*	2 3 4
	Clos Maggiore	*British, Modern*	3 4 5
	Simpson's in the Strand	*British, Traditional*	– – –
	L'Escargot	*French*	3 4 4
	Otto's	"	5 5 4
	The Petersham	*Italian*	2 2 3
	Decimo	*Spanish*	3 3 4
	Oscar Wilde Lounge	*Afternoon tea*	3 3 5
	RAI	*Japanese*	– – –
£90+	Milk Beach Soho	*Australian*	3 4 3
	The Ivy	*British, Modern*	2 3 3
	The Ivy Soho Brasserie	"	1 1 3
	Pivot	"	2 3 3
	Quo Vadis	"	3 3 5
	Bob Bob Ricard	*British, Traditional*	2 3 5
	Holborn Dining Room	"	2 2 3
	J Sheekey	*Fish & seafood*	3 3 4
	Margot	*Italian*	3 3 4
	Nopi	*Mediterranean*	3 2 3

CENTRAL | **AREA OVERVIEWS**

	Name	Cuisine	Ratings
	Mountain	*Spanish*	4 3 4
	Hawksmoor	*Steaks & grills*	3 3 3
	Zahter	*Turkish*	3 3 3
	Roka	*Japanese*	3 2 3
£80+	Balthazar	*British, Modern*	1 2 3
	Cora Pearl	"	3 3 3
	Dean Street Townhouse	"	2 2 3
	Ducksoup	"	4 4 3
	Jamie Oliver	"	2 2 3
	Noble Rot	"	3 3 3
	Sussex	"	2 2 3
	Rules	*British, Traditional*	3 3 5
	Burger & Lobster	*Fish & seafood*	3 3 2
	Fishworks	"	3 2 2
	The Oystermen	"	4 3 2
	Randall & Aubin	"	4 3 4
	The Seafood Bar	"	3 3 2
	Blanchette	*French*	3 2 2
	Story Cellar	"	3 4 4
	The 10 Cases	"	3 3 3
	Doppo	*Italian*	3 4 4
	Toklas	*Mediterranean*	4 3 4
	Lisboeta	*Portuguese*	3 2 2
	Maresco	*Spanish*	3 3 3
	Heliot Steak House	*Steaks & grills*	3 3 3
	Cecconi's Pizza Bar	*Pizza*	2 2 3
	Sucre London	*Argentinian*	2 2 3
	The Barbary	*North African*	5 4 4
	The Palomar	*Middle Eastern*	4 3 3
	Darjeeling Express	*Indian*	3 3 2
	Tamarind Kitchen	"	3 3 2
£70+	Paradise	*Sri Lankan*	3 3 2
	Andrew Edmunds	*British, Modern*	3 4 5
	Café Deco	"	3 2 2
	The Devonshire	"	3 4 5
	The French House	"	5 4 5
	Ham Yard Restaurant	"	2 3 4
	Indigo	"	3 2 3
	Nessa	"	3 3 2
	Noble Rot Soho	"	4 5 4
	The Portrait	"	3 3 3
	ROH, Amphitheatre	"	2 3 3
	ROH, Piazza Cafe	"	2 2 3
	ROH, Floral Hall	"	2 3 4
	10 Greek Street	"	4 3 4
	Cork & Bottle	*British, Traditional*	2 2 4
	The Delaunay	*East & Cent. European*	2 3 4
	Big Easy	*Fish & seafood*	2 2 3
	Parsons	"	4 3 3
	Mon Plaisir Restaurant	*French*	2 2 3
	Chotto Matte	*Fusion*	3 4 3
	Flesh and Buns	"	3 2 2
	Café Murano	*Italian*	3 3 3
	Da Mario	"	2 3 2

AREA OVERVIEWS | CENTRAL

	Vasco & Piero's Pavilion	"	3 4 3
	Barrafina Mariscos	Spanish	4 4 3
	Tapas Brindisa Soho	"	2 2 3
	Macellaio RC	Steaks & grills	2 2 3
	St Moritz	Swiss	2 2 3
	Rucola at The Conduit	Vegetarian	– – –
	Barshu	Chinese	5 3 2
	The Duck & Rice	"	3 2 2
	Donia	Filipino	4 3 3
	Colonel Saab	Indian	4 4 4
	Patara Soho	Thai	3 3 3
£60+	Tendril	Vegan	4 3 2
	Joe Allen	American	1 3 4
	Baudry Greene	British, Modern	3 4 4
	Double Standard	"	2 4 5
	Isla	"	2 4 4
	Kettners	"	2 2 4
	Ochre	"	2 3 3
	Riding House Bloomsbury	"	2 3 3
	VQ, St Giles Hotel	"	– – –
	Manzi's	Fish & seafood	2 2 2
	Le Beaujolais	French	2 2 4
	Boulevard	"	2 3 3
	Brasserie Blanc	"	2 2 2
	Brasserie Zédel	"	2 3 5
	Cigalon	"	3 4 4
	Le Garrick	"	2 3 3
	Palm Court Brasserie	"	2 2 3
	Caravan	Fusion	2 2 2
	INO	Greek	4 4 3
	Ave Mario	Italian	3 4 3
	Bancone	"	2 2 2
	Bocca di Lupo	"	4 4 3
	Dehesa	"	2 2 2
	Giovanni's	"	2 2 3
	La Goccia	"	2 2 3
	Grasso	"	2 3 3
	Notto	"	3 2 2
	Obicà	"	2 2 3
	Opera Tavern	Spanish	3 2 3
	Haché	Burgers, etc	3 3 2
	Rock & Sole Plaice	Fish & chips	3 3 2
	L'Antica Pizzeria da Michele	Pizza	4 2 2
	Homeslice	"	3 2 3
	Bébé Bob	Chicken	3 4 4
	Kapara by Bala Baya	Israeli	4 3 2
	Maison Bab	Middle Eastern	3 3 2
	Berenjak	Persian	5 4 4
	The Counter Soho	Turkish	3 2 3
	Yeni	"	3 3 3
	Lahpet	Burmese	4 3 2
	Chop Chop	Chinese	3 3 2
	Four Seasons	"	4 1 1
	New Loon Fung	"	3 2 1
	Orient London	"	4 3 2

CENTRAL | AREA OVERVIEWS

	Din Tai Fung	Chinese, Dim sum	3 2 2
	Cinnamon Bazaar	Indian	3 3 3
	Fatt Pundit	"	3 3 2
	Gunpowder Soho	"	3 3 2
	Masala Zone	"	3 3 4
	Tandoor Chop House	"	3 3 3
	Shoryu Ramen	Japanese	3 2 2
	Inamo	Pan-Asian	2 2 3
£50+	Hoppers	Sri Lankan	3 3 2
	Kolamba	"	3 2 2
	El Pastor Soho	Mexican	3 3 5
	The Black Book	British, Modern	3 4 4
	The Norfolk Arms	"	3 3 2
	Pierre Victoire	French	2 2 3
	Prix Fixe	"	3 3 3
	La Fromagerie Bloomsbury	International	2 3 2
	Casa Tua	Italian	2 2 2
	Ciao Bella	"	3 4 5
	Fumo	"	2 3 4
	Lina Stores	"	2 2 3
	Mele e Pere	"	3 4 4
	Pastaio	"	3 2 3
	San Carlo Cicchetti	"	3 2 3
	Blacklock	Steaks & grills	3 3 4
	temper Covent Garden	"	2 2 3
	Mildreds	Vegetarian	3 3 3
	Burger & Beyond	Burgers, etc	4 3 2
	MEATliquor	"	3 2 2
	Street Burger	"	2 2 3
	North Sea Fish	Fish & chips	4 3 2
	Cinquecento	Pizza	3 2 2
	50 Kalò di Ciro Salvo	"	4 2 2
	The Barbary Next Door	North African	4 4 2
	Miznon London	Middle Eastern	4 3 3
	Golden Dragon	Chinese	3 3 2
	Plum Valley	"	3 2 2
	Tao Tao Ju	"	3 3 2
	Dishoom	Indian	4 4 5
	Kricket	"	4 5 4
	Punjab	"	3 3 3
	Oka	Japanese	3 4 3
	Rasa Sayang	Malaysian	3 3 2
	YiQi	Pan-Asian	– – –
	Kiln	Thai	5 4 4
	Speedboat Bar	"	4 3 4
£40+	Chez Antoinette	French	2 2 2
	Gordon's Wine Bar	International	2 2 4
	Bar Italia	Italian	2 3 5
	Fadiga	"	3 4 2
	Flat Iron	Steaks & grills	3 3 3
	Patty and Bun	Burgers, etc	3 3 2
	Chick 'n' Sours	Chicken	4 3 3
	Bubala Soho	Middle Eastern	4 4 3
	Imad's Syrian Kitchen	Syrian	4 5 4

AREA OVERVIEWS | CENTRAL

	Dim Sum Duck	Chinese, Dim sum	4 3 2
	Dumplings' Legend	"	3 2 2
	Gopal's of Soho	Indian	4 3 2
	Sagar	"	3 2 2
	Bone Daddies	Japanese	3 2 3
	Eat Tokyo	"	3 2 2
	Kanada-Ya	"	4 3 2
	Koya-Bar	"	3 2 2
	Taro	"	2 2 2
	Singapulah	Malaysian	3 3 2
	Hare & Tortoise	Pan-Asian	3 3 2
	Viet Food	Vietnamese	4 3 2
	Bao Soho	Taiwanese	4 3 3
£35+	Audrey Green	Australian	3 2 3
	Café in the Crypt	British, Traditional	2 2 5
	Arcade Food Hall	International	2 2 2
	Rudy's	Pizza	3 4 3
	Baozi Inn	Chinese	3 2 2
	The eight Restaurant	"	4 2 2
	Wong Kei	"	3 2 2
	C&R Café	Malaysian	3 3 2
	Laxsa	"	4 2 2
	Plaza Khao Gaeng	Thai	5 4 3
£30+	Master Wei	Chinese	4 3 2
£25+	Kung Fu Noodle	Chinese	3 2 2
£20+	Bageriet	Sandwiches, cakes, etc	3 2 2
£15+	Maison Bertaux	Afternoon tea	3 4 5
	Liu Xiaomian	Chinese	3 2 2
£5+	Monmouth Coffee Co	Sandwiches, cakes, etc	3 4 3

Mayfair & St James's (Parts of W1 and SW1)

£650+	Sushi Kanesaka	Japanese	3 4 2
£390+	The Araki	Japanese	4 4 2
£380+	TAKU	Japanese	5 3 2
£350+	Ikoyi	West African	3 2 2
£310+	Alain Ducasse	French	2 2 3
£280+	Hélène Darroze	French	2 2 2
£270+	Maru	Japanese	5 4 3
£240+	Sketch, Lecture Room	French	3 4 5

FSA Ratings: from 1 (Poor) to 5 (Exceptional)

CENTRAL | **AREA OVERVIEWS**

£190+	Hide	*British, Modern*	3 3 3
	The Ritz	*British, Traditional*	4 4 5
£180+	Bacchanalia	*British, Modern*	1 2 3
£170+	Park Chinois	*Chinese*	2 2 3
£160+	The Cocochine	*British, Modern*	– – –
	Umu	*Japanese*	4 4 4
£150+	Ormer Mayfair	*British, Modern*	4 4 4
£140+	Grill by Tom Booton	*British, Modern*	3 4 3
	Estiatorio Milos	*Fish & seafood*	3 2 4
	L'Atelier Robuchon	*French*	2 3 2
	Pavyllon	*"*	3 3 3
	Amazonico	*International*	2 2 4
	34 Mayfair	*Steaks & grills*	2 3 2
	Ritz, Palm Court	*Afternoon tea*	3 4 5
	Kai Mayfair	*Chinese*	4 4 3
	Cubé	*Japanese*	4 4 2
	Novikov (Asian restaurant)	*Pan-Asian*	2 2 4
£130+	Corrigan's Mayfair	*British, Modern*	3 4 4
	The Twenty Two	*"*	– – –
	Bar des Prés	*French*	4 4 3
	Murano	*Italian*	4 4 5
	Nobu, Metropolitan	*Japanese*	4 3 2
£120+	Wild Honey St James	*British, Modern*	3 3 3
	The Game Bird	*British, Traditional*	3 4 4
	LPM (fka La Petite Maison)	*French*	4 3 3
	Gaia	*Greek*	3 3 3
	Il Gattopardo	*Italian*	3 4 4
	The Guinea Grill	*Steaks & grills*	3 3 4
	Claridge's Foyer	*Afternoon tea*	3 4 4
	Hakkasan Mayfair	*Chinese*	3 2 3
£110+	Charlie's at Brown's	*British, Modern*	3 5 5
	The Maine Mayfair	*"*	3 3 4
	Mount Street Restaurant	*"*	2 3 4
	Wiltons	*British, Traditional*	4 4 5
	Scott's	*Fish & seafood*	4 4 4
	Socca	*French*	2 3 3
	Brown's, Drawing Room	*Afternoon tea*	3 4 4
	Coya	*Peruvian*	3 2 3
	Jeru	*Middle Eastern*	4 4 3
	China Tang, Dorchester	*Chinese*	3 2 2
	Kanishka	*Indian*	3 3 2
£100+	Colony Grill, Beaumont	*American*	3 3 4
	Apricity	*British, Modern*	3 3 3
	Claridge's Restaurant	*"*	3 4 4
	Dovetale by Tom Sellers	*"*	2 1 3
	Bentley's	*Fish & seafood*	3 4 4

AREA OVERVIEWS | CENTRAL

	Sexy Fish	"	1 1 1
	Sketch, Gallery	French	2 2 4
	Scully	International	3 4 3
	MiMi Mei Fair	Chinese	3 4 4
	Gymkhana	Indian	4 3 3
	Veeraswamy	"	4 4 4
	Ginza	Japanese	3 3 3
	Koyn	"	3 4 4
£90+	American Bar, Stafford	American	3 3 3
	The Barley Mow	British, Modern	2 3 3
	45 Jermyn St	"	3 3 3
	Mary's	"	– – –
	Quaglino's	"	– – –
	Butler's, Chesterfield Mayfair	British, Traditional	3 3 3
	Maison François	French	2 3 4
	Al Duca	Italian	3 2 2
	Chucs Dover Street	"	2 2 3
	The Dover	"	3 3 5
	Franco's	"	3 3 3
	Ristorante Frescobaldi	"	2 2 2
	San Carlo	"	3 2 3
	Sartoria	"	2 3 3
	Theo Randall	"	4 4 2
	Goodman	Steaks & grills	3 2 2
	Hawksmoor	"	3 3 3
	Rowley's	"	3 2 3
	Fortnums, Diamond Jubilee	Afternoon tea	3 3 4
	Benares	Indian	4 4 3
	BiBi	"	5 4 3
	Chutney Mary	"	4 4 4
	Jamavar	"	3 2 2
	Chisou	Japanese	5 4 2
	Humo	"	4 5 4
	Roka	"	3 2 3
	Lucky Cat	Pan-Asian	2 3 2
£80+	Bellamy's	British, Modern	3 4 4
	Kitty Fisher's	"	2 3 3
	Little Social	"	2 2 3
	The Wolseley	"	2 3 4
	Burger & Lobster	Fish & seafood	3 3 2
	Fishworks	"	3 2 2
	Saint Jacques	French	3 4 3
	Cecconi's	Italian	2 2 3
	Delfino	Pizza	3 2 2
	Bombay Bustle	Indian	4 3 4
	Tamarind	"	4 3 2
	The Ivy Asia Mayfair	Pan-Asian	3 2 3
£70+	Field by Fortnum's	British, Modern	2 2 2
	Langan's Brasserie	"	2 3 2
	Café Murano	Italian	3 3 3
	Il Vicolo	"	2 4 2
	Sabor	Spanish	5 5 5
	O'ver	Pizza	3 4 3

CENTRAL | AREA OVERVIEWS

	Kiku	Japanese	3 4 2
	Patara Mayfair	Thai	3 3 3
£60+	123V	Vegan	3 3 2
	The Audley	British, Modern	3 3 3
	Noble Rot Mayfair	"	3 4 4
	The Windmill	British, Traditional	2 2 2
	Notto	Italian	3 2 2
	José Pizarro at the RA	Spanish	3 3 4
	Manthan	Indian	3 3 2
	Masala Zone	"	3 3 4
	Shoryu Ramen	Japanese	3 2 2
£50+	Casa do Frango	Portuguese	3 3 4
	El Pirata	Spanish	2 4 4
£35+	Fortnums, The Parlour	Ice cream	2 3 4

Fitzrovia & Marylebone (Part of W1)

£330+	Kitchen Table	British, Modern	4 4 4
£290+	Roketsu	Japanese	5 3 3
£270+	Mayha	Japanese	3 4 4
£230+	Lita	Mediterranean	2 2 3
£160+	Akoko	West African	5 4 3
£150+	Pied à Terre	French	4 3 3
£120+	Kol	Mexican	4 4 4
	Hakkasan	Chinese	3 2 3
	Nobu Portman Square	Japanese	4 4 3
£110+	The Chiltern Firehouse	American	2 3 5
	Berners Tavern	British, Modern	3 4 5
	The Ninth London	"	4 3 3
	Noizé	French	4 5 4
	Kima	Greek	4 4 3
	Locanda Locatelli	Italian	3 3 3
	Taka Marylebone	Japanese	3 3 3
£100+	Clarette	French	3 3 4
	Orrery	"	3 3 4
	Opso	Greek	3 3 2
	Lavo	Italian	3 3 4
	Arros QD	Spanish	3 3 3
	Donostia	"	3 2 3
	Palm Court, Langham	Afternoon tea	3 3 3
	Chishuru	West African	4 3 2
	Dinings	Japanese	5 3 3

AREA OVERVIEWS | CENTRAL

£90+			
	Cavita	Mexican	2 2 3
	Clipstone	British, Modern	3 3 2
	The Grazing Goat	"	2 2 3
	The Ivy Café	"	1 1 2
	Portland	"	3 4 2
	28-50 Oxford Circus	"	2 2 3
	Santo Mare	Fish & seafood	3 3 3
	Les 110 de Taillevent	French	3 4 3
	64 Goodge Street	"	4 5 4
	Meraki	Greek	3 3 3
	Norma	Italian	3 3 3
	ROVI	Mediterranean	4 3 3
	Zoilo	Argentinian	3 4 3
	The Bright Courtyard	Chinese	3 2 2
	Defune	Japanese	4 3 2
	Roka	"	3 2 3

£80+			
	Sunday in Brooklyn	American	2 2 3
	Brasserie of Light	British, Modern	2 3 4
	The Lore of the Land	"	3 4 4
	108 Brasserie	"	2 3 2
	Upstairs at The George	"	2 2 3
	Burger & Lobster	Fish & seafood	3 3 2
	Fishworks Marylebone	"	3 2 2
	La Brasseria Milanese	Italian	2 2 2
	Caffè Caldesi	"	3 3 2
	Blandford Comptoir	Mediterranean	3 3 3
	Carmel	"	5 3 4
	Royal China Club	Chinese	3 2 2
	Jikoni	Indian	3 2 4
	Pahli Hill Bandra Bhai	"	4 3 3
	Trishna	"	4 3 2
	Uli Marylebone	Pan-Asian	3 3 3

£70+			
	Daylesford Organic	British, Modern	1 2 2
	St John Marylebone	British, Traditional	4 4 2
	Fischer's	East & Cent. European	3 4 4
	Chotto Matte	Fusion	3 4 3
	Flesh and Buns Fitzrovia	"	3 2 2
	Twist Connubio	"	3 3 3
	1905	Greek	3 3 4
	Carousel	International	5 4 3
	Six by Nico	"	3 3 3
	Briciole	Italian	3 3 2
	Carlotta	"	1 2 4
	2 Veneti	"	2 3 2
	Bellazul	Mediterranean	3 4 3
	Ibérica	Spanish	2 2 3
	Lurra	"	4 4 3
	Pachamama	Peruvian	3 4 3
	Honey & Co	Middle Eastern	4 3 3
	Honey & Smoke	"	3 3 2
	Ottolenghi	"	3 3 3
	Ishtar	Turkish	3 2 3
	Royal China	Chinese	3 2 2
	Junsei	Japanese	3 3 2

CENTRAL | **AREA OVERVIEWS**

	Restaurant	Cuisine	Ratings
	Sushi Atelier	"	4 3 2
£60+	Studio Gauthier	Vegan	3 2 3
	Granger & Co	Australian	– – –
	The Wigmore	British, Traditional	3 4 4
	Caravan	Fusion	2 2 2
	Circolo Popolare	Italian	3 3 5
	Italian Greyhound	"	3 2 2
	Riding House Café	Mediterranean	2 3 3
	Boca a boca	Spanish	3 3 3
	Salt Yard	"	3 2 2
	Homeslice	Pizza	3 2 3
	Reubens	Kosher	3 2 3
	Kinkally	Georgian	– – –
	Chourangi	Indian	3 3 3
£50+	Hoppers	Sri Lankan	3 3 2
	The Wallace	French	1 2 5
	La Fromagerie Café	International	2 3 2
	Da Paolo	Italian	3 3 2
	Isola by San Carlo	"	3 3 3
	Lina Stores	"	2 2 3
	Relais de Venise	Steaks & grills	3 2 3
	Wulf & Lamb	Vegetarian	3 2 3
	MEATLiquor	Burgers, etc	3 2 2
	Golden Hind	Fish & chips	3 2 2
	Pizzeria Mozza	Pizza	4 3 3
	Delamina	Middle Eastern	3 3 3
	Zayna	Indian	4 3 3
	Oka	Japanese	3 4 3
	Laksamania	Malaysian	2 2 2
	Foley's	Thai	3 3 3
£40+	Via Emilia	Italian	3 2 2
	Flat Iron Marylebone	Steaks & grills	3 3 3
	Patty and Bun	Burgers, etc	3 3 2
	Florencio Pizza	Pizza	3 4 3
	Santa Maria	"	5 4 3
	Chettinad	Indian	3 3 2
	Roti Chai	"	3 2 2
	Sagar	"	3 2 2
	Bone Daddies	Japanese	3 2 3
	Monkey & Me	Thai	3 2 2
	Bao Marylebone	Taiwanese	4 3 3
£35+	Tommi's Burger Joint	Burgers, etc	3 2 2
	The Hunan Man	Chinese	3 2 3
	Ragam	Indian	4 3 1
£30+	Alley Cats	Pizza	3 3 3
£15+	Scandinavian Kitchen	Scandinavian	4 3 3
	Kaffeine	Sandwiches, cakes, etc	3 5 3
	Qima Cafe	"	4 3 4
	Tongue & Brisket	"	3 2 1

AREA OVERVIEWS | CENTRAL

Belgravia, Pimlico, Victoria & Westminster (SW1, except St James's)

Price	Restaurant	Cuisine	Rating
£250+	A Wong	Chinese	5 5 4
£220+	Muse	British, Modern	3 4 4
£200+	Nusr-Et Steakhouse	Steaks & grills	1 1 1
£180+	Brooklands	British, Modern	4 4 3
£170+	Dinner	British, Traditional	2 2 3
	Pétrus	French	3 3 3
£160+	Studio Frantzén	Scandinavian	4 4 3
	Imperial Treasure	Chinese	4 3 3
£150+	Cornus	British, Modern	– – –
	Mauro Colagreco	French	3 4 3
£130+	Dining Room, Goring	British, Traditional	2 3 5
	Azzurra	Italian	– – –
	Canton Blue, The Peninsula	Chinese	3 4 3
	Gouqi	Chinese, Dim sum	4 3 2
£120+	Paper Moon, OWO	Italian	2 3 4
	Santini	"	2 2 2
	Ekstedt at The Yard	Scandinavian	3 4 3
	Hunan	Chinese	4 3 2
£110+	Zafferano	Italian	4 4 3
	Boisdale of Belgravia	Scottish	2 3 4
£100+	Arlington	British, Modern	2 5 5
	Fallow St James's	"	4 3 4
	The Lanesborough Grill	"	3 3 4
	The Pem	"	4 3 2
	Cedric Grolet	Afternoon tea	2 4 3
	Crystal Moon Lounge	"	3 4 4
	Amaya	Indian	4 4 3
£90+	Ganymede	British, Modern	3 3 3
	The Ivy Victoria	"	1 1 3
	The Jones Family Kitchen	"	3 3 4
	Olivomare	Fish & seafood	4 3 2
	Harrods Dining Hall	International	– – –
	Chucs Belgravia	Italian	2 2 3
	Enoteca Turi	"	3 3 3
	Olivo	"	3 3 3
	The Campaner	Spanish	3 3 3
	Goya	"	3 3 2
	Tabisca	Steaks & grills	– – –
	The Cinnamon Club	Indian	4 3 5
	Quilon	Indian, Southern	5 4 2
	Sachi	Japanese	– – –

FSA Ratings: from 1 (Poor) to 5 (Exceptional)

CENTRAL | **AREA OVERVIEWS**

£80+	Blue Boar Pub	*British, Modern*	2 3 2
	The Thomas Cubitt	"	2 3 3
	Burger & Lobster	*Fish & seafood*	3 3 2
	Colbert	*French*	2 3 3
	Caraffini	*Italian*	3 4 3
	Sale e Pepe	"	2 2 2
	Wild by Tart	*Organic*	3 4 4
	Oliveto	*Pizza*	3 2 2
	Kahani	*Indian*	3 4 2
	Yaatra	"	4 3 3
£70+	Daylesford Organic	*British, Modern*	1 2 2
	Lorne	"	5 5 3
	La Poule au Pot	*French*	3 4 5
	Grumbles	*International*	3 4 3
	Motcombs	"	2 2 3
	Brumus	*Italian*	2 3 4
	Ibérica	*Spanish*	2 2 3
	Ottolenghi	*Middle Eastern*	3 3 3
£60+	Granger & Co	*Australian*	– – –
	Tozi	*Italian*	2 1 3
	Seafresh	*Fish & chips*	3 3 2
	Kazan	*Turkish*	3 3 2
	Toba	*Indonesian*	4 3 2
£50+	Casa do Frango	"	3 3 4
	Mildreds	*Vegetarian*	3 3 3
	Wulf & Lamb	"	3 2 3
	Cyprus Mangal	*Turkish*	3 3 3
	Ma La Sichuan	*Chinese*	4 3 3
	Shanghai Noir	"	3 4 3
£40+	Vincent Rooms	*British, Modern*	4 3 3
	Chez Antoinette	*French*	2 2 2
	Aloo Tama	*Indian*	4 3 2
	Sagar	"	3 2 2
	Bone Daddies	*Japanese*	3 2 3
	Café Kitsuné	"	– – –
	Kanada-Ya	"	4 3 2
	Taro	"	2 2 2
£25+	Bleecker Burger	*Burgers, etc*	2 2 1
£15+	Regency Cafe	*British, Traditional*	3 4 5

AREA OVERVIEWS | WEST

WEST

Chelsea, South Kensington, Kensington, Earl's Court & Fulham (SW3, SW5, SW6, SW7, SW10 & W8)

£230+	Bibendum	French	3 3 3
	Gordon Ramsay	"	2 2 1
£220+	The Five Fields	British, Modern	5 4 3
£180+	The Sea, The Sea	Fish & seafood	3 3 3
	Juno	Japanese	4 4 3
£130+	Wild Tavern	Italian	2 2 3
	Clap	Japanese	– – –
£120+	Zuma	Japanese	4 3 5
£110+	Clarke's	British, Modern	4 5 3
	Launceston Place	"	– – –
	Medlar	"	4 5 3
	No. Fifty Cheyne	"	3 3 5
	Yashin	Japanese	4 3 2
£100+	Elystan Street	British, Modern	4 4 4
	Kitchen W8	"	3 3 2
	Restaurant, the Capital	British, Traditional	3 3 2
	Le Colombier	French	3 5 4
	Daphne's	Italian	3 2 5
	Lucio	"	3 3 3
	Min Jiang	Chinese	5 4 5
	Dinings	Japanese	5 3 3
£90+	Bluebird	British, Modern	2 2 3
	Harwood Arms	"	4 4 3
	The Ivy Chelsea Garden	"	1 1 3
	28-50 Chelsea	"	2 2 3
	Myrtle	Irish	4 2 2
	Chucs	Italian	2 2 3
	Manicomio Chelsea	"	2 2 2
	Scalini	"	3 3 3
	Hawksmoor Knightsbridge	Steaks & grills	3 3 3
	Chicama	Peruvian	3 2 2
	Bombay Brasserie	Indian	3 4 2
	Chisou	Japanese	5 4 2
	Koji	"	3 3 3
£80+	The Cadogan Arms	British, Modern	3 2 4
	The Shed	"	3 3 4
	The Surprise	British, Traditional	2 2 4
	Bibendum Oyster Bar	Fish & seafood	3 4 4
	Josephine	French	4 4 4
	La Famiglia	Italian	2 2 5
	Cambio de Tercio	Spanish	4 3 3

274 FSA Ratings: from **1** (Poor) to **5** (Exceptional)

WEST | AREA OVERVIEWS

	Name	Cuisine	Ratings
	The Butcher's Tap and Grill	Steaks & grills	2 2 2
	Good Earth	Chinese	3 4 3
	Zaika of Kensington	Indian	3 4 4
	Akira at Japan House	Japanese	3 2 2
	Zheng	Malaysian	3 3 2
	The Ivy Asia Chelsea	Pan-Asian	3 2 3
£70+	Ixchel	Mexican	4 3 4
	The Abingdon	British, Modern	3 4 4
	Brinkley's	"	1 2 3
	Daylesford Organic	"	1 2 2
	The Enterprise	"	2 3 4
	Rabbit	"	2 3 3
	Maggie Jones's	British, Traditional	– – –
	Big Easy	Fish & seafood	2 2 3
	Wright Brothers	"	3 3 3
	Mazi	Greek	4 4 4
	Vardo	International	3 3 4
	Frantoio	Italian	3 2 3
	Jacuzzi	"	3 3 5
	Il Portico	"	3 3 4
	Belvedere	Mediterranean	2 2 4
	Daquise	Polish	2 2 3
	La Palombe	Spanish	– – –
	Tapas Brindisa	"	2 2 3
	Tendido Cero	"	4 4 3
	Macellaio RC	Steaks & grills	2 2 3
	Akub	Middle Eastern	4 3 4
	Royal China	Chinese	3 2 2
	Kutir	Indian	4 4 4
	Patara	Thai	3 3 3
£60+	The Anglesea Arms	British, Modern	2 3 3
	The Fox and Pheasant	"	3 4 4
	VQ	"	– – –
	The Admiral Codrington	International	3 2 3
	The Scarsdale	"	2 2 4
	Ziani's	Italian	3 3 2
	Ognisko Restaurant	Polish	3 4 5
	Volta do Mar	Portuguese	3 3 3
	Haché	Burgers, etc	3 3 2
	Ciro's (Pizza Pomodoro)	Pizza	2 2 3
	Maroush	Lebanese	3 2 1
	Masala Zone	Indian	3 3 4
	Shoryu Ramen	Japanese	3 2 2
	Go-Viet	Vietnamese	3 3 2
£50+	The Holland	British, Modern	3 3 3
	Los Mochis	Fusion	4 3 4
	Aglio e Olio	Italian	3 3 2
	Cicchetti Knightsbridge	"	3 2 3
	Da Mario	"	3 3 4
	Nuovi Sapori	"	3 3 3
	Riccardo's	"	3 4 3
	The Atlas	Mediterranean	3 4 4
	Street Burger	Burgers, etc	2 2 3

AREA OVERVIEWS | WEST

	Cinquecento	Pizza	3 2 2
	Made in Italy	"	3 2 2
	Rocca	"	2 3 3
	Best Mangal	Turkish	3 3 3
	Sichuan Popo	Chinese	4 3 2
	Dishoom	Indian	4 4 5
	Noor Jahan	"	3 4 3
	Pure Indian Cooking	"	4 3 3
	Oka	Japanese	3 4 3
	Sukho Fine Thai Cuisine	Thai	4 4 2
£40+	Flat Iron	Steaks & grills	3 3 3
	Santa Maria	Pizza	5 4 3
	Ceru	Middle Eastern	3 2 2
	Pravaas	Indian	– – –
	Bone Daddies	Japanese	3 2 3
	The Freak Scene	Pan-Asian	4 3 3
	Churchill Arms	Thai	3 4 4
	Phat Phuc	Vietnamese	3 3 2
£35+	Mali Vegan Thai	Thai	4 3 2
£30+	Alley Cats	Pizza	3 3 3
£25+	Big Fernand	Burgers, etc	4 3 2
	Stick & Bowl	Chinese	4 2 2

Notting Hill, Holland Park, Bayswater, North Kensington & Maida Vale (W2, W9, W10, W11)

£240+	The Ledbury	British, Modern	5 4 4
£230+	Core by Clare Smyth	British, Modern	5 5 4
£190+	104 Restaurant	British, Modern	5 4 4
£130+	Caractère	Mediterranean	3 3 3
£120+	Dorian	British, Modern	3 2 3
	Assaggi	Italian	4 4 2
£110+	London Shell Co	Fish & seafood	3 4 4
	Wild	"	2 3 4
£100+	Sumi	Japanese	4 3 3
£90+	The Princess Royal	British, Modern	3 3 3
	Straker's	"	3 4 3
	Vori	Greek	3 3 3
	Pollini	Italian	3 4 3
£80+	Sunday in Brooklyn	American	2 2 3
	Six Portland Road	British, Modern	3 4 3
	The Summerhouse	Fish & seafood	3 3 5

WEST | AREA OVERVIEWS

	The Cow	*Irish*	3 2 4
	La Brasseria	*Italian*	2 2 2
	Portobello Ristorante	*"*	3 2 3
	The Barbary	*North African*	5 4 4
	Uli	*Pan-Asian*	3 3 3
£70+	Daylesford Organic	*British, Modern*	1 2 2
	Gold	*"*	2 2 4
	The Ladbroke Arms	*"*	3 2 4
	The Park	*"*	3 4 5
	The Pelican	*"*	4 4 4
	Tsiakkos & Charcoal	*Greek*	3 4 3
	Mediterraneo	*Italian*	3 2 2
	Osteria Basilico	*"*	3 4 3
	Ottolenghi	*Middle Eastern*	3 3 3
	Mandarin Kitchen	*Chinese*	3 2 1
£60+	Bondi Green	*Australian*	3 3 3
	Granger & Co	*"*	– – –
	Orasay	*British, Modern*	4 3 4
	Cepages	*French*	4 3 4
	Edera	*Italian*	3 4 3
	The Oak W2	*"*	3 2 4
	Holy Carrot Portobello	*Vegetarian*	– – –
	Maroush	*Lebanese*	3 2 1
	The Counter	*Turkish*	3 2 3
	Four Seasons	*Chinese*	4 1 1
	Bombay Palace	*Indian*	4 4 2
£50+	The Cheese Barge	*British, Traditional*	3 3 3
	The Walmer Castle	*Scottish*	2 3 4
	temper Paddington	*Steaks & grills*	2 2 3
	MEATliquor	*Burgers, etc*	3 2 2
	Cinquecento	*Pizza*	3 2 2
	Miznon	*Middle Eastern*	4 3 3
	Fez Mangal	*Turkish*	3 3 2
	Pearl Liang	*Chinese*	3 3 3
	Empire Empire	*Indian*	3 3 3
	Noor Jahan	*"*	3 4 3
	Oka	*Japanese*	3 4 3
	Sushi Murasaki	*"*	3 3 2
£40+	Taqueria	*Mexican*	3 3 3
	Fish & Bubbles	*Fish & seafood*	– – –
	Ceru	*Middle Eastern*	3 2 2
	Fortune Cookie	*Chinese*	3 2 1
	Gold Mine	*"*	3 2 2
	Eat Tokyo	*Japanese*	3 2 2
	Med Salleh Kopitiam	*Malaysian*	3 2 2
	Med Salleh Viet	*Vietnamese*	3 2 2
£35+	Tab X Tab	*International*	3 4 3
£30+	Tavernaki	*Greek*	3 3 3

AREA OVERVIEWS | WEST

£25+	Electric Diner	American	2 3 4
	Normah's	Malaysian	3 3 1

£15+	Layla	Sandwiches, cakes, etc	3 3 3

Hammersmith, Shepherd's Bush, Olympia, Chiswick, Brentford & Ealing
(W4, W5, W6, W12, W13, W14, TW8)

£280+	Endo at The Rotunda	Japanese	5 5 4

£150+	The River Café	Italian	2 1 2

£110+	La Trompette	British, Modern	4 4 4

£90+	The Silver Birch	British, Modern	4 4 2
	Villa Di Geggiano	Italian	3 4 4

£80+	Sam's Riverside	British, Modern	3 4 5
	Le Vacherin	French	3 3 3
	The Melody Restaurant	International	3 3 3
	Cibo	Italian	3 5 3

£70+	The Havelock Tavern	British, Modern	2 2 2
	High Road Brasserie	"	2 3 4
	Annie's	International	3 3 4
	The Swan	Mediterranean	3 3 4
	Rayuela	Spanish	3 4 3
	Shikumen, Dorsett Hotel	Chinese	3 2 2

£60+	The Anglesea Arms	British, Modern	5 4 4
	Brackenbury Wine Rooms	"	2 4 4
	City Barge	"	2 2 4
	The Dartmouth Castle	"	3 3 3
	The Duke of Sussex	"	2 3 3
	Sam's Waterside	"	3 4 4
	Vinoteca	"	2 2 2
	Brasserie Blanc	French	2 2 2
	Le Petit Citron	"	2 3 3
	Giulia	Italian	4 3 3
	Mari Deli & Dining	"	4 4 4
	The Oak W12	"	3 2 4
	Pentolina	"	4 5 3
	Salt Yard	Spanish	3 2 2
	The Gate	Vegetarian	3 2 3
	Crisp Pizza	Pizza	5 3 3
	Indian Zing	Indian	4 4 3
	Rock & Rose	Pan-Asian	2 3 3

£50+	The Dove	British, Modern	2 2 5
	Kindred	"	3 3 3
	The Andover Arms	International	3 4 4
	Avanti	Mediterranean	3 3 4
	Zia Lucia	Pizza	4 4 4
	Chateau	Lebanese	3 4 2

FSA Ratings: from 1 (Poor) to 5 (Exceptional)

WEST | AREA OVERVIEWS

	Best Mangal	*Turkish*	3 3 3
	Copper Chimney	*Indian*	3 3 3
	Kricket	"	4 5 4
	Patri	"	3 3 2
	Potli	"	3 3 3
£40+	222 Veggie Vegan	*Vegan*	3 3 2
	Sam's Kitchen	*British, Modern*	3 4 4
	Faber	*Fish & seafood*	3 3 4
	Cottura	*Italian*	3 3 2
	Base Face Pizza	*Pizza*	4 5 2
	Napoli on the Road	"	3 3 3
	Oro Di Napoli	"	4 3 3
	Santa Maria	"	5 4 3
	North China	*Chinese*	3 3 2
	Sagar	*Indian*	3 2 2
	Shilpa	*Indian, Southern*	4 2 2
	Eat Tokyo	*Japanese*	3 2 2
	Kanada-Ya	"	4 3 2
	Makoto Sushi Bar	"	3 3 1
	Ta Ke Sushi	"	4 4 3
	Tosa	"	3 2 2
	Hare & Tortoise	*Pan-Asian*	3 3 2
	Chet's	*Thai*	2 3 4
£35+	Three Uncles	*Chinese*	4 2 2
	Poppy's Thai Eatery 2	*Thai*	3 2 3
£30+	Café Maja	*Polish*	3 2 2
	Persian Palace	*Persian*	3 2 2
£25+	Bleecker Burger	*Burgers, etc*	2 2 1
	Rhythm & Brews	*Sandwiches, cakes, etc*	2 3 4
	Tamp Coffee	"	3 4 3
	Strand Café	*Thai*	4 5 3
£20+	The Elder Press Café	*British, Modern*	3 3 3
£5+	Mr Falafel	*Middle Eastern*	5 2 1

AREA OVERVIEWS | NORTH

NORTH

Hampstead, West Hampstead, St John's Wood, Kilburn & Camden Town (NW postcodes)

£180+	INÉ	Japanese	3 4 3
£90+	The Ivy Café	British, Modern	1 1 2
	Landmark, Winter Garden	"	3 3 5
	Tish	Kosher	3 3 3
£80+	Bradley's	British, Modern	2 2 2
	Searcys St Pancras Grand	"	2 2 3
	L'Aventure	French	4 3 3
	Michael Nadra	"	3 3 2
	Midland Grand Dining Room	"	2 2 4
	Oslo Court	"	3 4 4
	Bull & Last	International	2 2 3
	Caldesi In Belsize	Italian	3 3 2
	Villa Bianca	"	3 2 3
	Carmel	Mediterranean	5 3 4
	Cinder	BBQ	3 3 3
	Good Earth	Chinese	3 4 3
	Kaifeng	"	3 4 3
£70+	Oak & Poppy	British, Modern	3 3 3
	The Parakeet	"	4 4 4
	Parlour Kensal	"	4 4 4
	The Wells Tavern	"	3 3 4
	Soutine	French	2 2 3
	Lemonia	Greek	2 2 2
	Morso	Italian	3 3 2
	The Rising Sun	"	3 4 3
	Ottolenghi	Middle Eastern	3 3 3
	Skewd Kitchen	Turkish	4 4 3
	Phoenix Palace	Chinese	3 2 3
	Patara	Thai	3 3 3
£60+	Terra Moderna	Australian	3 4 3
	Greenberry Café	British, Modern	2 2 3
	The Old Bull & Bush	"	2 2 4
	The Spaniard's Inn	International	2 3 4
	Anima e Cuore	Italian	2 2 2
	28 Church Row	Spanish	3 4 3
	Haché	Burgers, etc	3 3 2
	The Sea Shell	Fish & chips	4 4 3
	L'Antica Pizzeria da Michele	Pizza	4 2 2
	Roger's Kitchen	Caribbean	4 3 3
	Maroush Park Royal	Lebanese	3 2 1
	Green Cottage	Chinese	3 2 2
	Bonoo	Indian	3 3 3
	Jin Kichi	Japanese	4 4 3
	Singapore Garden	Malaysian	3 4 3
£50+	The Wet Fish Café	British, Modern	3 3 3
	L'Artista	Italian	2 2 3

FSA Ratings: from 1 (Poor) to 5 (Exceptional)

NORTH | **AREA OVERVIEWS**

	Emilia's Crafted Pasta	"	3 3 3
	Giacomo's	"	3 3 2
	Spagnoletti	"	3 4 3
	Mildreds	Vegetarian	3 3 3
	Zia Lucia	Pizza	4 4 4
	Crocker's Folly	Lebanese	3 3 4
	Saravanaa Bhavan	Indian	3 3 2
	Three Falcons	"	3 2 2
	Oka	Japanese	3 4 3
	Bang Bang Oriental	Pan-Asian	3 2 2
£40+	Ravel's Bistro	International	2 3 3
	Berbere Pizza	Pizza	3 3 2
	It's Bagels	Sandwiches, cakes, etc	4 2 2
	Golden Dragon	Chinese	3 2 2
	J M Oriental	"	4 4 4
	Great Nepalese	Indian	3 2 2
	Paradise Hampstead	"	3 4 2
	Vijay	"	3 4 2
	Café Japan	Japanese	3 3 2
	Eat Tokyo G2 (Shabu-Shabu)	"	3 2 2
	Sushi Masa	"	3 3 2
£35+	Nautilus	Fish & chips	5 4 1
	Three Uncles	Chinese	4 2 2
	Diwana Bhel-Poori House	Indian	3 2 1
	Kadiri's	"	5 4 2
	Ravi Shankar	"	3 2 2
	Sakonis	"	3 2 2
	SUDU	Malaysian	3 3 3
	East Pan Asian Restaurant	Pan-Asian	3 3 2
£30+	Crêpes à la carte	Sandwiches, cakes, etc	3 3 2
	Shayona	Indian	3 3 2
£25+	Pita	Middle Eastern	3 2 2
	Chutneys	Indian	3 3 2
	BONGA	Korean	4 3 2
£20+	Tofu Vegan	Chinese	4 2 2
£15+	Ginger & White Hampstead	Sandwiches, cakes, etc	3 3 4
	Roti King	Malaysian	5 3 1

Hoxton, Islington, Highgate, Crouch End, Stoke Newington, Finsbury Park (N postcodes)

£180+	Counter 71	British, Modern	4 5 3
£120+	Parrillan	Spanish	2 2 4
£110+	London Shell Co	Fish & seafood	3 4 4
£90+	Hot Stone	Japanese	2 2 2

AREA OVERVIEWS | NORTH

£80+	The Baring	British, Modern	4 3 3
	Perilla	"	4 4 3
	Saltine	"	2 3 4
	Prawn on the Lawn	Fish & seafood	4 2 2
	Salut	International	3 4 3
	Trullo	Italian	4 3 3
	Coal Office	Mediterranean	3 3 4
	Mangal 2	Turkish	3 2 2
£70+	Casa Pastór & Plaza Pastór	Mexican	2 2 3
	The Bull	British, Modern	3 3 3
	Frederick's	"	3 4 5
	Humble Grape	"	2 3 3
	Pig & Butcher	"	3 2 3
	Westerns Laundry	"	3 3 4
	Les 2 Garcons	French	4 5 3
	German Gymnasium	German	1 1 3
	Primeur	International	3 4 4
	Barrafina	Spanish	4 4 3
	Escocesa	"	3 2 2
	Ottolenghi	Middle Eastern	3 3 3
£60+	Granger & Co	Australian	– – –
	The Clarence Tavern	British, Modern	3 3 3
	The Plimsoll	"	4 3 4
	Porte Noire	"	3 3 4
	The Red Lion & Sun	"	3 3 3
	Rotunda, Kings Place	"	2 2 3
	St Johns	British, Traditional	2 3 4
	Kipferl	East & Cent. European	3 3 2
	Lyon's	Fish & seafood	3 3 3
	Bistro Aix	French	3 3 3
	La Petite Auberge	"	2 2 2
	Table Du Marche	"	3 3 3
	Caravan King's Cross	Fusion	2 2 2
	The Orange Tree	International	2 2 3
	Citro	Italian	3 4 2
	Osteria Tufo	"	3 3 3
	Terra Rossa	"	2 3 3
	Bar Esteban	Spanish	3 2 3
	The Gatehouse	"	2 2 2
	Chuku's	West African	3 3 3
	Arabica KX	Middle Eastern	2 3 3
	Supawan	Thai	4 3 3
£50+	Hoppers	Sri Lankan	3 3 2
	The Drapers Arms	British, Modern	3 2 3
	Granary Square Brasserie	"	2 3 4
	Haven Bistro	"	3 4 3
	Bellanger	French	1 2 3
	Caravel	"	3 4 4
	Le Sacré-Coeur	"	3 4 3
	FKABAM (Black Axe Mangal)	International	3 3 4
	The Flask	"	2 3 4
	La Fromagerie	"	2 3 2
	500	Italian	4 4 3

FSA Ratings: from **1** (Poor) to **5** (Exceptional)

NORTH | AREA OVERVIEWS

	Lina Stores	"	2 2 3
	La Lluna	Spanish	3 2 2
	Mildreds	Vegetarian	3 3 3
	MEATLiquor Islington	Burgers, etc	3 2 2
	Street Burger	"	2 2 3
	Toff's	Fish & chips	3 4 2
	Zia Lucia	Pizza	4 4 4
	Plaquemine Lock	Cajun/creole	4 3 4
	Jam Delish	Caribbean	3 4 3
	Gem	Turkish	3 3 2
	Dishoom	Indian	4 4 5
	The Tamil Crown	"	3 4 3
	The Tamil Prince	"	4 3 3
	Rasa	Indian, Southern	4 3 2
	OITA Wood Green	Japanese	4 4 3
	Sambal Shiok	Malaysian	3 3 2
	Farang	Thai	4 3 3
£40+	Le Mercury	French	2 2 2
	Frame	International	3 3 3
	Noci	Italian	3 2 3
	Sofalino	"	3 4 2
	Trevi	"	3 2 2
	Via Emilia	"	3 2 2
	Flat Iron	Steaks & grills	3 3 3
	Olympus Fish	Fish & chips	3 4 2
	Crudough	Pizza	3 4 3
	Santa Maria	"	5 4 3
	Yard Sale Pizza	"	3 3 2
	The Dusty Knuckle	Sandwiches, cakes, etc	5 3 3
	Sumak	Turkish	3 4 2
	Xi'an Impression	Chinese	5 2 1
	Kanada-Ya	Japanese	4 3 2
	Taro	"	2 2 2
	Dotori	Korean	4 3 2
	Cafe Bao	Taiwanese	4 3 3
£35+	Yum Bug	British, Modern	4 4 2
	Pizzeria Pappagone	Italian	3 4 4
	Testi	Turkish	4 2 2
	Afghan Kitchen	Afghani	3 2 2
	Shahi Pakwaan	Indian	3 2 3
	Viet Ngon	Vietnamese	4 3 2
£30+	Jolene	British, Modern	3 3 5
	Max's Sandwich Shop	Sandwiches, cakes, etc	3 4 3
£25+	Normans Cafe	British, Modern	3 4 3
	Bayleaf	Indian	3 3 3
£20+	Esters	British, Modern	3 3 2
	Vero Caffe	International	3 2 3
	Tofu Vegan	Chinese	4 2 2
	Hiden	Japanese	– – –
£15+	Hainan House	Chinese	– – –

283

AREA OVERVIEWS | SOUTH

SOUTH

South Bank (SE1)

Price	Name	Cuisine	Rating
£280+	Story	British, Modern	3 5 3
£240+	Hannah, County Hall	Japanese	4 4 3
£150+	Trivet	British, Modern	3 3 2
£130+	Sollip	French	5 4 2
	Hutong, The Shard	Chinese	2 2 5
£120+	Aqua Shard	British, Modern	2 2 4
	Oblix	"	- - -
	Parrillan	Spanish	2 2 4
£110+	Oxo Tower, Restaurant	British, Modern	1 1 2
£90+	The Ivy Tower Bridge	British, Modern	1 1 3
	Oxo Tower, Brasserie	"	1 2 3
	TING	"	3 3 4
	Seabird	Fish & seafood	3 2 4
	Le Pont de la Tour	French	3 4 4
	La Barca	Italian	3 3 3
	Hawksmoor	Steaks & grills	3 3 3
£80+	Elliot's	British, Modern	3 3 3
	The Garrison	"	3 3 3
	In Horto	"	3 3 4
	Sea Containers, Mondrian	"	2 2 4
	Skylon	"	2 2 2
	Roast	British, Traditional	2 2 3
	The Coal Shed	Steaks & grills	3 2 2
	Pique Nique	Chicken	3 3 3
	Baluchi, Lalit	Indian	3 3 3
£70+	Santo Remedio	Mexican	3 3 2
	Lasdun	British, Modern	2 2 2
	Swan at the Globe	"	3 3 4
	Applebee's Fish	Fish & seafood	3 2 2
	fish!	"	2 3 2
	Wright Brothers	"	3 3 3
	Casse-Croute	French	4 4 4
	Borough Market Kitchen	International	3 3 2
	Vivat Bacchus	"	2 2 2
	Cafe Murano	Italian	3 3 3
	Tavolino	"	2 2 3
	Barrafina	Spanish	4 4 3
	Pizarro	"	4 3 3
	Tapas Brindisa	"	2 2 3
	Macellaio RC	Steaks & grills	2 2 3
	O'ver	Pizza	3 4 3
	Paladar	South American	3 4 4
	Bala Baya	Middle Eastern	4 4 4

FSA Ratings: from 1 (Poor) to 5 (Exceptional)

SOUTH | **AREA OVERVIEWS**

£60+			
	Mallow	Vegan	3 2 4
	The Anchor & Hope	British, Modern	4 3 3
	40 Maltby Street	"	4 4 3
	Forza Wine	"	3 2 4
	The Garden Cafe	"	3 3 3
	Vinoteca Borough	"	2 2 2
	Brasserie Blanc	French	2 2 2
	Caravan Bankside	Fusion	2 2 2
	Bancone	Italian	2 2 2
	La Gamba	Spanish	2 1 2
	José	"	5 3 4
	Salt Yard Borough	"	3 2 2
	Arabica Bar and Kitchen	Middle Eastern	2 3 3
	Berenjak Borough	Persian	5 4 4
	Lahpet Larder	Burmese	4 3 2
	Gunpowder	Indian	3 3 2
	Sticky Mango Butler's Wharf	Pan-Asian	3 2 2
	Champor-Champor	Thai	3 2 2

£50+			
	El Pastór	Mexican	3 3 5
	Lupins	British, Modern	4 4 3
	Legare	Italian	3 4 3
	Bar Douro	Portuguese	3 3 4
	Casa do Frango	"	3 3 4
	Andanza	Spanish	3 3 2
	Meson don Felipe	"	2 2 3
	Burger & Beyond	Burgers, etc	4 3 2
	Kolae	Thai	5 3 4

£40+			
	Rambutan	Sri Lankan	4 3 3
	Tacos Padre	Mexican	4 3 2
	Camille	British, Modern	3 4 3
	Terry's	British, Traditional	2 4 4
	Mercato Metropolitano	Italian	3 3 4
	Padella	"	5 3 4
	Flat Iron Clink Street	Steaks & grills	3 3 3
	Patty and Bun	Burgers, etc	3 3 2
	Okan	Japanese	4 3 3
	Bao Borough	Taiwanese	4 3 3

£35+			
	Akara	West African	3 3 4
	Baozi Inn	Chinese	3 2 2
	Kanchana @ The King's Arms	Thai	3 2 3

£25+			
	Bleecker Burger	Burgers, etc	2 2 1

£15+			
	Roti King	Malaysian	5 3 1

£10+			
	Kappacasein	Swiss	5 3 2

£5+			
	Monmouth Coffee Co	Sandwiches, cakes, etc	3 4 3

AREA OVERVIEWS | SOUTH

Greenwich, Lewisham, Dulwich & Blackheath
(All SE postcodes, except SE1; also BR1)

£70+	Llewelyn's	British, Modern	3 4 3
	Toulouse Lautrec	French	3 3 4
£60+	Omni	Vegan	3 4 3
	The Camberwell Arms	British, Modern	5 4 3
	Forza Wine	"	3 2 4
	Franklins	"	2 3 3
	The Guildford Arms	"	3 3 3
	Levan	"	3 2 2
	Wilson's	"	3 4 4
	The Trafalgar Tavern	International	2 3 5
	Artusi	Italian	3 3 2
	Luciano's	"	3 4 3
	Manuel's	"	3 4 4
	Peckham Cellars	Spanish	3 3 2
	Kudu	South African	4 4 3
	Dragon Castle	Chinese	3 2 2
	Babur	Indian	5 4 3
	Everest Inn	"	3 3 2
	Yama Momo	Japanese	3 2 2
£50+	Brookmill	International	3 3 2
	The Yellow House	"	3 4 3
	Forza Win	Italian	3 3 4
	Marcella	"	3 3 3
	MEATliquor ED	Burgers, etc	3 2 2
	Street Burger	"	2 2 3
	Rocca	Pizza	2 3 3
	Kudu Grill	South African	3 4 3
	Heritage	Indian	3 3 3
	Kachori	"	3 4 3
	Kennington Tandoori	"	3 4 3
£40+	Peachy Goat	Vegan	3 3 4
	Trinco	Sri Lankan	3 2 3
	Lulu's	British, Modern	3 3 3
	Evi's (fka Souvlaki Street)	Greek	3 4 2
	Theo's	Pizza	4 3 3
	Yard Sale Pizza	"	3 3 2
	Ganapati	Indian	3 3 2
	Gandhi's	"	3 4 2
	Kokum	"	4 4 2
	Bone Daddies	Japanese	3 2 3
	Taro	"	2 2 2
	Mr Bao	Taiwanese	4 4 3
£35+	081 Pizzeria	Pizza	4 2 2
£30+	Everest Curry King	Sri Lankan	3 3 2
	Bar D4100	Pizza	4 3 3
£25+	La Chingada	Mexican	3 3 2
	Goddards At Greenwich	British, Traditional	3 3 2

FSA Ratings: from **1** (Poor) to **5** (Exceptional)

SOUTH | **AREA OVERVIEWS**

	Levante	*Turkish*	**4** **3** **2**
	Silk Road	*Chinese*	**5** **3** **2**
£5+	Monmouth Coffee Co	*Sandwiches, cakes, etc*	**3** **4** **3**

Battersea, Brixton, Clapham, Wandsworth Barnes, Putney & Wimbledon
(All SW postcodes south of the river)

£150+	Trinity	*British, Modern*	**5** **5** **4**

£110+	Chez Bruce	*British, Modern*	**5** **5** **4**
	JOIA	*Portuguese*	**3** **3** **4**

£90+	The Ivy Café	*British, Modern*	**1** **1** **2**
	Rick Stein	*Fish & seafood*	**2** **2** **3**

£80+	The Crossing	*British, Modern*	**3** **3** **3**
	Hatched	"	**3** **3** **3**
	The Pig's Head	"	**3** **3** **3**
	Darby's	*Irish*	**3** **3** **4**
	Riva	*Italian*	**3** **4** **2**
	Knife	*Steaks & grills*	**4** **4** **3**
	Good Earth	*Chinese*	**3** **4** **3**

£70+	The Laundry	*Australian*	**3** **3** **3**
	Brunswick House Café	*British, Modern*	**4** **4** **5**
	Humble Grape	"	**2** **3** **3**
	Trinity Upstairs	"	**4** **4** **4**
	Wright Brothers	*Fish & seafood*	**3** **3** **3**
	Augustine Kitchen	*French*	**4** **3** **3**
	Soif	"	**3** **2** **2**
	Brinkley's Kitchen	*International*	**2** **3** **3**
	Archway	*Italian*	**4** **4** **3**
	Fiume	"	**2** **2** **3**
	Numero Uno	"	**2** **3** **2**
	The Fox & Hounds	*Mediterranean*	**3** **4** **3**
	Tapas Brindisa	*Spanish*	**2** **2** **3**
	Macellaio RC	*Steaks & grills*	**2** **2** **3**
	Cilantro Putney	*Indian*	**3** **2** **2**
	Patara	*Thai*	**3** **3** **3**

£60+	The Apollo Arms	*British, Modern*	**3** **2** **3**
	Bistro Union	"	**3** **4** **3**
	The Black Lamb	"	**3** **2** **2**
	The Brown Dog	"	**3** **4** **4**
	Canton Arms	"	**3** **3** **4**
	Coppa Club Putney	"	**2** **2** **3**
	Crispin at Studio Voltaire	"	**3** **4** **3**
	The Light House	"	**3** **3** **3**
	Light On The Common	"	**3** **3** **3**
	Olympic Studios	"	**2** **2** **3**
	24 The Oval	"	**3** **4** **3**
	The Victoria	"	**3** **3** **4**
	The Waterman's Arms	"	**3** **2** **4**

AREA OVERVIEWS | SOUTH

	Fox & Grapes	British, Traditional	3️⃣4️⃣3️⃣
	The Plough	"	2️⃣2️⃣3️⃣
	Gazette	French	2️⃣2️⃣2️⃣
	Cent Anni	Italian	2️⃣3️⃣3️⃣
	Maremma	"	3️⃣3️⃣3️⃣
	Osteria Antica Bologna	"	3️⃣3️⃣2️⃣
	Pizza Metro	"	3️⃣2️⃣2️⃣
	Sorella	"	4️⃣2️⃣3️⃣
	Tozi Grand Cafe	"	2️⃣1️⃣3️⃣
	Haché	Burgers, etc	3️⃣3️⃣2️⃣
	Santa Maria del Sur	Argentinian	3️⃣3️⃣3️⃣
	Le Bab	Middle Eastern	3️⃣3️⃣2️⃣
	Cinnamon Kitchen Battersea	Indian	4️⃣3️⃣2️⃣
	Kibou London	Japanese	2️⃣2️⃣3️⃣
	Takahashi	"	5️⃣4️⃣3️⃣
	Tsunami	"	3️⃣2️⃣2️⃣
£50+	Home SW13	"	3️⃣4️⃣3️⃣
	El Pastor	Mexican	3️⃣3️⃣5️⃣
	Forty Four	British, Modern	4️⃣4️⃣3️⃣
	Home SW15	"	3️⃣4️⃣3️⃣
	The Telegraph	"	2️⃣3️⃣4️⃣
	Smoke & Salt	British, Traditional	5️⃣4️⃣3️⃣
	Lina Stores	Italian	2️⃣2️⃣3️⃣
	Little Taperia	Spanish	3️⃣3️⃣3️⃣
	Naughty Piglets	Steaks & grills	4️⃣4️⃣3️⃣
	MEATliquor	Burgers, etc	3️⃣2️⃣2️⃣
	Bravi Ragazzi	Pizza	4️⃣3️⃣2️⃣
	Made in Italy	"	3️⃣2️⃣2️⃣
	Pizza da Valter	"	4️⃣3️⃣3️⃣
	Zia Lucia	"	4️⃣4️⃣4️⃣
	Black Salt	Indian	3️⃣4️⃣2️⃣
	Kashmir	"	3️⃣3️⃣2️⃣
	Kricket	"	4️⃣5️⃣4️⃣
	Oka	Japanese	3️⃣4️⃣3️⃣
£40+	The Sun Inn	British, Traditional	2️⃣3️⃣4️⃣
	Ploussard	French	3️⃣3️⃣3️⃣
	Danclair's	International	4️⃣3️⃣2️⃣
	Noci	Italian	3️⃣2️⃣3️⃣
	Rosmarino	"	3️⃣3️⃣3️⃣
	Tokova Restaurant	Spanish	4️⃣3️⃣2️⃣
	Black Bear Burger	Burgers, etc	3️⃣3️⃣2️⃣
	Patty and Bun	"	3️⃣3️⃣2️⃣
	Yard Sale Pizza	Pizza	3️⃣3️⃣2️⃣
	Orange Pekoe	Sandwiches, cakes, etc	3️⃣3️⃣3️⃣
	tashas	South African	3️⃣2️⃣2️⃣
	Meza Trinity Road	Lebanese	4️⃣4️⃣3️⃣
	Balham Social	Indian	3️⃣3️⃣3️⃣
	Chook Chook	"	4️⃣4️⃣2️⃣
	Bone Daddies	Japanese	3️⃣2️⃣3️⃣
	Sushi Revolution	"	3️⃣4️⃣2️⃣
	Taro	"	2️⃣2️⃣2️⃣
	Tomoe	"	4️⃣4️⃣2️⃣
	Hare & Tortoise	Pan-Asian	3️⃣3️⃣2️⃣
	Awesome Thai	Thai	3️⃣3️⃣2️⃣

FSA Ratings: from 1️⃣ (Poor) to 5️⃣ (Exceptional)

SOUTH | **AREA OVERVIEWS**

	Cher Thai	"	4 4 3
	Kaosarn	"	3 3 2
	Bao Battersea	Taiwanese	4 3 3
£35+	Amrutha	Vegan	3 4 2
	Arcade Food Hall	International	2 2 2
	Watan	Afghani	3 3 3
	Forty Three Sichuan Kitchen	Chinese	4 3 2
	Three Uncles	"	4 2 2
	Ela & Dhani	Indian	3 4 2
	Daddy Bao	Taiwanese	4 3 3
£30+	Indian Ocean	Indian	3 3 3
£25+	Dropshot Coffee	British, Modern	2 3 4
	Milk	Sandwiches, cakes, etc	3 2 3
	Thai Tho	Thai	3 4 3
£15+	Roti King	Malaysian	5 3 1

Outer western suburbs
Kew, Richmond, Twickenham, Teddington

£130+	Petersham Nurseries Cafe	British, Modern	2 2 5
£110+	Scott's Richmond	Fish & seafood	3 2 4
£100+	The Dysart Petersham	British, Modern	5 4 4
£90+	The Ivy Café	British, Modern	1 1 2
	Al Boccon di'vino	Italian	4 5 4
£80+	Bingham Riverhouse	British, Modern	2 3 3
	A Cena	Italian	4 4 3
£70+	Le Salon Privé	French	3 3 3
	Bacco	Italian	3 2 2
	Tapas Brindisa Richmond	Spanish	2 2 3
£60+	Black Dog Beer House	British, Modern	3 3 3
	Petit Ma Cuisine	French	3 3 3
	Four Regions	Chinese	3 4 3
	Chatora	Indian	4 3 3
	Cah Chi	Korean	3 3 2
	Rock & Rose	Pan-Asian	2 3 3
£50+	Dastaan	Indian	5 4 2
£40+	Noci	Italian	3 2 3
	Newens	Afternoon tea	3 4 3
	Roots	Indian	4 4 3
£30+	Home	British, Modern	4 2 4

AREA OVERVIEWS | SOUTH

| £25+ | The Biriyani Centre | Indian | 5 4 3 |

EAST | AREA OVERVIEWS

EAST

Smithfield & Farringdon (EC1)

£220+	The Clove Club	British, Modern	3 3 2
£180+	Restaurant St. Barts	British, Modern	4 3 4
	Sushi Tetsu	Japanese	5 5 3
£170+	Club Gascon	French	4 3 3
£110+	Origin City	British, Modern	4 3 3
	The Quality Chop House	British, Traditional	3 4 3
£100+	Nest	British, Modern	4 4 3
	Luca	Italian	4 3 4
	Smiths of Smithfield	Steaks & grills	3 2 3
£90+	Bouchon Racine	French	5 5 3
£80+	The Jugged Hare	British, Modern	3 2 3
	St John Smithfield	British, Traditional	4 4 3
	Daffodil Mulligan	Irish	4 4 3
	Morchella	Mediterranean	4 4 4
	Moro	Spanish	4 3 2
	Lilienblum	Israeli	3 2 3
£70+	Bleeding Heart Bistro	French	3 4 4
	Apulia	Italian	3 3 3
	Ibérica	Spanish	2 2 3
	Macellaio RC	Steaks & grills	2 2 3
£60+	Granger & Co	Australian	– – –
	Sessions Arts Club	British, Modern	3 3 5
	Vinoteca	"	2 2 2
	Café du Marché	French	3 3 5
	Caravan	Fusion	2 2 2
	Trattoria Brutto	Italian	3 4 5
	Fare	Mediterranean	3 3 2
	Morito	Spanish	3 2 2
	Homeslice by Symplicity	Pizza	3 2 3
	Quality Wines	Sandwiches, cakes, etc	3 3 4
	Le Bab	Middle Eastern	3 3 2
	Berber & Q Shawarma Bar	"	4 4 2
£50+	Street Burger	Burgers, etc	2 2 3
£40+	Taqueria	Mexican	3 3 3
	Cloth	British, Modern	4 4 4
	Fish Central	Fish & seafood	4 4 3
	Noci	Italian	3 2 3
	The Eagle	Mediterranean	4 3 5
	Black Bear Burger	Burgers, etc	3 3 2
	Crudough	Pizza	3 4 3
	Bone Daddies	Japanese	3 2 3

AREA OVERVIEWS | EAST

£25+	The Shoap	Scottish	4 2 2
£20+	Daddy Donkey	Mexican	3 3 2

The City (EC2, EC3, EC4)

£190+	La Dame de Pic	French	4 4 3
£170+	Mei Ume	Japanese	3 3 2
£140+	Angler, South Place	Fish & seafood	3 4 2
£130+	Nobu Shoreditch	Japanese	4 3 3
£120+	City Social	British, Modern	3 3 4
	Sushisamba	Fusion	2 2 4
£110+	Fenchurch, Sky Garden	British, Modern	2 3 4
	Lutyens Grill, Ned	Steaks & grills	3 3 4
	Fazenda	Brazilian	– – –
	Coya	Peruvian	3 2 3
	Yauatcha City	Chinese	5 4 3
£100+	Duck & Waffle	British, Modern	2 2 3
	14 Hills	"	2 2 3
	Leroy	"	4 3 3
	Coq d'Argent	French	3 4 4
	M Restaurant	Steaks & grills	– – –
£90+	CORD	British, Modern	3 3 3
	Darwin Bras, Sky Garden	"	2 2 4
	Helix	"	2 3 5
	The Ivy City Garden	"	1 1 3
	1 Lombard Street	"	2 4 4
	Bob Bob Ricard City	British, Traditional	2 3 5
	Sweetings	Fish & seafood	3 3 4
	Cabotte	French	3 5 4
	Manicomio City	Italian	2 2 2
	The Don	Mediterranean	3 4 3
	Hispania	Spanish	3 2 4
	Goodman City	Steaks & grills	3 2 2
	Hawksmoor Guildhall	"	3 3 3
	Lucky Cat	Pan-Asian	2 3 2
£80+	Bread Street Kitchen	British, Modern	2 2 2
	The Mercer	"	2 3 2
	Stem + Stem	"	3 4 4
	The Wolseley City	"	2 2 3
	Burger & Lobster	Fish & seafood	3 3 2
	Bistro Freddie	French	3 2 4
	Luc's Brasserie	"	3 3 3
	Cecconi's, The Ned	Italian	2 2 3
	Piazza Italiana	"	3 3 3
	Llama Inn, Hoxton	Peruvian	2 4 4

FSA Ratings: from **1** (Poor) to **5** (Exceptional)

EAST | **AREA OVERVIEWS**

	Jang	*Korean*	– – –
	The Ivy Asia	*Pan-Asian*	3 2 3
£70+	Santo Remedio Café	*Mexican*	3 3 2
	High Timber	*British, Modern*	3 3 2
	Humble Grape	"	2 3 3
	Paternoster Chop House	*British, Traditional*	2 2 2
	Vivat Bacchus	*International*	2 2 2
	Gloria	*Italian*	2 4 5
	José Pizarro	*Spanish*	3 2 2
	Pachamama East	*Peruvian*	3 4 3
	Chinese Cricket Club	*Chinese*	3 2 3
	Brigadiers	*Indian*	5 3 3
£60+	Coppa Club Tower Bridge	*British, Modern*	2 2 3
	Vinoteca City	"	2 2 2
	Brasserie Blanc	*French*	2 2 2
	Gazette	"	2 2 2
	Caravan	*Fusion*	2 2 2
	Barbican Brasserie	*Italian*	2 3 2
	Caravaggio	"	2 3 2
	Eataly	"	3 2 2
	Obicà	"	2 2 3
	Popolo	"	4 4 4
	Terra Rossa	"	2 3 3
	Haché	*Burgers, etc*	3 3 2
	Homeslice	*Pizza*	3 2 3
	Haz	*Turkish*	3 2 2
	Cinnamon Kitchen	*Indian*	4 3 2
	Shoryu Ramen	*Japanese*	3 2 2
£50+	Los Mochis	*Fusion*	4 3 4
	The Wine Library	*International*	3 3 5
	Lina Stores	*Italian*	2 2 3
	Manteca	"	3 4 4
	Casa do Frango	*Portuguese*	3 3 4
	Blacklock	*Steaks & grills*	3 3 4
	Relais de Venise	"	3 2 3
	temper City	"	2 2 3
	Street Burger	*Burgers, etc*	2 2 3
	Pham Sushi	*Japanese*	2 3 3
£40+	Zapote	*Mexican*	4 4 2
	Padella Shoreditch	*Italian*	5 3 4
	Flat Iron	*Steaks & grills*	3 3 3
	Patty and Bun	*Burgers, etc*	3 3 2
	Koya	*Japanese*	3 2 2
	Sushi Revolution	"	3 4 2
	Hare & Tortoise	*Pan-Asian*	3 3 2
£35+	Three Uncles	*Chinese*	4 2 2
£30+	Dream Xi'an	*Chinese*	– – –
£25+	Bleecker Burger	*Burgers, etc*	2 2 1

AREA OVERVIEWS | EAST

| £5+ | Rosslyn Coffee | Sandwiches, cakes, etc | 4 4 3 |

East End & Docklands (All E postcodes)

£320+	Da Terra	Fusion	5 5 4
£220+	Cycene	Fusion	5 4 4
£150+	Behind	Fish & seafood	5 5 4
£140+	The Water House Project	British, Modern	5 4 4
£120+	Galvin La Chapelle	French	4 5 5
£110+	Brat at Climpson's Arch	British, Modern	4 3 2
£100+	Lyle's	British, Modern	5 3 2
	Pearly Queen	Fish & seafood	5 3 3
£90+	Brat	British, Modern	5 4 3
	The Ivy in the Park	"	1 1 3
	Casa Fofó	International	5 4 3
	Goodman	Steaks & grills	3 2 2
	Hawksmoor	"	3 3 3
	Roka	Japanese	3 2 3
£80+	Elliot's	British, Modern	3 3 3
	The Gun	"	2 2 4
	Burger & Lobster	Fish & seafood	3 3 2
	Smith's Wapping	"	4 4 4
	Planque	French	4 5 4
	Angelina	Fusion	5 3 3
	Cecconi's Shoreditch	Italian	2 2 3
	Brawn	Mediterranean	5 4 4
£70+	Humble Grape	British, Modern	2 3 3
	Rochelle Canteen	"	3 3 4
	Rogues	"	4 4 3
	Sune	"	4 5 4
	St John Bread & Wine	British, Traditional	3 3 2
	Big Easy	Fish & seafood	2 2 3
	The Melusine	"	3 3 2
	Six by Nico	International	3 3 3
	Oren	Mediterranean	4 3 2
	Ibérica	Spanish	2 2 3
	Elis	Brazilian	4 4 3
	Ottolenghi	Middle Eastern	3 3 3
	Royal China	Chinese	3 2 2
£60+	Chayote	Mexican	3 3 2
	Mallow	Vegan	3 2 4
	Barge East	British, Modern	3 3 4
	The Culpeper	"	3 2 4
	Jones & Sons	"	3 3 3

FSA Ratings: from 1 (Poor) to 5 (Exceptional)

EAST | **AREA OVERVIEWS**

	Papi	"	4 3 3
	Silo	"	4 4 4
	Cafe Cecilia	French	3 3 3
	Chez Elles	"	3 3 3
	Galvin Bistrot & Bar	"	2 2 2
	Provender	"	3 2 2
	Caravan	Fusion	2 2 2
	Il Bordello	Italian	3 3 4
	Obicà	"	2 2 3
	Ombra	"	3 4 4
	Morito	Spanish	3 2 2
	Le Bab at Kraft Dalston	Middle Eastern	3 3 2
	Berber & Q	"	4 4 2
	Haz	Turkish	3 2 2
	Lahpet	Burmese	4 3 2
	Café Spice Namaste	Indian	5 4 4
	Gunpowder	"	3 3 2
	Mambow	Malaysian	5 3 2
	Smoking Goat	Thai	5 4 3
£50+	Kolamba East	Sri Lankan	3 2 2
	Darkhorse	British, Modern	3 3 2
	ORANJ	"	3 2 4
	SlowBurn London	"	3 3 5
	Emilia's Crafted Pasta	Italian	3 3 3
	Blacklock	Steaks & grills	3 3 4
	Mildreds	Vegetarian	3 3 3
	Burger & Beyond	Burgers, etc	4 3 2
	Ark Fish	Fish & chips	3 2 2
	Pizza East	Pizza	3 2 4
	Zia Lucia Aldgate	"	4 4 4
	Acme Fire Cult	BBQ	2 3 2
	Smokestak	"	4 3 3
	TT	"	– – –
	Chakana	South American	3 3 3
	Delamina East	Middle Eastern	3 3 3
	Lucky & Joy	Chinese	4 3 2
	Dishoom	Indian	4 4 5
	Kricket	"	4 5 4
	Som Saa	Thai	5 3 4
£40+	Dalla	British, Modern	– – –
	Flat Iron	Steaks & grills	3 3 3
	Black Bear Burger	Burgers, etc	3 3 2
	Patty and Bun	"	3 3 2
	Yard Sale Pizza	Pizza	3 3 2
	The Dusty Knuckle	Sandwiches, cakes, etc	5 3 3
	Chick 'n' Sours	Chicken	4 3 3
	Bubala	Middle Eastern	4 4 3
	Mangal I	Turkish	5 3 2
	Koya Ko	Japanese	3 2 2
	Sushi Monster	"	3 2 2
	Taro	"	2 2 2
	Sông Quê	Vietnamese	3 3 2
	Bao Noodle Shop	Taiwanese	4 3 3

295

AREA OVERVIEWS | EAST

£35+	Bruno	*International*	– – –
	Crate Brewery and Pizzeria	*Pizza*	3️⃣2️⃣3️⃣
	Lahore Kebab House	*Pakistani*	4️⃣2️⃣2️⃣
	Tayyabs	*"*	4️⃣2️⃣2️⃣
£30+	Xi'an Biang Biang	*Chinese*	4️⃣3️⃣3️⃣
£25+	Bleecker Burger	*Burgers, etc*	2️⃣2️⃣1️⃣
	Singburi Royal Thai Café	*Thai*	4️⃣3️⃣2️⃣
£20+	Homies on Donkeys	*Mexican*	4️⃣3️⃣3️⃣
	The Yurt Cafe	*International*	3️⃣3️⃣4️⃣
	E Pellicci	*Italian*	3️⃣5️⃣2️⃣
	Tofu Vegan	*Chinese*	4️⃣2️⃣2️⃣
	YeYe London	*Pan-Asian*	3️⃣2️⃣2️⃣
£15+	Smokoloko	*BBQ*	4️⃣3️⃣3️⃣
	Big Night	*Japanese*	– – –
	Roti King	*Malaysian*	5️⃣3️⃣1️⃣
£10+	The Rib Man	*Burgers, etc*	5️⃣4️⃣ –
£5+	Brick Lane Beigel Bake	*Sandwiches, cakes, etc*	5️⃣2️⃣1️⃣

FSA Ratings: from 1️⃣ (Poor) to 5️⃣ (Exceptional)

MAPS

MAP 1 – LONDON OVERVIEW

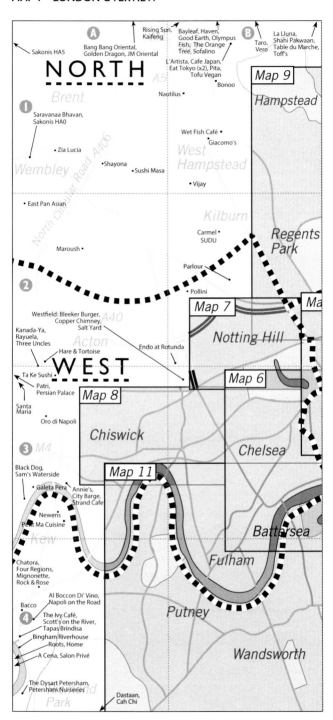

MAP 1 – LONDON OVERVIEW

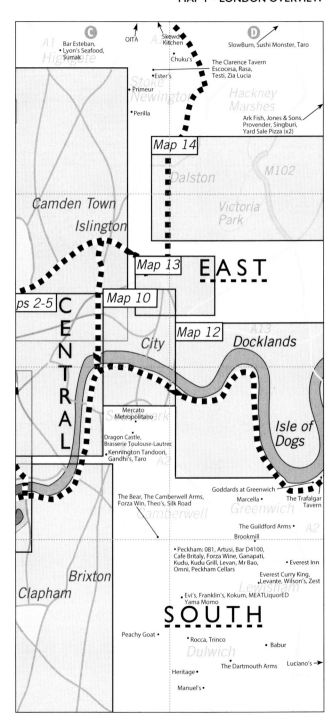

MAP 2 – WEST END OVERVIEW

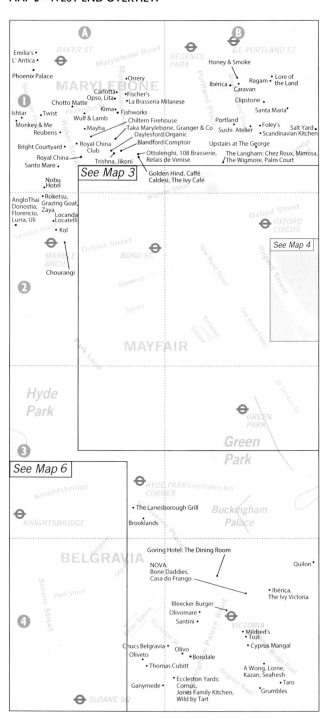

MAP 2 – WEST END OVERVIEW

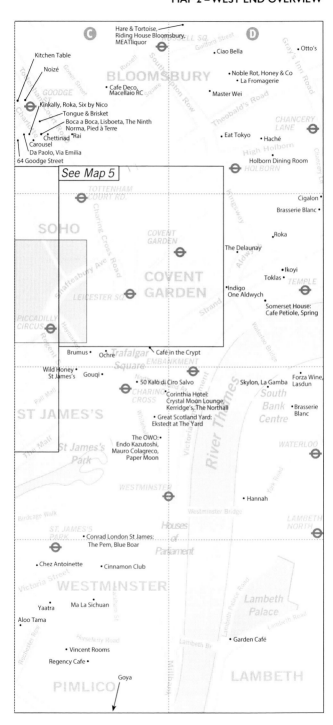

MAP 3 – MAYFAIR, ST. JAMES'S & WEST SOHO

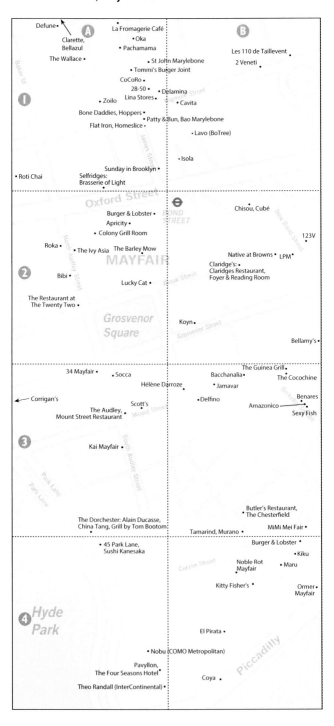

MAP 3 – MAYFAIR, ST. JAMES'S & WEST SOHO

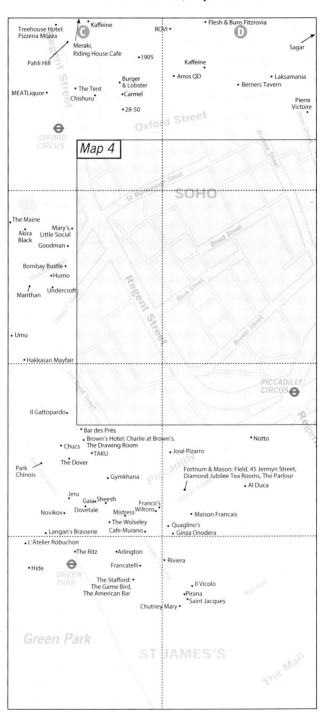

MAP 4 – WEST SOHO & PICCADILLY

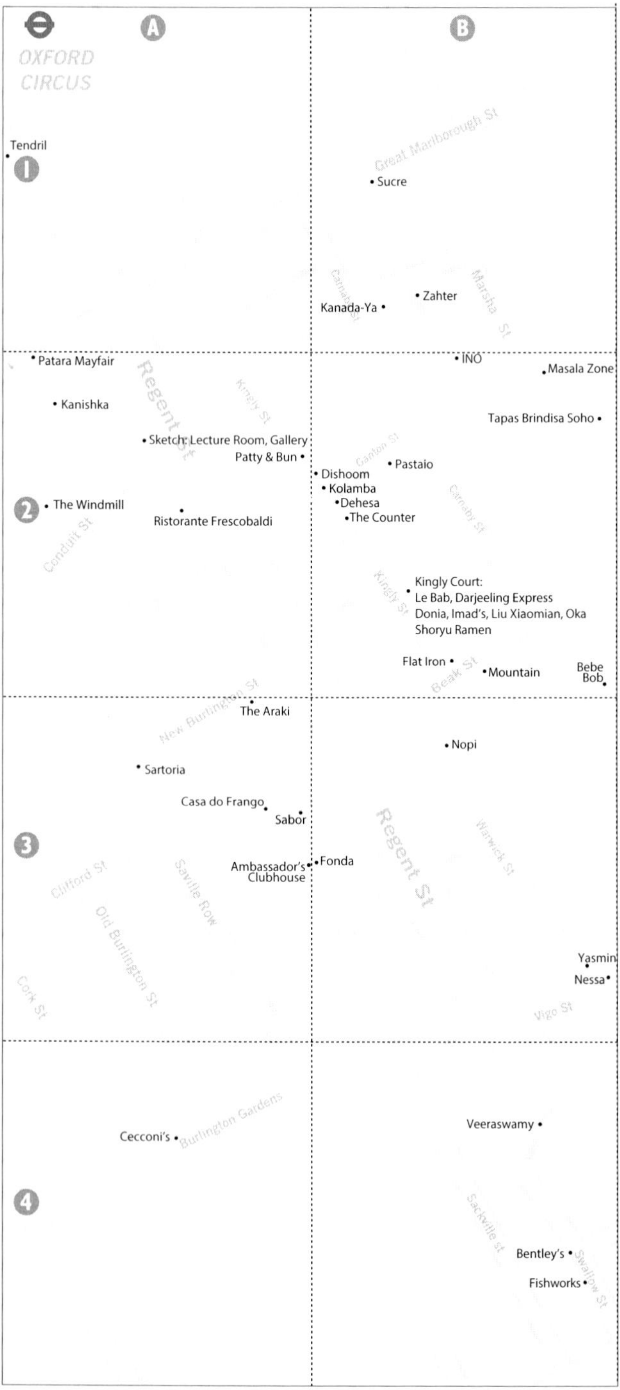

OXFORD CIRCUS

A1
- Tendril

B1
- Sucre
- Kanada-Ya
- Zahter

A2
- Patara Mayfair
- Kanishka
- Sketch: Lecture Room, Gallery
- Patty & Bun
- The Windmill
- Ristorante Frescobaldi

B2
- IÑO
- Masala Zone
- Tapas Brindisa Soho
- Dishoom
- Pastaio
- Kolamba
- Dehesa
- The Counter
- Kingly Court: Le Bab, Darjeeling Express, Donia, Imad's, Liu Xiaomian, Oka, Shoryu Ramen
- Flat Iron
- Mountain
- Bebe Bob

A3
- The Araki
- Sartoria
- Casa do Frango
- Sabor
- Ambassador's Clubhouse
- Fonda

B3
- Nopi
- Yasmin
- Nessa

A4
- Cecconi's

B4
- Veeraswamy
- Bentley's
- Fishworks

MAP 4 – WEST SOHO & PICCADILLY

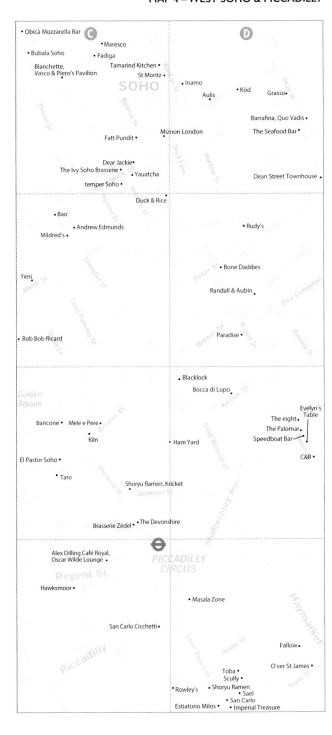

MAP 5 – EAST SOHO, CHINATOWN & COVENT GARDEN

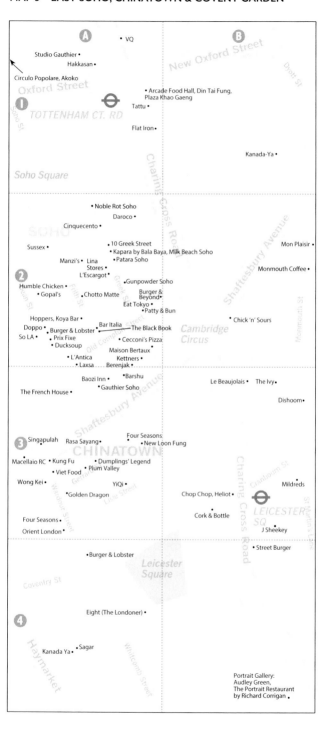

MAP 5 – EAST SOHO, CHINATOWN & COVENT GARDEN

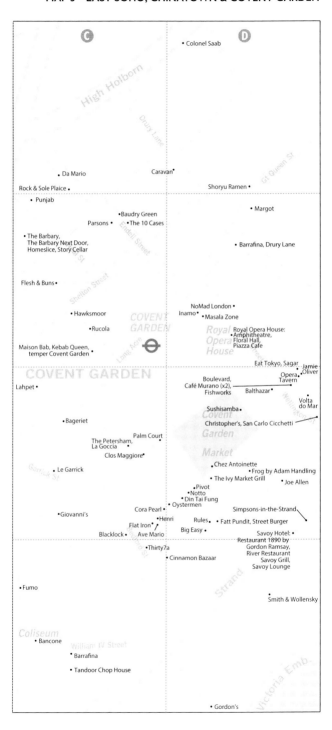

MAP 6 – KNIGHTSBRIDGE, CHELSEA & SOUTH KENSINGTON

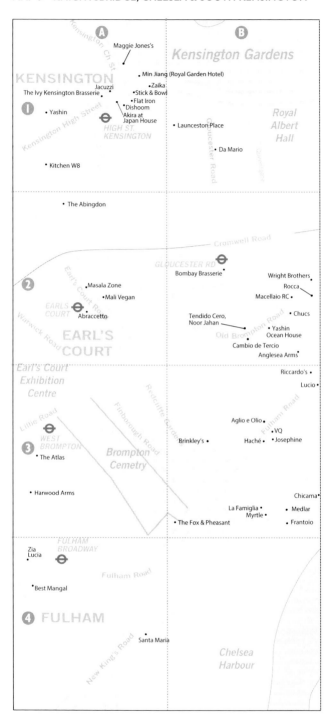

MAP 6 – KNIGHTSBRIDGE, CHELSEA & SOUTH KENSINGTON

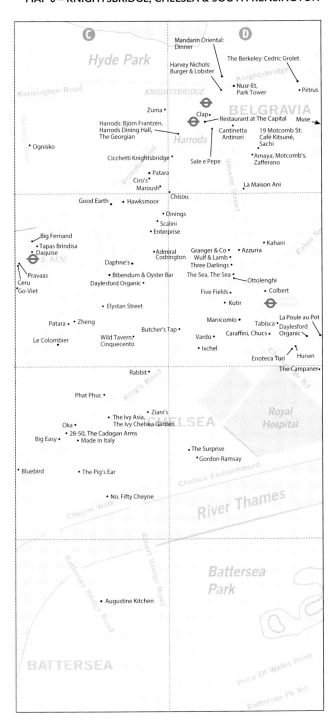

MAP 7 – NOTTING HILL & BAYSWATER

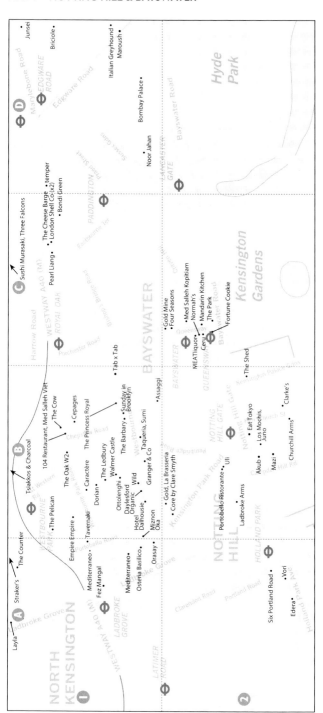

MAP 8 – HAMMERSMITH & CHISWICK

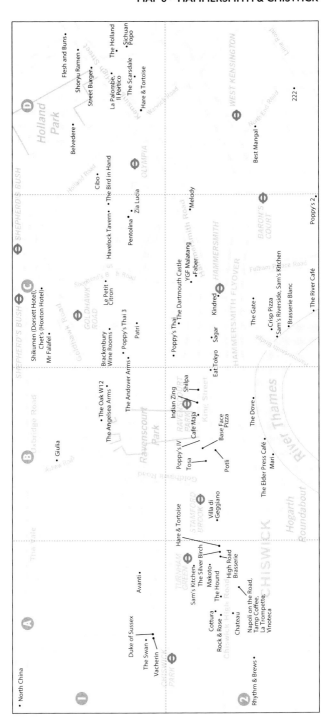

MAP 9 – HAMPSTEAD, CAMDEN TOWN & ISLINGTON

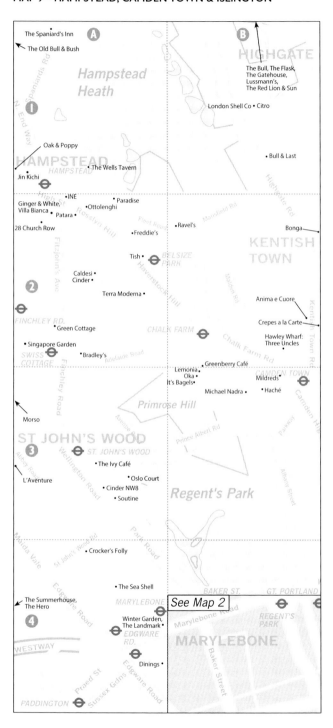

MAP 9 – HAMPSTEAD, CAMDEN TOWN & ISLINGTON

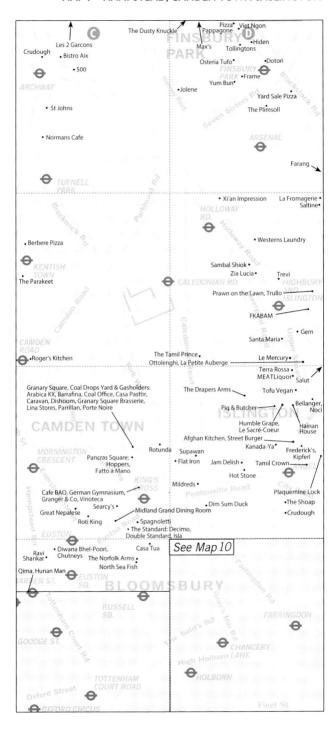

MAP 10 – THE CITY

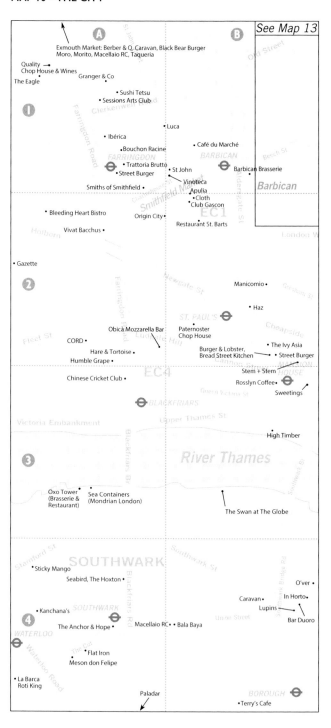

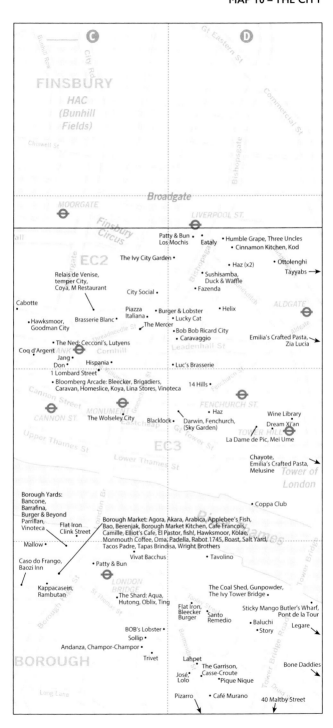

MAP 10 – THE CITY

MAP 11 – SOUTH LONDON (& FULHAM)

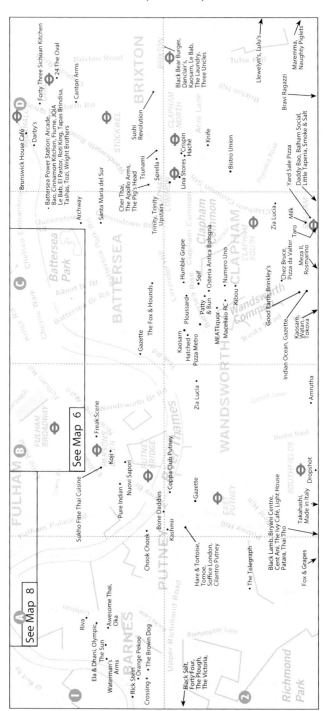

MAP 12 – EAST END & DOCKLANDS

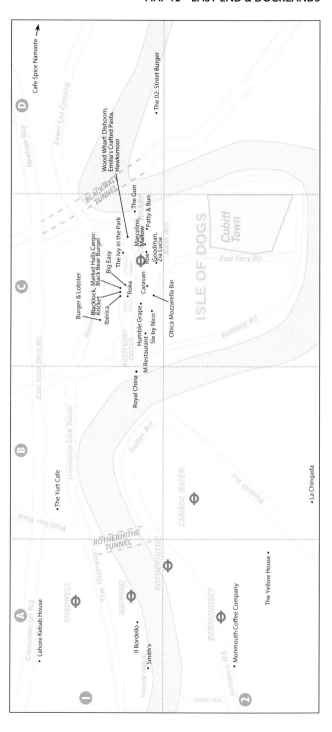

MAP 13 – SHOREDITCH & BETHNAL GREEN

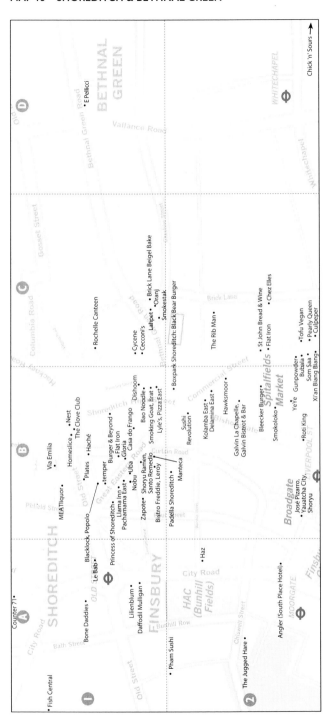